The Concept of International Legal Personality

To my parents,
and in memory of my grandmother
Janne Elisabeth van den Beukel-Boot

The Concept of International Legal Personality

An Inquiry Into the History and Theory of International Law

Janne Elisabeth Nijman

T·M·C·Asser Press
The Hague

Published by T.M.C.ASSER PRESS
P.O.Box 16163, 2500 BD The Hague, The Netherlands

www.asserpress.nl

T.M.C.ASSER PRESS' English language books are distributed exclusively by:

Cambridge University Press, The Edinburgh Building, Shaftesbury Road,
Cambridge CB2 2RU, UK,
or
for customers in the USA, Canada and Mexico:
Cambridge University Press, 40 West 20th Street, New York, NY 10011-4211, USA

www.cambridge.org

ISBN 90-6704-183-1

The cover illustration shows a painting, *Untitled*, by Nosratollah Moslemian (1951), which is at home with the author and reproduced with kind permission of the painter.

FOREWORD

This book is the report of a journey. The reader is invited to join the author on a trip in time and space. The trip takes its starting-point in 17th century Europe and the as yet confused post-Thirty Years War society. After some stops in the 18th and 19th century the author brings us to the post-World War I society which is as confused and is torn between ideals and despair. Then we make a stop in the post-World War II society when ideals seemingly have made place for trust in power but where we also get a glance of the fragile sapling of human rights law. And finally we pause in the post-Cold War world and try to cast a look into the future.

What is the purpose of this journey, what is the author in search of? As is clear from the title it is the concept of International Legal Personality which for many will have a rather formal and positive law connotation.

But the journey does not take us into the cabinets of Foreign Ministries or to conference-rooms or United Nations-buildings where the law is made nor to the court-rooms where the law is interpreted and modelled.

On the contrary, the trip leads us through the minds of men (and one woman) to find out what their view was, not on the concept of international legal personality, but on what the concept stands for: Who are the relevant actors on the international legal scene, who are the real addressees of international law, what can be found behind the 'mask', as the original meaning of the word 'persona' is?

And so the journey reflects not only a development of socio-political structures. The travel-story also presents a history of ideas but it does so with a very specific purpose. 'Past thought is made intelligible by its "re-enactment", and, by doing this, the historian provides us with knowledge we may use in thinking about human action', the author says. Or, as Alain Finkelkraut puts it: '*J'ai besoin des hommes anciens pour penser mon temps.*'

What makes the journey a fascinating one is the close interlinkage of – if not interaction between – social phenomena and the birth of conceptions and ideas: 'What could the author of this particular text, writing at that particular point in time and for the specific audience he addresses, actually have *intended* to communicate?' We see Hans Kelsen groping his way in the nineteen-twenties in an unstable, intolerant Vienna with its totalitarian tendencies to which his Pure Theory of Law is a reaction. The vicissitudes of the political system of the Third

French Republic – in particular during the *interbellum* – are the background for Duguit's and Scelle's legal thinking. The horrors of World War II lead both to the pessimistic realism of Niebuhr and Morgenthau and to the cautious idealism of Lauterpacht.

This contextual reappraisal of the concept of International Legal Personality as reflected in the history of international legal scholarship brings us finally to the beginning of the twenty-first century when world society finds itself in a new socio-political and conceptual quandary. At the end of her narrative (as she calls it) the author asks whether there is still a future for a concept like International Legal Personality which for so long has functioned as a beacon in a turbulent sea or – to use her own words – as the hinge of the meta-legal and the legal realm. While changing the symbol of the 'mask' for that of 'vocal cords' – which keeps us at any rate on stage – she hesitatingly comes to a positive reply.

Even if the final destination is not to the reader's liking, he will surely have made a memorable and rewarding journey.

The Hague, July 2004

P.H. KOOIJMANS
Judge, International Court of Justice

PREFACE

The crucial word in the phrase 'the concept of international legal personality,' must be personality or *personnalité*. It may have European origins – in the Latin word *persona* which in turn was derived from the Greek word used to indicate the theatrical mask – but the mask is a universally used attribute and symbol. It has an equally significant presence in African or Asian or many other cultures. It may moreover be hard to find a symbol which is equally universal with its often political connotations. Masks play a role in myths and stories both on and off stage, they become meaningful in the context of these stories and in relationships with others. The mask is an attribute used to represent, but also to *exclude* from representation. Often it functions as a symbol of authority in a closed system of representation, mostly with authoritarian and/or simplifying tendencies and rarely with positive or liberating effects. In the struggle for identity, casting off the mask liberates and sets free authenticity.

The mask is also used as a symbol or metaphor outside the theatre, for example, in poetry. It is given many meanings, among which that of the device to separate the internal from the external. Sometimes its role is political, as, for example, in what some have called the 'greatest poem of political protest ever written in English,' the 'Mask of Anarchy'. This poem was written in reaction to the 1819 massacre of St. Peter's Field[1] and the masks in the poem cover the faces of those who Shelley held responsible for the massacre: the political tyrants: 'I met murder on the way– / He had a mask like Castlereagh–.' (Who was Foreign Secretary at the time.) These rulers wear – again in the words of Shelley, this time from an earlier poem – the 'foul masks with which ill thoughts hide,' they wear the 'proud, angry looks' or 'false and hollow smiles,' which oppress truth and justice. Shelley censures the failing politicians and evokes an image of a 'masquerade' of murder, fraud and anarchy: 'And many more Destructions played / In this ghastly masquerade, / All disguised, even to the eyes, / Like Bishops, lawyers, peers, or spies.' Equally, the Mask of Anarchy shields off a political order based on fear and bloodshed, a polity which has become hollow, dark and unjust. Shelley portrays the heart of this polity as dark and empty. The only thing to prevent the eruption of chaos is fear; only the mask can bind the polity together. What will happen if the mask falls off or is cast aside and lays bare what was covered until then, the represented and the un-represented?

When the mask is removed, the law must be there as a safeguard, i.e., a body of law which is just and able to accommodate human plurality.

---

[1] R.H. Reiman and S.B. Powers (Eds.), Shelley's Poetry and Prose (1977), at 301-310.

Etymological remarks regarding 'personality' indeed tend to focus on the original meaning of *persona* as mask. Cicero however already used the word in at least three other distinct meanings,[2] among which that of 'distinction or dignity' (cf., 'personal style'), and this meaning soon became the basis for further transformation into the meaning of 'dignified personality' as used in relation to citizenship and representation. Contrary to the meaning of 'mask', this latter meaning does not exclude or hide the true self. 'Personality', conferring prestige and dignity, is used to indicate that 'some individuals had legal rights and obligations, and others did not.' In other words, it distinguished 'a free born citizen ... from the slave.' In addition, 'personality' acquired the meaning of 'a representative.'[3] Where *persona* as mask tends to indicate a lack of truthfulness and, in a way, misrepresentation, *persona* as dignity redirects us to the dignity of the human person and to the responsible powers of the citizen. It is the person who has the right to speak and act and as such to be a participant in the polity. It recognises that the individual is a person, has an individual personality, and is not merely one of the collective. Personality as the equivalent of selfhood is also used to indicate an ethical dimension. Legal personality can build on this meaning and come to indicate the self which asserts itself in political society and the legal order; an assertion which is of existential importance.

In international law, *persona* has become the concept which handles the question of who is an actor on the international stage, or: who is allowed to participate in international law and society, and who is not. The state has been identified by the fact that it wears a mask and the concept of international legal personality has often been interpreted as conferring quasi-statehood or quasi-sovereignty. International legal personality as worn by the state functioned as the mask used to separate completely internal life from external life on the international stage. However, throughout history, as the present study will confirm, alternative conceptualisations of ILP have been proposed. The history of the concept of international legal personality is also the history of the attempts to scrutinise and interpret the mask.

When the mask is cast aside, it reveals either a legal and political black hole or the autonomous individual who is free, free from the many forms of slavery, which Shelley described so well in 'The Mask of Anarchy'.[4] The difference lies in the presence of law and legal institutions which are just. The concept of ILP may have an important role here as the hinge between the legal and the meta-

[2] G.W. Allport, Personality: A Psychological Interpretation (1938), at 26: '(a) as one appears to others (but not really is) [i.e., the original significance of the mask]; (b) the part someone (e.g., a philosopher) plays in life; (c) an assemblage of personal qualities that fit a man for his work; (d) distinction and dignity (as a style of writing).'

[3] Id., at 28.

[4] The Mask of Anarchy, lines 205 *et seq.*; see, e.g., for an interpretation of 'free' as having the ability to use words, lines 299-300. See, for the exhortation that law should govern between the people or, as Ricoeur would call it, that a *juste distance* should be created between people, lines 327-330.

legal, the hinge which connects man's innate right to be a person to the international realm, i.e., a person with a voice who is directed by the law to the international institutional arena where he can be heard.

This is a book about international legal thinking, it is a project that deals with the concept of international legal personality not as it is functioning in international legal documents like treaties, statutes, or case law, but as an idea that has been used in international legal scholarship from Leibniz up to the present day. Legal practice and positive international law are evidently the basis for international law scholarship, however, this study focuses on texts theorising about international law and the international society. As such, the concept of international legal personality also guides us through other important themes in the history and theory of international law. It is not intended in this study, however, to give the impression that there a dividing wall or partition between theory and practice. On the contrary, the methodology that has been chosen aims at the interpretation of the (historical) meaning of an idea in *context*, i.e., in relation to the political, intellectual and jurisprudential context in which the scholar using the idea worked. As a result of the contextual approach chosen for this analysis the reader will search in vain for a static definition of international legal personality which may accompany him/her on this journey through the history and theory of international law. Instead, the meaning of the concept is defined by how it is used in the respective contemporary contexts. In the first chapter, I will further explain the methodology selected so as to caution the reader against simplification or anachronistic interpretations. Here, I wish to confront the question of significance or relevancy which may arise in response to my choice to present a study on 'the history of an idea.' Why is it relevant to study today how Leibniz, Kelsen or Chinkin used the concept of international legal personality in their scholarly texts and how by using it they gave it (historical) meaning? What can we learn from that?

It will teach us that the question of how to deal with 'new' actors, the question of inclusion and exclusion, has been central in the history of international law (scholarship). We will learn that the contemporary concern over non-state actors, which seems post-modern in nature, was actually also a concern of Leibniz', as he, too, needed to tackle the problem of how to accommodate new participants in established political structures without jeopardising stability or risking the complete breakdown of the established order. And he tackled it inspiringly, as at the same time he also pursued universal justice. It is arguable that the Pure Theory of Law is less useful for dealing with today's questions of mass society, but Kelsen's use of legal personality in his defence of democracy does help us to develop our own response to the enduring problem of how to serve democracy through (international) law. We will learn that the appeal for universality, the appeal for and of a global or universal legal system, belongs to the framework of international legal thinking itself, and is not merely the product of pre-modern or post-modern conceptions. We may arrive at the realisation that ILP does not by definition have its source in sovereignty; we may come to realise that it may well have an independent (meta-)legal source, completely distinct from sovereignty. Hopefully, a belief will be instilled that with our minds, through international legal thinking, alternative conceptions can be found and that by the re-conception of the identity of international law we can also re-conceive who is recognised 'in the eyes of international law' as an international legal person.[5] We could be reminded that with the emancipation of international law from (natural) theology and the concept of the universal human society, which has come to represent its modern identity as law created by sovereign states, international law was not merely given an independent identity, but was also cut off from its other source of origin, universal justice. Becoming aware of this unfortunate side effect may stir us to recover what we have lost. Reconnecting international law with justice may be helpful when we need to ponder the question of promoting the development of our global community and its legal and institutional structures. And such progress is not just a cosmopolitan fantasy, but is actually occurring, and traces of this development may be found in positive international law today. It is positive international law that indicates the relevance of 'the principles of justice' and the pursuit of justice for the development and interpretation of international law and institutions. It is this function that is so particular to the identity of international law, i.e., acting as an intermediary between morality and power politics. International law has always fulfilled this function and will be able to do so in the future if we keep wanting it enough, if we really set our minds to it.

How we conceive of international legal personality depends on how we conceive of and what we aspire for international law. The significance of this study therefore lies in the analysis of the conceptions of international law and international legal personality and in the enhancement of our understanding of these conceptions and how they were used to deal with contemporary (theoretical) problems.

Naturally, this study also took place in context. In the first place, thanks are due to the institutional context of the T.M.C. Asser Institute in The Hague, where I entered the Asser Dissertation Program in December 1996, and which I would like to acknowledge gratefully for its support and for giving me the opportunity each year to visit yet another 'non-state actors' conference. To my colleagues there, many thanks. Secondly, as part of the international context, I am grateful to the participants of the 1998 ACUNS/ASIL Summer Workshop 'Globalization and Global Governance: Changing Roles for State and Non-State Actors,' at Yale University, for their stimulating comments on methodology and the research on Chapter 3. In its final stage, Chapter 2 benefited from my stay as a Global Law Fellow and Visiting Fellow of the History and Theory of International Law Program of the Institute of International Law and Justice at NYU School of Law

[5] Art. 2, Montevideo Convention, i.e., Convention on Rights and Duties (Inter-American), 26 December 1933.

and from the discussion with participants of the History and Theory of International Law Seminar, Fall Term 2003. As a constant in the background, I must mention the reassuring presence of the Leiden University International Law Department, where Elsbeth de Vos in particular always made me feel that I was not working without an academic home.

I drew on this research and in particular on Chapter 4 for my article 'Sovereignty and Personality: A Process of Inclusion,' as published in *State, Sovereignty, and International Governance* (OUP, 2002). Similarly, Chapter 2 was the basis for the paper 'Leibniz's Theory of Relative Sovereignty and International Legal Personality: Justice and Stability *or* the Last Great Defence of the Holy Roman Empire' as published in the Working Paper Series of the History and Theory of International Law Program of the Institute for International Law and Justice (NYU Law School).

I would like to thank T.M.C. Asser Press, Marjolijn Bastiaans and Philip van Tongeren, for their expertise and kind cooperation on this book and Mieke Eijdenberg for her patient and persistent editing skills.

I am extremely grateful to Corinne van den Berg-de Keuning of Alfatext who has corrected my less than perfect use of the English language so very skilfully and professionally.

I also wish to express my gratitude to all my friends for having been so supportive throughout these years. My heartfelt thanks for respecting as well as disrespecting regularly my frequently self-imposed isolation. I hope to make it up to you.

My greatest debt is to my parents for their loving support at all stages of the project. This book is dedicated to them, thank you for listening to my stories, for sharing my excitement, and for encouraging me to think critically. This research could not have been done without the support of my brother and our wonderful coffee breaks during which we managed to mix debating serious issues with relaxing laughter. I also wish to mention my grandfather who was at the same time my 'first' teacher, passionate and patient enough to arrest the attention of a little girl with his historical narratives. This book is also dedicated to the memory of my grandmother who, with wisdom and exceptional wittiness, taught me that conventions are there to be scrutinised and that from this creative action arises. In a mysterious way, this wisdom stirred this study at multiple levels.

Responsibility for the views expressed herein, and for all errors and omissions, is fully my own.

Leiden, July 2004 Janneke NIJMAN

TABLE OF CONTENTS

LIST OF ABBREVIATIONS

Acad. Ed.	G.W. Leibniz, Sämtliche Schriften und Briefe, edition of the German (formerly Prussian) Academy of Sciences at Berlin, Darmstadt and Leipzig, 1923-.
AJIL	American Journal of International Law
Am.Pol.Science Review	American Political Science Review
ASIL	American Society of International Law
BYIL	British Yearbook of International Law
CEDAW	Convention on the Elimination of All forms of Discrimination Against Women
CEO	Chief Executive Officer
CPI	Corruption Perception Index
CSCE	Conference on Security and Co-operation in Europe
ECOSOC	Economic and Social Council
EJIL	European Journal of International Law
EPIL	Encyclopedia of Public International Law
EU	European Union
FTSE	Financial Times Stock Exchange
GA	(United Nations) General Assembly
HILJ	Harvard International Law Journal
ICAO	International Civil Aviation Organisation
ICCPR	International Covenant on Civil and Political Rights
ICJ	International Court of Justice
ICJ Rep.	International Court of Justice Reports
ICLQ	International and Comparative Law Quarterly
ILC	International Law Commission
ILO	International Labour Organisation
ILP	International Legal Personality
IMF	International Monetary Fund
Indian JIL	Indian Journal of International Law
IO	International Organisation
ITA	International Transitional Administration
IVR	Internationale Vereinigung für Rechts- und Sozialphilosophie
JNG	De Jure Naturae et Gentium

k.u.k.	Kaiserlich und köninglich
LPW	Leibniz Political Writing
LQR	Law Quarterly Review
MAD	Mutual Assured Destruction
MNC	Multinational corporation
Modern LR	Modern Law Review
NATO	North Atlantic Treaty Organisation
NGO	Non-governmental organisation
NILR	Netherlands International Law Review
Nordic JIL	Nordic Journal of International Law
OECD	Organisation for Economic Co-operation and Development
PCIJ	Permanent Court of International Justice
RCADI	Recueil des cours de l'Académie de droit international
RDI et Législation Comparée	Revue de droit international et Législation Comparée
RGDIP	Revue générale de droit international public
RIAA	United Nations Reports of International Arbitral Awards
SG	Secretary-General
TI	Transparency International
TNCs	Transnational corporations
UN	United Nations
UNTAD	United Nations Conference on Trade and Development
UNESCO	United Nations Educational, Scientific and Cultural Organisation
UNGA	United Nations General Assembly
Univ. of Col. Law R	University of Colorado Law Review
UNO	United Nations Organisation
Vanderbilt J. of Tr.L.	Vanderbilt Journal of Transnational Law
Virg.JIL	Virginia Journal of International Law
WB	World Bank
WEF	World Economic Forum
Wisconsin ILJ	Wisconsin International Law Journal
WTO	World Trade Organisation
WW	World War

Chapter 1
GENERAL INTRODUCTION

1.1. INTRODUCTION

The winter of 1996-1997, when I embarked on this research, was a time still characterised by an upbeat sense of change. Communism had collapsed only a few years earlier and as a consequence the dynamics of the international society had changed completely, creating a sense of hope. Hope that, for example, the United Nations would rise in authority and that the Security Council would at last be able to function properly now that it was no longer paralysed by Cold War antagonism. In many countries, the redistribution of world power also had quite an impact on domestic politics, especially in those formerly used as a battleground by the two super powers. However, the world was not only changing rapidly because of these events and in terms of international politics alone. The process we have come to identify as 'globalisation' challenges traditional (technological, economic, financial, environmental, criminal, political and social) structures worldwide and the challenge was initially applauded. New participants ascended to the international stage or were at least promoted from a silent to a speaking part and this resulted in a tendency to conclude that the state was in retreat. Governments and international organisations all reflected on the challenges which had to be met and the responses which had to be given. In the Netherlands, for example, foreign policy was reviewed to take account of the fact that states were under significant pressure, both from within and without.[1] In July 1997, a member of parliament officially asked the Dutch Minister of Foreign Affairs whether the nation state was indeed withering away. The Minister confirmed the erosion of certain state functions due to certain developments, such as globalisation, liberalisation and privatisation, which were gathering strength.[2] Notions such as good governance and democracy or political participation quickly came to the forefront of foreign policies and the United Nations launched a call for action through its Commission on Global Governance to reform the UN system, thereby implementing the shift from states to the people and linking the intergovernmental system and the international civil society in a renewed global network.[3] UN Secretary-General Kofi Annan stressed the importance of non-state actors to contemporary international life and officially called upon the UN

[1] Nota Herijking van het Buitenlands Beleid, Tweede Kamer der Staten-Generaal, Vergaderjaar 1994-1995, 24337, nr. 2 (1995).

[2] Handelingen van de Tweede Kamer, Vergaderjaar 1996-1997, aanhangsel, 1607, Vragen van Weisglas d.d. 1 juli 1997.

[3] UN Commission on Global Governance, Our Global Neighbourhood (1995). This report concludes hat the multitude of non-state global actors which has emerged, and their force and impact,

to make the 'global civil society ... a true partner in its work.'[4] Even a traditional organisation like the World Bank turned towards civil society movements and published a report entitled 'The State in a Changing World.'[5] As the global civil society continued its ascent, the world was seemingly hurled from the Westphalian order right into 'the Age of Non-State Actors.'[6]

Within this rapidly changing international context, the academic debate focused on the concept of sovereignty and the changing role of the state, now that it became evident that non-state actors were indeed gaining influence.[7] From all quarters, arguments to the effect that the state was nearing its end and that sovereignty had become more relative than ever before were put forward. To a student of international law, who in this changing international arena was starting on the

make it necessary for the nation state to adjust to the new global situation in order to improve global governance.

[4] In July 1997, UN Secretary-General Kofi Annan presents his report, 'Renewing the UN: A Programme for Reform' (A/51/950). 'The emergence of non-State actors has been of a growing influence on our changing environment. Non-governmental organizations are the clearest manifestation of what is referred to as "civil society", that is, the sphere in which social movements organize themselves around objectives, constituencies and thematic interests. ... Other actors have also taken on an increasing important role in shaping national international agendas. They include local authorities, mass media, business and industry, professional associations, religious and cultural organizations, and the intellectual and research communities.' Id., para. 207. Since 1997, the initiative to reform the institutional structures of the United Nations has advanced. In 2002, in his Report, Strengthening of the UN: an agenda for further change (A/57/387), the SG made additional proposals for much needed organisational change. It explicitly includes in its analysis and proposals for change the increased interaction between UN and civil society actors. In February 2003, the Secretary-General appointed a Panel of Eminent Persons on UN-Civil Society Relations to address the problems resulting from this increased interaction and participation and to issue a report in 12 months.

[5] See, World Bank President J. Wolfensohn on the Bank's relationship with civil society organisations: 'We are really interdependent. But we must build mutual trust. ... [and] accelerate and deepen the effort to work with existing and new *partners* – with specific measures for reaching out to the private sector NGOs and civil society.' As cited in M. Williams, International Organisations and the Environmental Social Movement, paper presented at Warwick conference. World Bank, The State in a Changing World, World Development Report 1997.

[6] J.T. Mathews, Power Shift 76(1) *Foreign Affairs* 50 (1997). See, e.g., on the end of the Westphalian Order and the need for a 'new Westphalian bargain' for the post Cold War world, J. Bryan Hehir, The Uses of Force in the Post Cold War World, presentation delivered at a conference at the Woodrow Wilson Center, June 1996, <http://www.clausewitz.com/CWZHOME/hehir.htm>. See, for revised version, Strategy and Ethics in World Politics, *in* R.L. Hutchings (Ed.), At the End of the American Century: America's Role in the Post-Cold War World 110 (1998).

[7] E.g., 'The State will become just one of many players in the international marketplace and will have to negotiate directly with foreign factors of production to solve domestic economic problems.' R. Rosecrance, The Rise of the Virtual State, 75(4) *Foreign Affairs* 60 (1996). See, e.g., on the information and telecommunications revolution, viewed as an aspect of the globalisation of the world economy which provides an increase in cross-border channels of communication and favours the position of non-state actors within the international system, R.O. Keohane and J.S. Nye, Jr., Power and Independence in the Information Age, 77(5) *Foreign Affairs* 81 (1998). See also, for a negative answer to the question whether technological globalisation spells the 'end of the nation state.' D. Archibugi and J. Michie, Technological Globalisation or National Systems of Innovation? 29(2) *Futures* 121-137 (1997).

journey towards a doctorate, the concept of international legal personality seemed an appropriate angle for an international law assessment of the evolution of international life. In international law, the relevant actors on the international legal stage have traditionally always been 'international legal persons,' or, in other words, entities subject to rights and duties under international law. Possessing international legal personality (hereinafter: ILP) meant that an entity 'existed' under international law and was recognised as having a separate legal identity. As such, it seemed a natural step to analyse the commotion, which had arisen over non-state actors, their status and the source of their authority, in terms of the concept of ILP. Turning to the concept of ILP, one may expect that this book will examine the contemporary role of ILP in international (state) practice. However, this is not the approach I chose to take. Instead, this book is an attempt to improve our understanding of the concept of ILP, how it is used in international legal thinking, and as such to contribute to the debate on the contemporary challenges faced by the international community and international law today from a historical-theoretical perspective.

My quest has been to locate ILP, and its source and the underlying theories that have developed around it, rather than to deliver technical, casuistic case assessments to determine whether, for example, non-governmental organisations (NGOs), transnational corporations (TNCs) or liberation movements should be considered international legal persons in the new international dimension. After I had read some recent literature on international law theory, I soon realised that the concept of ILP was not actually considered to be an issue at all. Although the debate provided evidence that interest in international law theory was on the increase (albeit very gradually and in quite specific ways), the concept of ILP was mostly absent from it.

The negation of the concept of ILP and of the fact that it could serve as a basis for inquiring into the fundamental aspects of international law in this new era is even more surprising now that it occurs at a time which is so preoccupied with identity and personality. Personality as a term today has a positive connotation: if someone or something has 'personality' it is appreciated for having a separate and distinctive identity. In those parts of the world where the age of individualism is in full swing, the individual pursues the construction and subsequent recognition of his own identity, his own personality. This process may at times cause people to lose sight of their roots and be cast adrift. However, at other times, it may also cause them to find in the farthest corners of this globalised world the missing building blocks for the construction of their identity and may thereby complete their roots. In the world process of globalisation, the Local and the Global configure and the (global) representation of (old and new) identities has already developed into a subject for serious study and academic debate. In law, including international law, the concept of 'legal personality' – *persona* – has traditionally been a concept that recognises the existence of these separate identities. It is the concept lawyers use to identify a certain actor as a separate and independent entity in law; ILP is the shield or mask which the law addresses and behind which an inner life takes place. The mask may present a pluralist 'culture' or a diverse society as an identifiable unit. In an age championing new global actors, both individuals and organisations, who have been given a voice on the international scene, and in an age which also favours distinctive personality – the capacity to both speak up and be spoken to – international law scholars seem to avoid the use or redefinition of their traditional language and seem instead to borrow from other disciplines. *Why?*

The attention that theory paid to ILP had already decreased after WWII, but especially after 1949, when the ICJ spoke out on certain aspects of the concept and dealt with them quite effectively, it went into a sharp decline. Since then, textbook writers have merely needed to quote from the Court's opinion to deal with the concept conclusively. Yet both the Court and these writers still admitted that the concept of ILP was controversial.[8] In its opinion, the Court seemed to take quite an open approach to ILP, which is especially interesting in the light of the contemporary transformation of international life. A connection is made between the doctrine of ILP – or the subjects-of-law doctrine – and the requirements of international life itself:

> The subjects of law in any legal system are not necessarily identical in their nature or the extent of their rights, and their *nature depends upon the needs of the community.* Throughout its history, the development of international law has been influenced by *the requirements of international life* ...[9]

If this is so, why is it that today the debate is dominated by contributions announcing 'The End of the Nation State' and analyses of 'The United Nations Facing the Crisis of the Nation State' or questions like 'Whatever Happened to Sovereignty?' and even contemplations on 'The End of Sovereignty?'[10] In a time when almost everything was proclaimed to be at an "end," even history, no such

---

[8] In the *Reparation for Injuries* case the ICJ contended that: '[International personality] is no doubt a doctrinal expression, which has sometimes given rise to controversy.' 1949 ICJ Rep. 178 (1949). See also, e.g., O'Connell referred to the discussion as 'the great debate on the nature of corporate personality, a debate that has been neither won nor lost, but only shelved.' D.P. O'Connell, International law 80 (Vol. I, 1970); Akehurst openly declared it a 'controversial area of the law,' M. Akehurst, A Modern Introduction to International Law 70, (6th ed., 1987); see also, Dominicé, *infra*, footnote 11.

[9] See *supra*, footnote 8. Emphasis added. As I understand it, 'international life' refers to the life of the international society: its nature, the changes it undergoes, the relationships that exist within it and the members who participate in it.

[10] J.-M. Guéhenno, The End of the Nation-State, transl. by V. Elliott (1995); K. Ohmae, The End of the Nation State: The Rise of Regional Economies (1995); R. Dupuy, The United Nations Facing the Crisis of the Nation State, *in* Nandasiri Jasentuliyana (Ed.), Perspectives on international law 201 (1995); B.R. Roth, What ever happened to Sovereignty? Reflections on International Methodology, *in* Ch. Ku and Th.G. Weiss, Toward Understanding Global Governance 69 (1998); See also, The End of Sovereignty? Round Table at the 48th Annual ASIL Meeting, 'The Transformation of Sovereignty,' ASIL Proceedings, at 71 (1994).

honours were paid to the fundamental concept of ILP.[11] But does this mean that the concept has become obsolete? We will discuss this question in chapter 5 which deals with 'The Concept of ILP Today: The End of the Subject?' This first chapter, however, is intended to convey how my fascination for the reasons behind the use of ILP came into being. The question *why* ILP is hardly ever used in contemporary international law scholarship gave rise to a need to look at things from a historical perspective. Examining what ILP meant and why it was used in the theory of international law in the past could contribute to our understanding of the concept of ILP today. After all, an analysis of the present and a theory concerning the future must evidently be founded on a certain understanding of the past. The past contains the elements that mark our approach to the future. If we misconstrue the past, we could be led astray in the future and this might unfairly limit our actions. Maybe the non-use of ILP today has to do with a false understanding of the concept's historical meaning, or at least this was the thesis that I started to work with soon after I received quite a number of comments in conference halls to the effect that 'ILP will get us nowhere.' After all, this reaction suggested that the theoretical controversy had run its course and that the concept of ILP was being rejected for its *obvious* obsolescence, despite the Court's statement that ILP depends on 'the needs of the community.' So this is how my quest for the historic meaning(s) of the concept of ILP began.

Before I now begin to outline the book, to account for the scope of the research, to explain the methodology used and to specify the research problem and its purpose further, I would like to make two final remarks concerning the progress of this study and the context in which it evolved.

First, many things have changed since I started my research. The international and the national political environment in which the research took place shifted from being situated in an atmosphere in which the dominant feeling was hope to finding itself in a time which is less optimistic about the future and which is once again dominated by concerns about peace, security and order in international life. Contrary to earlier assessments, the world today is not the multi-polar international system into which it was still expected to develop during the mid-nineties, but instead a world in which only one super power rules. International law is in crisis again and a demand for strong states is frequently expressed. This demand was already voiced before 11 September 2001, but in the past few years the call for a stronger state has become louder still and as a consequence the initial celebration of NGOs as the saviours of the new world has become more subdued. Notwithstanding their tremendously important role as the international legal system's watchdogs, their accountability – or the question: who controls the controllers? – has also become part of the debate. The realisation that compliance

---

[11] See also, e.g., C. Dominicé: 'Il est plus rare de rencontrer un effort de systémation.' 'Il s'agit d'un domaine où, dans la pratique, des vues très variés sont exprimées,' C. Dominicé, L'ordre juridique international entre tradition et innovation: recueil d'études 57 (1997).

with human rights requires a strong, well-functioning state rather than a weak, non-interventionist state has dawned for many and has recently frequently been held up as a warning. Statehood still appears to be the best political structure for international law to rely on for the implementation of its rules and the accomplishment of the goals of its institutions and this realisation flies in the face of the literature which only a few years ago announced the retreat of the sovereign state. The premise that the state should take a step back in order for international norms to flourish is now being replaced by, or at least adapted to, the premise that stable state structures are not by definition to be despised or to be viewed as a threat to democracy and to human rights and the implementation of international norms. To reduce state authority is not a goal in itself. In addition, international law at present tends to involve itself more in the internal exercise of state authority, now that normative concepts, such as 'good governance,' have begun to play a larger part in international relations. It moreover seems arguable that international law scholars have by now begun to realise that the onslaught on the concept of state sovereignty in the field of international relations does not automatically need to be followed by a similar comprehensive challenge of the institution of the state in international law. If international law still needs states in order to function, the international legal debate might as well include the internal aspects of these political communities.

Secondly, apart from having me travelling through the changing political context in which ILP took shape, this study also sent me on a more personal journey: I shaped this project, but as it came along it also began to shape me. Initially, my quest was – mostly instinctively – an idealistic one in which I hoped the individual human being would attain 'full glory' and become a direct and fully recognised participant in international law. However, going through the texts I had selected, such as for instance treatises by Kelsen and Niebuhr and Morgenthau, the authors' realism about human nature and the human condition as well as the world of power politics, and the background to their thinking, forced me to add some nuance to my initial position. A similar tension is discernible in international law theories on ILP: do only states have legal personality under international law or are individuals the true and exclusive international legal persons? This is a question loaded with moral and political ideology. Therefore, as the project unfolded, it developed – against all contemporary odds – into the kind of work which Hans Kelsen has so aptly described in the *Vorrede* of his *Hauptprobleme der Staatsrechtslehre*.

An dieser Stelle, wo auch Persönliches zu Worte kommen darf, ist es mir ein Bedürfnis, hervorzuheben, daß dieses Buch, an dem ich durch manches Jahr, über viele Hindernisse und Widerwärtigkeiten hinweg gearbeitet habe, für mich viel mehr geworden ist als die Bewältigung einiger spezialwissenschaftlicher Probleme: Diese Arbeit hat mir den lange und schmerzlich vermißten *Zusammenhang zwischen Fachdisziplin und Weltanschauung gezeigt*. Ich weiß, es wird viele befremden, daß ich einen Weg zu philosophischen Höhen aus einem Geistesgebiete such, das heute weiter von solchem Ziele entfernt ist, als irgendein anderes, so weit, daß jene Disziplin, die als solche berufen wäre, die Brücke zwischen Rechtswissenschaft und Philosophie zu schlagen, die Rechtsphilosophie, nur mit einem Tone der Geringschätzung genannt wird.[12]

1.2. Problem and Purpose

> Time present and time past
> Are both perhaps present in time future,
> And time future contained in time past.[13]

Looking at contemporary life, it is on the face of it perhaps hardly surprising that international legal scholarship tends to leave the concept of ILP by the wayside. ILP is so closely associated with statehood, while the issue which is currently debated is in fact that of '*non*-state actors.' However, this unwritten rejection of or disregard for a central and fundamental concept of international law such as ILP still demands clarification. It forces us to try to grasp the (implicit) interpretation of ILP which underlies the current response it elicits and to confront it with a conceptual history of ILP as determined by the paradigm of international law and, *in casu*, of ILP as we assume to have received it.

One of the tasks of legal scholarship is to speculate about possible and probable alternative futures for society. In my view, this is equally true for international law scholarship. It is the duty of the discipline of international law to contribute to the rethinking of the international society and its legal system and to provide alternatives for our collective future. The contemporary challenges to the theory and practice of international law provide the input for speculations on the possible future of international law. Selecting alternatives is at the same time debating their limitations or even their exclusion. This is as true for the contemporary debate as it is for past debates. The understanding of the concept of ILP that underlies the assessment that ILP is obsolete and useless when it comes to responding to the challenges of today and tomorrow is part of a specific view on the future of international law. Nonetheless, there is (always) room for alternatives. Today as in the past, the discourse on international law is fed by visions of alternative futures and we have to keep reminding ourselves of this when we turn to the legal discourses of the past. We have to realise that the dominant view or conception we receive was actually once one of many alternatives. When we consider other alternatives for the future, therefore, we would do well to inquire into the alternatives of the past.

Considering alternative futures requires a thorough understanding of the past. Or, as Toulmin has pointed out: 'The beliefs that shape our historical foresight represent ... our *Erwartungshorizonten*, or "horizons of expectation." Those horizons mark limits to the field of action in which, at the moment, we see it as pos-

[12] H. Kelsen, Hauptprobleme der Staatsrechtslehre XII (1911). Emphasis added.

[13] The first three lines of *Burnt Norton*, T.S. Eliot, in Four Quartets (reprint 1944 ed.) at 3 (1995).

sible or feasible to change human affairs, and to decide which of our most cherished practical goals can be realised in fact.'[14] The horizons of expectation will assist us in imagining the possibilities and limits of our alternative futures. In this study, I will therefore address the theoretical history of ILP in order to establish our horizon of expectation for ILP. The assumption of the value of studying the history of ideas is not uncontested. After all, 'we must learn to do our own thinking for ourselves.'[15] Yet, the study of history is '"for" human self-knowledge,' which is essential for shaping our ability to act today and for imagining alternative futures.[16] As Collingwood[17] put it: '[S]ince nobody knows what he can do until he tries, the only clue to what man can do is what man has done. The value of history, then, is that it teaches us what man has done and thus what man is.'[18] History can provide knowledge about human nature as it raises questions about past human actions, which can subsequently be answered through an interpretation of the available historical evidence.[19] As such, it is a process of thought in the historian's mind, the constant 're-enactment' of the 'historic inheritance of thought.'[20] Past thought is made intelligible by its re-enactment and in this way the historian provides us with knowledge which we may use in our thinking on human action. The Cambridge historian Quentin Skinner, who is directly indebted to Collingwood's ideas on the interpretation of historical thought,[21] also explains the relevance of the history of ideas in terms of self-knowledge:

> [T]he very reason for regarding such histories [of ideas] as indispensably 'relevant', [is] not because crude 'lessons' can be picked out of them, but because the history itself pro-

---

[14] S. Toulmin, Cosmopolis: The Hidden Agenda of Modernity 1 (1990). Hereinafter: Cosmopolis.

[15] Q. Skinner, Meaning and Understanding in the History of Ideas, *in* J. Tully (Ed.), Meaning and Context 66 (1988). Hereinafter: Meaning and Understanding.

[16] R.G. Collingwood, The Idea of History 10, rev. ed. 1993. Hereinafter: The Idea of History.

[17] During the first half of the 20th century, the British philosopher Robin George Collingwood (1889-1943) took a critical, anti-naturalist approach to history. He rejected the speculative or naturalistic theories of history, which perceived historical process as a natural process traveling in a meaningful direction, namely towards its ultimate rational and moral end, i.e., human destiny. In this perspective, history should be studied by the same scientific methods as nature, i.e., by searching for causal explanations in the interpretation of the historical process. Collingwood, however, held the opinion that the study of history was not a natural science to be researched based on the laws of strict causality, but one that should be studied by 're-thinking an agent's past action.' In other words, his rational model of explanation intended to show the rational necessity of a particular argument, thereby rendering the past intelligible by imaginatively demonstrating why a certain action was fairly rational or comprehensible at the time in response to a practical issue or dilemma.

[18] The Idea of History, at 10.

[19] Id., at 226. Collingwood on human nature: 'human nature, ..., is only a name for human activities ...' '[T]he historical process is a process in which man creates for himself this or that kind of human nature by re-creating in his own thought the past to which he is heir.'

[20] Id., at 227-228.

[21] Q. Skinner, A Reply to my Critics, *in* J. Tully (Ed.), Meaning and Context 234 (1988). See also, e.g., Skinner, 'Social meaning' and social action, *in* J. Tully (Ed.), Meaning and Context 80 (1988); Meaning and Understanding, at 55-56.

vides a lesson in self-knowledge. To demand from the history of thought a solution to our own immediate problems is ... to commit not merely a methodological fallacy, but something like a moral error. But to learn from the past – and we cannot otherwise learn at all – the distinction between what is necessary and what is the product merely of our own contingent arrangements, is to learn the key to self-awareness itself.[22]

Skinner expounds that historical study makes us aware of why we think what we think and have thought so far, and enables us to evaluate whether these ideas are still necessary and appropriate or whether they are simply of a highly contingent nature. It is a commonly accepted observation that our own thoughts and imaginations are constrained by society and its 'arrangements of social and political life.'[23] Rethinking inherited social and political arrangements and thereby rethinking the related past thoughts enables us to distinguish between necessary and adequate theories on the one hand and largely conditioned thinking which is needlessly based on social constraints rather than free imagination on the other.[24] The value of studying intellectual history therefore lies in the fact that since such studies concerns 'alien' problems and 'alien' societies they force us to step back 'from our own prevailing assumptions and structures of thought and to situate ourselves in relation to other and very different forms of life.'[25] As such, the study of history provides us with a 'sense of possibility':[26] by considering alternatives we are constantly given the opportunity to put our ideas and social structures to the test.

[A]bove all, we can hope to acquire a perspective from which to view our own form of life in a more self-critical way, enlarging our present horizons instead of fortifying local prejudices. ... it offers us a ... means ... of strengthening our present beliefs by way of testing them against alternative possibilities, or else of improving them if we come to recognize that the *alternatives* are both possible and desirable.[27]

Once more, we have returned to the question of the relevance of the past for imagining our alternative futures. To understand the past of ILP and assess the reasonableness of the interpretation of ILP in which its current negation is grounded, we thus have to recover the historic meaning*s* of this international legal concept, because ILP is neither a timeless nor a socio-politically independent concept. For although in both theory and practice the consensus is that ILP is one of the fundamentals of international law, scholarly positions have differed significantly as to its meaning and role. Opinions mainly diverge on the subject of primacy: some authors consider states to be the *primary* international legal persons, while others assign this role to individual human beings. We will deal with these

[22] Meaning and Understanding, at 67.
[23] Id.
[24] Id.
[25] A Reply to my Critics, at 286.
[26] Id., at 287.
[27] Id. Emphasis added.

various scholarly conceptions of ILP in the subsequent chapters. However, most writers today will agree that the standard account of the concept of ILP and the one underlying today's reaction stems from the Westphalian perspective. The current negation of ILP suggests that our discipline considers the concept as belonging to the "old" order.

As observed above, the origins of international law are traditionally traced back to the Westphalian Peace of 1648.[28] The decision to consider this date as the birth date of "modern" international law has determined the "traditional" understanding that international law is law binding upon sovereign states once they have accepted it. This Westphalian interpretation was still the widely held view in the early 20th century, as the following lines from the *S.S. Lotus Case* (1927) show, and more or less continued to be the basis of the international legal order for most of its remainder.

> international law governs relations between independent States. The rules of law binding upon States therefore emanate from their own free will as expressed in conventions or by usages generally accepted as expressing principles of law and established in order to regulate the relations between these co-existing independent communities or with a view to the achievement of common aims.[29]

Here, sovereignty is perceived as the central axiom of the inter-state society. It represents, in Brownlie's words: 'the basic constitutional doctrine of the law of nations, which governs a community consisting primarily of states having a uniform legal personality.'[30] In the Westphalian view of the nature of international law, ILP was habitually defined rather strictly as the legal personality of states alone. This traditional definition is the product of the perception that *true* international law only started with the Westphalian Peace. Only then did international law become "modern," i.e., construed on the basis of state sovereignty, as indeed in this view it should be. International legal concepts have been interpreted to fit the Westphalian inter-state model.[31] Even Grotius' work, which finds itself on

[28] H.G. Grewe, Fontes Historiae Iuris Gentium 183 *et seq.* (1988). See, e.g., L. Gross, The Peace of Westphalia 1648-1948, 42 *AJIL* 20-41, at 26 (1948). Also, A. Eyffinger, Europe in the Balance: An Appraisal of the Westphalian System, 54 *NILR* 161 (1998). A. Nussbaum, A Concise History of the Law of Nations 86 (1950), hereinafter: A Concise History.

[29] S.S. Lotus case, 1927 PCIJ (ser. A) No. 10, at 18. See also, the classical statement laid down in the *Island of Palmas* case, delivered by the Permanent Court of Arbitration in 1928: 'Sovereignty in relations between States signifies independence. Independence with regard to a portion of the globe is the right to exercise therein, to the exclusion of any other state, the functions of a State. The development of the national organization of States during the last few centuries and, as a corollary, the development of international law, have established this principle of the exclusive competence of the State in regard to its territory in such a way as to make it the point of departure in settling most questions that concern international relations.' (RIAA Vol. II, (Netherlands *v.* USA)), at 838.

[30] I. Brownlie, Principles of International Law 287 (1990, 4th ed.).

[31] The ICJ Opinion in the 1949 *Reparation for Injuries* case confirmed that the UN did indeed possess ILP. Although this firmly established the possibility of ILP attaching to a "non-state actor,"

the crossroads between medieval and modern thinking, has been interpreted in such a way that modern international law, which regulates the relations between independent sovereign states, had its origin in Westphalia, which made him the founding father of international law. This view on modern international law as a purely inter-state event evidently went hand in hand with the perception of the world society as a *Civitas Maxima*, or a 'society of sovereign states.'

The start of the modern era in both international law and politics is thus commonly dated around 1648, yet Reibstein has pointed out quite rightly that as far as international law is concerned this is the wrong conclusion:

> Die Frage nach dem Ursprung des modernen Völkerrechts ist falsch gestellt und kann nur einseitige, unbefriedigende Antworten finden, wenn man ein bestimmtes historisches Ereignis – und seien es so wichtige Ereignisse wie die Entdeckung Americas, die Reformation, die Veröffentlichung des Jus Belli ac Pacis oder der Westfälische Frieden – als Stichtag nimmt.[32]

A historiography of international law, which uses this method to date its "true" and "modern" origins, deprives it of a significant part of its conceptual heritage. Many international law concepts have their roots in the pre-Westphalian age of natural law and *jus gentium*. The development of state sovereignty into an absolute concept and the prime *rationale* of the international legal and political system have excluded other ideas (or interpretations) from the system. To relate the origin of modern international law to the specific historical event of 1648 is erroneous for two reasons. First, because it is based on a false perception of the European order of 1648 as an established order of 'modern' absolutely sovereign and independent states rather than on the understanding that the structures of the European political order were still changing and some of the Holy Roman imperial structures were still firmly in place. Secondly, because it rejects an important stream of thought as 'un-modern': the view of the world as a community of mankind based on natural law, the *communitas omnium gentium* or *Societas Humana* – a global human society. Until recently, the perpetual controversy over ILP had its origins in the discourse on the (desired) nature of the world society.

Precisely pinpointing the origin of modern international law is thus impossible, quite apart from being an exercise which is pregnant with ideology. The Westphalian Peace is used to mark the moment when the medieval *Respublica Christiana* was transformed into a society of sovereign states and when international law acquired its "true" identity after shaking off its natural law upbringing. A transformation may be symbolised by one specific historical event, but it can never be proclaimed its (only) cause, as this would restrict our understanding of history and oversimplify historic facts. Both the 1648 Peace Treaties and the fall

---

this particular instance of ILP was derived from that of the member states, i.e., its source was still statehood. Evidently, the Court's reasoning remained well within the classical framework.

[32] E. Reibstein, Völkerrecht: eine Geschichte seiner Ideen in Lehre und Praxis, Vol. I, 1957, at 363. Hereinafter: Reibstein Vol. I.

of the Berlin Wall in 1989 are frequently used to mark and define the beginning and the end of the modern age in international law. This is too strong a statement. In order to avoid oversimplification, I propose only to use these events as emblems of the respective transitions, not as their sole explanatory cause. Whether we have now indeed arrived in the age of the Post-Westphalian World Order remains open to debate, but that the world is undergoing a new transition is not, although the transition is not the prophesied instant leap from the Age of the Modern Nation State into the Age of Non-State Actors.

I am in full agreement with Reibstein on the impossibility of pinpointing the start of modern international law so precisely, but finding a starting point for the history of the idea of ILP seems less problematic. I propose to take the first appearance of the notion as the appropriate place to start. This takes us back to the final years of the 17th century, to one of the last remaining universal geniuses: G.W. Leibniz. Leibniz lived through the transformation of the medieval European society into the Europe of the modern state and tried to reconcile the old order with the new. He will make us realise that any realistic conceptual history of ILP should include its emergence in relation to a *relative* concept of sovereignty and the ideal of a universal human republic. Moreover, such a conceptual history should also include the Interbellum demystification of the state in response to its Hegelian glorification and the subsequent liberation of the individual. In short, the conceptual history of ILP should be considered less uniform than is currently thought or thought useful to remember. Our understanding of the conceptual history of ILP should reappropriate the heterogeneity which history has lent to the concept, because from this we may be able to shape new ideas or approaches to international life and the plane on which it takes place and the problems it has to tackle. What would be a reasonable horizon of expectation for the future, if any, of the traditional and fundamental concept of ILP?

Have we really come to the end of ILP? Or have we merely come to the end of a particular view of the concept of ILP? Even if the dismissive 'ILP will get us nowhere' is understandable against the background of an ever-changing international life and the messy participatory plurality of today, it is not necessarily correct as it is beyond doubt based on a specific perception of ILP, namely the Westphalian ILP dogma which stipulates that only states possess full ILP and that if other actors possess ILP it must be derived from the ILP of states. It is to be expected that the accepted view will be put to the test if the dynamics of the international community change.

At the end of this study, when we have traced the various historic meanings ascribed to the concept of ILP, we will indeed apply this test: what is the value of ILP at present? Alain Finkelkraut said: '*j'ai besoin des hommes anciens pour penser mon temps.*'[33] What can we learn from previous conceptions of ILP – what do they teach us about a possible or impossible role in and value to contem-

[33] A. Finkelkraut, La tolérance, notre dernier tyran?, The Pierre Bayle Lecture, 20 November, 1998.

porary and future international law? The concept of ILP either has value and a role to play or it is indeed rightly being ignored. In the end, the question as to its value will be related to the authority and justice of international law. The question will not so much be whether non-state actors may technically or justifiably claim ILP. Instead, the focus will primarily be on the concept of ILP as the legal concept that functions at the crossroads of the political, the moral and the legal; the concept as the hinge pin of the meta-legal and the legal realm.

In sum, there is ample reason to revisit the concept of ILP. We will thus first study the history of the concept in chapters 2, 3 and 4. Next, in chapter 5 we will as indicated deal with the (absence of) the concept of ILP in contemporary international law scholarship. The structure of the surveys in these chapters will follow from the methodology chosen, which I will address hereafter. Finally, while taking into account the historical findings, I will try to give my own views on the value of ILP to (the foundation of) international law, even today.

1.3. METHOD

1.3.1. **Introduction**

'*When you make sense of something, it tends to disappear. It is only mystery which keeps things alive ...*'[34] In order words, if something has a clear and well-defined meaning it loses its presence and its history can no longer be written... This is of course not a new idea. But is it what happened to the concept of ILP as it stands today? Without getting ahead of the conclusions, the question here is how to record the history of an idea that lacks a well-defined meaning. The objective I have set out, i.e., to uncover the historic meaning of the concept of ILP at certain specific moments in time, appears to be evidence of a certain faith in the act of interpretation and in the 'human subject'. Holding this faith is presently considered quite unfashionable among (a certain group of) academics and artists. Many have claimed that we have arrived in a place 'beyond the subject.' We are urged to accept that the idea of the (knowing) human subject is *passé*, as is the traditional author, whose demise we must also mourn, as the reader has replaced him in his capacity of the productive locus of meaning. Text apparently only emerges from inter-textuality and is not written by a composing mind, which intends to communicate something to his readers. Today, the 'dead author' does not care how his text is understood or interpreted; the reader may as well interpret it wildly or even contrary to the original ideas of the author. This perspective is frequently chosen in, *inter alia*, philosophy, the human sciences and the arts.[35] In the introduction to a book on the sculptor George Segal, we find the following striking comment:

---

[34] B. Okri, Astonishing the Gods 30 (1995).

[35] The post-modern claim that the human subject is a completely fictional character will be touched upon in chapter 5, 'ILP Today: The End of the Subject?'

In recent years, there has been much fashionable talk of the "death of the author", as if works of art came into being solely through a collision of circumstances rather than filtering through the mind, temperament and experience of individuals in response to the conditions in which they each find themselves.[36]

As my choice of quote suggests, I am not convinced that a work – whether it is a scholarly study or a sculpture – comes about 'solely through a collision of circumstances.' On the contrary, the sculptor is involved and makes a difference, he communicates. The image of the sculptor is not only appropriate, it is also a traditional metaphor for dealing with the relationship between the scholar, and even the scientist, and his work.

The sculptor reveals something meaningful that lies hidden in a piece of marble; hidden, yet already there. Just as the sculptor lays bare the hidden figure, the scholar discovers and exposes the concealed, but meaningful narrative. In the first four lines of one of his sonnets, Michelangelo expressed his view on sculpting. Reason or nature has defined the shape of the figure that is to be carefully freed from the marble and the sculptor's mind already knows the concept hidden within: 'No block of marble but it does not hide / The concept living in the artist's mind- / Pursuing it inside that form, he'll guide / His hand to shape what reason has defined.'[37] Scholars are faced with enormous amounts of information: social, historical, philosophical, legal, and so on and so forth. It is the raw material, which needs to be shaped. Like the sculptor, who in the words of Henry Moore, 'ha[s] to wait until an idea came that fitted the shape of the stone and that was seen, the idea, in that block,'[38] a scholar has to slowly discover the narrative inside the raw material at hand. The scholarly enterprise is an active one, it consists of researching the material by paying attention to its structure and cohesion: cellular or dense, pure or diluted, with strong lines or (recurrent) patterns, cut in various places while left untouched in others.[39] Research determines where to

[36] M. Livingstone, Retrospective George Segal 17 (1997).

[37] Michelangelo Buonarroti, *Non ha l'ottimo artista alcun concetto*, First four lines from a poem to Vittoria Colonna, *in* G. Bull (Ed.) Michelangelo, Life, Letters, and Poetry 153 (1987).

[38] J. Bronowski, The Ascent of Man 115 (1980). (1st ed., 1973.) Quotation of a reflection by Henry Moore: 'To begin with, as a young sculptor, I could not afford expensive stone, and I got my stone by going round the stone-yards and finding what they would call a "random block." Then I had to think in the same way that Michelangelo might have done, so that one had to wait until an idea came that fitted the shape of the stone and that was seen, the idea, in that block.' Hereinafter: The Ascent of Man.

[39] In defining the line between jurisprudence and socio-psychology as well as the two different methodologies needed to investigate these two fields (of *Sollen* and *Sein*), Kelsen stated: 'die Methode in der Wissenschaft [ist] so etwas ... wie die Technik in der Kunst ...' and although he admitted that 'es [sind] auch nicht die schlechtesten Künstler ..., die von ihrer Technik keine Ahnung haben,' in his view, the right methodology did matter. But he wondered 'vielleicht ist das Verhältnis zwischen Weg und Ziel wissenschaftlicher Forschung geradezu ein umgekehrtes, indem es nicht der Weg ist, der zum Ziele führt, sondern das Ziel, das sich irgendeinen Weg bahnt. Vielleicht gilt auch hier Hamerlings tiefes Wort, das der ihren verlorenen Eros suchenden, nach Weg und Steg fragenden Psyche entgegentönt: Was dich führt zum Gotte ist der Weg nicht, ist das Wandern!' H. Kelsen, Über Grenzen zwischen juristischer und soziologischer Methode, Vortrag gehalten in der Soziologischen Gesellschaft zu Wien 1-2 (1911).

split, cut or polish. The sculptor-scholar will attempt to reveal the story enclosed within the information, unravel the structure, show the interaction and establish a reasonable, convincing argument.

However, what is revealed is also a personal history, as not only the texture of the marble but also the imagination of the sculptor influences the result. He who studies something by his action influences the outcome of this study.[40] The metaphor thus equally expresses the second aspect of the academic and scientific enterprise: every sculptor-scholar will undoubtedly reveal a statue that is *different* to some extent from that of other sculptor-scholars, even if they had the same materials to work with. Bronowski elaborated on this metaphor in connection with physics:

[T]he metaphor tells the truth about the relation of discovery that exists between man and nature; and it is characteristic that philosophers of science (Leibniz in particular) have turned to the same metaphor of the mind prompted by a vein in the marble. In one sense, everything we discover is already there: a sculptured figure and the law of nature are both concealed in the raw material. And in another sense, what a man discovers is discovered *by him*; it would not take exactly the same form in the hands of someone else – neither sculpted figure nor the law of nature would come out in identical copies when produced by two different minds in two different ages. Discovery is a double relation of analysis and synthesis together. As an analysis, it probes for what is there; but then, as a synthesis, it puts the parts together in a form by which the creative mind transcends the bare limits, the bare skeleton, that nature provides.[41]

The metaphor of the sculptor expresses the duality of the relationship between the scholar and his object of study. Over the past few decades, we have come to accept this duality. Our quest for understanding will never bring us absolute and perfect knowledge, however, it is not completely arbitrary either: what we find is relatively or tolerably objective.[42] I am of course well aware that the metaphor is

[40] This view, on the relationship of discovery that exists between man and nature, is at first glance rather remote from this legal study, yet the discovery of early 20th century quantum-mechanics had a tremendous influence on the 20th century perception of knowledge which made itself felt far beyond the realm of physics. The electron riddle consists of the apparently irreconcilable aspects of the electron as both a particle and a wave. When perceived as a wave, the electron appears to be/act like a wave. However, when perceived as a particle, it behaves as a particle would. Are we able to distinguish reality from perception? Knowledge of the world appears to be merely an *interpretation* of the world. This became known as the Principle of Uncertainty, which had a great epistemological impact quite beyond the natural sciences and can be found in rather extreme as well as lay versions which all claimed that objective knowledge or absolute certainty was impossible. For more details concerning its undeniable impact during the 1960s, see Cosmopolis, at 139-174.

[41] The Ascent of Man, at 115.

[42] Together with Bronowski, we may need to realise that: 'what physics has done is to show that that [the method of the artist] is the only method to knowledge. There is no absolute knowledge. And those who claim it, whether they are scientists or dogmatists, open the door to tragedy. All information is imperfect. We have to treat it with humility. That is the *human condition*; and that is what quantum physics says. I mean that literally.' Id., at 353. Emphasis added. Realising that all information is imperfect, however, should neither keep us from conducting research, nor plunge us

mostly used to describe the relationship of discovery that exists between man and nature and I certainly do not intend to argue that the methodology of the natural sciences should be applied to social sciences as well. Yet, the sculptor metaphor suits the hermeneutic enterprise surprisingly well and is indeed quite instructive as far as the present study is concerned. The historical narrative of ILP is already "there" – buried inside the raw research material – and needs only to be revealed, although the account of the history of ILP which I propose to give will be 'tolerably', but never 'exactly' alike to the narrative of others who might be exploring the subject.[43] I reject the scepticism voiced by some concerning the very possibility of (historical) knowledge, but I do not presume to lay claim to giving the one and only account of the concept of ILP. Still, the narrative offered is intended to convince, both in method and in substance, and both rhetorically and logically. The relative or tolerable objectivity of the product lies in the fact that it is based on pre-existing material and on a verifiable process of interpretation. Much depends on the method, i.e., on how the process of interpretation is performed, to prevent an arbitrary outcome.

For the appropriate methodology, we turn to the history of ideas. Scholarship in the history of ideas aims to create understanding of past human philosophies by imaginatively analysing the available or retrievable knowledge and uncovering the historic meaning of ideas. Law is a more or less coherent set of ideas. ILP is one of these ideas: it is not a thing (nor does it refer to one), but a product of contemplation and language.[44] Words and concepts do not have eternally fixed meanings. Their meaning is determined by how they are used. Law is a social phenomenon, legal thought stems from the fact that we are social creatures. Man lives within society and this requires social interaction. Ideas are thus conceived in response to social and political life and in (intellectual) discussion on these subjects. Legal theory is inscribed with ideas about this socio-political context. A scholar in the field of international legal theory expounds his arguments while confronting the socio-political and legal reality that surrounds him – a reality made up of both domestic and international life and formed by the controversies

---

into unjustified scepticism. The Principle of Uncertainty or Tolerance also comprehends the idea that despite the fact that the world is never '*exactly*' the same we may still recognise the objects in it because they are '*tolerably*' alike. 'In the act of recognition a judgement is built in – an area of tolerance or uncertainty.' Therefore, even if nothing can be described with certainty, the resulting uncertainty is not absolute either. The act of recognition provides us with an instrument of judgement, which enables us to gain understanding. Id., at 365. Emphasis added.

[43] *Supra*, footnote 42. Collingwood argued that historical knowledge is indeed possible by the 're-enactment of past thought,' i.e., understanding by re-enacting past thinking, and stated: 'Everyone brings his own mind to the study of history, and approaches it from the point of view which is characteristic of himself and his generation. ... [T]his does not reduce history to something arbitrary or capricious. It remains genuine knowledge.' As cited in the Editor's Introduction to The Idea of History, J. van der Dussen (Ed.), at xii.

[44] The expression ILP does not refer to an actual thing – no factual or material entity can be designated as its bearer. ILP belongs to what Wittgenstein termed the '*large* class of cases' for which it is true that the meaning of the notion is its use in the language, *in casu* the language of international legal scholarship. L. Wittgenstein, Philosophical Investigations (1953), section 43.

discussed in the jurisprudence of his time. Consequently, since developments in both the socio-political and the jurisprudential context affect the theoretical arguments concerning the concept of ILP, these contexts have to be included in the methodological approach. If we were to ignore the context, we would almost certainly misunderstand the concept. As we are concerned with an inquiry into legal *thinking* and in order to avoid arbitrariness, we will therefore use the methodology of Quentin Skinner for the purpose of this study. His approach to the history of ideas basically consists of the *contextualisation* of the historic texts in question. It is my intention to contribute to a *contextual* reappraisal of the history of international legal scholarship on ILP, while guarding against the danger of over-simplification or what Collingwood has called 'scissor-and-paste history.'[45]

1.3.2. **A contextual approach**

'*A theory in its day helps to solve the problems of the day.*'[46] If law is studied within its unique context, legal theory should also be studied this way. Let me first cite three experts from our tradition who seem to support this view. In *Lloyd's Introduction to Jurisprudence*, it is stated that 'law ... reflect[s] the ideologies of its place and time, ... the close relation of law to the social structure inevitably brings into prominence the ideological context of legal theory.'[47] Wolfgang Friedmann in his book *Legal Theory* also explained that 'legal theory reflects the political beliefs of a particular society, and translates them into legal propositions and problems.'[48] In his view, legal theory will always to some extent be intertwined with both philosophy and political ideology: 'all legal theory must contain elements of philosophy – man's reflections on his position in the universe – and gain its colour and specific content from political theory – the ideas entertained on the best form of society. For all thinking about the end of law is based on conceptions of man both as a thinking individual and as a political being.'[49] Indeed, although a very difficult concept to grasp, human nature plays an important, albeit mostly implicit, role in legal theoretical reasoning, even within international law. Finally, the historian of international law, Reibstein, has also stressed the importance of the *Umstände* – the context – in his study of the emergence of modern international law. According to Reibstein, there has not

[45] By 'scissors-and-paste history,' Collingwood meant the kind of history which is 'constructed by excerpting and combining the testimonies of different authorities.' The Idea of History, at 257. This is the kind of evidence I have tried hard to avoid. It has not been my objective to cut excerpts from statements on ILP from the canonical dialogue and paste them into international law, but rather to get a sense of its use in four different periods by describing the views of a few chosen scholars and placing them within a broader context than the strictly legal one which we are usually presented with when the theory of international law is addressed.

[46] The Ascent of Man, at 140.

[47] M.D.A. Freeman (Ed.), Lloyd's Introduction to Jurisprudence 2 (6th ed., 1994). Footnotes omitted.

[48] W. Friedmann, Legal Theory 420 (2nd Impression Revised, 1947).

[49] W. Friedmann, Legal Theory 3 (5th ed., 1967).

been one specific historical event (*Umweltselement*) that can be called the origin of this development and which would therefore merit exclusive attention. Instead, any study of the origins of a particular development should include contextual elements, such as the political and cultural movements which were influential at the time as well as the concrete historical problems and circumstances.[50] In other words, by its very *nature* we cannot write the history of legal conceptual thinking without placing the historic texts in the broader context that informed them. Since it is the purpose of this inquiry to generate understanding of a number of written statements on the concept of ILP, I will study these pieces of international law scholarship *in context*. Consequently, this history of ILP is not a traditional history of an isolated continuous canonical exchange of positions throughout the ages, but a history of ILP composed of four episodes in conformity with the idea that:

> The history of thought should be viewed not as a series of attempts to answer a canonical set of questions, but as a *sequence of episodes* in which the questions as well as the answers have frequently changed.[51]

The *questions* also *change*: contextual factors interfere with the contemplation of the law and influence the scholarly agenda concerning which problems and questions to confront. Awareness of this circumstance is an important fundamental attitude to adopt when one starts to write the history of a legal concept. This assumption, however, does not mean that we should consider these episodes as systems (both social systems and systems of thought) that are completely closed or that we should deny the existence of intellectual links between the ages; after all, concepts evolve through time. Yet, the emphasis is not on continuity, but rather on approaching legal arguments as contemporary positions. This view of the history of (legal) thought as a 'sequence of episodes' and of the intellectual (legal) debate as a sequence of contemporary debates springs from the perception that every age has its own issues and struggles, which determine the use of words and concepts. The meaning of a concept changes over time and depends on the episode and the (linguistic and practical) context in which it is used. By taking a contextual approach to the present inquiry, we aim to bring about a better understanding of the various conceptions surrounding ILP.[52] Skinner's methodology tells us how we should responsibly perform such an inquiry into the historic meaning of a text.

A responsible interpretation of historic arguments requires an analysis that situates the argument within the contemporary contexts – contextualisation – as

[50] Reibstein, Vol. I, at 363.

[51] Id., at 234. Emphasis added.

[52] Skinner: 'To discover from the history of thought that there are in fact no such timeless concepts, but only the various different societies, is to discover a general truth not merely about the past but about ourselves as well.' Meaning and Understanding, at 67.

each historic text is 'an intended act of communication'[53] on things which lie outside the text itself. When trying to grasp the meaning of an historic text, we must respect these intentions, just as we expect in our everyday lives to encounter respect for what we actually intend to communicate when we engage in the act of speech. Much has been written on the concept of meaning, but this is not the place to enter this discussion or to address the vast amount of literature on the validity of interpretation. The choice to attach value to the scholar's original intentions when searching for the message in a text which he composed is not only a hermeneutic choice, but also a moral one. In interpreting a text, the interpreter constructs the text's meaning. As Hirsch has argued, with any such construction 'an interpreter, like any other person, falls under the basic moral imperative of speech, which is to respect an author's intentions. That is why, in ethical terms, original meaning is the "best meaning."'[54] Since Hirsch, many discussions have taken place on the original meaning as the best meaning and on how to find it, but the idea of showing a basic measure of respect for the author's intentions should still be put into practice whenever we try to understand a particular concept that is expressed in a scholarly text.

Having indicated the underlying reasons for taking a contextual approach – first, to avoid arbitrariness in seeking out the true meaning of an idea or a concept or the true nature of a legal theory and how it is bound up with the contemporary context and secondly, to ensure respect for the author's intentions – I will now elaborate on the procedure of Skinner's methodology and how it will be applied to the present study. To put it briefly, Skinner's methodology acknowledges that the circumstances in which a text was conceived should be included in the hermeneutic process of obtaining a responsible and valid interpretation. However, he does not derive from the wider context any *direct* explanatory *cause(s)*, but merely considers a certain amount of knowledge of this context a prerequisite for understanding the scholar's intentions. He recognises the relevance of context to the content of an argument and indicates how the context should be incorporated in any analysis of the argument which is later performed. This methodology is therefore not only useful in the field of social and political thought, but also constitutes a valuable method for analysing the meaning and context of international legal thinking in general[55] and the conceptual history of ILP in particular.

[53] Q. Skinner, Motives, intentions and the interpretation of texts, *in* J. Tully (Ed.), Meaning and Context 77 (1988). Hereinafter: Motives, intentions and the interpretation.

[54] E.D. Hirsch Jr, Three Dimensions of Hermeneutics, III (2) *New Literary History* 245-261, at 261 (1972): on the 'ethical' choice of 'original meaning' over 'anachronistic meaning' as the 'best meaning.' See also, Motives, intentions and the interpretation, at 68-78; Meaning and Understanding, at 55-67.

[55] On this point I agree with Cotterrell, who stated: 'Quentin Skinner's influential interpretive outlook on political theory has much relevance for an understanding of normative legal theory: "[legal] life sets the main problems for the [legal] theorist, causing a certain range of issues to appear problematic, and a corresponding range of questions to become the leading subjects of debate." This view does not entail that theoretical ideas are to be treated as "a straightforward outcome of their social base," but they are certainly to be read in terms of their wider intellectual context.' R.

In defining the purpose of this inquiry and in indicating the considerations as regards the appropriate method to write a history of ILP, the terms 'meaning' and 'historic meaning' have been used several times. It has even been mentioned in passing that the meaning of any concept is determined by the context in which it is used. This perspective has its origin in the philosophy of language, more in particular, in the ideas which were submitted by Wittgenstein and further developed by a great many philosophers of language, among whom J.L. Austin who we will shortly discuss. Skinner's understanding of language and meaning evidently lies at the heart of his views on how the history of ideas should be approached.

Wittgenstein established that 'the meaning of a word is its use in the language'.[56] In general, knowing the use of a word entails knowing its meaning. Words and expressions may continue to exist unchanged, but over time, they may also begin to obtain different meanings as they are used in different ways. A text or, generally, any act of speech (i.e., any act involving language) emerges within a specific context or, as Austin called it, a 'speech situation', which determines the purpose and meaning of the act.[57] Wittgenstein's adage, '*words are also deeds*',[58] was further refined when Austin distinguished two separate acts within the performance of one speech act.[59] Besides the actual speaking of words or writing down of sentences with a certain meaning and reference, i.e., the locutionary action, Austin also discerned the performance of an '"illocutionary act," i.e., the performance of an act *in* saying something as opposed to the performance of an act *of* saying something.'[60] He claimed that 'to perform a locutionary act is in general, ..., also and *eo ipso* to perform an *illocutionary* act ...To determine what illocutionary act is so performed we must determine in what way we are using the locution,' i.e., as a warning or a question, as advice, or to urge, protest, argue, etc. [61] Austin termed this idea concerning the different functions of language or the different ways in which language is used the 'doctrine of "illocutionary force."'[62] The illocutionary force or point of the speech situation is taken to be the determinant of its *meaning*. As words and concepts have no fixed or timeless essence, the quest for their meaning must necessarily aim for the

Cotterrell, The Politics of Jurisprudence, A Critical Introduction to Legal Philosophy 17, 14-20 (1989). Cotterrell quotes and describes statements made by Skinner himself.

[56] L. Wittgenstein, Philosophical Investigations, section 43, see also, section 30.

[57] J.L. Austin, How to do things with words 138 (1962). Hereinafter: How to do things with words.

[58] Wittgenstein in *Culture and Value* as cited by Tully as the motto of the book by J. Tully (Ed.) Meaning and Context: Quentin Skinner and his Critics x (1988).

[59] I leave aside here the third act which Austin distinguished, namely the perlocutionary act, i.e., what is *brought about by* the speech situation, e.g., persuasion, surprise, alarm or emotion on the part of the listener or reader.

[60] How to do things with words, at 99.

[61] Id., at 98.

[62] Id., at 99.

illocutionary point – what was the author *doing in* using these words? – i.e., the intention with which the speech act is performed. In order to be able to understand what the author was *doing in* writing, the author's intentions must be uncovered and these intentions can only be found through situating the particular linguistic action within its context.

Skinner's methodology, however, challenged the *orthodox contextual* approach. This approach, together with the *textual* analysis method, was, in his view, entirely inadequate.[63] The first because it oversimplified the relationship between context and meaning, the second because it completely denied the relevance of such a relationship.[64] The textual analysts are, however, right to the extent that they claim that language, for example, as a tool for expressing legal or political thought, is the vehicle for handing down through history 'a fairly stable vocabulary of characteristic concepts.'[65] At the same time, the textual method relies on the erroneous idea that words or concepts perennially keep the same meaning. Though obviously necessary for purposes of communication, a stable vocabulary is potentially dangerous when 'stability' is understood in the non-nominististical sense. Consequently, to avoid reading anachronistic explanations or (culturally) conditioned interpretations into an historic text, the study of the history of ideas must break free from what is termed the 'unconscious application of paradigms' (i.e., the constellations of absolute presuppositions which organise our thinking) in the study of ideas.[66] In order to escape from this hermeneutic

---

[63] Meaning and Understanding, at 30 *et seq.*; see also, Motives, Intentions and the interpretation of texts, at 69-78.

[64] Meaning and Understanding, at 29-63. The textual analysis considers a text 'the self-sufficient object of inquiry and understanding.' Id., at 30. The text is seen as the sole and autonomous key to understanding its meaning, it is completely intelligible within itself and without its context. Based on this assumption, it ignores the nature of language and misunderstands 'meaning.' The *orthodox contextual* approach, as Skinner argues, contains another misconception. In this view, a historical text should be interpreted and understood '*in terms* of its social context,' since the text has its direct origin in the social context. Id., at 58-59. This is also false: what caused a text to be written should not be equated with what was actually *done in* writing a statement. The relationship between text and context is much more complex. Writing a text is performing a linguistic act, knowledge of a text's context helps us to understand the act but the context does *not* by itself constitute the *causal* explanation for the act.

[65] The concept of the present inquiry may be considered such a characteristic or central concept of the language of international legal theory. See below.

[66] Meaning and Understanding, at 32, (text to) n. 17 and 18. Skinner demonstrates four types of consequences of the unconscious application of paradigms: the mythology of doctrines, which presupposes that every writer had available a complete doctrine on every possible issue, even when it was not explicitly discussed; the mythology of coherence, which is based on the assumption that a writer's thoughts should form one coherent system and that, if this system is difficult to discern, it should be constructed by means of abstracting his ideas as far as necessary for showing the "inner coherence;" the mythology of prolepsis, in which form of analysis the text is teleologically explained to the extreme – the future meaning is read in the historic text; and, finally, the mythology of parochialism, which causes oversimplification by misdescribing a text's reference (e.g., mistaken assumption of an author's intention to refer to another text and assume influence) or a text's meaning (misdescribing by means of misleading familiarity). Id., at 32-49.

trap, consisting of the preconditioned nature of our thinking and our expectations, a text should be firmly placed within its historic and intellectual context. However, this should not be done in the orthodox way, because this would erroneously equate 'knowledge of the causes of an action' with understanding the action itself. This would be a gross oversimplification. Skinner's alternative conceptualisation of the relationship between meaning and context does more justice to the complex nature of this relationship: to understand the meaning of a linguistic act and to avoid writing 'historical nonsense,'[67] Skinner places intentionality at the heart of his methodology.

With this concept of intentionality, we have returned to the illocutionary point of a speech act. Skinner makes an express distinction between the author's *motives* and his *intentions* and he uses the latter for his methodology.[68] The concept of intention is based on the Austinian analysis of a speech act. The intention of the author is formed by what he intended to *do in* writing a text: it is the illocutionary force within that text.[69] Knowledge of the author's intentions may thus assist in determining the meaning of a text. In Skinner's approach, therefore, it must be '*amongst* the interpreter's tasks ... [to] recove[r] ... the writer's intentions *in* writing what he writes.' In other words, what the author was doing in writing is an essential factor for interpreting the meaning of a text.[70] Therefore, when we examine the context of a particular linguistic act, it is not because we believe this will offer a direct causal explanation of it, but rather because it gives us 'an ultimate framework for helping to decide what conventionally recognizable meanings, in a society of *that* kind, it might in principle have been possible for someone to have intended to communicate.'[71] As the text is an intended act of communication which responds to its context – and which thus necessarily has a '*conventionally* recognizable meaning; otherwise it would be unintelligible – addressing the timely context of the text is essential for uncovering the author's intentions and the historic meaning of the text. Skinner provides two hermeneutic rules for revealing the author's intentions and finding a credible interpretation.

In the first place, we have to 'focus not just on the text to be interpreted, but also on the prevailing *conventions* governing the treatment of the issues or themes with which the text is concerned.'[72] In other words, we must situate the

---

[67] Id., at 50.

[68] An author's motive is 'a condition antecedent to, and contingently connected with, the appearance of his work.' As such, an author's motive stands outside his work, and is consequently irrelevant for determining the meaning of his work. Motives, Intentions and the interpretation of texts, at 73.

[69] Skinner points out that the author's own statements concerning his intentions may not be the final authority on the issue and that, moreover, 'it may sometimes be appropriate to discount his own statements about them. ... [as he] himself may have been self-deceiving about recognizing his intentions, or incompetent at stating them.' Id., at 77.

[70] Id., at 76.

[71] Meaning and Understanding, at 64.

[72] Motives, Intentions and the interpretation of texts, at 77. Emphasis added. See also, Q. Skinner, Some Problems in the Analysis of Political Thought and action, *in* J. Tully (Ed.) at 102-104. Hereinafter: Some Problems.

text within its *linguistic* or *ideological context* to which at the same time it is a response, and thereby 'survey'[73] what Tully has called 'the collection of texts written or used in the same period, addressed to the same or similar issues and sharing a number of conventions.'[74] Here, the ideological context refers to the language of politics or, for our purposes, law, which was in use at a certain time and place and is defined by these 'conventions,' which may be considered as the 'relevant linguistic commonplaces uniting a number of texts,' as Tully explained.[75] Without links to these conventions or commonplaces, a text would be incommunicable and unintelligible.[76] Authors respond to this linguistic context: they associate with and dissociate from these conventions. If they would not do this, they would simply be unable to communicate. Surveying the linguistic context is thus an essential step in understanding the conventions of the time in which a particular text or speech act is situated.

The second hermeneutic rule that Skinner provides, tells us to 'focus on the writer's mental world.'[77] If we want to understand the author's intentions, we have to understand the 'practical context'[78] to which he responded and about which he held opinions and beliefs. The particular political problems of his time and the relevant features of the society in which he lived help to understand in what way the linguistic act was a social or political act. Moreover, it is often attempted to influence reality by trying to change the perception of the act and make it something more or other than an act embedded in language. A linguistic act is thus considered to include a social or political act which either challenges or confirms the actual practice of contemporary national and/or international political life. We have to consider a historic text in relation to the appropriate 'practical' context in which the argument it contains was made in order to understand what is *done*. What is done could be, for example, providing legitimisation for certain practices, or conversely, challenging them. Certain terms may be used to either support or undermine social, political, moral or legal practices and when they are successful, they cease to be merely descriptive, but in addition obtain an 'evaluative dimension', which influences conventions and awareness.[79] These 'evaluative-descriptive terms' evidently play an important role in language as they are the *locus* of change: 'It is essentially by manipulating this set of terms that any society succeeds in establishing and altering its moral identity.'[80] To understand such manipulation one has to have some clue about the practical context in which these social and political acts are carried out. Finding the relevant pieces

[73] This requirement to 'survey' the linguistic context has caused this approach to be referred to also as a 'survey approach.' See, J. Tully, The Pen is a Mighty Sword, *in* J. Tully (Ed.), at 6.

[74] Id., at 9.

[75] Id. As examples Tully names: 'shared vocabulary, principles, assumptions, criteria for testing knowledge-claims, problems, conceptual distinctions and so on.'

[76] Some Problems, at 103.

[77] Motives, Intentions and the interpretation of texts, at 78.

[78] For Tully on the 'practical context,' see pages 10-12.

[79] Some Problems, at 110.

[80] Id., at 112.

of the jigsaw, i.e., the author's mental world, the intellectual climate of his time and the common beliefs of social and political life, is therefore an important part of the process of interpretation. Here, I would like to add that works of *art* can sometimes also be extremely useful, including for an inquiry such as this one, for shedding light on the broader context. 'Art does indeed register or picture, sometimes prophetically, the movement of the *Zeitgeist*. The way we grasp the world changes, and the artist knows first, like the animals whose behaviour foretells an earthquake.'[81] For example, the 15th and 16th-century woodcuts entitled 'The Emperor and the Pope,' which express what became known as the 'two swords theories,' are witness to the political situation at the time and depict the pope and the emperor who headed the Holy Roman Empire entangled in such a way as to create a complex and delicate balance by which some measure of stability and justice was secured. Further examples are Peter Paul Rubens' *The Consequences of War* (1638) and Max Ernst's *The Horde* (1927), which each in their own way express the reality of the crises that gripped Europe at these times.[82] Spender's poem *Vienna* (1934) and Auden's *The Age of Anxiety* (1948) also give evidence of the spirit of the times in which they were created, namely a spirit of passion and intensity. Due to these prophetic qualities, art as a form of human experience or knowledge can indeed serve as a well of knowledge and assist us in our efforts of interpretation and understanding.[83]

The present inquiry into (the history of) the concept of ILP is an inquiry into how ILP was *used* in (past) international legal scholarship. It will thus deal with a number of scholars who used the concept at various moments in time:

> [W]e should study not the meanings of the words, but their use. For the given idea cannot ultimately be said in this sense to *have* any meaning that can take the form of a set of words which can then be excogitated and traced out over time. Rather the meaning of the idea must *be* its uses to refer in various ways. ... [T]here *is* no determinate idea to which various writers contributed, but only a variety of statements made with the words by a va-

---

[81] I. Murdoch, Metaphysics as a Guide to Morals 4 (1992, Penquin ed. 1993). 'Art is informative and entertaining, it condenses and clarifies the world, directing attention upon particular things. This intense showing, this bearing of witness of which it is capable, is detested by tyrants who always persecute or demoralise their artists. Art illuminates accident and contingency and the general muddle of life, the limitations of time and the discursive intellect, so as to enable us to survey complex or horrible things which would other wise appal us. It creates an authoritative public human world, a treasury of past experience, it preserves the past.' Id., at 8.

[82] See, for reproduction of two woodcuts, e.g., A. Vagts, The Balance of Power: Growth of an Idea, 1(1) *World Politics* 90-91 (1948). P.P. Rubens, *The Consequences of War* (1638), Palazo Pitti, Florence, Italy; Max Ernst, *The Horde* (1927), Stedelijk Museum Amsterdam, The Netherlands.

[83] I do not intend to involve myself in the debate concerning the hermeneutics of art, as this goes far beyond the scope of this study. But I will say that I do not agree with Collingwood where he claims that art exists solely in the artist's mind, which means that in order to understand it we have to re-experience or re-create it. I rather concur with Gadamer's view that art exists as '*Wirkungsgeschichte*' – a sequence of interpretations – and that the experience of art is individual and subjective, that we experience art with our being rather than by methodical cognition. Be that as it may, here I intend to use art as 'historical evidence.'

riety of different agents with a variety of intentions, then what we are seeing is equally that there *is* no history to be written, but only a history necessarily focused on the various agents who used the idea, and on their varying situations and intentions in using it.[84]

1.3.3. Contextualisation of the concept of ILP

In order to fulfil our hermeneutic duties in this study of the concept of ILP, the following four chapters will be used to contextualise the scholarship of a number of international jurists. We will examine how ILP was used by these scholars in their writings and in the ideological and practical contexts of their time. In order to *understand* the concept of ILP, the question of 'what did/does ILP *mean*?' has been rephrased and now reads 'how is/has it been *used*?,' in other words: what was the scholar *doing in* making this statement about ILP? The core question we need to ask when we try to understand a historic statement concerning ILP will therefore be: What did the author of this particular text, writing at that particular point in time and for the specific audience he addresses, actually *intend* to communicate?[85]

Each chapter therefore first addresses the contemporary contexts so as to provide an insight into both the conventions of the international law scholarship of the time and the more general questions and conventions that were current and provided the background for this international law scholarship. What were the political, intellectual or legal problems and issues at stake in the period concerned? By relating scholarship to context, and thereby to what is conventional and what is *at stake*, we attempt to grasp the intention of the scholar, or the *point* of the scholar's argument on ILP. In other words, what were the scholar's intentions in using the concept of ILP in his writing? Was the particular scholar attacking a particular opinion or, conversely, justifying or even promoting one?

The following questions and many more like them will all either explicitly or implicitly be part of the analysis when we examine what a particular scholar was doing in writing on international law and on ILP in particular. What role did ILP play within the broader thinking (or, the mental world) of the particular scholar who used it? What was the concept's position within the scholarly debates of the particular period? Was ILP a subject of general interest or was it totally disregarded? Was there a receptive audience, vivid discussion, controversy, or mere silence maybe? To confront what kind of (international) political problems and which controversies in jurisprudence was the concept of ILP used? The separate examinations of each scholar's concept of ILP will all follow the same hermeneutic pattern.

This book does not contain the history of the canonical dialogue on ILP, but a history of its use during certain periods in time only. This means that the book covers four episodes in which a particular intellectual climate prevailed and in

[84] Meaning and Understanding, at 56.
[85] Id., at 63.

which specific practical political problems and social issues were at stake. These elements characterise the various contexts of the various schools of thought of each time. In each chapter dealing with a separate period, we will examine the then current views on ILP in relation to a central theme emerging from these contexts as well as from the international law scholarship at the time in question. All chapters start with an outline of the political and general intellectual context in place at the time in order to give us some idea of the socio-political acts that this context may have required or provoked. Subsequently, the conventional context will be surveyed, that is to say, a survey will be given of the collected jurisprudential writings addressing ILP so that in the next stage of the research we may understand where the scholar is linking up with the prevailing conventions and where he is manipulating their change.

The fundamental usefulness of the concept of ILP to international law language has long been beyond doubt, even if the concept's meaning has been controversial. Knubben has rightly pointed out that '*die Völkerrechtssubjekte das wesentlichste Merkmal zur Bestimmung des Völkerrechtsbegriffes bilden.*'[86] ILP has become a truly fundamental notion in defining international law. Because of this, it is likely that ILP is used as a descriptive-evaluative term. When used in a conventional descriptive way, ILP legitimises the prevailing opinions and practice, but if used in a more evaluative way, the concept may serve to provoke change, to de-legitimise the old and bring about new beliefs and practices. After all, any speech act also includes a socio-political or legal-political act. The discovery of the hidden act is an important part of our hermeneutic undertaking and requires at least some knowledge of the scholar's mindset as regards both international law and the broader socio-political reality. The chapters that follow will be structured along the lines of the hermeneutic procedure as it has been explained above.

The problem, purpose and method of this contextualisation exercise evidently also determine its scope. In order to avoid embarking on – in the words of Quentin Skinner – an 'absurdly ambitious enterprise,' this study is restricted to an examination of the notion of ILP as it was upheld by a total of ten different scholars in international law. The concept of ILP has been part of the language of ILP since 1693. It therefore makes sense to start there, with G.W. Leibniz, who used the concept first.

Our initial focus on Leibniz will give direction to the historical introduction of this study. Leibniz' first use of the notion of ILP in the late 17th century occurred at a time when Europe's political structure was still shifting from the medieval or pre-modern order to the modern or Westphalian order. Contrary to the general image often used, this transition did not end in 1648, as our research of Leibniz' conceptualisation of ILP will confirm. In any event, the historical introduction will discuss the emergence of the concept of ILP and invite us to review our prejudice that ILP is a concept totally intertwined with the modern or

[86] R. Knubben, Die Subjekte des Völkerrechts 1 (1928).

Westphalian concept of absolute sovereignty. The book next takes up the history of ILP in the early 20th century, albeit with the necessary references to 19th-century international legal theory which it so often challenged. This part exceeds the nature of a mere historical introduction. It is a study in itself which forces us to rethink some of our most readily used assumptions. It also places the particular emphasis on the emergence of the concept of ILP against the more general background of the scholarship which both preceded and followed this event. The objective is to change the current understanding that the concept of ILP is of purely "Westphalian" origin and to demonstrate that in reality ILP's roots lay in both legal idealism and political realism. In addition, the research shows that the 20th-century struggle between legal idealism and political realism continues to influence conceptual thinking on ILP today.

The historical introduction is not inconsistent from a methodological point of view. It simply follows the contextual approach, where the history of ILP unfolds in a 'sequence of episodes', rather than in 'an isolated continuous canonical exchange.' I hope this study will encourage others to fill the gaps.

Next, this study will go in search of alternatives to and for ILP, after which an evaluation is presented in the final chapter. The answer to the question 'Has ILP become obsolete?' should in my view be both 'Yes' and 'No.' The value of ILP for international law theory today and for international law theory in the future lies in its function of forming an essential link between the international legal system, democracy and the individual.

Chapter 2
HISTORICAL INTRODUCTION: LEIBNIZ AND THE EMERGENCE OF THE CONCEPT OF ILP

2.1. INTRODUCTION

The focus of this historical introduction is on Gottfried Wilhelm Leibniz (1646-1716). Evidently though, Leibniz's ideas are part of a long history which can be traced back to the theories advanced by Grotius and Hobbes, who preceded Leibniz on the subject of international relations and law and runs all the way up to the 18th-century aftermath of the concept's introduction when Leibniz influenced scholars like Wolff, Vattel and Kant. Here, however, Leibniz's thinking will be positioned horizontally rather than vertically and the 'episode' we will discuss is emphatically the emergence of ILP. In the next chapter we will deal with the 'de-mystifying' episode in the sequence of the concept's history.

Leibniz was the first writer to use the term 'international legal person'[1] – or rather '*persona jure gentium*' – and he included it in the *Praefatio* to his *Codex Iuris Gentium diplomaticus* (1693).[2] The fact that the term does not reappear in the *Praefatio* to a similar collection from 1700, i.e., the *Mantissa Codicis juris Gentium diplomatici*,[3] does not mean that Leibniz' first use of it was merely random. In the first edition of the *Codex Iuris Gentium diplomaticus*, it is already emphasised by the use of italic print. This *Codex* is a collection of over 200 historical public acts and treaties dating from 1096 to 1497 with which Leibniz aimed to assist scholars as well as practising diplomats and their sovereigns. He intended this work to 'serve the art of politics, that of history, that of erudition in general, but above all to [serve the] understand[ing of] the law of nations.'[4] Leibniz considered it particularly necessary to contribute to the clarification of the law of nations and its relation to natural law: 'the title *Codex Iuris Gentium* was adopted precisely because of this objective.' In his opinion, 'the notions of law and of justice, even after having been treated by so many illustrious authors,

---

[1] '[T]he scholar who ... was the first to use the technical term of "international person" ... was Leibniz' J.H.W. Verzijl, International Law in Historical Perspective, Volume II: International Persons (1969), at 2.

[2] G.W. Leibniz, Codex Juris Gentium diplomaticus, Hanover, 1693; here, I will use the transl. of P. Riley (Ed.), Leibniz Political Writing (1989), hereinafter: LPW, and refer to it as Codex.

[3] Letter to Wilhelm de Beyrie of April 7, 1693 (Hanover), *in* Acad. Ed., I, 9er Band, (N. 241), at 391: shows Leibniz' original intention to publish another two volumes in addition to the Codex. The *Mantissa*, however, was never followed by a third volume.

[4] Codex, at 170. At this stage in the development of the law of nations, the term 'nations' was used to translate *gentium*, which the French translated more accurately by *(droit des) gens*.

have not been made sufficiently clear.'[5] In the *Praefatio*, he explained his ideas on justice and the law of nations and thereby introduced the concept of ILP.

The *Codex Iuris Gentium diplomaticus* was published almost half a century after the Westphalian Peace of 1648, which is so often presented as the instant starting point of the "modern" European order of absolutely sovereign states, but which was actually a time when political structures were still largely in transition. On the one hand, the political structure of the Holy Roman Empire headed by the Emperor and Pope was still in place, although it was beginning to show signs of weakening. On the other hand, new actors, namely the German princes, who sought increased power and independence, wanted to be part of the European political order at the highest level. These circumstances put a strain on the political structures and challenged them to change. The reality of the changing structure of the European political order created the need for a theory that could make the accommodation of these new actors possible. In an attempt to facilitate the changes that seemed necessary, i.e., stretching the political order to include new actors yet preventing it from breaking down altogether, Leibniz developed a theory of the law of nature and nations or, as he preferred to call it, a *universal jurisprudence*, that was politically realistic and normative at the same time.

Leibniz' universal jurisprudence must be positioned in the natural law tradition. Since the 16th century, international jurisprudence had been gradually evolving from a branch of moral philosophy into an independent discipline. Spanish scholastic writers, like Francisco de Vitoria (1480-1546) and Francisco Suarez (1548-1617), were among the first to contribute to this evolution by their separate treatment of *ius gentium*. It took until 1661 for the first chair on 'The Law of Nature and of Nations' to be created at Heidelberg University, where Samuel Pufendorf (1632-1694) was the first to hold it. He was initially mainly assigned to teach and comment on Grotius' *De Jure Belli ac Pacis* (1625), the book that became a cornerstone for the 'emancipation'[6] of international law theory from scholastic theology and the identification of the law of nations. In a prelude to the analysis of Leibniz' use of ILP we inevitably encounter Hugo Grotius (1583-1645) and Thomas Hobbes (1588-1679). Leibniz managed to reconcile their opposing psychological assumptions by incorporating both the altruism described in Grotius' work and the egoism alleged by Hobbes into the idea that it is in one's own interests to take account of and possibly even serve the interests of others. We will find that this is indeed a fundamental and leading element of his universal jurisprudence. Theological-political and practical-political influences have been crucial to the formulation of Leibniz' thinking in general and to the coining of the concept of ILP in particular. As such, they are essential building blocks of our analysis here. In other words, in order to understand the historical meaning of

[5] Id.; see also, Leibniz' letter to Abbé Jean-Paul Bignon of October 1693: 'Je n'ay rien de commun avec le celebre Grotius, que la qualité d'estranger, et peut estre la volonté de contribuer encor quelque chose à l'eclaircissement du droit des gens comme j'ay fait par l'essay d'un Code diplomatique d'Actes publics...' Acad. Ed., I, 9er Band, (N. 396), at 590.

[6] A Concise History, at 105-106.

the concept of ILP as used in the *Praefatio*, the concept is placed within the contemporary context rather than within the centuries-long tradition of natural law theory. I must therefore analyse how the particular arguments made in this text fit in with the broader context of Leibniz' moral and political ideas and the political reality in Europe and the Holy Roman Empire. We will find that his concept of justice animated his views on politics and that his professional involvement in the political game substantially influenced his opinion on the *ius gentium*.

I intend to demonstrate that Leibniz' introduction of the notion of ILP resulted from an original attempt to preserve the universal (medieval) structures propagated by the Pope and Emperor while accommodating the emergence and inclusion of new participants in the diplomatic community and on the European stage. We will see how ILP's introduction related to Leibniz' attempt to restore stability and to prevent the outbreak of another European war as well as to his longing for mutual understanding and harmonious relations. For this purpose, I will briefly outline the political, intellectual and jurisprudential context that Leibniz worked in. Subsequently, the coining of the concept of ILP will be assessed in the light of the issues at stake at the time. It will be established that the introduction of the concept of ILP was a timely event originating in the need to reconcile moral idealism and European political reality and intended to legitimise the participation of the free German Princes on the international stage. This chapter will be concluded by taking a brief look at the 18th-century aftermath of the introduction of ILP.

2.2. The Post-1648 European Context[7]

2.2.1. **Restoration of communication and political modernisation in Europe**

The first half of the 17th century was not a time of localised skirmishes, but of widespread war and 'general crisis.' Social and economic conditions during this period were critical and highly uncertain.[8] The plague and other epidemic diseases struck frequently and agricultural decline and years of drought caused a

---

[7] For the general characterisation I am greatly indebted to Toulmin's analysis in Cosmopolis, in particular, at 45-137. *Op .cit.*, chapter 1, footnote 14.

[8] Cosmopolis, at 17. Also, N. Davies, Europe: A History 569 (1997), hereinafter: Europe: A History. See, more thoroughly on this subject, e.g., E.J. Hobsbawm, The Crisis of the Seventeenth Century, *in* T. Aston (Ed.), Crisis in Europe (1560-1660): Essays from *Past and Present* 5 (1965), on the general crisis in the European economy; see also, G. Parker, Europe in Crisis 1598-1648 (1979); Parker, N.G. and Smith, L.M. (Eds.), The General Crisis of the Seventeenth Century (1978), at 6: the crisis consists of 'two contemporaneous but separate phenomena: one, a series of individual political confrontations, some of which developed into revolutions; the other, a truly "general crisis" in the demographic and economic development of the world.' See, on social revolts also after 1648, Hobsbawm, at 12. See also, G. Pagès, who regarded the War as a 'turning point between medieval and modern times.' He perceived this War as part of a 'larger crisis' consisting of the process of change from medieval to modern times. *In* Rabb (Ed.), The Thirty Years' War 33 (1972, 2nd ed.).

food shortage that lasted for decades; population growth slowed down significantly and some populations even declined.[9] Europe increasingly slipped into a climate of religious intolerance resulting in the religious wars, the worst of which was the Thirty Years' War.[10] From 1618 onwards, war did not only shake what is now Germany but the whole of Europe to its foundations. The (medieval) Holy Roman Empire was in crisis and even though it managed to persist in name until 1806,[11] it was actually fragmenting into a new Europe of gradually ever more independent states during the 17th century. Since the war's heritage was one of ruin, the second half of the 17th century was characterised by a struggle for reconstruction, both politically and intellectually, and a search for social stability, renewed social solidarity and a precarious balance between (enforced) religious conformity and tolerance. The end of the Thirty Years' War marked the end of the general crises of the 17th century and indeed heralded the onset of a process leading to new equilibrium in Europe. After 1648, the European powers found a new *modus vivendi*.

The 1648 Peace Treaties of Münster and Osnabrück had to bring an end to the "religious" Thirty Years' War and prevent religion from ever becoming the international source of conflict again. The 1648 Treaties reaffirmed the principle *cuius regio, elius religio*, which had already been agreed upon in 1555 in the Treaty of Augsburg. It was determined that religion was an internal issue, outside the scope of the international realm. The Catholic and Protestant princes and towns had to live side by side within the Empire.[12]

The Westphalian Peace Treaties, traditionally identified as the beginning of the 'new' order, actually neither caused nor terminated but rather confirmed the process of political transformation which also continued after 1648. Lately, the Westphalian Treaties have been mostly referred to as the origin of the "modern," i.e., inter-state, political and legal order in Europe. Indeed, the Treaties acknowl-

---

[9] J. de Vries, Economy of Europe in an Age of Crisis (1600-1750), at 4-13 (1976). During the Thirty Years' War, 35 percent of the German population was killed. By contrast, the populations of both England and the Dutch Republic kept growing substantially until the 1660s. Id., at 5. See also, Parker, *op. cit.*, at 17-28.

[10] It is often argued that the Thirty Years' War should be considered a religious war, as otherwise its occurrence is simply incomprehensible. C.J. Friedrich, The Age of the Baroque 1610-1660 (1952), reprinted *in* Rabb (Ed.), at 53-57.

[11] See also, on the crisis within the Empire, Pagès, at 34-38. Pagès mentions why in Germany, 'modern Europe managed to establish itself only at the price of thirty years of war.' He states: 'One cannot understand the Germany of that period if one forgets that survivals from the middle ages lasted longer there than anywhere else and also that this country was in the middle of a Europe much further advanced than itself.' Rabb (Ed.), at 33. During Leibniz' professional life, the Habsburg dynasty reigned: Leopold I (*reg.* 1658-1705), Joseph I (*reg.* 1705-11) and Charles VI (*reg.* 1711-40) succeeded each other as Holy Roman Emperor. At the same time, moreover, the spiritual monarchs occupying the Holy See were Pope Innocent X (*reg.* 1644-55), Alexander VII (*reg.* 1655-67), Clement IX (*reg.* 1667-69), Clement X (*reg.* 1670-76), Innocent XI (*reg.* 1676-89), Alexander VIII (*reg.* 1689-91), Innocent XII (*reg.* 1691-1700) and Clement XI (*reg.* 1700-21).

[12] Article V, Friedensvertrag des Kaisers mit Schweden/ Osnabrück, *in* W.G. Grewe (Ed.), Fontes Historiae Iuris Gentium: Sources Relating to the History of the Law of Nations, Vol. 2 (1988), at 193.

edged and consolidated the process of the fragmentation of Christendom as well as of the formation of states in Europe. As such, they formed the trusted foundation for the emerging new European order, which had to prevent a repetition of chaotic times and bloody conflicts and was meant to establish stability.[13] However, one should not pass over that this is true mainly because the Treaties of 24 October 1648, dealt with the 'internal' imperial problems and conflicts between the Emperor and the *Reichstände* (Estates)[14] and with those among the (religiously opposed) *Reichstände* themselves. As such, it laid down a new constitutional basis for the Holy Roman Empire.[15] Article VIII(1) of the Peace of Osnabrück, which determined the constitutional position of the *Reichstände*, re-established the *Reichstände* in their old rights.[16] Article VIII(2) recognised the international capacity or sovereignty of the *Reichstände* where it stipulated that 'above all, each of the Estates of the Empire shall freely and for ever enjoy the Right of making Alliances among themselves, or with Foreigners, for the Preservation and Security of every one of them.' However, the article continues, 'provided nevertheless that these Alliances be neither against the Emperor nor the Empire, nor the public Peace, nor against this Transaction especially; and that they be made without prejudice in every respect to the Oath whereby every one of them is bound to the Emperor and the Empire.'[17] The right of making alliances and the right of warfare were thus not without limits. However, the sovereignty of the Emperor was further constrained by the necessary cooperation and consent of the Diet or *Reichstag* in the creation of law on a number of significant issues.[18] The constitutional controversy over the relationship between the Em-

---

[13] Westphalia was an attempt to once and for all settle all Europe's outstanding issues, Rabb: 'whatever the reality, the people of the seventeenth century believed that that was what had been accomplished. It was now assumed that a new, permanent, settled situation had been established, and for more than a century all further treaties, however extensive, were regarded merely as a rounding out of what had been laid down at Westphalia.' Rabb, Introduction to *The Thirty Years' War*, at xvii.

[14] After 1648, the three *Reichstände* are represented in the *Reichstag*, which consists of: (1) the *Kurfürstenrat*, i.e., the college of Imperial Electors; the rank of Elector conferred upon those bearing the title, the right to vote in case of Imperial succession and co-determine who should be elevated to the rank of new Emperor; (2) the *Fürstenrat*, i.e., the college of princes, and (3) the *Städtetag*, i.e., the conference of the free Cities and Towns. For the inclusion of the *'freien Reichstädte'* as among the *Reichstände*: see, Art. V(29) of the *Peace Treaty between the Emperor and Sweden/Osnabrück, in* W.G. Grewe (Ed.), Fontes Historiae Iuris Gentium: Sources Relating to the History of the Law of Nations, Vol. 2 (1988), at 194).

[15] Id., at 199-200: Art. XVII stipulated that the Peace treaty would serve as a perpetual law of the Empire.

[16] Art. VIII(1): 'And in order to prevent for the future all Differences in the Political State, all and every the Electors, Princes, and States of the *Roman* Empire shall be so establish'd and confirm'd in their antient Rights, Prerogatives, Liberties, Privileges, free Exercise of their Territorial Right, as well in Spirituals and Temporals, Seigeuries, Regalian Rights, and in the possession of all these things, by virtue of the present Transaction, that they may not be molested at any time in any manner, under any pretext whatsoever.' Id., at 197.

[17] Id.

[18] Id. First part of Art. VIII(2) reads: 'That they enjoy without contradiction the Right of Suffrage in all Deliberations touching the Affairs of the Empire, especially in the matter of interpreting

peror and the Empire was thus stifled by a formal distribution of power.[19] Any claim to absolute sovereignty by the Emperor was from now on much more difficult to sustain legally. The ambivalence of the political situation is visible in the position and nature of the *Reichstag*. The *Reichstag* resided permanently in Regensburg from 1663 onwards. On the one hand this permanency contributed to the further consolidation of this institution as a kind of parliament in the constitutional order, i.e., as the representative body of the *Reichsstände*. On the other hand however this permanency also resulted in a loss of flexibility and pace which are unavoidable disadvantages of *Gesandtenkongresses*.[20] Its slow pace was indeed also due to the many conflicts over ceremonial issues.

The popular historiographical narrative of modern international law, which dates back to 1648 when the European order of modern sovereign states came into being and the Treaties put an end to the 'statehood' of the Holy Roman Empire, is thus severely undermined if we take the 'internal' imperial political reality into account.[21] In fact, the struggle for sovereignty had not yet been resolved, the dualism between the Emperor and the Princes continued to dominate imperial (and thus European) politics during the decades that followed. The interpretation of the Peace of Westphalia as guaranteeing the Empire's fall may well be coloured by hindsight.

If the 1648 Treaties were to stand a fair chance of establishing 'a Christian and Universal Peace, and a perpetual, true, and sincere Amity'[22] between all the former enemies, a climate of tolerance and mutual respect and at the very least of open (diplomatic and inter-religious) communication would be essential. Only open communication would lead the way out of the quagmire of theological disputes and political conflicts. Since the beginning of the 15th century, diplomatic communication had become increasingly important and permanent missions had

---

Laws, resolving upon a War, imposing Taxes, ordering Levies and quartering of Soldiers, building for the public Use new Fortresses in the Lands of the States, and reinforcing old Garrisons, making of Peace and Alliances, and treating of other such-like Affairs; so that none of those or the like things shall be done or receiv'd afterwards, without the Advice and Consent of a free Assembly [i.e., the Diet or *Reichstag*] of all the Estates of the Empire...' Article VIII(4) provided the Free Towns of the Empire with the right to political representation in the *Reichstag* and the right to vote. Id., at 198.

[19] See also, M. Stolleis, Geschichte des öffentlichen Rechts in Deutschland, Vol. 1 Reichspublizistik und Policeywissenschaft 1600-1800 (1988), at 225-226. Hereinafter: Geschichte des öffentlichen Rechts.

[20] Id., at 227 and 229.

[21] See also, id., at 228: 'Die völkerrechtlich inspirierte These, das Reich sei 1648 als «Staat» untergegangen und habe als Verein souveräner Staaten forexistiert, ist weitgehend als unhistorisch abgelehnt worden. Die Zeitgenossen, an denen sich des Historiker zu orientieren hat, waren sich über die Forexistenz des Reichs als «Staat» einig, so mängelbehaftet dieser auch sein mochte; sie haben «die Möglichkeit der völkerrechtlichen Beurteilung des Reiches meist nicht einmal erwogen».' Footnotes omitted.

[22] Article I, Peace Treaty between the Emperor and France/ Munster, *in* W.G. Grewe (Ed.), Fontes Historiae Iuris Gentium: Sources Relating to the History of the Law of Nations, Vol. 2 (1988), at 184; see also, Peace Treaty between the Emperor and Sweden/Osnabrück, id., at 189-190.

gradually been established. By the time of the Westphalian peace talks, diplomatic practice had developed from a temporary missionary approach into a system of more permanent postings. The religious division among European princes and monarchs caused diplomatic immunity to be a pure necessity: embassies and diplomats had to be protected regularly against religious riots in protest of their confessional denomination. But the timely significance of *Gesandtschaftsrecht* goes further than that. The European princes and monarchs, who wished visibly to express their prestige and autonomy, considered their ability to dispatch permanent ambassadors as proof of these attainments. As such, the changing European diplomatic life reflected the process of political modernisation and of its needs and problems. The controversy with regard to the status of the Dutch delegates – whether they were permitted to use the title of 'Excellency' – during the peace negotiations in Westphalia is a point in case. The permission to use the title would 'have been an expression of the sovereign status of their country.'[23] In other words, the diplomatic ceremonial controversies were indicative of a changing political order in which new actors claimed sovereignty. Nonetheless, it was still too early to speak of an inter-state order. Moreover, the transitory nature of international relations was clearly reflected by the fact that the sovereigns who concluded the treaties did so in their '*personal* capacity,'[24] and the treaty obligations they took upon themselves were assumed as personal obligations.[25]

In brief, the post-1648 European and imperial political structures, which were based on the Westphalian Treaties, continued to develop. The dual nature of the Treaties made the internal politics of the Empire susceptible to external influences. The inclusion of France (Treaty of Munster) and Sweden (Treaty of Osnabrück) in imperial politics was intended to prevent the Emperor from expanding his power and claiming absolute sovereignty. Thereby, the fragmentation of sovereignty in the Empire was preserved and diplomatic controversy was consequently guaranteed.

Leibniz was born in Leipzig on 21 June 1646, two years before the conclusion of the Westphalian Peace. In 1668, after concluding his studies in, among other things, philosophy, mathematics and law in Leipzig and Jena, Leibniz started his

---

[23] The Epochs, at 185. Grewe reports that the French and the Spanish – after initially denying the Dutch delegates' right to the title – later accepted its conditional use, after the Emperor had given the Dutch his permission on the condition that they reached a peace agreement with Spain, which they did on 30 January 1648.

[24] Id., at 196, and at 361: '[Only] [i]n the course of the eighteenth century, treaties gradually ceased to be considered as personal obligations of the sovereign. This was the case even though, as before, it was the monarchs themselves who appeared as the contracting parties. However, the monarchs began to be listed – in the text of a treaty and in its preamble – not by their names, but only by their most important titles. By this practice it was expressed, significantly, that the contracting parties did not only engage themselves personally, but also the State which they represented and embodied.'

[25] See also, J. Ray, La Communauté Internationale d'après les Traités du XVIe Siècle à nos Jours, 3 *Annales Sociologiques*, Ser. C, (1938), at 18-20.

almost 50-year-long career in governmental service at the Court of one of the most powerful rulers of the Empire, Prince-Bishop Johann Philipp von Schönborn, the Elector of Mainz. He left for Paris in 1672 and lived and studied there until 1676. In 1677, Leibniz resumed public service at the Court of the Duke of Brunswick-Lüneburg in Hanover – at the centre of the Empire – where he worked in various capacities for 40 years. The Duke was one of the prominent princes of the Empire (*Reichsfürsten*), although he was not a *Kurfürst* like Leibniz' former employer. The Duke's power was territorially based, rather than exclusively determined by old feudal rights. The ambitions of the *Reichsfürsten*, who were pushing to expand their power and rights and who continually claimed sovereignty, furthered the process of state building and political modernisation. Although they opposed the principle of absolute sovereignty when it came to the position of the Emperor, their actions were initially driven by the desire to consolidate their own power and (absolute) sovereignty.

Leibniz was a skilled diplomat and he did not flinch from the problems at stake. In his capacity of advisor to the *Reichsfürsten*, Leibniz was directly confronted with the urgent need of restoring and harmonising the diplomatic and inter-religious channels of communication in Europe. For most of his (professional) life, Leibniz served various German Principalities in various capacities: as an in-house philosopher, a jurist, a diplomat, a counsellor, an historian, a librarian, etc.[26] But his position at the prominent Court of the House of Brunswick-Lüneburg perfectly placed him to witness the confusion over diplomatic and ceremonial practices which was symptomatic of the changing political constellation both in and outside Germany.[27] At the peace conference of Nijmegen, the Duke of Brunswick-Lüneburg claimed his equality to the Electors and argued that he had a right to participate and be represented by his ambassadors during the international negotiations.

As a result of his position, Leibniz was called upon to address the *Gesandtenfrage* – the issue of diplomatic representation and ceremonial – which presented itself so clearly during the Nijmegen peace negotiations (1677-1679) between the Emperor and France. He discussed the issue in many of his works, often anonymously, like in the case of the *Entretien de Philarete et d'Eugène Sur la question du temps agitée à Nimwegue touchant le droit d'ambassade des Electeurs et Princes de l'Empire* (1677).[28] This treatise is written as a fictional

[26] MacDonald Ross, at 23. In addition to the court of Brunswick-Lüneburg, Leibniz at some point served at the court of Berlin, where the Duke of Brandenburg resided, and at the court of the Holy Roman Emperor, as well as at Peter the Great's court in St. Petersburg. See Riley's Introduction to LPW, at 2.

[27] The following remark suggests that Leibniz moreover enjoyed this task. Codex, at 170: 'It is pleasant then to be admitted to solemn events, to observe ceremonies, to know the changes in things, in rules, in customs and in legal norms, over several centuries; and to wonder at the changes of human genius and of languages amidst the very simplicity of our old people and their *naïvétés*.'

[28] In the preface to the 2nd edition, the title is slightly different and mentions also the right to sovereignty: Entretien de Philarete et d'Eugène sur la question du temps agitée à Nimwegue touchant le droit de Souveraineté et d'Ambassade des Electeurs et Princes de l'Empire; see, Acad. Ed., IV, 2, at 289 and 293. Hereinafter: Entretien de Philarete et d'Eugène.

dialogue between a representative of a prominent German Prince and an ambassador of the Elector of Brandenburg and makes it poignantly clear what the question was, namely: '*si les Princes de l'Empire ont droit d'envoyer des Ambassadeurs à Nimwegue, et si ces Ambassadeurs y doivent estre traités comme ceux des Roys et Electeurs, ou Princes d'Italie.*'[29] This question is answered with an unequivocal confirmation. The treatise also illustrates that the issue had already stirred controversy before Nijmegen.[30] The debate on the right to diplomatic representation was of course a debate on and a claim to (the right to) sovereignty and Leibniz had to formulate a legal argument to support the legitimacy of his employer's (controversial) claims. To further this cause, Leibniz also published a more theoretical legal work on the sovereignty of the Princes, *Caesarinus Fürstenerius* (1677),[31] which became the subject of much debate at the universities and to which we will return later.

The controversy surrounding Ernst-August, the Duke of Brunswick, is evidence of the fact that the (legal) status of the newly participating representatives needed further clarification.[32] In spite of the participation of (the delegates of) the leading German Princes in the diplomatic conference for the preparation of the 1648 Treaties and the subsequent recognition of their capacity to conclude the treaties and Alliances, which granted them the new status of independent actors on the international plane, the legal status of the Electors and leading German Princes as well as the status of their delegates was neither equal nor unequivocally determined yet. This was the reason why tension mounted at the Nijmegen Conference over Ernst-August's claim of equality to Kings and Electors. The French, however, wished to continue to discriminate between Electors and Princes and refused to recognise the Duke's representatives as ambassadors. Consequently, Ernst-August assigned Leibniz to the task of assuring his elevation to the imperial rank of Elector. The Electorate was a privilege which was originally granted to only a few Houses. Despite the changing political situation, the Duke evidently considered the rank of *Reichskurfürst* to be preferable to the rank of *Reichsfürst*. Eventually, the campaign on Ernst-August's behalf was successful and in 1632, the Duke was designated the 9th Elector of the Holy Empire, of the Electorate of Hanover.[33]

In brief, the controversy surrounding ceremonial practices was a symptom of the prevailing confusion over the rules of political *representation* at and *partici-*

---

[29] Id., at 296-297.

[30] See, e.g., 316-317.

[31] Caesarini Fürstenerii de Jure Suprematus ac Legationis Principum Germaniae (1677), Acad. Ed. IV, 2, at 3. Here, in an English transl.: Caesarinus Fürstenerius (1677), in LPW, at 111 *et seq*.

[32] See also, J. Walter Jones, Leibniz as International Lawyer, 22 *BYIL* 3 (1945): 'The Duke had not yet attained the rank of an Elector, and at the opening of the negotiations which ended in the Treaty of Nijmegen, 1679, there had been much dispute as to the ceremonial honours and precedence to be shown to those free princes of Germany who were not Electors and who complained that their representatives were accorded a lower place than those of such Italian rulers as the dukes of Modena and Mantua.'

[33] See also, Riley's Introduction to LPW.

pation in international conferences and diplomatic life which had resulted from the political modernisation of Europe. The diplomatic practice had to adapt to newcomers and reestablish mutual respect and international understanding and thereby contribute to the establishment of European and Imperial stability and to the prevention of conflict. But at the same time, the constitutional structure of the Empire was at stake. The power and (legal) status of the German princes, their relationship with the Emperor and the Electors (in terms of sovereignty) and the relationship between the Emperor and the Electors itself featured prominently on the political agenda. Leibniz was well aware of the urgent need for clarification of these issues and devoted much of his time to this. In the next section we will discuss the conceptual world and intellectual conventions among which his work was carried out.

2.2.2. At the crossroads to modernity: rationalism and the cosmopolis

Rationalists like Leibniz and Descartes (1596-1650) before him, lived in troubled times rather than amidst tranquillity.[34] The uncertainty ruling the 17th century was in fact one of the major contributing factors to, first, the rise of rationalism and, second, the unification of the natural and moral-political order into one stable *cosmopolis*. We will briefly outline these two developments and indicate their relevance to Leibniz' work.[35]

First, it would be difficult to overestimate the influence of the Thirty Years' War on the development of Modern Thinking. The rise to supremacy of the human faculty of reason was a natural and necessary response to the general crisis and religious wars. The exposure to – social, economic and political – insecurity and the prevailing uncertainty over religious matters as well as over the foundations of human knowledge fuelled the objectives and intellectual programmes of rationalists like Descartes and Leibniz.[36] In order to prevail in the fight for theological supremacy the most effective weapons would be independent, general and universal truths that would ring true to all opposing camps and could serve as a starting point for all reasoning. This was also the objective of Descartes' 'reflections [namely, to] ope[n] up for people in his generation a real hope of *reasoning* their way out of political and theological chaos, at a time when no one else saw any-

[34] See, for a revision of the traditional interpretation of Modernity as a purely 'rational' enterprise, which goes back to the (erroneous) historical assumption that Modernity came about at a time of social comfort and prosperity, with merely 'rationalist' origins (as such negating modernity's humanist origins), Cosmopolis, at 30-44 and 45-87. See also, Europe: A History, at 471.

[35] See also, S. Brown, The Seventeenth-century intellectual background, *in* N. Jolley (Ed.), The Cambridge Companion to Leibniz 43-66 (1995).

[36] Following Toulmin's analysis of the 17th century here I will leave aside the content of the underlying philosophical debates among Cartesians, anti-Cartesians, Newtonians, Spinozists, etc., like the one on "substance" or the idea of a (providential) God, and will describe Leibniz' intellectual context in necessarily more general terms which may to some extent fail to satisfy the philosophically trained reader, but will also keep the text accessible for readers with a legal background.

thing to do but continue an interminable war.'[37] The 17th-century philosophical '*Quest for Certainty*'[38] – as Toulmin termed it – was an attempt to escape *uncertainty*: Rationalist theories had to *replace* the more practical, sceptical humanist approach that was rooted in tolerance, diversity and the acceptance of uncertainty. In the eyes of the rationalists, the humanist approach had failed. They now turned to Universal Reason to guide them to certainty and stability:

> the 17th-century triumph of rationalism, and the Quest for Certainty to which it gave rise, did not happen out of a clear blue sky, but were intelligible responses to a specific historical crisis. Viewed in context, that is, the rationalist move of decontextualizing the problems of science and philosophy, and using the methods of formal logic and geometry as a basis for rational resolution of physical and epistemological problems, was more than a worthwhile experiment in philosophical method. It was also a smart political move: a rhetorically timely response to the general crisis of the 17th-century politics.[39]

A rational method was considered one that unfolded like mathematical reasoning. It did not cite tradition, theological or mythological elements, or Church authority as building blocks. Descartes hoped that the Euclid's geometrical model or axiomatic system would overcome all conflict. After Descartes it became the dominant model for scientific reasoning.[40] This switch of method was part of the broader intellectual counterpart of the 17th-century crisis: rationalism and decontextualisation were necessary in order to re-establish a *dialogue* which was detached from the political and religious controversies of the time. The rationalist pursuit of 'the light of reason' would uncover certainty, uniformity and order.

Just as Descartes dreamed of 'an ideal *method*' to establish theological and epistemological certainty and indisputable truths, so – against a background of reconstruction and the restoration of diplomatic communication and amidst the dynamics of European and Imperial politics – Leibniz searched for *unity* and *universal harmony*. He presented a number of concrete proposals for tackling the contemporary practical problems and for (re-)establishing open diplomatic and inter-religious communication. For instance, Leibniz wrote many essays which attempted to establish some common theological ground, which all religious opponents could agree to, with the aim of reuniting the Christian churches under one Papacy.[41] Moreover, himself a Lutheran in practice, Leibniz was in continuous dialogue with Catholicism and as such he was well placed to take on the task

---

[37] Cosmopolis, at 71.

[38] Id., at 10. This central phrase in Toulmin's analysis is actually the title of the 1929 Gifford Lectures by John Dewey in which it was 'claimed that the debate in philosophy had rested, ever since the 1630s, on too passive a view of the human mind, and on inappropriate demands for geometrical certainty.'

[39] Id., at 80.

[40] Id., at 72-80.

[41] Riley's Introduction to LPW, at 1; See also, Cosmopolis, at 101: 'his longlife mission as a theological "ecumenist."' Also, G. MacDonald Ross, Leibniz 6 (1984), hereinafter: MacDonald Ross.

of bridging the gap. His determination to restore the dialogue between Protestants and the Catholic Church, and his plea for the foundation of ecumenical Councils,[42] bear witness to his life-long ideal of Christian reunification as well as to his concern for and involvement in the restoration of European unity in general, for which aim inter-religious dialogue was a bare necessity.

Another of Leibniz' concrete endeavours was his search for 'an ideal *universal language*' which could restore communication and overcome conflict and misunderstandings.[43] Leibniz realised that as many issues as possible should actually be kept outside the delicate realm of religion. Therefore, he considered it necessary to put together a *universal encyclopaedia*, one single system of all knowledge, and to create a *universal language – characteristica universalis* – to serve as the means by which to communicate about the encyclopaedia and as a tool for finding common ground. In his analysis, the world's *diversity* of languages and cultures was the primary source of misunderstanding, and therefore of conflict and mistrust.[44] Since the universal language would be an *exact* language, it would be *neutral*, i.e., unaffected by theological, cultural or political opposites, and therefore *authoritative*.

> [The system] will constitute a new language which can be written and spoken. This language will be very difficult to construct, but very easy to learn. It will be quickly accepted by everybody on account of its great utility and its surprising facility, and *it will serve wonderfully in communication among various peoples*.[45]

On top of that Leibniz developed a calculator. By attributing not only characters, but also numbers to every possible idea or concept, reasoning became a relatively simple calculus exercise which would result in *true understanding*. People could now *calculate* rather than *fight* their way out of their differences by means of an instrument that would help them find identical answers and that would thus prevent or even end all conflicts.[46] Leibniz had a vision of homogeneity in human reasoning and intended to provide 'the greatest instrument of reason' by his unification of mathematics and philosophy.[47] The whole programme was a supremely

---

[42] Leibniz mentioned these councils in, e.g., a Letter to Bossuet, *in* LPW, at 140. See, e.g., the Preface to *Caesarinus Fürstenerius*, where Leibniz considers that the Emperor should arrange the ecumenical Council's meetings, *in* LPW, at 111. See also, Cosmopolis, at 98-105.

[43] Cosmopolis, at 98-105. Toulmin explained that '[in] reading the philosophical response to the disasters of the early 17th century, the crucial figures were Descartes and Donne: for the period after the Thirty Years' War, it is helpful to consider, rather the life of Gottfried Wilhelm, Freiherr von Leibniz.' Id., 99-100.

[44] See also, D. Rutherford, Philosophy and Language, *in* N. Jolley (Ed.), Cambridge Leibniz Companion, at 230 (1995).

[45] As cited in Cosmopolis, at 100. Emphasis added.

[46] There is one obvious fundamental point of criticism of Leibniz' universal language argument: what he set out to accomplish, i.e., a mutual understanding between languages and among cultures, is at the same time that which necessarily precedes the whole exercise.

[47] The binary numbers (the system whereby every number is a combination of 0 and 1), which he invented to indicate the value (or degree of perfection) of concepts and perform calculations with,

rationalist project. It required making the best analysis and arriving at the soundest judgment guided by *reason.* By the faculty of reason, humanity would come closer to perfection, as Leibniz optimistically contended. The re-establishment of stability, however, depended equally upon the organisation of the domestic societies of the Empire and of Europe in general.

Secondly, in the intellectual attitude to or view of the world in this age, nature and society were united in one harmonious structure, as, after all, both originated from (the laws of) reason. Toulmin tried to express this vision by the notion of '*cosmopolis*,' which turned on the conviction that humanity had to copy the Divine order given by Creation and had to re-create this order within society in order to establish stability. The hierarchy and stability apparent in the structure of the natural world set the example for the organisation of a human society aiming to achieve the same result. The aim of capturing the natural and the moral-political world in one single conceptual language and explanatory structure was a joint endeavour. Politics and mathematics were practised to serve theology and cosmopolitical structuring. The Rationalists intended to 'purify' human reasoning[48] and sought a comprehensive approach to make the world rationally intelligible (although it was conceded that man might never reach the point where it would be). One overall rational logical structure, the macro-*cosmos*, which incorporates the micro-*cosmos* (i.e., the individual) and the *polis* (the in-between level of man-made society) would lay bare the harmony of creation and of the laws of nature.[49]

After 1655, the *cosmopolis* idea became part of the effort to construct new *stable* societies after the decline of feudality.[50] The Europe of nations and their sovereigns, which was horizontally organised, gradually replaced the medieval,

---

connected mathematics with metaphysics. Cosmopolis, at 101. Leibniz wrote: 'I dare say that this is the highest effort of the human mind; and, when the project is accomplished, it will simply be up to humans to be happy, since they will have an instrument that exalts the reason no less than the telescope perfects our vision.' As cited in Cosmopolis, at 104.

[48] Cosmopolis, at 104. See, Europe: A History, at 507. 'The Wars of Religion offered fertile soil for the fragile seeds of reason and science.'

[49] Europe: A History, at 510. 'Together with the fruits of the Scientific Revolution and the rational method of Descartes, it [the "natural light of reason"] formed the core of an ideology which held centre stage from the 1670s to the 1770s. It led to the conviction that reason could uncover the rules that underlay the apparent chaos of both the human and material world, and hence of natural religion, of natural morality, of natural law.' Id., at 597

[50] Cosmopolis, at 98. Leibniz explained that: 'Between 1660 and 1720, few thinkers were *only* interested in accounting for mechanical phenomena in the physical world. For most people, just as much intellectual underpinning was required for the new patterns of social practice, and associated ideas about the *polis*. As a result, enticing new analogies entered social and political thought: if, from now on, "stability" was the chief virtue of social organization, was it not possible to organize political ideas about *Society* along the same lines as scientific ideas about *Nature*?' Id., at 107. An illuminating analogy had it that God was 'the Great Clockmaker' and the laws of nature, whose mysteries were slowly being unveiled, were expressions or prescriptions of God's will. Europe: A History, at 510. Around 1650, the universe was also pictured as a ladder or a huge pipe organ. Kepler (1571-1630) described the cosmos by means of musical analogies, with planets as notes on

vertical, organisation of society.[51] For the sake of stability and hierarchy, there had to be a "God on earth" to serve as the pinnacle of the national social structures. The development of the nation state benefited from the fact that the transnational Church under the authority of the Pope lost influence to national churches.[52] Moral and religious authority passed from the Pope to the regional sovereign or prince. In the cosmopolitical world, the sovereign was thought to have been "appointed" by God. As God's replacement on earth, he became the new centre of power: 'the Sun around which the State's motions turned: even the personal embodiment of the State itself.'[53] In the new structure, the sovereign was no longer the feudal landlord, but became the symbol of the people and the unity of the nation. This new role of the sovereign, combined with the centralisation of political and military authority, decided the development of the European states;[54] the age of absolutism was dawning.

With the intellectual mood or world view bringing the socio-political organisation and the natural order together inside analogous systems, the Sun, as the centre and binding force of the solar system, became the symbol of unifying power, the icon of supreme unity itself, the legitimisation of (the sovereign's) supreme power. Although absolutism differed throughout Europe, the cosmopolitical connotation was, nevertheless, shared, as in France *le Roi-Soleil* (Louis XIV,1643-1715) ruled and in Spain *el Rey de las Planetas* (Philip IV, 1621-1665). Nature was understood as an expression of God's Rationalism. The King was obliged to establish in his state the same stability and hierarchy which God had created in the *Cosmos*.[55] The *polis* therefore had to be modelled on the *Cosmos*; hierarchy became justifiable and God was the 'ultimate source of change in both Orders.'[56] Both the human and the natural order were ruled by a similar set of rational laws and so harmony was re-established in the idea that all was part of one rational order.

Similarly, in his quest for unity and harmony, Leibniz perceived the natural and moral-political world as one single system.[57] Although at first glance the world seemed to be in chaos, Leibniz believed in a universal system of 'pre-es-

---

the heavenly scale. According to his system, planet Earth's tune was *mi fa mi*, which he explained (during the Thirty Years' War) as follows: 'this vale of tears is ruled by *mi*sère et *fam*ine.' A. Rood, Alchemie en Mystiek, Het Hermetische Museum 90, 89-97 (1997).

[51] Cosmopolis, at 96-97. See also, Europe: A History, at 516.

[52] See, e.g., Cosmopolis, at 91-93. Also, The Rise and Fall of the Great Powers, at 70.

[53] Cosmopolis, at 94-95.

[54] See, e.g., The Rise and Fall of the Great Powers, at 70, 75.

[55] W. Shakespeare, King Lear Act IV, 3: 'It is the stars, / The stars above us, govern our conditions.'

[56] Cosmopolis, at 127. 'Behind the inertness of matter, they saw in Nature, as in society, that the actions of 'lower' things were subordinate to oversight and command by 'higher' creatures, and ultimately by the Creator. The more confident one was about 'subordination and authority' in Nature, the less anxious one need accordingly be about social inequalities.' Id., at 128.

[57] This perception of cosmopolitical unity is also illustrated by Leibniz' drawing accompanying a poem he wrote on the occasion of the illness and recuperation of Louis XIV, *Devise sur la Reconvalescence du Roy*. Drawing of April 1687, *in* Acad. Ed., IV, 3er Band, N. 128, at 841-842.

tablished harmony' hidden in its depths.[58] His philosophical attitude is best summarised in the words of Jaspers: 'We can speak of a basic frame of mind that resides in the notion of harmony.' His 'trust in order, reasonableness, [and] the harmony of things' shaped every project he undertook.[59] The unity, coherence, and consistency that inspired his thinking – from the lowest level of the composition of the soul up to the structure or composition of the political organisation in Europe as a whole – is typical of this cosmopolitical view. The cosmopolitical 'pre-established' harmony Leibniz discerned sprang from the designation of God as the 'Architect' of the natural world and the 'Law-Giver' of the moral-political world: in God nature and humanity were united.[60]

This profound conviction of pre-established harmony between the natural and the moral-political realm constituted the deepest source and underlying principle of all Leibniz' constructional thinking. Riley rightly points out that '[s]ince ... Leibniz is a supremely architectonic thinker who wants to relate everything to "first philosophy," one cannot just cordon off his moral and political thought from his metaphysics and theology: that is precisely what he himself did not do.'[61] Riley demonstrates that Leibniz' theory of justice cannot be separated from his metaphysical speculations on the concept of substance and their consequences for the conception of the human soul as part of the entire (moral) universe. Riley placed Leibniz' theory of substance and the soul – eventually laid down in the *Monadology* (1714) – at the heart of his study of Leibniz' 'universal jurisprudence' and shows that the former sustains the latter.

Within Leibniz' philosophy, the 'monad' is the smallest possible unit of rational substance; monads exist in degrees and in a hierarchical order.[62] The rational

---

[58] 'What is below is like what is above.' Europe: A History, at 530. E.g., Leibniz was also attracted to alchemy. See, MacDonald Ross, at 5, 15-6; also, R. Ariew, G.W. Leibniz, life and works, *in* N. Jolley (Ed.), at 21. He was mainly preoccupied with its theoretical aspects. Alchemy belonged to a time in which it was attempted to discover unity between the macro- and microcosmos, it 'is from the outset a theory of how the world is related to human life' rooted in the idea that both the human body and the universe 'are made of the same materials, or principles, or elements.' Bronowski, at 138.

[59] K. Jaspers, Leibniz, *in* The Great Philosophers Vol. III (Engl. ed., 1993), at 173 and 183. More fully the quote reads: 'We can speak of a basic frame of mind that resides in the notion of harmony, in intrinsic accord with the will of God, in the trust that everything is in order; and we can say right away that this basic frame of mind is precisely the ineradicable certainty of the rationality of God and the universe and that, therefore, rational cognition is the only way into the ground, and that, therefore, from the beginning rational construction from logical premises was, for Leibniz, the form of his philosophy.' Moreover, once when making some observations concerning a number of schools of philosophy Leibniz concluded his remarks with the words: 'I flatter myself that I have discovered the harmony of the different systems.' As cited in, Sheldon, Leibniz's message to us, VII (4) *J. of the History of Ideas* 386 (1946).

[60] Leibniz, Monadology (1714), transl. G.R. Montgomery (1992), Discourse on Metaphysics and the Monadology, §§ 80, 89. Hereinafter: Monadology.

[61] P. Riley, Leibniz' Universal Jurisprudence: Justice as the Charity of the Wise 5 (1996). Hereinafter: Leibniz' Universal Jurisprudence. Metaphysics is referred to as first or pure philosophy.

[62] By stating that the 'created Monads may be called Entelechies, because they have in themselves a certain perfection,' Leibniz links up with the Aristotelian tradition in which *entelechia* is a teleological force in nature, including human nature.

human soul is a monad of the highest degree, a 'spirit,' not only capable of feeling and 'accompanied by memory,'[63] but by its reason able to discover the eternal and universal truths:

> [T]he knowledge of eternal and necessary truths is that which distinguishes us from mere animals and gives us reason and the sciences, thus raising us to a knowledge of ourselves and of God. This is what is called in us the Rational Soul or the Mind.

The 'rational soul' is the 'image of the Deity himself ... [hence] capable of knowing the system of the universe.' In other words, the human 'mind' enables man to separate right from wrong, just from unjust, true from untrue, and to act upon this knowledge. These capacities to tell the difference and to act accordingly define man's humanity. They enable him to be 'self-conscious' and 'to enter into a sort of social relationship with God.'[64] With mankind, God has created spiritual bodies and although 'the soul follows its own laws, and the body has its own laws,' '[t]hey are fitted to each other in virtue of the pre-established harmony between all substances, since they are all representatives of one and the same universe.'[65] The final causes in the moral realm, like the efficient causes in the natural world, will "naturally" bring about 'progress' towards perfection, i.e., towards God: '[f]or he is not only the Architect and the efficient cause of our being, but he is also our Lord and the Final Cause, who ought to be the whole goal of our will, and who, alone, can make our happiness.'[66]

This rather optimistic idea of inevitable progress is related to the capacities of the human mind and its desire for perfection and justice. Since God was perfect, he created a world as close to perfection as it could possibly be,[67] and it was in the nature of all things and all beings to strive to perfect the perfection. In other words, Leibniz argued that it was human nature to try to perfect oneself and others. Justice, as we will see below, Leibniz defined as wise charity or the inclination to favour the good of others, "the general good." Because of man's moral capacity and his (social) direction towards God or the general good, he was a citizen of 'the city of God.' All human minds together, i.e., 'the totality of the spirits,' inhabited 'the City of God, that is to say, the most perfect state under the most perfect monarch. This city of God, this truly universal monarchy, is a moral world within the natural world.'[68] Man inhabited this moral world and his desire for perfection led him in the direction of *universal justice*.

---

[63] Monadology, §§ 1-19.

[64] Id., § 29 and §§ 83-84. These eternal and universal truths are fixed like the numbers in the arithmetic or geometric system, see, Leibniz, Opinion on the Principles of Pufendorf (1706), *in* LPW, at 71.

[65] Id., § 78. See also, §§ 86-87, and § 79: The laws of the soul are 'the laws of final causes through their desires, purposes and means.'

[66] Id., §§ 87-90

[67] Id., §§ 53-55.

[68] Id., §§ 85-86.

In brief, the cosmopolitical designation of God as Architect and Monarch formed the foundation underlying the all-connectedness of the Leibnizian universal system. His theory of justice based on the human rational soul which was essentially directed at God cannot be separated from his metaphysical theory of substance. In this theory, the rational soul qualified man for citizenship of the Christian Republic. In Leibniz' universal jurisprudence, each monad of the highest degree was a 'person' with moral and social awareness. The rational mind defined human nature, it made a person human. The (moral) concept of personality thus formed an essential link between the natural and the moral-political world. Or, to conclude in Riley's words:

> [Leibniz] is, to be sure, concerned as a metaphysician with substance as such, but always wants to show that without (naturally immortal) substances or persons there can be no moral concepts, no "subjects" of universal justice, no "citizens" of the divine monarchy or City of God.[69]

We will return to Leibniz' concept of universal justice below. Here, it suffices to conclude that at a time when intellectual life was characterised by profound rationalism and a cosmopolitical attitude including the wish to unite all things within one harmonious system, and at a time when sovereignty became *the rationale* of the socio-political realm, not unlike God in his capacity as *the foundation* of the moral realm, Leibniz' theory of substance, which was also a theory of the human soul, attained fundamental moral-political significance. Leibniz' famous optimism was moreover based on the idea that man was not only capable of knowing the system of the universe but that with this knowledge and by his nature man was also endowed with the ability 'to *imitate* it somewhat by means of architectonic patterns,' i.e., by his own *actions* within his own sphere of human society.[70] The responsibility to act justly is therefore part of man's moral personality.

Let us now turn to the jurisprudential context and in particular to Grotius, Hobbes and Samuel Pufendorf, so that afterwards we may evaluate Leibniz' argument on the desired European (and Imperial) order against this background.

2.2.3. **Jurisprudential context: identifying international legal scholarship**

2.2.3.1. *Prelude – Grotius and Hobbes*

Both Grotius and Hobbes lived and worked amidst the chaos and insecurity of the Thirty Years' War, and Hobbes had fled Britain because of the Civil War there. Thus, almost naturally one could say, they raised the questions of how to create order and establish legitimate power and authority in order to bring about lasting

---

[69] Leibniz' Universal Jurisprudence, at 51, at 5: Riley summarized 'in short the *Monadology* is a theory of personality.'

[70] Id., § 83. Emphasis added.

peace. Leibniz generally referred to Grotius with approval and admiration.[71] Hobbes' views, however, he generally regarded as severely conflicting with his own, although he agreed with Hobbes on the subject of the state's duty to establish order and security for its people and also shared his belief that a tendency to be selfish was inherent in human nature.

Grotius' *De Jure Belli ac Pacis* (1625) bears witness to the general scientific transition from casuistic reasoning to more systematically constructed arguments.[72] At a time when the Euclid's system of axiomatic reasoning was coming into fashion, Grotius considered himself to be the first to approach the law of nations systematically. With this systematic approach he intended to increase respect for the law of nations and heighten its authority as a proper branch of the law.[73] However, Leibniz' respect for Grotius was inspired rather by the substance of his argument than by the way in which it was advanced. The significance of Grotius for Leibniz' thinking, Riley explains, is to be found in Grotius' contribution to the revival of the Platonic notion of justice to which Leibniz' frequent citing of Grotius' words, – 'measureless as is the power of God, nonetheless it can be said that there are certain things over which that power does not extent ... just as even God cannot cause that two times two should not make four, so he cannot cause that which is intrinsically evil, to be not evil' – seems to point. Indeed, Leibniz consistently criticised Hobbes and Pufendorf for contending that justice is what is done by a supreme power, as this implies that justice is based on will and power.[74] But there are even more specific traces in Leibniz' universal juris-

[71] See, e.g., 'Hugo Grotius, that excellent man,' Leibniz' Caesarinus Fürstenerius (1677), *in* Acad. Ed., IV, 2ter Band (1677-1687), N.1, at 3. Here, in Riley's LPW transl., at 111-120. Hereinafter: Caesarinus Fürstenerius. See also, Opinion on the principles of Pufendorf, 'the discernment and erudition of the incomparable Grotius,' LPW, at 65. See also, e.g., Letter to Abbé Jean-Paul Bignon, *op. cit.*, footnote 5.

[72] Cosmopolis, at 78. This development would, e.g., lead to Ch. Wolff's work entitled 'The Law According to the Scientific Method' (or rather Jus Gentium Methodo Scientifica Pertractatum) first published in 1749 and which was methodologically based on geometry.

[73] 'Up to the present time no one has treated [that body of law which is concerned with the mutual relations among states or rulers of states, whether derived from nature, or established by divine ordinances, or having its origin in custom and tacit agreement] in a comprehensive and systematic manner; yet the welfare of mankind demands that this task be accomplished.' ... 'Such a work is all the more necessary because in our day, as in former times, there is no lack of men who view this branch of law with contempt as having no reality outside of an empty name.' H. Grotius, De Jure Belli ac Pacis, Prolegomena, § 1 and 3, at 9 and in § 58, at 30: 'With all truthfulness I aver that, just as mathematicians treat their figures as abstracted from bodies, so in treating law I have withdrawn my mind from every particular fact.'

[74] Leibniz' Universal Jurisprudence, at 33-34. See, e.g., for Leibniz' critical remarks on the way 'De Jure Belli ac Pacis' was written, *in* Caesarinus Fürstenerius, LPW, at 114. See, e.g., for Leibniz' use of Grotian thought, i.e., that there is a natural obligation to take care of oneself and of others even in case God (Pufendor's divine law-giver) does not exist, in his critique of Hobbes and Pufendorf, The Principles of Pufendorf, LPW, at 71. Leibniz expressed his 'astonish[ment]': 'will he who is invested with the supreme power do nothing against justice if he proceeds tyrannically against his subjects; who arbitrarily despoils his subjects, torments them, and kills them under torture; who makes war on others without cause?' Id., at 70.

prudence of crucial concepts of Grotius' theory. The first of these is the fundamental concept of *appetitus societatis*, which is man's natural desire and need to live in a society. The second is the establishment of agreement among the free wills of man, the establishment, therefore, of common consent. In Grotius' view, the *ius gentium* was the entirety of legal norms that all nations have in common and that apply to the relations among political communities and their rulers. It stems from the two concepts mentioned: natural reason and free will. A third element of Grotius' theory concerns sovereignty. The individual human being was fully included in the Grotian system of the law of nations and sovereignty was considered a personal capacity of the ruler of the state rather than belonging to the state itself. Sovereignty conferred upon rulers full legal competence. In this scenario, the correlative right to good governance was merely an *aptitude*, but it was still conceptually indispensable to the establishment of another right, namely the right to rebel, which I will finally touch upon briefly.

Grotius considered social life as a *sine qua non* for human existence.[75] For this reason, man was naturally predisposed to pursuing a peaceful social order.[76] From this perspective, the source of natural law is human nature itself: the *appetitus societatis* together with the faculty of reason. These enable man to decide what would serve both his own and his fellow man's interests, i.e., what would be in accordance with human nature, and, conversely, what would be contrary to natural law. Grotius defined natural law as a 'dictate of right reason.'[77] Human *nature* was able to distinguish between the just and the unjust through *right* reasoning: *just* was that which was in conformity with the nature of man and the public good, i.e., the good of the community to which he wished to belong.[78] Injustice was done if an act was committed which was contrary to the nature of the community of *rational* human beings and which consequently threatened peace and order.[79] Because of its 'universal cause,' this 'common sense of mankind'[80] was indeed the law of the *Societas Humana*. Because the *capacity* of knowing the difference between just and unjust and the *capacity* of acting accordingly were attributed to the human *individual*, man was the moral and political actor of this world. The *ius gentium* ultimately spoke to the conscience of – and thus applied to – every member of humanity, whether sovereign or subject, whether individually or collectively organised; it was the law of the univer-

[75] Grotius recalled Seneca's warning against the solitary life: 'Take us *singly*, and what are we? The prey of all creatures, their victims ...' Man has 'no might of claws or of teeth [which] makes him a terror to others, naked and weak as he is, his safety lies in fellowship.' Seneca, On Benefits IV xiii para. 1, Loeb Classical Library, at 241. Emphasis added. Here, Seneca rejects the perception of individualism as atomism; man living outside human society loses his humanity and is a human being no longer, because he has lost an essential part of his nature. De Jure Belli ac Pacis, Prolegomena, § 16, at 15.

[76] Id., Prolegomena, § 6 and 7, at 11-12.

[77] Id., Book I, Ch. I, §10, at 38 *et seq*.

[78] Id., Prolegomena, § 44, at 25.

[79] Id., Book I, Ch. I, § 3, at 34-35.

[80] Id., Book I, Ch. I, § 12, at 42-44.

sal human society. As the primary source of the law of nations was natural law and the source of natural law was human nature, the individual took up a central position in Grotius' theory of the law of nations. Besides providing its source, it was also its ultimate addressee.

Grotius recognised that the terms 'natural law' and 'the law of nations' were often confused, and went on to explain that his perception of *ius gentium* also included *voluntary* law.[81] The voluntary law of nations was no different from the natural law of nations in respect of the kind of relations they governed, as both applied to the relations between political communities (*civitas*) and to the relations between the rulers of these communities, the heads of state.[82] However, because voluntary law had a different source, a different method was required for finding its rules. The voluntary law of nations was the law that 'almost' all political communities had in common and that originated in the *free will* of the people of these communities. 'Almost' universal consensus was evidenced by enduring custom and tacit agreement as witnessed and described by experts.[83] If used separately from natural law, *ius gentium* consisted of this voluntary law of the universal community. At the time when Grotius expounded his theory, the universal community was shifting away from feudalism and towards the Westphalian order and as a result, so was the law of nations or *ius gentium*. Grotius still perceived the universal community as populated with 'persons,' as a society made up of sovereigns and their subjects, who were united in the natural bond of mankind. Treaty obligations were still entered into by sovereigns in their personal capacity, even though the modern state – *civitas* or political community – was already emerging.

Grotius' concept of sovereignty was an indication of the *internal* situation: it indicated what was the highest power (*summa potestas*) *within* the 'perfect association,' i.e., the "state."[84] The best state was the one aiming for perfection, which meant the attainment of the common good or the happiness of *all*. Grotius defined the 'people' as a composite artificial body – a *corpora artificialia* – in which separate members were united in 'spirit.' This way, 'a single essential character' existed among them. This essential character 'is the full and perfect union of civic life, the first product of which is sovereign power; that is the bond which binds the state together.'[85] He distinguished between the *general* and the *specific* bearer or subject ('*subiectum*') of this highest or sovereign power: just as the human body was the subject of the sense of sight and the eye was its particular subject, so the *civitas* – the political community – was the general subject of

[81] Id., Book I, Ch. I, § 11 and 14 (1), at 41, 44; Ch. II, § 4 (1), at 57. It is commonly accepted that Grotius' use of the terms was sometimes confusing: 'Grotius, like scholastics, has no single term for international law. ... [and] [a]gain like the scholastics, Grotius is more interested in natural law touching international relations than in the volitional *jus gentium*.' A Concise History, at 104.

[82] Id., Prolegomena, § 1 and 17, and Book I, Ch. I, § 14 (1), at 44.

[83] Id., Book I, Ch. I, § 14.

[84] Id., Book I, Ch. III, § 7, at 102-103.

[85] Id., Book II, Ch. IX, § 3, at 310-311.

the sovereign power and the sovereign its specific subject.[86] This distinction offered a framework for the recognition of a right to rebel under the law of nations, although Grotius was reluctant to acknowledge this right, and understandably so if we take the instability of the time into account. In principle, the *civitas* cannot "legitimately" rise up against the supreme power. This means that sovereignty did not reside with the people in such a manner that it included an absolute right to rebel.[87] The actual rights of sovereignty belonged to the ruler, but they were not unconditional.[88] Grotius considered rebellion legal under natural law if the sovereign ruler 'transgress[ed] against the laws and the State,' 'manifestly abandoned his governmental authority' or 'showed himself [to be] the enemy of the whole people.'[89] Grotius had been appointed as the official historiographer of the States of Holland in 1601 and his particular assignment was to describe, or rather, to justify, the Dutch uprising against the Spanish government.[90] Unsurprisingly, he came to the conclusion that the Dutch Republic, which was the product of this rebellion, had resulted from a revolt against tyranny and was therefore based on legitimate (natural law) grounds.[91]

It should be noted in the context of this study, that Leibniz often endorsed Grotius' argument on the right to rebel. The right to rebel is relevant here in the

[86] Id., Book I, Ch. III, § 7, at 102-103. Also, Book II, Ch. IX, § 8(1), at 314.

[87] Id., Book I, Ch. IV, § 7 (15), at 156.

[88] Id., Book I, Ch. III, § 8, at 103 *et seq.*

[89] Id., Book I, Ch. IV, §§ 8-14, at 156-159.

[90] This historical study partly found expression in Grotius' *Annales et Historiae* (1657).

[91] On the Prince of Orange's initiative, the States General renounced the sovereignty of the Spanish King on the basis of *bad oppressive governance* and offered the rights, duties and privileges of (the constitutionally regulated) sovereignty over the Netherlands to a new sovereign, the duke of Anjou. In 1581, with the Act of Abjuration (*Plakkaat van Verlatinge*) the States General 'repudiat[ed] Philip II and his heirs in perpetuity.' J.I. Israel, The Dutch Republic: Its Rise, Greatness, and Fall 1477-1806 (1995), at 209. It should moreover be noted that at the time the States General was the assembly composed of the representatives of the United Provinces, which was dominated by the province of Holland. This representation was organised on the basis of the Dutch social classes, i.e., the nobility and the regent class as representatives of the cities. J. Huizinga, How Holland became a Nation (1924), *in* Verzamelde Werken 2 (1948), at 278: 'Each province was governed by its States, which means Estates, composed of representatives of the towns and of nobles, the clergy having dropped out as an Estate by the Reformation.' The repudiation of the old and the adoption of the new sovereign was largely a personal affair: the personal ties of rights and privileges between the representatives of the classes and the lord of the land were first renounced and subsequently re-established between the representatives and the new lord whereby the latter swore an oath to abide by the rules and customs in force. The Dutch Republic, at 209: 'Furthermore, the Act of Abjuration required new oaths of allegiance to be taken from all office-holders and magistrates, as well as the civic militias, whereby holders of office had to swear that they no longer held themselves to be bound by their former oaths of loyalty to the Spanish king and "swear further to be true and obedient to the States against the king of Spain and his followers."' Anjou's sovereignty and authority were merely formal and never really effective. After he left in 1583 and died in 1584, the States in 1585 offered the sovereignty over the Netherlands to the King of France, Henri III, who declined, and subsequently to the British Queen Elizabeth, who also refused. Consequently, the *rebellious* United Provinces – after spending a few years as an English protectorate – reluctantly transformed into a Republic.

sense that if it was indeed a recognised right under the positive law of nations and attributed to the governed as a group, this group could conceptually qualify for international legal personality. To understand how Grotius could, in principle, deny the existence of a right to resist, yet at the same time acknowledge its moral legitimacy on certain occasions it is useful to introduce the gradual distinction between *facultas* and *aptitudo*.[92] *Facultas* conveys an active quality in its most perfect form: a legal competence or right based on either natural or positive law. *Aptitude* is a less perfect state of being, it concerns 'dignity' or 'worthiness,' and legal claims cannot be based on it. It is the passive rather than the active quality of competence; it indicates the 'potential' to act. Having sovereignty has the legal meaning of having full competence, i.e., *facultas*, and as such provides the highest legal claim to the power to rule a political community, a right that is conferred upon the *ruler* by the people, or, in the case of the Dutch Republic, by the social classes which had naturally united to form the *civitas*. Both qualities relate to justice: *facultas* to 'corrective justice' and *aptitude* to 'distributive justice.' Grotius claimed that the aptitude of the represented for being the recipients of 'good governance' fell within the category of distributive justice: it was a (passive, but nonetheless powerful) right that could not be legally enforced. However, in cases of gross injustice, it could turn into a (natural) *legal* right to revolt against tyrannical rule. This would happen as follows. If the head of state completely failed to live up to the standards of good governance, the aptitude would become a *facultas* and the represented would acquire the natural legal right to revolt. Aptitude therefore means having passive rights under natural law, but not the capacity to enforce them. In case of severe injustice, however, the moral (potential) quality may change into a proper natural right.

It can be concluded that Grotius did not formulate an explicit concept of international legal personality. However, every member of the *societas humanas*, whether sovereign or subject, was, in a *personal* capacity, subject to (the) natural law (of nations).

Personality is more expressly a significant element of Hobbes' political philosophy. In *Leviathan*, he dedicates a key chapter to the concept of personality, namely the final chapter of the first part, '*Of MAN*,' which is linked to the next part, '*Of COMMON-WEALTH*.' This may be considered an indication of the concept's function: it is the essential link between the natural world of chaos and the civil world of organised peace. The concept is necessary to be able to transcend the former and reach the latter. Hobbes gives the following definition of the concept of person:

> A PERSON, is he *whose words or actions are considered, either as his own, or as representing the words or actions of an other man, or of any other thing to whom they are attributed, whether Truly or by Fiction.*

---

[92] De Jure Belli ac Pacis, Book I, Ch. I, §§ 4-8, at 35-37.

When they are considered as his owne, then is he called a *Naturall Person*: And when they are considered as representing the words and actions of an other, then is he a *Feigned* or *Artificiall person*.[93]

In Hobbes' theory, the concept of person plays an essential role in the creative process of the state. In the beginning there is chaos; an unorganised crowd of 'natural persons' live in a natural state of war.[94] However, as the crowd begins to realise that peace and order are the preconditions for the effective pursuit of their individual interests and the protection of their property, they surrender their liberty by concluding a covenant among themselves that creates a Sovereign Power, an 'artificial person,'[95] who has the authority to represent and command them.[96] The crowd thus transforms into a regulated group, which is subordinate to the Sovereign Person, *ergo*: the generation of 'that great LEVIATHAN called a COMMON-WEALTH, or STATE.'[97] The (artificial) personality of the Sovereign of the Common-wealth is an essential condition for the creation of the state, or, in Hobbes' own words: 'the Essence of the Common-wealth; which (to define it,) is *One Person*, ... And he that carryeth this Person, is called SOVERAIGNE, and said to have *Soveraigne Power*; and every one besides, his SUBJECT.' This definition suggests that the state is also a person, as the Sovereign Power is said to 'carry the one person of the commonwealth.' However, in the next chapter Hobbes explains more clearly that the Sovereign Person has 'the *Right* to *Present* the Person of them all, (that is to say, to be their *Representative*).'[98] The multitude is transformed into one Commonwealth, but does not thereby become one Author. In fact, Hobbes expressly denies the personality of the state: 'the Common-wealth is *no Person*, nor has capacity to doe any thing, but by the Representative, (that is the Soveraign;).'[99] The Sovereign is a *conditio sine qua non* in Hobbes' theory of

---

[93] Th. Hobbes, Leviathan, Ch. XVI, Penguin class ed, at 217.

[94] Leviathan, Ch. XIII, at 185-6: the life of man in a state of nature is not social, but '*solitary*' and miserable. The state of nature is a state of total war: '[men] are in that condition which is called Warre; and such a warre, as is of every man, against every man.'

[95] Ch. XVII, at 227: 'The only way to erect such a Common Power, ..., is, to conferre all their power and strength upon one Man, or upon one Assembly of men, that may reduce all their Wills, by plurality of voices, unto one Will: which is as much as to say, to beare their Person; and every one to owne, and acknowledge himselfe to be Author of whatsoever he that so beareth their Person, shall Act, or cause to be Acted, in those things which concerne the Common Peace and Safetie; and therein to submit their Wills, every one to his Will, and their Judgements, to his Judgment. This is more than Consent, or Concord; it is a reall Unitie of them all, in one and the same Person, made by Covenant of every man with every man, in such a manner, as if every man should say to every man, *I Authorise and give up my Right of Governing my selfe, to this Man, or to this Assembly of men, on this condition, that thou give up thy Right to him, and Authorise all his Actions in like manner.* This done, the Multitude so united in one Person, is called a COMMON-WEALTH, in latine CIVITAS. This is the Generation of that great LEVIATHAN, or rather (to speak more reverently) of that *Mortall God*, to which wee owe under the *Immortall God*, our peace and defence.'

[96] Leviathan, Ch. XVII, at 223: '[W]ithout the terrour of some Power ... without the Sword,' peace would not be possible and the state would collapse.

[97] Id., Hobbes' Introduction, at 81.

[98] Id., Ch. XVII, at 228.

[99] Emphasis added.

the creation of the state; without the Sovereign, there can be no state or civil society. For statehood, we need the artificial Person who is a covenanted Actor on behalf of the state which he creates by his existence.[100] The unity of the multitude depends on the multitude being united in the one person of the covenanted Actor, although the united multitude is not itself one Author, but 'many Authors.' In brief, Hobbes claimed that as a result of the creation of the Sovereign, the artificial person, by a group of natural persons, chaos and war would be transformed into the peace of a regulated group subject to absolute Sovereign power. The state was 'instituted' with the sole purpose of defending peace and order,[101] and it so happened that absolute sovereignty served this purpose best.

In addition to the use of personality in connection with the political notions of authority, representation and the capacity to act and take responsibility, Hobbes highlighted the theatrical model or image it is connected to:

> *Persona* in latine signifies the *disguise*, or *outward appearance* of a man, counterfeited on the Stage; and sometimes more particularly that part of it, which disguiseth the face, as a Mask or Visard: And from the Stage, hath been translated to any Representer of Speech and action, as well in Tribunalls, as Theaters. So that a *Person*, is the same that an *Actor* is, both on the Stage and in common Conversation; and to *Personate*, is to *Act*, or *Represent* himselfe, or an other; and he that acteth another, is said to beare his Person, or act in his name;[102]

The connection of the concept of person with the image of the *mask* was thus once more brought to the fore. And *persona* was, indeed, a mask in this context: when worn by the Sovereign, it turned him into the artificial person in whom the crowd became a state. In summary, therefore, Hobbes claimed that a state was founded when natural persons by covenant authorised one central power to be their representative and "wear" the "mask" of the Sovereign Actor in whom the multitude was united.

In conclusion, however, Hobbes' use of personality could not, of course, include the concept of ILP,[103] as Hobbes did not recognise the law of na-

---

[100] Ch. XVI: 'A multitude of men, are made *One* Person, when they are by one man, or one Person, Represented; so that it be done with the consent of every one of that Multitude in particular. For it is the *Unity* of the Representer, not the *Unity* of the Represented, that maketh the Person *One*. And it is the Representer that beareth the Person, and but one Person: and *Unity*, cannot otherwise be understood in Multitude.'

[101] Following this line of thinking, Hobbes came up with a negative definition of freedom as the 'absence of external impediments' as these 'oft take away part of mans power to do what hee would.' Id., Ch. XIV, at 189. His contractarian theory of the state is based on a rather atomistic concept of human nature. After all, man only became a social being by contract, solely to pursue his own ends. This became the canonical representation of the negative concept of political liberty. Id., Ch. XXI, at 261 *et seq*. The republican or positive concept of liberty as the inclusion of the people in the political processes and the creation of law is not one Hobbes embraced.

[102] Id., Ch. XVI, at 217. Hobbes refers to Cicero here.

[103] In Hobbes' theory, legal persons (or '*Persons in Law*') 'are made by authority from the Sovereign Power of the Common-Wealth.' Id., Ch. XXII, at 274-275. Legal persons are subordinate to the law, the authority of the representative they have established is limited by law, the Sovereign

tions.[104] Hobbes' conception of absolute sovereignty[105] together with his negation of the separate existence of a legal order among and above sovereigns and their nations, foreshadowed the development of the international law discipline in the 19th century, as the next chapter will briefly describe. The image of the *mask* would continue to be attached to the concept of personality and – by shifting from the Sovereign to the state and from the national to the international context – would remain linked with the concept of ILP.

Leibniz however challenged Hobbes on these issues, sometimes using Pufendorf as a straw-man, and presented a different concept of sovereignty which also supported rather than undermined the law of nations.

2.2.3.2. *The other German advisor – Samuel Pufendorf (1632-1694)*

Leibniz and Samuel Pufendorf were two prominent representatives of the *Reichspublizistik*, which was a tradition of legal scholarship that dealt with Imperial constitutional and public law, also in relation with political philosophy, and which after 1648 mainly dealt with the question: who is the Sovereign: the Emperor, the Electors or perhaps the *Reichstag* (i.e., the collectivity of the *Reichstände*)?[106] The parallels between Pufendorf and Leibniz are many: both studied numerous subjects, among which Mathematics, Theology and Law, both attended, although not simultaneously, the Universities of Leipzig and Jena, and at the University of Jena both were pupils of Erhard Weigel (1625-1699), who combined two branches of science – natural law and mathematics – and who taught ethics by means of the Euclidean geometrical method.[107] Like Leibniz, who throughout his life acted as an advisor to various European rulers, Pufendorf

---

must recognise the legal persons and it is he who prescribes the limits of their representative's power by law.

[104] The law of nature is the liberty which both men and nations have to act in self-preservation when living in a state of nature. Law only exists if peace and security are guaranteed by the Common *Power*, the Sovereign who rules on the basis of the fictitiously concluded covenant. In Hobbes' view, authoritative power makes law (as without sovereignty there can be no law) and thus he identified the law of nations with the law of nature: 'the law of nations, and the law of nature, is the same thing.' In his view on the law of nations, Right is equated with Power. Leviathan, Ch. XXX, at 394. This position of positive law theory foreshadowed Austin's (19th-century) legal theory and doctrine on sovereignty.

[105] See, e.g., Ch. XXII, at 275: In (national) legal persons, 'the power of the Representative is always Limited: And that which prescribeth the Limits thereof, is the Power Sovereign. For Power Unlimited, is absolute Soveraignty. And the Soveraign, in every Commonwealth, is the absolute Representative of the subjects, and therefore no other, can be Representative of any part of them, but so far forth, as he shall give leave ...' In the international context there is no sovereign and therefore no authority to create either international law or international legal persons.

[106] See, e.g., Geschichte des öffentlichen Rechts, *op. cit.* footnote 19, at 230 *et seq.*

[107] See, MacDonald Ross, at 4. 'Throughout his life Pufendorf remained gratefully devoted to this eminent teacher.' See also, W. Simons' Introduction to On the Law of Nature and Nations (1688), transl. De Jure Naturae et Gentium (1672) in the Classics of International Law (ed.), at 12*a* (1934). Hereinafter: JNG. Although Pufendorf 'formally' broke with this method in De Jure Naturae et Gentium (1672), its structure is still present in the way he reasoned. Id., at 14 *a*.

was involved in the practical aspects of Imperial and European politics. In 1658, Pufendorf earned his living as a tutor in Denmark in the service of the Swedish ambassador. When war broke out between the two countries shortly after his arrival, he was imprisoned by the Danish authorities and recourse to diplomatic protection was denied him.[108] In 1670, Pufendorf ended a nine-year stay at the University of Heidelberg in order to take up residence at the University of Lund, in Lutheran Sweden. Two years later, he published *De Jure Naturae et Gentium*.[109] Leibniz and Pufendorf corresponded intermittently from 1674-1693.[110]

From 1677 until his death in 1694, Pufendorf dedicated his professional life to being a full-time advisor to several royal courts. First, he became the privy councillor and historiographer of Charles XI, the King of Sweden. In 1688, Frederick William, the Great Elector of Brandenburg, invited him to the Court in Berlin, where he served Frederick William's son, Frederick III, until his death. From 1618 onwards, Brandenburg and Prussia were both governed by the same Sovereign.[111] In 1640, Frederick William (r. 1640-1688) succeeded to the title of Elector of Brandenburg and Duke of Prussia and while in the former capacity he was officially an imperial subject, in the latter he was not. Frederick William was a "modern," "enlightened absolutist" protestant ruler who built his state at the expense of the 'universal' authoritative structures of the Emperor and Pope. The celebrated description of the imperial institution as a 'monstrous' political organisation however pre-dates his service to both the King of Sweden and the Great Elector of Brandenburg: 'l'Allemagne est un corps irregulier & confus & qu'il s'en faut de bien peu que ce ne soit un monstre en politique.'[112] As early as 1664 under his pseudonym *Monzambano*, Pufendorf analysed the (problematic) state of imperial politics in clear terms:

> Ce qui cause des grands maux à l'Allemagne, & qui est une source de trouble & de malheurs pour elle; c'est que Caesar [il] travaille incessamment à reduire l'Empire sous les veritable loix d'une Monarchie, au lieu que les Estats tout au contraire font ce qu'ils peuvent pour conserver & pour augmenter leur liberté. ... 'les autres Princes de l'Allemagne, sont si faschés de voir les Electeur si puissans, & si riches que leur jalousie passe quelque fois jusques à la querelle & au bruit, & va si avant, qu'ils n'ont point de

---

[108] During his eight months in captivity, he wrote *On the Elements of Universal Jurisprudence* (1660).

[109] A second edition appeared in 1684, and a third in 1688, published in Amsterdam, of which The Classics of International Law (ed.) is a photographic reproduction.

[110] K. Müller and G. Krönert (Eds.), Leben und Werk von G.W. Leibniz (1969), at 37.

[111] Until 1618, Prussia had *not* been part of the Holy Roman Empire. In the Middle Ages, Prussia was the land of the Teutonic Knights. Europe: A History, at 556 *et seq.* In 1701, Frederick Willem III crowned himself King of Prussia.

[112] Pufendorf, L'Estat de l'Empire d'Allemagne de Monzambane (1669), at 310 and 348; this is a French transl. of Pufendorf's work: Severinus de Monzambano, De statu imperii Germanici (1664). See also, id., at 277: 'l'irregularité de cet Estat;' id., at 346: 'L'Allemagne ne peût ester qu'un Estat bien infirme.' Leibniz referred to Pufendorf's qualifications of the Empire in, e.g., Caesarius Fürstenerius, at 119.

honte d'usurper, contre toute forte de justice, & de droit beaucoup de choses, qui ne leur appartiennent pas; ...[113]

Religious differences that tended to result in wars caused problems both within and outside the emerging states. Unlike Leibniz, Pufendorf did not strive to reconcile these differences by means of a single ecumenical programme or to reinforce the universal authoritative structure.[114] Pufendorf never opposed the definitive break-up of the medieval universal political structures; he simply considered this break-up inevitable. In his opinion, a political constellation was either a united state with one sovereign or an alliance of states. Any division of sovereignty was impossible.[115] Moreover, to restore the Empire and turn it into a regular and unified state was, in his eyes, practically impossible as it would require a 'complete turn-around and total revolution' and would consequently result in horrible disorder: 'on ne pourroit jamais remettre l'Allemagne dans son premier Estat, qu'avec des difficultés extremes qu'avec des travaux insurmontables, & qu'en causant des confusions & des desordres horribles.'[116] Pufendorf therefore did not expect that the re-unification and reinforcement of the Empire would promote peace and order among the Imperial and European powers. He did, however, subscribe to the view that religion as a potentially explosive and divisive element within the Empire and Europe at large should be brought under control. In order to serve as the guideline in politics among the rulers and to transcend the religious differences between them and in order to preserve peace and order within the Westphalian system, international politics should operate on the basis of one (neutral) natural law system.

Starting from man's natural reason and his existential desire to associate (sociability), Pufendorf built a whole system of rights and duties of necessary natural law upon the obligation to support society, or at least upon the prohibition to harm one's fellow man. He followed Grotius in the idea that man was essentially sociable, although Pufendorf believed that man was sociable out of a concern for his own safety and well-being, instead of out of his love for society. It was true, he believed, that the Divine creator had established a state of fellowship among all men, but since by nature man loved himself more than society, 'it does not at once follow that man is led by nature to a civil society.'[117] On the contrary, man was not civil by nature: by nature, man needed law in order to be capable of being civil. Since man was thus both social and anti-social, he could not live without either society or law, for then he would be 'miserable' and 'degrade[d].'[118]

[113] L'Estat de l'Empire d'Allemagne, at 310 and 352-353.

[114] In 1679, Pufendorf under the pseudonym Basilii Hyperate, published a critical work on the Roman Catholic Church and its claim to sovereignty, 'Historische und Politische Beschreibung der geistlichen Monarchie des Stuhls zu Rom.'

[115] See also, Geschichte des öffentlichen Rechts, at 234.

[116] L'Estat de l'Empire d'Allemagne, at 311 and 369.

[117] JNG, Book VII.I.3, at 952.

[118] Id., Book II.I.8, at 153.

The human condition made society necessary: man needed social life within a state to protect him from his fellow man. This is how the social contract became the origin of the domestic civil society. Man used to live in an insecure state of nature until the 'multitude' agreed, first, to unite and to form a state – an association of the people – and, second, by a subsequent covenant, to subject itself to a sovereign, which made man into a citizen. The sovereign to which the multitude subjected itself thereupon became the Commander of the law and, as such, was bound to complete the natural law already present within the societies.[119]

In Pufendorf's theory, the state was thus unequivocally defined as a 'moral person,'[120] distinct from both the sovereign ruler and those he rules, and with a will of its own directed at securing a common peace.[121] The state was the public composite moral person in whom 'supreme authority is found ... by which ... it lives and is animated,' like man by his '*soul*.'[122] This supreme political authority or sovereignty indicated the capacity to use 'natural strength, through which a subject can be coerced by the threat of some evil ...to obey its commands.' In Pufendorf's view, states were 'unintelligible without supreme sovereignty' and therefore 'states ... and *supreme sovereignty came from God* as the author of natural law.' His contribution to the emerging perception of sovereignty as a somehow sacred state of being is evident.[123] The analogy of the indivisible,

---

[119] Id., Book VII.II and III. Contrary to Hobbes' theory, Pufendorf claims that the creation of the state took *two* covenants. First the multitude united into an association designed to defend their security and after this association had chosen a form of government a second covenant was made which arranged for the Sovereignty of the ruler, monarch or assembly, and the subjection of what had then become 'citizens' to this supreme authority. Only the second pact completes the creation of the state and confers civil duties upon the subjects. However, this second pact is not a transfer of sovereignty from the united multitude to the sovereign, which would suggest a kind of popular sovereignty, it is in fact the *creation* of sovereignty.

[120] To be precise, Pufendorf started the construction of his theory on the Law of Nature and of Nations with metaphysics and the formation of moral entities by the unification of individual men and 'by reason of that union, [whatever] they want or do, is considered as one will, one act, and no more.' Id., Book I.I.13, at 13,the state being an example of a 'general,' 'public,' and 'civil' society.

[121] 'And as it is distinguished and marked off from all individual men by one name ... And so the most convenient definition of a state appears to be this: 'A state is a compound moral person, whose will, intertwined and united by the pacts of a number of men, is considered the will of all, so that it is able to make use of the strength and faculties of the individual members for the common peace and security.' JNG, Book VII.II.13, at 984.

[122] In natural law thinking, the 'soul' enabled man to relate to God and to know the eternal and universal truths emanating from reason. Having a soul was indeed a requirement for falling under God's law, the law of nature. Pufendorf's concept of sovereignty is therefore not detached from the moral realm, nor is it exclusively a political notion concerning power. See also, *supra*, on Leibniz and the rational soul which enables man to relate to God and Perfection. According to Leibniz, the soul was a simple rational substance, but with multiplicity within this simple unity. Similarly, the Emperor is sovereign, but the Princes he governs are also Sovereign; another example of division or 'plurality' within unity. Pufendorf's concept of the soul is a single undivided unity and sovereignty – the 'soul of the state' – is therefore absolute. See also, for 'plurality' within the imperial union, Entretien de Philarete et d'Eugène, *supra*, footnote 28, at 291: 'conciliant la pluralité des souverainetés avec l'unité de la Republique de l'Empire.'

[123] JNG, Book VII.III. 1 and 2, at 1000-1. Emphasis added.

single 'soul' served Pufendorf in his criticism of the weakness of the Holy Roman Empire and in his legitimisation of the authority and independence of the newly emerging states and their absolutist Sovereigns. The Empire lacked the required 'single soul' and undivided will to be a regular state and by the label of 'irregularity' the imperial political constellation could be discredited and undermined.[124] The imperial system was described as a weak, disintegrating political institution made up of regular states which each had a soul of their own. Pufendorf thus dealt quite a blow to the imperial structure of divided political authority and the excuses made used by the German princes to support their claim to absolute sovereignty and convince of the need to reinforce their states.

Although Pufendorf considered sovereignty to be 'absolute,' he rejected the idea that absolute Sovereigns were allowed to display 'unjust or intolerable' decision-making behaviour: '[f]or surely we do not establish states to the end that we may neglect natural law, and do everything according to our wicked lusts.' On the contrary, the whole point of the state was 'that the security and safety of every man may be better guarded by uniting the resources of many, and that therefore there may be opportunity for the safe exercise of natural law.'[125] The created Sovereign, whether 'one simple person, or one council, composed of a few or all citizens,'[126] however, had a supreme authority in which his subjects did not share. His governance was not subject to the approval of the people, the Sovereign was 'not accountable.' In fact, he was 'sacrosanct.'[127] However, although sovereignty did not always come with the corollary of accountability, as this, it was thought, would only contribute to disorder, the sovereign still had a duty under natural law to defend the internal and external safety of his subjects and a duty to act in a manner beneficial to the state and to promulgate laws to that end. Like Grotius, Pufendorf recognised that there was – if only in very rare cases – a moral right to rebel against *tyrannical* rule.[128] However, tyranny was defined so restrictively that the legitimacy of political rule was based upon the needs and happiness of the subjects in theory only. In politics, all depended on the enlightenment of the ruler. The citizens were obedient subjects who did not participate in their own governance, unlike in the 'republican' definition of citizenship.

---

[124] 'We hold that the *regularity* of states lies in this: that each and every one of them appears to be directed by a single soul, as it were, or, in other words, that the supreme sovereignty, without division and opposition, is exercised by one will in all the parts of a state, and in all its undertakings. From this it is not difficult to gather what an *irregular* state is.' JNG, Book VII.V.2, at 1024. Emphasis added.

[125] Id., Book VII.VI.7, at 1064. It was the highest and most absolute liberty found within the state: 'to decide by their own judgement about the means that look to the welfare of the state. ... [I]t is the right to prescribe such means for citizens, and to force them to obedience.' Id.

[126] Id., Book VII.V.3 and 4, at 1024-1025.

[127] Id., Book VII.VI and VIII, at 1055 and 1103 *et seq.*

[128] Id., Book VII.VIII, at 1106 *et seq.* A revolt against tyranny is legitimate when it springs from self-defence and self-preservation. Anything even slightly less than tyranny was not a legitimate cause for revolt against the ruler.

Even in this perception of the state as a 'person,' independent of both sovereign and subjects, and with a will and "face" of its own, the state still did not have *personality* in *international* law, because Pufendorf denied the existence of a law of nations which was separate from natural law. He 'fully subscribe[d]' to the Hobbesian definition which stated that the law of nations was nothing more than the laws applicable among nations that lived in a state of nature and were fighting for self-preservation. As no supra-sovereign commander had as yet emerged onto the international scene, a (positive) law of nations could not exist.[129] States and their sovereigns lived in a 'state of nature,' which was therefore a non-'civic state', i.e., a state in which there were no civic or legal duties towards others.

In conclusion, Pufendorf's search for a moral and political philosophy of the Imperial system and his persevering perception and promotion of a new Europe of sovereign states lent his theory its strangely "modern" identity. His characterisation of Sovereignty as the "sacred" soul of the state quite unintentionally foreshadowed the future glorification of the state. In the 19th century, the moral – natural law – dimension of the notion of sovereignty was abandoned in favour of its purely political meaning of unrestricted power. Pufendorf's rejection of the Holy Roman Empire as a state may be considered an example of the linguistic or ideological context. Riley argued that: 'a great many seventeenth-century theorists devoted their efforts to the (theoretical) destruction of all the medieval *collegia* existing below the level of the state, as well as the 'universal' authorities existing above the level of the state.'[130] Pufendorf's description of the Empire as an organisation or system of sovereign states is recognised as reflecting the general view in a 'brilliant and provocative' manner.[131] His support of an absolute and undivided concept of sovereignty as well as his denial of the existence of a separate law of nations were conceptual impediments to the introduction of ILP in his theory. Put differently, for the purpose of Pufendorf's (practical and theoretical) argument, ILP was not an appropriate or necessary concept. Against the background of this brief introduction to the conventions of the jurisprudential context – we may consider Pufendorf's views as representative of the prevailing view of his time – the originality of Leibniz' defence of the Holy Roman Empire as a (federal) state and his argument on *relative* sovereignty and ILP stands out clearly.

2.3. Introduction of ILP within Leibniz' Universal Jurisprudence

Leibniz' introduction and definition of ILP reads as follows:

He possesses a *personality in international law* who *represents the public liberty*, such that he is *not subject to* the tutelage or the power of anyone else, but has in himself the

[129] Id., Book II. III, at 226.
[130] Riley's introduction to LPW, at 29.
[131] See also, Geschichte des öffentlichen Rechts, at 235.

power of war and of alliances; although he may perhaps be *limited by the bonds of obligation* towards a superior and owe him homage, fidelity and obedience. If his authority, then, is *sufficiently extensive*, it is agreed to call him a potentate, and he will be called a *sovereign* or a sovereign power; ... Those are counted among sovereign powers, then, and are held to possess sovereignty, who can count on sufficient freedom and power to exercise some influence in international affairs, with armies or by treaties ...[132]

First, the words 'personality in international law' were a translation of *persona jure gentium*. Leibniz did not use *persona iuris inter gentes* here even though he did use the term *iuris inter gentes* to indicate international law. Likewise, in spite of the fact that the *Codex* was a collection of positive law, Leibniz chose the title *Codex Iuris Gentium* instead of *Codex Iuris inter gentes*, which would have been the obvious choice.[133] *Ius gentium*, the law of nations, and *iuris inter gentes*, the law between nations and their Sovereigns, were both in use but it could be said that they referred to different concepts of law.

Second, this definition of ILP immediately brings to light the contemporary tension with regard to the concept of sovereignty in relation to which ILP here emerged. ILP depended on sovereignty, but according to Leibniz sovereignty was a relative concept. On the one hand, in order to posses international personality one had to 'represent the public liberty' and have supreme public power, which included 'the power to exercise some influence in international affairs.' On the other hand, one could be subjected to an even higher power and have obligations towards it. Leibniz introduced the notion of ILP in direct relation to this *relative* concept of sovereignty.

To understand the emergence of ILP, we must first recall the political realism which Leibniz displayed by recognising both the German Emperor's and the German Princes' claims to sovereignty. Leibniz' relative conception of sovereignty was the perfect solution to this dilemma. At the same time it accomodated another political reality in Europe: the powerful and expansionist King of France.

Secondly, because we can only fully grasp the originality of Leibniz' reasoning if we consider his moral ideology, we must examine Leibniz' defence of the ideal of a unified *Respublica Christiana*, and of the Holy Roman Empire as the approximation of this ideal, and analyse his concept of the law of nations in relation to natural law and justice. He was the 'last thinker of great stature to defend the Empire,' but, since he also took account of political reality, he was at the same time the 'apologist' of the sovereignty of the German Princes.[134] It is from this balancing act between idealism and apology that the concept of ILP was born.

---

132 Codex, at 175. Emphasis added.

133 In 1651, Richard Zouche published a textbook with '*ius inter gentes*' in the title. See, The Epochs, at 25.

134 Riley's Introduction to LPW, at 1, 26.

2.3.1. Political realism: the concept of relative sovereignty

With the *Codex*, Leibniz continued the line of reasoning already set out in the *Caesarinus Fürstenerius* ('Prince-as-Emperor,' the pseudonym under which Leibniz published this work in 1677), which dealt with the sovereignty of the Princes.[135] In this work, Leibniz presented quite an original position. His objective, as Riley has pointed out, was 'the redefinition of the concept of sovereignty in a way which would *allow the minor German princes to be treated as sovereigns* in international negotiations.'[136] This redefinition was refined in the *Codex*. The Codex was, however, also prompted by another practical political objective: the medieval documents brought together in the *Codex*, which were intended as authoritative precedents, were '*supporting the position of the Empire* against the claims of the French.'[137] In other words, these two texts should be read against this practical-political background of the appearance of new actors on the international stage and French expansionist politics. In 1677, Leibniz observed that to write on sovereignty was a delicate and tricky endeavour:

> In explaining the concept of sovereignty, I confess that I must enter into –and this is remarkable, dealing as it does with so important and common a concept – a field which is thorny and little-cultivated. The reason for this is that, because of a deplorable mania, those who undertake to write [on sovereignty] have eyes only for what is ancient, [and] of which vestiges scarcely survive, while they are not interested in more modern things.[138]

First, the words 'more modern things' at the end of this observation may be read to refer to the undeniable importance of the German Princes in international politics after the conclusion of the 1648 Treaties. Given the practical problems of ceremonial and diplomatic practices as well as the political instability as a result of the Princes' struggle for sovereignty, political reality demanded the recognition of the supremacy of the Princes in their territories and the accommodation of their representation at and participation in international affairs. More concretely: the advocacy of the sovereignty and equality of the German Princes in general and of the Duke of Brunswick in particular required solid underpinning and legitimisation. Both the *Entretien de Philarete et d'Eugène* and the more legal theoretical *Caesarinus Fürstenerius* serve this cause.[139]

---

[135] See *supra*, footnote 71; the original title of this work is: De Jure Suprematus ac Legationis Principum Germaniae.

[136] Riley, LPW, at 111. Emphasis added.

[137] Riley's Introduction to the Codex, LPW, at 165. Emphasis added. See, for Leibniz' objections to French foreign policy, Codex, at 166-169.

[138] Caesarinus Fürstenerius, *op. cit.* footnote 71, at 113.

[139] In the Dialogue between the two diplomats, Philarete and d'Eugène, Leibniz examined what exactly distinguished the Electors from the prominent Princes and argued that the issue of diplomatic privileges actually belonged to the realm of the law of nations: it is related to what Electors and Princes have in common, i.e., their independence and sovereignty in/over their Estates, rather than to what sets them apart, i.e., the right to choose the Emperor. Moreover, it explains how the sovereignty of a Prince is compatible with the obligations he owes to his superior the Emperor.

Secondly, also relevant to the redefinition of sovereignty was the drawback involved in strengthening the position of the German princes, namely their (potentially) arbitrary use of power. Leibniz pointed out the possibility that the Princes 'without regard of what is permitted and what is not, are disposed to sacrifice the blood of the innocent to their particular ambition, and often push [them] into criminal actions.' To prevent such abuses from occurring, i.e., to secure order and peace among the Princes in the German political constellation, Leibniz favoured 'constrain[ing] them, by a greater authority, ... by the authority which [he] believe[d] reside[d] somehow in the universal Church, and in the Holy Empire, and in its two heads, the Emperor and a legitimate Pope, using his power legitimately.'[140] In order to maintain this power and authority, Leibniz strove to preserve the 'two-headed' structure of the Holy Roman Empire as this might counterbalance the drawback mentioned.

Thirdly, the Empire's position was affected by France's expansionist stance both within and outside Europe. This issue, which was given particular emphasis in the publication of the *Codex*, is also relevant in the sense that it indirectly supports a second concept of sovereignty. Leibniz' attachment to the continuation of the Holy Roman Empire and the position of the Emperor cannot be explained from his idealism alone – although this was indeed of crucial importance – but must also be considered against the background of the balance of power in Europe at the time, a balance which had formed the foundations of Europe's stability since the Westphalian peace treaties. For this reason, Leibniz defended the Empire's position against the absolutist French monarch Louis XIV. German rulers and peoples alike lived in fear of French domination and French expansionism.[141] The Thirty Years' War had caused Germany's position to weaken significantly. After the War had ended, France had still succeeded in annexing German territory, among which the city of Strasbourg in 1681, in spite of the Peace of Nijmegen (1678-1679). These acts had a profound effect on Leibniz and seemed to have roused his anger.[142] The balance of power was further disturbed by the fact that the German Princes were unable to keep up with France's expanding colonial power outside Europe. To compensate for the negative impact on the European power balance, which jeopardised the hard-fought peace and stability, Leibniz came to the defence of the Holy Roman Empire and pleaded its resurrection. This was based on a realistic political calculation: a united Empire would be better capable of standing its ground against the French, because 'there is strength in unity,' or so Leibniz must have thought.

---

[140] Id., at 112.

[141] Riley, Introduction to LPW, at 33 *et seq.* In this light, Riley explains, we should also read Leibniz' suggestion to Louis XIV to conquer Egypt (in *Consilium Aegyptiacum* (1671)). Rather than attack a Christian power like the United Provinces, he advised France to attack the Ottomans in Egypt, which he hoped would spare Europe, i.e., the Christian 'universal monarchy' from another devastating war. Egypt would sufficiently distract France to make it less of a threat to Europe.

[142] Codex, at 166, 'the almost ridiculous fact that a truce was established a little after a peace treaty.' See also Leibniz as cited by Riley: 'the king needed it for the security of his kingdom; that is to say, to better maintain what he had stolen from the Empire ...,' *in* Introduction to LPW, at 36.

These political factors must have encouraged Leibniz to redefine sovereignty and international participation. As Princes, Kings and the Emperor all claimed sovereignty and the (diplomatic) privileges that came with it, the clarification of the matter depended on a new concept of sovereignty, which would serve all parties and prevent further embarrassments, such as befell the Duke of Brunswick in 1676. Correspondence actually shows that Leibniz indeed received letters supporting his intention to offer clarity on the issue of (legal) status and diplomatic ceremonial as apparent from his exposé in the *Praefatio* as well as in the sequel of the *Codex*.[143]

In the *Praefatio*, Leibniz built on and refined his 1677 exposé on the concepts of sovereignty and state in terms of the law of nature and of nations. His argument on the sovereignty of the Princes and the relations among the Imperial and European powers became increasingly connected with justice.

To begin with, Leibniz introduced a new theory of sovereignty in the *Caesarinus Fursteneriu*s.[144] He distinguished between the 'lord of the territory' and the 'lord of the jurisdiction,' who has 'the right of deciding cases or of handing down judgments,' which generally includes the right and capacity to take mild coercive action against 'obstinate private persons [*imperium*] ... by using a few officers of justice, or even, if necessary, by calling citizens together for help.'[145] Secondly, he explained that sovereignty consisted of a substantial and a gradual element. Sovereignty required: a) the right of territorial hegemony, i.e., being 'lord of the

[143] In 1692 and 1693, Leibniz wrote many letters to collect pieces for the Codex. He also received many letters praising his project as 'very useful' and 'promising' and offers of assistance. Some of these letters pay express attention to the issue of diplomatic ceremonies and privileges. See, e.g., C.D. Findekeller, who, in a letter to Leibniz dated 30 December 1692 which he sent from Dresden, wrote: 'Avanthier Monsieur d'Ilten apres avoir receu son creditif comme Ministre Electoral de vostre Ser^me^ Maistre, fut introduit à l'audience de S.A. E^le^ en conformité d'un Ministre d'une teste Couronneé, car chez nous il n'y a pas de distinction dans l'introduction d'un Minsitre d'un Roy ou d'un Electeur. Le lendemain il depescha un Courrier à vostre Cour. Le Gr. Escuiyer de Danemarc Mr Haxthausen, qui est icy, peut bien avoir eu en Commission de son Roy, de traverser cette Investiture, mais voyant à present, que c'est une affaire faite, il fait bien, de n'en plus parler, chez nous l'on me mande, que les autre Opposants ne reposent pas cela, et qu'ils viennent de conclure un *Foedus* avec Danemarc, sous pretexte du maintien des Droits des Princes de l'Empire.' Excerpt from a letter by Findekeller as published *in* Acad. Ed., I, 9er Band, at 225-226. On 21 May 1693, C.J. Nicholai von Greiffencrantz wrote the following in a letter to Leibniz: 'Les Ceremonies passées à des solemnitez, seront sans doute le point le plus delicat et le plus éembarasée de vostre ouvrage. Vous sçavez, que dans les siecles passés elles n'ont gueres été reglées, et nous trouvons, par example, encore au siecles passé des rencontres, où des Princes les Principaux de l'Empire, ont sans dispute cedé la place à des Plenipotentiaires des Electeurs, non point en actes de ceremonie, mais à des repas ou festins, Ce qui ne se feroit point au temps où nous sommes.' Id., at 452-453. See also, von Greiffencrantz' letters of July 1693 and February-March 1694, id., at 531-532, and Acad. Ed., I, 10er Band, at 272-274 and 324-327. See also Leibniz in a letter he wrote to P. Pellisson-Fontanier on 3 July 1692 which was published *in* Acad. Ed., I, 8er Band, at 127.

[144] This new conceptual thinking on (the plurality of) supreme power and its basis did cause, *inter alia*, the Elector of Brandenburg to protest against the newfangled theory. See, e.g., Lotte Knabe's Introduction, Acad. Ed., IV, 2er Band, at XXI.

[145] *Caesarius Fürstenerius*, at 115-116. See also, *Entretien de Philarete et d'Eugène*, at 305.

territory,' and b) a 'large' territory, as only '*larger* powers' had the capacity to participate in international affairs.

Concerning the first, substantial, requirement, Leibniz defined the legal meaning of the notion of 'territory:'

> *Territory* is a name common to a state or a dominion or a tract of land. But in addition to its fundamental meaning, it *also expresses the aggregate of laws and rights*, so that just as inheritance and patrimony involve the whole of the things and rights in some family or dwelling, so territory signifies the whole of laws and rights which can come to obtain in an inhabited portion of the earth.[146]

Within a territory, a variety of laws and rights may be applicable and these rights may be distributed over a number of 'lords' within this territory. The person who has the right of territorial hegemony is the 'lord of the territory' with a right to limited military power. The lord of the territory may lack the right of supreme jurisdiction and of judging capital crimes or the right to take mild enforcement action against private persons, he may even lack the right of taxes or coining, however, if he has 'the right to assemble a military force which is sufficient for keeping the whole dominion in its duty' – the right and power to maintain an army that is mighty enough to be employed 'against an entire community' and thus to secure domestic order and stability – he has what Leibniz called territorial hegemony:

> It is *essential only* that he have in readiness the power to obtain from his subjects, either by his dignity or, when necessary, by *force majeur*, whatever rights do remain his. For even if all other rights or royalties are taken from him, it is enough that there remain sufficient jurisdiction to preserve his authority over his subjects, and enough revenue to sustain his household, in keeping with his rank, and to support the ministers of his power.[147]

Territorial hegemony was therefore the 'highest right of *forcing* or *coercing*' within a territory, higher than the right to use force against a few rebellious citizens or on certain 'stubborn people.' In Leibniz' opinion, this highest right of force 'can be retained even without soldiers, merely by men's opinion, that is by their obedient reverence, by the *dignity* (of the ruler), which can accomplish just as much, and often more, than force itself – so long that the common opinion of the subjects is that one ought to *obey*.'

The second (gradual) requirement that only the lords 'who hold a *larger* territory' were sovereign and were thus, as '*larger powers*,' entitled to significant military power meant that only these lords had the right and capacity to conduct international relations. As such, sovereignty is a relative, gradual concept. Sovereign rulers differ from other 'lords of territory' only *by the degree*, not the nature, of their rank.[148]

---

146 Id., at 114.

147 Id., at 115-116.

148 Id., at 114-117: '[A]lthough smaller territories of this kind are customarily called *souverainétés*, the term in its more usual sense is somewhat more narrowly restricted, and those per-

Leibniz stressed that this specific capacity of larger powers to participate in international (diplomatic) life and to handle issues 'concerning the law of nations (*ius gentium*)' was indeed the qualifying faculty.

Souverain ou Potentat est celuy qui se peut faire considerer en Europe en temps de paix et en temps de guerre, par traitez, armes et alliances. ... c'est cette faculté qui fait prendre part aux privileges du droit des gens, c'est à dire à l'égard des ceremonies, du rang, des Ambassades, des declaration de guerre, des cartels, du respect qu'on doit aux Souverains, de l'inviolabilité de leur personne, et de tout ce qui est receu entre les Potentats par la raison reconnue generalement de tout temps, ou par la coustume introduite de nos temps entre les peuples civilisés et sur tout entre les Chretiens de nostre Europe.[149]

Leibniz consistently argued that the German Princes fulfilled these requirements and thus qualified as sovereigns: 'the German princes can do all these [things – they have all of the required capacities].' With sovereignty as a relative concept, Leibniz nevertheless had to distinguish between the counts and the Princes of the Empire.[150] Neither the 'counts' nor the 'lords of tiny territories' – 'of some village or burg' – were 'powerful enough' to be sovereign. And of course political stability would not be served by further political fragmentation, which could render diplomatic relations almost ineffective. Lords of small territories could therefore not qualify as sovereigns.

Here, it seems that Leibniz' concept of state also came into play.[151] In 1677, he explained that '[a] state would seem to be a fairly *large* gathering of men, begun in the hope of mutual defense [*sic.*] against a large [external] force, such as is usually feared, with the intention of living together, including the foundation of some administration of common affairs.'[152] To qualify as a *respublica* or state,

---

sons only are called sovereigns or potentates who hold a *larger* territory and can lead out an army. And this it is, *finally, which I call supremacy*. The French too, I think, when they are discussing matters concerning the law of nations [*ius gentium*] – peace, war, treaties – and call some persons sovereign, are not speaking of lords of tiny territories which even a wealthy merchant might easily buy for himself, but of those *larger* powers which can wage war, sustain it, survive somehow by their own power, make treaties take part with authority in the affairs of other peoples: (in short), powers which are somehow exempt from the commerce of private persons and which, as human affairs now stand, cannot easily fall to lower persons, or persons of lesser standing (excepting the election of ecclesiastical princes). Thus it is that those who occupy this summit are honoured by the *other major* powers, and by the lords of lands and peoples and the masters of human affairs, as brothers and persons of equal condition (although, perhaps, of lesser power by a considerable degree), and are considered to differ from those men *by the degree*, not the nature, of their rank.' Emphasis added.

[149] Entretien de Philarete et d'Eugène, at 306.

[150] Id., at 115.

[151] Leibniz located the origins of the state not so much in a pact or original contract, but in *nature*. As Leibniz did not consider man purely egoistic by nature, like Hobbes believed, he did not support the view that man could only become civilised by contract either. Instead, Leibniz argued that man was by nature a rational soul seeking perfection and the happiness of others and that society was born from nature, not from contract.

[152] Id., at 114.

the gathering should therefore be *large*. In Leibniz' view, smaller gatherings would sooner resemble the ('Aristotelian') *polis*, which he proceeded to name *civitas*. In other words, the size of the territory determined whether it was a city or a state, and whether the lord of the territory was powerful enough to be a *sovereign person*. Having enumerated the capacities one needed to possess in order to qualify for sovereignty (i.e., the right to territory and military power and (thus) the capacity to conduct international relations) and having ascertained that '[t]he German princes can do all these [things],' Leibniz concluded that 'the union notwithstanding' they are *sovereign*.[153]

This was the conception of sovereignty that underpinned Leibniz' argument in the *Praefatio*, where he repeated that if a ruler's 'authority, then, is *sufficiently extensive*, it is agreed to call him a potentate, and he will be called a *sovereign*.' ... '[T]hose are counted among sovereign powers, then, and are held to possess sovereignty, who can count on *sufficient* freedom and power to exercise *some* influence in international affairs, with armies or by treaties.' In the relative meaning that Leibniz contributed to the concept, a sovereign was he who had the capacity to wage war, the capacity to conclude treaties, in brief, he who had 'sufficient freedom' and was powerful enough to participate with at least 'some influence' in international affairs together with other major European powers.[154] Note that sovereignty was thus a capacity of *individual* rulers. It was the individual who was the lord of a territory and thereby the bearer of the right of sovereignty, *not* the state.

Leibniz balanced his advocacy of the sovereignty of the Princes with a defence of the imperial *majestas* and the unity of the Holy Roman Empire. He argued that the Emperor and the Empire had a 'tres grand pouvoir sur les Electeurs et Princes.' Leibniz contended that the Empire qualified as a state and that the Emperor had imperial *majestas*. Here, *majestas* means superiority, which is different from sovereignty.[155] Sovereigns, i.e., rulers with sufficient military power, may be subordinate to rulers with *majestas*, which is the central *locus* of authority. '[L]a Majesté est le droit de commander sans pouvoir ester commandé,' Leibniz explained. It is a right to 'supreme jurisdiction.'[156] Because he had imperial *majestas*, the Emperor was able to ensure the unity of the Empire.

Contrary to the contemporary conventions, Leibniz regarded the Empire as a 'union' of regions, which each had a *sovereign* lord of the territory. 'For a union, it is necessary that a certain administration be formed, with some power over the members; which power obtains as a matter of ordinary right, in matters of great

---

[153] Id., at 117. See also, Leibniz in A letter to P. Pellisson-Fontanier, *op. cit.* footnote 143, at 127.

[154] See *supra*, citation to footnote 132.

[155] In other words, Leibniz disagreed with Bodin, who regarded *majestas* as sovereignty, i.e., absolute power, when for Leibniz *majestas* and sovereignty were two distinct concepts.

[156] Entretien de Philarete et d'Eugène, at 308. Here, *majestas* approaches the notion of 'lord of jurisdiction.' See, e.g., for *majestas* in Reichspublistik, Geschichte des öffentlichen Rechts.

moment, and those which concern the public welfare. Here I say there exists a *state*.' Leibniz explained that a confederation of regions or Princes would not create a new and independent legal person. However, a *union* of territories which all recognised one administration and a coordinating power for the purpose of 'public welfare' would be a state. In a way similar to the founding of a 'company, a new civil person is formed.'[157] And indeed in earlier writings, from around 1670, we find Leibniz describing the Empire in such terms: 'das Reich soll eine *Persona Civilis* sehn'[158] and '*Respublica est persona civilis*.'[159] The *Caesarius Fürstenerius* continued this line of reasoning and also claimed that the Holy Roman Empire was a state with its own supreme ruler and an administration which, in the case of this union, had authority over its composing members, but whose superiority or *majestas* did not invalidate the sovereignty of the Princes, i.e., the union members. This theory concerning the Empire left the existing universal structure intact and gave the Emperor the following powers which the Princes lacked:

> The position of the [Holy Roman] Emperor is a little more elevated than one commonly thinks; Caesar is the defender, or rather the chief, or if one prefers the secular arm of the universal Church. All Christendom forms a species of republic, in which Caesar has some authority – from which comes the name, Holy Empire, which should somehow extend as far as the Catholic Church. Caesar is the commander [*Imperator*], that is, the born leader of Christians against the infidels: it is mainly for him to destroy schisms, to bring about the meeting of [ecumenical] Councils, to maintain good order, in short to act through the authority of his position so that the Church and the Republic of Christendom suffer no harm.[160]

The Emperor stood at the head of an imperial administration which had a certain degree of authority over the Princes and was concerned with the public welfare of the Empire. He was expected to establish unity, to defend and command the Empire against external enemies, to preserve the 'public peace' and to 'administer justice' among the Princes and Dukes. As the secular arm of the Universal Church, the Emperor was the universal authority in the Christian Republic and this 'elevated' him to 'greater' authority over the members of this 'Republic.'

---

[157] Caesarius Fürstenerius, at 117. Emphasis added.

[158] Securitas Publica (1670), *in* Acad. Ed., IV, 1er Band (1667-1676) N.5, 133-214, at 135: 'Denn das Reich soll eine *Persona Civilis* sehn. Gleich wie nun in einer *persona naturali* oder menschlichen Leibe sich die *Spiritus*, das Blut and die Glieder finden, also ist in der *persona civili* ein *perpetuum consilium*, welches den Verstand and die Spiritus, ein perpetuum aerarium, welches geblüth und adern, ein *perpetuus miles*, welcher die Glieder repraesentirt, von nöthen, und gleichwie die Glieder von dem Bluth sich nähren, das Blut nicht ohne der *spirituum* Bewegung sich reget, also kan der *perpetuum miles* ohne stetswerendes aerarium nicht verpfleget, das *aerarium* sowohl als *miles sine consilio perpetuo* in ordentlicher Bewegung nicht erhalten oder regiert werden.'

[159] Leibniz, Georgius Ulicovius Lithuanus (1669), Propos. XLII, *in* Acad. Ed., IV, 1er Band (1667-1676) N.1, 3-98, at 37. See also, e.g., Leibniz, Severinum de Monzambano (1668-1672), *in* Acad. Ed., IV, 1er Band (1667-1676), N.32, at 500 *et seq*.: '*Civitas est una persona moralis*.'

[160] Caesarinus Fürstenerius, at 111.

The Emperor enjoyed a 'species of primacy analogous to the ecclesiastical primacy [of the Pope].' He was the sovereign of the Holy Roman Empire, endowed with the highest legitimate power the Empire could bestow, and this made him a major power in Europe.[161] By calling the Empire a 'union,' a federal state *avant la lettre* as it were, Leibniz made a hugely original contribution to the debate, which was nothing less than the '*Entwicklung einer ständisch orientierten Bundesstaatstheorie*.'[162]

Leibniz' theory of relative sovereignty enabled him to argue that the Emperor possessed the highest legitimate authority of the Empire and, at the same time, that the German Princes enjoyed (a certain level of) sovereignty in spite of the fact that they were united within the same Empire. It also enabled him to label both the Empire and the Princely Territories 'states.' He thus managed to develop an original conceptual solution to the pressing political issues referred to earlier.

First, the concept of relative sovereignty provided a solid legal-political basis for the Princes' claim that they should be included in international diplomatic life. Now diplomatic relations could be maintained between all rulers with sufficient power to influence peace and security in Europe and Germany. When the status of the various European powers was clarified, diplomatic confusion would most likely decrease and political stability increase. The princely claim to international *representation* and *participation* could now be firmly based on their sovereign status.

Secondly, the relative interpretation of sovereignty served to preserve the universal structure in which the Empire was a state and the Emperor a sovereign. Leibniz argued that this would benefit German "internal" *stability*. He believed that one of the values and functions of the Holy Roman Empire was to keep in check any Princes who failed to govern their people in such a manner that these could pursue happiness and were treated justly. As the imperial *majestas*, the Emperor had the authority to constrain the Princes and to administer justice among them. As will be explained below, in Leibniz' system of universal jurisprudence the source of this authority was *justice*.

Last but not least, supporting the Empire's position of strength also served to preserve "external" stability, which would benefit from a clear balance of power in Europe. After all, a united Holy Roman Empire would be in a stronger position to respond to French expansionism.

It may be argued that this Leibniz' theory was the obvious conceptual response to the practical political issues of the time, but this would not do justice to the *originality* of his argument. We know that Leibniz' concepts of state and sovereignty differed significantly from the 'conventional' definitions. Pufendorf in the same context had called the Empire 'monstrous,' but Leibniz rejected any interpretation of sovereignty as an *undividable* and *absolute* highest power.

---

[161] Id., at 111-112.

[162] Schneider, as cited in, Geschichte des öffentlichen Rechts, at 237.

The learned men, ... who have treated this subject, have exceeded the bounds in both directions: some admitting the unity of the state, have believed that liberty or supremacy are abrogated in the individual members; others, conceding the liberty of the individual members, have thought that there is constituted not one state, but an alliance.

Leibniz was aware of the fact that distributing sovereignty could also bring conflict and perhaps even the disintegration of the very structure his theory was intended to perpetuate. For this reason, he restricted the application of his theory to larger powers and territories only. This was further proof of his opposition to Pufendorf's and Hobbes' 'fallacy,' as in Leibniz' view, 'prudence and moderation' would prevail, not chaos and anarchy.[163] Leibniz' faith in prudence and moderation can only be understood when read in conjunction with his theory of justice and his concept of the law of nature and of nations, which I will now discuss, after the following brief summary of the above.

The fragmentation of power in the Holy Empire was evidently a fertile breeding ground for anarchy and chaos, the outbreak of which had to be avoided at all costs. However, keeping the Empire afloat was not widely considered to be the best approach. In fact, its dissolution was mainly considered to be more conducive to peace[164] and Leibniz seemed to be the only one who argued in favour of its continued existence. Leibniz' personal theological-political ideal of a reunified Republic of Christendom as set out below will help us to understand why he dissociated from the conventional attitude that the Empire had to be abolished.

2.3.2. **Universal justice: natural law and the law of nations**

Leibniz' argument on the position of the German and European powers was further refined in the course of his work from the *Caesarinus Fürstenerius* to the *Praefatio* (to the *Codex*). The precise nature of this refinement is its treatment of the subject in relation to his theory of justice and the law of nature and of nations. I have already stressed the significance of Leibniz' moral ideals for his introduction of the notion of ILP and for his views on sovereignty and the need to perpetuate the Holy Empire. These opinions can only be explained from Leibniz' theory of universal *justice*.

Earlier, where we recognised the moral-political significance of Leibniz' theory of substance for his universal jurisprudence, i.e., the system of law of the universal community of spirits (human and divine), it was concluded that for Leibniz every human mind or person was a 'subject' of universal justice or a citizen of the City of God. Throughout his lifetime, Leibniz' dedication to the ideal of the City of God made him favour the reinforcement of the Christian system in Europe, the *Respublica Christiana*. The Holy Roman Empire – which he considered to be a prime example of a *Respublica Christiana* – was the closest existing

[163] Id., at 117-120. In the omitted footnote, Riley mentions other writers besides Pufendorf.
[164] See *supra*, section 2.2.3.

political approximation of the moral-theological ideal of the City of God.[165] For Leibniz, this ideal lay at the foundation of the legitimacy of the authority of the Pope and the Emperor. They were the defenders, one religious and one profane, of the *common good* of Christendom and their authority derived its legitimacy from their position or *responsibility* to defend the Church and the Republic of Christendom.[166] In the *Praefatio* to the *Codex*, Leibniz again emphasised the perpetual 'common bond' that linked the whole of Christendom and stated that it was 'not without reason' that prior to the schism that divided Catholics and Protestants it was 'accepted' to contemplate 'a kind of common republic of Christian nations.' For the 'common good of Christendom,' it was actually quite reasonable to strive for the reunion of Catholics and Protestants into a universal society based on justice.[167] Leibniz thus held on to the ideal of

> a kind of common republic of Christian nations ..., the heads of which were the Pope in sacred matters, and the Emperor in temporal matters, who preserved as much of the power of the ancient Roman emperors as was necessary for the common good of Christendom, saving [without prejudicing] the rights of kings and the liberty of princes ...[168]

In spite of the religious schism, the Holy Empire was still the best structure to defend the common good of Christianity and as such a *just* political constellation on the basis of which the authority of the various Sovereigns was *legitimate*.

Leibniz envisioned a European system based on justice as 'universal benevolence.' In this political theory, *justice* was the source of legitimate power and authority. The argument that sovereign power was intended to conform to the demands of *justice* was supported by the fact that the suppression of the arbitrary use of power was generally a key element in Leibniz' work, albeit that it only found elaboration in terms of international law in the *Codex*. Two years after his apologia for the sovereignty of the Princes, Leibniz, in a new work entitled *Portrait of the Prince* (1679), went on to describe the counterpart of sovereignty, so to speak, namely the duty to serve justice.

Leibniz' theory of political order in the national sense and as between sovereigns relied upon the (Platonic) ideal that the wise should rule, since they were best placed to attain the necessary knowledge of the eternal natural truths and, therefore, better equipped to manage political and ethical life within society and to govern justly.[169] In *Portrait of the Prince*, Leibniz stressed the importance of the virtues of justice for the Princes and their rule. 'Since the order of states is

---

[165] See, e.g., Leibniz, Observations on the Abbé de St Pierre's 'Project for the Perpetual Peace' (1715), *in* LPW, at 181. 'I find that M. l'Abbé de St Pierre is right to consider the Empire as a model for the Christian society.'

[166] See *supra*, text to footnote 160.

[167] See, e.g., P. Schrecker, Leibniz's Principles of International Justice, VII (4) *J. of the History of Ideas* 484-498 (1946). See also Riley's introduction to LPW.

[168] Codex, at 174-175.

[169] See, e.g., Letters to Th. Burnett, *in* LPW, at 191 *et seq.*

founded on the authority of those who govern them,' their authority to command and to be obeyed was 'founded no less in nature than in law.' Leibniz therefore cautioned that 'princes must be above their subjects by their virtue, and by their natural qualities, as they are above them by the authority which the laws give them to reign according to natural law and civil law.' The Princes enjoyed a position of superiority over their subjects because nature had instilled in them great virtues; their authority was *legitimate* because they ruled virtuously and wisely and thus served *justice*, at least, in theory. Leibniz realised, however, that it was not necessarily the wise who ruled and that the civil law basis of power could run counter to the natural (law) basis of authority.[170] 'No one is unaware, either, of the force of laws which have caused so many bad princes to reign, without any other support than that of the laws.' It was therefore rather out of a concern for the possible rule of the corrupt that '[i]t is necessary that the dominance of princes be equally based on the advantages of nature, on virtue, and on the laws, to bring to an end the struggle of virtue and of merit against fortune, in order to ensure public tranquillity,' and that a situation should be avoided where a power under civil law, which could go against natural law, would triumph.[171] Here, Leibniz' unceasing concern for stability – for *public tranquillity* – makes itself felt as does the objective that the sovereign must rule not merely on the basis of civil law but also on that of natural law, all for the sake of stability, wise rule and the promotion of justice.

The idea, therefore, that politics should be based on natural law and that power should reign in accordance with natural law in order to secure stability and justice is the core of Leibniz' argument. The 'goal' of the Princes 'must always be the public good, the glory and repose of peoples.' Because of their task, they 'must not only have the virtues which perfect a man with regard to himself, ... [but] also have those which dispose them to do, with respect to others and to the people, everything which pertains to the duty, the glory and the greatness of sovereigns, such as justice, clemency, liberality, magnificence and generosity. *Justice is, of all these virtues, the most necessary to princes.*' Leibniz placed further emphasis on its importance by stating that: '[t]he others are the ornaments of this

[170] Portrait of the Prince (1697), *in* LPW, at 85: 'It may happen, however, that though nature wishes that those to whom she has given many great qualities and who have the most virtue always rule over others, the laws of many states ordain, on the contrary, that children be the heirs of the goods and of the power of their fathers, because as a result of the prudence of legislators and of human weakness, the civil law is often contrary to natural law; but the empire of great princes has always been founded on the advantages of nature and of fortune, on the authority of virtue and on the power of law.'

[171] Leibniz in this respect commended the double legitimacy of the ruler of Hanover, Johann Friedrich of Brunswick-Lüneburg, who he served and for whom this work was written: 'This is the advantage which is visible in the person of Your Most Serene Highness. His authority is doubly legitimate: it is based on the law of nature, which requires that the most perfect command the others, since he is above his subjects by his virtue and by his natural qualities; it is established by the civil law, since he was borne the son of a prince in a hereditary state; it is based on the divine law which commands peoples to obey their sovereigns.' Id., at 86.

glory, but [justice] is essential, being in states what reason is in nature.' He explained that:

For if reason, which is in God to direct his power, is the cause of the natural disposition of creatures, and if it conserves the admirable harmony of the universe, *justice establishes the political order*, and allows the union of men in monarchies and republics to subsist. It is *the social tie* which can only be established by these three political virtues: friendship, justice, and valor. If the first, which makes goods common, could be observed, the second would be useless; and if men did not always estrange from justice, valor would not be necessary to defend states. But the weakness of human nature not being able to suffer that civil life be founded solely on friendship, it was necessary to arrive at a division of goods, common by nature, and to conserve it through (legal) justice, which must be applied by force against those who dare to violate the laws. [172]

In Leibniz' political philosophy, it was neither power that established the political order nor a social contract that determined the legitimacy of the ruler. In his view, it was *justice* which was at the basis of a *political order* and of political power. *Legitimate* authority both within a political community and it its external relations could therefore only be based on *justice*: only power that was exercised justly was legitimate.

The constraint of power by natural law had always been a key element in Leibniz' political philosophy and as his universal jurisprudence envisioned an all-comprising universal structure and society these constraints also applied here, both internally and externally. The universal jurisprudence did not separate the internal order from the external inter-sovereign order in the sense that in both spheres the sovereign had to conduct his affairs *justly*. In their international conduct the Princes' were equally bound to observe the principles of justice:

sovereigns and peoples must be restrained by respect for the laws, and since the peace of states with neighbors is ordinarily maintained by the motive of mutual fear, it is necessary that princes rule equally by [justice] and by laws, like Your Most Serene Highness, who has so much solicitude for justice that he wishes that it be rendered without exception of persons and without drawing a distinction between subjects and foreigners.[173]

However, to count fully upon the enlightenment of the Princes and their virtuous observance of justice would have been naïve and to count exclusively on civil law to restrict their power would have been inadequate. Therefore Leibniz did neither. The recognition of the Princes' authority required a correlative moral responsibility (i.e., that their actions should be guided by wisdom and should be directed towards justice) which had to be strictly enforced. In the *Praefatio*, Leibniz transferred the moral-political idea of the correlative responsibility to the international *legal* realm. By the attribution of 'personality in the law of nations'

---

[172] Id., at 98. Emphasis added.
[173] Id., at 98.

Leibniz did not only put his faith in morality and justice, but also developed a universal *legal* system, which would contribute to *just* actions.

According to Leibniz' universal jurisprudence, *justice* was the source of *natural law*. Natural law that applied to sovereign rulers constituted the *ius naturae et gentium* and these rulers had to conduct their international affairs on the basis of the law of nature and of nations. Leibniz distinguished three degrees of natural law which followed from three degrees of justice: commutative, distributive and universal justice, of which the latter was the highest-ranking. To live in accordance with the virtues of justice meant to apply 'reason[ably]' or 'wisely' the command to 'love everybody.' Wisdom was the knowledge of perfection and of the eternal and necessary truths of nature and reason the appropriate tool to acquire this knowledge and to make it universally available to all mankind.[174] 'Wise love' was Leibniz' interpretation of (the activity of) justice: justice as 'universal benevolence' or 'charity guided by the dictates of wisdom.' This 'willing the good' for everybody came down to 'converting the happiness of another into one's own'; this was what Leibniz called 'disinterested love.'[175]

Underlying this concept of justice is the reconciliation of two psychological premises, namely of Grotius' perception of human nature as social and rational with Hobbes' view on man as primarily selfish and living a calculating life.[176] Leibniz brought these two opposing views together in the concept of *disinterested love*, which is a combination of altruism and egoism claiming that the interests of others are our own interests. Leibniz recognised the selfish tendency in human nature to which Hobbes had concluded. But he also recognised that the rational soul enabled man to have a relationship with God and to acquire knowledge of the eternal and necessary truths, i.e., the dictates of nature, and to transcend his egoism, as essentially, by his very nature, he could only ultimately seek God.

Seeking God means seeking perfection, in the moral sense of the word. This natural desire for perfection consisted of 'find[ing] pleasure in the perfection of another.'[177] Leibniz *equated* the love for God with loving the public good: 'to

[174] See, for Leibniz' critique of Pufendorf's position that only through revelation man is able to know what justice is, Opinion on the Principles of Pufendorf (1706), *in* LPW, at 68-69. Pufendorf, unlike Leibniz, contended that justice came from the free employment of the divine will. Natural law is the commandment of the sovereign God. This type of 'despotism' and uncertainty was unacceptable to Leibniz, as he believed that the eternal and universal truths from which justice stems are accessible to every human being through reason. '[J]ustice follows certain rules of equality and of proportion (which are) no less founded in the immutable nature of things, and in divine ideas, than are the principles of arithmetic and of geometry.' Supreme justice and goodness are in (the essence of) God; they are not randomly deployed. Through the faculty of reason, man is capable of knowing and acting justly and truthfully. Id., at 70-71.

[175] Codex, at 171.

[176] See also, G. Brown, Leibniz's moral philosophy, *in* N. Jolley (Ed.), Companion 412-413 (1995).

[177] Felicity, *in* LPW, at 83. 'Pleasure' is defined as 'knowledge or feeling of perfection, not only in ourselves, but also in others, for in this way some further perfection is aroused in us.'

contribute to the public good and to the glory of God is the same thing.'[178] To seek God by loving wisely and act upon it contributed to the common good: 'when one is inclined to justice, one tries to procure good for everybody.'[179] This was an essential feature of Leibniz' theory of justice: by identifying the religious with the socio-political in his notion of justice, he formed a system whereby theology, morality and politics were all part of a gradual continuum.

Justice in this sense was therefore an active and social concept: it involved the promotion of the common good and public happiness. Justice here included mutual respect for the interests of others as well as a commitment to society. To act *justly* was a social virtue, as Leibniz explained: 'Justice is a *social* duty (*Tugend*), or a duty which preserves society.'[180] *Just* acts could only be social; they benefited society naturally. Natural law, which had justice as its source and was the law of natural societies, was thereby also the law which aimed to preserve or promote the common good and public happiness.[181] Each degree of justice was a source of (a principle of) the law of nature (and of nations).

First, Leibniz considered that universal justice 'commands us to live honorably (or rather piously),' which meant to live as a good citizen of the City of God. Universal justice and the natural law that flowed from it was concerned with man's relations with God or perfection. But as offering God his due was the same as serving the (universal) common good, it also related to man's relationship with humanity at large.[182] In the hierarchy of the natural societies ruled by God the universal monarchy was the highest natural society,[183] it 'binds the whole human race together.' It was higher than the natural societies of states: 'all

---

[178] Excerpts from three letters to Th. Burnett (1699-1712), *in* LPW, at 191. Without God – without this characteristic of man to seek God by natural inclination – it is impossible to reconcile altruism with egoism. It is more convincing that man seeks God than that he is by nature inclined to aim for the happiness of others, as, after all, man is also a natural egoist, as Leibniz conceded. See also: Memoir for Enlightened Persons (mid 1690s), *in* LPW, at 105: 'to contribute to the glory of God, or (what is the same thing) to the common good.'

[179] Felicity, *in* LPW, at 83.

[180] Leibniz, On Natural Law, *in* LPW, at 77.

[181] Id., at 77. 'A society is a union of different men for a common purpose. A natural society is one which is demanded by nature. The signs by which one can conclude that nature demands something, are that nature has given us a desire and the powers or force to fulfil it: for nature does nothing in vain. Above all, when the matter involves a necessity or a permanent utility: for nature everywhere achieves the best. The most perfect society is that whose purpose is the general and supreme happiness. Natural law is that which preserves or promotes natural societies.'

[182] 'In this way we can think of all men living in the most perfect state, under a monarch who can neither be deceived in his wisdom nor eluded in his power; and who is also so worthy of love that it is happiness [itself] to serve such a master.' Codex, at 173. See also, for a summary of the *Monadology* argument even before appearance of the latter, Memoir for Enlightened Persons, § 9, *in* LPW, at 105.

[183] 'The sixth natural society is the Church of God .... Its purpose is eternal happiness.' On Natural Law, at 79. Besides natural law, Leibniz contended that there was also a 'divine positive law' governing the relations between the citizens of this perfect state. This law consisted of the 'sacred Scriptures' and 'sacred canons accepted in the whole Church and, later, in the West, the pontifical legislation, to which kings and peoples must submit themselves.' Codex, at 174.

countries, finally, would stand under the Church of God.' '[T]he whole human race ... constitutes a community under the rule of God:'[184] a *universal society of humanity*. The highest degree of natural law flowed from universal justice and it was 'among things to be desired, that the law of nature and of nations [*ius naturae et gentium*] should follow the teachings of Christianity.' For this reason, Leibniz interpreted the natural law principles springing from justice in the light of 'the divine things of the wise,' that is 'according to the teachings of Christ.' The highest universal laws of nature were the 'eternal laws of the divine monarchy.'[185] Every person, Leibniz felt, was a subject of this law, whether Prince or subject, and thus morally obliged to be a good citizen of the City of God. The *law of nature and of nations* – as Leibniz explicitly pointed out – had universal justice as its highest source.

Secondly, the next (lower) source of the *law of nature and of nations* was distributive justice or 'strict charity': it 'strives for ... that while each benefits others as much as he can, he may increase his own happiness in that of the other. [This] right tends toward happiness.' Leibniz pointed out that Grotius called a right of this degree of law and justice 'a moral claim [*aptitude*], not a legal claim [*facultas*];' such a right gave 'no ground for [legal] action in compelling us to fulfil them.' The command of distributive justice 'to give each his due' was not a legal, but a moral duty. The concomitant claim was therefore an *aptitude*, unless positive law included obligations of a distributive kind.[186] In some cases, it might be necessary to 'depart from [strict right]' for the sake of the 'greater good.' To 'distribute our own or public goods' out of 'respect of persons' – as this second natural law principle ordered – underlined the social character of justice.[187]

The third source of the *law of nature and of nations* according to Leibniz' was the lowest degree of justice, commutative justice. From it sprang the principle of 'strict right [*ius strictum*]' that 'no one is to be injured, so that he will not be given a motive for a legal action within the state, nor outside the state a right of war.' Strict natural law gave to those affected an enforceable legal claim. At the inter-sovereign plane, compliance with the strict natural law principle to injure no one would prevent other sovereigns from obtaining the legal claim (*facultas*) to warfare. If not injured, one had no legal right to start a war and peace was 'conserv[ed].' In other words, the law of nature and of nations springing from commutative justice was legally binding and the prohibition to inflict harm in-

---

[184] On Natural Law, at 79-80.

[185] Codex, at 174.

[186] Codex, at 172-173. '[I]t is here that the political laws of a state belong, which assure the happiness of its subjects and make it possible that those who had a merely moral claim acquire a legal claim; that is, that they become able to demand what it is equitable for others to perform.' This statement also reflects that Leibniz gave a much wider interpretation of state duties than Hobbes, who only considered the duty to provide security, whereas Leibniz included the ruler's duty to act in accordance with the commands of distributive justice.

[187] Codex, at 173. See also, Portrait of the Prince, at 99: 'Princes must not only render to each that which belongs to him, by justice, and pardon sometimes by clemency: they must also distribute their riches by liberality.'

tended to prevent the emergence of a rightful claim to warfare and aimed to secure stability and peace.[188] Evidently, as only a strict right could be the origin of legal claims, distributive and universal justice were practically speaking less relevant in international relations. Nonetheless, the natural principles flowing from these degrees of justice were also taken into account when the notion *ius naturale et gentium* was used.

After having determined the three principles of the law of nature and of nations as they originated in the three sources or degrees of justice (universal, distributive, and commutative), Leibniz further established that these principles were '[t]he basis then of international law [*iuris fecialis inter gentes*].'[189] The *ius naturale et gentium* and the voluntary law of nations were not coordinate, but gradually different. The voluntary law of nations had to follow *ius naturae et gentium*, as it drew on the 'eternal right [or law] of rational nature.' From this distinction it is also clear that Leibniz used *ius naturae et gentium* for the law of nature and *of* nations and '*iuris fecialis inter gentes*' for the positive or voluntary law *between* nations as created by sovereigns in their personal capacity and by mutual consent, as expressed through custom (*usus*) or (tacit) consensus. In the creation of this voluntary law, *iuris fecialis inter gentes*, the sovereign rulers had to follow or conform to the principles of the *ius naturae et gentium*. In other words, voluntary law created by sovereign rulers was to operate within the limits of the natural law system. Consequently, any arbitrary exercise of power would be contained by the law (of nature). Leibniz was always quite clear about his concern over the possible abuses of power, which included a healthy mistrust of positive inter-sovereign law.

Even though his *Codex Iuris Gentium* was a collection of positive legal acts, Leibniz still openly expressed his low opinion of positive law. In the *Praefatio*, he could not resist the opportunity to criticise its authority.[190] His scepticism is evident where he observed that 'today, in truth, we would not be wrong in many cases to say that rulers play cards in private life and with treaties in public affairs.' Natural law was eternally and universally the same and accessible to every individual, whereas positive law was not without the flaws of secrecy and arbitrariness, because, as Leibniz observed, 'both the attractions of women and the splendor of gold often have more force than the laws and testimonies.'[191]

In spite of his loathing of the arbitrariness of legal and political acts, Leibniz recognised their relevance as the expression of power and politics and understood the need to edit and publish them. (International) positive law communicated historical facts to the future, bore witness to social changes and thereby increased

[188] Codex, at 171-173.

[189] Codex, at 175.

[190] Id., at 167, Leibniz remarked: 'Some will be surprised that an editor of acts and treaties should discourse in his preface on the weakness of paper chains; and will retort that esteem for public acts must diminish if it is recognized that sovereigns have secret intentions quite different than those which are declared.'

[191] Id., at 165-168.

certainty in history.[192] Besides its role in the provision of historical certainty, Leibniz pointed out another advantage of positive law. The principles of the law of nature were of eternal and universal value, but the voluntary law of nations 'changes according to time and place.'[193] Natural law reflected the unity of mankind, while the voluntary law of nations could reflect 'the diversity of the world of men.'[194] Consequently, its natural and positive law sources enabled the law of nations to combine the universality and certainty of natural law with the cultural plurality and historical development of humanity.

A brief summary of the above will conclude this section. Leibniz' perceived the law of nations as a collection of natural law principles flowing from justice and the voluntary law of nations. The natural law ties of the law of nations prevented it from relying on the arbitrary use of the power of the state. Instead, in order to be "right" [not *Gesetz*, but *Recht*], it had to be just, or it had to at least be in accordance with the three principles of justice enumerated above. The general obligation to serve justice was incumbent upon every person within the pre-established harmonious cosmopolitical order: because of his moral personality, every individual had the moral responsibility to act *justly*. For the sovereigns of Europe, this meant among other things that it was their responsibility to conform to the law of nature and nations. From this point of view, therefore, the law of nations was not the law of a society of absolutely sovereign states, but rather the law 'among those who participate in the supreme power (of whom there may be more than one, even in the same state).'[195] The 'international society' was a personal and diverse society of *relative* sovereigns existing within the universal natural society of humanity. Because of the power and authority which sovereigns possessed, they were on the one hand well equipped to promote the general good of humanity, as this required power, but on the other hand, this power had to be used in accordance with the law. Those 'powerful enough' to *participate* in international life were governed by the law of nations, which conferred upon them a certain *responsibility* to conduct their international affairs within the limits of the law.

2.3.3. Conclusions on the emergence of ILP: reconciling realism and idealism, sovereignty and justice, and participation and responsibility

It has been established that Leibniz was a realist in his political assessment of (the distribution of power in) Germany and Europe, but rather more of an idealist in his thinking on morality and law. In conjoining his politically realistic concept of

---

[192] Id., at 169: 'Collections of public acts are thus the most trustworthy part of history, and they transmit to prosperity, as do coins and inscriptions, the certainty of facts.'

[193] Id., at 174.

[194] Id., at 170.

[195] Codex, at 174.

relative *sovereignty* with his ideal of a *justice*-based European order, Leibniz introduced the notion of '*persona jure gentium*' (ILP). This idealism of universal justice contrasted with his advocacy regarding the position of the German Princes, but this apparent contradiction was resolved as follows: the mainly morally motivated support for the universal structure was brought into line with the practical political need to open up European society to the newly participating powers on the international stage and the need to clarify their position. The introduction of ILP was a refinement of Leibniz' argument on the position of the Princes, their sovereignty and their responsibility to serve justice, in *legal* terms. Leibniz stipulated that ILP was the prerogative of those whose 'authority, then, is sufficiently extensive,' to be called sovereign.[196] ILP was thus attributed to (relative) sovereigns and by possessing ILP they were conceptually connected with or included in the system of *ius gentium*.

Now we are able to answer some key questions concerning the meaning and role of ILP in Leibniz' thinking, such as "Why was the term ILP first used at the particular time that it was?" "Why did Leibniz need the term and how did it connect with his ideas in general and with his ideas on politics and international relations in particular?" "What was his objective when he made his argument concerning ILP?" In short, we can now come to understand the meaning Leibniz gave to the concept when he introduced it; in other words, we can now retrieve what he was *doing in* using ILP. In using ILP for the first time, Leibniz intended to *legitimise* the participation of the sovereign Princes in international life and simultaneously to subject these (newly) sovereign powers to the rule of law and the responsibilities of justice.

The argument that Leibniz used ILP to subject sovereign power to the requirements of justice is supported by the fact that this fits in with his earlier work on sovereignty and justice, which we discussed above, and by the fact that the suppression of the arbitrary use of power was a significant theme in his (moral-political) writings. In the *Praefatio*, ILP it finally found its full legal conceptual form.

Leibniz' intention to clarify the issue of international diplomatic communication and participation has been amply discussed: by attributing ILP to the (relative) sovereign he pursued the objective of regulating sovereign participation in terms of the law of nations. The military power of rulers may have formed the basis of their international influence and sovereignty, but it was ILP by which their participation on the international plane was finally recognised under the law of nations and thereby legitimised. However, this same ILP also brought duties under the law of nations.

ILP in this view was thus the legal counterpart of the more political notion of relative sovereignty. Sovereignty and ILP were not attributed to the state, but to its ruler. The state was considered a natural society in which rights and laws applied. The sovereign whose 'authority is ... sufficiently extensive' to represent

---

[196] See *supra*, footnote 132.

public liberty, 'who can count on sufficient freedom and power to exercise some influence in international affairs, with armies or by treaties,' had ILP. The people did not have ILP either. Leibniz had no sympathy for democracy, as, in his view, democracy was a political order that was all too susceptible to chaos and instability and was incapable of serving justice well.[197] ILP was thus a *personal* attribute of the sovereign ruler. His wise and virtuous use of power would ensure that the public good was represented and considered, even on the international stage. All European sovereigns, regardless of rank, from Emperor to minor Prince, were obliged to observe the natural and voluntary law of nations if they were capable of exercising even the tiniest degree of international influence.

In other words, the recognition of the Princes' participation in diplomatic life and international (inter-sovereign) relations due to their possession of ILP meant that sovereign persons who were powerful enough to threaten the peace and overturn stability had to comply with the law of nature and of nations and that this was how inter-sovereign war could be prevented. After all, the first – strict – principle of the law of nations stipulated that unless the other party was the first to inflict harm, there was no right to wage war. In other words, even then, only war in self-defence was legitimate. It was never permitted to harm another sovereign or his state territory first. The right of sovereignty thus came to exclude the absolute right to wage war, because the (natural) law of nations placed this external constraint upon the sovereign. Earlier it has been pointed out that as sovereigns, the Emperor, King, Prince or other ruler had both a right and a responsibility to act as an enlightened sovereign, who dispensed charity wisely. He was morally responsible for the wise government of his people and for conducting his international affairs in accordance with the demands of justice. This is where the sovereign responsibility for the promotion of justice became a legal responsibility to the extent that as an international legal person a sovereign ruler should conform to *ius gentium.*

Considering Leibniz' desire to limit the arbitrary use of power and his intention to encapsulate all power in the universal natural law system, ILP was used to confirm and capture in a legal notion the ruler's subjection to the law of nations. It was used to give *sovereignty* a counterpart in *responsibility*. Sovereignty was thus not only relative in the sense that it applied to those with a sufficient *degree*

---

[197] We have seen that both Grotius and Leibniz, even Pufendorf, agreed that in very rare and exceptional cases the civil community had a right under the law of nations to revolt against tyranny. Leibniz actually referred to *De iure belli ac pacis* in this respect: 'I ... remain in agreement with Grotius, that one can resist a tyrant in some circumstances, when he is a monster who seems to have vowed public ruin.' This, however, did not give the civil community a legal claim to good governance, only a moral one, until some excessive misuse of power was committed against the community by the ruler, who would thereby violate natural law and change the aptitude into a *facultas*. Leibniz' Letter to Landgraf Ernst of Hesse-Rheinfels, *in* LPW, at 185. Footnote omitted. Considering the rather explosive political situation in Europe at the time, Leibniz' subsequent comment is not without logic: 'However, I hold that it is a greater perfection to be able to suffer without resistance, and it is this that one must advise as much as one can – men being only too much given to violence.' Id., at 187-188.

of force and related competences, but also in the sense that sovereign powers were externally restricted by the law of nations. By having ILP, rulers not only had powers or rights, but also the *legal* responsibility to use their authority in accordance with the law of nations as springing from justice. Those who possessed international personality had international powers, such as the right to wage war, the right to conclude treaties and the right to conduct international relations, but they also had the duty to use these rights in conformity with the law of nature and of nations. Consequently, the use of power was contained by law and any abusive, corrupt or arbitrary use of power was (in theory) prevented. By subjecting the sovereign powers to the *ius naturale et gentium* they were obliged to use their power and authority justly; it legitimised their power and authority.

By considering every person with relative sovereignty a *persona jure gentium*, Leibniz defined the concept in such a way that every ruler 'powerful enough' to influence international life and affairs was bound by the law of nations and obliged to act legitimately and justly. The use of a personality *jure inter gentes* would not serve this purpose. Personality *jure gentium* created the capacity to establish *ius inter gentes* and to enter into treaty relations, on the condition that these capacities were used in accordance with *ius gentium*. In other words, because Leibniz used personality *jure gentium* instead of personality *jure inter gentes*, the concept did not merely validate the international capacity of the Princes to enter into treaty relations and alliances and the capacity to wage war in defence in terms of international law, but also implied that being a sovereign and having ILP included the responsibility to use power in accordance with the law and, given that power, authority and the law stem from justice, in accordance with the demands of justice. ILP was not merely a technical concept used to indicate formal subjection to the law of nations, but also, as was to be expected from Leibniz' universal jurisprudence with its natural-law based concept of international law, a substantial or material concept, which added to the capacity to act the capacity to act responsibly and justly.

It may thus be concluded that Leibniz used the concept of ILP to serve the dual purpose of, first, recognising the *legitimate participation* of the new actors and, secondly, subjecting all authority in Europe with some degree of military power to the rule of the law of nations.

Finally, by situating the *Praefatio* in the political, intellectual and jurisprudential context charted in this chapter, it has been established that Leibniz intended to contribute to the rationalisation of international relations; an intention that was fuelled by the tense and unstable contemporary situation in Europe, where diplomatic confusion caused by political upheaval was the norm. Leibniz' contribution was the redefinition of the supreme *rationale* of international life – sovereignty – in such a way that the status of the new actors could be clarified and diplomats would be spared further embarrassments. It has been demonstrated that Leibniz' relative concept of sovereignty served practical political considerations, but was also highly original at the time and that this originality was for the main part the result of the moral ideology that guided his (political) thinking. The originality of

Leibniz' ideas on sovereignty and personality will become even more evident if we compare them to the ideas that prevailed before. Pufendorf, for example, denied the separate existence of the law of nations and supported the rise of the modern state and absolute sovereignty. For this reason, he did not have to create a concept such as ILP and therefore the concept never emerged in the context of his work. In other words, the notion of ILP was connected with Leibniz' general cosmopolitical ideas and especially with his ideas on politics and international relations because of Leibniz' objective of bringing all power and force under the rule of (international) law.

The concept of ILP thus on the one hand legally sanctioned the sovereign's power, but on the other hand also restricted it by the rule of law, which necessarily served the cause of justice. And so it has become clear that Leibniz used the notion of ILP as a response to new political developments, a response which at the same time allowed him to hold on to his own convictions and the old universal structure. Therefore the 'best meaning' of the concept of personality in international law as Leibniz used it is *legitimate participation* which in Leibniz' universal jurisprudence cannot be separated from justice: legitimate (i.e., including *just*) participation in international relations. As such, the concept of ILP in Leibniz' work had a 'descriptive' as well as an 'evaluative dimension.'[198] The new term seemed to provide for legitimisation while at the same time challenging political practice by urging the (new) sovereigns to conduct themselves morally and/or legally. In this sense, ILP emerged in an attempt to guide the German imperial society and the European inter-sovereign society towards a heightened 'moral identity' and the promotion of universal justice.

2.4. THE 18TH-CENTURY INTERLUDE

At the end of the 17th century, a new 'Europe' consisting of new national entities could be seen to emerge against the background of the steadily declining Holy Empire. European politics continued on its course to rationalism, culminating in the beginning of Modernity:

> [the] commitment to 'rationality' was extended into the practical realm, when the political and diplomatic system of the European states was reorganized on the basis of *nations*. From then on, at least in theory, the warrant for a sovereign monarch's exercise of power lay less in the fact of an inherited feudal title than in the will of the people who consented to his rule: once this became the recognized basis of state authority, politics could also be analysed in the new 'rational' terms.[199]

Eighteenth-century enlightened despotism which, influenced by the ideal of the public good, required the despot to govern in the people's best interests, formed

[198] See *supra*, chapter 1, text to footnote 80.
[199] Cosmopolis, at 9.

the next step in the longer process of Enlightenment. After the recognition of the institution of the state during the 17th century, the 18th century 'rationalised' the need to further develop constitutionalism and respect for individual rights and freedoms.

Throughout this chapter, we have followed two threads, a moral-ideological and a practical-political one. These ultimately came together to explain why the concept of ILP emerged at the particular time and place that it did.

As we considered ILP in context, it became clear that the concept did not emerge "accidentally," but that it was an essential tool in reconciling Leibniz' re-valuation of the position of the German Princes with his commitment to harmony and unity. Leibniz' perception of the law of nations, his concept of sovereignty and his use of ILP proved even more original when set off against the ideas of Pufendorf.

However, in the 18th century, after its introduction, ILP did not immediately go on to become a household notion in the vocabulary of the law of nations. The concept did not feature in Wolff's or Vattel's systematic books on the law of nature and the law of nations and it was absent from the 18th century's most famous book on international peace: Kant's *Zum ewigen Frieden*, even though Wolff, Vattel and Kant were all significantly influenced by Leibniz. However, ILP as a *personal* attribute still belonged to a world that was rapidly being abandoned in the ongoing political modernisation. The formation and consolidation of the modern state prevented ILP, in the meaning in which Leibniz had used it, from making a breakthrough.

In *Jus Gentium Methodo Scientifica Pertractatum* (1764), Christian von Wolff (1679-1754), who was a pupil of Leibniz' and a follower of his philosophy, made an important contribution to the concept's transition from the *personal* to the *state-centred* phase of international law. He distinguished the *civitas maxima*,[200] the society of states as a universal super-state or common-wealth, from the universal human society, the *societas humana*, which Leibniz had still approached rather symbiotically. For Leibniz the Empire had been both a state and a structure that included the Empire's sovereign members. Wolff also regarded the *civitas maxima* as a kind of including structure, as well as as a new – if fictitious – moral person. The *civitas maxima* was based on 'a pact or quasi-pact' with the common good as its purpose. This international legal community of states was ruled by both natural law, i.e., the necessary law of nations (*jus gentium naturale* or *jus gentium necessarium*) and by the voluntary law of nations (*jus gentium voluntarium*), which was laid down by the 'fictitious ruler of the community' as an expression of the will of the community's members. This fictitious ruler was the personification of right reasoning at the international level. In Wolff's view, the law of nature differed in accordance with the subject it applied to, i.e., the hu-

[200] Chr. von Wolff, Jus Gentium Methodo Scientifica Pertractatum (1764), Classics of International Law, Vol. 13, 1934. See, e.g., Prolegomena, § 7 *et seq.*, and 11 *et seq.*

man individual or the state.[201] States as moral persons are bound by both the necessary law of nations and the voluntary law of nations. Like individuals, states have inherent natural rights. The right of a sovereign state to non-interference by other states is one of them.[202] As 'the law of nations is originally nothing else than the law of nature applied to nations, which are considered individual persons living in a state of nature,'[203] moral persons are legal persons under the law of nations and, in the case of the voluntary law of nations, they are also legal persons with additional positive legal rights and obligations as agreed to by the nations. The notion of moral personality helps to distinguish the nation from its individual members.[204] Consequently, states are the exclusive subjects of the laws of the *civitas maxima*. This is indeed a fundamental idea in Wolff's theory: the only subjects of the law of nations – as the laws of this *civitas* – were states. The state is a moral person which is 'naturally' bound by the universal law of nations, i.e., the necessary law of nations and the voluntary law of nations, and by agreements and customary law if these were consented to. Despite the fact that the notion *personae jure gentium* was not used literally, it was nonetheless conceptually present and changing from a personal notion into one concerning states.

Emmerich de Vattel (1714-1767) proceeded on the basis of the theory of his mentor, Wolff. However, he considered the idea of the *civitas maxima* as a superstate with a fictitious legislator as rather unrealistic and rejected it as such. Instead, he worked with the concept of the society of states. He further developed the idea that the state is an entity with a set of natural rights, This resulted in the doctrine that the state by its sovereignty has fundamental rights under international law. Vattel and Kant both regarded the state as the moral person conducting international relations,[205] but they disagreed on the relevance of the *internal*

[201] 'But since, indeed, nations are *moral persons* and therefore are subject only to certain rights and duties, which by virtue of the law of nature arise from the *social contract*, their nature and essence undoubtedly differ very much from the nature and essence of individual men as physical persons. When therefore the duties, which the law of nature prescribes to individuals, and when the rights, which are given to individuals to perform the duties, are applied to nations, since they can be such only as are allowed by their subjects, they must be suitably changed by them, that they may take a new form. And *thus the law of nations does not remain the same in all respects as the law of nature*, in so far as it controls the acts of individuals. What therefore stands in the way of treating it separately as a law peculiar to nations ?' Id., Preface, at 5. Emphasis added. Also, Prolegomena § 3, at 9-10.

[202] Id., § 256, at 131.

[203] Id., § 156, at 84.

[204] 'Every nation owes to every other nation that which it owes to itself, in so far as the other does not have that in its own power, while the first nation without neglect of duty toward itself can perform this for the other. ... This is a general principle, which of itself embraces within its scope all duties toward other nations. ... But ... the moral person is to be distinguished from physical individuals, that is, the nation as a nation is to be looked at, but not those who are of a certain nation, individually.' Id.

[205] Vattel, The Law of Nations or the Principles of Natural Law applied to the Conduct and to the Affairs of Nations and of Sovereigns, Classics of International Law transl. of 1916, at 3. Emphasis added. Hereinafter: Vattel's Law of Nations. Wolff also considered the nation or state a moral

political system to international law theory and the establishment of world peace. Vattel considered the kind of government present within a state to be a question outside the scope of the law of nations. As long as the government that was in place pursued the common good or public happiness, it made no difference to the international society whether it took the shape of a monarchy or a democracy.[206] He used the state's moral personality as a dividing concept and paved the way for dualism and absolute sovereignty. His theory marked the emergence of the modern perception of *ius gentium* as the voluntary law between sovereign states only. The moral personality of the state depended on sovereignty in the framework of the law of nations and was connected with the selection of participants in the 'great society.'[207] A law of sovereigns is a law that applies to the public authorities of the moral persons called states. It is a law that is binding between states. Only sovereign moral persons can participate in the great society governed by the law of nations.[208] The law of nations is no longer (natural) law that applies to (sovereign) individuals, but consists of the *positive* law that is exclusively applicable between independent sovereign states.

In Kant's political philosophy, domestic peace and international peace were mutually dependent. He argued that, in order to secure peaceful relations among the members of the universal society or federation of states, the internal political structure of the state had to be *republican.* A republican constitution is based on the supremacy of law and peace can only exist in an environment ruled by

person, but he always expressed this in the smaller script he used to explain his main lines of reasoning. Vattel immediately mentioned the moral personality of the nation or state in the second paragraphs of the Introduction and the first chapter. The overall similarity in wording and structure of the first general opening sections of the two books is striking. See, Kant, Perpetual Peace, Section 1, *in* H.S. Reiss (Ed.), Kant Political Writings (1991) at 94; hereinafter: Perpetual Peace; see also, The Metaphysics of Morals, § 53, id., at 165.

[206] Vattel: 'This is not the place to consider in detail what should be the character of [a State's] constitution and these [fundamental, public, and civil] laws, for a discussion of that belongs to the field of public law and politics.' They have to be established 'wisely,' but the form should be chosen by the Nation itself and each political society should suit itself best. It concerns a duty of the Nation towards itself, and the Law of Nations concerns rights and duties among Nations. Vattel's Law of Nations, at 17.

[207] 'Every Nation which governs itself, under whatever form, and which does not depend on any other Nation, is a *sovereign State.* Its rights are, in the natural order, the same as those of every other State. Such is the character of the moral persons who live together in a society established by nature and subject to the Law of Nations. To give a Nation the right to a definite position in this great society, it need only to be truly sovereign and independent; it must govern itself by its own authority and its laws. ... The Law of Nations is the law of sovereigns; free and independent States are moral persons, whose rights and obligations we are to set forth in this treatise.' Id., at 11-12, section 4 and 12.

[208] In the Preface, Vattel explains: 'There is no doubt of the existence of a natural law of Nations, inasmuch as the Law of Nature is no less binding upon States, where men are united in a political society, than it is upon the individuals themselves. Now an exact knowledge of this law can not be had by a mere understanding of what the Law of nature prescribes for individual persons. When a law is applied to different subjects it must be applied in a manner suited to the nature of each subject.' Id., at 3a. Here Vattel also indicates the influence on his work of Grotius, Wolff and Hobbes.

law.[209] A social contract transforms the 'natural' freedom of man into civil liberty: the freedom of every citizen as an equal member of the state. This civil liberty of all men is established and guaranteed by law. The individual is a formal concept: under a republican constitution every subject is a *citizen* and as such a co-legislator. Freedom in the form of political participation is the primary right of the citizen. His participation in law-creation as a member of the polity makes him a free person who obeys his own laws and not merely those of the sovereign ruler.

To serve peace effectively, the law of nations should actually be the law of a federation of free states. Kant points out that this is not the same as a federation of peoples because that would indeed imply a single super-state, an '*international state*' or '*civitas gentium*.'[210] The law of nations, or as Kant called it 'international right,' is the law applicable to the relations between independent sovereign states. Kant proposed that sovereign states should form a 'League of Nations' under the rule of law. In addition, Kant introduced the concept of a *ius cosmopoliticum*, a cosmopolitan right. Just as Leibniz had believed in a 'universal republic of spirits,' inhabited by God and all men, Kant believed there was a universal republic called the *cosmopolis*. The *ius cosmopoliticum* provides rights for the citizens of the universal state of mankind.[211] These citizens can be both individuals and states. The *ius cosmopoliticum*, i.e., the law applicable to the relations among states and individuals as members of the *cosmopolis*, confers upon every human being the legal status of world citizenship, or legal personality under cosmopolitan law.

By the end of the 18th century, both Vattel and Kant had offered alternatives with respect to the law of nations, elements of which had already been present in Leibniz' theory. As it turned out, Vattel's approach was the most successful and the most commonly practised, as the glorification of the absolute sovereignty of the state during the 19th century serves to indicate. The concept of the state as a moral person with an independent will would burgeon in Hegelian and Post-Hegelian thinking during the 19th century. However, some Kantian ideas may also be found, especially in Kelsen's pure theory of law, which reacts against the 19th-century mystification of the state and the reification of legal personality.

---

[209] This is laid down in the first definite article for perpetual peace: 'The civil constitution of every state ought to be republican. The only constitution resulting from the idea of the social compact, upon which every good legislation of a nation ought to be founded, is a republican constitution.' Perpetual Peace, Section 2, at 99.

[210] Id., Section 2, at 105.

[211] Id., Section 2, at 98.

Chapter 3
DEMYSTIFYING ILP: BRIERLY, KELSEN AND SCELLE

> Nous nous trouvons actuellement à un des moments les plus angoissants de l'histoire de l'humanité. De profondes transformations, ainsi que des crises, des malaises se manifestent dans les principaux ordres de l'activité. Il y a un grand changement dans la psychologie des peuples[1] et dans la vie internationale. Il y a une crise des formes de Gouvernement. On ne sent que trop la crise économique. Il existe aussi une crise du Droit des Gens ...[2]

3.1. Introduction

In this chapter, I will assert that the concept of ILP was demystified in the international legal scholarship of the early 20th century. To sustain this claim, I will analyse how three specific scholars used ILP and show how they redefined the concept in their arguments. Such an investigation cannot be performed properly without at least some reference to the preceding age and, more importantly, to the broader context. This chapter will therefore also briefly describe some of the most relevant historical developments, the main practical-political issues of the time and the debate they generated in intellectual circles, and the jurisprudential context in which the scholars in question worked. However, in this section I will first give an outline of the present chapter.

The 'long nineteenth century,' which is generally perceived as having started with the American and French political revolutions, ended in 1914. During this 'era of unparalleled peace in the western world,'[3] Euro-centric western civilisation transformed its authoritarian monarchist societies into capitalist-driven, bourgeois societies with public institutions shaped by political liberalism. Then WWI caused the 19th-century European political structure of the congress system, which had been in place since 1815, to collapse. The first part of the subsequent 'short twentieth century,'[4] the Interbellum period (1919-1939),[5] showed

---

[1] Alvarez explains: 'Par cette expression il faut entendre tout ce qu'il y a d'immatériel dans la vie des peuples: sentiments, sous leurs divers aspects, caractères, états d'esprit, mentalité, doctrines, idéaux.'

[2] A. Alvarez, Exposé de Motifs et Déclaration des grands principes du Droit International Moderne 5 (1936). Also, A. Alvarez, La Psychologie des Peuples et la Reconstruction du Droit International Le Problème de la Paix (1936).

[3] E. Hobsbawm, The Age of Empire (1875-1914) 9 (1994). Hereinafter: The Age of Empire.

[4] E. Hobsbawm, Age of Extremes: The Short Twentieth Century 1914-1991, (1994). Hereinafter: Age of Extremes.

[5] Although the present chapter has this particular period as its focal point and most texts dealt with here therefore date from these years, this temporal demarcation has, however, not been strict to the point of excluding certain texts written just before WWI or during one of the World Wars.

signs of both heartfelt optimism and profound pessimism, but can most accurately be described as the 'Twenty Years' Crisis.'[6] It was in every respect (economically, politically, socially and psychologically) an extremely difficult and turbulent period in the history of Europe and the world. International life was generally perceived to be in transition and international law in 'crisis.'[7]

Interbellum international law scholarship[8] was very active in confronting the crisis in international law, so that it became rich, imaginative and often innovative. It was evidently marked by the disaster of the First World War and the social and political problems of the decades that followed and by the failure of the League of Nations and the rapidly increasing threat of yet another war. Many scholars felt that the classical international law views of their 19th-century predecessors were in dire need of some careful scrutiny. Interpreting international social life by using the language of international law, inter-war jurists frequently addressed the concept of international legal personality in their contributions to the scholarly debate. This chapter is concerned with three scholars who by their theories intended to tackle and overcome the crisis and who all in their own way redefined ILP in the process. The scholars in question are J.L. Brierly (1881-1955), Hans Kelsen (1881-1973) and Georges Scelle (1878-1961). In order to understand their conception of ILP and to appreciate how original their ideas truly were, we will look at their texts on ILP and re-situate these works in the political, intellectual and jurisprudential context of their time in an attempt to discover what they were *doing* in putting forward their arguments. Having thus determined the principal purpose of this chapter, two important issues in terms of the thesis of this chapter still remain to be introduced. In the first place, the considerable attention paid to ILP at the time was due to a general development in inter-war international legal scholarship, i.e., the attempt to reconstruct international law and theory, which evidently gave rise to considerable debate on whether to endorse pre-war classical doctrines or to try something fundamentally different. Secondly, when placing this debate within its proper context, we come to realise that the close and careful attention devoted to the position of the individual in international law by the most scrutinous of scholars is really the contemporary response to one of the most important issues of the time, namely the

[6] E.H. Carr, The Twenty Years' Crisis: 1919-1939 (1939), hereinafter: The Twenty Years' Crisis. Hobsbawm labelled the period from 1914-1945 the 'Thirty-one Years' War' to indicate the similarities with the Thirty Years' War of the 17th century. Age of Extremes, at 52. See also, on Europe in crisis, N. Davies, Europe: A History 938-998 (1997) (hereinafter: Europe: A History) and Toulmin in Cosmopolis.

[7] A. Alvarez, (Motifs) *op cit.* footnote 2, at 5. Also, De Louter's qualification of the status of international law: '*une crise pathologique*,' J. de Louter, La Crise de Droit International, 26 *RGDIP* 77 (1919). See, for transformation, Alvarez, at 5 and 6. Also, Bourquin observed a general feeling of 'transformation,' Règles Générales du Droit de la Paix, 35 *RCADI* 5 (1931-I), hereinafter: Bourquin-1931.

[8] See, e.g., for a general introduction to the period, W.G. Grewe, History of the Law of Nations: World War I to World War II, 2 *EPIL* 839 *et seq.* (1995). Also, A Concise History, *op. cit.* chapter 1 footnote 28, at 238 *et seq.*

crisis that democracy found itself in and the threat this posed to human individuality and freedom. The two main themes of this chapter are the reconstruction of international law and theory and the connection of international law thinking with the widely felt concern over democracy and human individuality which was reflected in international law scholarship.

First of all, the international legal scholarship of the Interbellum period in general possesses a strong ontological dimension. In response to attacks on its actual existence or to scepticism about its use and value, scholars argued that international law was in fact really law and not merely a moral code.[9] The failure of the "old" international legal, political and diplomatic order evoked quite fundamental discussions concerning the principle of state sovereignty and the binding nature of international law. As mentioned above, WWI left behind a general feeling of transition and a perceived need to reconstruct the order of the world. Jurists advocated that a role be set aside for international law within this new order and they were involved in the reconstruction of both law and theory in the hope of preventing another war. This general characterisation of inter-war international legal scholarship should, however, be refined further and I would therefore like to distinguish here between "restoration" and "revision."[10]

With the term *restorative* scholarship, I refer to those scholars who argued that the "old" order had to be restored, albeit with some adaptations. We will elaborate on their work below; suffice it here to cite Theodore Woolsey's remark: 'Readjustment of existing principles to new conditions may be necessary, ... while reconstruction in the sense of the evolution of new principles and their application to a new world order, is unnecessary and unlikely. ... My conception ... of reconstruction and international law, is of the old system of law with new teeth ...'[11] Restorative scholars basically endorsed 19th-century legal positivism

---

[9] See, e.g., J.E. Harley, The League of Nations and the New International Law (1921), where in the concluding chapter he enumerated the defects of the 'old machinery' preceding the establishment of the League of Nations and concluded his general argument with a defence of the nature of international law as truly law and not merely a 'code of ethics.' It breathes the spirit of hope and new beginnings. Id., at 59. Also, Politis, who opened the Lectures he delivered at Colombia University in July 1926 with an observation on post-WWI 'sceptic[ism]... to ... the existence of international law.' N. Politis, The New Aspects of International Law 1 (1928). He observed soon thereafter that 'international law ha[d] already entered, or [wa]s to enter, on a new phase of its evolution.' Id., at 2. [Hereinafter: The New Aspects].

[10] See, for contemporary analyses of interbellum scholarship as a project of reconstructing international law: M. Koskenniemi, From Apology to Utopia, The Structure of International Legal Argument 132 fn. 1, *et seq.* D. Kennedy, A New Stream of International Law Scholarship, *in* Beck and Arend and Vander Lugt (Eds.), International Rules 233 (1996); originally published in *Wisconsin ILJ* (1988). Also, D. Kennedy, International Law and the Nineteenth Century: History of an Illusion, 65 *Nordic JIL* 385-420 (1996). See also, N. Berman, Modernism, nationalism, and the rhetoric of reconstruction, XIII *Current Legal Theory* 33-60 (1995). I realise that Koskenniemi, Kennedy and Berman all use 'reconstruction' to refer to scholarship involved in thorough renewal, but the term 'reconstruction' at the time was used more generally and was not exclusively or by definition used to refer to renewal or modernisation.

[11] T.S. Woolsey, Reconstruction and International Law, 13 *AJIL* 187 and 189 (1919).

and continued the tradition of voluntarism and the doctrine of sovereignty that went with it. In their attempts to restore international law, ILP was used to preserve its classical identity. Although their approach often drew on Hegelian and Austinian thinking, not all restorative scholars went so far as to negate international law altogether.

Revisionist scholarship challenged this rather conservative attitude. Its contributors consisted of a fairly heterogeneous group, but their desire to fundamentally *revise*, i.e., to renew and modernise the conception of international law itself in order to meet the "new" conditions of international life, justifies putting them in the same category.[12] After the discipline's initial self-doubt and 'self-questioning,'[13] these initiatives were often undertaken in a spirit of optimism whereby it was for example observed that international law was entering a 'new phase of its evolution.'[14] In their attempts to 'rehabilitat[e]'[15] the role and importance of international law, one of the fundamental issues the revisionists had to deal with was the problem of legal personality in international law. They severely criticised the classical conception(s) of ILP and some scholars even relinquished the concept altogether.

I will illustrate how ILP functioned in both *restorative* and *revisionist* arguments on international law. The concept was used respectively to restore the classical identity of international law and to claim a *new* – modern – identity for international law. With respect to this objective, *revisionist* scholarship was often accused of losing sight of the reality of international life and frequently labelled

---

[12] Alvarez, Brierly, Verdross, Kelsen, Krabbe, Scelle and Politis (among others) were all involved in this *revisionist* project. Alvarez, Motifs, at 8-9 (Also, Psychologie). See, e.g., Politis, who began his 1925 Course at The Hague Academy by declaring 'le droit international arrive à un véritable tournant de son histoire,' spotting in the collapse of classical international law an opportunity for 'la reconstruction du droit international sur de nouvelles bases.' N. Politis, Le Problème des limitations de la souveraineté et la théorie de l'abus des droit dans les rapport internationaux, 6 *RCADI* 5 (1925-I). Also, D.J. Jitta, The Renovation of International Law (1919), in which Jitta proposes the renovation of international law on the basis of 'the reasonable principles of international social life' of the 'juridical community of mankind,' at 194-195. Also, G.C. Wilson, The Modernization of International Law, XIX *Am.Pol.Science Review* 268 (1925).

[13] M.N. Shaw, International Law 29 (3rd ed. 1991).

[14] See, The New Aspects, where Politis also observed that: 'the initial wave of discouragement was swiftly followed by that confidence in the future which has manifested itself in the movement for a complete *revision* of international law.' Id., at 2. Emphasis added. See also, C. van Vollenhoven, De Drie Treden van het Volkenrecht (1923), in which it was argued that a new phase, the third stage, of the law of nations was beginning, at 89. See also, R. Pound; in a lecture delivered at Leiden University in 1923 he stated that he had observed a 'revival of faith in the efficacy of effort.' He condemned the 'juristic pessimism of the immediate past,' and urged (international) legal scholars to have 'juristic faith' and display 'creativity' in legal theory. He argued the need for revision based on a new social philosophical theory of international law. R. Pound, Philosophical Theory and International Law, 1 *Bibliotheca Visseriana* 89 (1923). Also, Harley, *op. cit.* footnote 9.

[15] Brierly used the phrase 'the need of rehabilitation' in 1924 in the Inaugural Lecture which he delivered at the University of Oxford. See, J.L. Brierly, The Shortcomings of International Law, *in* Lauterpacht and Waldock (Eds.), The Basis of Obligation in International Law and other papers 68 (1958).

'utopian' or 'naïve day-dreaming.'[16] Viewed in the proper context, which is what we intend to do in this chapter, the tendency of Interbellum scholarship to construct a *new* international law was, however, closely related to the adverse contemporary socio-political developments that also marked other disciplines. Their work reflects the common concern about the changing social environment and the consequences of these changes, in particular where democracy was concerned.

Therefore and in the second place we will also address the broader context. The general intellectual reaction to the Great War and the subsequent crisis may be compared with the scholarly quest for universal harmony after the Thirty Years' War.[17] Once again, the 'old' European political order had collapsed and needed to be replaced by a new world order and once again, Europe was in the grip of social, political and economic instability. The cultural and intellectual impact of these developments manifested in a widespread renewed interest in rationalism and formalism, as apparent, for example, in art and philosophy.[18] In most disciplines, it was felt that a fresh start had to be made to serve as the basis for a new order which would provide certainty and stability:

Between the Wars, serious-minded European intellectuals faced the same task as had faced Leibniz after 1670: to find a neutral basis of communication between former en-

[16] 'Since 1919, ... theories of international law have become more markedly utopian than at any previous time.' The Twenty Years' Crisis, at 224. G. Schwarzenberger, Power Politics, A Study of International Society xv, 2nd ed. (1951).

[17] See *supra*, chapter 2.

[18] In art, the modernist spirit of logical (re)construction was discernible in movements such as the Dutch *De Stijl*, the German *Bauhaus*, the French *Purists*, or the Russian *Constructivists*, all searching for order based on the purity of geometric rationality. Abstract, geometric forms were considered 'ideal' as all (rational) human beings around the world could understand them. Batchelor and Fer and Wood (Eds.), Realism, Rationalism, Surrealism, Art between the Wars (1993), at 27, 17, 154, 140-141, 19-30. Hereinafter: Art between the Wars. These artists presented 'a utopian vision of universal harmony' (B. Haskell, The American Century: Art & Culture 1900-1950, at 284 (1999) reaching out to what they perceived was the 'higher' part of human nature, i.e., logical reason, in an attempt to contribute to the moral reconstruction in Europe and the advancement of civilisation. In the Purist Manifesto of 1920, as published in the journal *L'Esprit Nouveau*, it was formulated as follows: 'Logic, born of human constants and without which nothing is human, is an instrument of control and, ... permits one to go ahead with certainty ...' Art between the Wars, at 19. The architect Le Corbusier (who was also the painter C.-E. Jeanneret) considered architecture a 'pure creation of the spirit,' and this new spirit he described as '*imagination* and *cold reason*.' (Le Corbusier, as quoted by Bachelor and Fer and Wood (Eds.), at 29 and 28.) '[T]he new building would not simply provide the physical material for a reconstructed Europe, but would serve moreover as the basis of a moral and spiritual reconstruction.' Id, at 29. Also, at 20 and 26-27. In philosophy, the rationalist spirit was found in the Logical Positivism of the *Wiener Kreis*. Their philosophical program aimed to construct from scratch an abstract universal model, based on formal logic, for structuring every scientific theory in a uniform way. They considered rationality as abstract and pure, independent of any particular context and believed that the human mind was capable of knowledge through individual experience and learning. Cosmopolis, at 154-159.

emies, devise a rational method for comparing ideas from different nations, and build transnational institutions that could prevent a renewal of international war.[19]

The post-WWI endeavour of *revising* international law varied in accordance with the scholar who undertook it. However, they all performed it against the same background and attempted to formulate a response to the general crisis and in particular to the dangers which democracy was exposed to. Bearing this fact in mind will result in a better understanding and fuller appreciation of their thinking. The *crisis of democracy and its threat to the individual* thus consitutes both the thread and the interpretative theme of this chapter.

The position of the individual amidst the (irrational) forces of mass society was a serious concern of many novelists, sociologists, political scientists, psychologists, journalists and jurists. They each from their own perspective struggled to preserve democracy and individual freedom and identity in mass society, and tried to find a balance between the solidarity claims made by society and the autonomy of the individual. *Revisionist* scholars in particular were concerned with these issues. Their preoccupation with the position of the individual in international law and the (inter)national society contributed to the lavish attention paid to the concept of ILP.[20] In numerous cases, the position and status of the individual was discussed using the 'personality' and 'subjects of law' vocabulary.[21] The theoretical debate on the *new* position of the individual[22] fit in well with the *revisionist* desire to renew international law and to change its identity. The classical fixation on sovereignty and the state had to make way for the new idea that the true, *modern*, objective of international law was the protection of the human individual.

It is the thesis of this study that the *revisionist* rejection of the classical concepts of sovereignty and personality was not only legally-theoretically motivated, but also practically-politically. It was the product of a scholarly struggle in aid of democracy and individual human freedom and against the former *mythologies* in international law, which tended to ignore these values. Interbellum international legal scholars, as the heirs of the 19th-century international legal language that

---

[19] Cosmopolis, at 157-158.

[20] See, e.g., J. Spiropoulos: 'Le problème de la position de l'individu dans la vie juridique internationale est à l'heure actuelle un des problème les plus discutés de notre discipline.' Spiropoulos, l'Individu et le Droit International, 30 *RCADI* 195 (1929-V).

[21] In his course, l'Individu et le Droit International, at the Hague Academy of International Law in 1929, Spiropoulos at length discussed the various conceptions of the individual's position in international law. His course illustrates how the topic was frequently treated from a personality perspective. Id.

[22] N. Politis, The Status of the Individual in International Law, *in* The New Aspects, at 18. See, on the issue of giving individuals access to the PCIJ, N. Politis, How the World Court has functioned, 4 *Foreign Affairs* 447-8 (1925-6). Also, E.M. Borchard, The Access of Individuals to International Courts, 24 *AJIL* 359 (1930). Also, on the emancipation of the individual, Bourquin-1931, at 33-47.

reified,[23] even *mystified*, the collective, the state, its sovereignty and personality, were confronted with a reality in which dangerous forces threatened democracy and the individual. Those who continued on the basis of this language and ignored the changed social reality did so out of a desire to *restore* the sovereign state to its exclusive status of only subject of international law around which the whle discipline centred. However, their views were challenged by scholars who emphasised the importance of the protection of the individual and who considered the European democratic crisis part of the social reality which international law had to deal with. For this reason, the *revisionists* rejected the classical conceptions of sovereignty and personality for being authoritarian and anti-democratic. In 1929, Spiropoulos captured the new 'mood' of the scholarship of his age as follows:

> Ce fut l'évolution des idées en matière de droit public qui fournit *le motif décisif de l'orientation nouvelle*. Depuis que le dogme de la souveraineté absolue a été ébranlé, depuis que l'État a été dépouillé de toute *personification mystique*, enfin que la conviction se fait jour que *l'État n'est pas une fin en soi*, mais simplement un moyen de satisfaction de besoins individuels on commence à se rappeler que tout droit – par conséquent le droit des gens lui-même – n'existe en dernière analyse que pour *la protection des individus*.[24]

After this introduction of the purpose, themes and thesis of this chapter, I will now first deal with the contemporary context in order to put Interbellum international legal scholarship into a broader (intellectual) perspective. Secondly, I will describe the general use of ILP in Interbellum scholarship and the use of ILP in the work of Brierly, Kelsen and Scelle. I chose to focus on these particulars scholars because of their original, unconventional approach to ILP and the profound influence they had on 20th-century international law scholarship. All three of them rejected the 'old' anthropomorphic and *mythical* thinking about the state and legal personality.[25] They lived in different countries, belonged to different intellectual traditions and they all had their own *modus operandi* and objective, but they were united in their commitment to international law and individual human freedom.

---

[23] See *infra*, section 3.2.3.1. 'Reification' is a Machian term which means 'to attribute reality to abstract and general terms. ... It involves assuming the existence of entities which are 'metaphysical'.' See, Janik and Toulmin, Wittgenstein's Vienna 123 (1973); hereinafter: Wittgenstein's Vienna. See also, Carty's definition: to reify means 'to consider or to make an abstract idea or concept real or concrete.' A. Carty, Critical International Law: Recent Trends in the Theory of International Law, 2 *EJIL* 67 fn 1 (1991).

[24] See *supra*, footnote 20, at 197. Emphasis added.

[25] See, e.g., H. Kelsen, General Theory of Law and State (1945), at 93, 108, on the mythological theory regarding legal personality and the legal person as a superman. See, on Kelsen's attempt to free law and jurisprudence/legal science from mythological elements, i.e., from 'the grandiose normative mysticism of natural thought', e.g., J. Boyle, Ideals and Things: International Legal Scholarship and the Prison-house of Language, 26 *HILJ* 350 (1985). See, on Scelle in this respect, H. Thierry, The Thought of Georges Scelle, 1 *EJIL* 193 (1990).

3.2. THE CONTEMPORARY CONTEXT OF INTERBELLUM SCHOLARSHIP

3.2.1. Political context: democracy endangered

The Interbellum period cannot be properly understood without briefly referring to the preceding century. The 19th century had been a relatively peaceful time in Europe. The balance of power that had been put in place after the defeat of Napoleonic France by the Congress of Vienna (1815) had secured a reasonably stable system in which the European states evolved from rather meagre political institutions established upon an original contract into socio-political organisations with many tasks to fulfil within society. This international stability created room for internal political change – and halfway the century, in 1848, revolutions did indeed challenge many European societies – and for rapid economic and industrial development. The modernisation of society, in particular of agriculture, liberated many peasants from their ties to the rural areas, but they soon found that in the industrialising cities their new freedom mainly brought uncertainty, a lack of rights and extreme poverty. The labour and socialist movements became active, powerful and, eventually, effective in advocating the improvement of the workers' position and they canvassed against the mentality of *laissez-faire* individualism. In France, governmental instability, syndicalism and the dominance of parliament paralysed and undermined democracy and the state itself. After the 1848 revolts, substantial social reforms were carried out throughout Europe during the second half of the century.[26] The newly emerging social forces were so powerful that 'the masses' became a matter of great public and political concern during the last decades of the 19th and the first decades of the 20th century.[27] The democratisation of the bourgeois liberal societies brought the interests of the impoverished masses and their hostility towards bourgeois liberalism to the forefront and this delayed the reluctant extension (into universality) of (male) suffrage until the late 19th- early 20th century,[28] and even then it was mainly introduced to prevent widespread social revolution. The tension and problems the bourgeois liberalists had to contend with over 'mass politics,' democracy and legitimacy thus first surfaced in the early 20th century.[29] This was how the '*politi-*

[26] The Age of Empire was also 'the era when massive organized movements of the class of wage-workers created by, and characteristic of, industrial capitalism suddenly emerged and demanded the overthrow of capitalism.' The Age of Empire, at 10.

[27] Europe: A History, at 759, 779-780 *et seq.*

[28] Europe: A History, Appendix III, Indices of Liberalization, 1791-1948, at 1295.

[29] Also, The Age of Empire, at 84 *et seq.* The problems in question were serious and concerned the preservation of unity and the very existence of the state. They were 'already urgent in multinational politics confronted with national movements. In the Austrian empire it was already the central problem of the state, and even in Britain the emergence of mass Irish nationalism shattered the structure of established politics.' Id., at 95-96. See, for the role of war demagogy as a way to acquire legitimacy through mass loyalty, id., at 103-104. The problems were worst in Austria: 'when the masses entered the political stage pursuing their own concerns, they were hostile to all that bourgeois liberalism stood for. Nowhere was this more obvious than in Austria, where the Liberals by the

cal significance of irrationality' was discovered.[30] Political and economic liberalism did not only stimulate political reforms, but also contributed to the process of the codification of law and the adoption of constitutions at the end of the 19th century, thereby causing the positive law systems to expand.

The relative stability of international life relied upon the Congress system,[31] which was 'designed to prevent change in a world where the forces of change had only been contained by a whisker,'[32] and indeed, the map of Europe remained reasonably unchanged until 1914. Changes did occur, however, when Italy was united in 1861 and again when Germany was reunified under the Emperor, the Prussian King William I, in 1871. A contributing factor to both these transformations was one of the century's strongest sentiments: nationalism. The nationalist sentiment either contributed to the institute of the state or, if it was ethnic in nature, opposed it and aimed to create a nation instead.[33] The glorification of the nation and/or state tended to be mystical. Nationalism increasingly gave rise to intolerance, hostility and aggression towards ethnic minorities during the late 19th century.[34] Despite the mounting tension, multinational empires managed to maintain their unity. The Russian Empire persisted throughout the century, as did the Ottoman Sultanate, while the Austro-Hungarian Empire – the *k.u.k.* – was established in 1867 and under the rule of Francis-Joseph I lasted until 1916. In France, the Second Empire (since 1851) was succeeded by the Third Republic (as of 1870) which, despite its instability, lasted until 1940.

In Europe, tension increased due to the rivalry between France and Germany and as a result of developments in the East where the Ottoman Empire had begun its decline and the Russians had begun their expansion, filling the other European powers with fear. This so-called 'Eastern Question ... gave rise to the independence of the Balkan nations, to the Crimean War (1854-6), and to a chain of complications which eventually sparked the fatal crisis of 1914.'[35] Outside Europe, colonial peoples suffered the consequences of imperialist oppression and exploitation by various rival European industrial economies.[36] In the 'colonial' world, the map changed drastically.[37] Eventually, France and Britain overcame their ri-

---

end of the century were reduced to a small isolated rump of city-dwelling comfortable middle-class Germans and German Jews. The municipality of Vienna, their fortress in the 1860s, was lost to radical democrats, anti-Semites, the new Christian Social party [of the demagogue Karl Lueger (1844-1910)] and eventually the Social Democrats.' Id., at 104 and 91.

[30] Id., at 105. Emphasis added.

[31] Europe: A History, at 865 *et seq.*

[32] Id., at 762.

[33] Europe: A History, at 812-815. Also, on late 19th-century nationalism, Age of Empire, at 142-164.

[34] Id., at 817, 822 *et seq.*; see, for anti-Semitism, at 844, 846-847.

[35] Europe: A History, at 869. See, for the astounding manner in which territory was distributed at the Congress of Berlin (1878) and the explosive dangers this included, id, at 871.

[36] Id., at 848 *et seq.* Also, Age of Empire, at 56 *et seq.*

[37] As a break with the situation during the first three quarters of the 19th century, a 'systematic attempt to translate [the economic and military supremacy of the capitalist countries]' into 'formal

valry and concluded the *Entente Cordiale* (1904); three years later Russia joined them. The opposing bloc, the so-called Triple Alliance, consisted of Germany, Austria and Italy. In August 1914, a little over a month after the assassination of the Austro-Hungarian Archduke in Sarajevo by conspirators among the Serbian anti-imperial mob, war could no longer be avoided and Europe exploded.

During the Interbellum period, 'Europe never escaped the shadow of war.'[38] Of this period, three developments are particularly relevant: the problem of the 1919 peace agreement; the worldwide economic crisis and, finally and closely related to these two, the socio-political crisis that attacked the structures of the domestic societies and centred round the position of the European masses.

First, there was the problem of the Versailles peace agreements. By 1919, four empires had collapsed: the Hohenzollern German Empire, the Habsburg Austro-Hungarian monarchy, Romanov Russia and the Ottoman Sultanate, which caused Europe to fragment into over thirty internationally recognised independent states.[39] Bearing in mind the power of nationalism in the years before the war, the re-mapping of Europe in 1919 was largely based on – or at least lip service was being paid to – the principle of national self-determination. At the same time, the new borders were drawn as a '*cordon sanitaire*' to prevent communism from further seeping into.[40] This also explains why not only the Weimar Republic (1918-1933), but also Russia, originally one of the Allied Powers, was excluded from the peace conference. By participating in the Great War, the US had abandoned isolationism and established world supremacy, which it made felt in the Paris negotiations. In spite of Wilson's promise of an open peace openly negotiated, five treaties (among which the Treaty of Versailles and the Covenant of the League of Nations) were drafted and 'imposed' by the Allied Powers upon the defeated Central Powers. The peace '*Dictat*' included the war-guilt clause, which declared Germany solely responsible for causing the war. The settlement was a dangerous powder keg in a recently reshuffled Europe suffering from nationalist tension and facing economic depression. It utterly failed to establish international

conquest, annexation and administration' was made between 1880 and 1914. The empires divided the world into 'zones of influence'. Age of Empire, at 57-59.

[38] Europe: A History, at 938. WWI had been fought in a true hell on earth, by endless trench warfare, vanquishing almost an entire generation of European young men and causing the civilian population to starve. The Allied Powers (Russian Empire, France, Great Britain, Italy, Romania, Serbia, Belgium, Portugal, Greece and Montenegro) and the Central Powers (Germany, Austria-Hungary, Turkey and Bulgaria) together lost nearly 8.5 million men in the fighting and an estimated 21 million soldiers were wounded. Another 5 million civilians lost their lives. See, Europe: A History, at 1328-1329. Also, The Age of Extremes, 'both sides ... resorted to starving the other's civilians', at 28.

[39] Europe: A History, Map 25 The New Europe, 1917-1922, at 939 (1997). Some, however, became part of Soviet Russia (after 1923: the USSR) after several wars.

[40] The Age of Extremes, at 32. See also, R.S. Baker, Woodrow Wilson and World Settlement, Vol. II, at 64 (1923). The Paris peace conference cannot be understood without taking into account the Russian problem, i.e., the threat of communism spreading towards Europe. The *cordon sanitaire* consisted of six states: Finland, Estonia, Latvia, Lithuania, Poland and Rumania.

stability and did not offer any possibility for reconciliation. Obstructing Germany's re-integration into the European and world economy further contributed to the instability.

The worldwide economic crisis was actually closely related to this obstruction. The Allies had placed the financial burden of the war entirely upon the Weimar Republic.[41] After the Republic in 1921 refused to continue to pay the other states' way, numerous negotiations were spent trying to find an equitable division of the debt.[42] However, the resulting reparation agreements (1924-26) did not achieve this and the German attempts at restoration remained severely thwarted. This led to disastrous internal socio-political developments in Germany, namely rapidly increasing militarism and extremism. The swift worldwide financial and economic deterioration during the 1920s was, however, not exclusively caused by Germany's problems, but also by Soviet Russia, when it declared the promissory notes (which had been issued as proof of the Tsarist loans) worthless, and by the USA, which initially insisted on the full repayment of all inter-Allied debts. The European societies had to secure their own recovery. Their economies were under tremendous pressure: huge inflation figures and mass unemployment characterised the years up to the Great Crash on Black Thursday (24 October 1929) on the NY Stock Exchange. The hope and jubilation of the period just after the war were by then quickly fading. The world's institutional structures for financial and monetary co-operation were unable to halt the economic decline and the world economy slipped into the Great Depression. The depression which was not simply restricted to the economic sphere; it also affected the political and psychological outlook of the people of Europe. This put enormous pressure on the domestic socio-political structures.

The impact of WWI was not restricted to the international level. At home, European states also needed to reconstruct their socio-political structures and to deal with the forces challenging their stability. European societies were struggling with the erosion of their hierarchical, class-based, social structures. Europe's urbanised and industrialised society of the early 20th centrury was the result of over a hundred years of technological progress. Since the 19th century, power and wealth, although for the most part still firmly in the hands of the upper class, had been trickling down to the middle classes and upper working class. But while the middle classes slowly emancipated themselves and took advantage of the blessings of capitalism, the lowest classes did not. On the contrary, amidst and in spite of (economic) modernisation, their social and economic position was deteriorating rapidly until it seemed quite hopeless. We have already noted that at the end of the 19th century and the beginning of the 20th century, the lives of the lowest

---

[41] This was done against the advice of, e.g., the well-known economist Keynes. See, e.g., The Age of Extremes, at 31.

[42] The whole war effort had cost the parties over $200 billion and had caused over $30 billion in damage. The financial burden of restoring Europe was almost impossible to bear, but the Allies nevertheless presented the Weimar Republic with a 132 billion gold mark bill.

classes were marked by poverty, unemployment, epidemics, migration, poor living conditions, a high death rate, etc., which were the harsh consequences of the economic *laissez-faire* policy. WWI further acerbated these problems and when the War ended the crisis continued. The European 'masses' were the ones most afflicted by the economic crisis of the 1920s and 1930s. The darkness, anxiety and despair which characterised their lives at the time were impressively communicated by Dorothea Lange's photographs 'The White Angel Breadline' (1933) and the famous 'Migrant Mother' (1936).[43] The social realities of massive unemployment and poverty caused the loss of individual identity in the endless bread lines and employment queues. The disastrous socio-economic situation confirmed many in their conviction that the social and political structures had to change. Hobsbawm put it as follows: 'the old world was doomed. The old society, the old economy, the old political systems had, as the Chinese phrase it, "lost the mandate of heaven." Humanity was waiting for an alternative.'[44] And so, in the course of the 1920s and 1930s, totalitarianism, both the fascist and the communist kind, occurred not only in Germany or Stalinist Russia, but extended its power to no less than 18 other countries.[45] The war had accelerated the changes in the position of the 'masses' in the European societies. For the first time, warfare had been a 'mass' event with mass-mobilisation and mass-production of ammunition and army supplies. This had generated jobs, which closely involved the civilian population in the war effort.[46] This needed continued mass-support and so the power of public opinion in national politics and international life became apparent. As a result, propaganda developed into a recognised policy instrument and continued to fulfil this role after the War. It was not only applied to manipulate the enemy population, but also used in the European democracies to mobilise 'mass national feeling' in order to keep the public motivated or at least prepared to continue the fight.[47] This mobilisation of patriotism further enhanced the political relevance of the masses and, after the war, the political parties which became increasingly organised canvassed for their support. At the same time the labour unions strengthened their position further and a powerful post-war social position was secured. The European public had become highly disillusioned as a result of the war and, during its aftermath,[48] at the time when the masses found their voice, the voices were those of despair and a bitter longing for new beliefs.

[43] B. Haskell, The American Century: Art & Culture 1900-1950, at 254, 248-250 (1999). Hereinafter: The American Century. Also, 'The Unemployed at the New York Municipal Lodging House during the Depression' (1930), id., at 215.

[44] The Age of Extremes, at 55.

[45] Europe: A History, Appendix III, 'The Dictatorships of Inter-War Europe, 1917-39' at 1320.

[46] The Age of Extremes, at 44-52.

[47] Id., at 29 and 50.

[48] Id., at 52: 'Such hopes as [WWI] generated – of a peaceful and democratic world of nation-states under the League of Nations; of a return to the world economy of 1913; even (among those who hailed the Russian Revolution) of world capitalism overthrown within years or months by a rising of the oppressed, were soon disappointed. The past was beyond reach, the future postponed, the present bitter ...'

The 'despair of the masses' over their poverty, their state of unemployment and their poor living conditions, coupled with the failure of the politicians to improve their lot, eventually drove the masses into the arms of the fascist alternative.[49]

In short, the post-WWI decades were an unstable and chaotic time. The European societies came under severe pressure. The forces of mass politics, forces that the bourgeois liberal democracies were not yet capable of challenging, endangered democracy. Shocked by the war and deeply depressed by the harsh economic situation, the people's general susceptibility to mass emotion increased and in many European states democracy was replaced by authoritarian regimes which manipulated the masses. 'Collectivist creeds,'[50] like nationalism, communism, or fascism, spoke to 'the masses' and contributed to their (metaphysical) formation and existence. After the war, the uneasiness over the developments taking place in mass society and the profound concern over the threats to individuality and personal freedom surfaced everywhere and completely dominated intellectual life.[51]

3.2.2. Between hope and fear: the public's reason versus the irrationality of the masses

3.2.2.1. *Introduction*

In 1927, the Surrealist Max Ernst painted *The Horde*.[52] It shows a group of earth-brown anthropomorphic figures with 'red and orange highlights ambiguously danc[ing] or fight[ing] against a stark [vivid] blue sky.'[53] This was Ernst's symbolic representation of the unconscious human mind. He used the image of the horde as an allegory of the *irrational*. But the painting also unites themes of the revolt against the western philosophy of rationalism with that of mass revolution, a synthesis which is characteristic of Surrealist thinking.[54] Surrealism was heavily influenced by Freud and psychoanalysis and therefore desired that any revolution to take place should in the first place be a revolution of the mind. The mind had to break away from the rationalist tradition of European thinking and this breaking away would free the unconscious or the irrational from its repression by logic and Reason.[55] The psychoanalytical thread was joined with Marxist

---

[49] P. Drucker, The End of Economic Man: The origins of Totalitarianism (1939).

[50] Europe: A History, at 835.

[51] Davies, at 855-856 and 859-860. Some early 20th century intellectuals panicked over the threat posed by the masses.

[52] Stedelijk Museum Amsterdam. See also, Art between the Wars, *op. cit.* footnote 18, at 52, 53, 54, 194, and 197. Another painting by Max Ernst, of 1941, bears the exact same title as Freud's book Totem and Taboo (1912-13).

[53] W.A. Camfield, Max Ernst: Dada and the Dawn of Surrealism 158 (1993). '*The horde* is a truly monumental painting ... [I]t stands as one of the powerful premonitions of the violence that was to engulf Europe once again a decade hence.'

[54] J. Russel, Max Ernst: Leben und Werk 84 (1966). Also, Art between the Wars, at 194.

[55] See, Art between the Wars, at 49-51; H. Lewis, The Politics of Surrealism 17-23, 28-34 (1988). Hereinafter: The Politics of Surrealism.

socio-political ideas and the rhetoric of 'revolution'. In his painting, Ernst visualised the dual programme of the surrealist revolution, namely the socialist emancipation of the masses and the liberation of the human mind.[56] The Surrealists reached out to the masses in an attempt to spread their ideas among them; they were confident of the masses' revolutionary force.[57] Ernst's depiction of the *mass* as the *personification of irrationality* aptly illustrates the connotations of the term and image 'mass' as it was used during this period.[58]

Ernst's painting may be regarded as a reflection of the dominance of the mass-image and idea in Interbellum intellectual and cultural life. However, Ernst believed that the rise of the masses would lead to social change in the shape of a social revolution which would emancipate the masses. He alos believed it would secure the final victory of the irrational. This optimistic view of the situation was not widely shared. On the contrary, the image of 'the horde' as representative of the irrational element in society might have been a shared concept but, rather than being celebrated, it mainly induced fear, concern, panic and rejection,[59] some of which also resonates in Eliot's lines from The Waste Land (1922): 'What is that sound high in the air/ Murmur of maternal lamentation/ Who are those hooded hordes swarming/ Over endless plains, stumbling in cracked earth.'[60] The masses were mostly used as an image or metaphor to express the (contemporary) denial of man's human individuality and to represent the cause of the crisis of European civilisation.[61] The image of the horde or mass referred to the most primitive form of society.

---

[56] The Politics of Surrealism, at 173-174; Art between the Wars, at 49-51. Between 1924-1929, the Surrealists published their own periodical entitled *La Révolution surréaliste*.

[57] Breton et al., *La Mobilisation contre la guerre n'est pas la paix: Les Raisons de notre adhésion au congrès contre la guerre*, [1933], as quoted in, The Politics of Surrealism, at 121.

[58] The Surrealist movement celebrated the irrational or unconscious and sympathised with the masses for being revolutionary, although individual liberty was beyond doubt equally significant to these artists. Their complicated relationship with the Communist Party was rooted in their conviction that 'liberty for the individual was just as important to them as mass revolution'. The Politics of Surrealism, at 174, and throughout the entire book.

[59] Take for instance British writers like D.H. Lawrence, W.B. Yeats, T.S. Eliot, A. Huxley, V. Woolf or H.G. Wells. Their fear of the masses caused them to disparage modern newspaper culture and mass culture in general; often they went as far as opposing the promotion of literacy and deliberately tried to widen the gap between the masses and those who 'truly understood' their literature. It was their understanding that civilisation was under threat from mass values and therefore they opposed 'the progressive intentions of democratic educational reform.' Moreover, '[t]he intellectuals could not, of course, actually prevent the masses from attaining literacy. But they could prevent them reading literature by making it too difficult for them to understand – and this is what they did. The early twentieth century saw a determined effort, on the part of the European intelligentsia, to exclude the masses from culture. In England this movement has become known as modernism. In other European countries it was given different names, but the ingredients were essentially similar, and they revolutionized the visual arts as well as literature.' J. Carey, The Intellectuals and the Masses 15-17 (1992). In this perspective, the masses were demonised and viewed as the cause of the general declime.

[60] T.S. Eliot, The Waste Land (1922), lines 366-369.

[61] The Intellectuals and the Masses, *supra* footnote 59, at 21.

Earlier, I indicated that the altered social environment during the Interbellum period and especially the widespread concern with respect to the threat the masses posed to the (still fledgling) European democracies had a significant effect on the international law scholarship of the time. Today, the phrase 'the masses' may sound somewhat anachronistic, but its frequent use during the period under discussion is indicative of the period's intellectual atmosphere and best captures the general perspective on the crisis. Interbellum intellectual analyses of the period continually blame the rise of the masses for the disruption of the socio-political structures and the overturning of certainties and declare the masses a peril to democracy.

I will not go into detail as regards the modernist attitude of contempt for the masses or its opposite, the celebration of the masses. I will, however, describe the resulting intellectual struggle between hope and fear. A balance had to be found between the two in order to find ways to adapt society to the new challenges, if society was not to stand still or worse, lapse into chaos. The intellectual challenge consisted of retaining faith in democracy and in the public as the essential element in the democratic system, while the public could at the same time be considered the system's worst enemy. It might turn *democracy* into *mobocracy.*

I will start with the optimistic views of Wilsonianism, which put great faith in democracy and in the rationality of human nature and considered public opinion the voice of reason and a necessary force in confronting the world crisis. After this, I will discuss a number of scholars from various disciplines who regarded the 'mass' as a threatening social and political reality.

3.2.2.2. *The public: voice of reason*

Initially, the optimism of Wilsonianism could be called rationalism where it argued that the new international order had to include the voice of the public. In the Wilsonian idealistic outlook, the public's voice was the expression of objective reason. According to US President Woodrow Wilson, the new order should take a rational approach to international affairs and should be based on the doctrines of liberal democracy and national self-determination. These ideas also dominated US conduct at the negotiations on the creation of the League of Nations. The League was to be the one good thing to emerge from the European war and in order to live up to this standard it had to assume 'with duties and responsibilities that would make it the source of order in the reconstruction of the world out of chaos.' Wilson put it as follows: 'Europe is being liquidated ... and the League of Nations must be the heir to this great estate.' He considered the organisation as 'the key' to the whole Paris peace settlement, 'for it was the concrete symbol of the whole struggle between the 'new order' and the 'old order'.'[62] The League was, however, predominantly the product of American idealism and optimism:

[62] Wilson cited in R.S. Baker, Woodrow Wilson and World Settlement, Vol. I, at 225 and 235 (1923).

the British and French negotiators were much more sceptical about the new order and new diplomacy.[63] The aspirations to rehabilitate international law were nonetheless included in the Covenant's preamble as the parties confirmed that 'the understandings of international law' were to be 'the actual rule of conduct among Governments' and declared that they would maintain justice.[64] In his 'Four Points' address (1918), Wilson already anticipated this: 'What we seek is the reign of law, based upon consent of the governed and sustained by the organized opinion of mankind.'[65] This reference to the principle of democratic governance and the *opinion of mankind* as the basis of the international legal order is indeed striking. It shows that public opinion had become a frequently addressed issue in the inter-war discussions on international relations and on the League in particular:[66]

> ... the whole concept of the League of Nations was from the first closely bound up with the twin belief that public opinion was bound to prevail and that public opinion was the voice of *reason*. If "open covenants openly arrived at" could be made the rule, the plain public could be relied on to see that the contents conformed to the requirements of that reason which was the *highest morality*. The new order must be based ... on "the thought of the plain people here and everywhere throughout the world, the people who enjoy no privilege and have very simple and unsophisticated standards of right and wrong." It must be "sustained by the organized opinion of mankind."[67]

The highest attainable morality was thus related to the rational force of public opinion. Here, the public is not (yet) feared as the incarnation of the irrational, this lack of fear being by nature a fundamental American perspective.[68] Liberal democratic faith in the *rational* nature of public opinion and in *reasoning* as a guarantee against war in Wilsonian thinking and diplomacy was extended to the international level.[69] The people were the new voice in international affairs, they

---

[63] Id., Vol. II (1923). Also, H. Kissinger, Diplomacy 221 (1995).

[64] Wilson stressed the importance of the principle of self-determination from the very start of the League's founding process. Concluding the 'Fourteen Points' address, he stated: 'An evident principle runs through the whole programme I have outlined. It is the principle of justice to all peoples and nationalities, and their right to live on equal terms of liberty and safety with one another, whether they be strong or weak. Unless this principle be made its foundation no part of the structure of international justice can stand.' Fourteen Points from his address to the Joint Session of Congres, January 8, 1918, *in* R.S. Baker, Woodrow Wilson and World Settlement, Vol. III, at 42 (1923).

[65] Id., at 45. 'Four Points' Address at Mount Vernon, July 4, 1918.

[66] See, e.g., Schindler, GG Wilson, Van Vollenhoven, Schwarzenberger, etc., *infra* 3.2.3.2.b.

[67] Wilson, as cited in The Twenty Years' Crisis, at 45. Emphasis added.

[68] Wilson based his programme for world peace and reconstruction on traditional American policy. His 'new world order' was basically a generalisation of the Monroe Doctrine, in its positive aspects. He extended this Doctrine to encompass the whole world. As such it had to contribute to the 'new attitude of mind.' *Supra* footnote 64, Vol. I, at 325-332; see also, Vol. II, at 63.

[69] See, for similar faith in the value of public dialogue and the intelligence of public opinion, the American political scientist Mary Parker Follett (1868-1933). In her book, The New State (1918), she examined how to reconcile unity with plurality, collectivism with individualism. She claimed that there was human 'individuality' and that 'diversity' could be enjoyed in collective life. The

expressed what was 'rational'. It is important to note the use of language: the choice of words displays optimism and the word 'public' was generally used as a positive adjective to opinion. It was said that effective public opinion would prevent another war and this view found favour among many American politicians.[70] This new role for international public opinion was based on a rather idealistic faith 'in the essential peaceful nature of man and an underlying harmony of the world.'[71] As said, this was a predominantly American affair, since most European politicians were much more sceptical about human nature and its potential danger to world order. In any case, the Wilsonian view of 'public opinion as objective reason' shows not only boundless faith in liberal democracy, but also reveals the total absence of any fear of the phenomenon known as 'the masses'.[72] In Europe, it was not only the politicians who were less positive and optimistic: many scholars also disagreed with the role attributed to public opinion in the American view. Karl Jaspers, for example, regarded '[t]he Peace Conference at Versailles [a]s symptomatic of the general condition of the world,' in which abstract principles and public opinion ruled. He gloomily qualified the new order as a 'job-lot of idealism.'[73] In Europe, 'public opinion' was vigilantly watched and considered the collective expression of irrationality.

3.2.2.3. *The irrationality of the masses: threatening democracy and individuality*

In European intellectual circles, numerous writers expressed their concern over the position of the individual in mass society and the preservation of his individuality, freedom and individual rights and duties. It was also admitted that as a result of the war the US had gained the status of a great power, while Europe had lost its.

After WWI, intellectual life flourished. It grappled with the general confusion of the time, and the sense of crisis and pessimism with respect to European

---

question was how to liberate instead of supressing the individual in collective life? 'The New State' was a valuable contribution to theory at the time. It considered the relationship between the individual and the collective and discussed participatory democracy at a time when democratic participation was frequently caricatured as mass rule and consequently forcefully rejected at times.

[70] President Taft also declared that international public opinion had an important corrective affect on the behaviour of states. See, The Twenty Years' Crisis, at 42.

[71] Diplomacy, *supra* footnote 63, at 222.

[72] This optimism on the new role of international public opinion was shared by British intellectuals, such as Buckle and Norman Angell. The latter believed that the war was caused by 'a failure of understanding', as cited in The Twenty Years' Crisis, at 35. If the masses would be properly educated, human reason would reveal to the people the absurdity of war and a similar grasp of reality could be reached through the objectivity of *Reason*. Norman Angell's faith in 'good reasoning' as the solution to war was of course also approached with scepsis, e.g., in The Twenty Years' Crisis, at 53: 'It may turn out to be untrue that if men reason rightly about international politics they will also act rightly, or that right reason about one's own nation's interests is the road to international paradise.'

[73] K. Jaspers, Man in the Modern Age 109 (1957, orig. publ. in 1932 entitled: Die geistige Situation der Zeit). Hereinafter: Man in the Modern Age. First English transl. published in 1933.

civilisation.[74] Europe had had a clear intimation of its own mortality, as Paul Valéry claimed in *La Crise de l'esprit* in 1919: '*nous savons maintenant que nous sommes mortelles.*'[75] By the early 1930s, images like 'a whirlpool' or 'the crater yawning beneath our Western society' were used to give expression to the problems and chaos of modern life.[76] In 1935, Huizinga wrote: 'We are living in a demented world. And we know it. It would not come as a surprise to anyone if tomorrow the madness gave way to a frenzy which would leave our poor Europe in a state of distracted stupor, with engines still turning and flags streaming in the breeze, but with the spirit gone.'[77]

How to respond to the absurdity of war, the incomprehensibility of chaos and the irrationality of society and its inherent dangers? The crisis of Western civilisation and democracy were understood to be part of the same modern phenomenon: mass-man and strong social forces stemming from mass emotions. The primitivism of mass-man threatened both civilisation and democracy.[78] Ortega y Gasset explained in *La Rebelión de las Masas* (1930): 'Civilisation is, before all, the will to live in common. A man is uncivilised, barbarian in the degree in which he does not take others into account. Barbarism is the tendency to disassociation.' Since '[t]he mass ... does not wish to share life with those who are not of it,' it constitutes a fundamental danger to liberal democracy, which, as Ortega y Gasset stressed, rests on the idea of the peaceful co-existence of the majority with minorities and of the strong with the weak.[79] Mass-man desires homogeneity, he rejects all that is not like or part of the mass. And since heterogeneity and pluralism are essential to a democratic system, he is a threat to democracy. For this reason, the psychology of mass-man became every intellectual's concern.

Although the present research must restrict itself to dealing with only a handful of these intellectuals, it must be made clear that, regardless of whether we discuss Ortega y Gasset, Freud, Jaspers or Mannheim, all considered the contemporary political crisis a crisis at both the social and the individual level of life and it marked the intellectual contributions of all of them.

The contemporary importance of the issue of the individual versus the masses in intellectual life may be illustrated by an 'open letter' which Albert Einstein wrote to Sigmund Freud (1856-1939) in the *Warum Krieg?* series (1932). This series had been initiated by the *Comité permanent des Lettres et des Arts* of the

---

[74] O. Sprengler had of course already written about the decay of Western civilisation in his 1918 book *Untergang des Abendlandes*, but it took a few more years before the idea of a cultural crisis became widespread.

[75] P. Valéry, La Crise de l'esprit, XIII *La Nouvelle Revue Française* 321-337 (1919).

[76] Man in the Modern Age, at 33; see also, Mannheim, at 5.

[77] J. Huizinga, In de Schaduwen van Morgen: een diagnose van het geestelijk lijden van onzen tijd 1 (1935), translation by Huizinga, In the Shadows of Tomorrow (1936), at 15.

[78] See, e.g., in addition to the examples below, also Valéry in 1919: 'Nous avons étourdiment rendu les forces proportionelles aux masses!' *Supra* footnote 75, at 336-337, on the balance between the social and the personal and between individuality and collectivity.

[79] J. Ortega y Gasset, The Revolt of the Masses 54-55 (1950 ed., 1932 transl.).

League of Nations and gave 'den repräsentativen Vertretern des Geisteslebens' the opportunity to discuss issues which were considered of interest to the League and to general intellectual life.[80] Einstein asked:

Wie ist es möglich, daß die soeben genannte Minderheit (s.c. der Herrschenden) die Masse des Volkes ihren Gelüsten dienstbar machen kann, die durch einen Krieg nur zu leiden und zu verlieren hat? ... Wie ist es möglich, daß sich die Masse durch die genannte Mittel (i.e. die Minderheit der jeweils Herrschenden habe vor allem die Schule, die Presse und meistens auch die religiösen Organisationen in ihrer Hand) bis zur Raserei und Selbstaufopferung entflammen läßt? Gibt es ein Möglichkeit, die psychische Entwicklung der Menschen so zu leiten, daß sie den Psychosen des Hasses und des Vernichtens gegenüber widerstandsfähiger werden?[81]

How is it possible that the masses, who will only suffer from war, follow their leaders in their policies of hatred and annihilation; why is the human psyche willing to follow and serve its leaders to the point of its own destruction? Freud's response to Einstein's penetrating questions reflected the views which he had already expounded in his 1921 work *Massenpsychologie und Ich-analyse* and in *Das Unbehagen in der Kultur* of 1930.

In *Massenpsychologie und Ich-analyse*, Freud concentrated on the individual's loss of 'distinctiveness', 'freedom' and 'independence' as part of the mass.[82] He explained how human mental processes change when the individual becomes part of a collective (mind): due to the suggestibility induced by group life – a kind of hypnotising effect – the individual loses his critical faculties and, as the individual's *unconscious* personality begins to dominate his *conscious* personality, he is no longer guided by his own will and sense of responsibility.[83] As Le Bon had done earlier,[84] Freud described the 'group mind' in terms of delusion and fallacy: primitive, impulsive, instinctive, violent, extreme, led by the unconscious, exaggerating, excluding reason and lacking any interest in the truth; it is considerably less intelligent or even plainly simplistic, and highly susceptible to

[80] S. Freud, Warum Krieg? (1932), *in* Gesammelte Werke, Vol. XVI, at 12 (1950). Hereinafter: Warum Krieg?

[81] Id. A. Einstein, Letter of 30 Juli 1932, as cited in the introduction to Freud's response.

[82] S. Freud, Group Psychology and the Analysis of the Ego 25 and 35 (Standard ed. J. Strachey, 1959). Hereinafter: Group Psychology.

[83] Id., at 9-11, 23, and 70. See, for Freud's grave concerns over the social influence of this psychological mechanism, 'how much every individual is ruled by those attitudes of the group mind...' Id., at 63.

[84] Considering the social and political developments we mentioned earlier it will not come as a surprise that one of the first key works on mass psychology dates back to the late 19th century. One of these is Le Bon's La Psychology des Foules (1895), which discussed the mental condition of an individual human being in a group (or: mass) and examined the kind of extreme behaviour which a group or mass is capable of. The book unleashed a stream of publications on mass psychology and its impact on socio-political life. This was the starting point of the debate on the problems of mass society as many intellectuals became aware of the findings in this field. This explains how Le Bon's book also found its way into international legal scholarship.

illusions and rhetoric.[85] But contrary to Le Bon's approach, Freud analysed social or group phenomena and processes in terms of the *individual* mind; unlike the influential 19th-century *Völkerpsychologie*, his modern psychology was not a psychology of the objectified group mind. This is important to remember when we will deal with Kelsen's appreciation of Freud's theory below. In order to correct the social disadvantages of the psychological processes that govern individuals who are part of a group, Freud proposed to 'procure for the group precisely those features which were characteristic of the individual and which are extinguished in him by the formation of the group', i.e., to enhance the level of organisation of the group.[86] Controlling the dangers of mass-life and mass-society required the leadership of a thoroughly responsible and well-educated intellectual elite, which aspired to truth and would not abuse its powers.[87]

The importance that Freud attributed to this elitist leadership was rooted in his understanding that groups, including societies or states, were formed by a collective love of and submission to an authoritative father figure, i.e., the leader. [88] Freud distinguished groups with a leader and groups without a leader. In the leaderless groups, the leader had been replaced by 'an idea, an abstraction', but these could still be personified by a secondary leader.[89] There are two psychological ('libidinal') processes operating in the individual mind and these remain the same, regardless of whether they follow a leader or a '*leading idea*'. The processes are 'substitution' and 'identification.' Groups formed under the leadership of an abstraction, however, are much more 'stable and lasting' than the groups of which the members have substituted their ego-ideal for a leader figure and thus identify with each other on the basis of this substitution.[90] The leaderless groups tend to be better organised and more institutionalised.

Freud pictured mass life as the revival of an earlier stage in human society, namely that of the primal horde in which man lived as 'a *horde* animal, an individual creature in a horde led by a chief.'[91] This evidently goes back to his Oedi-

---

[85] Group Psychology, at 6-25, and 62.

[86] Id., at 24-25. See also, for Freud's critical view on the public and his personal feelings of isolation and vulnerability in groups or masses, D.J. Fisher, Reading Freud's *Civilization and Its Discontents*, *in* LaCapra and Kaplan, Modern European Intellectual History 271 (1982).

[87] See also, Warum Krieg?, at 12. At the same time, Freud was rather sceptical about the probability of such an elite.

[88] Group formation requires a bond between individuals that unites them into a collective and holds them together. Freud argued that the type of leader is decisive in this process in which the individual overcomes his primary hostility towards people: the individual identifies with other members, as they all substitute their 'ego ideal' for the same leader (father figure). Identification is the original form of an emotional tie with other people and a substitute for the libidinal tie. '[It is] based upon an emotional common quality, ... the nature of the tie with the leader.' Group psychology, at 42-56, 78-86. See also, J. Brunner, Oedipus Politics, Freud's Paradigm of Social Relations, *in* M.S. Roth (Ed.), Freud: Conflict and Culture 81 (1998).

[89] Group psychology, at 40-41.

[90] Id., at 78-79.

[91] Id., at 68. Emphasis added. See, for the entire argument, id., at 69-77.

pus theory on the genesis of human society and civilisation[92] and explains why Freud's concept of society was 'inevitably depicted as divided into masses/sons on the one hand and leaders/fathers on the other.'[93] This picture of mass-society was certainly threatening, but at the same time Freud recognised that the individual could only attain civilisation if he lived in a group or society. Ultimately, society is the only instrument capable of channelling and correcting barbarism and primitive impulses.[94] Positive elements of society, like social structures and the 'rule of law' and religion, are necessary to control mass-society's negative effects on the individual.[95]

In any case, Freud's findings on the changes in the psychology of the individual mind *caused* by group life have been the subject of profound controversy ever since Freud suggested them,[96] but the impact these ideas had on his contemporaries, both in his own field and outside psychology, and the discussions they stirred up were unparalleled during the 1920s and 1930s. In Kelsen's view, Freud's psychoanalysis-based social theory was 'exceptionally brilliant and far-seeing.'

One of Freud's most vehement opponents was Karl Jaspers (1883-1969), the psychiatrist-philosopher, who fundamentally disagreed with Freud's description of man as '*die Marionette seines Unbewußten.*'[97] Their intellectual quarrels go beyond the scope of this section,[98] but like Freud, Jaspers was concerned with the individual in modern mass-society and he focused on the preservation of the individual self. He discussed this issue from a philosophical perspective in *Die geistigen Situation der Zeit* (1932).[99]

---

[92] According to this theory, the primal tyrannical father is killed by his sexually frustrated sons, who subsequently form a society based on a social contract instigated by the internalised parental authority. By this murder, human society developed from the original, primal stage into the next 'totemic' phase: 'a community of brothers'. Group psychology, at 69 and 86-89. See also, Civilization, *infra* footnote 94, and Warum Krieg?

[93] J. Brunner, Oedipus Politics, Freud's Paradigm of Social Relations, see *supra* footnote 88, at 91.

[94] S. Freud, Civilization and Its Discontents 48-49 (1930), (Standard ed. transl. J. Strachey, 1961), hereinafter: Civilization. See also, Group Psychology, at 44: 'in the development of mankind as a whole, just as in individuals, love alone acts as the civilizing factor in the sense that it brings a change from egoism to altruism.'

[95] Civilization, at 48-49. See also, Warum Krieg?.

[96] D.J. Fisher, Reading Freud's *Civilization and Its Discontents*, see *supra* footnote 86, at 252.

[97] K. Jaspers, Die geistigen Situation der Zeit 154 (1932 ed., 1965 print). See also, *supra* footnote 73.

[98] Freud's doctrine justifies man and life as it *is*, a line of reasoning which Jaspers rejected. Man had to transcend these realities and 'learn to contemplate human existence as something different from them.' Man is *human* exactly because he is able to rise above these natural impulses. Freud's conception of man, Jaspers argued, prevents man from becoming himself, 'he is to return to that nature in which he no longer needs to be man.' Man in the Modern Age, at 168.

[99] On the meaning of the term 'masses' and how it relates to the term 'public'. Jaspers said the following: 'If we use the word "masses" as a synonym for the "public," this denotes a group of persons mentally interlinked by their common reception of certain opinions, but a group vague in its

Jaspers observed that the individual was increasingly reduced to a mere 'cog' in the machinery of a technologically advanced, economically rationalised mass-society, which only aim was to supply the 'masses' with their material needs and to maximise the welfare of the largest possible 'whole.'[100] Man's life-order (*Daseinsordnung*) was reduced to a '*technischer Massenordnung*' and this resulted in conflict between the mass-order and human individual life. Forced to live in this unyielding world, man is overwhelmed by 'a feeling of powerlessness.'[101] In the technical life-order, the individual is slowly being annihilated by mass-man. His meaning is limited to serving the 'whole', with total disregard for human individuality.[102]

The individual is merged in the function. ... The individual consciousness is absorbed into the social, so that, in exceptional instances, the individual has joy in work without any tinge of selfishness. It is the *collectivity* that matters; and what to the individual would be tedious, nay intolerable, becomes endurable to him as part of the collectivity, in which a new stimulus inspires him. He exists only as "we." Essential humanity is reduced to the general; to vitality as a functional corporeality, to the triviality of enjoyment.[103]

Jaspers observed that the problem of the annihilation of the individual occurred at several levels. First, at the individual level, where the question was raised how to preserve human individuality and prevent the sacrifice of selfhood.[104] Secondly, at the political level, as democracy itself was at stake. Jaspers expressed his ambivalence in respect of the masses as follows: 'We infer ... that the masses must rule, and yet we find they cannot rule', because '[e]ven an articulated mass always tends to become unspirited and inhuman. It is life without existence...'[105] But even political life cannot be lived unless it involves some representation of '*existence*.'

---

limits and its stratification, though at times a typical historical product. The "masses," however, as an aggregate of persons who are articulated in some apparatus of the life-order in such a manner that the will and the peculiarities of the majority among them are decisive, constitute the unceasing operative and effective power in our world-the power which manifests itself no more than transiently in the "public" or in a "mob".' Id., at 37.

[100] Id., at 39-54, 75, 83.

[101] Id., at 3.

[102] Id., at 14, 42, 51. Also, at 35. See also, for the idea of the individual serving the whole, at 75.

[103] Id, 47-48. Emphasis added. See also, at 37-58.

[104] 'Man is faced by the problem whether he will fatalistically submit to the sway of the mighty forces which appear to determine everything that happens, or whether, after all, paths are discernible along which he can walk freely because on them the writ of the aforesaid powers no longer runs.' Id., at 34.

[105] Id, at 37, 40, and at 38, where he criticised the notion of 'public opinion:' 'The "public" is a phantom, the phantom of an opinion supposed to exist in a vast number of persons who have no effective interrelation and though the opinion is not effectively present in the units. Such an opinion is spoken of as "public opinion," a fiction which is appealed to by individuals and by groups as supporting their special views. It is impalpable, illusory, transient, "tis here," "tis there," "tis gone;" a nullity which can nevertheless for a moment endow the multitude with power to uplift or to destroy'.

Jaspers advanced his *Existenzphilosophie* to counter the development of the individual's usurpation by the massess.[106] Instead of willingly becoming an exponent of mass will and losing one's selfhood, freedom and human dignity, all members of society, regardless of whether they are leaders or subordinates, must strive to preserve their individual existence or existential life. Only then can individual personality and responsibility be guaranteed. Existential life consists of the realisation of the true self, both in individual and in social life: man alters reality by becoming himself. He makes his being 'actual' through the communication and employment of his individual will and thinking.[107] The underlying mental cause at the individual level of the universal and complex crisis of lost humanity is the loss of the individual true self.[108] However, the individual has the ability to limit the damage caused by mass-rule by refusing to be reduced to a mere 'function'. For this he must remain aware of and continue to express his individual 'self'.

At the political level, the expression of selfhood is equally important. By means of both his mental self-creation and the state, the human individual 'can regain consciousness of the origin and the aim of human existence.' Even in politics, therefore, which depends on the union of wills and deals with 'the concreteness of life on the whole,' the individual has (or should have) the opportunity to express his selfhood. By means of the will of the state, man shapes his individual and collective destiny.[109] For this reason, all individuals should actively participate in politics and by doing so prevent the body politic from turning into a state governed by demagogic rulers spouting sweeping rhetoric for the purpose of mobilising mass emotion. Politics give shape to man's social existence and for this reason Jaspers argued that man's destiny had to be bringing about an 'historical transformation of life'. Man needed to assume the burden of responsibility, he had to participate and thereby give shape to (the socio-political) collective reality.[110] Jaspers recognised how difficult it would be to achieve these aims and was therefore not surprised to see that the masses seemed to prefer Communism and Fascism as easier options.[111]

In other words, in Jaspers' view, the underlying cause of the general crisis could be found at the level of the individual. For this reason, Jaspers focused on human nature in his response to the crisis. He defined the central issue as follows:

---

[106] Jaspers considered 'the general mood of [his] time' as destructive, (Id. at 173) and Marxism, Freudianism and ethnological theory as particularly destructive. He belived these theories were products of mass life, which put their 'faith in Nothingness.' Id. They pictured man as a conditioned being, completely stripped of free will, and denied his ability to shape his own destiny. Id., at 173, and 166-174.

[107] Id., at 175.

[108] Id., at 84-88.

[109] Id., at 87 and 89.

[110] Id., at 91-95.

[111] Id., at 98.

The essential problem of the political history of our time is *whether the masses of mankind can be democratised*, whether average human nature is such as to enable each to *accept his share of responsibility as a citizen* equally aware with all others of what he is doing, and ready as a part of his daily life to take his share in deciding fundamental political issues.[112]

To prevent totalitarians from seizing power and creating a life-order governed by deviously inspirational demagogic leaders and ruled on the basis of technical and economic interests, mass-society must be democratised. All individuals must participate in the political decision making. In other words, they must all behave like true citizens and assume their civic responsibility. Realising one's individual self is an act of independence, not intended to please the crowd. It is the 'lonely' path of the individual who 'stands steadfast against the almost overwhelming power which, from generation to generation, works to enforce its blind will against the will of the lonely doer, and which in each generation, works in a peculiar way to itself – to-day the hero has to safeguard himself against the impalpable masses.' By acting this way man can remain an individual instead of becoming the 'executan[t] of the mass-will.'[113] For this reason, Jaspers considered the emancipation and education of the individual *self* – the *Existenz* – the answer to the crisis facing humanity.

To conclude this concise illustration of the concerns and preoccupations of the Interbellum period, I will briefly touch upon a work entitled *Mensch und Gesellschaft im Zeitalter des Umbaus* by the sociologist Karl Mannheim (1893-1947). The book was published in 1935, two years after the German people signed over their right to democracy.[114] He attributed this catastrophe to 'the failure of the liberal democratic machinery in the Weimar Republic ... to solve the problems of modern mass society.' He explained that the liberal democratic crisis of mass-society was a wider phenomenon. At the core of Mannheim's analysis is the correlation between the social and the individual. He agreed with the need for a new psychology that could transform man and also proposed a new type of social planning that could transform society. Both were neceassry to tackle the disintegration of liberal democracies and the rise of totalitarianism.

The core element of Mannheim's analysis was his conclusion that the general crisis was the result of an imbalance between the *rational* and the *irrational* (both in individual and in social life). The technological development of man and modern society had overtaken their moral-psychological development, causing a lack of rationality and morality in mass-society. The balance urgently needed to be redressed.[115] In this, however, it was important not to take a *functional* approach to

[112] Id., at 107. Emphasis added.

[113] Id., at 189.

[114] The English ed. was published in 1940, entitled: Man and Society in an Age of Reconstruction.

[115] '[M]ass society ... produces all the irrationalities and emotional outbreaks which are characteristic of amorphous human agglomerations ... it favours a great number of irrational impulses and

rationalisation, because this would not free the individual from the mass and mass-emotion. On the contrary, it would allow democracy to remain the captive of uncontrollable eruptions of mass feeling. To halt the danger inherent in the phenomenon of the *Stimmungsdemokratie*,[116] an educational approach was needed which would emancipate the individual and liberate him.[117] The extension of the suffrage had to be followed by a campaign to educate the masses. Man had to be taught how to be a democratic citizen, with rights and obligations. He had to be acquire the ability to form and express (responsible) opinions.[118] In Mannheim's view, the new social planning together with the new psychology would help realise this educational goal: 'In this way we are keeping in the foreground both the highest good of society and the peace of mind of the individual.'[119]

Mannheim's views on the problems of mass-society and its threats to democracy resemble Jaspers' arguments for democratising the masses. Both agree on the importance of educating and emancipating the individual. Where Jaspers sought the solution in individual *Existenz*, Mannheim pointed to social planning for the transformation of society from a democracy of the few into a mass democracy of responsible individual citizens. '[I]t must constantly be kept in mind that the transition from a minority democracy to an organized mass democracy does not take place spontaneously but must itself be planned.'[120]

3.2.2.4. *Conclusion*

During the early decades of the 20th century, the image of the *mass* generally came to represent barbarism and the irrational forces in socio-political life which endangered democracy. It thereby became a symbol and a catch phrase in the expression of serious and widespread concern. The optimism of liberal democracy, which was so apparent in Wilsonianism, was generally absent in Europe, despite Wilsonianism's initial influence on international relations. More than by the idea that the public represented rationality and morality, the European intellectual debate was dominated by the role of the masses in causing the current crisis of civilisation and democracy.

Ortega y Gasset and Freud suggested the rule of an educated elite. Freud further stressed the importance of social and legal structures and institutions to hold

---

suggestions and produces an accumulation of unsublimated psychic energies which, at every moment, threatens to smash the whole subtle machine of social life. ... the more modern mass-society is functionally rationalized the more it tends to neutralize substantial morality ...' See, Man and Society in an Age of Reconstruction, at 61, 67.

[116] Id., at 45.

[117] Id., at 359. Also, at 114, 195-196, 222-224.

[118] He stressed that in mass democracy 'public opinion' should be based on well-thought out ideas and healthy criticism from an educated public in an articulate society, not on public mood swings. Id., at 111, 222-224.

[119] Id., at 222.

[120] Id., at 114.

barbarism at bay and reduce the individual's susceptibility to mass-induced 'hysteria'. Jaspers and Mannheim both argued that mass-man needed to be educated and mass-society democratised by turning man into an individual citizen with political rights and responsibilities. Only the liberation of the individual from the masses would prevent mass societies from becoming totalitarian.

The problem of mass society and its threat to democracy and individual liberty were thus at the heart of the intellectual debate during the Interbellum period, as is evidenced in many important works and analyses of the time. This is important to remember when we examine the writings on international law produced during this crisis.

3.2.3. Jurisprudential context

3.2.3.1. *Introduction: the 19th-century legacy*

Two 19th-century developments have been of crucial importance to the course of international law scholarship, especially to (both restorative and revisionist) Interbellum theories. The first development was that legal positivism had become the elected approach of mainstream thinking, which had resulted in the glorification of the sovereign state.[121] The second development was that a transformation had taken place in the law of nations which took it from a thoroughly European to a truly universal set of rules.

As regards the first development, Vattel's approach was further followed in the direction of positivism. Natural law was increasingly marginalised and relegated to the realm of personal conscience: actual common consensus ousted reason as the primary source of the law of nations and positivism characterised late 18th and 19th-century legal thinking. During the 18th century, international legal personality had gone from being a personal (individual) attribute of the King or Prince to being an attribute of the state. Every sovereign state was now the recognised holder of fundamental rights under the law of nations. More importantly, it could no longer cease to exist at the international level after internal changes of government. Soon, the responsibilities of statehood were thought of more lightly than the rights it had brought to states. The late 18th-century French Revolutionaries, however, challenged 'the rule that the international legal personality of a State preserved its identity even in case of a domestic constitutional upheaval.' They 'adhered to the postulate that »the sovereignty of peoples cannot be bound by the treaties of tyrants«.'[122] Within the law of nations, however, this ideal gained insufficient support at the time and absolute sovereignty with ILP as a barrier between the domestic and the international order continued to prevail. Nonetheless, the 'dynamic force' of some of the ideas governing the French

---

[121] See, A Concise History, at 222 *et seq;* also, The Epochs, at 503 *et seq.*
[122] The Epochs, at 413.

Revolution did leave 'inextinguishable tracks' on 19th-century international law, of which the 'full emancipation of the sovereign nation-State' was one of the most important. The idea that the sovereignty of the people was transferred to the international level established the principles of national self-determination and non-intervention as absolute sovereign rights of *states*.[123] As Grewe observed, the ideologists of the Revolution 'completed the process of rendering the doctrine of sovereignty absolute;'[124] a development that had been set in train by Vattel. In other words, contrary to what one would expect, it was not the position of the individual human being, but that of the individual sovereign state which was strengthened by the political philosophy of individualism. In accordance with the sovereign equality of all peoples, all members of the international legal community of civilised nations enjoyed the same fundamental natural rights and duties and the law of nations depended fully on national sovereignty and common consent for its creation. With the accumulation of sovereign rights and the increase of power, the state began to consider itself above the law. Its legal personality in the classical sense depended upon absolute sovereignty. Consequently, the question of the status of the law of nations – is it truly law or merely power and politics – always hovered in the background. The two best-known 19th-century opponents of the legal nature of the law of nations were the British legal theorist John Austin (1790-1859) and the German philosopher Georg W.F. Hegel (1770-1831).

Austin distinguished positive law, i.e., law that is properly called law, from morality or natural law, without, however, denying the latter's existence. He defined 'law proper' as a 'command'[125] given by a sovereign (person or persons) and concluded that '[s]trictly speaking, every law properly so called is a *positive* law.'[126] Therefore, 'law proper' did not exist at the international level, as it could not possibly operate among equal states. The law of nations had to be considered to belong to the realm of 'positive morality', which amounts to a denial of the independent existence of the law of nations as real law: 'international law is law improperly termed law.'[127] However, as an expression of international positive morality, the rules of the law of nations were nevertheless valuable. In *The Providence of Jurisprudence Determined* (1832), Austin argued that '*positive* international law' should have been called '*positive* international *morality*,' since it was law '*set by [the] general opinion*' of the society of nations and not by a sovereign.[128]

---

[123] See, for self-determination as a sovereign right of nations, id., at 420-421.

[124] Id., at 414-415.

[125] J. Austin, The Province of Jurisprudence Determined (1832), W.E. Rumble (Ed.), at 10 *et seq.* and 109 *et seq.*

[126] Id., at 110.

[127] Id., at 20.

[128] Id., at 112, 123-124. See, for Austin's criticism that Grotius and Pufendorf confused morality with law, id., at 160. See also, H. Wheaton, who believed that Austin's negation of the legal nature of international law was justified: Elements of International law (6th ed., 1855), at 18.

In the 19th century, a shift occurred in the concept of state: from being perceived as a collection of individuals it went to being viewed as a kind of organism, with a mind of its own, in which every human mind participated. As such, it was understood that the individual could only be free and realise his true self when he was part of the collective. In Hegelian thinking, the state and sovereignty were exalted and Hegelian ideas were therefore used to deny that international law could be true law or they were used to justify only granting international law the status of external state law.[129] 'The nation-state is mind in its substantive rationality and immediate actuality and is therefore *absolute power on earth*,' from which it follows, according to Hegel, 'that every state is sovereign and autonomous against its neighbours.' State sovereignty was considered absolute and international law depended exlusively and entirely on the sovereign will: 'what really happens is that international relations in accordance with treaty alternate with the severance of these relations.' International law was completely at the whim of the sovereign. Hegel continued: 'It follows that if states disagree and their particular wills cannot be harmonized, the matter can only be settled by war.' [130] This was not particularly disturbing to Hegel, who considered war to be a 'part of the international political game.' The state was seen as the ultimate cause which individuals could serve and maybe even had to sacrifice their lives for, because war was a necessary fact of life.[131] Hegel defined individual freedom as self-sacrifice: 'a self-sacrifice which yet is the real existence of one's freedom; the maximum self-subsistence of individuality, yet only as a cog playing its part in the mechanism of an external organisation ...', the self-sacrifice to serve the ultimate and absolute goal: the sovereignty of the state.[132] It is 'the supreme duty' of the individual to be 'a member of the State.' Only as a member of the state, the 'individual himself has objectivity, genuine individuality, and an ethical life. Unification pure and simple is the true content and aim of the individual, and the individual's destiny is the living of a universal life.' [133] The state was the God individual man had to serve by self-sacrifice, or, as Hegel put it: 'The march of God in the world, that is what the State is.' And so, the state became 'a secular deity.'[134] We might say that the state had donned a divine mask: in its absolute power and supremacy it had been declared sacred. The "divine mask" identified

---

[129] See, e.g., A. Lasson, System der Rechtsphilosophie (1882), at 394 and 402: 'Zwischen den Staaten als souveränen Wesen ist zwar ein eigentlicher Rechtszustand nicht möglich ... ... der Character eigentlichen Rechtes bleibt ... dem Völkerrechte ... für immer entzogen.'

[130] G.W.F. Hegel, The Philosophy of Right, (1967, transl. Knox), at 213 and 214.

[131] Id., at 209: Hegel stated that war cannot simply be rejected as 'an absolute evil'. In fact, at times it is, in his view, even a 'necessity,' 'healthy for the ethical state of peoples' and preventive of corruption in nations.

[132] Id., at 211.

[133] Id., at 156.

[134] Id., at 279 and 285.

each state as a sacred and sovereign personality, as an independent unit completely distinct from other states.[135]

An important exponent of the 19th-century Hegelian-inspired theory on statehood was Otto Von Gierke. Both Georg Jellinek's inorganic theory of the state and von Gierke's organic one were, on the one hand, the subject of scrutiny and repudiation by revisionist scholars and, on the other hand, a source of inspiration for their restorative contemporaries. In the organic theory, the will of the state is considered to have *substance*, to exist – in a socio-psychological sense – as the true, collective will of the people. The will forms the basis of the state and its (legal) personality. Von Gierke advanced the theory that the personality of the state was *real*. He considered the state as a real entity with a life and will of its own. He *reified* the social and legal personality of the state, as he did with any group personality.[136] According to Gierke, the individual needs to be part of the collective consciousness and will (the Hegelian *Volksgeist*) in order to find direction and be *free*. This collective consciousness of the people was represented by *die Staatsseele*, and subsequently given a physical presence, *Staatskörper*. In legal thinking, the state was also regarded as a mystical anthropomorphic person and its deification was 'legalised' in the shape of the state as a legal personality. Gierke's socio-psychologically-based concept of state and its substantive legal personality became 'an important stepping-stone towards that merger of the individual in the collective, which is an essential and vital aspect of modern totalitarian government.'[137] The three revisionist scholars whose work we will discuss below understood the (political) danger inherent in these views and instead desired the liberation of the individual from the collective.

Georg Jellinek (1851-1911) also based his concept of state on the idea of a collective will, but regarded this will as an abstraction or fiction and not as a thing of substance or reality. In his view, the will of the state was not composed of the will of individuals, but of the will of state *organs*. *Der Organwille ist Staatswille*. '*Staat und Organ [sind] eine Einheit*,' in fact, the state *is* its organs. The personality of the state is a fiction. It is the organs that represent the state, state and organs are one.[138] The inorganic doctrine of the state recognised the su-

---

[135] In Hegel's theory, the state is considered the personification of morality and its sovereignty is necessary to determine individual morality. The individual rights of man were not really relevant because individual freedom could only be realised if by complete submersion in the state.

[136] Interbellum revisionists frequently used Otto von Gierke's ideas to set off their own arguments, for example the ideas contained in his 'Das Wesen der menschlichen Verbände' (1902), at 10: 'Dass das Recht, indem es die organisirten Gemeinschaften als Personen behandelt, durchaus nicht in einen Widerspruch zur Wirklichkeit tritt, sondern der Wirklichkeit adaequaten Ausdruck verleiht? Sind vielleicht die menschlichen Verbände reale Einheiten, die mit der Anerkennung ihrer Persönlichkeit durch das Recht nur das empfangen, was ihrer wirklichen Beschaffenheit entspricht? Mit Vielen antworte ich: Ja! Und mir scheint, dass Jeder so antworten muss, der mit der individualistischen Gesellschaftsauffassung gebrochen hat und das menschliche Gemeinleben als ein Leben höherer Ordnung betrachtet, dem sich das Einzelleben eingliedert.'

[137] W. Friedmann, Legal Theory, see also, *infra* chapter 4.

[138] G. Jellinek, Allgemeine Staatslehre (1905), at 546: 'Der Staat kann nur vermittelst seiner Organe existieren; denkt man die Organe weg, so bliebt nicht etwa noch der Staat als Träger seiner

premacy of the state will and considered the state to be the '*Bewahrer und Fortbilder des Rechts.*'[139] Only the state had the power to limit its power (the *Selbstverplichtungs-Theorie des Staates*), both internally and externally.[140] This quite invalidates Jellinek's compromise between state sovereignty (as the independent and highest *Gewalt*) and international law.[141] Indeed, he concluded himself that the law of the society of states was '*ein anarchisches Recht.*'[142]

In any event, both organic and inorganic theorists based their theory of the state on state will. Voluntarism was, after all, the dominant view in the late 19th and early 20th century. In these theories the state was pictured as a meta-juridical person who wore its legal personality like a divine mask to separate the state from the law and in acknowledgment of the state's absolute sovereignty. As sovereignty continued to expand and positivism overtook the law of nations, the ideas of the French Revolution concerning the position of the individual 'lay dormant until 1919, when they experienced an astonishing rebirth.'[143] But until then, neither Kant nor the French Revolution could prevent the concept of legal personality from being used as a barrier for keeping the law of nations from penetrating into the domestic sphere.

The second of the two 19th-century developments which determined the course of international law scholarship in the Interbellum theories was the transformation of the law of nations from a fully European into a universal international law, the law of a global system of 'civilised nations.' After 1815, the law of nations was no longer based on the idea of Christian unity, but rather on the idea of civilisation. The international legal community comprised only civilised nations and the admission of new members was based on the required level of civilisation. In this respect, the abolition of the slave trade became 'the formal criterion for the required, minimum standard of civilisation.' Latin American and Asian States joined the system in the course of the 19th century.[144]

Legally speaking, 'civilised' nations separated themselves from 'barbarian peoples' by considering themselves the exclusive sovereign international legal

---

Organe, sondern ein juristisches Nichts übrig. Dadurch unterscheidet sich das Organverhältnis von jeder Art der Stellvertretung. Vertreter und Vertretender sind und bleiben zwei, Verband und Organ sind und bleiben eine einzige Person.'

[139] Id., at 155.

[140] If the state and the law are separate and the state is a sovereign meta-juridical entity, the question arises if the law is binding upon the state. In answer to this question, Jellinek formulated the legal doctrine of self-limitation, see, id., at 462 *et seq.*, and at 464: '[Der Staat] befielt im Gesetze auch den ihm als Organe dienenden Personen, ihren Organwillen dem Gesetze gemäß zu gestalten. Da aber der Organwille Staatswille ist, so bindet der Staat durch Bindung der Organe sich selbst.'

[141] Id., at 364 *et seq.*, at 366: 'das Völkerrecht ist der Staaten, nicht aber sind die Staaten des Völkerrechtes wegen da.' Id., at 465: 'Auch im Völkerrecht bleibt rechtlich der Staat nur seinem eigenen Willen unterworfen.'

[142] Id., at 368.

[143] The Epochs, at 414.

[144] Id., at 445 *et seq.*

persons. For this reason, the recognition of a state's international legal personality depended on whether it was recognised by other civilised nations as 'sufficiently' civilised to be included in the Family of Nations. Recognition became a formal constitutive act and the international legal personality of states fully depended upon it. The right to recognise other state as equals was similarly exclusive to (civilised) sovereign states. In this view, the Hegelian-Austinian theory that the law of nations emanated entirely and exclusively from the free will of sovereign states found application.[145] The tendency to claim racial superiority which was inherent in the civilisation approach contributed to the imperialistic notions at the root of the international system. However, this racial and colonial thinking increasingly met with opposition and the idea of civilisation as the foundation of international law began to lose ground in the early 20th century.

In short, in the 19th century and during the first decade of the 20th century, the personification of the state in international law was no longer the 'liberal and progressive devise' for conferring duties on the state as it had on the King or Prince under the natural law of nations. Instead, it had 'come to be associated with the assertion of unlimited rights of the State over the individual.' In the mainstream perspective on international law, which was voluntarism, ILP was used in a 'reactionary and authoritarian' way,[146] which tainted its reputation for the future.

3.2.3.2. *The concept of ILP in Interbellum international legal scholarship*

From the introduction above we learned that the considerable scholarly attention devoted to the concept of ILP was mainly due to two interrelated developments. The legal theoretical conflict between Restorers and Revisionists concerning the identity of international law and the character of the international society had ineluctably invaded the doctrine on ILP and divided scholars on the topic of what were the *true* subjects of international law or the *original* international legal persons.[147] The great interest taken in the (new) position of the individual must be

[145] See also, id., at 500.

[146] The Twenty Years' Crisis, at 189. See also, Nussbaum on sovereignty, who indicates the same response to the 19th century conception of the state and its sovereignty: 'a strong aversion to state omnipotence, as epitomized in the concept of sovereignty, evolved and was fomented by the pacifist movement that made sovereignty responsible for the horrors of war. In this setting, new doctrines emerged which attacked the notion of sovereignty at its very roots. More particularly, attempts were made to *sever the law from the state ideologically, with the higher dignity in the law*.' A Concise History, at 282.

[147] This is evidently due to the fact that the role of ILP in the definition of international law is decisive, while at the same time consensus on its content has not yet been attained: '[L]es sujets forment l'element essentiel, la marque caracteristique de toute conception et de toute definition de ce droit, ... [mais] la determination des sujets est, dans le domaine du droit des gens, incomparablement plus difficile que dans d'autres domaines juridique ... Le droit international n'etablit, en effet, aucune regle generale sur la caracterisation de ses sujets. Ordinairement, les systemes juridiques, ... etablissent ce qu'on pourrait appeler le signalement de leurs sujets. ... Le droit international positif, au contraire, est muet sur ce point, dont l'importance saute aux yeux. ... La doctrine, a son tour, est

related to the broader context of the general and serious concern regarding the threat to democracy and its consequences for individual human life. I will now discuss the response of contemporary international legal scholarship in this context of political crisis. It will become clear that Restorers and Revisionists were divided on the position of the individual and used the concept of ILP either to include or exclude actors from international law.

a. Restoration

Restorative scholarship continued in the Voluntarist tradition, which relied on the personification of the state so that it could be said to have its own *will* and be regarded as a sovereign state *person* who could exercise this will in order to create law. This anthropomorphic theory of the state and its sovereignty and (legal) personality contributed to the mystification of the state and to the oppression of the individual in the service of the state person. This mystification, which we typified earlier as a characteristic of 19th-century thinking, decreased after WWI, also in restorative scholarship, but the related classical interpretations of the state and its sovereignty were retained and some traces of the mystification of the state remained.[148] The existence of international law was not denied. In fact, the restorative scholars believed in the legal nature of *positive* international law[149] and considered it (or its systemisation) the only worthy object of legal study.[150] In their view, the purpose of international law was to regulate the (peaceful or non-peaceful) conduct of the members of the community of sovereign states. Restorative scholars, such as Triepel, Anzilotti, Cavaglieri, Heilborn and (to a lesser extent) Oppenheim, consequently defended the thesis that 'States are the sole subjects of international law' or 'Only sovereign states have (full) ILP'.[151]

pleine d'incertitudes en cette matiere.' M. Siotto-Pintor, Les Sujets du droit International autres que les Etats, 41 *RCADI* 251-253 (1932-III). Emphasis added.

[148] See, e.g., E. Kaufmann, Règles Générales du Droit de la Paix, 54 *RCADI* 324-325, 340, 351-365 (1935-IV), hereinafter: Kaufmann-1935; Kaufmann, however, argued that the role of the state and the importance of state sovereignty had increased instead of decreased, *inter alia*, due to the economic and industrial revolution of the 19th and early 20th century and the internationalisation of social concerns on the one hand and the nationalisation of international social and economic life on the other. See, D. Anzilotti, Cours de Droit International Vol. I, at 47 (1929), hereinafter: Anzilotti-1929.

[149] Oppenheim, who did not join in the radical break with classical positivism, wished to liberate international law doctrine from the 'tyranny of phrases', e.g., the doctrine of state sovereignty. Instead, he argued a return to the actual rules. It could be said that this was already an attempt to 'reconstruct' or perhaps defend the independent existence of international law, even though Oppenheim argued along traditional positivist lines. L. Oppenheim, The Future of International Law 58-63 (1921), (transl. of a 1911 German text). Hereinafter: Oppenheim-1921.

[150] See, e.g., Anzilotti: 'L'object de la science du droit est le droit positif; sa tâche première est de déterminer et d'expliquer les règles en viqueur, en les ordonnant sous la forme logique d'un système.' Anzilotti-1929, at 19 and 8.

[151] H. Triepel, Les Rapports entre le Droit Interne et le Droit International, 1 *RCADI* 82 (1923), hereinafter Triepel-1923; Anzilotti-1929; A. Cavaglieri, Règles Générales du Droit de la Paix, 26 *RCADI* 318-319 (1929-I), hereinafter: Cavaglieri-1929; P. Heilborn, Les Sources du Droit Interna-

In order to understand how restorative scholars used ILP, we will briefly examine four characteristics of their scholarship and show how ILP played a role in them. This separate treatment of the four aspects in question is to some degree artificial, as each of the four elements inherently includes the other three. The four elements are: 1) the endeavour to reconcile international law with sovereignty; 2) the complete separation of the state from the law (also found with the voluntarists), whereby the state is perceived as a social phenomenon pre-dating (international) law; 3) a general adherence to dualism; and 4) the featuring of the concept of ILP in the characterisation of international society as an inter-state society.

First, in spite of the fact that many (revisionist) scholars blamed sovereignty for the failure of the old order, restorative scholars tried to reconcile sovereignty with international law. Oppenheim, for example, conceived of sovereignty as 'absolute independence,' which, in his view, was not diminished by the state's subjection to international law.[152] International law was defined as the law *between* and not above the sovereign states.[153] It is exclusively created by the (either express or tacit) declaration of the 'common consent,' '*la volonté collective*,' '*la volonté commune*' or '*la volonté concordante*' of sovereign states.[154] Like Jellinek, the restorative scholars argued that international law was a 'self-imposed order',[155] both based on and limited by sovereignty. Accordingly, although the existence of international law was expressly confirmed, the (classical) doctrine of sovereignty maintained its central and dominant position. The sovereign and formal act of recognition was still considered decisive for the question whether a state could acquire ILP and be welcomed into the Family of Nations.[156] 'By sov-

---

tional, 11 *RCADI* 5 (1926-I), hereinafter: Heilborn-1926; P. Heilborn, Subjecte des Völkerrechts, *in* K. Strupp (Ed.), II Wörterbuch des Völkerrechts und der Diplomatie 685 (1925), hereinafter: Heilborn-1925; L. Oppenheim (R.F. Roxburgh Ed.), International Law: A Treatise 18-19 (1920), hereinafter: Oppenheim-Roxburgh. See also, e.g., Kaufmann-1935, at 324-325; S. Séfériadès, Principes Généraux du Droit International de la Paix, 34 *RCADI* 294-295 (1930-IV), hereinafter: Séfériadès-1930.

[152] 'Sovereignty as the highest earthly authority, which was allegiance to no other power, does not exclude the possibility that the sovereign should subject himself to a self-imposed order, so long as this order does not place him under any higher earthly power. All members of the international society thus subject themselves in point of fact to the law of nations without suffering the least diminution of their sovereignty.' Oppenheim-1921, at 11, 20.

[153] Oppenheim-Roxburgh, at 19; Triepel-1923, at 81; Cavaglieri-1929, at 318; Heilborn-1926, at 5; Kaufmann-1935, at 320-325; The PCIJ confirmed this position in 1927 in the *Lotus* case, PCIJ Ser. A. 10, at 18 (1927), *op. cit.*, chapter 1. Restorative scholars did (often explicitly) confirm that international law existed, see, e.g., Anzilotti-1929, at 67 and 88; Cavaglieri-1929, at 316 and 321; Kaufmann declared sovereignty a 'condition sine qua non' for the international order and argued that international law depended on sovereignty. Kaufmann-1935, at 351, and 398-399.

[154] Subsequently in: Oppenheim-1921, at 15-17.; Cavaglieri-1929, at 322; Triepel-1923, at 82-83, 87; Anzilotti-1929, at 44-46, 48 and 67. Triepel's 'volonté commune' is formed by the (express or tacit) union – 'vereinbarung' – of the wills of a number of states, this collective will is binding upon the individual states who participate in the accord. See also, Heilborn-1926, at 15.

[155] Oppenheim-1921, at 11. See also, Cavaglieri-1929, at 322.

[156] See, on the Family of Nations attributing ILP through recognition, e.g., Oppenheim-Roxburgh-1920, at 194-195; Also, Cavaglieri-1929: 'international legal society' attributes ILP.

ereign will only' was how things were done in practice and this practice had now transformed into law.[157] Before ILP could be acquired by recognition, there had to be a social autonomous group which possessed both internal and external sovereignty and the will and ability to serve as a member of the Family of Nations.[158] Some continued to add the prerequisite of civilisation: only *civilised* sovereign states were fit to acquire ILP.[159] The acquisition of ILP through recognition and subsequent Family of Nations membership was thus still used to include or exclude an entity from the international society. To possess ILP, according to Oppenheim, meant to possess a 'body of qualities,' encompassing the 'equality, dignity, independence, and territorial and personal *supremacy*' of the state. By gaining membership of the international community, the new International Legal Person recognised these same qualities or fundamental rights in every other member. 'The States are International Persons because they recognise these qualities in one other, and recognise their responsibility for violations of these qualities.'[160] And so, state sovereignty and international law were reconciled in the use of ILP.

Secondly, as their view of the act of recognition has already revealed, restorative scholars generally considered the state as an actual, social – meta-juridical – entity, which was neither defined nor founded, but still presupposed, by international law.[161] Cavaglieri stated: '*l'État est un phénomène social, avant d'être un phénomène juridique.*'[162] Triepel maintained that the state had a *real* personality: '*L'État est une véritable personnalité, il est une personnalité indépendante,*

[157] Anzilotti however criticised this practice which started from a non-legal conception of the state and attributed ILP to this entity simply because according to non-legal analysis it is a state. Anzilotti: 'ainsi à l'investigation normative, propre à la science du droit, on substituait, en la faussant, un concept étranger qui en prédéterminait les résultats.' Anzilotti-1929, at 124. He argued that it should first be established who were subjects of international law and after whether the 'state' fulfilled the requirements. Anzilotti thus pointed to the automatic identification of the (non-legal) state with the international legal person, which from a theoretical point of view, was not properly based in reasoning. Id., at 124-125. However, the problem was soon solved by accepting that 'state' was a legal notion. 'Si l'on veut parler d'Etats dans le droit international, et l'usage de ce mot a certainement des avantages, au moins de simplicité, il doit être bien clair que ce sont les Etats du droit international, non pas ceux de la sociologie, de l'histoire, ni non plus ceux du droit public interne: l'Etat, pour le droit international, vaut en tant que destinaire des normes et en tant que sujet de l'ordre juridique, que cette conception coïncide ou ne coïncide pas avec celle qui est propre aux autres disciplines.' Id., at 125. See also, Cavaglieri-1929, at 321; Séfériadès-1930, at 293-297. It should be borne in mind that the Montevideo Convention was not signed until 1933.

[158] See, e.g., Oppenheim-Roxburgh, at 194-196; Cavaglieri-1929, at 342; Séfériadès-1930, at 295.

[159] Oppenheim-Roxburgh, at 31-33, 125, 135, 180-181 (1920). Cavaglieri criticised this criterion and claimed that the only criterion for admission to the international society should be and was the acceptance of the general rules of international law. See, Cavaglieri-1929, at 327-329.

[160] Oppenheim-Roxburgh, at 194-195. Emphasis added.

[161] See, e.g., Oppenheim who said that the social reality of international life, i.e., international interaction, is a 'pre-supposition of the International Personality of every State.' Oppenheim-Roxburgh, at 235-237. See also, Anzilotti-1929, at 122; Cavaglieri-1929, at 320.

[162] Cavaglieri-1929, at 321, 340-342.

distincte de la somme des individus qui le composent.'[163] He stressed that the state was a real and independent person. Redslob also considered the state not just an 'artificial being', but a real and mystical person: '*L'Etat est un produit de la nature; dans les arcanes les plus profonds de sa personnalité s'accomplit le grand mystère primordial et indéchiffrable qu'est l'éclosion de la vie.*' International law is therefore by nature 'contract law', created by the joint wills of states, and these wills are '*toujours conscientes, cristallines, précises, pour la bonne raison qu'elles emanent d'organismes à la structure solide et parfaitement agencée.*'[164] ILP is used to transform the collective – the state – into a closed unit under international law. In the work of, for example, Kaufmann this masking function of ILP is also expressed:

> l'Etat n'entre en cause dans le domaine international que comme une unité: c'est la *conception unitaire de l'Etat* qui régit le droit international. Il s'ensuit que la distinction des pouvoirs publics entre les différents organes et autorités d' ordre constitutionnel, législatif, gouvernemental, administratif ou judiciaire, telle qu'elle est prévue et organisée par le droit interne, ne regarde pas le droit international, qui n'est intéressé qu'à l'attitude observée par l'Etat en tant qu'unité.[165]

The concept of ILP was thus essential in giving to the social group, i.e., the state, a united identity and to the internally constituted sovereign will a 'presence' in international law. The constitutional organisation of the state is merely presupposed by international law.[166] The internal order is needed for the formulation of a uniform and sovereign state will. This is necessary to enable the state to operate as a united entity in the international legal order.[167] The limit of international law was situated at what Anzilotti called the *point of attachment*, the point where it granted ILP to the state. Anzilotti explained that in his view ILP operated to supply the collective with unity.[168] As the origin of the sovereign will and the type of internal (political) organisation in place were considered irrelevant to international law,[169] the classical doctrine of '*le principe de la continuité de la*

---

[163] Triepel-1923, at 87.

[164] R. Redlob, Théorie de la Société des Nations 9-10 (1927). Hereinafter: Redlob-1927.

[165] Kaufmann-1935, at 398.

[166] Triepel-1923, at 95.

[167] See also, Heilborn-1925, at 685: 'Erst durch die Organisation erlangt das Volk die Möglichkeit einheitlichen Wollens und Handelns, wird es eine Person, d. h. ein Rechtssubject.'

[168] Anzilotti-1929, at 122-123, at 42: les normes considèrent le groupe comme une unité, et non pas quant à ses parties composantes; elles font du groupe une *unité de rattachement*, de telle façon que le pouvoir accordé, le devoir imposé, ne sont pas le pouvoir et le devoir d'individus isolés, mais de la collectivité, quand bien même, formellement, il serait possible de fragmenter la subjectivité de ces entités en un complexe de droits et d'obligations individuels. En réalité il ne semble pas que pour comprendre la personalité internationale des agrégats humains il y ait beaucoup à ajouter au précepte romain en vertu duquel *l'universitas* est simplement une unité d'attribution juridique.'

[169] See, e.g., Cavaglieri-1929, at 340-342 and 365-366. '[Le] droit international ... règle les rapports entre États et les prend tels qu'ils sont, sans se préoccuper des causes et des élémants sociologiques qui en ont déterminé la formation, ni les principes d'organisation intérieure qu'ils sont donnés. Tout cela est *prius* pour le droit international ...' Id., at 340, 342. Also, Séfériadès-1930, at 295.

personnalité internationale de [l']État'[170] persisted. This meant that changes in the internal political regime or constitution of a state would not have any impact on the identity of the state as an international legal person and, as such, as a respected member of the Family of Nations. The continuity of ILP provided certainty and stability in the world order, irrespective of the internal situation in the states. ILP was thus used to maintain the strict separation between the domestic and the international order, which automatically brings us to the third element, that of duality.

Scholars such as Heilborn, Anzilotti and Cavaglieri supported Triepel's dualist theory[171] that national and international law governed completely different legal orders, because they regulated different 'social relations.' Domestic law existed within national societies, and its subjects were individuals, legal persons and national administrative entities. These subjects are subordinate to the commands of the state as laid down in the enacted laws. International law, however, was defined as regulating interaction *between* 'equal' states. It was exclusively created by and addressed to states, in other words: only states had ILP. As the national and the international order stem from different legal sources (the will of the state on the one hand and the *Vereinbarung* of sovereign wills on the other) and as both have different subjects, they are two completely distinct legal systems. An international legal rule can only apply within the national order if it has been 'appropriated' by this order, i.e., if it has been transformed into a national rule.[172] Anzilotti underlined the importance of ILP in this respect:

> [L]es normes internationales prennent le caractère juridique dans les ordres internes que par le moyen de la réception ...: le principe contraire est exclu par la distinction des ordres juridiques et par la conception de l'Etat comme unité d'attribution juridique, dans laquelle se manifeste sa personnalité international.[173]

In this role, ILP prevents international law from addressing individual human beings; it is used as a barrier rather than an intermediary. In other words, ILP is used as an obstacle which prevents international law from reaching all the way down to the individual inside the collective.

As to the fourth element, we may conclude from the above that as far as Restorative scholars were concerned, the international society had maintained its classical identity as a society of sovereign (civilised) states, governed by a law which Jellinek called practically anarchical: '*La societé des Etats est une societé* non

[170] Cavaglieri-1929, at 366; Redslob-1927, at 12-13;

[171] Anzilotti-1929, at 50-65. In his opinion, the national and international legal orders are distinct, since they are based on different fundamental norms: 'Emanant de normes fondamentales autonomes, le droit international et le droit interne sont, par suite, des ordres séparés.' Id., at 51. See also, Cavaglieri-1929, at 319 and 342; Heilborn-1926, at 5-11; Oppenheim-1921, at 25-26. See, for a different approach, which is neither dualist nor monist, Kaufmann-1935, at 437-439.

[172] Triepel-1923, at 83-84.

[173] Anzilotti-1929, at 134.

organisée *dont les membres sont les Etats organisés, reconnus comme sujets du droit international.*'[174] The position of the individual in this constellation was that of the object, rather than the subject of international law.[175] Some restorative scholars nevertheless accepted the notion of 'derived or limited ILP' – '*sujet secondaire* or *fragmentaire*' – to identify the '*germes d'Etat*'. These could be nations, insurgents or belligerents. Some recognised the ILP of international organisations as a kind of 'derived ILP', while others at the same time vehemently denied that the League of Nations could have ILP.[176] Oppenheim took the middle road: 'The League of Nations is an International Person *sui generis* besides the several states.'[177] With respect to the prerequisite of 'sovereignty' (which one had to have before one could be an ILP), exceptions were only made in the case of Colonies or Dominions who were members of the League of Nations or eligible for membership in accordance with Article 1 of the Covenant.[178] Since positive international law did not address nationalities or minorities, they were not recognised as international legal persons.[179] Anzilotti rejected the ILP of social groups like tribes and nomadic people, although together with Heilborn he admitted that tribes could have 'derived ILP' if they had concluded agreements under international law with the colonising state.[180] The attribution of ILP to individuals, state agents and organs, international associations, or peoples was unanimously rejected.[181] Similarly, the right of self-determination of peoples was generally denied to be a rule of positive international law; at most, it was seen as a political principle.[182] States exclusively determined who were the subjects of international law and, by using ILP as a means for unifying the social collective called 'state' into one legal entity, the international society admitted or excluded new members. *Restorative* scholarship identified the international society as the society of states and rejected the much-debated idea of a 'universal federal state' as the end of international law itself.[183]

In sum, it can be concluded that restorative scholarship followed the voluntarist tradition. By linking ILP exclusively to the state person, these scholars used

---

[174] Heilborn-1926, at 14.

[175] Oppenheim-Roxburgh, at 457-461. This also denies that minority rights (i.e., the right to protection) as included in the Minority Treaties are international rights. Id., at 458 fn. 2. Also, Anzilotti-1929, at 132-136; Triepel-1923, at 81; Kaufmann-1935, at 415; Heilborn-1926, at 5-11. Illustrative of this conventional perspective on the position of the individual is also the fact that the 'Wörterbuch des Völkerrechts und der Diplomatie' of the 1920s does not include a section on 'the individual in international law.' Nevertheless, Heilborn stated in his contribution: '*Auch das Völkerrecht ist um der Menschen willen da.*' Heilborn-1925, at 685.

[176] Heilborn-1926, at 15-16; R. Erich, La Naissance et la Reconnaissance des États, 13 *RCADI* 438 (1926-III). Hereinafter: Erich-1926.

[177] Oppenheim-1921, at 125.

[178] See, e.g., Anzilotti-1929 at 124-125; Heilborn-1925, 684-685; Kaufmann-1935.

[179] See, e.g., Oppenheim-1921, at 458; Erich-1926, at 437; Anzilotti-1929, at 127-131, 135.

[180] Anzilotti-1929, at 127-131, 135, and at 130: 'l'Etat colonisateur établirait par voie de *fiction* la personnalité dans la tribu barbare, faisant ainsi entrer dans le domaine du droit international l'acte constitutif du protectorat.'

[181] Heilborn-1925, 684-686. See also, *supra* footnote 180.

[182] Kaufmann-1935, at 366-7; Heilborn-1925, at 685.

[183] Oppenheim-1921, at 12-13; Anzilotti, at 47.

the concept to reaffirm the classical identity of the international society and international law, after the cataclysm of WWI. Consequently, they considered that international law was based on power and that it derived from and was limited by the sovereign power of states, including the power to apply limits to international law. The recognition of ILP was used as an instrument to include or exclude members from the civilised Family of Nations. Further, in conformity with most of their predecessors, restorative scholars valued ILP for guaranteeing international continuity – and thereby certainty and stability – irrespective of internal political developments. They also applauded its masking function, which was to prevent the intrusion of the international order into the domestic order. ILP remained the mask beyond which international law should and could not reach.

b. Revision[184]

The revisionists' endeavour to helpt international law find a way out of its crisis by redefining its identity was connected with their desire to protect democratic values and the individual. Around this time, the question of the influence of democracy on the development of international law and the prevention of another war surfaced in earnest.[185] Democratic countries tended to be less aggressive in their international conduct, as Kant, speaking from the perspective of his own discipline, had already observed. But was this still true in mass society?[186] International legal scholars also struggled with the issues of democracy and individuality in mass society. The new socio-psychological findings were important factors in the revisionist rejection of the traditional perception of the sovereignty and personality of the state. But their influence did not stop there. Below, these aspects will be discussed in more detail. However, it can already be stated that the problem of the individual versus the collective was considered one of the most relevant issues of the time.[187]

---

[184] The term is used by Politis, see *supra* footnote 14, and Pound, see *supra* footnote 14, at 79.

[185] See, e.g., J.S. Reeves, La Communauté Internationale, 3 *RCADI* 42 (1924). Hereinafter: Reeves-1924.

[186] Luchaire gave a course on 'la Coopération Intellectuelle International' at The Hague Academy, in which he raised the issue whether a civilisation dominated by the moral and material power of the 'masses' tends to diminish the prestige as well as the achievements of the intellectual elite. A question often answered in the affirmative by people who are anti-democratic, so he stated. See, for his treatment of 'La démocratie et l'intelligence,' Les Principes de la Coopération Intellectuelle International, 9 *RCADI* 342-345 (1925). See also, D. Schindler, Contribution à l'étude des Facteurs Sociologiques et Psychologiques du Droit International, 17 *RCADI* 233-322 (1933-IV), hereinafter: Schindler-1933. Schindler perceived the masses as emotional, irrational, simplifying and often displaying nationalist and mythical tendencies. As such, their influence on international relations through public opinion should be monitored closely; he considered Wilson's suggestions on the international role of public opinion 'a serious problem'.

[187] See, e.g, Brierly, Kelsen, Luchaire, Nippold, Pound, Schindler. See also, Alvarez: 'Les peuples, comme les individus, ont une âme et, par suite, une psychologie. ... Elle est ... le résultat de la vie social; et c'est cette psychologie collective qui forme et modèle, en grande partie, la psychologie individuelle.' He distinguished, however, between the psychology of people and the

Van Vollenhoven, for example, did not dispute the need for democracy, but considering the direction into which mass society was developing, he doubted whether the democratic involvement of the people culd indeed contribute to the establishment of a new and peaceful international law. Would the public really be able to take that leap and establish a rule of law binding upon every state?[188]

Nippold was also clearly aware of the difficulty of the dilemma. Like Alvarez, Le Bon, Kelsen, Reeves and Schindler[189] he considered the susceptibility of the masses to suggestion as one of the most important problems of the time. In 1924, during his course at the Hague Academy, Nippold wondered whether too much hope and faith had been put in the participation of the people in international politics:

On avait, *en nourrissant ces espérances, négligé quelques point importants*: d'abord on avait oublié que la mentalité des peuples importe beaucoup plus que la constitution des États. Ensuite on avait négligé de tenir compte de *la suggestibilité des masses*. ... Les conditions de cette «suggestibilité» peuvent fort bien n'être pas les mêmes dans tous les pays; *l'éducation politique* d'un peuple peut certainement jouer un rôle dans le degré de sa «suggestibilité»; mais il est certain que des meneurs habiles, souvent aussi sans scrupules, peuvent, grâce à une adroit propaganda, tromper des peuples entiers sur des questions de politique internationale et même les empêcher absolument de connaître la vérité. ... La dernière guerre nous a malheureusement fourni en abondance des exemples où ce cas s'est présenté, même dans des pays de vieille démocratie et dont l'éducation politique n'est plus à faire.[190]

WWI had demonstrated the force of this susceptibility even in established democracies. Nippold also referred to socio-psychological elements which had played a role in past failures of democracy and could easily do so again.[191] Therefore, rather than simply expecting politics – even 'democratic politics' – to

psychology of the masses and stated that the first should indeed be taken seriously both as a factor in international life and as a relevant factor in the reconstruction of international law, Alvarez-1936, at 12-14, *et seq.*

[188] See, e.g., Van Vollenhoven, *supra* footnote 14, at 70-85: 'Die den aantocht van het derde volkenrecht vertragen, die machten schuilen onder de millioenen-massa zelf. De aanstaande vrede zal democratisch moeten zijn ...' 'Maar al het tot hiertoe bepleitte is veel te ingewikkeld voor den grooten hoop. De stormachtige drang naar een volkenbond, zegt men, moet uitgaan van de millioenenmassa; doch wie zal der millioenenmassa aan het verstand kunnen brengen de plichtenleer van Grotius en het verraad van Vattel, de illusie van de tsaar en de vondst van Bryan?' Id., at 82. 'Het derde volkenrecht maakt het niet alleen mogelijk, maar maakt het noodig, het dilemma – bandeloosheid óf gebondenheid der staten – zóó scherp te stellen, dat heel het kiezersvolk in alle landen het kan beantwoorden met ja of neen. ... Wil de massa, ten koste zelfs van offers, de plichtenleer van Grotius toegerust zien met de ontbrekende organisatie, dan is een geordende wereld verzekerd; wil of durft of kan men dat niet, dan blijft de aarde een menschenpoel.' See also, Schindler-1933, at 234-235.

[189] Id., at 103. Also, Alvarez-1936, at 13; Kelsen-1922, at 19; Reeves-1924, at 82-90; Schindler-1933, at 299 *et seq.*

[190] O. Nippold, Le Développement historique du Droit International depuis le Congrès de Vienne, 2 *RCADI* 20 (1924-I). Emphasis added. Hereinafter: Nippold-1924

[191] Id., at 20 and 102-103.

achieve international legal progress, Nippold argued that every effort should be put into strengthening the 'moral conscience' of the public and of the ruling parties. The public should be (politically) educated to make them immune from their inherent susceptibility.[192] Jaspers and Mannheim had alos argued the importance of extending political education to the people.

After WWI, morale was difficult to lift and mutual confidence was painfully lacking among governments, peoples and states. Only a form of politics based on 'solidarity' and a sense of duty towards the international community might be able to change this. But could this be achieved? '*Il est permis d'en douter.*'[193] In any case, it demanded the social and political education of the masses and could therefore take generations. Nippold therefore claimed that the organisation of international cooperation had to be taken up without delay. In the late 1930s, Q. Wright even had visions of a 'new world order' based on a global organisation in which not only national governments would participate but in which 'every important group with a distinctive public opinion ought to have some representation whether that group is national, regional or universal.'[194] Finally, the conviction that an organisation for international judicial dispute settlement could further contribute to the recovery of the 'conscience of mankind' was not exceptional either.[195]

Some authors, like, for example, Reeves also pointed out positive aspects of the influence of democracy and public opinion on international politics.[196]

> Toutefois, le développement du droit international montre que si la démocratie n'a pas fait naître de conceptions nouvelles, elle a du moins contribué à l'échange et à la vulgarisation des idées. Par là, elle est la source de l'idée juridique et tend à déterminer les conditions des relations entre États.[197]

---

[192] Id., at 21.

[193] Id., at 102.

[194] Q. Wright, as quoted in R.P. Hillmann, Quincy Wright and the Commission to study the Organization of Peace, 4(4) *Global Governance* 489 (1998).

[195] J.S. Reeves, International Society and International Law, 15 *AJIL* 374 (1921). Hereinafter: Reeves-1921. See also, Alvarez for the idea of 'une *conscience internationale* de caractère juridique,' based on the idea that the egoistic instincts of the individual are corrected by social life. In his view, collective psychology dimmed the individual natural instincts. In international social life, an international conscience could gradually emerge, which had the potential to correct the egoistic national psychology of the people, because it was not authority, but 'public international legal conscience' that was the source of the fundamental principles of international law. This law now had to become a social law taking account of international interdependence and sociability and as such correcting nationalist sentiments while in fact under threat from these same sentiments. Moreover, the new international law should become less purely legal and be inspired by international psychology and international social life: a '*Droit psychologique international.*' Alvarez-1936 La Psychologie des Peuples, at 23, 60, 73, 81, 101, 103.

[196] 'Dans la démocratie, un gouvernement est moralement obligé de refuser son consentement à toute entreprise internationale qu'il pense ne devoir pas être tout au moins approuvée et soutenue par l'opinion publique du pays.' Reeves-1924, at 89.

[197] Id., at 42.

The Wilsonians also argued that if the public could democratically control the positions taken by the state in international affairs, it could represent the rational and the moral in international life. However, this idea rather lost its appeal where public opinion tended to be no more than mass emotion. The scholarly views on 'public opinion' reveal the tension that existed (as already evidenced by Nippold and Reeves) between faith in the people's participation in international politics, on the one hand, and fear and concern over the emergence of a mass opinion and its possible destructive tendencies, on the other.[198] The emancipation of the individual, to be achieved by means of, *inter alia*, political education, was considered an important factor in preventing mass rule and the decline of democracies into mobocracies. For the purpose of the renewal or modernisation of international law, the involvement of the public was considered desirable, but only a very thin line divided public opinion as generated by rational individuals from public opinion as emanating from the masses, a fact which also greatly troubled the revisionists.[199]

The legal theoretical argument in favour of a new international law and the socio-politically inspired fight for democracy conjoin in the revisionist attack on the classical conception of international law and in the redefinition of ILP in particular. Revisionist scholars, like Alvarez, Le Fur, Jitta, Krabbe, Politis, Verdross and Van Vollenhoven, were in complete agreement concerning the 'transformation' of international life.[200] They considered it their task to revise international law and theory in order to suit it to modern international life.[201] In this endeavour

[198] Id., at 82: 'L'opinion, de toute évidence, ne signifie pas un jugement rationnel ou une série de jugements rationnels. Elle est généralement basée sur les goûts ou les répulsions préexistantes, sur des préjugés et des préventions. L'opinion de la masse est une chose différente de la somme des opinions individuelles d'une majorité numérique. La majorité est supposée l'exprimer à un moment donné; ...' See, e.g., for further indications of the increased importance of public opinion in international and state policy, Wilson, *supra* footnote 13, at 274.

[199] Based on the psychological traits of the masses and their consequences for 'public opinion,' Schindler argued that international diplomacy should not take place under the 'control or pressure' of public opinion. The obligation under the Covenant to publish any treaties that are concluded is of course completely valid and valuable. Schindler-1923, at 312-313. Reeves-1921, at 374. 'The international law of the future, deriving a renewed vigor on the basis of international agreement from the creation of an international court of justice, must seek to interpret the actualities of international life, for in that way mainly, if not solely, can it become the "expression of the organized opinion of mankind."' Id. The openness required by the Covenant of the parties involved in an international conflict to some extent took the relevance of the public into account. It was hoped that the Court would become the voice of mankind's legal conscience.

[200] Bourquin-1931; Politis-1925, at 5. See also, e.g., De Louter, *supra* footnote 7, at 76. Also, Reeves: '[In August 1914, in a way, the old international law came to an end, for the invasion of Belgium and the retribution which is being exalted for that invasion and its results give a new and solider basis for international law than the world had ever before afforded.' Reeves-1921, at 373.

[201] See, e.g., Descamps: 'Faut-il s'attarder alors à tenter de reconstituer [l]e [vieux] moule [éclaté], tant bien que mal, en rassemblant ses débris? Ne convient-il pas, au contraire, de donner à la science en partie transformée un cadre nouveau répondant à des institutions nouvelles? Il semble bien que les hommes de progrès ne doivent pas hésiter à choisir cette dernière voie.' E.E.F. Descamps, Le Droit International Nouveau, l'influence de la condamnation de la guerre sur l'évolution juridique internationale, 31 *RCADI* 402 (1930-I). Also, Bourquin-1931, at 8.

they severely criticised their rather more conservative contemporaries. This critique of restorative scholarship can be placed in a logical order in accordance with the four elements singled out above. The revisionists: 1) generally rejected the doctrine of state sovereignty;[202] 2) rethought the traditional concept of the state; 3) considered the national and international legal orders to be one; and 4) commonly typified international society as being, in fact, a global human society. Moreover, our examination clearly brings to light the serious concern present among the revisionists regarding democracy in mass society and the latter's threat to the individual. The objective of the new international law was to protect democratic values and to bring about *l'émancipation internationale de l'individu.*[203] Accordingly, international law was not defined as the law which exclusively governed relations between states, but as a law that in the final instance includes norms which spring from and regulate human conduct as well:

> [O]n proclame la nécessité, pour donner au droit international le caractère démocratique réclamé par notre époque, de mettre à sa base, à la place de l'idée aristocratique qui subordonne l'homme à l'État, des principes fournis par l'étude des rapports de l'individu avec ses semblables.[204]

In the revision of international law, the shift away from state sovereignty and towards the individual included the attempt to go from authoritarianism to democracy, from the subordination to the liberation of the individual and to the promotion of his interests.

A clear illustration of the fact that the revisionists challenged the traditional doctrine of state sovereignty is found in the following quote from Le Fur:

> Nous assistons aujourd'hui à la naissance d'un nouvel ordre international, où l'on tente de remplacer la notion de souveraineté absolue de l'État, – c'est-à-dire, au fond, de la considération exclusive de son intérêt ou de ce qu'il croit l'être, avec la force comme mesure de réalisation,-par un droit international à base de justice, où, par conséquent, en cas de conflit, une solution de droit remplace celle de la force.[205]

In the view of the revisionists, the new international order had to be based on law and justice, rather than on power and absolute state sovereignty. The traditional conceptions of sovereignty and international personality, which were traditionally exclusively attributed to the state, were generally identified as part of the 'old' international law and were therefore discredited by the revisionists.[206] Sover-

---

[202] See, e.g., Van Vollenhoven: 'Monsieur de Vattel, ... stik in souvereiniteit en verdwijn.' Van Vollenhoven, *supra* footnote 14, at 51.

[203] Bourquin-1931, at 46. See also, (text to) footnotes 20-24.

[204] Politis-1925, at 8.

[205] L. Le Fur, La Théorie du Droit Naturel Depuis le XVIIe Siècle et la Doctrine Moderne, 18 *RCADI* 400-401 (1927-III). Hereinafter: Le Fur-1927.

[206] Id.

eignty, the former *rationale* of international law, was regarded as a principle that led to acts of aggression or individual reprisals[207] and that should therefore be replaced. As the old concept of ILP was so intertwined with the supremacy of the state, it was denounced as useless and even 'dangerous,'[208] or as a meaningless imaginary concept which results in vague and metaphorical formulations.[209] Consequently, the attack on sovereignty included a new use of ILP: not as a quality attributed to the sovereign state, because it was precisely this kind of thinking which had brought about the reification and mythologisation of the state, but as a quality which could only be attributed to the one real, tangible entity there was: the human individual. In this vein, Le Fur declared that: '*La personnalité juridique doit être la simple traduction juridique de la personnalité réelle, qu'elle doit être reconnue à tout individu.*'[210]

The observations of the American scholar Roscoe Pound reflect the relevance of the contemporary problems surrounding the issue of mass society in this respect. In a lecture he gave at Leiden University in 1923, he demanded a thorough review of the role of sovereignty, because when sovereignty passed from the King to the 'collective entity,' i.e., the people, international law left the realm of individual relations, and from then on:

> It had to do with the conduct and relations of a greater or smaller but fluctuating group of men who acted in the name and to an increasing degree in the fear of an indefinite collectivity, with all the irresponsability and proneness *to act on suggestion and instinct rather than reason which psychology has taught us is characteristic of the crowd.* ... It was expected to govern whole populations, not by acting upon single individuals therein, but taking each population as a legal unit, and it was expected to do this through the juristic assumption that each population as a collective person was accountable and amendable to legal reason as such.[211]

Taking the contemporary political context into consideration, a conceptual review of ILP was urgently needed in order to cope with ongoing developments. The situation had become especially pressing since the publication of the findings

---

[207] Le Fur-1927, at 413-414, Van Vollenhoven, 58-59 and 71.

[208] See, e.g., Politis' tirade: 'Now the personality of States is a pure fiction, which has ceased to be useful. No doubt in the past it rendered, like sovereignty, incontestable services. ... But when the State's ends were attained, or at any rate when they were directly recognized to be necessities of national and international existence, the idea of personality, which, with that of sovereignty, had until then served as a peg, became useless, cumbrous and even dangerous. It is absolutely false, both in the organic and the juridical aspect. ... Reality shows that what we call the will of the State is the will of the men who govern it. The personality of the State is only a metaphor to make people understand that the acts of Governments are distinct from their private acts. But the metaphor itself is useless. For what enables us to distinguish between the public and private acts of Governments is not the capacity in which they claim to be acting, but the rule of law which they are obeying.' Politis-1928, at 13-14: 'the fiction of a collective will attributed to the not less fictitious personality of the State.'

[209] L. Duguit, Traité de droit constitutionnel, Vol. I, xviii (1927).

[210] Le Fur-1927, at 404.

[211] Pound, see *supra* footnote 14, at 78. Emphasis added.

concerning mass psychology.[212] Clearly, 'the juristic dogmatic fiction ... treating the mass of a population collectively as the equivalent in moral responsibility of an individual man' was fallacious.[213] The moral responsibility of the individual was getting lost in the crowd and, therefore, in order to protect it, ILP had to be redefined and attributed to individuals rather than to collective entities.

Now that sovereignty had been disposed of, the classical (meta-legal) concept of the state had to be dealt with and a variety of alternatives were offered in order to arrive at something other than 'an international law which conceives of states as absolute units, essentially equal, mutually exclusive, with the point of contact in time of peace largely formal and decorative', because this type of international law 'w[ould] not fit with the facts of international life.'[214] The conceptual function of ILP, used to conceive of the state as a closed and masked 'absolute unity' in international law, was thus rejected. Modern international law simply could not embrace this concept, for, as Pound had explained, the units in question were hopelessly irresponsible. Democracy and internal state politics were actually highly relevant to modern international life and law, so it was argued.

Les sujets du droit international moderne ne sont pas un groupe d'unités irresponsable, vivant chacune dans un état de nature, mais bien les États fonctionnant entre eux, chacun d'eux gouvernés par des êtres humaines, de capacité et de pouvoir limités, responsables devant leurs peuples de l'exercice de leurs fonctions, même lorsque ces dernières comportent des actions internationales. Partout le peuple peut détrôner les puissants sinon «exalter les humbles».[215]

Modern international law needed to break with the traditional exclusive attribution of ILP to the reified and deified state in order to put an end to the exaltation of the state at the expense of the position of the individual. The personification of the 'Will of the State' as the unified will of the collective which was directed towards a common objective tended to submerge the individual in the state and prevented him from having his own say on the international stage. The concept of legal personality came under close scrutiny and it was concluded that it had only served to create an artificial and absolute separation between the state and the individual citizens of which it is composed. DeVisscher observed: '*Il a favorisé*

---

[212] Id., at 79: 'The *need of revision* was not perceived since psychology had not as yet revealed the hollowness of the assumption that a moral order among sovereign kings could become a moral order among sovereign peoples by mere political changes and constitutional provisions.' Emphasis added.

[213] Id., at 79: 'In truth a moral order among states is not the simple matter which the analogy of the individual man has made it appear. There are many difficulties, psychological, economic and biological that make the analogy of the politically organized society to the individual human being wholly misleading.'

[214] Reeves-1921, at 369.

[215] Reeves-1924, at 42.

dans le droit public l'éclosion des théories absolutistes.'[216] Consequently, democracy demanded that the individual be given a clear identity under the law and that it was recognised as such and that a stop be put to the personification of the state and the subsequent oppression this made possible.

As to the third element, revisionist scholars generally opposed the strict separation of the international and the domestic legal order and maintained a monist view, which mainly involved the replacement of state sovereignty with the notion of the sovereignty of international law: '*Il n'y a qu'une seule souveraineté absolue, celle du droit.*'[217] The international and national legal orders were thus understood to be *one single* universal order emanating from the same source. For Kelsen the ultimate source was the *Grundnorm*, while Jitta constructed the unity of law on the basis of 'the juridical community of *mankind*, [a] system of reasonable principles for the international intercourse of men...' He perceived mankind as a 'juridical community,' and the state as the 'local representative of the public power of mankind.' The state's sovereignty was derived from the community of mankind, not the other way around. Krabbe understood '*le sentiment du droit dans l'homme*' to be the *exclusive* source of all law, and adhered to the supremacy of international law. Politis and his fellow sociological scholars declared law to be a product of social reality. Verdross contended that the international community was sovereign, which would make state sovereignty a relative concept and would subject states to the law.[218]

Fourthly, revisionist scholars tended to define the *modern* identity of the international society and the law that governed it in terms of the individual. In their view, international legal reasoning should not start from the notion of the state as a person but from the reality of the individual. The state is viewed as the necessary backdrop for the social and international life of man on this earth, but the idea of the state as the actual purpose of individual, national or international life is rejected. Some even rejected the state as a subject of international law alto-

---

[216] 'C'est dans le système de la personnalité-fiction légale que ce régime de concentration a trouvé son expression la plus radicale et aussi son expansion la plus redoutable. Les origines de ce système sont politiques; son inspiration est nettement étatique. C'est parce qu'on entend subordonner à la décision souveraine de l'Etat toute personnification des groupements sociaux que l'on a conçu cette personnification comme l'oeuvre de la concession légale. C'est parce que sur la personnalité juridique, par lui créée de toutes pièces, l'Etat entend exercer un droit non seulement de control, mais d'absolue disposition, parce qu'il ne veut connaître qu'elle, que s'est implantée l'idée *d'une séparation absolue et à tous égards définitive entre la personnalité juridique et les individualités composantes.* Etroitement soudé au postulat purement politique de la concession légale, le système de la fiction a été longtemps aux mains de l'Etat un instrument de gouvernement.' Emphasis added. Ch. De Visscher, La Technique de la Personnalité Juridique en Droit International Public et Privé, 17 *RDI et Legislation Comparée* 475-476 (1936).

[217] Le Fur-1927, at 414.

[218] D.J. Jitta, The renovation of International Law 1 and 193-5 (1919); H. Krabbe, L'Idée Moderne de l'État, 13 *RCADI* 571, 577 (1926-III); A. Verdross, Le Fondement du droit international, 16 *RCADI* 319 (1927-I).

gether, while others would merely concede that the individual was a subject of international law besides it.[219] There is only one *real* personality behind the fiction of the state, i.e., the personality of the individual, and ILP should be the translation of that reality in legal terms.[220]

In brief, revisionists used ILP in the deconstruction of traditional state and sovereignty doctrines; personality became a notion attributed to the individual rather than to the state. Without personality, the state was stripped of its mythological adornments and rediced to an instrument of individual and social moral life. It was denied that the state had any *reality* as such: only individuals were real entities and as such recognised as legal persons. Consequently ILP ceased to be the mask that shielded the internal from the external order, and both orders were now argued to be part of one universal legal order in which the individual was subject to both national and international law. Where the collective was considered to have irresponsible tendencies, the individual was seen to represent rationality and moral responsibility. In order to preserve the representation of morality and justice at the international level and within international law and, therefore, in order to participate, the individual had to be protected and emancipated and democracy needed to be defended. Nevertheless, the tension between hope and concern also left its mark on revisionist scholarship.

c. Conclusion

In both restorative and revisionist scholarship, the concept of ILP played a significant role as a means of either restoring the old identity of international law or establishing a new one. With respect to the new identity of international law, the attribution of ILP to the individual was induced by the contemporary developments in mass society: the suggestibility of the masses, the threat this implied to the representation of moral responsibility in the world, and the participation of the individual, in short, the problems of democracy in mass society. The personification of the state was emphatically rejected as authoritarian and anti-democratic, and, therefore, dangerous. The same ambivalence which we found in the broader intellectual context concerning the 'rationality of the public', on the one hand, and the concern regarding the 'irresponsibility and irrationality of the collective (mental) life of the masses' on the other also surfaced in (revisionist) interbellum international law scholarship. The revisionists' use of ILP – its attribution to the individual human being, the description of the individual's position by means of traditional international law terms, such as 'international personality' and 'subject of law', which had historically always been used when writing about

---

[219] See, e.g., C. Van Vollenhoven, Sprongen in de Ontwikkeling van het Gewoonterecht (1912), *in* Mr. C. Van Vollenhoven's Verspreide Geschriften 32 (1934). Also, Lauterpacht, Règles du Droit de la Paix, 62 *RCADI* 101, 207-243 (1937-IV).

[220] Politis-1925, at 6.

the state – in their attempt to confer legitimacy and credibility upon their (socio-political or ideological) ideas contributed to the position of the individual. On the one hand, the revisionists associated with tradition, as they sought a connection with the prevailing scholarly convention that defined international society and its law as the society and law of international legal persons, but, on the other hand, by completely redefining ILP, they also attempted to provoke radical changes in the identity of international law and in the position of the individual.

3.3. James Leslie Brierly (1881-1955)[221]

> We may be appalled by the claims that the state is making today in many countries. It is rejecting alike the claims of the individual on the one hand and of the world community on the other, and exalting itself as the final goal of humanity. Unless one can believe that this idolatry of the state will prove to be a temporary phase, it is idle to talk of the international rule of law; it must be as fatal to international peace as it has already been in the countries concerned to individual liberty.[222]

3.3.1. **Introduction**

James Leslie Brierly's scholarly writings seem to be fundamentally motivated by hope, probably often against his better judgement, or at least by an attempt to be hopeful. In his eyes, it was essential to maintain faith in the rule of law and in the approaching end to the exaltation of the state. His optimism was by no means naive; it was, however, driven by a deep sense of morality.[223] At first glance, this might not be so apparent due to his questioning style of analysis, which seemed rather to reject than suggest answers, his crushing honesty on the defects of international law, and the ceaseless emphasis on the contemporary needs of international life.[224] But being the legal scholar that he was, Brierly considered it his

[221] See, e.g., C.H.M. Waldock, James Leslie Brierly (1881-1955) – a Biographical Note, *in* Lauterpacht&Waldock (Eds.), The Basis of Obligation in International Law and Other Papers by the late James Leslie Brierly ix-xiii (1958). See for reference to this book, hereinafter: Lauterpacht and Waldock (Eds.). Also, H. Lauterpacht, Brierly's Contribution to International Law, *in* Lauterpacht and Waldock (Eds.), at xv-xxxvi. See also, C. Landauer, J.L. Brierly and the Modernization of International Law, 25 (5) *Vanderbilt J. of Tr. L.* 881-917 (1993).

[222] J.L. Brierly, The Rule of Law in International Society (1936), *in* Lauterpacht and Waldock (Eds.), at 263. Hereinafter: Rule of Law.

[223] See also, Lauterpacht, Brierly's Contribution, *supra* footnote 221, at xxxv.

[224] See, e.g., Brierly, The Basis of Obligation in International Law, *in* Lauterpacht and Waldock (Eds.), The Basis of Obligation in International Law and Other Papers by the late James Leslie Brierly, at 1 and 3 (1958). This is the original English version of the course 'Le Fondement du caractère obligatoire du droit international' as delivered in 1928 (See, 23 *RCADI* 467 (1928)). Hereinafter: The Basis of Obligation. See, for law in relation to society: 'Law and society are correlative terms, and it is trite learning that neither can exist without the other.' Rule of Law, at 250. '[A]fter all law is not an isolated phenomenon, but only part of the general texture of society; you cannot take it out of its social context, thinking to improve it, without destroying its vitality; you can de-

moral duty to contribute to the 'rehabilitation' of international law[225] and the construction of a 'saner' international order, [226] and to suggest that in natural law could be found a 'vista full of hope for legal science.'[227]

Brierly had joined the army in 1914 and served his country during the First World War. After the war, he returned to his academic career. He was appointed to the Chair of International Law and Diplomacy at Oxford – his old University – in 1923.[228] His inaugural lecture on this occasion, *The Shortcomings of International Law*,[229] may be regarded as his research agenda for the following years. It poses questions, which he subsequently dealt with in various articles and it also shaped his Hague Academy course on *The Basis of Obligation in International Law* (1928) and his famous textbook, *The Law of Nations* (1928).

In *Shortcomings*, Brierly confronted the crisis of international law and searched for the deeper causes of the weak and subordinate role international law played in international society.[230] His diagnosis reached beyond the common explanation of the lack of effective sanctions and focused on the inordinately wide scope of the *domain reservé*.[231] International law failed in its aim to preserve international peace because the 'reserved domain' doctrine prevented the most important and inflammatory areas of conlict from being regulated by law.[232] In Brierly's view, this obstacle to international legal progress was the legal reflection of the 'irrational force of nationalism', together with the rational calculation and protection of national interests, i.e., 'reasonable nationalism.'[233] The irrationalism pervading international law deserved a strong response and Brierly was simply unable to resign himself to the passiveness of the 'wait and see' attitude widespread among those who wished for some sense of internationalism to spring up. Brierly therefore appealed to international legal scholarship to show that states *needed* international law to protect their interests and mutual relations. To

velop it only as one of the functions of a growing society.' Brierly, The Judicial Settlement of International Disputes (1925), *in* Lauterpacht and Waldock (Eds.), at 107. Hereinafter: Judicial Settlement. Also, J.L. Brierly, The Legislative Function in International Relations (1931), *in* Lauterpacht and Waldock (Eds.), at 212.

[225] Brierly, The Shortcomings of International Law, *in* Lauterpacht and Waldock (Eds.), at 68. First published in *BYIL* 1924. Hereinafter: Shortcomings.

[226] Brierly in the Preface to: The Law of Nations: An Introduction to the International Law of Peace (1928). Hereinafter: The Law of Nations.

[227] See also, The Basis of Obligation, at 67. See, for Brierly's hopeful commentary on the League of Nations, The Law of Nations, at 222.

[228] Waldock' Biographical Note, Lauterpacht and Waldock (Eds.), at ix.

[229] Shortcomings, at 68.

[230] See also, The Law of Nations, at 52 *et seq*.

[231] Shortcomings, at 68, 71. See also, The Law of Nations, at 53-4.

[232] Id., at 71. One year later Brierly commented on 'domestic jurisdiction' as the 'new catchword' introduced by the League's Covenant. He said that 'we are warned against any encroachment on the province of the new fetish, about which, however, little seems to be generally known except its extreme sanctity.' Brierly, Matters of Domestic Jurisdiction, *in* Lauterpacht&Waldock (Eds.), at 81. First published in *BYIL* 1925. Hereinafter: Domestic Jusrisdiction.

[233] Shortcomings, at 71.

make this an even more compelling option, 'the quality of international law' had to be improved, i.e., it should be made to meet more fully the needs of the international society. In fact, Brierly ascribed a dual function to international law: it should be both stable and flexible, maintaining established values and creating new ones. This duality was required in order to deal with – or meet the demands of – (continuously changing) international life. In order to develop international law further, its flexibility should be enhanced, which was an absolute priority in the eyes of this British scholar.[234] However, the rather functional definition of the quality of law which Brierly promulgated must not give the impression that his perception of law was merely functional; on the contrary, he ultimately found the basis of law in morality and turned, for the urgently needed 'active principle of growth', to natural law, or, in his words, to 'reason'.[235] In 1924, Brierly concluded that the (political) problem of the wide scope of domestic jurisdiction could only be solved by 'the reconsideration and restatement of some of the fundamental postulates of the law.'[236]

In the following years, Brierly took up this challenge, committing himself to, *inter alia*, the revision of two fundamental postulates: the doctrine of sovereignty and the question of the basis of law. This revision has been the legal theoretical goal of his scholarship, although the urgency with which he pursued it clearly stemmed from the contemporary problematic political situation of his time. The emergence of this situation is here blamed on nationalism, but, as will become clear below, Brierly's approach displays a more general concern about the perceived threat to democracy and the relationship between the individual and the collective. As his legal philosophical remarks show, Brierly was deeply concerned for the position of the individual, as, in his view, reason and morality could only function at the individual level. In *Shortcomings*, Brierly deplored the anti-social effect of ('irrational')[237] nationalism, which was represented in the law by the doctrine of *domain reservé*, and argued in favour of the 'progressive diminution of th[e] 'reserved domain', and the annexation of part of it at any rate by the domain of law.'[238] Brierly's position on this matter revealed one of the

[234] Brierly's attitude towards the project of the codification of international law where he feared this would decrease international law's flexibility also reflects this concern. See, e.g., Shortcomings, at 74; 'the principles of international law are not susceptible of precise formulation.' Also, Brierly, Règles Générales du Droit de la Paix, 58 *RCADI* 21 (1936-I). Hereinafter: Règles Générales. He was a member of the committee of experts for the codification of international law, which was appointed by the Council of The League of Nations, as of 1924.

[235] Shortcomings, at 73-74; The Basis of Obligation, at 8, 18. In his textbook, Brierly treats 'Reason' as one of the sources of the law. 'Those who administer law must meet new situations not precisely covered by a formulated rule by resorting to the principle which medieval writers would have called natural law, and which we generally call reason.' The Law of Nations, at 44-45.

[236] Shortcomings, at 75.

[237] Id., at 71.

[238] Id. In the following year, Brierly discussed the problem of the extent of domestic jurisdiction, and accepted that Australian immigration policy fell within its scope, but was horrified by the idea that the Armenian massacres should also come under domestic jurisdiction. Brierly: 'every state would be a gainer if gradually and with proper consideration of each step these interferences [of

guiding ideas and objectives in his work over the next few decades, namely the establishment of a clear presence of reason through law in an attempt to control irrationality.[239] Whether it had the face of chaos, 'anarchy,'[240] mythical nationalism and racism, legal conceptions glorifying force, or 'the emotions and prejudices of masses of men,' [241] law should put a stop to all moral decline. Brierly conceived of law as 'applied reason': '*le droit, quand il est fidèle à sa propre essence, n'est rien d'autre que la raison appliquée aux problèmes de la conduite humaine et ne saurait vivre dans un monde voué à tout ce qui est contraire à la raison.*'[242] Faith, for him, was bound up with reason:[243] '[f]or us..., a rational universe, even if we cannot prove it to be a fact, is a necessary postulate both of thought and action ...'[244]

3.3.2. **Brierly's concept of international law**

Motivated by the idea that international law and theory had to be 'reform[ed],' i.e., adjusted to the reality of international life, Brierly's approach had a strong *revisionist* character. This, however, does not become readily apparent from statements such as: 'by international law we mean the body of principles which regulates the conduct of states in their relations with one another.'[245] This choice of words evidently closely resembles the definitions given by *restorative* scholars, such as Oppenheim.[246] Lauterpacht was nonetheless correct in applauding Brierly for his 'progressive' and 'innovative' contributions to international law. Brierly connected with the respectability conveyed by traditional wording, but manipulated the definitions by redefining the basis of international law, i.e., the source from which the body of principles originates, as well as the concept of the nature of the state. Here we will focus on his conception of international law, and

common international action or pressure] with domestic jurisdiction, which will certainly continue, were regulated, and the matters themselves converted into matters of international law. This process has in fact begun under the machinery of the Covenant; it offers no sensational success, but it is one of the most promising features of the international outlook today, and it calls not only for our willing co-operation, but above all for the exercise of a wise patience.' Domestic Jurisdiction, at 81.

[239] '[E]n même temps que s'effectue ce recul moral de l'idéal d'une communauté internationale vers celui d'un chaos de souveraineté rivales, nous assistons à un recul intellectuel basé sur la propagation de mythes tels que ceux de nation, de race, et sur la glorification de la force comme étant une fin en elle-même, recul qui mène à l'abaissement de la raison et à l'exaltation des éléments irrationnels et émotifs de la nature humaine. Aucun état d'esprit ne pourrait être plus étranger à la légalité, car le droit, quand il est fidèle à sa propre essence, n'est rien d'autre que la raison appliquée aux problèmes de la conduite humaine et ne saurait vivre dans un monde voué à tout ce qui est contraire à la raison.' Règles Générales, at 233.

[240] See, e.g., The Law of Nations, at 55.

[241] Domestic Jurisdiction, at 81.

[242] Règles Générales, at 233.

[243] See, e.g., Règles Générales, at 232-235. See also, The Law of Nations (5th ed.), at 57: here Brierly is more explicit.

[244] The Law of Nations, at 14.

[245] The Basis of Obligation, at 1-2 and 48.

[246] See *supra* section 3.2.3.2.

in the next section deal with his redefinition of the state and of the concept of ILP.

Although progressive, Brierly's thinking was never radical (yet still always fundamental), but on the contrary rather moderate or 'pragmatic.'[247] To start off a concise overview of Brierly's ideas, the following statement, made in 1924, will serve to show the break he made with voluntarism and reveal the *revisionist* trajectory he subsequently took up.

A system of law that encourages the maximum of will may be tolerable at certain times, as in the nineteenth century; but we are more and more finding it intolerable in the twentieth, and it has already almost ceased to be the theory, as it certainly has ceased to be the practice, of our municipal law. Yet we continue to proclaim it as the *unchallengeable* basis of international law, though it is rapidly passing away also from the structure of international society. To do that means that we are consenting to a divorce between the law and the ideas of justice prevailing in the society for which the law exists; and it is certain that as long as that divorce endures, it is the law which will be discredited.[248]

As his lecture *Shortcomings* had already made clear, Brierly systematically challenged the voluntarist basis of international law. A clean break with voluntarism was necessary in order to stop international law from being further discredited. The 'divorce between justice and international law' had to be halted immediately. In his revisionist search for a non-voluntarist, non-antropomorphical and demythologised conception of international law, Brierly first needed to define a new basis for international law from which a revised conception of international law could subsequently be drawn. For this he focused on the falseness of the notion of sovereignty and opposed the idea that states did not dwell in a 'political' context.

Brierly challenged the 'unchallengeable.' The two traditional theories on the binding nature of international law, i.e., the naturalist doctrine of the fundamental rights of states in a 'state of nature,' and the positivist doctrine of state consent, could not possibly meet with Brierly's approval given that they stemmed from a false notion of sovereignty.[249] To Brierly's mind, the doctrine of sovereignty was a misrepresentation of reality. For this reason, he rejected the attempts of his *restorative* contemporaries, naturalists and positivists alike, to reconcile international law and the doctrine of state sovereignty.[250] He analysed the history of this

[247] Brierly defended the 'pragmatic' approach: 'The lawyer is entitled to take a pragmatic standpoint and to assume that when a certain course of conduct is generally felt by those to whom it applies to be obligatory, it is obligatory for him; in such an assumption he does not claim any ultimate truth or even anything objectively valid outside the system with which he is concerned.' The Law of Nations, at 51.

[248] Shortcomings, at 80. Emphasis added.

[249] The Basis of Obligation, at 3-18; The Law of Nations, at 33-39.

[250] 'Our traditional theories of sovereignty ... at bottom are quite irreconcilable with conceptions of international society or international law ...' Judicial Settlement, at 99. '[I]t is meaningless to say

doctrine closely and concluded that it was a misleading concept with 'absolutist associations,'[251] and an inadequate theory when it came to representing the nature of political authority and characterising the mutual relations among states.[252] Brierly stressed that international practice had demonstrated that state power was never absolute and that states were never completely independent, but were, on the contrary, interdependent. International life, in his eyes, should therefore not be characterised as a state of nature, but rather as a phenomenon concerning *political* relations among states which derive their competence from international law. States co-exist in a political condition and not in a free and absolutely sovereign condition.

Brierly argued that, in keeping with their traditional doctrine of sovereignty roots, both naturalists and positivists advocated 'the maximum of will.'[253] As Brierly found such voluntarism 'intolerable,' he had to find a new foundation for international law, and having discovered it, he argued that eventually it was the same as that of *all* law:[254] morality – '*nous sommes moralement obligés d'obéir au droit.*'[255] The problem of the binding nature of law, whether domestic or international, is a moral problem. People conform to law because they believe it to be morally right. Ultimately, it is in man's rational nature to behave morally. In *The Law of Nations* (5th ed.) Brierly expressly stated that:

---

that [states] are sovereign.' The Law of Nations, at 62. Like Van Vollenhoven, Brierly considered Vattel's influence 'a disaster for international law,' due to his 'exaggerated emphasis on the independence of states.' See, The Law of Nations, at 33, 31. Any reconciliation of international law with sovereignty involves the negation of law itself. Brierly criticised the PCIJ judgment in the *Lotus* case for its traditional, voluntarist conception of international law and its emphasis on the 'independence' of sovereign states. States are not independent, on the contrary, they are bound by international law and their competence derives from it. See, e.g., The Basis of Obligation, at 11; Règles Générales, at 146-147.

[251] The Basis of Obligation, at 43.

[252] Brierly did not distinguish the internal from the external aspects of the institute 'state' or its sovereignty: 'a state cannot be properly understood unless it is seen as a whole. It is not two separable entities according as it functions internally and externally, but one entity regarded from two different aspects.' States are institutions coexisting in a political condition, *not* in a state of nature, and are therefore not fully interdependent. The Basis of Obligation, at 30.

[253] See *supra*, quote to footnote 248.

[254] For his inquiry into the basis of the obligation of law in general, Brierly considered Duguit's theory of 'solidarity' and Krabbe's theory of the 'sense or feeling of right'. Id., at 56-64.

[255] Règles Générales, at 34. In 1928, Brierly stated: '[T]oo often we have been tempted to forget that the connection between law and morals is really much more fundamental than their distinction, and that the ultimate basis of obligation to obey the law cannot be anything but moral. Just as the problem of the obligatory character of international law is only one aspect of the problem of the obligatory character of law in general, so this in its turn is only one aspect of a still wider problem, the problem of obligation in general, and this is a problem of ethics. ... It simply means that if we ask why we ought to obey rules of law simply because they *are* rules of law, the answer is that there is a rule of morality of which that is the content.' The Basis of Obligation, at 65-66. Many scholars tend to view Brierly's perspective as the product of unrealistic idealism, but it must be pointed out that he does not expecting too much of the law itself and stresses that it all comes down to human morality and the actions based upon it. In his view, the individual is the only entity that is able to represent morality within society and to act upon it.

The ultimate explanation of the binding force of all law is that man, whether he is a single individual or whether he is associated with other men in a state, is constrained, in so far as he is a reasonable being, to believe that order and not chaos is the governing principle of the world in which he has to live.[256]

Given that the basis of obligation in all law, including international law, is found in human reason, it naturally follows that, contrary to the predominant view as expressed by the restorers, Brierly recognised that international and domestic law were fundamentally (‘*en essence*’) identical and united.[257] This realisation is the source of his monist approach to the relationship between the international and domestic legal orders. Consequently, although the ‘international legal reformer’ Brierly did not think it likely that ‘in any literal sense a “world-state”’ would soon arrive, he did, however, recognise ‘that the world as it exist[ed] ... constitute[d] in some true sense a single society.’[258] A statement he made a few years earlier is even clearer. In 1928, Brierly argued the ‘return to [the international juridical community] of Grotius,’ i.e., the re-adoption of the concept of international society comprising a ‘community of *Civitatis*’ as well as ‘a community of *genus humanum*.’[259]

Brierly, in this manner reconstructed international law by giving it a new basis, which was non-voluntarist and ethical and which, with its roots firmly planted in morality, also counteracted the ‘divorce’ between justice and law which was discrediting international law. By reinforcing its credibility, international law would become more relevant and more widely used; only by rendering its use more compelling and by restoring confidence in the rule of law would the scope of the *domain reservé* be reduced and would ‘nationalism’, or rather nationalist-driven international conduct, be controlled by international law. I will now elaborate on Brierly’s concept of ILP, which is so closely related to his approach of the state.

3.3.3. Personality and the state: towards an anthropocentric approach

Immanent in Brierly’s vision of the law as outlined above, is his *anthropocentric* approach to international law, which actually goes back to his repudiation of the continuing exaltation and glorification of the state to which the opening quote also referred. Earlier, we have already indicated that the second fundamental revision, which Brierly argued in favour of, was related to the traditional idea of the state. To his mind, the idea of ‘the state as a personality,’ which both naturalists and positivists advanced, was utterly ‘false.’[260]

---

[256] The Law of Nations (5th ed.), at 57.

[257] Règles Générales, at 35-42; The Law of Nations, at 50; Judicial Settlement, at 97 and 102-105.

[258] Rule of Law, at 250, 254 and 250.

[259] The Basis of Obligation, at 52.

[260] The Law of Nations, at 62; The Basis of Obligation, at 19.

[A]ctually states are not persons, though it is often convenient to personify them; they have no wills except the wills of the individual human beings who direct their affairs; and they exist not in a political vacuum but in continuous political relations with one another. The subjection of states to law needs no special philosophical explanation other than that by which we explain the subjection of individuals to the law of the state; the differences between that law and international law are important, ... but they do not lie in metaphysics nor in any mystical qualities of the entity called state sovereignty.[261]

As regards Brierly's concept of ILP, three elements must be singled out: 1) Brierly strongly felt that to the entity called 'state' should *not* be attributed any kind of 'mystical qualities;' 2) Brierly consequently rejected the image of the state as a 'person' and redefined it as an 'institution;' and 3) Brierly observed that *only* individual human beings have the capacity to display a will of their own, *not* states.

First, Brierly understood that the theories concerning the sovereign state which had been submitted by the political philosophers of the past were actually all 'advocac[ies] of a cause.'[262] Since none of them considered the international order as the 'cause' to advocate, all of them failed to take sufficient account of inter-state relationships. Brierly, who, as we have seen above, positioned himself as an advocate of the international order, concluded that international legal theory, which had for centuries been closely intertwined with the doctrine of the sovereign state, should distance itself from its heritage. Sovereignty had some truth to it, Brierly admitted, but the traditional theories were not very helpful in the advocacy of international law and order. The political philosopher who Brierly most forcefully attacked was Hegel, whose political cause had been the national state. Hegel, he repeatedly declared, had done untold damage to international law as a result of the *mystification* of the state which had been inspired by his ideas.

As can be gleaned from the opening quotation, Brierly abhorred the 'idolatry of the state.' He rejected any kind of glorification of the state that was practised as 'an end-in-itself' or the goal of human civilisation.[263] In his view, Hegel's ideas had given rise to a notion of the sovereign state as an absolute, autonomous substantial being and, even, as the realisation of the ethical ideal of the fully autonomous 'Will.'[264] Defined as sovereign persons, states were not subjected to any kind of moral standard, as they themselves were considered the moral incarnation of spirit (*Geist*), or, to repeat Hegel's own words, 'the march of God in the world.'[265] The calamity of the First World War greatly contributed to the general repudiation of the idea of absolute sovereign and independent state persons.

[261] The Law of Nations, at 34 and 62-63.

[262] The Basis of Obligation, at 29. Bodin and Hobbes were motivated by the need for internal order, Locke and Rousseau were both concerned with liberty, and Hegel was inspired by the national state.

[263] See, e.g., The Basis of Obligation, at 29.

[264] See *supra*, section 3.2.3.1. See also, The Basis of Obligation, at 29.

[265] See *supra*, footnote 134.

Much of the optimism concerning the moral nature of states had faded. The idea of states as persons, possessing a will that was not susceptible to external limitation,[266] had become an obstacle to the emergence of a new concept of sovereignty and to the development of international law. Consequently and with the aim of liberating international legal theory from this heritage of Hegelian thought, Brierly took the offensive:[267]

Of all writers on the state [Hegel's] influence on the theory of international law has probably been the most far-reaching, and certainly it is still the most devastating; for even cynicism may be refuted by argument and observation of the facts, but hardly mysticism.[268]

Since Hegel the belief in the state as a super-person has remained until our own time practically unshaken, with disastrous effects not only on the clearness of our thought on political affairs, but on action. The mysticism in which Rousseau and Hegel enveloped it has only deepened ... by the process which has raised nationalism almost into a religion or fanaticism.[269]

Hegelian mysticism had entirely pervaded the concept of personality. The state person was conceived of as substantial, transcendent and mystical. Above all, the mysticism of Hegelian thinking had struck the position and liberty of the individual a fatal blow.[270] The individual was reduced to serving the state and obliged to sacrifice himself in service to this secular deity. Man had lost his freedom, his independence and individuality and even his humanity in serving the state as the 'end of humanity.' Brierly was profoundly troubled by this loss of individual liberty and morality and concluded that any kind of mythological or mystical qualities or perceptions had to be avoided in theories concerning international law. The political problems of his time required a theory of state and sovereignty that was different from the theories that had arisen out of the historic political causes of the past which were no longer at issue. Brierly attributed the mythologisation and mystification of the state and its sovereignty to the idea of personality and for this reason challenged the notion of the 'state *person*.'

Secondly, Brierly treated the presence of irrational elements in the political process as a contemporary political problem. The tendency in early democratic theories (like Rousseau's) to appoint the people *collectively* as the theoretical *locus* of sovereignty – political authority – and thus to accept, in practice, the majority as

[266] Brierly in particular considered the doctrine of self-limitation, which was still very influential among *restorative* scholars, as a theory that was inherited from Hegel and was quite disastrous for international law. The Law of Nations, at 37; The Basis of Obligation, at 13 and 35.

[267] Brierly held forth on Hegelian thought and its consequences quite frequently. See, e.g., The Basis of Obligation, at 13, 29, 30, 35-36, and 46. See also, The Law of Nations, at 37.

[268] The Basis of Obligation, at 36.

[269] Id., at 29.

[270] See also, opening quotation, text to footnote 222.

the sovereign, in Brierly's understanding took insufficient account of the irrational psychological elements of the problems of government (in mass society).[271] This tendency was itself a danger to democracy and human freedom, the irrational elements in society needed to be faced and neutralised. The theory of state sovereignty has historically had to deal with two problems at once: a) a legal problem consisting of the formal validity of law, i.e., the identification of the legislature, the formal test that enables us to pronounce a rule actually binding; and b) the political-philosophical problem of explaining the nature of the state's political authority.[272] Brierly considered the former (legal) problem part of the latter, the political issue of authority and its organisation.[273] To explain the nature of political authority, one has 'to inquire into *the forces that determine* the action of the juridical sovereign.'[274] These are the socio-political forces influencing political action and authority: in absolutist regimes, law-making and law-enforcement were in the hands of one single entity; in democratic societies, however, these functions were divided with the result that the identification of juridical sovereignty within the state was often an impossible task. To conclude that the real sovereignty was thus vested in the people as a whole was, however, 'unsatisfactory' in Brierly's view, as this conclusion actually attributed sovereignty to the majority, and secondly, failed to take into account that the popular will is expressed though a variety of organs and not in a unified, or uniform, manner.

The suggested alternative, the *hypothesis of the state person*, however, was equally unsatisfying as an explanation of political authority. In Brierly's view, this alternative involved a misrepresentation for three reasons. i) To begin with, there was the false psychological assumption that authority over the individual human will should proceed from a separate and 'superior will.' To invent 'an hypothetical person' to attribute this superior will to and thus 'make the logical structure complete' was utterly wrong, in Brierly's view, and only confirmed the 'anthropomorphical bias of the human mind.'[275] ii) The nature of the (internal and external) political authority of the state (i.e., sovereignty) is no different from any other form of authority. It is neither absolute nor unlimited,[276] nor is it based on force, although it has the right to use force in exceptional cases if necessary. To understand sovereignty as the absolute and exclusive right to use (arbitrary) force is a 'misconception.'[277] iii) 'Obligation can be created only if we can con-

[271] The Basis of Obligation, at 41.

[272] Id., at 36-46.

[273] Id., at 38. Brierly does not favour the use of the notion 'juridical sovereignty,' he found it merely 'confusing' and felt that '[I]t is better to admit frankly the simple fact, namely, that in some constitutions there is no absolute and ultimate authority over the law, and therefore there is no sovereign in the juridical sense.' It remains true, however, that to prevent 'anarchy' and establish 'certainty', a legal system requires an organ which declares the law. It is the political organisation of authority which determines whether an organ is a law-making authority. Id.

[274] Id., at 39. Emphasis added.

[275] Id., at 40.

[276] Id., at 43-45.

[277] Id., at 45.

vince ourselves that the externality of the superior will or the superior force is an illusion.'[278] In other words, if in our understanding we conform to or obey an internal force of morality that has been laid down in an external rule, we do not need a 'person' to derive law and authority from. Brierly elaborated on the relationship between will and authority by following the reasoning of Professor Korkonov, who stated that:

> authority depends not on the will of the ruler, but upon the *consciousness* of the subject. If this is so, there is no need of attributing will to the state and of personifying it in order to explain the state's authority.[279]

Brierly concluded that the source of authority is *submission* chosen by the individual, *conscious* subject. Submission is thus a *rational* decision. In the contemporary mass politics of the time, the rational will proved to be not the only human capacity playing a role. The early democratic theories ignore the irrational elements of human behaviour and political participation, which makes them somewhat problematic:

> Early democratic theory certainly exaggerated the extent to which the ordinary man either acts or thinks on purely rational grounds; it failed to make proper allowance either for the psychological effects of suggestion and prejudice; or for the complexity of the individual's problems, or for the little attention that even a moderately intelligent and public-spirited individual can devote to public affairs. It assumed that the task of reformers was merely to liberate man from his chains, and that the citizen would then stand revealed, ready and able to take his share in the rational direction of public affairs. We are beginning to understand that this is not so; that the psychological elements in the problems of government are much less simple that we thought; and that rational will of any kind, interested or disinterested, plays only a limited part in them.[280]

The irrational elements of the political process have to be acknowledged. Brierly accepted Lippmann's image of the public as a possible *phantom* within a democratic state.[281] The democratic process of producing public policies is chaotic, it is both rational *and* irrational. As Lippmann observed, 'the making of one general will out of a multitude of general wishes is not a Hegelian mystery, but an art well known to politicians.'[282] Political authority is, thus, not always or solely based upon rational will. The individual rational will, Brierly observed, turned out to play 'only a limited part' in public affairs. Since the source of authority is not will, but subjection, the invention of the 'hypothetical person' with a superior will to explain political authority was entirely unnecessary. Authority actually

---

[278] Id., at 46.

[279] Korkunov, as cited in: The Basis of Obligation, at 41. Emphasis added.

[280] Id., at 41.

[281] Id. Lippmann published The Phantom Public in 1925. See also, for the image of the public as a phantom, Jaspers, *supra* section 3.2.2.3.

[282] Lippmann, as cited, in The Basis of Obligation, at 42.

emanates from many different sources of submission.[283] Modern democratic theory equally needed to take the irrational side of the story into account more; Brierly, however, concluded that since public opinion was not purely rational and because the will was not the sole determining factor in the political process, political authority could not simply be explained by the will of the hypothetical state person.

As the hypothetical person proved unhelpful in explaining state authority, Brierly wondered how then to explain the nature of the state: the *organisation* of government on a specific territory and a population living on this territory. Brierly proposed an alternative to the idea of state personality: the state as an '*institution*' which exists '*within* society, but it is not ... the *form* of society.'[284] The notion of institution was taken from the French scholar Hauriou.[285] His own elaboration on the term, in *The Law of Nations*, reveals Brierly's aim to cut the state down to size and stress its relational or functional nature:

> it is a *relationship* which men establish among themselves as a means of securing certain objects, of which the most fundamental is a system of order within which their activities can be carried on. ... A state should not be confused with the whole community of persons living on its territory; it is only one among a multitude of other institutions ... though obviously it is one of tremendous importance; none the less it is not an all-embracing institution, not something from which, or within which, all other institutions and associations have their being.[286]

Although in some way they were both appalled by the same idolatry and irrational social forces, Brierly did not join Kelsen in his identification of the state with the legal order,[287] but instead defined the state as an institution – a system of relationships – aiming to realise security and order within society so as to enable the relationships to function properly. The state is the institution which has the exclusive use of force within society. Law does not create the system of order but helps sustain it.[288] The institute 'state', being an organisation of government, produces law. It is an instrument to organise society and order human relationships.[289] Law serves order in society and therefore has to be obeyed; non-compli-

---

[283] Brierly enumerates tradition, prejudice, loyalty, interest, apathy, in fact, almost any idea that influences the human mind. Id., at 42.

[284] Brierly cited MacIver with approval, Id., at 47.

[285] 'Une institution est une idée d'oeuvre ou d'entreprise qui se réalise et dure juridiquement dans un milieu social; pour la réalisation de cette idée, un pouvoir s'organise qui lui procure des organes; d'autre part, entre les membres du group social intéressé à la réalisation de l'idée, il se produit des manifestations de communion dirigées par les organes du pouvoir et réglées par des procédures.' Cited in, The Basis of Obligation, at 48. For a discussion of Hauriou's thought, see, e.g., M. Simonovitch, Les Théories contemporaines de l'Etat 269 *et seq.* (1939).

[286] The Law of Nations, at 56.

[287] See *infra* section 3.4. on Kelsen.

[288] J.L. Brierly, The Outlook for International Law 75 (1944). Hereinafter: The Outlook.

[289] Brierly's approach to international law indeed closely resembled Pound's 'social-engineering' approach. See, e.g., Brierly, International Law as a Subject of Education (1926), *in* Lauterpacht and Waldock (Eds.), at 128-129, 132. Hereinafter: Subject of Education.

ance is only an option in the rare case where we consider a legal rule to be so immoral that the fact that it is law is no longer enough to keep us from breaking it. In this relationship between law and the state, the latter, being an institution, is no longer a tight billiard-ball unity, but has become an instrumental (or procedural) entity.[290] The anthropomorphical conception of the state was pessimistic and lacked flexibility, but in Brierly's understanding the state, perceived as an institution, was an expression of its 'dynamic' nature – a 'product of evolution.'[291] The institute 'state' offered hope and opportunity. Brierly avoided using any metaphor that could again result in rapid reification or mythologisation. The state is made up of *relationships* among individual human beings and law is one of the effects – 'sequel[s]' – of the order which man has created. Instead of considering the state as a goal in itself, it is reduced to a *means* of securing other goals. Perceiving the state as an institution instead of a mystical moral person returned the state to the realm of the individual human being and made its reinforcement possible, as well as a strengthening of international law.

Brierly's contemplation of democracy reveals an inner struggle. Kant had argued that a republican state would be less willing to wage war. Brierly tended to agree. At the same time, however, the idea of a majority ruling mass society was hardly a comfortable or reassuring one; it would doubtless culminate in harm to the essence of democracy. 'We infer, ..., that the masses must rule, and yet we find they cannot rule' as Jaspers put it. A precondition for democratising the masses is the creation of a system, which accepts that every individual is vested with both rights and duties, and which thereby accepts individual responsibility. In this vein, by defining the state as an institution, Brierly stressed the importance of individual human choice and argued in favour of a political philosophy based on the individual, instead of on shifting majorities.

In the third place, looking at Brierly's redefinition of the state, the shift away from traditional anthropomorphic thinking into a more anthropocentric direction is elusive. It brings us to the final element singled out above: *only* the *individual* has the capacity to display a will. This element was already partly discussed with regard to Brierly's explanation of authority, but I will now elaborate it further. An absolute key feature of Brierly's approach is, as Lauterpacht rightly submitted, the position he attributed to ethics. Brierly distinguished law from morality; law is obeyed because it is law, i.e., produced by the state organisation and ultimately backed up by force. A legal obligation can be enforced by means of the legal order and within this order the duty to obey is 'absolute',[292] apart from the exceptional case, which was mentioned above, where the rule is such that compliance itself would be immoral. Law serves order in society and we accept the duty to obey in order to avoid 'social evil.' However, at which point do we feel that

[290] Brierly's agreement with Kelsen should be viewed in this context. Règles Générales, at 47.
[291] The Basis of Obligation, at 6.
[292] Id., at 66.

compliance is immoral? Man acts morally because our individual conscience tells us to and moral obligations speak to our sense of responsibility. There is a thin line dividing the two, in Brierly's approach.[293] As we have seen earlier, he determined that the problem of obligation was ultimately a problem of ethics.[294] The problem of authority was eventually resolved by the explanation of 'submission', an act which, in the end, only an individual can perform. Both law and ethics are ultimately only directed at the individual and it is the individual who ultimately opts to comply with them. In Brierly's view, law can only help to sustain order but for man to submit to it, it must also be just; for Brierly, ultimately, it all comes down to individual choice.[295] Law's 'final appeal' is to the individual!

> Law exists for individuals in society, and it must make its final appeal to the individual, and not to any collective, conscience, for the latter does not exist. In that forum the voice of law can never claim an unconditional primacy; for no system of law has an *absolute* value, and there are no rules, either of law or morals, which are absolutely independent of the situation in which the individual is called upon to make a choice.[296]

Individually, man is considered a reasonable being, a (partly) rational being. Social psychology had demonstrated the for the most part negative influence of collective experience. Brierly succeeded in avoiding the problem of the negative effects which the collective 'mind' purportedly had on (international) law by conceiving of law as an instrument which appealed to the individual and which had its ultimate foundation in individual human morality. The collective conscience, 'the group mind'– primitive, destructive and threatening as mass psychology had shown it to be – is simply denied existence; for Brierly, only the individual conscience has relevance in law. The individual is called upon to participate and make a rational choice. This choice to submit to the law and to what is socially right should therefore be based on a moral choice which is made individually and consciously. Inevitably, and acknowledged by Brierly, we have now moved outside the sphere of law:

---

[293] Brierly called upon international lawyers to refrain from 'mark[ing] off law as such somewhat too rigidly from ethics and from politics ... it is easy to forget that its connexion with those subjects is really something far more fundamental *sub specie aeternitatis* than the difference between it and them; that, in fact, the boundary lines which we draw around the subject of law only exist for convenience of our specialized study. ... in truth ethics, politics, jurisprudence, are only three branches of a single wider study, that of human conduct in society, and that the ultimate foundation of them is all the same.' Subject of Education, at 132.

[294] The Basis of Obligation, at 65. Some have rejected this view as lacking realism, but ultimately perceiving it as a moral problem which all individuals have to face as it affects international life just as much as their own life is, on the contrary, highly realistic, as this shows a complete absence of any false hope as to the law.

[295] In 1947, in relation to international law, Brierly stressed the individual right to private judgment: 'the right of private judgement according to the guidance of each man's conscience,' a right which only totalitarianism could deny. As cited in Lauterpacht, Contribution, at xix.

[296] The Basis of Obligation, at 66.

[T]he problem how to reconcile the right of the individual conscience to judge of the individual's duty, with the right of the community to enforce upon him what others judge to be his duty, I confess that I can see no general principle of solution. Ultimately, I suppose, we must fall back on metaphysics, and say that we believe duty to be duty ... It may not always be easy to feel intellectually assured that such a belief is founded in reality, but it is a belief upon which even the most sceptical acts every minute of his life.

Therefore, as lawyers, we ultimately arrive at a point where we must simply have faith in natural law and believe in this truth that we actually have a natural tendency to act morally:

We are all of us compelled to act as if we are convinced of the reality of an objective order, both physical and moral, if we are to go on living and acting at all. This no doubt is to believe in natural law, but I confess that to me the modern resurgence of natural law theories seems to open *a vista of hope* for legal science.[297]

3.3.4. The *true* subjects of international law

Brierly's anthropocentric approach to international law – ultimately addressing the individual and having its basis of obligation in morality and individual choice – has obvious consequences as regards the question of the *true* subjects of international law. Brierly observed that '[i]t has been possible to regard states as the subjects of international law only because we have personified them.' If Brierly preserves the notion of ILP, it is still clear that it has been detached from the state-personality idea. States have no personality, no consciousness. Only individuals are conscious beings and are capable of willing and acting, although these acts may, however, be attributed to institutions. In order to ensure that the personification of the 'state-institution' is not a misrepresentation, but a true expression of its character, Brierly examines the three possible interpretations.[298] He rejects both the 'fictional'[299] and the 'individualist'[300] interpretation of the personality concept. The first because it leads to the glorification of the state as a separate omnipotent entity 'without taking account of the lives and purposes of its members.'[301] The second, the individualist theory, is false as it actually entails

[297] Id., at 67. Emphasis added.

[298] Brierly took the three theories on legal personality from Raymond Salleilles' 1907-8 Comparative Civil Law Course on legal persons, *De la personnalité juridique*, published in 1910.

[299] He comments that '[t]his abstraction is conceived as living a life and pursuing purposes of its members. This system leads straight to the omnipotence of the state, to the theory of sovereignty; it is the system which leads it nowhere.' Id., at 49.

[300] Brierly cites Saleilles and contends that the individualist interpretation is 'erroneous' for being oppressive: '[c]ette thèse tend à supprimer l'état, purement et simplement, les citoyens, pris comme un total d'individualités, se substituant à lui, et par suite la masse des intérêts individuels en conflit, suivant celui qui devient le plus forte, primant l'intérêt général; c'est la thèse majoritaire.' Id., at 50.

[301] Id., at 49.

the oppressive rule of the majority, counting only the masses within society, if not the state.

Brierly adhered, however, to the 'realist theory': '*nous avons l'État par et pour les individus. L'État est une unité formée d'individualités, lesquelles n'ont pas disparu de la scène.*'[302] This adherence may come as a surprise, as we saw Brierly rejecting the idea of personality altogether, but the realist theory of *legal* personality has three elements of truth, as Brierly acknowledged. i) First of all, the individuals forming the institution 'do not disappear from the scene'. ii) Secondly, the 'unifying' function of personality is preserved. In this scenario, however, the state is not perceived as a fictitious unity. Instead, through ILP, international law recognises the unity of the state. iii) Thirdly, only one aspect of individual human personality is included in the institution that is the state. The state is composed of individuals and can only exist in the service of and through these individuals, not the other way around! The institution of 'the state' is simply the precondition for social life, and only a very small part of the human personality is realised by means of the 'state-institution'. Having thus reduced the importance of the state and emphasised the significance of individual personality, Brierly concluded that the dogma that states are the exclusive subjects of international law was not 'sacrosanct;' '[I]t is not a principle, but essentially a rule of expediency, and mainly a rule of procedure.'[303] The ILP of the state is simply a legal instrument to connect the individual members of the institution with the international legal system. The orthodox doctrine, which only accepted states as international persons, was also erroneous in that it could only classify a wrong suffered by an individual in a foreign state as a wrong suffered by the home state itself. Brierly illustrated his position with the contemporary changes in international life at the time in order to demonstrate that individuals did have rights and duties under international law. And although he realised that these changes could somehow be explained by traditional theory, he argued in favour of a revision: 'there is no reason why international law should not become, if it is not already, a law of which subjects are indifferently either states, or other institutions such as the League of Nations ..., or, finally individuals.'[304]

Recognising that the individual who has suffered a wrong has a right of its own would prevent the 'mysterious but powerful abstraction [of] national honour' becoming part of conflicts between states. Similarly, within international economic relations, the identification of a state's interests with the interests of an individual could be avoided. Brierly considered both these issues threatening to international peace. 'That a broadening of the notion of international personality would make for peace seems to be certain.'[305] Eight years later, Brierly stated in even clearer terms: '*en dernière analyse, seuls les individus sont susceptibles*

[302] Brierly cites Saleilles, id., at 50.
[303] Id., at 51.
[304] Id., at 52.
[305] Id.

d'être sujets d[u] droit [international] ...' While in 1928, Brierly recognised the ILP of the institute 'state', in 1936, he stressed more firmly that the individual is the ultimate subject of international rights and duties:

Mais si nous nous abstenons, ainsi, de porter la guerre dans le camp adverse, il importe que nous ne tombions pas dans l'hérésie de considérer l'Etat comme un sujet du droit, indépendamment des membres qui le composent. Une des données que la nature impose à la science juridique, c'est que les ordres donnés par la loi, pour avoir un sens, doivent s'adresser à des êtres humains individuels, qui seuls peuvent penser, vouloir ou agir; d'où il s'ensuit qu'une théorie de la personnalité morale ... ne doit pas nier qu'en dernière analyse, c'est à l'individu que toute loi s'applique et que, par conséquent, même si les Etats sont le plus souvent les Membres immédiats de la société internationale, elle se résout en dernier lieu en individus, puisque les droit et les obligations des Etats ne peuvent être autre chose que les droits et les obligations des individus qui les composent.[306]

To complete this elaboration on Brierly's concept of (legal) personality and its connection with the political problem of democracy and individual liberty, Brierly's warning to the 'men in the masses' deserves some final attention. Like many of his fellow intellectuals, Brierly struggled with the democratic idea of public opinion and the reality of mass psychology, as we have seen. How to preserve a rational public opinion and prevent it from becoming a channel for irrationality? Initially, Brierly was still rather hopeful with respect to the moral strength of public opinion.[307] During the first few years after the war, public opinion was considered a peacekeeping force, partly due to the fact that it was understood to have played a beneficial role in the establishment of the League. However, the social climate changed and also influenced Brierly. Moreover, it is difficult to pinpoint exactly when Brierly read Lippmann's *The Phantom Public* (1925), but according to the references he made to this work, he seemed to have agreed with the analysis.[308] In his 1928 course, the initially hopeful mood regarding public opinion had turned into concern, as we have seen earlier.[309] In 1944, Brierly reflected on the disastrous situation in Europe and the role public opinion had played in the rise of totalitarian regimes:

We need have no delusions about the rationality or the dependability or even the pacific tendency of men in the mass to see that one at least of the conditions on which the future of international law and co-operation depends is the liberation from this new and terrible subjection.[310]

---

306 Règles Générales, at 47.

307 'Incomparably [the Covenant's] greatest service was to create an organisation, which, as its authors rightly foresaw, would render conciliation easier and prompter, because it would be capable of bringing moral pressure to bear on a refractory state by focusing upon it the newly discovered but immensely powerful force of international public opinion.' Domestic Jusrisdiction, at 88. Also, at 91.

308 See, e.g., The Basis of Obligation, at 41-42; The Outlook, at 107.

309 See *supra* text to footnote 279 and 280.

310 The Outlook, at 107-108.

In order to secure a future for international law and to establish and preserve international peace, the manipulation of public opinion had to be prevented by means of the dissemination of reliable data and the protection of the individual freedoms of speech and thought, as well as the freedom of press and information. That is the only way to prevent public opinion from becoming the incarnation of irrationality. Having said that, Brierly immediately made the link with the domain and subjects of international law. To conceive of states as the only subjects of international law involves a limitation that cannot be upheld. A rational and reasonable public opinion depends completely on the responsibility of every single individual. In 1944, Brierly considered the dogma of state personality as a continuing obstacle to the progress of international law and the liberation of the individual.[311] The notion of the state as a sovereign person contributed to keeping the doctrine of domestic jurisdiction and non-intervention firmly in place. Brierly argued, as he had done 20 years earlier in the *Shortcomings*, that the scope of domestic jurisdiction should be narrowed. In this respect, Brierly stated that he considered the proposals for an international bill of human rights 'attractive both on political – ... – and humanitarian grounds.'[312] In that particular style of his, both honest and questioning, he discussed the problems with regard to the bill's enforcement and the institutionalisation of an international authority with (universal) jurisdiction to judge violations. And although he thus focused on the difficulties, his reasoning nevertheless confirms the conclusion which Brierly drew in 1936 that ultimately the *individual* is the *true* subject of international law.

3.3.5. **Conclusion**

It may be concluded from Brierly's legal-theoretical as well as his practical-political goals that the idea of (legal) personality lay at the heart of his thinking.

By detaching ILP from the idea of state personality, Brierly was able to *demythologise* the state and, with it, the concept of ILP. By attributing ILP to the state institution, Brierly was able to connect the individual to the international legal order and show that in the final analysis it was actually the individual to whom ILP was attributed.

---

[311] 'Hitherto the impact of international law on the lives of individual men and women has not been direct or immediate; it has reached them only through the medium of the state of which they are members. This characteristic, though international lawyers have sometimes been inclined to erect it into an immutable dogma, is really a survival from the original character of international law as law between personal monarchs or sovereigns; after the personified state had taken the place of the personal monarch it was maintained because it was on the whole found to be convenient that the collectivity to which an individual belongs, and not the individual himself, should be treated as the subject of the rights and duties which make up international law. But one of the consequences of the rule has been that the manner in which a particular state chooses to treat its own subjects has hitherto been considered by the law to be a matter of domestic jurisdiction and not of international concern ... today the appalling vista which totalitarianism has opened out is forcing us to question the expediency of maintaining this limitation on the range of law.' The Outlook, at 108.

[312] Id.

As part of his legal theoretical endeavour, Brierly vigorously attacked the idea of personality in order to undermine the orthodox theories and he based these attacks on the concept of obligation in international law. By relocating this basis in human reason and morality, Brierly undertook a fundamental revision of the law. When sovereign will ceased to be the central focus, it was no longer necessary to hold on to a fictional 'person.' Secondly, his attack on personality aided the reconsideration of the concept of state. The definition of the state as an institution, within which political authority operates, and the rejection of absolute sovereignty enabled Brierly to argue that states are not an end in itself, but a means, and that entities are bound by international law. The legal theoretical arguments are directed by Brierly's political causes, i.e., to defend individual liberty against the suffocating collective and international peace against the 'idolatry' inflicted on the state and the rise of totalitarianism.

As the ultimate addressee of international law, the individual human being, through his private judgment, his conscious, moral choice, gives Reason a presence in the world. By accepting that states, organisations and individuals alike are endowed with ILP, Brierly dismantled the orthodox international personality dogma and made ILP into a *technique*, which linked the individual and international law.

3.4. Hans Kelsen (1881-1973)[313]

> Zieht man den auf der politischen Schaubühne das religiöse oder soziale Spiel Tragierenden ihre *Masken* vom Gesicht, dann ist es nicht mehr Gott, der belohnt und straft, der Staat, der verurteilt und Krieg führt, dann sind es Menschen, die anderen Mensch Zwang antun ....[314]

3.4.1. **Introduction**

In 1933, Hans Kelsen wrote that within the Pure Theory of Law the concept of legal personality evolved from a *Substanzbegriff* (a substantive concept) into a *Functionsbegriff* (functional concept) or *Relationsbegriff*.

> The Pure Theory of Law, recognizing the concept of person as a substantive concept, as the hypostatisation of ethico-political postulates (freedom and property, for example), re-

---

[313] See, e.g., R.A. Métall, Hans Kelsen. Leben und Werk (1969), hereinafter: Métall. Also, R. Walter, Hans Kelsen – Ein Leben im Dienste der Wissenschaft (1985); N. Bersier Ladavac, Hans Kelsen (1881-1973) Bibliographical Note and Bibliography, 9 *EJIL* 391-400 (1998).

[314] H. Kelsen, Gott und Staat (1922/23) [hereinafter: Gott und Staat], *in* Klecatsky and Marcic and Schambeck (Eds.), Die Wiener rechtstheoretische Schule: Schriften von Hans Kelsen, Adolf Merkl, Alfred Verdross (1968), at 177. Hereinafter: Die Wiener Schule.

solved this concept in the spirit of Kantian philosophy, where all substance is to be reduced to function.[315]

The two questions that immediately spring to mind, and which we will address here, are, first, *why* was Kelsen committed to bringing about this evolution? and, second, *how* did he accomplish this (essentially Kantian) transformation? This distinction, between why and how, is usually ignored and as a consequence Kelsen's theory is often considered excessively 'formalistic' and detached from the social reality within which the law operates.[316] However, when the distinction *is* introduced, this perception proves fundamentally mistaken. The Austrian – Viennese – context in which Kelsen lived has, in fact, significantly influenced his theory of law and state. In this respect, Kelsen has declared that:

> Angesichts des österreichischen Staates, der sich aus so vielen nach Rasse, Sprache, Religion und Geschichte verschiedenen Gruppen zusammensetzte, erwiesen sich Theorien, die die Einheit des Staates auf irgendeinen sozial-psychologischen oder sozial-biologischen Zusammenhang der juristisch zum Staat gehörigen Menschen zu gründen versuchten, ganz offenbar als Fictionen. Insofern diese Staatstheorie ein wesentlicher Bestandteil der Reinen Rechtslehre ist, kann die Reine Rechtslehre als eine spezifisch österreichische Theorie gelten.[317]

In order to find the answers to the questions of *why* and *how* Kelsen accomplished this legal theoretical shift, we will in particular examine them in relation to the Viennese socio-political and cultural-intellectual context.

With regard to *why*, the recognition and subsequent rejection of the concept of the person as a hypostatisation of the *ethical-political postulate of freedom* is an important first clue. My discussion of Kelsen's theory begins where the discussion of the broader Interbellum context in section 3.2 ended. At that point it was claimed that *the* issue at stake at the time was the contemporary crisis of democracy in modern mass society and its threat to the individual and his freedom. We have considered Ernst's paintings and the writings of Freud, Jaspers, Mannheim and Ortega y Gasset as examples of the prevailing intellectual climate, which oscillated between hope and fear concerning the role of the general public and the tension between individual and collective life. The same issue came up in the pre-

---

[315] H. Kelsen, The Pure Theory of Law, 'Labandism', and Neo-Kantianism. A Letter to Renato Treves (1933), in S.L. Paulson and B. Litschewski Paulson (Eds.), Normativity and Norms, Critical Perspectives on Kelsian Themes 174 (1998). Hereinafter: A Letter to Renato Treves.

[316] J.M. Kelly, A short History of Western Legal Theory 359 (1992). Also, Kennedy-1995, at 35-39, 45-47.

[317] H. Kelsen as cited in Métall, at 42. In the present inquiry, the emphasis will primarily be on the Austro-Viennese context. See, for a study of Kelsen's Pure Theory of Law in the German-Weimar context, D. Dyzenhaus, Legality and Legitimacy: Carl Schmitt, Hans Kelsen and Hermann Heller in Weimar (1997). The focus on the Austro-Viennese context is more than justified, not just by this quote from Kelsen but also by the fact that his quest for a Pure Theory of Law had already started with the publication of *Hauptprobleme der Staatsrechtslehre* in 1911, and that thus, by the early 1930s, Kelsen had been working on it for twenty years.

vious section when we discussed Brierly. In this section, it will become evident that the socio-political dynamics menacing democracy also played a significant part in the development of Kelsen's legal theory, not in the least when we consider *why* he deemed it necessary to revise the general conception of the law and the state, as well as the concept of legal personality. Kelsen experienced the threats to democracy and individual freedom at first hand and faced the political developments by formulating a legal theory that was free of all political and moral elements – perhaps paradoxically? We will see that in the politically strained and unstable Austro-Viennese context, which was virtually on the brink of chaos and civil war, a pure and formalistic concept of law and a concept of state viewed as *order* made perfect sense.

In the preface to his *Reine Rechtslehre*, Kelsen defended his strict separation between legal science and natural and social science and between law and politics, and his argument is fairly clear-cut: the independence of legal science and law itself simply has to (and, indeed, will) succeed because it serves social interests that are more powerful than politics: i.e., *social stability* and peace.[318] With the Pure Theory of Law, Kelsen took a stand against politics, ideology and justice within law and legal science. His objective was to achieve radical – and purifying – change: 'to free legal science of all foreign elements.' He consequently opposed the 'ideological character' of both traditional positivist and natural law theories, because, in his view, *both* schools had continuously failed to sever the ties between law and ideology or metaphysics. Even positivism he found to be insufficiently complete in its positivist orientation at a time in history that was *not* 'comparatively quiet,' but, on the contrary, lacked 'a relative balance of power among the various social factions.' To transcend the struggle of power politics among the (for example, antagonistic Austrian) social factions, legal science should be 'completely positivistic' and the concept of law freed from all 'ideological biases' and 'political interests.' Kelsen stressed that legal science or theory was a 'specialized field of enquiry' dealing with the phenomenon of law, which is *purely* normative and deals exclusively with 'ought', as distinct from nature or 'is', and as distinct from the realm of morality.[319]

Kelsen's opposition to both positivism and natural law theory is also marked by his arguments against 'ontological dualism.' Dualism in natural law theory served the ideology of the 'conservative legitimisation' of positive law by a divine natural law system. Dualism in positivist jurisprudence has contributed to the false distinction between, for example, law and state.[320] The dualism of law and state, the image of the state as a real and separate entity 'marching as God on

[318] H. Kelsen, Introduction to the Problems of Legal Theory (1992), at 4, this is a translation of the first edition (1934) of the *Reine Rechtslehre: Einleitung in die Rechtswissenschaftliche Problematik* by S. Paulson and B. Litschewiski Paulson (Eds.), hereinafter: Problems of Legal Theory.

[319] Id., at 7-22, at 14: 'The problem of the Pure Theory of Law is the specific autonomy of a realm of meaning.'

[320] Id., at 37.

earth', proved to be ethically entirely unbeneficial. In Kelsen's view, the ontological distinction between law and the meta-juridical state person was politically and morally threatening to democracy, rather than supportive of it. In his view, the traditional legal theories had been politically discredited because of this concept of state. It will become clear that Kelsen's attempt to purge the concept of law from politics and morality and his desire to identify law and state were as much politically as juridically motivated. In brief, Kelsen's challenge of the prevailing theories resulted in true *revisionist* legal scholarship in defence of democracy.

For understanding *how* Kelsen transformed the concept of legal personality – by means of the act of *reduction* –, an investigation into Viennese intellectual life will prove insightful, particularly where the act of reduction is related to the Kantian-inspired discussion on the epistemological problem of the practice of substantiating and personifying notions. During the 19th century, the notion of the state as a moral person had developed into the notion of the state as a sacred substantiated entity which was entirely above the law, adding to the state's glorification. In the light of the political developments, it was deemed necessary to reduce the substantiated concepts and to correct the epistemological fallacies they had caused. In line with this general intellectual project, Kelsen reduced the concept of legal personality to its proper limits, i.e., to that of 'a singular unity' rather than of a – '*veiled*' – spiritual *mythological* body.[321] To be able to grasp fully this act by Kelsen, we need to turn to the debate on language and epistemological problems and, in particular, to the ideas of the Viennese intellectuals Mauthner and Mach, and the German philosophers Vaihinger and Cassirer. We will discuss the first two when we paint the Viennese background and the latter two when we focus on Kelsen's reduction of legal personality. Any examination of their ideas needs, however, to be necessarily brief and will exclusively serve to illustrate Kelsen's conception of legal personality. I will show that Kelsen's revision of the concept of legal personality was part of the endeavour to escape the metaphysically contaminated conceptions of state and law and, as such, was an attempt to *demythologise* international law and the concept of legal personality, in particular.[322]

In brief, I clearly do not subscribe to the idea- underlying various introductions to Kelsen and his theory – of the '*Lebensfremdheit*' of his scholarship, nor do I agree that it had its origins in '*luftleeren Raum.*'[323] Instead, I intend to dem-

[321] H. Kelsen, Das Verhältnis von Staat und Recht im Lichte der Erkenntniskritik (1921), *Die Wiener Schule*, at 99. Hereinafter: Staat und Recht im Lichte der Erkenntniskritik. See also, Kelsen, Allgemeine Staatslehre 11 (1925). Hereinafter: Allgemeine Staatslehre. See also, H. Kelsen, Von Wesen und Wert der Demokratie, 47 *Archiv für Sozialwissenschaft und Sozialpolitik* 57 (1920/21), hereinafter: Von Wesen und Wert der Demokratie.

[322] See, on the mythological stage international law still found itself in, Staat und Recht im Lichte der Erkenntniskritik, at 101-102. Also, Problems of Legal Theory, at 108: international law as a primitive legal system.

[323] Métall, at 110 and 106. Or to use Kelsen's expression of this criticism: 'that by remaining entirely free of all politics, it stands apart from the ebb and flow of life and is therefore worthless in

onstrate that Kelsen's redefinition of legal personality was influenced by the contemporary socio-political and intellectual developments in Austria and mainly in Vienna, the city where Kelsen lived half of his life. The treatment of Kelsen's thinking in this section follows a by now fairly well-known track. First, we will briefly address the socio-political and intellectual Viennese context of his time. Subsequently, we will concentrate on Kelsen's conception of (international) law and pay special attention to the four elements, which we have previously used to analyse Brierly's scholarship as well as Interbellum scholarship in general, in order to uncover the particularly *revisionist* characteristics of his scholarship. Finally, in the paragraph on Kelsen's formulation of the concept of legal personality, the various threads will come together and I will reveal what Kelsen meant by his use of the concept of legal person in his writings.

3.4.2. **The Viennese Context**

... behind each "book" there is a man with his conflicts.[324]

3.4.2.1. *Introduction*

Hans Kelsen lived in Vienna (from early childhood to the age of 49) during the time when it was evolving from being the dazzling first city of the Austro-Hungarian Empire to being the capital of the Austrian Republic.[325] During WWI, he experienced, at first hand, the final decline of the *kaiserliches und königliches* Habsburg Empire in his capacity of close and trusted advisor to the Minister of Defence concerning questions of both constitutional and international law as well as issues of a more political nature.[326] Realising that the *k.u.k.* army and the House of Habsburg were the only two elements keeping the Empire together, Kelsen expected it to collapse soon and felt that a transformation was unavoidable. During the last month of WWI, he worked on a procedure for the calm and peaceful transformation of the Empire into a confederation of nation states, either with or without the Emperor as the Head of State, to avoid further economic and political decline. Kelsen was therefore involved from the very beginning in the political, constitutional process to somehow preserve as well as radically transform the political constellation in such a way that unity and a solid foundation of the state would prevent the various nationalities from reaching a state of active antagonism. After the war, Kelsen returned to the Law Faculty of the University of Vienna and became Professor of Constitutional and Administrative Law there

---

terms of science.' Problems of Legal Theory, at 3. By then, Kelsen had been developing the Pure Theory for over two decades.

[324] H. Kelsen, General Theory of Law and State 430 (1945).

[325] See, e.g., on 'Wiener Welt' between 1848 and 1914, Europe: A History, at 849-850.

[326] Métall, at 18-28. Kelsen was, in particular, assigned to prepare the division of the joint Austro-Hungarian army in the light of a post-war constitutional reform.

in 1919. His involvement in state affairs, however, continued, as in October 1918 he was assigned to the drafting of the new constitution, which had to establish a parliamentary democracy with a sufficiently centralised authority so as to prevent the *Länder* from disintegrating.[327] The constitution of the German-Austrian Republic was proclaimed on 1 October 1920. The following year, Kelsen became a member of the Republic's Constitutional Court. During the 1920s, political tension in Austria mounted to dangerous and even state-threatening levels. In 1930, the political conflict between the progressive left and the conservative Catholic faction caused Kelsen to leave the Court. He moved to Cologne to teach public international law. In 1933, Kelsen left Germany for Geneva, where he lived until 1940 when he immigrated to the USA.

Various sources on the intellectual-cultural milieu of Vienna during the 1900-1930s reveal that Kelsen was a prominent and respected participant in the city's intellectual and cultural life.[328] When Kelsen left the Constitutional Court, and ultimately Vienna, this attracted considerable attention in the newspapers. In an attempt to prevent Kelsen's departure, a group of 24 Viennese intellectuals stated in the *Neue Freie Presse* of 10 July 1930 that his leaving would be a great loss to Vienna's intellectual life.[329] Viennese intellectual life during these decades was extremely rich and, in fact, too diverse to do justice here in this brief overview. Discussions in these circles were also marked by the tense political environment in which they took place. Problems as regards communication and mutual understanding in the multi-national (i.e., multi-cultural and multi-lingual) Empire were already quite profound before 1914. Since 'problems of identity and communication plagued Viennese society at every level – political and social, individual and even international,' language, communication, mutual understanding and, following naturally, epistemological issues, required urgent attention. The Empire's minorities used their individual languages as *the* instrument to assert their own identity: 'language was the basis of social as well as political identity in the bitter struggles for civil rights which marked the final years of Habsburg rule before the cataclysm of 1914.'[330] This earned language a place on the philosophical agenda where it remained to influence post-WWI thinking. Paraphrasing Toulmin's statement on the 17th-century Rationalists, one could say that the main task incumbent on Viennese intellectuals after WWI consisted of finding a *depoliticised* means of communication. Against the background of this quest for *demyth-*

---

[327] Id., at 34 *et seq.*

[328] See, e.g., Wittgenstein's Vienna, at 15, 133, 241; P. Op de Coul (Ed.), Tekens van Moderniteit: Wenen in het Interbellum 8, 29-30 (1998); Musil also reports Kelsen's whereabouts in his diaries of these years, R. Musil, Tagebücher, Aphorismen Essays und Reden 315, 344, 352, 543 (1955 ed. by A. Frisé – Gesammelte Werke); Also, Musil in 1939 in a letter to a friend, R. Musil, Prosa, Dramen späte Briefe 750 (Herausgabe by A. Frisé 1957). See also, C. Jabloner, Kelsen and his Circle: The Viennese Years, 9 *EJIL* 368 (1998).

[329] Métall, at 57.

[330] Wittgenstein's Vienna, at 65. For Karl Kraus' response to the dehumanising forces dominating Viennese society and the importance this had for the intellectual involvement in the crisis of language, see, chapter 3. 'Language and Society: Karl Kraus and the last days of Vienna,' id., at 67-91.

ologised and/or *depoliticised* language and communication, Kelsen's concept of law, stripped of all political elements, is much less surprising. With regard to the political problems in the multinational Empire and subsequently the Austrian State, the notions of nation (or: *Volk*) and state came under especially close scrutiny. Nominalism was strong among Viennese intellectuals like Mauthner and Kraus, writers with whose ideas Kelsen was familiar. In the next section, I will briefly characterise both the political and the intellectual context to the extent necessary for an analysis of Kelsen's transformation of both the concept of law and legal personality.

3.4.2.2. *'The polluted political atmosphere'* [331]

Until 1916, Vienna was the capital of an Empire which encompassed eleven constituent nations.[332] As Kelsen's autobiographical notes elucidate, the Pure Theory, because of its roots, may indeed count as a specifically Austrian theory. This is explained best against the background of the Dual Monarchy's multi-national nature. The specifically Austrian character of Kelsen's theory is precisely its supra-national character, even 'radically universalistic character.'[333] This is indeed in conformity with the contemporary Viennese 'supranational, cosmopolitan consciousness,' which was 'the dynasty's only hope for surviv[ing]' the problem of the multitude of nationalities.[334] Political nationalism was now 'mass-based,' putting significant pressure on the political system.[335] The irrational force of self-destructive *Kriegsbegeisterung* had been allowed to surface in the Empire.[336] As the Liberals failed to modernise the Empire, they lost power to the Social Democrats and Catholic Conservatives who came to dominate politics around the turn of the century. German nationalism mushroomed in Habsburg society and only served further radicalisation. The Emperor continued to Germanise the bureaucracy, even though minorities were already extremely poorly represented and this elicited an even stronger response from non-German nationalists.[337] Politics de-

[331] A Letter to Renato Treves, at 172. See *infra* footnote 337.

[332] Wittgenstein's Vienna, at 38.

[333] Kelsen stated that the Pure Theory was of a 'radically universalistic character,' A Letter to Renato Treves, at 172.

[334] Wittgenstein's Vienna, at 41.

[335] Id., at 58, 49-66.

[336] J. Koch, Tussen Habsburg en Hitler: Cultuur en politiek in Oostenrijk, 1918-1938, *in* P. Op de Coul (Ed.), Tekens van Moderniteit: Wenen in het Interbellum (1998), at 12. Hereinafter: Tussen Habsburg en Hitler.

[337] With regard to feelings of nationalism it is interesting to note that Kelsen was attacked for having produced an 'un-German' theory of law. Kelsen in August 1933: 'The Pure Theory of Law first made the Kantian philosophy really fruitful for the law by developing it further rather than inclining to the letter of Kant's own legal philosophy. If one recognizes in Kant's work a truly German philosophy, then the Pure Theory of Law is the most German of all legal philosophies developed in Germany since Kant. I address this to those who do not understand the Pure Theory of Law and therefore believe that they can successfully combat it in the politically polluted atmosphere of our time by describing it as 'un-German'.' A Letter to Renato Treves, at 172.

veloped into mass politics under the spell of demagogic and collective creeds. Already *before* the War, Vienna therefore experienced 'the problems of alienation in modern mass society, which spread throughout the rest of Europe only after World War One.'[338] Living in Vienna, Kelsen witnessed these problems early on in his career, at the formative stage of his thinking. Hence, the genesis of the Pure Theory coincided with the turbulent final years of the Empire and its evolvement continued after the War and the foundation of the Austrian Republic, at a time when the stability of the state and its democratic system were under permanent threat.

During the 1920s, Austrian democracy turned into what could be termed a *Stimmungsdemokratie*. Tension mounted and from 1923 onwards all political parties had their own special assault groups. The political situation at that time may be characterised as a 'latent civil war'[339] as the social forces raging among the masses intermingled with the fierce internal confrontations between Red Vienna and Catholic conservative Austria. The result was an extremely explosive cocktail that continued to endanger the unity of the Austrian Republic for years.

The Social Democrats in their political programme held on to the Liberal 'ideals of reason and progress,' counting on socio-economic progress and democratic reforms.[340] The Nationalist and Catholic movements were, however, anti-liberal, class-based and demagogic, and they supported a reactionary form of Catholicism as the state's driving philosophy.[341] These movements were strongly represented in most parts of Austria, with the exception of Vienna. Since the entry into force of the new constitution, the Social Democrats were no longer part of the government and their power had been reduced to the city of Vienna and its bordering areas. Due to the way in which the representation was geographically distributed, the internal political conflict between the progressive Social Democrats and the conservative Catholics was, at the same time, a conflict between Vienna (urban) and the rest of the country (rural).

The internal political schism was tremendously harmful to the process of developing a common state identity.[342] Before 1914, the Habsburg society had already undergone a crisis of both individual and social identity due to the Empire's nationality problems, but in the period from 1918 to 1938 the Austrians also failed to develop an independent Republican identity due to the overwhelming support for the cause of joining Germany, especially in, for example, Tyrol

[338] Wittgenstein's Vienna, at 61.

[339] Tussen Habsburg en Hitler, at 19.

[340] Wittgenstein's Vienna, at 50 and 53.

[341] Id., at 48-49. Also, Tussen Habsburg en Hitler, at 17.

[342] 'None of the pre-1914 Powers collapsed more completely as a result of the war than did the Austro-Hungarian Dual Monarchy; nor did any other city see its *raison d'etre* more suddenly destroyed than Vienna. As Austria lost its *Imperial identity*, and had to construct a *Republican identity* from scratch [emphasis added], the simultaneous defeat of Newton's natural philosophy-the basis of the Modern Cosmopolis-by Einstein's relativity physics, called for equally 'constructive' efforts in science and the arts. It is no wonder, then, that in Vienna, of all places, the cultural ambitions of the 17th century were revived with special enthusiasm.' Cosmopolis, at 157. Emphasis added.

and Salzburg.[343] The Paris international Peace Treaties, however, prohibited this option from ever being made a reality, a prohibition that had come about under pressure from France, in particular.[344] The recently formed Austrian State had trouble finding a new and unifying state identity, which could set it apart from the strong pro-German nationalist tendencies. This was also reflected in the conservative Catholic government's '*Anlehnung an das faschistiche Italien.*'[345] The lack of a state identity of its own evidently affected the stability and solid foundations of the newly established state. The political developments consequently hindered the process of healthy state building and the strengthening of democracy. On the contrary, they bore every trait necessary to fall prey to some kind of (nationalist, communist, or fascist) *Massenwahn*. The former 'other half' of the Dual Monarchy, Hungary, moreover, fell victim to totalitarianism as early as 1922, which the Viennese could not have failed to notice. Kelsen witnessed this conflict between the Viennese Social Democrats and Conservative rural Austria from very close up.

In 1927, Kelsen, himself a Viennese citizen and a member of the judiciary, if not a Conservative, was a witness to the mass uprising against the judiciary.[346] The situation had become volatile and susceptible to the influences of collective emotion after a worker had been wrongly convicted. As a result, on 15 July, socialist Vienna staged a revolt against the right-wing, conservative-dominated judiciary. In his memoirs, Elias Canetti reports his experiences of being caught up in the crowd demonstrating in front of the Viennese Hall of Justice.[347] This made such an impression on him that he defined the event as '*seit dem Tode des Vaters der einschneidendste [Tag] meines Lebens*,'[348] and looked back on it as the day which had caused him to spend the next 30 years analysing the phenomenon of the masses and eventually publish the socio-psychological study *Masse und Macht* in 1960.[349]

What had started as a legal conflict (the *Ehedispens* cases[350]) during the late 1920s concerning issues of divorce, dispensation and the permission to remarry in an Austria that was for the most part Roman Catholic, had changed into a situ-

[343] Tussen Habsburg en Hitler, at 16-20. There, 98.8 and 99.3% of those entitled to vote supported unification with Germany.

[344] Id., at 18. See, Treaty of St Germain, Art. 88: 'independence of Austria is inalienable'.

[345] Métall, at 48.

[346] The revolt was caused by a court decision in which a murderer was found not guilty of killing a worker, a decision that was celebrated by the government party as being fair and just. The Viennese workers spontaneously revolted against this miscarriage of justice and gathered in front of the Hall of Justice. 'Es war eines von jenen nicht zu häufigen öffentlichen Ereignissen, die eine ganze Stadt so sehr ergreifen, daß sie danach nie mehr dieselbe ist.' E. Canetti, Die Fackel im Ohr, Lebensgeschichte 1921-1931, at 274 (1980 ed., Carl Hanser Verlag). Hereinafter: Die Fackel im Ohr.

[347] Elias Canetti (1905-1994), writer of the socio-psychological study 'Masse und Macht' and other essays; Nobel Prize winner of 1980.

[348] Die Fackel im Ohr, at 276. See also, on the mass revolt, Métall, at 48.

[349] Die Fackel im Ohr, at 274-282.

[350] See, Métall, at 47-57.

ation that opened up a chasm between the City and rural Austria and that resulted in Kelsen's departure from the Court, since it was he who had led the Court's action to validate divorce and the possibility to remarry. The developing legal practice with regard to divorce threatened the authority of the atate as well as the people's faith in the Austrian state apparatus, as the state on the one hand validated marriages through its administration, while, on the other hand, these same marriages could be determined invalid by the state's judiciary.[351] Evidently, this crisis of authority was unacceptable and the authority of the state needed to be restored immediately. The Constitutional Court decided to recognise the decisions from the Executive and to overrule the lower judiciary. The internal political conflict then escalated: the Catholic Government, i.e., the Executive, unleashed an attack on both the Legislature (in the Austrian parliament the Social Democrats formed a strong minority) and on the Constitutional Court. The *Ehedispens* cases in fact served to disguise the broader conflict concerning constitutional reforms and the dissolution of the Constitutional Court, which, once dissolved, could be filled with new, more Conservative, judges. The Catholic Conservative party in effect blackmailed the Social Democrats into either accepting constitutional reform together with the Court's dissolution or relinquishing their last bastion of power, the city of Vienna, by accepting considerable limitations upon the city's autonomy. In 1929, '*Die Meute war gegen Kelsen losgelassen*,'[352] when the Catholic press attacked his person by making sexual and anti-Semitic insinuations and alleging that he had had a hand in the Court's decision to recognise the competence of the Executive in the questions concerning marriage and thus allow the possibility of divorce. The conflict did eventually result in the dissolution of the Court and the judges were discharged from office as of 15 February 1930, in complete accordance with the wishes and intentions of the Catholic Party, which had succeeded in blackmailing the Social Democrats into lending their support.[353]

After Kelsen had left the country,[354] the situation escalated further: the Austrian parliament was sidelined in April 1933, and in February 1934 democracy ended in bloodshed when once again Red Vienna revolted against the conserva-

[351] Kelsen: 'Derselbe Staat, der durch seine Verwaltungsbehörde die Schließung einer Ehe ausdrücklich erlaubte, erklärte durch seine Gerichte eben diese Ehe für ungültig. Die Autorität des Staates konnte kaum in ärgerer Weise erschüttert werden.' Kelsen's autobiographical notes, id., at 51.

[352] Id., at 54.

[353] Kelsen: 'Der Gerichtshof erfüllte lediglich seine Aufgabe, die bestehende Kompetenzgrenze zwischen Gericht und Verwaltungsbehörde aufrechtzuerhalten. ... sein pflichtgemäßes Eintreten für das bestehende Recht und die auf diesem Recht beruhende Autorität des Staates, fürte zu seiner Auflösung.' Id., at 54.

[354] Being known to sympathise with the Social Democrats, although not a Party member, Kelsen was offered to return as a judge. He refused, as it would have been impossible to function properly in a Court in which 12 of the 14 judges were appointed by the Government of Catholics and Nationalists. Moreover, the appointment of members of the judiciary by the governing political parties was an absolute disgrace to democracy.

tive Catholic government. This time, 1500 workers were killed, and '*the word "Freedom" was choked by the rope*,' as Spender lamented, afraid for '*this Vienna, emerging upon Further terrible ghosts from dreams.*'[355]

As the most distinguished constitutional lawyer in the country and drafter of the Republican constitution, as well as a Viennese citizen, Kelsen had, from an early stage and from close up, been a prime witness to the problems of the state, i.e., the threat to social stability, the danger to the individual citizen and the erosion of individual freedom in modern (mass) society. Since the final years of the Empire, the socio-psychological dimensions of the internal political tension and the (factional, i.e., nationalist) antagonism encountered in Austria necessarily undermined the hitherto firmly rooted belief that the state was a socio-psychological unity. The prevailing (German) theories of state endangered the Austrian situation and were generally wrong in cognitive terms. Under these circumstances, a state, in order to preserve stability, would need to exclude all social and socio-psychological factors from its self-definition and identity.

The importance attributed to (the rejection of) social psychology in Kelsen's scholarship stems from his critique of legal theory, as well as from his way of dealing with actual political problems. Kelsen had discussed the problems of the *Massenseele* in relation to democracy and the nature of the state from relatively early on. In 1911 already he contended that jurisprudence had to be liberated from socio-psychological notions, such as 'the collective consciousness' and 'the collective will', which had developed into 'independent, metaphysical substances' and had forced an unwelcome entrance into legal theory. The psychological collective will in the legal role of the 'Will of the State' is an idea that Kelsen abhorred: it is '*ein Phantom.*'[356] In his defence of parliamentary democracy, Kelsen's line of argument on the law and the state came to the fore: in legal theory, the will is a purely legal construction, i.e., the legal order itself. The powers of the legislature are based on the constitution and not on the social phenomenon of the people. Kelsen went on to discuss the relationship between social psychology and the law and jurisprudence and the concept of the state in many of his earlier writings. In August 1921, Kelsen visited Freud in Seefeld (in the North of Tyrol), where they went hiking together.[357] In 1922, Kelsen responded extensively to Freud's theory of mass psychology, for example, in *Der Begriff des*

---

[355] S. Spender, Vienna 34 and 42 (1934), poem narrating the socialist workers' uprisings of February 1934 against the (pro-Italy, pro-Fascist) conservative Catholic Chancellor of Austria, E. Dolfuss, who had been elected in 1932. The uprisings amounted to a three-day civil war in which even the air force was ordered to participate. In February 1934, the Social Democrats were declared illegal.

[356] Kelsen, Über Grenzen zwischen juristischer und soziologischer Methode 29 (1911).

[357] E. Jones, The Life and Work of Sigmund Freud 79-80 (Vol. 3, 1957). Another scholar influenced by the Freudian idea of a 'totemistic' society and social evolution was the Russian legal historian Paul Vinogradoff (1854-1925). See, Historical types of International Law: lectures delivered in the University of Leiden, *Bibliotheca Visseriana* (1923).

Staates und die Sozialpsychologie. Mit besonderer Berücksichtigung von Freuds Theorie der Masse and in *Der Soziologische und der Juristische Staatsbegriff*, and also in his *Allgemeine Staatslehre* and in *Vom Wesen und Wert der Demokratie.*[358] In the midst of the internal political tension, Kelsen crusaded to defend political and moral relativism and parliamentary democracy. In his view, the parliament was the place to debate moral and political issues from different ideological perspectives on the basis of mutual respect and the recognition that absolutist values go hand in hand with autocracy. He believed that only moral and political relativism were compatible with democracy and served social stability much better, by means of the inclusion of minority positions, than the authoritarian practice of excluding non-ruling social groups from politics altogether. Kelsen explained: '*Der Relativismus ist daher die Weltanschauung, die der demokratische Gedanke voraussetzt.*'[359]

Bearing this political context in mind, we will see that the idea of the state as a legal order as derived from the Pure Theory does indeed have social and political relevance. In this view, law is a technique for creating social stability and securing order. In defence of democracy, concepts of sovereignty and the state that were distinct from the glorification of the sovereign or the mythical state person were essential. After all, the latter propositions would easily lead to a state of totalitarianism, in which the individual would merge into the collective and be rendered powerless and unfree; democracy would turn into *mob*ocracy.

---

[358] Der Begriff des Staates und die Sozialpsychologie. Mit besonderer Berücksichtigung von Freuds Theorie der Masse, VIII *IMAGO-Zeitschrift für Anwendung der Psychoanalyse auf die Geisteswissenschaften* 97 (1922); Der Soziologische und der Juristische Staatsbegriff (1922); Allgemeine Staatslehre (1925); Also, Kelsen in 1927: Der Staatsbegriff und die Psychoanalyse, Almanach Internationaler Psychoanalytischer Verlag Wien (1927), Die Wiener Schule, at 135-141. See also, Von Wesen und Wert der Demokratie, at 50-85. Kelsen published a 2nd rev. ed., in 1929. Emphasis added. Kelsen explicitly stated that the social revolution incited by WWI now required a review of democratic political values and an examination of what they were developing into.

[359] Von Wesen und Wert der Demokratie, at 83. Kelsen elaborated that: 'Die für die Demokratie so charakterische Herrschaft der Majorität unterscheidet sich von jeder anderen Herrschaft dadurch, daß die eine Opposition – die Minorität – ihrem innersten Wesen nach nicht nur begrifflich voraussetzt, sondern auch politisch anerkennt und in den Grund- und Freiheitsrechten, im Prinzipe der Proportionalität schützt. Je stärker aber die Minorität, desto mehr wird die Politik der Demokratie eine Politik des Kompromisses, wie auch für die relativistische Weltanschauung nichts charakterischer ist, als die Tendenz zum vermittelnden Ausgleich zwischen zwei gegensätlichen Standpunkten, von denen man sich keinen ganz und vorbehaltslos und unter völliger Negation des anderen zu eigen machen kann. Die Relativität des Wertes, den ein bestimmtes politisches Glaubensbekenntnis aufrichtet, die Unmöglichkeit, für ein politisches Programm, für ein politisches Ideal – bei aller subjektiven Hingebung, bei aller persönlichen Ueberzeugung – absolute Gültigkeit zu beanschruchen, zwingt gebieterisch zu einer Ablehnung auch des politischen Absolutismus, ... der Absolutismus ... jede ... ausschließenden Gruppe ... ... Das ist der eigentliche Sinn jenes politischen Systems, das wir Demokratie nennen, und das darum dem politischen Absolutismus entgegenstellt werden darf, eil es der Ausdruck eines politischen Relativismus ist.' Id., at 83-84.

3.4.2.3. *Intellectual context: conceptual monsters*

> Die meisten Menschen leiden an dieser geistigen Schwäche, zu glauben, weil ein Wort da sei, muß es auch das Wort für etwas sein; weil ein Wort da sei, muß dem Worte etwas Wirkliches entsprechen.
>
> *Fritz Mauthner*

In the section above on the general jurisprudential context, it has been indicated that during the 19th century the concept of legal personality underwent a process of reification. This means that an abstract or metaphysical term is endowed with *reality*, or given actual, substantial existence.[360] Notions such as the state and sovereignty, and *Volk* and *Geist* thereby developed from merely abstract, metaphysical notions into extremely powerful political instruments capable of spawning (nationalist) mass movements.[361] And even in the inorganic theory, the personification of the state – albeit it as an abstraction – led to the fundamental notion of the state as a meta-juridical entity: the state as a divine person above the law. In the European and, in particular, Viennese context of the early 20th century, the threat emanating from the political consequences of this philosophical practice to attribute reality to metaphysical notions contributed to the rising criticism of the 'metaphysical' in general. In discussions, the terms 'mystical' and 'mythological' were frequently used to put the metaphysical in a bad light and to stress the irrational nature of metaphysical realism. Progressive Viennese intellectuals, who during the final years of the Dual Monarchy had already discerned the dangers looming on the horizon, turned against this practice of producing, what Ernst Mach called, 'conceptual monsters.'[362]

Ernst Mach's ideas were highly influential at the time: '[f]rom poetry to philosophy of law, from physics to social theory, Mach's influence was all-pervasive in Austria and elsewhere.'[363] Mach's position in the epistemological debate was

---

360 Wittgenstein's Vienna, at 123.

361 Here, I would like to refer to the opening lines of Ernst Cassirer's book The Myth of the State (1945), where he introduces his objective to resolve or analyse the modern (totalitarian) political myths, which amidst the post-WWI crisis had developed into such powerful political weapons because '[i]n desperate situations man will always have recourse to desperate means – and our present day political myths have been such desperate means,' by observing that 'in the period between the first and the second World Wars, we have not only passed through a severe crisis of political and social life but have also been confronted with quite new theoretical problems. We experienced a radical change in the forms of political thought. ... Perhaps the most important and the most alarming feature in this development ... is the appearance of a new power: the power of mythical thought. The preponderance of mythical thought over rational thought is obvious.' Language played an important role because of its magical power or function. Being used 'magically' with the purpose of 'produc[ing] certain effects and ... stir[ring] up certain emotions,' language could, amidst the desperate circumstances, become a powerful political weapon and contribute to the loss of individual responsibility and to moral subjectivity to the collective. Thus, the individual as the autonomous moral subject no longer acted as his own law-maker and consequently, from the Kantian perspective, freedom was lost. In totalitarian systems, the leader plays the role of the magician. Id., at 3, 279, and 283 *et seq*.

362 Wittgenstein's Vienna, at 123.

363 Id., at 133.

'sceptical' and anti-metaphysical. In his view, metaphysics actually amounted to mysticism and did not belong to the realm of science or philosophy. Mach perceived knowledge as the collection or sum total of sense data, 'elements' that can actually be 'sensed' and, therefore, empirically known. He contended that it was science's task to *reduce* knowledge to these elements.[364] Its function was to bring about the 'reduction' of knowledge to the most efficient and simple description of experience, also known as Mach's principle of the economy of thought. Knowledge of the 'elements' is possible, but beyond that – transcending the elements and thus entering the realm of metaphysics – cognition is impossible and would put one on the road to mysticism. Mach's critique of the mystifying force of reifications – the 'conceptual monsters' – as well as the idea of reduction deeply influenced both Fritz Mauthner and Hans Kelsen[365] and Mach's ideas left visible traces in their work.

As a Viennese journalist, the legally trained Fritz Mauthner's job was to observe the contemporary political situation and as such he came across the mystifying, mythologising use of language in politics. He lashed out against the tendency to reify and formulated a nominalist critique of language:[366]

> The immediate stimulus to Mauthner's nominalist "critique of language" was his reaction against the political witchcraft he saw being exercised all around him by the use of such grandiose abstract terms as Volk and Geist. ... Mauthner came to epistemology and the theory of language through marrying a liberal antiauthoritarian position in politics to a Machian empiricism in philosophy.[367]

Mauthner's nominalism was therefore not simply a linguistic issue, but was rooted as much in his anti-authoritarian political convictions. When Mauthner argued, for example, that all philosophical problems are in essence problems of language ('Philosophy is theory of knowledge. Theory of knowledge is critique of language')[368] we may add that in this case a critique of language also included a critique of politics. Mauthner agreed that the human mind naturally tends towards

---

[364] Janik explains Mach's perception of abstract knowledge: 'Abstract conceptions, ideas, representation, are similarly reduced to sense data, by being identified as species concepts which enable us to deal with groups of "elements" efficiently.' Id., at 134.

[365] See, Wittgenstein's Vienna, at 133. See, for Kelsen's own confirmation of Mach's influence on his theory, A Letter to Renato Treves, at 174. See, e.g., for Kelsen's and Mach's critique of the *Substanzbegriff*, Staat und Recht im Lichte der Erkenntniskritik, at 101-102.

[366] Nominalism traditionally considers names and words as corresponding to individual entities and sense experiences. Concept or abstract words should be understood as descriptions of collections of these individual elements. Mauthner went one step further and argued 'names are at best *metaphors* for what the senses perceive.' '[H]e was, [therefore] sceptical about our capacity to know the world.' Wittgenstein's Vienna, at 122. Mauthner viewed his own work as belonging to the British tradition of nominalism and empiricism, (he considered himself indebted not only to Kant but also to Locke and mainly to Schopenhauer). Id., at 123.

[367] Id., at 121-122.

[368] F. Mauthner, *Wörterbuch der Philosophie: Neue Beitrage zu einer Kritik der Sprache* xi, as cited *in* Wittgenstein's Vienna, at 122.

reification, but this tendency should be vigorously opposed for being a source of 'practical injustice and evil in the world.'

In science, these ["conceptual monsters"] include such misleading notions as force, laws of nature, matter, atoms and energy; in philosophy, substance, objects and the absolute; among religious ideas, God, the devil and natural law; in politics and social affairs, obsession with notions like the Race, the Culture, and the Language, and with their purity or profanation.[369]

The 'conceptual monsters' were not only monstrous because of their epistemologically misleading quality, but also due to the part they played in politics. By reifying a metaphysical abstraction into an actual, existing entity, it becomes substantially static, fixed, concrete and can thus be easily turned into a source of exclusion and intolerance. The reified concepts of state and sovereignty were therefore considered monstrous notions that sustained absolutist power, authoritarian thinking and moral absolutism, having been given an independent existence in the factual world and been endowed with human properties, like the ability to will and act. As such, the metaphysical, which is in essence unknowable, is treated as a factual 'thing', with 'properties', which can be the object of sensory knowledge.

Mauthner sought an alternative and the approach he proposed may be explained by his view on language: 'there is no such thing as *language*, but only individual human beings who use language.'[370] Mauthner demonstrated that the way in which language is used, the meaning attributed to certain terms, results in the recognition of entities – things – which in reality are not factual or substantive, but merely functional abstractions. Kelsen's appreciation of Mauthner's reasoning may be gleaned from the page-long quote from Mauthner's study on Schopenhauer and the will in Kelsen's *Staat und Recht im Lichte der Erkenntniskritik* (1921).[371] Mauthner felt, as did Mach, that knowledge of the 'will' is only possible in the form of knowledge of the action of someone 'willing' something. We cannot know the pure will, only the will functioning. For this reason, Mauthner propounded the 'heterogenetic theory of will', in which the will is not a primary and homogeneous fact of the mental life of man, but conceived of as a product or sum of psychological factors, rendering it secondary and abstract.[372] The will is not a concrete substantial object, cognisable as such, but is,

---

[369] Id., at 123.

[370] Id., at 126.

[371] Staat und Recht im Lichte der Erkenntniskritik, at 136-137. Mauthner demonstrated that Schopenhauer had also reified the abstract notion of will. In asserting that there exists an object to the word, a practice Mauthner called 'word superstition' (*Wortaberglauben*), 'in attempting to reach beyond the word *will* to a real entity-namely, the Will, ... Schopenhauer too had committed the fallacy of reification.' Wittgenstein's Vienna, at 125.

[372] Staat und Recht im Lichte der Erkenntniskritik, at 135-136. '... daß der sogenannte *Wille* als Kraft ein mythologisches Abstraktum ist, in seinen einzelnen Erscheinungen jedoch nur ein *Gefühl*, also ein Gefühlseindruck, der sich den spezifischen Sinneseindrücken nur durch seine Unbestimmt-

on the contrary, only discernible in its functioning as a composition of willed actions. Similarly, so we will see, Kelsen attacked the substantiated will of the state and dissolved it into a legal order composed of the individual will of citizens, which, because of the norms they promulgate and adhere to, together form the state will. The parallel is immanent: there is no such *thing* as will, law or state, only individual human beings who use law and create law. For our understanding of Kelsen's inner and outer way of thinking, the problem of reification or *Hypostasierung* and Mauthner's criticism of this practice are quite insightful. It is fair to say that Mauthner's theory of language and Kelsen's theory of law were both affected by the 'polluted political atmosphere.'

During the 1920s, Kelsen was not the only member of the Viennese school of law to be familiar with Mauthner's ideas.[373] Kelsen explicitly referred to Mauthner's thinking on quite a number of occasions,[374] where he agreed that reifying or mythologising language did indeed pose a profound epistemological problem in legal theory because of its tendency towards falsification.

> Die Technik d[er] Hypostasierung mit ihrer Verdoppelung des Erkenntnis-Gegenstandes und ihrem Gefolge von Scheinproblemen ist durchaus die gleiche, die schon in der *mythologischen* Naturanschauung sich betätigte, die hinter jedem Baum eine Dryas, hinter jeder Quelle einen Quellgott, hinter dem Mond Luna und hinter der Sonne Apollo vorstellte. Vom Standpunkt der Erkenntniskritik stellt sich diese mythologische Methode, die schon kraft unserer substantivischen Sprache – wie sie Fritz Mauthner erkannt und genannt hat – noch tief in alle Wissenschaften, insbesondere aber in die Geisteswissenschaften hineinragt, als die zu überwindende, weil fehlerhafte Tendenz dar, die von der Erkenntnis allein zu bestimmenden, durch Erkenntnis allein bestimmbaren *Relationen* in feste *Dinge*, die Function in *Substanz* umzudeuten.[375]

Consequently, Kelsen began to speak out against the practice of reification (*Substanzialisierung*) in legal theory and against the resulting 'metaphysical realistic' state concept, in particular.[376] Legal theory and its conceptual constructions

---

heit underscheidet.' Mauthner, as cited, *in* Staat und Recht im Lichte der Erkenntniskritik, at 136-137.

[373] See, e.g., A. Verdross, Eine Antinomie der Rechtstheorie, *in* Die Wiener Schule, at 1379; A. Merkl, Die politische Freiheit als Gegenstand wissenschaftlicher Erkenntnis, *in* Die Wiener Schule, at 736.

[374] See, e.g., Kelsen, Der Staatsbegriff und die Psychoanalyse (1927), *in* Die Wiener Schule, at 212. In 1925, in the opening line of *Allgemeine Staatslehre*, Kelsen referred to Mauthner's remark that the word 'state' had become meaningless, at 1, see, on Mauthner in relation to the legal subject, id., at 62. Also, H. Kelsen, Das Problem der Souveränität und die Theorie des Völkerrechts 18ff (1920), hereinafter: Das Problem der Souveränität.

[375] Der Staatsbegriff und die Psychoanalyse (1927), at 212.

[376] See, e.g. Kelsen, Problem der Souveränität, at 19ff: 'Sofern die herrschende Lehre den Staat als "Person," als "Träger" des Rechts vorstellt, leistet der Begriff des Staates der Rechtswissenschaft die analoge Funktion wie der Begriff der Substanz der Naturwissenschaft. Auf diese sehr interessante Parallele verweist Sander ... Er nennt den Staat die "kategoriale Beharrlichkeitsform des funktionalen Zusammenhanges von Rechtssätzen." Es handelt sich bei der Staatsperson eben um nichts anderes als um den personifikativen Ausdruck für die Einheit eines Systems von Rechts-

(*Begriffsbildung*) were, in Kelsen's view, still mired in this primitive, mythological phase and held captive by '*unserer substantivischen, durchaus anthropomorphen Sprache.*'[377]

When dealing with the personality of the state in his early work, Kelsen not only referred to Mauthner, but also to the neo-Kantian German philosopher Hans Vaihinger. The latter dealt with the process of doubling – *Verdoppelung* – the object of cognition, which occurs when an abstract concept is reified into a separate entity, and the confusing effect this produced. Vaihinger, in his book *Philosophie des Als-ob*, established that this was characteristic of the act of 'personifying fictions'.[378] Vaihinger's book was the subject of Kelsen's article *Zur Theorie der juristischen Fictionen* (1919). In this article, Kelsen concentrated on the epistemological value of fictions as an instrument of cognition in law and as a valuable tool for knowing the legal reality. I will deal with his argument on the concept of 'person' in this regard below. Suffice it here to say that Kelsen greatly appreciated Vaihinger's theory, particularly since it explained how 'personifying fictions' tend to substantiate the abstract notion, i.e., attribute to it '*ein reales Dasein.*' In legal theory, the concept of 'person' had a similar function. Although they are epistemological tools, personifying fictions tend to *Realsetzung* and as such, they *falsify*: the object of cognition, i.e., the legal order, is doubled into the separate entity of the state. In line with the Kantian perspective and like Mauthner, Vaihinger contended that personifying fictions were '*notwendige Folgen des inneren Mechanismus des Denkorgans selbst.*'[379] Even though Kelsen distanced himself from Mach and Vaihinger in 1933,[380] and ceased his express references to their work and to that of Mauthner, the main features of his thinking had, by then, already crystallised, shaped during his formative years in the 1910s-1920s. These decades had marked the formulation and foundation of the Pure Theory of Law. Afterwards, the terms in which he couched his observations on the concepts of law, state and person never changed significantly.

---

normen. Solche Besinnung ist dringend notwendig gegenüber den *Exzessen eines metaphysischen Realismus*, so wie er neuestens wieder in dem Werke Kjelléns 'Der Staat als Lebensform', 1917, zum Ausdruck kommt, wo behauptet wird, 'daß die Staaten, wie wir sie in der Geschichte verfolgen und uns in der Wirklichkeit unter ihnen bewegen müssen, sinnlich vernüftige Wesen sind – genau wie die Menschen.' Emphasis added. See also, id., at 73: 'Nach der Durchschnittsvorstellung der Juristen ist der Staat eine Art seelisch-körperliche Realität, die einen bestimmten Raum ausfüllt.'

[377] Allgemeine Staatslehre, at 62. With references to Mauthner, see also, Problem der Souveränität, at 18. Also, without reference to Mauthner but for similar rejection of the anthropomorphic tendency of legal language, Problems of Legal Theory.

[378] H. Vaihinger, Die Philosophie des Als Ob, System der theoretischen, praktischen und religiösen Fiktionen der Menschheit auf Grund eines idealistischen Positivismus 50-52, 391 *et seq.*, 406-407 (1913).

[379] H. Kelsen, Zur Theorie der juristischen Fiktionen (1919), *in* Die Wiener Schule, at 1220. Hereinafter: Zur Theorie der juristischen Fiktionen.

[380] Kelsen stated: 'it is altogether correct that the theory of the basic norm finds a certain support in Mach's principle of economy of thought and in Vaihinger's theory of fictions, nevertheless, owing to misunderstandings that have arisen from these references, I no longer wish to appeal to Mach and Vaihinger.' A Letter to Renato Treves, at 173-174.

3.4.2.4. *Conclusion*

In the instable political environment and the wavering democracy in Austria during the first three decades of the 20th century, the epistemological and the political were quite visibly intertwined in the Viennese debate. The old conceptions of state and sovereignty with their mythological tendencies were in urgent need of revision, being as they were incompatible with and a threat to the values of freedom and democracy. This intellectual challenge was tackled especially after WWI. Motivated by his desire to defend democracy, tolerance and moral relativism, Kelsen used a legal language which had been purged of any metaphysical connotations in order to be able profoundly to revise a great number of legal concepts. In keeping with this context, if perhaps a trifle paradoxical considering the contents of the Pure Theory of Law and State, Kelsen's theory rested on an ethical-political and an epistemological pillar. The following words from Kelsen on the rejection of the state as a meta-juridical person confirm this perspective:

Die Fernhaltung aller Politik ist zwar eine heute allgemein anerkannte Forderung der positivistischen Rechtswissenschaft. Allein erfüllt kann sie nur werden, wenn auf den Begriff eines metarechtichen Staates verzichtet wird. Und dieser Verzicht ist, weil er das Operieren mit zwei beziehungslosen Erkenntnissystemen aufhebt, nicht nur eine logisch-erkenntnistheoretische, er ist auch eine *ethische* Notwendigkeit.[381]

Once we have stopped to consider the complexity and dynamics of the political-philosophical context, Kelsen's endeavour to 'decontextualise' the concept of law is entirely comprehensible. His purely formal and magnificently logical construction may be regarded as a true example of the post-WWI return to formalism, which aimed to confront social instability and uncertainty. The concept of law as order served to challenge chaos, support democracy and guarantee individual freedom, thereby paving the way for tolerance and moral relativism. In general, after WWI, the revival of humanism was deferred and pure rationalism (e.g., as promoted by the Vienna Circle) dominated the scene, but in Kelsen's case, the values of humanism were *underlying* or driving factors in formalism. Taking account of the findings in psychoanalysis and socio-political philosophy, the developments in epistemology (in particular those concerning the mythological dimension of reified abstract terms and the falsity of personifying fictions) have been essential to Kelsen's argumentation on the concept of personality, as we will see below.[382] His anti-metaphysical position, visible in his attempt to purify legal reasoning and free it from anthropomorphic and mythological elements, goes hand in hand with his constant concern over the instable political situation and the weakness of the Austrian democracy. Before we focus on how epistemology

[381] Kelsen, Der soziologische und der juristische Staatsbegriff 252 (1922).

[382] See also Vaihinger on the misuse of abstractions in Hegelian philosophy, see *supra* footnote 378, at 393.

and politics come together in Kelsen's reasoning concerning legal personality, we must first explore his general position on international law.

3.4.3. **Kelsen's concept of international law**

Law is a hierarchical system of norms which reaches all the way down from the hypothetical basic norm, *die Grundnorm*, to the individual normative relationship where it links legal condition with legal consequence. The legal system is a coercive order wholly constructed of 'ought-propositions'. When such a proposition is violated, coercive action is taken against the person who committed the illegal act. The specific meaning of law is therefore this 'ought', the purely normative meaning. Kelsen's theory unifies all law into a single universal legal system: 'This basic norm *qua* common source constitutes the unity in the plurality of all norms forming a system.'[383] In the Pure Theory, the basis of international law is a 'presupposed' basic norm that enables us to understand international law as a legal system which is positioned above the states and thereby provides the states' legal systems with the (international law) principle of effectiveness as their 'relative basic norm.'[384]

Kelsen view of the relationship between law and power was different from that of the 'old' positivists. He rejected the positivist doctrine of voluntarism which determined that the *factual* condition of sovereign state *power* was the source of *law*, because this doctrine confused the 'is' and the 'ought' and ultimately led to the negation of international law. In Kelsen's view, it is not power that constitutes law, but law that authorises power, or rather recognises its legitimacy if government power is effective. This way, power is no longer above the law, but neither is the state subordinated to law. Rather, it is a case of power being transformed into competence and international law enjoying supremacy over the state's legal systems.

[I]nternational law, by legitimizing power that is actually establishing itself, authorizes the coercive system set up by this power, that is, authorizes it in so far as it actually becomes affective. This principle of effectiveness, a principle of international law, functions as the basic norm of the various state legal systems; the constitution adopted by the first legislator, historically speaking, is valid only on the presupposition that it is effective, that reality corresponds by and large, to the system unfolding according to constitutional provisions. ... ... What this really means is that a coercive system directly under international law is to be regarded, in terms of international law, as a legitimate, binding legal system – or, in other words, that the community constituted by such a system is to be regarded as a state – for precisely that area where the system has become continuously effective, that is, where reality corresponds, by and large, to the system.[385]

---

[383] Problems of Legal Theory, at 55.

[384] Id., at 62.

[385] Id., at 61.

Hereby Kelsen challenged both the conventional view that international law was – to use Jellinek's words – '*ein anarchisches Recht*'[386] and the ultimate voluntarist complete denial of the legal nature of international law.[387] Kelsen defended the position that international law was *truly* law, and that international law was, indeed, a coercive system. The international community enforces its legal norms through its 'subsystems,' i.e., the individual states, each of which constitutes a centralised legal system. The states as subsystems in turn all participate in the creation of international law.[388]

Let us now briefly deal with the four elements which were previously used to characterise Brierly's work, although here we will discuss them in a different order: first the state, then sovereignty, then monism, and finally the universal community. Kelsen's interest in international law cannot possibly be viewed separately from his work in the field of constitutional law. We may best enter his world by first assessing his concept of the state.

From the introduction, it has already emerged that Kelsen rejected the state *qua* person and the notion that any state could be above the law. But what then is the state if it is something other than a '*Makroanthropos*' or '*Übermensch*'?[389] And what is the 'Will of the State' if it is not something *real*, not the actual will of a state person? Moreover: '*Wie ist der Staat als Verband von Menschen möglich?*'[390] In the early 1920s, Kelsen's quest was for the nature of the *Verbindung* – the connection – between the people who lived together in a state. Should it be characterised as a *causal* connection, as the social sciences suggested?

Early on in his career, in *Hauptprobleme der Staatsrechtslehre* (1911), Kelsen had already expounded that the socio-psychological idea of the will is '*unbrauchbar*' in legal theory. Kelsen pointed out the error in Jellinek's inorganic theory, which was that the 'Will of the People' was considered identical to the 'Will of the State'. This erroneously intermingled sociology (to which the concept of *Volk* belongs) with jurisprudence (to which the concept of state belongs).[391] The unified will of the state, i.e., of *Volk*, constituted the essence of the

---

[386] See *supra*. text to footnote 142.

[387] Problems of legal theory, at 116-117.

[388] Id., at 122-124.

[389] Kelsen used these terms in many of his writings, see, e.g., Der soziologische und der juristische Staatsbegriff, at 3; see, Kelsen's response to a piece by A. Hold-Fernek which he gave the title Der Staat als Übermensch: Eine Erwiderung (1926); see also, Problems of Legal Theory, at 97.

[390] Der soziologische und der juristische Staatsbegriff, at 3.

[391] Hauptprobleme der Staatsrechtslehre, 97 *et seq.*, at 99-100: 'Juristisch betrachtet wäre das Volk, wenn ihm ein 'Wille' zuerkannt wird, ebenso Person wie der Staat, der ja auch nur, sofern er willen begabt ist, als Rechtssubject gilt. Ist aber das 'Volk' eine vom Staate verschiedene Person und die Rechtsordnung teils Wille des Staates, teils Wille des Volkes, dann ist von einer einheitlichen Staats- und Rechtskonstruction keine rede ...' Id., at 162: ' ... das diese Untersuchungen ergeben haben: daß der Begriff des Willens im ethisch-juristischen Sinne etwas völlig anderes bedeutet, als der einen tatsächlichen Seelenvorgang beinhaltende Begriff der Psychologie überhaupt bedeuten

unified state personality and of legal personality in general. The legal will was thus formed and defined in a socio-psychological manner.[392] Von Gierke's concept of the will of the state as a collective will formed by a collective consciousness was, if possible, even more contrary to the principle strictly adhered to by Kelsen of the distinction between *Sein* and *Sollen*. In Kelsen's view, Gierke regarded the will of the state '*als eine massenpsychische Tatsache*.' According to Kelsen, however, to identify society with the state was obviously also incorrect, as society was '*eine völkerpsychologische und soziologische Einheit*', while the state was *not*.[393] The organic concept of state also confused the social and the legal.[394] Kelsen rejected the idea of the organic unity of the meta-physical collective will and declared it – as a sociological fact – an unfit basis for a legal construction.

Considering the socio-political context, with Vienna as the capital of the multinational Empire and, later on, of the divided Republic, Kelsen obviously needed to take a totally different approach. The 'Will of the State' is the legal order itself, so Kelsen consistently maintained, ever since he had qualified it as such; it is a 'figure of speech', used to indicate the legal system of the state through which law is created.[395] The attention which Kelsen initially devoted to social psychology thus related to his rejection of the 'Will of the State' as the basis of the state person in both the organic and the inorganic theory of state, whether as a reality or as an abstraction.[396] But this attention only increased as the general interest in social psychology grew, especially after Freud's entry upon the Viennese scene, and as the problems concerning the unity and identity of the state, which we discussed above, intensified in Austria after WWI.

Freud's psychology of the *individual* focused on the individual mind in the analysis of man among the masses, rather than on the independent and separate *Massenseele*, which tended to be physically hypostatised into a new individual with qualities of its own. Freud does not make this mistake, Kelsen observed.[397] We have already seen that Freud explained the state by means of his libido

---

kann, daß unter Wille im ethisch-juristischen Sinne kein psychischer Akt, sondern eine zum Zwecke der Zurechnung vollzogene Konstruktion zu verstehen ist.'

[392] Kelsen quoted the inorganic theorist of state, Gerben: 'das Volk ist die natürliche Grundlage der Staatspersönlichkeit. Das will sagen, daß der Staat um dieses Volkes willen vorhanden ist, daß er das Volk in seiner politischen Gestaltung darstellt. Das Volk ist aber nicht die Summe der einzelnen jetzt lebenden Menschen, sondern das in geschichtlicher Gemeinschaft geistig verbundene Ganze ... Id., at 173-174.

[393] Id., at 165.

[394] 'Ihr methodischer Fehler, der in der Vermengung soziologischer und juristischer Betrachtung besteht, zeigt sich nirgends deutlicher, als gerade hier, wo sie eine zweifellos gesellschaftliche Tatsache, den Gesamtwillen, der Konstruktion eines Rechtsbegriffes, der Staatsperson, zu Grunde legt.' Id., at 167-168.

[395] Id.; see also, e.g., Problems of legal theory, at 104.

[396] Hauptprobleme der Staatsrechtslehre, at 162 *et seq*. See, for Kelsen's criticism of Von Gierke and his *Völkerpsychologische* Will of State, id., at 164 *et seq*., for a critique of Jellinek's theory, id., at 172 *et seq*.

[397] Der soziologische und der juristische Staatsbegriff, at 21-22.

theory, in the same way that he explained other social groups. From the socio-psychological perspective, the state was understood as a social phenomenon caused by the 'psychic interaction' between the people in the group. We have already learned of Kelsen's particular appreciation of Freud's social theory, but we have yet to find out which elements exactly, if any, Kelsen adopted and how he incorporated them in his thinking. In one of his many writings dedicated to the question of the nature of the state and, in this particular instance, to Freud's theory on the issue, Kelsen raised the '*für das Problem des sociologischen Staatsbegriffs maßgebende – Frage: ob auch der Staat eine psychologische Masse sei ... ob auch der Staat – als soziale Gruppe, als sozialpsychische Realität aufgefaßt – jene 'libidinöse Struktur' aufweist.*'[398]

Even though Kelsen generally valued Freud's findings, it is still not surprising – taking into account Kelsen's ideas on the purity of law and legal science coupled with his aversion to metaphysics and mysticism – that Kelsen firmly rejected any definition of the state being other than purely legal. Nonetheless, he took serious account of Freud's social theory and its concept of state, and in particular of the possibility that the state was the *idea* which might function as the object to substitute the *Ichideal* of the individuals united in this leaderless group.

Kelsen brought to the fore Freud's distinction between temporarily and long-term stable masses, whereby the latter are much more organised and institutionalised and therefore less regressive and primitive by nature.[399] We have indeed seen that Freud argued that the primitive masses should be assigned or should develop the qualities of the individual, i.e., self-awareness, a critical mind, a sense of responsibility and a conscience, qualities which the individual members of the group lost when they merged to become the short-term masses. Kelsen, however, considered this argument a flaw in Freud's reasoning. In his view, it constituted a clean break with Freud's psychological approach of the *individual.*[400] To conceive of the state as well-organised pseudo-masses, or as a stable, institutionalised, collective, new type of individual ran counter to Freud's own individualism, so Kelsen felt. He oreover pointed out that in Freud's definition of the masses the principle of identification was essential. Only a group of people connected by the two libidinal principles could be the 'masses' in the socio-psychological sense. The principle of identification, however, failed in the case of the state, as citizens, according to Kelsen, generally did not identify with each other to the necessary extent, and this failure to identify made it impossible for the state to also be the masses, either ephemerally or artificially. If the state were to be defined as the *idea* assuming the role of the leader in a leaderless, stable, artificial, well-organised group, the state would be perceived as just another social phenomenon like 'religion' or 'nation'.[401]

---

[398] Der soziologische und der juristische Staatsbegriff, at 27-28.
[399] Id., at 29.
[400] Id., at 29-30.
[401] Id., at 31-33.

Considering the Austro-Viennese background and its political problems, social instability and antagonistic religious, nationalist, social and political groups, Kelsen's rejection of the use of anything even slightly sociological or psychological to explain the state makes perfect sense. With the *Kriegsbegeisterung* of the early 1910s, and the post-WWI problems concerning the unity and identity of the state, a concept of state encompassing psychological, sociological, ideological and other non-legal elements inherently threatened the state itself. In *The Conception of the State and Social Psychology*, Kelsen touched upon the tension between the forces of disintegration and the nature of the state, stressing the dangers of socio-psychological concepts of the state:

> [I]f the state were actually founded on them [i.e., on psychic interactions], [this] would cause it inevitably to fall headlong into a bottomless pit of economic, religious and national antagonism?[402]

Indeed, in the face of so much diversity and pluralism, the unity and stability of the state were best served by a neutral definition, and for this reason Kelsen favoured a purely legal definition of the state. The state was neither a social nor a psychic phenomenon and the connection that established its unity was *not causal*, but purely *normative*. Of course, we have already quite extensively dealt with Kelsen's rejection of the sociological concept of the state and, in particular, with his rejection of Freud's theory, but the issue was one which greatly concerned Kelsen at the time and which especially related to his revision of the concept of legal personality. It also demonstrated that Kelsen was not just correcting the old positivism, but was in fact responding to the contemporary issues at stake, which had also been addressed by Freud. The position of the state in Kelsen's concept of international law was inseparable from his rather more domestically driven thinking about the nature of the state and his concern for the democratic system.

The state as a person, who may or may not observe the law and may or may not be a *Rechtsstaat*, the conventional concept of the state as a '*reales Faktum, als Macht oder Gewalt*' was in Kelsen's theory replaced by a state that was order – legal order; the state was a legal system. In *Das Problem der Souveränität und die Theorie des Völkerrechts* (1920), Kelsen disqualified the mythologisation or hypostatisation in the conceptualisation of the state: '*als ob der Staat noch etwas anderes wäre als eine Menschen verpflichtende Ordnung* ...'[403] He identified the state with the coercive order, the legal order: *Staatsbegriff und Rechtsbegriff verschmeltzen*. The state as a normative order was Kelsen's answer to the issues of state identity and power.[404] During the decades that followed, Kelsen defined

---

[402] H. Kelsen, The conception of the State and Social Psychology, V *The Internat. J. of Psycho-Analysis* 5 (1924), translation of 1922 IMAGO article, see *supra* footnote 358.

[403] Das Problem der Souveränität, at 16-18.

[404] Kelsen: 'L'idée qu'il y aurait entre l'État et les individus, et par suite d'État à État, des rapports qui ne seraient pas des rapports entre individus est une simple illusion, qui ne s'explique que par l'inadmissible hypostase de l'État en un surhomme.' Kelsen, Les Rapports de Système entre le Droit Interne et le Droit International Public, 14 *RCADI* 281 (1926-IV). Hereinafter: Les Rapports de système.

the state in his Pure Theory not as an entity, but as the personification of the state's national legal order, which led to the identity between law and state.

Kelsen's argument concerning the nature of the state – 'free of metaphysics and mysticism' – went against the common practice of justifying a state's conduct by law; law is thus considered essentially different from the state. The state as a person meant the state in the sense of power, inherently inclined to abuse the law. Such conceptions of state were false because the state and the law were, in fact, inseparable, as Kelsen contended in his arguments against the old and prevailing theory of state. Kelsen's equation of the law with the state makes the state into a legal person and renders it the same by nature as every other legal person:

Die Person des Staates is nur in vergrößtem Maßstabe was jede andere juristische Person, aber auch jede physische Person ist: die Personification von Rechtsnormen.[405]

We will return to the personification of the state in the next section, but with regard to Kelsen's concept of international law, suffice it here to conclude the following. In the first place, the state was not defined in the conventional way as a meta-legal or anthropomorphic entity. On the contrary – and highly originally – it was defined in purely normative terms. Secondly, Kelsen intended to prevent the misuse of the law for the purpose of justifying state behaviour. Finally, the state existed because of law; in other words, law reigned supreme over power, and international law was – to recall an earlier quote – the law that 'authorised' the state. The state was a 'subsystem' of and under the international legal system: it was limited by international law and at the same time 'an organ of the international legal community.'[406] These conclusions automatically introduce the second element: Kelsen's concept of sovereignty.

Kelsen could not have been clearer on sovereignty, as, for example, when he stated: *Die Souveränitätsvorstellung freilich muß radikal verdrängt werden.*[407] He did not give in to the *restorative* – in fact, the conventional – urge to reconcile international law with state sovereignty, whether absolute or relative,[408] which basically meant the denial of international law. Still, the *convention* in international law theory was that sovereignty existed and that it played a fundamental role. On the one hand, therefore, Kelsen firmly, consistently and frequently rejected the concept of sovereignty as an exclusive attribute of the state – sovereignty to indicate supreme state power[409] – as a falsehood and irreconcilable with international law,[410] thus *dissociating* himself from the convention concerning

405 Das Problem der Souveränität, at 20.

406 Problems of Legal Theory, at 122.

407 Das Problem der Souveränität, at 320.

408 Les Rapports de système, at 311-313.

409 Kelsen remarked that sovereignty was often used as if it concerned 'une propriété sensible d'un objet perceptible ou tout au moins susceptible d'être appréhendé par une expérience psychique.' Les Rapports de système, at 255.

410 See, for Kelsen's rejection of traditional concepts of sovereignty, e.g., id., at 249-262.

sovereignty. On the other hand, however, he revised the concept of sovereignty to assume the meaning of the primacy of law, international law, and by doing so he retained sovereignty as part of his theory, thereby in effect still *associating* with the convention, albeit in the strictest possible sense:

Discuter sur la souveraineté de l'État, c'est raisonner sur des hypothèses de science juridique. Le problème n'est pas une problème d'observation, mais *d'interprétation* de certains faits; et bien des interprétations sont possibles, selon qu'on part de l'hypothèse que l'État est un ordre suprême, c'est-à-dire souverain, ou qu'on admet au contraire la suprématie d'un ordre supérieur à l'État, – du droit international. [411]

Interpretation is, however, a matter of choice: either the state is sovereign or international law is, either the national legal order is sovereign or the international legal order is. Interpretation may even be a political choice, as Kelsen would be the first to admit, having opted for the primacy of international law from a "anti-imperialist" perspective.[412]

In *Das Problem der Souveränität*, Kelsen explained how the choice between the sovereignty of the state legal system and the sovereignty of the international legal system was both an epistemological or cognitive choice and an ethical-political choice. As regards the first choice, this involved choosing between a subjective and an objective cognitive perspective. The first perspective, i.e., the primacy of the state legal order, led to *solipsism*:[413] the perspective of the sovereign state order induced states to consider other states as *Teilordnungen* – as component parts – of their own state order, with the result that the latter '*sich über alle anderen staatlichen Rechtsordnungen als Universalordnung ausdehnt.*' This was therefore a path that led to the negation of international law and '*zur Behauptung des reinen Machtsstandpunkt.*' In the objectivist theory of the primacy of international law, the legal systems of the individual states were *Teilordnungen* of the international law system. The ethical-political dimension of the cognitive choice is evident:

Wie die egozentrische Position einer subjektivistischen Erkenntnistheorie in einem ethischen Egoismus (wenn solcher noch als Ethik bezeichnet werden kann) verwandelt ist, so paart sich die Rechtserkenntnishypothese des Primates eigener staatlicher Rechtsordnung mit Staatsegoismus einer imperialistischen Politik.[414]

---

[411] Id., at 255. Emphasis added.

[412] See, Problems of Legal Theory, at 124: where Kelsen indeed points out the 'political import' of the Pure Theory.

[413] Das Problem der Souveränität, at 315: 'Die Ausschließlichkeit der Souveränität, die Einzigkeit des souveränen Staaten-Ich ist nur die Analogie, ist mehr als die Analogie der unentrinnbaren solipsistischen Konsequenz des Subjektivismus. Die subjektivistische Völkerechtstheorie, die dem Staat als Subjekt die übrige Rechtswelt als Object entgegensetzt und der Anerkennungstheorie dieses Object als Funktion des Subjekts auflöst, findet bei der nicht zu übersehenden Relativität des Gegensatzes von Subjekt und Object ihre natürliche Fortsetzung und Ergänzung ...' Also, Problems of Legal Theory, at 116.

[414] Das Problem der Souveränität., at 315-317, at 318: 'Zweifellos sind Hegel und sein Schüler Lasson Vertreter einer objektivistischen Weltanschauung. Aber Hegels Kollektivismus blied be-

Kelsen reshaped the issue of state sovereignty and power into one of the 'primacy' of law and went on to phrase the ensuing legal question concerning the primacy of either national or international law as an epistemological question and ultimately as an ethical-political one, to which his answer was:

> Die Rechtseinheit der Menschheit ... ... das ist der politische Kern der juristischen Hypothese vom Primate des Völkerrechts, das ist aber zugleich der Grundgedanke des Pazifismus, der auf dem Gebiete der internationalen Politik das Gegenbild des Imperialismus darstellt. So wie für eine objektivistische Lebensanschauung der sittliche Begriff des Menschen die Menschheit ist, so ist für eine objektivistische Rechtstheorie der Begriff des Rechts identisch mit dem des Völkerrechts und gerade darum zugleich ein ethischer Begriff.[415]

A choice had not been made, the two perspectives continued to co-exist and as a consequence international law found itself in an ambivalent transitory stage and international law theory was engaged in a 'tragic conflict' on the matter, as Kelsen observed. Kelsen nonetheless discerned some progress in the objectivist direction. The subjectivist theory of international law had sounded the retreat and with the victory over the state sovereignty dogma: '[*wird*] *die Existenz einer objektiven, von aller "Anerkenning" unabhängigen, über den Einzelstaaten stehenden Völker-, richtiger Weltrechtsordnung, einer* civitas maxima *sich durchsetzen. ... Als unendliche Aufgabe aber muß solcher Weltstaat als Weltorganisation allem politischen Streben gesetz sein.*'[416] And so Kelsen arrived at the conclusion that state sovereignty should be 'radically pushed aside' and that the focus should be on the establishment of a truly international law community approaching a *civitas maxima* or world state.

The above has also served to clarify Kelsen's position in the debate on monism and dualism, now that Kelsen apparently treated the problem of sovereignty as a problem concerning the relationship between domestic law and international law. Kelsen opted for the primacy of the international over the national legal order and regarded the latter together with the former as part of one universal order, thereby rejecting the prevailing or conventional dualist view, but also the particular monist view which defended the primacy of state law.[417]

---

kanntlich im Staate stecken. ... Ist eine schärfere Zuspitzung des Staats- oder Volksindividualismus möglich als die Vorstellung einer "auserwälten" Nation, als die Hegelsche Idee, daß der Weltgeist in einer Nation allein seinen Thron augeschlagen habe? Welch schrankenloser Imperialismus muß von einer solchen Vorstellung ausgehen.'

[415] Id., at 319.

[416] Id., at 320.

[417] See also, Les Rapports de système, at 261 *et seq*. Monism that gives primacy to the national legal order conceives of international law as external national law and therefore: '[la théorie de la primauté de l'ordre étatique] part de l'idée et elle aboutit à l'idée qu'il n'existe qu'un seul État. ... Elle montre de plus qu'il ne peut y avoir plus d'un État souverain ...' Id., at 296, 289-298, 297: '[L]'hypothèse de la primauté de l'ordre étatique équivaut à la négation d[u] droit [international].' Id., at 276-277 and 288: '[L]a construction dualiste ... aboutit à faire de ce qu'on appelle le droit

There were, however, two concepts in particular that connected and structured Kelsen's monist construction: the idea of *Stufenbau*, or: the hierarchy of the order of the universal legal system, and the *Zurechnung*. In the hierarchy of law, all norms were connected: the unity of the legal order 'consists in the chain that emerges as one traces the creation of norms, and thus their validity back to other norms, whose own creation is determined in turn by still other norms.' And so, ultimately, this led 'to the basic norm ... and thus to the ultimate basis of validity, which establishes the unity of this chain of creation.'[418] In other words, the higher norm determined the creation of a lower norm, with creation standing for the process as well as the content. The universal legal order stretched from the *Grundnorm* all the way to the ultimate extensions of individual relations and 'persons,' natural and legal alike. This therefore also resolved the duality between public and private law.[419]

As the principle of causality functioned in nature, so did the principle of *Zurechnung* or 'imputation' function in law.[420] The human will was free and consequently man had a choice whether to act or remain idle. In other words, in the realm of the ought-proposition, it was not causality, but imputation, which connected reality to the legal norm. Norms stipulated what ought to be done in response to any particular action. In other words, the consequence was attributed to the action. The *Zurechnung* therefore went to the essence of the law. Law was ultimately a regulation of human conduct, and therefore the *Endpunkt der Zurechnung* had to be man himself. However, *Sein* and *Sollen* belonged to completely different realms which did not overlap or mingle. As a consequence, the human will was indeed the culmination of attribution. However, the human will in the field of law should not be confused with the human will in psychology.[421]

---

international tout simplement une sorte de morale ou de droit naturel, et non pas un droit véritable, au sens plein du mot, au sens ou l'on qualifie le droit interne de «droit positif» Seul le droit interne pourrait alors définir ce qui est droit et ce qui ne l'est pas. ... Dans ces conditions, la construction dualiste implique la négation de la nature juridique du «droit international»'. See also, Problems of Legal Theory, at 107 *et seq.*

[418] Problems of Legal Theory, at 64.

[419] See also, e.g., on dualism in private and public law with its tendency to favour autocracy instead of democracy and to absolutise the opposition between law and power. The Pure Theory resolved this duality, in an attempt to relativise the opposition between law and power and, as such, it tried to break down the ideology that is connected with this duality. See para. 44 and 45.

[420] See also, Kausalität und Zurechnung, at 685.

[421] Die Zurechnung, der die einzelne normgemäße oder normwidrige Handlung oder Unterlassung nur Durchgangspunkte sind, sucht sich – figürlich gesprochen – im Innern des Menschen einen Endpunkt: diese, im Innern des Menschen gedachte, als Endpunkt der Zurechnung fungierende Konstruktion – und nichts anderes – ist es, was die Terminologie der Ethik und Jurisprudenz als "Wille" bezeichnet.' Die Lokalisering des Zurechnungsendpunktes 'Wille' muß keineswegs notwendig in das Innere des "Menschen" erfolgen; die ethisch-juristische Einheit der Person muß durchaus nicht immer mit der zoologisch-psychologischen zusammenfallen. ... der Wille der Ethik- und Jurisprudenz ist eine unter dem Gesichtspunkte der Norm, des Sollens vollzogene Konstruktion, der im realen Seelenleben des Menschen kein konkreter Vorgang entspricht. ... sondern, eine zum Zwecke der Zurechnung vollzogene Konstruktion zu verstehen ist.' Id., at 145-146, and 162.

In law, the human *will* was the legal construction or point at which the *Zurechnung* was aimed. As early as 1911, Kelsen determined the concept of 'person' as a *Zurechnungs-Subject*. The subject of attribution was by no means a simple biological-psychological entity, '*sondern zu einem außerhalb der Welt tatsächlichen Geschehens gedachten normativen Konstruktionspunkte.*' The law tended to personify the will and as such represented it as a 'person'. In other words, the notion of person in the field of law was the expression of a legal order – a bundle of norms attributed to the legal will. '*Denn die organisch-teleologische Einheit "Mensch" ist keineswegs an und für sich identisch mit "Person". Nur als Zurechnungssubjekt ist der Mensch Person.*' [422]

Finally, as will be abundantly clear by now, Kelsen in these early Interbellum years viewed the world not only as a universal legal system but also as possibly ultimately destined to develop into a world state. Over the years, however, Kelsen watered down his remarks on the world state, stating, for example, in 1934 that '[a]t the present time, however, there can be no talk of a world state.'[423] Yet his position on the matter during the first few years after WWI is revealed by his comments on the possibility of a *civitas maxima*, which have been quoted above, and even as late as 1944, Kelsen could see no other way of securing international peace than by means of the establishment of a world federation.[424] However, when Kelsen spoke about progress towards a world state when he equated the state with law, he was merely referring to the further evolution of the universal legal order, or, in other words, to the development of international law. After all, when sovereignty would no longer stand in the way, the proper development of international law would be possible and this, in Kelsen's view, was the only way of securing world peace, i.e., by means of the primacy of the law over power.

In brief, against the background of the Austro-Viennese 'polluted political atmosphere' with its problems of social and political instability, antagonism between social groups, and the threats to political freedom and the democratic system at large, Kelsen's definition of the state in *purely* legal terms and his rejection of

---

[422] H. Kelsen, Hauptprobleme der Staatsrechtslehre 74 (1911). Personification took place through attribution, the concept was therefore already purely normative and not determined by any element from the realm of *Sein*: 'Allein man verschließe sich nicht der Erkenntnis, daß auch der Mensch erst durch die Zurechnung zur Person wird, und daß auch hier nur durch die Zurechnung eine Summe von natürlichen, physikalischen, chemischen und psychischen Prozessen personifiziert, d. h. zu einer normativen Einheit erhoben wird.' Id., at 83.

[423] Problems of Legal Theory, at 111.

[424] '[T]o unite all individual States ... in a World State, to concentrate all their means of power, their armed forces, and put them at the disposal of a world government under laws created by a world parliament. If States are allowed to continue their existence only as members of a powerful world federation, then peace among them will be secured as effectively as among the component States of the United States of America or the Cantons of the Swiss Republic.' Kelsen, Peace through Law 5 (1944).

any socio-psychological concept of the state, whether restorative or contemporary, refutes any assertion that Kelsen's theory lacked a sense of reality. On the contrary, the Pure Theory of Law with its monist construction and the primacy of international law as a revisionist contribution to (international) legal theory took thorough account of the developments in both national and international life. In the midst of the Austro-Viennese intellectual context with its demythologising objectives and ensuing epistemological approaches, taking an anti-ideological, anti-metaphysical theoretical stance, with the intention of keeping law away from ideological and political disputes about what was 'right' in which each side tended to make its own (moral and political) values the absolute norm, was acutely appropriate. The attempt to find a pure and neutral legal language, or rather a definition of law, actually linked epistemological with ethical-political considerations and as such bore evidence of being a response that was closely related to the there and then, rather than estranged from it all. This is especially true when it comes to Kelsen's revision of the concept of legal personality, as will be shown hereafter.

When we take the contextual factors into account, therefore, we are able to understand Kelsen's intentions regarding the contemporary *conventions* of international law scholarship, in particular where the prevailing voluntarist dogmas of state sovereignty and international law were concerned. When writing about international law, Kelsen was not merely engaged in revising traditional theory. His intentions were as much to perform a political as a linguistic act in defence of law and democracy. In international scholarship, the concepts of sovereignty and the state were (and still are) key notions, or what we have described as 'evaluative-descriptive terms.' By redefining such evaluative-descriptive terms as state and sovereignty, Kelsen intended to *change* the perception of (and thus eventually the practices of) (inter)national political life. He intended to communicate a vision of the construction or reconstruction of the identity of the society, whether domestic or international. When asked what Kelsen was *doing in* writing in this way, I conclude that by denying the primacy of the state and its absolute sovereignty, he challenged the mythologising, authoritarian practice of the glorification of the state and the marginalisation, or even negation, of international law. By redefining sovereignty and giving it primacy in international law and by equating the law with the state, Kelsen intended to contribute to change, to renewal, to the establishment of peace, stability, and *especially* democracy, by means of the victory of law over power (and politics).

We will now turn to his concept of legal personality, by which we will find that values of tolerance and democracy conjoin with epistemological views in a *usage* of the concept of legal personality as an evaluative-descriptive term: used with the intention to defend these values, corresponding to the epistemological criteria, in an action as much political as legal by nature, resulting in the inclusion of the individual in the international legal system.

3.4.4. Kelsen's concept of legal personality: democracy and reduction[425]

3.4.4.1. *Introduction*

By now we have accumulated the necessary building blocks to wind up this argument and to sustain that Kelsen's revision of legal personality was an act of *unmasking*, the *Entschleierung* of the gods.

First, having dealt briefly with the practical political context, it was made clear that Kelsen lived in a country marked by internal antagonism, social and political instability, the endangerment of the unity and identity of the state and a democracy that was increasingly under threat. By positioning Kelsen's serious and prolonged consideration of Freud's social theory and his concept of state against this background, we have come to understand that to ground the state in a socio-political basis would mean to endorse the old theory and its inclination towards authoritarian rule and that this would pose an immediate threat to the state itself. The inclusion of non-legal elements would mean an irresponsible welcoming of antagonism into the very institution of 'the state' itself. Internationally, tension was also mounting, as power politics tended towards colonial international law (thinking) and the list of European states which were falling prey to authoritarian and totalitarian rule grew.

Secondly, we have established that among Viennese intellectuals a resentment of *Substanzierung* had emerged. We have seen that, in his criticism of hypostatisation and its mythological tendencies, Kelsen concurred with Mauthner's critique of language. Just as 'Matter', 'Atom', 'Force' and 'Soul' were reified and doubled in the process, the state person had been hypostatised into a separate substantive entity, 'bearer' of rights and duties. This practice of *hypostatisation* had spawned 'conceptual monsters', spouting rhetoric with harmful political overtones. Fully in line with Kelsen's condemnation of hypostatisation, the Viennese intellectuals considered *anthropomorphism* to be a 'cardinal sin.'[426] When Kelsen concluded in the *Reine Rechtslehre* (1934) that:

> [T]he concept of legal subject or person [i]s simply an artificial aid to thought, a heuristic concept created by legal cognition – under the pressure of a personifying, *anthropomorphic* legal language .... 'Person' is simply a personifying expression for the unity of a bundle of legal obligations and legal rights, that is, the unity of a complex of norms. ...[427]

the rejection of the traditional concept of legal personality could not have been stated any more clearly. His words were a firm attack upon what Kelsen called

[425] I consistently focus on the formative years of the Pure Theory and of Kelsen's conception of (international) legal personality because the writings of these years are the most enlightening concerning this conception which persisted in the years thereafter. The analysis of Kelsen's concept of legal personality in international law is basically the same as that of the concept in national law.

[426] Wittgenstein's Vienna, at 138.

[427] Problems of Legal Theory, at 46-47 *et seq*. Emphasis added. See also, *supra* footnotes 375-377.

the *Exzessen eines metaphysischen Realismus.*[428] Having already dealt with Kelsen's appreciation of Mauthner's ideas, we will here elaborate further on the contribution of the ideas of Vaihinger and Cassirer to Kelsen's thinking.

In the third place, set against the background of the conservative restorative doctrine of voluntarism, which was still the conventional, dominant view of international law, we have established that Kelsen's approach to international law was profoundly revisionist by nature.

Finally, it has become clear that Kelsen paradoxically did not embark on his project to liberate law and legal science from politics without ethical-political intentions. His rejection of the old conceptions of state, sovereignty and law was equally sustained by an ethical-political choice in favour of democracy or rather a defence of the individual against collective (post-Hegelian) freedom. I will thus show that Kelsen, by attacking the conventional concept of personality, intended to defend democracy as well as *individual* freedom and responsibility. We will now continue the epistemological thread of this narrative and demonstrate how Kelsen brought about the demystification of ILP by means of reduction.

3.4.4.2. *Hypostatisation and reduction*

The method Kelsen adopted to reduce the concept of legal personality was rooted in his critique of 'personifying fictions' and their falsifying and mystifying character. Having set the stage earlier by addressing Kelsen's familiarity with the ideas of Mauthner, we now have to deal with Vaihinger and Cassirer and their influence on Kelsen's epistemological shift towards a *Funktionsbegriff* in order to be able to demonstrate convincingly the *demystification* of ILP.

In 1919, in his article *Zum Theorie der juristischen Fictionen* Kelsen discussed the concept of legal personality in the light of Vaihinger's philosophy. Vaihinger's analysis of (personifying) fictions was crucial to the development of Kelsen's theory about the concept. Fictions are constructed for the purpose of *knowing*: a fiction is an epistemological tool. Kelsen extended Vaihinger's definition of the use of fictions in order to include as the possible objects of cognition, besides objects belonging to actual empirical reality, also non-factual objects.[429] Legal fictions are used for the purpose of knowing law, i.e., for the cognition of the legal order. Kelsen agreed with Vaihinger's general finding that the fiction (in general) was determined by 1) purpose, and 2) means. Kelsen extended the purpose for legal fictions: fictions may be used to know the factual reality – *Sein* – but also the normative realm of *Sollen*. The method to attain the objective was the

[428] See *supra*, footnote 376.

[429] If a fiction by definition should contain a factual – real – element, it would be harmful to legal theory: 'dann kann auf dem Gebiete einer Wissenschaft, deren Erkenntnisse nicht auf die Wirklichkeit bezogen sind, eine Fiktion stets nur eine unzulässige und gänzlich unnütze, bloß schädliche Entgleisung sein.' Zum Theorie der juristischen Fictionen, at 1217.

same: '*eine Fälschung, ein Widerspruch, ein Kunstgriff, ein Umweg und Durchgangspunkt des Denkens.*'[430]

Its contradiction of reality was the main characteristic of the epistemological fiction (the *Als-Ob* construction); something was 'as if', or, in other words, was not in conformity with the object of cognition, but was used to improve the understanding of the latter. A legal epistemological fiction was a detour inconsistent with – but aimed at the cognition of – the legal order.

Dealing with Vaihinger's theory, Kelsen concentrated on the concept of 'person'.[431] The concept had traditionally been interpreted to refer to an independent being, separate from the legal order, who was the bearer of rights and duties. In conventional legal scholarship, Kelsen discerned an '*ausgesprochenen Tendenz zur Realsetzung der Person.*'[432] The subject of law, both natural and legal, was hypostatised and reified. He examined whether the use of the 'person' as an epistemological instrument in conventional legal theory could be passed off as relatively harmless or should be taken seriously. In Kelsen's view, the concept of 'person' did indeed falsify the epistemological representation during the process of being used, as it *doubled* the object of cognition. This was a particular feature of what Vaihinger termed '*personifikativen Fiktionen*'.[433]

Sie entstammen dem unseren Vorstellungsapparat von jeher beherrschenden antropomorphistischen Personifikationstrieb, jenem »unverwüstlichen Hange des Menschengeschlechtes«, alles rein Gedankliche in der Form der Person, des Subjektes, zu hypostasieren und so zu veranschauen.

The principle of hypostatisation operated within the personifying fiction and transformed a phenomenon into a Thing or Personality. The first or most original representation of substantiality was, in Vaihinger's view, Personality. The history of the concept of the legal person or subject equally showed this transformation, as Kelsen explained:

Es kann gar nicht nachdrücklich genug hervorgehoben werden, daß der Begriff des Rechtssubjektes von derselben logischen Struktur ist, wie die characteristischte aller personifikativen Fiktionen, der Begriff der Seele, oder der Begriff der Kraft ...[434]

However, it had the same doubling effect. The concept of 'person' eventually included the duplication of law, and in the case of the state person this appeared as the separate existence of the state as a legal order and the state as

[430] Zur Theorie der juristischen Fiktionen, at 1216.

[431] 'Fictionen des auf Erkenntnis des Rechtes, auf geistige Bewältung der Rechtsordnung gerichteten Denkens. Fictionen der Rechtstheorie. Ein solche Fiktion, ein Hilfsbegriff, eine Hilfkonstruction ist z. B. der Begriff der Rechtssubjektes oder der Begriff des subjektiven Rechtes.' Id., at 1218.

[432] Id.

[433] See *supra*, text to footnote 378.

[434] Zur Theorie der juristischen Fiktionen, at 1219.

an entity.[435] Kelsen agreed that personifying fictions stemmed from the '*Mechanismus des Denkorgans selbst.*'[436]

The general psychological reason why man showed this tendency to substantiate, related to man's preference for stability and certainty. This was also true, in Kelsen's opinion, for the concept of the state, theories on which were rooted in a '*konservativen Zug der menschlichen Natur.*'[437] The tendency of the human mind to hypostatise had been a particularly Kantian concern.[438] Human reason tended to transcend the experience that was gathered and to construct 'meaning' beyond the limits of experience; however, this was not knowledge, even though it was not meaningless either. Metaphysical thinking was natural to the human mind as was the tendency to personify, but the *doubling* that resulted from this personification and that was subsequently recognised and legitimised through the use of language had to be rejected. Kelsen extensively quoted Kant on this tendency to reify,[439] and transplanted the Kantian insights to legal theory in order to address the idea of the state person.

The state as person was acceptable as long as it was not hypostatised into a real entity, but simply understood as the expression of the systematic unity of all law. As such, the use of the concept of the (state) person was legitimate since it simply functioned as an aid to thought, and in this role, the personification was legitimate.[440] In other words, Kelsen could accept the simplified representation of the state as person provided that the fictitious character and the doubling remained perfectly clear. Unfortunately, this clarity was lost in Kelsen's view. Vaihinger argued that if the fictitious nature of a personification was not clear and doubling had set in, a correction of the fiction needed to be performed. Vaihinger did not, however, consider such a correction necessary with respect to legal fictions. Kelsen, on the other hand, mourned the loss of the fictitious nature of the state person and the legal person.

---

[435] See also, Les Rapports de Système, at 246: '[L]e dualisme de l'État et du Droit n'est qu'un des nombreux exemples de dédoublement de l'objet de la connaissance, dont est remplie l'histoire de l'esprit humain. Ce qui n'est qu'un moyen de la connaissance pour appréhender son objet, une représentation auxiliaire qui permet de mettre de l'unité dans la multiplicité et la diversité des relations-la personnification-on l'hypostasie, on en fait un objet doué d'une existence propre, en dédoublant l'objet originaire de la connaissance; on crée ainsi un problème purement apparent, celui des rapports de deux objets qui en réalité n'en font qu'un.'

[436] Zur Theorie der juristischen Fiktionen, at 1220.

[437] Staat und Recht im Lichte der Erkenntniskritik, at 103.

[438] See the extensive quote from Kant, *in* Staat und Recht im Lichte der Erkenntniskritik, at 112-113.

[439] Id., at 112-113. Kant on reification: 'Die Vernunft kann aber diese systematische Einheit nicht anders denken, als daß sie ihrer Idee zugleich einen Gegenstand gibt, der aber durch keine Erfahrung gegeben werden kann; ... ... *Aus einer solchen psychologischen Idee kann nun nichts anderes als Vorteil entspringen, wenn man sich nur hütet, sie für etwas mehr als bloße Idee, d.i. bloß relativisch auf den systematischen Vernunftsgebrauch in Ansehung der Erscheinungen unserer Seele gelten zu lassen.*' Kant as cited by Kelsen, id.

[440] Kelsen: 'Die Personifikation der systematischen Einheit ist jedenfalls durch *Kant* selbst als zulässiges Hilfsmittel des Denkens legitimiert.' Id.

In conventional legal scholarship, the concept of 'person' had failed to remain true to its fictitious character and as such to the absolute requisite of contradiction – the 'as-if' situation – and therefore, a correction was necessary. To characterise this correction in Kelsen's own words, what was needed was '*eine Reduktion des Personenbegriffs auf seine natürlichen Grenzen, durch Selbstbesinnung der Rechtswissenschaft, durch das Klarstellen seiner logischen Struktur.*'[441] The task was thereby set. The practice to understand the world in substantiated concepts had led to a mythological perception of the world.[442] In order to replace this mythological world view, the *Substanzbegriffs* were to be reduced to their proper singularity. This posed the challenge of dissolving the opposition between the state entity and state law through the liberation of law from the concept of personality as a *Substanzbegriff* and through its replacement with a *Relationsbegriff*, i.e., the equation of law with the state.[443]

The 'Viennese' critique of the use of reified notions was thus also applied by Kelsen to the theory of state and law and to the idea of liberating theory by reduction. In this respect, Kelsen also consulted Ernst Cassirer's *Substanzbegriff und Functionsbegriff.*[444] Natural science and philosophy also displayed a tendency to attribute more or a higher worth to 'things' than to non-substantiated phenomena.[445] The concept of state had undergone a similar process. Therefore the reduction of this concept could be exercised analogously to the reasoning employed in natural science, although it was evidently not identical to the method of natural philosophy or physics.[446] In *Substanzbegriff und Functionsbegriff*, Cassirer developed an epistemological analysis of the history of natural scientific reasoning. Kelsen maintained that the reification in legal theory of the state as personality conformed to the general tendency found in science and he contended that its reduction was a natural next step in its development.[447] Kelsen argued that the epis-

---

[441] Zur Theorie der juristischen Fiktionen, at 1222.

[442] See also, Staat und Recht im Lichte der Erkenntniskritik, at 101 and 108.

[443] See also, id., at 104-105: 'indem hier der Versuch unternommen wurde, den Begriff des vom Recht verschiedenen Staates aus seiner Hypostasierung herauszulösen und auf einen bloßen Einheitsausdruck für den Systemzusammenhang des Rechtes zu reduzieren, somit also den *reinen*, von aller verdoppelnden Substanzierung befreiten *Rechtsbegriff* wiederherzustellen, wird für den Bereich der Rechtswissenschaft etwas ganz ähnliches unternommen, was Avenarius mit der Auflösung des Substanzbegriffes für die Weltanschauung überhaupt anstrebt und was er »die *Restitution des natürlichen Weltbegriffes*« nennt.'

[444] E. Cassirer, Substanzbegriff und Functionsbegriff: Untersuchungen über die Grundfragen der Erkenntniskritik (1910).

[445] Staat und Recht im Lichte der Erkenntniskritik, at 102-103.

[446] 'Nur ihre Argumentation gegen den Substanzbegriff und deren reinigende Wirkung auf die Naturwissenschaft soll für die Rechtswissenschaft fruchtbar gemacht werden.' Id., at 105.

[447] 'Was Cassirer für die Grundbegriffe der Naturwissenschaft wie Atom, Äther, Materie, Kraft, Seele usw., das ist in ganz analoger Weise auch für den Begriff des Staates zu leisten: sie aus Substanz- in reine Funktionsbegriffe zu wandeln, zu leisten: *daß die Tendenz zu diesem Wandel in der Entwicklung der Wissenschaft selbst liegt.*' Id., at 105. See, on the doubling effect of cognition: 'Statt *hinter* der Welt der Perzeptionen ein neues *Dasein* zu erdichten, das doch immer nur aus den

temological purification process, which had already been taking place in natural science for over two centuries, should be applied analogously to legal theory:

»Die *Abwehr* der metaphysischen Ansprüche ist es, die die Theorie zunächst zu leisten hat«, sagt *Cassirer* von der Entwicklung der Physik; und für die Rechtswissenschaft galt es zunächtst die soziologisch-psychologischen, die naturrechtlichen – kurz: die *metarechtlichen* Ansprüche *abzuwehren:* »und diese Abwehr kann nur dadurch geführt werden, daß die *empirischen* Grundlagen der exakten Wissenschaft immer genauer und deutlicher bloßgelegt werden«; für die *Rechtswissenschaft*: daß die Einschränkung auf die rein positivrechtlichen Elemente, die Reinheit der juristischen Methode immer schärfer betont wird.[448]

Kelsen applied Cassirer's analysis of the atom to the state: instead of as a real thing with concrete features it should be conceived of as a '*gedachten* Ansatzpunkt *für mögliche Relationen« aus einem Teil des Stoffes zu einem bloßen ideellen »Subjekt für bestimmte Änderungen ...*' Cassirer could accept that the atom was represented as a 'subject' provided that it was defined as a 'starting point for possible relationships.' The atom was thus no longer a substantiated thing, but was understood as a 'point' which actually represented a system of relationships. The same could be said of the state person, argued Kelsen, as both were *not* indivisible objects but rather virtual points of unification. The parallel drawn between the atom and the state is indeed illuminating:

Wie dieses so ist auch jener eine »Idee«, nicht die Idee des Rechtes im soziologisch- oder naturrechtlich-ethisch metaphysischen Sinne, sondern eine *logische* Idee, die Idee der Einheit des Rechtes, »eine Idee, die zum Zwecke der Ordnung der Erscheinungen konzipiert ist, aber mit diesen Erscheinungen selbst methodisch nicht auf der gleichen Stufe steht«.[449]

To recall a point made above, let us reiterate that as early as 1911, Kelsen stated in his *Habilitation* that the concept of 'person' was a normative entity or *Zurechnungs-Subject*. The subject of attribution was in any event not a biological-psychological entity, '*sondern zu einem außerhalb der Welt tatsächlichen Geschehens gedachten normativen Konstruktionspunkte.*'[450] Influenced by Cassirer, the argument was further refined. Kelsen rejected a 'metaphysical', but accepted a 'logical' differentiation between law and the state:[451] the state person should be conceived of as a logical idea representing the unity of law. Kelsen thus reduced the legal concept of person to an expression of legal relationships (*die Reduction der Person des Staates ebenso wie der sogenannten physischen*

Materialien der Empfindung aufgebaut sein könnte, begnügt sie sich damit, die allgemeingültigen intellektuellen Schemata zu entwerfen, in welchen die Beziehungen und Zusammenhänge der Perzeptionen sich vollständig darstellen lassen müssen.' Id., at 107.

[448] Id., at 114.

[449] Id., at 105-106.

[450] See *supra*, text to footnote 422. Id., at 83.

[451] Id., at 107.

Person auf Rechtssatzbeziehungen).[452] In the field of law, the person, whether physical or legal, was a legal notion meaning the point of attribution of legal *relationships* involving rights and duties.

As the starting point for possible relationships and subsequently as the personification of the normative *Zurechnungspunkt*, 'person' was thus redefined as a *relational* concept. The concept of the (state) person could therefore be sustained in legal theory provided that *this* was the *meaning* it was given.[453] Kelsen stressed that the legal subject was *not* man – the human individual – but the 'person' – the personification of part of a legal order and, in the case of the state, the personification of a complete legal order.[454]

3.4.4.3. *The de-deification of the state*

In order to be able to fully grasp what Kelsen was doing in revising the concept of person and arguing 'reduction through identification' (state = law), we have to address another parallel which Kelsen drew, i.e., that between theology and legal theory and between their respective objects of cognition, namely the idea of God and the concept of the state. The main problem that theology tried to solve was in Kelsen's opinion strikingly similar to the main problem that the theory of the state had to tackle: the relationship between God and the world he had created – or nature – resembled the relationship between the state and its law.[455] This parallel turns out to be highly illustrative. In orthodox theology, God in the first place was understood as transcendental, as separate and above the world, just as the state was conventionally conceived of as being above and separate from the law. God was an *Absolutum*, omnipotent even, as Catholic doctrine declared, and similarly, the doctrine of sovereignty had made the power of the state absolute. Omnipotence was the condition which made God God, just as sovereignty was the condition defining the state as a state. Both God and the state were the *prima causa* to their systems or orders: God equalled '*die absolute Substanz*' and the

[452] Id., at 131.

[453] 'Ob das Bild der »Person« mehr oder weniger geeignet ist, die Einheit auszudrücken, scheint mir nicht von irgendeiner Relevanz zu sein. Schließlich kommt es nur darauf an, was man ihm für *Bedeutung* beimißt. ... die Einheit des Rechtes ... als Einheit eines Urteilszusammenhanges...' Id., at 112 ff.

[454] Id., at 131. The state as '*Makroanthropos*' – in the organic theory of the state – considered the state and the human being to be phenomena of the same realm, i.e., that of nature. The state and the 'person', whether physical or legal, belonged to the same existential sphere, the normative, but only because both were personifications of legal orders. Id. See also, *supra* footnotes 389-391.

[455] Kelsen (the principle of the economy of thought comes from Mach): 'Wenn eine Analogie zwischen dem Mikrokosmos der Rechtsordnung und Makrokosmos der Ordnung des Universalismus zulässig ist – und sie ist keineswegs neu und schon dem primitiven bewußt – dann steckt in der grandiosen Personifikation aller das Universum beherrschenden Normen, sofern sie als ein sinnvolles, widerspruchsloses System gedacht werden, dann steckt in dieser Idee eines persönlichen einheitlichen Gottes die gleiche oder doch eine verwandte Ökonomie des denkens, wie in der juristischen Konstruktion eines einheitlichen, persönlichen Trägers der staatlichen rechtsordnung, der staatsperson, des persönlichen, einheitlichen Staates.' Kelsen, *Über Staatsunrecht*, as cited in Staat und Recht im Lichte der Erkenntniskritik, at 114-115.

state equalled the '*absolute Rechtssubstanz.*' Similar to theology, where God was believed to be completely separate from – transcendental to – the world, in traditional state theories, the state was ascribed a separate meta-legal nature. And so, the 'state person' as sovereign represented the will of the state as the absolute power and source of law.

Der Staat als absoluter Wille im Sinne einer obersten Quelle des Rechtes findet seinen Ausdruck in der Vorstellung des Staates als Person, und zwar hier zunächst als metarechtliche Person (zum Unterschied von der der Rechtsordnung unterworfen gedachten Person des Staates). Als »Person« wird der Staat in dieser Hinsicht insofern vorgestellt, als er gegenüber den veränderlichen Funktionen des Rechtes als ruhende »Substanz«, als einziger und einheitlicher Träger des Rechtes gedacht wird. Zur Einheit und Einheitlichkeit des Staates tritt aber, als Konsequenz der Souveränität, die Einzigkeit hinzu: die Souveränität des einen Staates ist unvereinbar mit der eines anderen, und der Staat – sofern er wesentlich souverän ist – einzig.[456]

The concept of person or personification is vital to both legal theory and theology:

Das Urschema aller Substantialität is die Personalität«, sagt schon Vaihinger. Und so tritt auch die absolute Substanz in der Staatslehre ebenso wie in der Theologie als Person auf.

...

Wie der Staat so ist Gott als Persönlichkeit: Wille.[457]

Epistemologically, since the principal tendency of cognition is to aim at systematic unity, this separation or dualism is problematic. In theology, the connection was found in Christ, the incarnation of God on earth, both completely God and completely human. The Church established the dogma of the self-limitation of God, and the legal doctrine of the self-limitation of the state worked in roughly the same way.[458] Kelsen explained that just as theology had the 'Zwei Naturen Theorie', the theory of the state had the 'Zwei Seiten Theorie': the state person as both the sovereign power and the legal subject limits himself.[459] Any theological perception deviating from the one described above was declared a heresy. Any deviating legal theoretical position was non-conventional. Kelsen nevertheless took the non-conventional road. The problems were similar and so was the solution: reduction from two to one.

The equation of God with the world, '*Gott und Welt sind* einer *Wesenheit*,'[460] is considered 'pantheism' in orthodox theology.[461] Since its early days, the

[456] Id., at 115.

[457] Id., at 117 and 118.

[458] 'Dem Dogma von der Mensch – oder Weltwerdung Gottes entspricht haargenau die Theorie von der Selbstverplichtung des Staates.' Id., at 120.

[459] See *supra* Jellinek, text to footnote 140.

[460] Pohle, as cited in, Staat und Recht im Lichte der Erkenntniskritik, at 141.

[461] There are two forms of pantheism: 1) *Pankosmismus*, God is dissolved into the world; 2) *Akosmismus*: the world is dissolved into God. Id. Similarly, there are two ways to overcome the dualism of state and law.

Christian Church has opposed pantheism, because it was based on an *un*-personal idea of God. Pantheism, nevertheless, restores unity to the divided system by overcoming dualism. Kelsen sought a way to overcome the problem of dualism in the theory of law and the state[462] and borrowed the solution which advocated that one should recognise[463] '*die jeweilige Rechtsordnung als Staatsordnung, ... oder die jeweilige Staatsordnung als Rechtsordnung.*' The importation of this solution was possible because of the *logical* parallel between God and the state and the actual relationship between them:

Der die Menschen durch Gesetzesbefehl leitende König ist das Urbild für die die Natur lenkende Gottheit. Politisch-juristisches Denken geht naturwissenschaftlicher Erkenntnis nicht nur voran, sie weist ihr auch die ersten Wege. ... Das System von Staat und Recht ist das bestimmende Vorbild für das System von Gott und Natur. Auf einer gewissen Stufe der religiösen und politischen Entwicklung fallen die Vorstellungen von Gott und Staat geradezu zusammen: Der National-Gott ist einfach die in der Personifikation vergöttlichte Nation; es ist der Zustand, in dem die religiöse und die rechtliche Organisation, in der Kirche und Staat identisch sind.[464]

This argument included clear political aspects. The *Substanzbegriff* tended to make things 'absolute',[465] as the evolution of the concept of sovereignty in the theory concerning law and the state had proven. By using the parallel between God and the state, between theology and legal theory, Kelsen illustrated that the epistemological perspective and the ethical-political perspective conjoined in the problem of the relationship between law and the state.[466]

... das Kernproblem der Politik: das Verhältnis zwischen Individuum und Staat, und alle hier möglichen und versuchten Lösungen zum Teile wörtliche Wiederholungen jener Spekulationen sind, die die Theologie und insbesondere die religiöse Mystik über das Verhältnis von Gott und Einzelseele angestellt hat. Die Einheit zwischen den beiden entgegengesetzten Polen herzustellen, die Zweiheit als eigentliche Einheit aufzuzeigen, ist das Ziel des religiösen wie des politischen Denkens. Und auch die Wege zu diesem Ziel sind die gleichen: Entweder geht man vom Einzelindividuum aus, um das Universum in ihm aufgehen zu lassen, oder man geht vom Universum aus, um das Einzelindividuum in ihm aufzulösen. Individualismus und Universalismus sind die beiden Urschemata für die religiöse wie für die politische Theorie.[467]

---

[462] 'Worauf es ankommt, ist vor allem die Erkenntnis, daß, solange Staat und Recht als zwei von einander verscheidene Wesenheiten behauptet werden, für die Staats- und Rechtstheorie die gleiche Alternative gilt, vor die Feuerbachs Kritik des Gottesbegriffs die Theologie stellt: weil Gott die Natur und die Natur Gott aufhebt, darum: »Entweder Gott oder Natur! Ein drittes, Mittleres, ein beide Vereinigendes gibt es nicht.«' Staat und Recht im Lichte der Erkenntniskritik, at 141-142.

[463] This was possible because, Kelsen argued: 'Zwischen »Gott« und »Staat« besteht nicht nur eine logische Parallele, sondern auch manche reale Beziehung.' Id., at 142.

[464] Id., at 142.

[465] Id., at 103.

[466] 'Und genau so wie in der Theologie ... tritt in der Staatslehre das Problem der Vereinigung von Staat und Recht in einer eigenartigen Vermengung des ethisch-politischen mit dem erkenntnistheoretischen Gesichtspunkt auf.' Id., at 121.

[467] Id., at 132.

Traditionally the concept of the state tended to favour autocratic and absolutist orders, which did not in the least aim to establish a democratic legal order.[468] The state was allowed to do as it pleased. The interpretation of the state as a legal order, however, opened up the way to the democratic constitutional state.

In this respect, Kelsen's dissolution of the dualities of the subjective right and objective law as well as of private and public law is significant, as it also had an important political dimension. After all, the essence of exercising a legal right is the expression of a will, and, in the case of political rights, this means 'the power to influence the formation of the will of the state.' The 'will of the state' is the personification of the system of norms, the legal order: 'it is simply the phenomenal form of the legal norms making up the legal system – that is to say, statutes.' The citizens who are subject to the legal system are thus directly or indirectly participating in legislation, and that is 'the essential characteristic of the democratic form of state.'[469] Kelsen's unification of private and public law in one legal order which addressed 'persons' and thereby resulted in a relational concept of person was therefore as much a political as a legal theoretical act.[470]

3.4.4.4. *Freedom and democracy*

In 1932, at The Hague Academy, Kelsen opposed the conventional – restorative – concept of ILP which claimed that only states had legal personality under international law:

> [C]ette thèse, acceptée par la plu-part des théoriciens du droit international [que]: seuls les Etats sont sujets du droit international, est théoriquement fausse, et même, une fois rectifiée théoriquement, elle reste encore contraire au droit positif.[471] ... Comme tout droit, le droit international est ..., lui aussi, une réglementation de la conduite humaine. C'est à l'homme que s'adressent les normes du droit international, c'est contre l'homme qu'elles dirigent la contrainte, c'est aux hommes qu'elles remettent le soin de créer l'ordre. ... La "personne" en tant que sujet de droits et d'obligations n'est que l'expression personnifié de l'unité d'un système de normes réglementant des actions humaines, de l'unité d'un ordre total (Etat) ou partiel (autres personnes juridiques et «personnes physiques»).[472]

---

[468] Id., at 147.

[469] Problems of Legal Theory, at 45.

[470] 'If [political rights] are characterized by the fact that they grant to the right-holder a role in forming the will of the state, then even the subjective right of the private law is a political right, for here, too, the right-holder participates in forming the will of the state. ... if both the subjective right of the private law and the political right can be subsumed under one and the same concept of legal right, it is simply because the same legal function – the law-creating function – is expressed in both; that is to say, in both cases, those subject to the law participate in creating the law.' Id., at 46.

[471] H. Kelsen, Théorie Générale du Droit International Public, Problèmes Choisis, 42 *RCADI* 145-146 (1932-IV). Hereinafter: Théorie Générale. See also, Les Rapports de Système, at 243-244.

[472] Théorie Générale, at 142-143.

The idea that only states could have ILP was false. It was based on the old assumption that the state was a substantive meta-legal being and thus ignored the fact that international law was as much a regulation of individual human behaviour as any domestic legal order. Moreover, it wrongly perceived the 'person' as a biological-psychological being, rather than a purely normative construction. Kelsen's remarks on the concept of legal personality have provoked a certain amount of confusion. Part of the criticism of Kelsen's failure to perceive law contextually has been that he "unrealistically" 'eliminate[d]' sovereignty and personality from international law. The idea that he simply did away with the concept of ILP is, however, not correct.[473] And indeed, to speak of 'elimination' might be pushing the matter too far, but it is true that Kelsen obviously rejected the conventional meaning of the concept. What his comments on the subject of ILP *do* show is how the individual human being and international law are connected in the concept of legal personality. Having redefined the concept of person into a relational concept, Kelsen had broken down the hypostatisation of the ethical-political postulate of freedom and by replacing it with the concept of person as the personification of a bundle of norms, individual freedom was liberated, at least in theory.

When Kelsen chose to reject the old concept of legal person because it was the hypostatisation of the postulate of freedom, this was at the same time a repudiation of the Hegelian idea of individual freedom: only as part of the state could man realise his freedom, individuality, and morality. Self-awareness and individual freedom were only possible collectively, within a rational state community. It was this idea of freedom that the prevailing concept of legal personality and the state's legal personality, in particular, had hypostasised. The findings of social psychology seemed only to give increased warning against collectivism. The irrationality of mass behaviour and mass decision making only served to bring the question of how law could contribute to the protection of individual freedom and a stable social order further to the fore.

In *Vom Wesen und Wert der Demokratie*, we find evidence of how Kelsen viewed the relationship between the political dimensions of the tension between the individual (will and freedom) and the collective (will and freedom) on the one hand and the concept of the state person on the other:

Die im Grunde genommen unrettbare Freiheit des Individuums tritt allmählich in den Hintergrund und die Freiheit des sozialen Kollektivums in den Vordergrund. Der Protest gegen die Herrschaft von meinesgleichen führt im politischen Bewußtsein zu einer Verschiebung des Subjektes der – auch in der Demokratie unvermeidbaren – Herrschaft: zur Konstruktion der anonymen Person des Staates. Von ihr und nicht von äußerlich

[473] See, e.g., Schwarzenberger (1940), at 73. 'Kelsen eliminates the State as a legal personality ...' '[This] theor[y] suffer[s] from an element of wishful thinking which anticipates desirable changes in the political reality where the sovereign State is still firmly entrenched, and where the gap between theories and social facts merely produces bewilderment and dissolution.' With this remark he referred as much to Kelsen as to Scelle.

sichtbaren Menschen läßt man das Imperium ausgehen. Ein geheimnisvoller Gesamtwille und eine geradezu mystische Gesamtperson wird von den Willen und Persönlichkeiten der einzelnen losgelöst. Diese fiktive Isolierung vollzieht sich nicht so sehr gegenüber den Willen der Untertanen, als vielmehr gegenüber den Willen derjenigen Menschen, die die Herrschaft faktisch ausüben, und die nunmehr als bloße Organe eines hypostasierten Herrschaftssubjektes erscheinen. So verdeckt der Schleier der Staatspersonifikation das dem demokratischen Empfinden unerträgliche Faktum einer Herrschaft von Mensch über Mensch.[474]

Kelsen described how in political theory the idea of individual freedom and its realisation developed in relation to the state. He feared that if individual freedom was replaced by the sovereignty of the people as a collective, individual human and civil rights would be lost and so '*fungieren die Grundrechte der Demokratie als Minoritätsschutz und sichern die Gleichberechtung auch demjenigen, der nicht die politische, religiöse oder nationale Ueberzeugung der Mehrheit teilt.*'[475] Kelsen was a fierce defender of the system of parliamentary democracy, firmly based on a constitution which defined the people as a unity and thus protected the unity of the state against possible tension arising among a variety of groups. With so much diversity, the unity of a people could not be based on social psychology but was only possible if it was presented as an organisation or legal order. In order to save democracy and individual freedom it was essential to arrive at new concepts of the state and the person. The threat emanating from the problem of the individual versus the masses was countered by the purification of law and the state in an attempt to protect democracy as well as individual rights and responsibilities.[476] By the Pure Theory of Law Kelsen conjoined the values of tolerance, relativism and democracy.

The essential characteristic of the democratic form of state is that people subject to the statutes participate in legislation, in contradiction to the autocratic form of state, which excludes its subjects from any participation in forming the will of the state. ... ... The will of the state is expressed no less in the individual norm of the judicial decision than in the general norm of the statute. And if both the subjective right of the private law and the political right can be subsumed under one and the same concept of legal right, it is simply because the same legal function – the law-creating function – is expressed in both; that is to say, in both cases, those subject to the law participate in creating the law.[477]

With the dualities between private and public law and between objective law and subjective right resolved, a legal right might thus be 'an institution of a capitalist

[474] Von Wesen und Wert der Demokratie, at 57.

[475] Id., at 59.

[476] 'The essential problem of the political history of our time is whether the masses of mankind can be democratised, whether average human nature is such as to enable each to accept his share of *responsibility* as a *citizen* equally aware with all others of what he is doing, and ready as a part of his daily life to take his share in deciding fundamental political issues.' Jaspers, *supra* footnote 73, at 107.

[477] Problems of Legal Theory, at 46.

legal system, or ... a fixture of a democratic legal system.' One was entitled to participate in the creation of either an individual norm or a general norm. The positive (Kantian) concept of individual freedom defined as each citizen's participation in the creation of the law and the formation of the will of the state was thus given a legal foundation and framework. These legal rights and obligations were established by law and the concept of person was simply used to indicate the unity of the complex of these norms. 'In other words, the human being belongs to the community constituted by a legal system not in its entirety, but only in certain of his acts and forbearances, namely, those that are governed by the norms of the community's legal system.' 'Person' was a legal notion and it operated in the same way for physical and legal persons:

> The assumption that the legal person is a reality different from individual human beings, a reality, yet curiously imperceptible to the senses, or a supra-individual social organism made up of individual human beings – this is the naïve hypostatization of a thought, of a heuristic legal notion. Just as the 'physical' person is hardly the human being, so the legal person is hardly a supra-human being.[478]

In brief, the state was a legal order, democracy was participation in the state and therefore in the creation of law, and every individual had the right to participate, which made him a legal subject as well as a legislator. Every legal person was the personification of a legal order, which was a level in the hierarchy of law, extending from the basic norm and from the level of international law downwards, ultimately down to the human individual. The individual human person was thus the final destination of attribution as well as the starting point of the creation of the 'will of the state'. The concept of legal personality had the same function in national law as in international law: it was purely normative by nature.

3.4.5. Conclusion: *Entschleierung*

Having placed Kelsen's Pure Theory of Law and his argument in favour of the equation of law with the state against the background of the particular political situation of the Dual Monarchy and, subsequently, of the Austrian Republic's polluted political atmosphere, we may conclude that the Pure Theory sought a legal answer to the (contemporary) problems concerning the identity of the state, political stability and a threatened democracy. The epistemological analogy of the state and the atom and the absolute separation of *Sein* und *Sollen* were instrumental and essential to this equation. The parallel between theology and legal theory was equally vital to Kelsen's solution to the problem, which was reduction for the purpose of equation. Due to Kelsen's strict distinction between *Sein* und *Sollen*, the person, whether natural or legal, became the personification of a bundle of norms attributed to the same subject.

---

[478] Id, at 47-49.

The ILP of the state therefore ceased to function as the *Schleier* of the deity. Instead, the state was a legal person – a subsystem – addressed by international law and through its identity of legal person, international legal norms were able to connect with the ultimate lowest levels of the universal legal order. Personality was demythologised, reification rejected and ILP only acceptable as a legal construction. In our attempt to grasp the meaning of Kelsen's inter-war comments on the concept of legal personality, we have examined these statements in relation to the (legal) philosophical and the more practical political context in which they were made. In reference to the first, Kelsen's points were innovative but clear: it was necessary to overcome dualism and the connected mythological or metaphysical elements in legal theory. This would at the same time serve to support democracy. Kelsen's conception of legal personality was influenced by these goals. By 'person', Kelsen did *not* mean the individual human being – the physical person – but the *Zurechnungspunkt*, or: the point of attribution. By dissolving the duality between the physical person and the legal person into the singularity of the 'person' *as* a 'point of attribution,' it became a functional concept useful for cognition. From an epistemological perspective, this use of the concept of person, as a '*durchgangspunkt des denkens*' – '*ein Mittel der Logic*', an '*erkenntnismittel*,' i.e., a tool for cognition, was considered legitimate. '*[D]er Begriff der Rechtssubjektes' ist ein 'erkenntnistheoretische Fiction der Rechtswissenschaft.*'[479]

Secondly, Kelsen responded to the political problems which he witnessed by means of his argument in favour of a pure theory of law detached from the socio-political surroundings, i.e., by arguing a pure concept of law. This legal theoretical exercise was therefore as much a socio-political and ethical-political exercise. By equating the state with the legal order, Kelsen ensured that the state's rights and competences were never absolute but always based on and limited by (international) law. Every individual, enjoying 'personality' in the legal sense, participated in the formation of the will of the state, i.e., in legislation. In conformity with the Kantian republican theory of the state, every individual, because he was a person, was both legislator and legal subject, or, in other words, a citizen! And because international law ultimately addressed individual human beings this meant that they were also entitled to legal personality under international law. Consequently, just like citizenship gives the individual rights and responsibilities, so personality as a point of attribution, which indirectly links the individual – via the democratic constitutional state – to the international legal order, also gives rights to the individual and couples these with the responsibility to maintain and improve the international legal order: '*C'est à l'homme que s'adressent les normes du droit international, c'est contre l'homme qu'elles dirigent la contrainte, c'est aux hommes qu'elles remettent le soin de créer l'ordre.*'

During the modernist Interbellum period humanism might have been in retreat, but Kelsen's formalistic approach, de-deifying the state and laying down a

[479] Zur Theorie der juristischen Fiktionen, at 1216-1218.

concept of the state which linked every individual to the universal framework of law, in fact seems quite humanist by nature. The demystification or *Entschleierung* of the state person through the attribution of a new meaning to the concept of person, which is a key evaluative-descriptive term of (international) law language, was accomplished along the lines of contemporary epistemological insights and was aimed against the traditional conventions of legal language. As was stressed before, the sheer originality of the Pure Theory of Law and Kelsen's concept of legal personality can only be fully understood against the background of the prevalent practical political problems, the endangered democracy and the tendency to worship the reified collective will and freedom. By following a train of thought running on the dual track of both the epistemological and ethical-political aspects of the legal discussion and of the concept of legal personality in particular, Kelsen did not only revise (international) legal theory, but, in redefining legal personality, also defended democracy and fought to liberate individual freedom and responsibility.

3.5. Georges Scelle (1878-1961)[480]

> Sans doute nous trouvons-nous actuellement dans une période de régression parallèle dans le domaine interne et dans le domaine international, mais un rideau d'arbres ne saurait voiler la forêt. Cette régression des libertés individuelles se traduit, d'ailleurs, par une régression du fait social lui-même et un recul dangereux de la civilisation. Le monde entier souffre d'une sorte d'anarchie moyennâgeuse [sic.] faite de tyrannies étatiques. La fiction de la personnalité collective reparaît dans les dogmes et les mystiques, avec une virulence qui pourrait bien, d'ailleurs, n'être que la fièvre d'agonie de formes politiques et juridiques en train de se transformer pour s'adapter à des besoins nouveaux. Économiquement et politiquement, la société humaine, constituée et reliée par des phénomènes de solidarité inéluctables, cherche l'ordre et paix. Elle ne peut les trouver que dans des institutions sociales élargies et se subordonnant les États.[481]

3.5.1. **Introduction**

The French scholar with whom we conclude this chapter on the Interbellum demystification of the concept of ILP is the *realist* jurist Georges Scelle. Being characterised as a realist would meet with Scelle's approval, although the characterisation is not uncontested: in the historiography of international law

[480] See, e.g., Ch. Rousseau, Georges Scelle, 65 *RGDIP* 5 (1961); H. Thierry, The Thought of Georges Scelle, 1/2 *EJIL* 193 (1990); A. Cassese, Remarks on Scelle's Theory of 'Role Splitting' (dédoublement fonctionnel) in International Law, 1/2 *EJIL* 210 (1990); Id., L. Condorelli, Scholie sur l'idiome scellien des manuels francophones de droit international public, at 232; Id., R.J. Dupuy, Images de Georges Scelle, at 235; Id., A. Tanca, Georges Scelle (1878-1961), at 240.

[481] G. Scelle, Précis de Droit des Gens, Principes et Systématique, Vol. II Droit Constitutionnel International, at 294 (1934). Hereinafter: Précis II. Vol. I, Introduction, le milieu intersocial, 1932, hereinafter: Précis I.

theory Scelle has, on the contrary, been portrayed as an *idealist*. The discrepancy between these two portrayals is intriguing, even more so because it touches upon this chapter's overall theme: the crisis of early democracy within modern society and the endangered position of the individual.

In his article on Scelle's thinking, Thierry tends to support the view that the themes in Scelle's work 'did not take account of the strength of destructive and evil forces, of the herd instincts and fanaticism which brought about the Second World War ....' He recognises that even though he never closed his eyes to the reality around him, Scelle, 'against all odds', as Thierry points out, retained his idealist outlook.[482] The idealism attributed to Scelle's scholarship is mainly due to the social solidarity principle which I will discuss below and which he chose to cast as the foundation of law at a time when the world went through a critical stage or, in Scelle's own words, experienced a '*période de régression parallèle [des libertés individuelles] dans le domaine interne et dans le domaine international.*' Scelle evidently acknowledged the ongoing general decline of social life or 'sociability' and the crisis of civilisation. Upon close reading of the passage cited above, it becomes clear that he considered these developments to be the expression of a parallel – internal and external – crisis of individual liberties. *That*, in his eyes, was the fundamental issue to be confronted and challenged: the political crisis of individual liberties.

Scelle did not take up this challenge while blind to, what he called, '*les psychoses collectives.*'[483] On the contrary, although his methodology and choice of words at first glance suggest differently, when we realise that it fits in with a tradition in French political and public law thinking that featured actively in the debate on the crisis of democracy and individual liberties during the Third Republic, things start to fall into place. So by seeing Thierry's point and recognising Scelle's idealism (indeed, to disregard it would seriously interfere with our understanding of his work), rather than simply confirming Scelle's lack of attention to contemporary herd instincts and destructive social forces, it will become clear that Scelle was indeed aware of the developments taking place within modern mass society. However, it is equally important to realise that in the French political context, the state had, put boldly, posed more of a threat to the individual than the mass had to the state.

Turning to the specific context of the Third Republic, we will come to understand that the constitutional or institutional approach which Scelle chose to defend individual liberties, actually aimed to challenge the political reality of the parallel crisis by strongly appealing to *individual* competence, i.e., to the socially guaranteed power and duty to act,[484] and to effort.[485] He used ILP not only to

---

[482] Thierry, *supra* footnote 480, at 194 and 196.

[483] G. Scelle, La doctrine de L. Duguit et les fondements du droit des gens, 1-2 *Archives de Philosophie du droit et de Sociologie juridique* 105 (1932). Hereinafter: La doctrine de L. Duguit.

[484] Précis II, 'Droit Constitutionnel International,' at 3.

[485] Even though their theoretical perspective differed fundamentally, there is a parallel here with Kelsen who also valued and defended the importance that individual action and responsibility have for political developments.

demystify international law and downsize the state but also to subject all power under the law by conceiving of power in terms of (an) (individual) competence that is attributed and conditioned by law: only individuals possess (international) legal personality. It is a defence of individual liberties against the abuse of (state) power by those who rule. Instead of frowning over Scelle's method, we will begin to understand that in centre-left France the crisis of democracy and the unstable political situation in the Third Republic were generally analysed in terms of '*l'absolutisme de gouvernants [parlementaires]*' and the relation between the *Chef d'Executive* and the parliament. Just like the internal decline of individual liberties in France required a political *institutional* response, so, in this stage of parallel crisis, a similar response was necessary at the international level. We find the foundation of Scelle's comprehensive approach in the opening quote: human society constituted and existing by the phenomena of solidarity searches for order and peace, which it can only find or to which it can only progress by having the *right institutions*, i.e., here, subordinating states. This institutional approach is however at the same time an individualistic approach.

In brief, I agree with Kooijmans' conclusion on the 'strongly *individualistic* character' of the sociological school of law[486] and suggest that Scelle's doctrine on legal personality may best be understood by situating it not just in the international context but equally in the democratic crisis in Third Republic France with its strong social tension and persistent political divide. Scelle's pupil René Jean Dupuy has also confirmed Scelle's awareness of the social forces with which dangerous propagandists were playing, thereby posing a threat to democracy. However, Scelle trusted the resilience of society and the law it creates:

> Georges Scelle savait fort bien que le jeu spontané de l'éthique peut être profondément bouleversé par les propagandes. Si cette déformation est considérable dans les Etats totalitaires, elle n'est pas absente des autres. Mais à travers la complexité du jeu des forces sociales, la formule «*ubi societas, ibi jus* » lui semblait toujours vraie.[487]

By combining realistic observations with visionary idealism, Scelle has made a highly original contribution to the tradition of international law theory. Moreover, even though the sociologist's vocabulary that he used would initially seem to suggest otherwise, Scelle's scholarship supports our underlying theme concerning the *revisionist* endeavour to modernise international law and defend *individual* autonomy and freedom. It substantiates the thesis that international law theory was employed to confront the crisis of democracy and to contribute to human progress by assisting in the emancipation of the individual and his social environment.[488]

[486] P.H. Kooijmans, The doctrine of the Legal Equality of States: an Inquire into the Foundations of International Law 159 (1964). Emphasis added.

[487] R.J. Dupuy, *op. cit.* footnote 480, at 237.

[488] Précis II, at 17: 'Il n'y a pas de progrès humain sans un minimum d'émancipation individuelle et collective.' In the footnote, Scelle adds: 'L'émancipation est une réalisation juridique aussi vieille que le Droit lui-même, et contemporaine des institutions d'asservissement qui ne furent elles-mêmes que des réglementations des compétences.'

It is indeed accepted practice to label Scelle's work as a 'demystification project.' The quotation heading this section already revealed in Scelle's own words his intention to contribute to the transformation of international law and to adapt it to the new demands of international life and to the rejection of mystical and anthropomorphic tendencies in classical international law theory and in particular to the rejection of the contribution to such tendencies by the concept of ILP. In 1961, Rousseau also typified Scelle's work as the '*grande entreprise de «démythification» ou de démystification – de l'Etat*', observing that '*il tenta dans l'ordre international procédait directement de l'analyse de Duguit – son seul et vrai maître.*'[489]

In order to be able to fully understand Scelle's demystification project in relation to ILP, it is not enough to know that his work is anti-metaphysical. It particularly requires a basic understanding of Léon Duguit's ideas. The concept of social solidarity has contributed to the confusion concerning the position of the individual in relation to the social phenomenon of collectivities. But like Duguit, Scelle, as a true realist, was only prepared to acknowledge the human individual as a *real* being and denied such reality to the collective. In order to overcome the old voluntarist (subjective) doctrines concerning the state and state sovereignty, Scelle needed a non-voluntarist approach, in other words, an *objective* approach, which he found with Duguit. This approach may be social by nature, but it is *not* collectivist: in no way do either Duguit or Scelle recognise the existence of a collective consciousness or collective personality. The present analysis will emphasise the *competence* attributed to the *individual* in controlling the state through his involvement in society's formulation of the law.

The originality and vitality of Scelle's theory have been repeatedly acknowledged and confirmed, even up to today.[490] Here however our contextual approach aids the understanding of Scelle's theory of (international) law and his conception of ILP as aimed at the development and improvement of international constitutional law in order to limit both domestic and international power. When we take this context seriously in analysing the notion of ILP, a rather more constitutional angle automatically presents itself. We will primarily base our argument on the fundamental parts of the *Précis de Droit des Gens principes et*

---

[489] Rousseau, *op. cit.* footnote 480, at 11.

[490] In 1990, the *European Journal of International Law* kicked off its unrivalled series on The European Tradition in International Law with articles dedicated to Scelle and his work. *Supra*, footnote 480. See also, M. Koskenniemi, The Gentle Civilizer of Nations: The Rise and Fall of International Law 1870-1960 (2002), at 266-352. Koskenniemi provides an analysis of Scelle's outlook on international law (theory) by relating it to contemporary French political theories, such as (radical) solidarism, internationalism as a means of best serving French national interests, and he linked Scelle's thinking especially to that of Durkheim, Duguit and Bourgeois, Pillet, Renault, Alvarez, Politis, and others. Koskenniemi insightfully positions Scelle next to his more conservative colleague, Le Fur. While both agree on the dangers inherent in German positivist international law theories, Le Fur defended the nation state at a time when this institution was under threat, whereas Scelle turned to federalism and international solidarity to provide the answer to the internal and post-WWI international crisis.

systématique I and *II* (1932-34).[491] It is my conviction that we can only begin to understand Scelle when we realise that contemporary political internal problems were also central to his thinking. Segal has already pointed out that, besides the fact that the contemporary international context called for a reaction against voluntarist thinking, the domestic context also influenced the perspective on public (international) law:

[L]'idée de l'État de droit (Rechtsstaat) qui semble en recul à l'heure actuelle, idée essentiellement démocratique, a gagné de plus en plus du terrain pendant les premières décades du vingtième siècle. L'idée démocratique triomphant et exerçant son influence toujours plus effective sur la vie nationale, ne pouvait pas s'accommoder des conceptions volontaristes du droit, fruit de l'absolutisme étatique et gouvernementales. *La sauvegarde et la défense des droits des citoyens contre les abus et l'arbitraire des gouvernants est devenue le problème essentiel du droit public*. Pour atteindre ce but, il était nécessaire que le droit fût considéré comme étant *au-dessus des gouvernants*, qu'il les oblige malgré et même contre leur volonté. Cette *tendance de défendre les droits individuels contre l'oppression de l'État* est d'une importance capitale pour toutes les doctrines qui s'opposent au subjectivisme juridique; pour quelquesunes, c'est la principale raison d'être.[492]

Clearly, Scelle is one of those scholars who participated in this endeavour to uphold democratic values. As Cassese has pointed out, Scelle actually conceived of the international community as 'in fact a society of rulers (*une société de gouvernants*) who try to perpetuate their authority by clinging to the postulate of state sovereignty.' He explains that '[p]rogress, in Scelle's view, can be made in the international community only if one moves towards *restraining* the authority of *rulers* and succeeds in establishing a set of international agencies or bodies capable of bringing the international legal order into line with the basic configurations of state systems.'[493] The international society had to develop from a rather primitive into a more constitutionally and institutionally complex structure.

It will thus become clear that the demystification of the concept of ILP and the subsequent attribution of ILP to individuals in general and to rulers in particular – '*les gouvernants étatiques [sont les] principaux sujets du droit des gens*'[494] – served a dual cause. On the one hand, Scelle faced up to the domestic crisis of the

[491] We will also consider another text which is relevant for understanding Scelle's approach to ILP and international law in general: Théorie et Pratique de la Fonction Exécutive en Droit International (1936), 55 *RCADI* 87-202 (1936). Hereinafter: La Fonction Exécutive. I tend to understand this text as forming an integral part of the Précis I and II, because, at various instances in these two volumes (Le milieu intersocial and Le droit des gens constitutionnel), Scelle refers to what according to his plan should have become Chapter IV: La fonction executive in part III: Le Droit des gens administrative, but which never appeared as such. See, e.g., Vol. I, at 59, 69, and 312; Vol. II, at 31-32, 102, 131, 134, 203, 310, 327, 402.

[492] S. Segal, Les fondements du droit dans la doctrine de M. Georges Scelle, IX *Revue internationale de la théorie du droit* 186-187 (1935). Emphasis added.

[493] Cassese, *op. cit.* footnote 480, at 216. Emphasis added.

[494] La Fonction Exécutive, at 91.

French democratic system and, on the other hand, formulated a response to the crisis of international law and in particular to the claim that international law does *not exist* as long as there is no executive to enforce its rules; a defect which he remedied by attributing *international* competences to *national* state executive officers, i.e., the famous doctrine of the *dédoublement fonctionnel.* The concept of ILP serves to pursue both goals.

In the following outline of the political and intellectual context in which Scelle worked, the crisis of democracy and its threat to individual liberties is the issue at stake.

3.5.2. **French Context: The Third Republic (1870-1940)** [495]

3.5.2.1. *The political context: l'absolutisme des gouvernants*

Scelle was born in 1878, only a few years after the Third Republic had come to replace the authoritarian regime of the Second Empire (since 1852). The internal decline of democracy and individual liberties during the early 20th century to which Georges Scelle referred was rooted in the constitutional structure of the Third Republic itself. The Third Republic had its origins in international war, civil conflict and political tension between Republicans (left-wing) and conservative Monarchists (right-wing) sympathisers.[496] From 1871 to 1875, when all constitutional laws were finally in place, France vacillated between a republican and a monarchical identity and even after it had been constitutionally recognised, the republican identity was never entirely beyond dispute. Especially during the Republic's early years, the anti-republican movement was still quite strong and monarchist sympathies were particularly widespread among the army and the clergy.

The 1875 constitutional laws had been a compromise between republicans and monarchists.[497] Consequently, these laws in the first place contained the ingredients for the *political institutional imbalance* that came to characterise the Third Republic's political life largely due to the ambiguous position of the Head of

---

[495] See, e.g., W. Fortescue, The Third Republic in France 1870 – 1940: Conflicts and Continuities (2000). Hereinafter: The Third Republic. J.-M. Mayeur, La vie politique sous la Troisième République 1870-1940 (1984, éd. du Seuil). Hereinafter: La vie politique.

[496] During the final years of the Empire, the lack of democracy and of an effective system of civil and labour law rights resulted in the genesis of working class consciousness. When a proper representation of their interests failed to materialise, rural and urban France started to drift apart. The political opposition between leftists and conservatives came to coincide to a considerable extent with the divide between urban (Paris in particular) and rural France.

[497] The position of the President was, on the one hand, 'declared irresponsible,' on the other hand, 'he was, through the influence of the monarchists, given the powers of a constitutional king on the English or Orleanist model.' At the international level, moreover, the President 'played almost as important a role as the ministers.' For instance, '[h]e could sign treaties of alliance, which, unlike treaties of commerce and of peace, needed no parliamentary ratification.' Th. Zeldin, France 1848-1945, Vol. I, Ambition, Love and Politics, 593-594 (1973). Hereinafter: France.

State. A second consequence of the fact that the constitutional laws were a compromise between republicans and monarchists was that contrary to the revolutionary tradition a *Déclaration des droits* was lacking, since consensus had been lacking on the issue of individual fundamental rights.

Let us start with the *political institutional imbalance* which existed in the relationship between the executive branch, i.e., the cabinet and the President of the Republic – *le chef de pouvoir exécutif* –, and the legislative branch. The relative weakness of the executive and especially of the President, on the one hand, and the increasingly powerful position of the parliament, on the other hand, resulted in a situation of *parliamentary absolutism*.

Initially, the 1875 constitutional laws were intended as temporary laws while awaiting a permanent constitution that some hoped would turn France back into a monarchy. As a temporary compromise, the laws merely organised the three branches of power and distributed competences among them. The legislative power was placed in the hands of a National Assembly, made up of a Chamber of Deputies and a Senate, which together elected the President of the Republic by majority vote for a 7-year term. The executive power was invested in the Cabinet rather than in the Presidency and the Cabinet was 'at the mercy' of the deputies.[498] Yet, the President did have the right to appoint and dismiss ministers, and he tested the limits of this right with some regularity. The controversy over the state's identity – republican or monarchist – had become an inherent part of the temporary constitutional structure by the mixed character given to the head of state, the President of the Republic. This ambiguity was carried over into the Third Republic's political institutional practice largely because of the mixed conception of the executive:

> [L]a conception de l'exécutif aujourd'hui officiellement admise tient le milieu entre autres conceptions : celle de l'exécutif, simple agent de l'assemblée, et celle de l'exécutif indépendant.[499]

Duguit's spoke of '*une sorte de roi élu*,' a king without power '*un fantôme sans pouvoir effectif*.'[500] The institutional dominance of parliament grew out of the continuing controversy over the kind of President France needed: for many a strong Executive had monarchical overtones and was therefore suspicious. During the Second Republic (1848-1852), Napoleon III – the independent *chef de pouvoir executive* – had turned the republic back into an empire and thereby negatively influenced the conception of the strong executive as anti-republican and non-parliamentary. During the first few decades of the Third Republic, there-

---

[498] J.D. Bragger, Constitutional Laws of 1875, *in* P.H. Hutton (Ed.), Historical Dictionary of the Third French Republic, at 237. Hereinafter: Historical Dictionary.

[499] J. Barthelémy, Le Role du Pouvoir Exécutif dans les Républiques Modernes (1906/7), at 414. Hereinafter: Le Role du Pouvoir Exécutif.

[500] L'Etat, Les Gouvernants et Les Agents (1903), at 327-328.

fore, the republicans in their doctrines advocated a weaker position for the executive and a strong parliament, representative of the sovereignty of the people, as the most democratic solution imaginable. This geneally remained the position of the republicans in the subsequent series of confrontations and crises that shaped political and institutional France during the early years of the Third Republic. The monarchists, on the other hand, tended to argue in favour of strengthening the Presidency. A number of political crises further defined the process of government in general and affected the relationship between the legislature and the executive in particular.[501] The increasing dominance of parliament, however, failed to create political stability. On the contrary, political processes were increasingly plagued by governmental instability and recurring struggles for authority between the President and the parliament.[502]

First, there was the '*seize mai*' crisis which was symbolic of the ongoing disagreement between the conservative President MacMahon and the mainly republican Chamber. This constitutional conflict erupted on 16 May 1877 when the President dismissed *premier-ministre* J. Simon without the approval of the Chamber. The conflict ultimately affirmed 'the primacy of the legislature over the executive.'[503]

Secondly, there was the *Boulanger* Affair (1886-89), which developed into a crisis concerning among other things a proposed revision of the constitution, which aimed to enhance the powers of the President and to abolish the Senate. It resulted in a confirmation of the *status quo*, as the revision was not successful.[504]

Thirdly, another defining crisis during the Third Republic was the *Dreyfus* affair (1894-1906).[505] The affair once more revealed the gap of opinion between

---

[501] P.H. Hutton, Politics, Historical Dictionary, at 784-789. Hereinafter: Hutton.

[502] 'The Third Republic was one of the most confusing and paradoxical of political regimes. It was supposed to mark the advent of democracy, but it produced disconcertingly little fundamental change in the structure of the state, which remained monarchical, or even *ancien régime*, in many ways. Its vision ... ... was a free, egalitarian and fraternal society, in which constant discussion of common interests would lead all classes to a higher sense of solidarity and justice. But in practice it gave power to an oligarchy of discredited professional politicians, who maintained their dominance by placating the particularist interests of their more influential constituents and by closing their eyes to the corruption which surrounded them. The exceptional longevity of the regime is difficult to reconcile with its equally unprecedented instability.' France, at 570.

[503] Hutton, at 785; France, at 595. See also, The Third Republic, at 33: Although the constitutional laws indeed conferred 'the right to appoint and dismiss government ministers' on the President 'it was widely understood that a government should not be dismissed by the president unless it had been defeated in a vote of confidence in the Chamber of Deputies.' The '*seize mai*' crisis consolidated this understanding and thereby the predominance of the Chamber.

[504] Hutton, at 785. Also, The Third Republic, at 43-46.

[505] The *Dreyfus* affair demonstrated that the state could not only fail, but could even crush individuals by a sequence of state failures. The state repeatedly failed to uphold justice, while the army involved itself in fabricating false evidence against Dreyfus and ignoring evidence against another officer. The traditionally anti-semitic catholic clergy supported the anti-Dreyfussards and the parliament, which was controlled by the liberal bourgeoisie, consistently turned a blind eye. The parliament continually refused to grant a retrial until the very end of the affair in 1906, although in 1900 a pardon was accepted. Meanwhile, the state made use of the anti-semitic sentiments among the French to make Dreyfus the scapegoat of an embarrassing espionage situation.

right-wing and left-wing supporters where the 'fundamental question of the definition of France's national identity and of the character of the French Republic'[506] was concerned. Earlier, the *Panama* affair had already brought home to many that Parliament had become a corrupt forum of businessmen instead of a legislature that served the public and the common good.[507] But it was the *Dreyfus* affair that would throw a long shadow over French society and remain a political factor even after WWI, although it also 'symbolized the victory of modern over traditional French society by affirming the Republicans' obligation to protect individual liberties, abide by democratic procedures, promote equal opportunities in public life, and ensure the separation of church and state.'[508] During this period of political and intellectual turmoil, Scelle studied law at the University of Paris. He lived in the city during the late 1890s – early 1900s and obtained his *doctorat* in 1906.

One more political incident should be mentioned here. It concerns an affair that took place just before the *Cartel de Gauche* came to power in 1924. President Millerand was forced to step down after the Chamber had accepted Herriot's motion demanding that the President resigned for overstepping the limits of his authority and negating the rights of the parliament.[509] Again the Republican ideal of a strong legislative power with a dependent and weak executive was victorious, while the idea of reform for the purpose of strengthening the President's authority failed to succeed.

This tension flared up at particular instances in the political history of the Third Republic and was never completely absent in the periods in between.[510] Politically critical situations continued to occur as Presidents tested the limits of their powers. However, the 'dominance of the deputies' was confirmed and remained a distinctive feature of French politics.[511] Gradual change could be perceived after WWI, when arguments in favour of reinforcing the executive were also made in defence of democracy against *parliamentary absolutism.*

In the late 1920s and early 1930s, the general perception that the idea of strengthening the position of the executive was suspect changed. Or, rather, the realisation dawned that 'a lessening of the intrusion of the legislative into the realm of the executive, [and] the abolition of meddling by the deputies with the bureaus of public administration' might be necessary.[512] This realisation led to

---

[506] The Third Republic, at 50.

[507] Id. See also, on the corruption of Parliament, France, at 576-84.

[508] Hutton, at 785. The separation of church and state was arranged by a law of 9 December 1905.

[509] La vie politique, at 277-279.

[510] See, e.g., La vie politique, at 218-220 and 229 (on the years just before WWI); at 252, 262-263 (on the years 1919/20), at 339-341 (on the year 1934).

[511] For the dominance of the deputies and the permanency of the parliamentary sessions, the excessive use of the deputy's right to initiate legislation, and the system of parliamentary commissions, see, e.g., France, at 584 *et seq.*

[512] J. Benda, The Enemies of Democracy in France, 13 *Foreign Affairs* 291 (1934/5).

intense political and intellectual debate. The firm position of the Republicans during the major crises had resulted in a weakening of the executive and a strengthening of the legislature. In the 1930s, however, some Republicans based themselves on the dominant position of the parliament to push for constitutional reforms.[513] The international (political) uncertainty and economic crisis of the early 1930s increased the pressure on the politicians. However, the governmental instability for which the Third Republic is now known prevented politicians from responding effectively to the social needs. According to the constitutional structure, the Chamber had the power to dismiss the Cabinet and as politically it had the upper hand it used this power quite freely. Approximately every six months a new Cabinet had to be installed. Still, although the 1920s may have been less turbulent then the 1930s,[514] figures unambiguously reveal that the realisation of ambitious (political or social) reforms also proved very difficult in that period. This means that between 1919 and 1940 there were 'forty-two governments, each of which lasted on average no longer than six months.'[515] Especially during the early 1930s the parliament performed very weakly and proved incapable of forming the majority decisions necessary to fight the Depression.[516] The internal political instability and the inability to respond effectively to the problems of the time focused the debate on the Republic's institutional problems.

---

[513] La vie politique, at 334.

[514] After WWI, it appeared that the dominant position of the Radicals had waned. During the 1920s until 1932, moderate right-wing governments ruled France, with only one exception, namely the Government of Edouard Herriot (1924-25), which only lasted eleven months, mainly because the Socialists who had won the elections together with the Radicals under the joint name of *Cartel de Gauche*, refused to actually join the Cabinet. Under this Government, Georges Scelle served as the director of the cabinet of Justin Goddart, the Minister of Labour. See also, Rousseau, *op. cit.* footnote 480, at 9. This government recognised moreover *le droit syndical pour les fonctionaires*. The Herriot Cabinet ended with the *Affaire Scelle*. After ten months (14 juin 1924 – 17 april 1925) at the Ministry of Labour, the Minister of Education appointed Scelle as Professor of Law of the Paris Faculty. The University of Paris had, however, already endorsed the faculty council's designation of Louis Le Fur for the post. The issue at stake was evidently the independence of the university, but, as Rousseau observed, the conflict was 'politically exploited.' We should bear in mind that Scelle was identified with left-wing politics, while Le Fur was more acceptable to right-wing sympathisers, and because the manifestations of the (extreme right-wing) *Action française* students became quite violent the Faculty had to be closed for a while. The real causes of the Cabinet's decline were however of a financial and budgetary nature. The government had moreover been evidently unstable from the start since no Socialist minister had taken a seat in it. Koskenniemi's eminent piece of scholarship makes further elaboration on more biographical issues like the '*affaire Scelle*' rather redundant at this point. The Gentle Civilizer, at 316-317. Also, Rousseau, at 9.

[515] Between democracy and autocracy, at 206. The political instability of the Third Republic regime is a subject of academic dispute. Some say the ministerial instability was counterbalanced by the stability of the dominance of the deputies.

[516] Id. From 1934 onwards, the French Left scouted for candidates with whom to establish some kind of left-wing alliance. Eventually, the Radicals joined the so-called Popular Front. When the Popular Front won the 1936 parliamentary elections, social reforms finally seemed possible. The resulting government however already collapsed in 1937.

The other major consequence of the fact that the 1875 constitutional laws were a compromise intended for a brief period of time was that the 1875 *constituants* had failed to incorporate a *Déclaration des droits*. This silence on civil liberties was to a large extent due to the lack of consensus on the substance of these liberties, still '[*l*]*e régime ne tarde d'ailleurs pas à consacrer, par une série de lois, les principales libertés* ...' *However*, '*il ne suffit pas de proclamer des droits, encore faut-il en garantir effectivement l'exercice. Or, sur ce terrain, l'œuvre de la Troisième République demeure inachevée* [*incomplete, defective*].'[517] The constitution lacked such fundamental norms as the individual fundamental rights or liberties at a time when the need to protect the individual right of every citizen particularly against the abuse of power by the Chamber deputies was pressing and the institutional system itself offered no solutions.

Pour protéger efficacement les libertés contre les abus du législateur, il aurait fallu, d'une part, que l'on pût se référer à des normes opposables à celui-ci; d'autre part, que fût organisé un contrôle de constitutionalité. Or, aucune de ces conditions, strictement complémentaires, n'est remplie.[518]

Besides omitting individual liberties, the 1875 did not include an incontestable ground for a procedure of constitutional control either. Unsatisfied with the situation, 'Hauriou et Duguit eurent beau soutenir que la Déclaration de 1789 avait valeur positive.' Others argued that the *Déclaration* still had to be incorporated in the constitutional texts. '*Rien n'y fit. La Déclaration demeura ineffective*.' The lack of a constitutional procedure was due to the sovereignty of the parliament: '[*l*]*a souveraineté de la loi, héritée de la Révolution, y mettait obstacle*.' Another aspect of the institutional imbalance was that: '*dans le contexte de la République parlementaire, il était difficile d'imaginer une lutte entre législateur et juge qui ne tournât pas à l'avantage du premier. L'instauration d'un contrôle efficace supposait donc une modification du droit positif*.' Nonetheless, some Chamber deputies introduced proposals to create a Supreme Court, which would have to deal with individual complaints by citizens that their rights had been violated by the legislative or executive. None of these proposals was accepted and the constitutionality of the laws which the parliament promulgated remained untested apart from by the parliament itself. Giving any other organ the power to test these laws would be tantamount to denying the supremacy of the law and the legislative. It was generally considered that this would affect the sovereignty of the national will. Obviously, Third Republic *parliamentary absolutism* also manifested itself here.[519]

In brief, in the political constellation of the Third Republic, the Chamber of deputies had superior power. Together with the Senate, it elected the President of the

[517] M. Morabito, Histoire constitutionnelle de la France (1789-1958), 7th ed. 2002, at 326.
[518] Id., at 327.
[519] Id., at 328 and 380.

Republic and could dismiss Cabinets by a vote of no confidence. On the one hand, this corresponded to the republican tradition of the sovereignty of the people as represented by the parliament. On the other hand, however, the resulting weakness of the executive affected the system of checks and balances between the branches of power and contributed to governmental instability. Also, because there was no other body to challenge it, the power of the Members of Parliament was not sufficiently restrained. This imbalance, together with the phenomenon of *syndicalism*,[520] was a recurring and defining factor in the political reality of the Third Republic. The emphasis which is generally placed on the role of syndicalism in Scelle's work will not be repeated here. The phenomenon of syndicalism should be considered more part of the larger picture of disenchantment over the political (institutional) organisation of the Third Republic and its failure properly to defend the individual liberties against the absolutism and abuse of power of the Members of Parliament, *les gouvernants*. This is the practical context in which I wish to position my analysis of Scelle's concept of international law and ILP.

3.5.2.2. *Intellectual context: debating the decline of democracy and individual liberties*

Against the background of the political crises which continually put French democracy and the French state to the test, the debate on the Republic's political institutional structure and the need for its reform continued and in fact often dominated the intellectual agenda. Moreover, in the early 1930s, the failure of politics to respond effectively to the international political uncertainty and economic depression increased the pressure on the political institutions and heated up the debate.[521] Le Fur and Barthélemy analysed the French democratic crisis and both advocated a strengthening of the executive in order to salvage democracy.[522] Leon Duguit argued the opposite, but with the same objective, namely

---

[520] See for a concise description, Papayanis, Syndicalism, *in* Historical Dictionary, at 991: Syndicalism aimed to change the capitalist and political structures which ignored the workers' interests; revolutionary syndicalists believed that it would take a revolution necessary to accomplish this change, while more moderate syndicalists favoured structural change through the representation of workers' interests by trade or labour unions. The changes would most probably have to be enforced by strikes. 'According to syndicalist theory, labor organisations were prototypes for the organization of postrevolutionary society. This new society would be federal in structure, would favor voluntary associations of producers, and would depend on trade unions and Bourses du travail for the administration of local communities.'

[521] La vie politique, at 334.

[522] See also, e.g., E. Giraud, La Crise de la Démocratie et le Renforcement du Pouvoir Exécutif (1938), at 7: '*L'Executif est le point faible de la démocratie.*' Id., at 85: 'une partie de l'opinion démocratique voit, dans l'Exécutif, un suspect et croit à la nécessité de l'affaiblir. Il faut faire justice de ces préjugés.' However, strengthening the position of the Executive was also in Giraud's opinion the only way to prevent a general dictatorship from taking over. Id., at 71: 'Ce sont les défaillances et les insuffisances de la démocratie qui ont engendré la dictature. On n'évitera celle-ci qu'en rénovant la démocratie.'

defending democracy and individual liberties. All the participants in the debate at least agreed that in order to remedy the failings of democracy and halt the decline of individual liberties, a fundamental *institutional* response was required.

In 1931, Barthélemy[523] published *La crise de la démocratie contemporaine*, a comparative study of European democracies in crisis in order to learn whether these crises stemmed from similar roots or had shared characteristics.[524] In his view, the French crisis was caused by a decline of parliamentary democracy and individualism. Individualism was particularly threatened by syndicalism, which he regarded as: '*la lutte de l'intérêt grégaire* [the struggle of the horde interest] *des masses contre l'individualisme* moral, social et politique.'[525] The *idea* of democracy itself was in crisis: 'la foi est morte.'[526] Among intellectuals, Barthélemy observed an increasing degree of scepticism concerning parliamentary democracy.[527] He tentatively positioned anti-parliamentarism as being primarily present in the drawing rooms of Paris, but also expressed serious concern about French public opinion in general, which also seemed to have lost faith in parliamentary democracy and had embraced less democratic political movements. Barthélemy contended that this democratic crisis should be treated as a crisis mainly of parliamentary authority with a resulting lack of leadership. The institutionally dominant, but practically ineffective legislature needed to be counterbalanced by a true executive power: 'Le régime parlementaire ne peut fonctionner que si à la tête du gouvernement, il y a véritablement un chef.'[528] In the Third Republic, the nation was sovereign and had delegated the exercise of its sover-

---

[523] Barthélemy was not only a professor at the Paris law faculty, but had also been active in politics as a Member of Parliament for the *Bloc national*, in which his centre political party, *l'Action républicaine et sociale*, participated. See *infra*, footnote 21: La vie politique, at 260. Koskenniemi points out that Barthélemy somehow went from being one of the leading liberal constitutional lawyers of the 1920s and 30s to a member of the Vichy Government. The Gentle Civilizer, at 313.

[524] J. Barthelémy, La crise de la démocratie contemporaine (1931). He analysed the political situations in Italy, Spain, Poland and Russia. Hereinafter: La crise de la démocratie contemporaine.

[525] Id., at 12, 146 *et seq.*, 190, and 211. Barthélemy believed that syndicalism had to be contained. Bringing the representation of particular economic interests within a democratic political system would harm the primacy of politics and of the public interest, which are both essential to any democracy. It therefore required effective channeling to prevent syndicalist dictatorship from taking over France. His opinion differed significantly from Duguit's and Scelle's, who were more positive and considered syndicalism as a possible answer to the malfunctioning of democracy. Barthélemy found the *Conseil national économique* less than successful. The *Conseil* was the consultative organ to the government in which both workers' syndicates and employers' organisations were represented and in the establishment of which Scelle was actively involved during his time at the Ministry of Labour.

[526] Id., at 12-13. Emphasis added.

[527] Id., at 134-135.

[528] Id., at 141. Id., at 139: 'Le parlementarisme actuel souffre d'une crise de leadership.' He pointed to various factors to explain the failure of the parliament, such as the quality of the Members of Parliament which had been dropping for years and continued to do so; the danger that professional *syndicates* would take up social positions between the individual and the state; the poor quality of the decisions and documents produced by the parliament; the excessive length and frequency of parliamentary sessions.

eignty to the parliament. The dominant position of the parliament was, however, undermining political stability and democracy: '*le contrôle [parlementaire] détruise l'autorité*.' According to Barthélemy governmental authority had to be strengthened by limiting the excessive control exercised by the Chamber and by strengthening the executive power, in order to halt the '*régression de la liberté démocratique*'.[529]

Similarly, in 1934, Le Fur published his analysis of the contemporary French crisis, *La démocratie et la crise de l'Etat*, in which he distinguished 'une triple crise, la crise de la démocratie politique et sociale, la crise du régime parlementaire ... enfin la crise de l'Etat lui-même.'[530] However, in his view, *law* not politics should be supreme within a democracy. To defend the autonomous will of *individual* citizens against majority dominance,[531] supremacy should not be entrusted to the majority but rather to law and morality. Since Le Fur had no faith in what he termed the '*sentiment autonome de justice des masses*' and intended to defend parliamentary democracy as the political system which best served liberty, equality, and the public good,[532] he argued that natural law had to be the basis of individual conduct and national and international political and social life. To save democracy and to ensure that every individual was recognised as an end in itself, Le Fur, surpassing Barthélemy, argued that the abusive 'new feudalism' of the Chamber deputies had to be controlled and that the executive's independence had to be strengthened by means of the *direct* national election of the *chef de l'Etat*. According to Le Fur, the misuse of (parliamentary) power demanded an urgent institutional response: 'sinon il est à craindre que, en présence des abus d'un système où, selon le mot de Jaurès, les députés cherchent à se « tailler des fiefs d'absolutisme dans la souveraineté nationale », on ne soit acculé par un coup d'Etat ou une révolution à un brusque changement de régime.'[533] The debate on (how to remedy the) 'crisis of democracy and individual liberties' thus centred on the absolutism of the Members of Parliament and the weak position of the Republic's President.

---

[529] Id., at 153-154, emphasis added. In 1931, Barthélemy still preferred '*des réformes* dans *l'Etat*' to the '*Réforme* de *l'Etat*,' but after 1934, he accepted the argument that a mere change of, e.g., the Chamber's working procedures would not be enough to reinforce governmental authority and that institutional reforms were indeed necessary. La vie politique, at 336.

[530] Le Fur, La démocratie et la crise de l'Etat (1934), *in* Les Grands Problèmes du Droit 530-583 (1937). Hereinafter: La démocratie et la crise de l'Etat.

[531] It was discussed whether a proportional system should replace the constituency voting system, as the latter falsified the representative nature of the Chamber. Due to constituency voting, the parliamentary *majority* represented only a *minority* of French citizens.

[532] According to Le Fur, a true democracy is neither purely liberally individualist nor purely collective in nature, but reconciles the rights or interests of the individual with the interests of society and the authority of the governmental powers. Democracy is the right of being governed *well*, i.e., the right of the governed to *good* governance, to a fair balance of interests and sound control of governmental powers to ensure that the common good is served and power not abused. La démocratie et la crise de l'Etat, at 582-583.

[533] Id., at 577-581.

By the 1930s, the problem had become a classic one in the public law debate in France. As the problem of the position of the executive and its relationship with the legislature was rooted in the ambiguity of the 1875 constitution, the debate could refer to contributions from the earliest years of the 20th century, such as, for instance, Léon Duguit's *L'État, Les Gouvernants et Les Agents* (1903),[534] and Joseph Barthélemy's *Le Role du Pouvoir Exécutif dans les Républiques Modernes* (1906). Both expressed their concern about the decline of democracy and the threat to individual liberties, but proposed different ways of dealing with these problems. They agreed that the constitutional system's conception of the executive was ambiguous, as it neither proclaimed the President a fully independent *representative* of the nation('s sovereignty), a *gouvernant*, nor reduced him to a mere parliamentary *agent*. Moreover, although the 1875 Constitution may have intended to create a system of *collaboration* between the executive and the legislative, the (temporary) political organisation it had actually laid down had in reality led to a dominant position of the Chamber deputies and a purely symbolic head of the executive. Barthélemy and Duguit disagreed, however, on how to redress this institutional imbalance. Barthélemy argued that the position of the President of the Republic should be strengthened in his quality of the *représentant de la volonté nationale*.[535] He contended that a 'relative' separation of state powers, including the recognition of a relatively 'independent' and 'active' (and thereby more 'collaborative') executive,[536] would serve the *individual liberties* best: a 'restored' President was needed to defend 'les libertés individuelles et les intérêts supérieurs de la nation' against 'les abus du Parlement.'[537]

[534] Also, its preceding volume, L'État, le droit objectif et la loi positive (1901).

[535] Le Role du Pouvoir Exécutif, at 731. Id, at 627 and 717-718, Barthélemy: 'L'exécutif actuel n'agit pas en *représentant* comme l'avaient voulu les constituants de 1875. Mais grâce à sa haute situation et à son irrévocabilité il joue comme *agent* supérieur un rôle utile, je dirai même indispensable à la République.' Emphasis added. In 1906 like in 1931, Barthélemy argued that to re-balance the political situation, the 'political weakness' of the executive had to be repaired by the enhancement of his authority and the limitation of the controlling position of the legislature. To enhance the President's authority, he should be strengthened in his quality of *représentant* of the people. He explained that the president had 'assez de *pouvoirs:* c'est le *pouvoir* qui lui manque. Et le pouvoir, ce ne sont pas les textes, quelque hautes qu'en soient les conceptions, quelque habiles qu'en soient les dispositions, ce ne sont pas les textes qui le donnent: C'est le peuple.' Increasing the President's (parliamentary) independence by moderate reform would empower the executive in its task of supervising the parliament and make him more than a mere dependent parliamentary *agent*. Id., at 731-735. Bearing in mind France's recent political history and its monarchical tendencies, reforms should not aim to introduce direct universal suffrage for the presidency as this involved the risk of making the President's position too powerful and could once more plunge France into despotism. Instead, the '*collège électorale*' which elects the President could be made to include non-parliamentary delegations of each General Council of France and Algerie.

[536] Id., at 736-738.

[537] Id., at 747-748. Also, Barthélemy, Traité de Droit Constitutionnel (1933), at 77: the '*prétensions absolutistes des parlementaires*' against which the individual freedoms had to be protected.

The details of the contributions to the debate must remain outside the scope of this section. However, they do not merely serve to demonstrate that institutional problems were at the heart of the Third Republic's crisis of parliamentary democracy and its threat to individual liberties. Behind this more practical-political debate on the position of the Republic's President, or rather intertwined with it, but on a deeper level, lie the theoretical questions of the concepts of state personality and national sovereignty. These concepts were central to the then prominent German state theories and were now being scrutinised by French scholars against the background of the Third Republic and its political institutional problems.[538] Barthélemy explained the relevance of the concept of state personality for the practical issue of the position of the Republic's executive. He explained that questions of whether the executive power is a *représentant* or *fonctionnaire*, whether it is a *organe direct* or *indirecte*, a *gouvernant* or *agent*, *parlementaire* or *non parlementaire*, rely upon the postulate of state personality:

> Quand on se demande si l'exécutif est *représentant*, on suppose qu'il existe une personne juridique, la nation, qui a délégué à certains corps ou individus la mission de vouloir pour elle. La nation, réalité personnelle, distincte des individus qui la composent, resterait titulaire du droit de souveraineté; elle en déléguerait l'exercice à des mandataires qui la représenteraient ... – Si l'on admet ce principe, on reconnaît nécessairement le caractère de mandataire de la nation au Parlement, qui exerce en son nom le pouvoir législatif. ... Le pouvoir exécutif sera-t-il un représentant investi du pouvoir d'exprimer la volonté souveraine de l'Etat; ou bien aura-t-il simplement une commission, un emploi; simple agent d'exécution des volontés du Parlement, n'aura-t-il d'autre titre que celui d' « officier », de « commissaire » de l'Assemblée?[539]

In other words, to ask whether the executive is a *représenant* presupposes that the nation is a legal person independent of its members, with a right to sovereignty which it delegates to the parliament *as well as* to the executive. The nation is thus not only represented by the parliament but also by the executive in the expression of its sovereignty and national will. In this case, the executive is not a dependent agent or *fonctionnaire*, but a representative and *gouvernant*. How to perceive the state in terms of its *organs*, including those exercising executive power, and either direct or indirect state organs, also depends on the postulate of the state personality. The distinction between a President-*gouvernant* and a President-*agent*

---

[538] Duguit's main objective in *L'État, le droit objectif et la loi positive* was to refute the conventional (German) conceptions of the state and of law, id. at 1: 'nous voulons faire avant tout une oeuvre négative, montrer que l'Etat n'est point cette personne collective, investie d'un pouvoir souverain, que le droit n'est point cette construction édifiée de toutes pièces par les juristes sur le fondement peu stable du droit individuel ou de l'omnipotence de l'Etat, que tout cet ensemble de fiction et d'abstractions s'évanouit à la simple observation de la réalité.' Id., at 290: 'L'idée, que l'Etat est le représentant sur la terre de la loi morale et se trouve chargé comme tel de la sanctionner, est insoutenable et à peu près unanimement abandonnée.' Le Role du Pouvoir Exécutif, at 28-29: Barthélemy considered Jellinek's organic theory 'd'esprit monarchique' and 'd'inspiration antidémocratique.'

[539] Le Role du Pouvoir Exécutif, at 20 *et seq.*

goes primarily to the principle of the separation of state functions and the balance of power.[540] The idea of a parliamentary executive clearly relied upon the basic conception that the state-person delegates his sovereignty to the parliament to use as it sees fit, whereas a non-parliamentary (independent) executive would violate this sovereignty. In any case, the constitutional questions raised by the practical political problems that destabilised a young democracy reveal that at the time ideas concerning the political institutional organisation went hand in hand with theories on state personality.

In the context of the present study of Scelle's conception of ILP, Duguit's theory must be briefly referred to. Duguit was among the scholars who argued in favour of a procedure to test the constitutionality of laws as a way to guarantee individual liberties and to protect the individual citizen against the abuse of power. Here, however, we focus on his even more fundamental response to *l'absolutisme des gouvernants* and *l'aménie du Président*, which was his complete redefinition of the concepts of the state and law. Indeed, it was his fundamental conviction that the political problems threatening French democracy required a completely new approach, addressing the problems at a more fundamental level than conventional theories which continued to recognise such unrealistic notions as the state-person and its right to sovereignty. He rejected the conventional legal notions, or fictions, of the mandate and the state organ derived from – and presupposing the – state personality.[541] After WWI, in the preface to the 1920 edition of the *Traité*, Duguit observed:

Il n'est pas douteux que, sauf de très rares exceptions, les juristes publicistes allemands, en édifiant leurs théories, souvent ingénieuses, ont été avant tout déterminés par le désir de fonder sur des bases d'apparence juridique la souveraineté illimitée de l'Etat, *l'absolutisme des gouvernants* à l'intérieur et la politique de conquête et de rapine à l'extérieur. Il est indispensable de dénoncer cette tendance ... depuis que j'écris, mon effort constant a été de les combattre.[542]

---

[540] At a time of parliamentary absolutism, the question of how to control and counterbalance the power of the Deputies raised the issue of the strict separation of state powers and/or the distribution of these functions over *gouvernants* and *agents* as an effective approach. Since the Third Republic Presidency had a rather mixed character, the dilemma was imminent: being both *gouvernant* and *agent*, the President had (a degree of) legislative power – and could therefore create generally binding rules – and was involved in the implementation of these rules by taking concrete and specific decisions or formulating administrative decrees by which he could establish *subjective* legal situations. It was difficult to distinguish between these legislative and administrative acts and the political responsibility for administrative acts was not clear because these acts escaped parliamentary control. Moreover, there was alos the possibility that the parliament would exercise control (through collaborative procedures) over administrative acts, which would be an abuse of their power. The *absolutism* of the *gouvernants* raised the question whether a stricter separation of powers – all three part of one indivisible sovereign state-person and/or even each power a legal person in itself – was necessary to rebalance the failing democracy and adjust the system to the modern *republican* age. Or rather than separation, the *collaboration* should be improved.

[541] L'État, Les Gouvernants et Les Agents, at 53.

[542] Traité I (1927 ed.), at xii. Emphasis added.

Duguit, driven by realism, individualism[543] and the intention to defend democracy against the metaphysical and absolutist tendencies inherent in these concepts, firmly rejected the notions of state sovereignty and personality.[544]

Relevant here are Duguit's propositions that: 1) the *fiction* of the delegation of the will had to be replaced by the *fact* of social *solidarity* as the basis for the representation of the people by the *gouvernants*. The President should not be considered a *représentant*, but a simple *agent*; 2) only the *individual* conscience and will were *real;* there was no national or collective will. The law sprung from social solidarity; 3) democracy demanded that individuality and the individual free will were protected against those in power, or: the state.

As to Duguit's first proposition, Duguit applied his general rejection of mandatory representation to the political realm and to sovereignty. He rejected the legal fiction of representation by mandate as this presupposed the existence of two legal persons, and also assumed that the delegation of such a personal individual faculty as the will was actually possible.[545] A person cannot exercise another person's will or right. Duguit challenged the idea that the national sovereign will is represented by the parliament through mandate.[546] However, in the philosophy of the 1875 Constitution, the deputies of the Chamber were representatives of the nation, which was a legal person separate from its individual members. The nation had a right to sovereignty, which it exercised by its mandatories. According to Duguit, the French political institutional system could not be based on this *false* principle of mandatory representation nor accept the related unaccountability of the Members of Parliament. In his view, the concept of legal personality was to blame. The idea that the collective personality of the parliament represents the sovereign national personality by mandate meant that the individuality of the Members of Parliament was absorbed by the collective personality of the parliament so that no individual responsibility remained. But, of course, deputies should never be immune.[547]

Moreover, Duguit repeatedly denied that sovereignty was a subjective right. Subjective rights do not exist, not even for individuals. The individual members

---

[543] Here I refer to his methodological individualism. Duguit rejected the individualist (legal) doctrine as it failed to solve the problem of how to limit state sovereignty, Traité I, at 633 and 715.

[544] L'État, le droit objectif et la loi positive; L'État, Les Gouvernants et Les Agents; see also, Traité I, e.g., at vii, 3, 74, 585-586, 633, 719. See also *supra* footnote 538 and *infra* footnote 569 and 570.

[545] L'État, Les Gouvernants et Les Agents, at 8-9: 'On ne peut exercer le droit d'un autre, puisque ce serait exercer le pouvoir de vouloir de cet autre. Quand on veut légitimement, on exerce toujours son droit propre, car on manifeste sa volonté, non la volonté d'un autre, et l'exercice d'un droit est toujours une manifestation de volonté. L'idée de représentation est donc fausse en soi, puisqu'elle a pour point de départ une chose fausse.' Representation by mandate is a fiction, which if applied to politics and the national sovereign will may lead to 'l'esclavage,' e.g., id., at 15-16.

[546] As mentioned earlier, Duguit also rejected the state concept which was used in the organic theory because this also recognised the state as a person. The notion of mandatory representation traditionally dominates French doctrine, id., at 47-48.

[547] L'État, Les Gouvernants et Les Agents, at 150.

of the electorate do not have a subjective right to vote. Instead, they have an objective *duty* to vote and are thereby competent to vote.[548] As the *gouvernants primaires*, the majority appoints the *corps représentatif* or the *gouvernants secondaires*, i.e., the Members of Parliament. In Duguit's theory, representation relies on the principles of solidarity.[549] Political representation is rooted in social solidarity between the individual Members of Parliament and the individual members of the electorate: 'il n'y a point séparation complète, indépendance absolue du parlement et du corps électoral, que l'un et l'autre sont unis ensemble par les liens d'une étroite solidarité ...' Social solidarity thus determines the legal position of the deputy. Because the parliament is not a legal person, in legal terms there are only *individual* Members of Parliament with objective powers limited by the solidarity that united them with the *gouvernants primaires.*

Le député peut vouloir; mais il ne peut vouloir juridiquement et efficacement qu'à la condition que son acte de volonté soit déterminé par le but de maintenir et d'accroître la solidarité qui l'unit aux membres du corps électoral. En d'autres termes, son pouvoir objectif est limité par le pouvoir corrélatif qui appartient à l'électeur.[550]

Contrary to the theories based on the concept of the state person, Duguit thus retains the individuality and individual *responsibility* of the deputy. His was a fundamentally legal response to the *absolitisme des gouvernants,* beyond mere institutional procedural measures.

Between the legislature and the executive there is no 'delegation' of will from mandator to mandatory either.[551] Instead, the principle of solidarity requires that, to act legitimately, the executive must depend on the will of the legislature.[552] For the sake of a well-functioning political society, tasks must necessarily be divided among the three state powers or social functions, which have to cooperate and which derive their duties from objective law. In this way, the relationship be-

---

[548] L'État, Les Gouvernants et Les Agents, at 127-128; see also, Traité I, at 631.

[549] Individual human beings are both equal and different, both individual and social beings. They necessarily cohabit in a society with the aim of limiting individual hardship. According to Duguit, the society or social solidarity are not the result of a *contrat social*, but are necessary *facts*. Individuals are equal in the sense that they naturally share aspirations and needs (*solidarité par similitude*), but these can also fundamentally differ. To realise both these similar and different needs and desires, the society establishes a (political) organisation and distributes the necessary 'aptitudes' and 'competences' (*solidarité par division de travail ou organique*). In this perspective on man and society, *individualisation* and *socialisation* go hand in hand. As the members of society have to divide the work and evidently also have different needs, thoughts and wills, the society could diversify. L'État, le droit objectif et la loi positive, at 23 *et seq*.

[550] L'État, Les Gouvernants et Les Agents, at 233-234.

[551] Id., at 342 *et seq*.

[552] The executive expressed its own will, but its consciousness was influenced by the solidarity mechanism of the will of the legislature and the people. For an act to be a legitimate legal act, irrespective of whether it is performed by the governors or the governed, its purpose should be to serve social solidarity, i.e., it should be in conformity with objective law.

tween the executive and the legislative is not hierarchical, but *collaborative*, precisely as the 1875 laws intended.[553]

However, strengthening the executive by remodelling the French President to resemble the American President would involve the risk of '*une dictature*'[554] instead of saving democracy and protecting individual liberty. The hybrid nature of the French presidency – both representative and agent – was indeed problematic in terms of (judicial) control and political *responsibility*.[555] Duguit concluded that the President's could no longer be the *représentant* of national sovereignty. The institution of the President-*gouvernant* had to be abolished:

Nous avons montré que l'institution de la présidence était en soi une antimonie [*sic.*]. Les conséquences en apparaissent nettement. Représentant et gouvernant, le chef d'Etat est en même temps un agent administratif; d'où les difficultés inextricables qui se produisent, les conflits, les discussions, et tout cela au détriment des situations individuelles. Ces conflits, ces discussions ne disparaîtront que le jour où la loi politique positive, mise en harmonie avec les faits, *supprimera* la présidence de la république comme organe *gouvernant*.[556]

Duguit also stressed the importance of improving the functioning of the parliament:

---

[553] See *supra*. It is also relevant for assessing the quality of the President that Duguit considered the principle of the strict separation of state powers 'false'. He believed it had monarchical overtones. L'État, Les Gouvernants et Les Agents, at 344. The constitutional laws did not include any separation of powers either. On the contrary, they laid down that the relationship between the executive and the legislative power should be collaborative. The idea of 'une puissance souveraine, une et trois pouvoirs, est une conception métaphysique ... [et] inadmissible.' Duguit found it confusing and inaccurate: 'Pour moi, ..., il n'y a pas plus de pouvoir exécutif qu'il n'y a de pouvoir législatif. Il y a des agents judiciaires et des agents administratifs ...' Traité II, at 688. The principle of the separation of powers may have been formulated to protect the individual against 'l'arbitraire des gouvernants et des administrateurs', but, according to Duguit, law itself can provide this function. L'État, Les Gouvernants et Les Agents, at 363 *et seq.*

[554] Id., at 360.

[555] Id., at 329: '[Le chef d'Etat, il] n'est pas un simple agent administratif chargé d'assurer, sous le contrôle du parlement, l'exécution des lois; il n'est pas seulement le chef de la hiérarchie administrative; il est plus que cela; il est gouvernant; il est un organe direct, disent les fervents de la théorie juridico-organique; il est un *représentant* disait la constitution de 1791. Notre président de la république est tout cela. Il ne faut point y voir un agent administratif nommé par le parlement, mais un *représentant* de la souveraineté nationale. Le congrès qui le nomme n'est point la réunion des chambres; ..., le parlement, des deux chambres réunies, fait fonction d'assemblée électorale; il élit au nom du peuple souverain le président de la république. Celui-ci est un représentant sortant d'un suffrage populaire à plusieurs degrés. Les conséquences de ce caractère sont importantes.' Id., at 333: 'Nous croyons avoir établi que le chef de l'Etat est autre chose et plus qu'un administrateur. Sans doute, il fait des actes administratifs; mais le règlement statuant par voie générale n'est pas et ne peut pas être un acte administratif. Le président de la république est un gouvernant collaborant avec le parlement à l'accomplissement des fonctions politiques. Il est exactement ce qu'était le monarque dans la monarchie parlementaire.' The problem is that acts resulting from the President exercising the legislative function in collaboration with the parliament (e.g., by a *general* public order or regulation) cannot be monitored by administrative tribunals, as no law designates the President as an administrative authority and agent: '*il est alors un pouvoir politique échappant au contrôle des tribunaux* ...' Emphasis added. Id., at 334.

[556] Id., at 372. Emphasis added.

La présidence de la république est une institution décorative, un symbole qui plaît au peuple. ... En réalité, le pouvoir politique appartient en France exclusivement à deux organes de représentation, le sénat et la chambre; c'est par une organisation plus complète et plus savante de ces deux corps représentatifs qu'on donnera au pays une constitution positive harmonique à son état social.[557]

As to Duguit's second proposition, in Duguit's legal-political theory individualism and realism go hand in hand. Only the individual human being is capable of solidarity.[558] The individual human being is the only *real* entity with an individual conscience and will which makes him capable of sociability and 'willed' action towards a (social) goal. '*Individual* human beings are the only *realities* of the *social* world.'[559] Collective consciousness, collective will and collective personality simply do not exist: states, peoples, tribes, or any other group can never have legal personality. In fact, the existence of *subjective* rights is completely denied in his theory.[560] Only *objective* law exists and this only addresses the individual conscience and will.[561]

In this perspective, the voluntarist basis of law is eliminated: law is *not* the commanding force of the sovereign national will.[562] *Objective* law is actually defined as an *objective social reality* which emerges from the social solidarity of the collective; it is the 'eternally changing' product of social solidarity.[563] Duguit also based his rejection of law-as-a-command on the fundamental idea of individual autonomy and the claim that no individual will is superior to another.[564] In other words, equipped with a conscience and a will, every individual is capable of pursuing social solidarity and thus also capable of acting in conformity with objective law and producing a legal effect or situation.[565] An act is legitimate if it

---

[557] Id., at 328-329.

[558] Social solidarity is *not* a *collective* thought or consciousness, it is an *individual* state of mind, even though it is the foundation of every group, including political communities and nations. It is the individual who realises that happiness is better pursued as a group with individuals who have similar as well as different needs and goals.

[559] L'État, le droit objectif et la loi positive, at 29.

[560] Traité I, at 198: 'Il y a un droit objectif qui s'impose aux individus et seulement à eux, dans leurs rapports sociaux et leurs rapports internationaux. Il n'y a pas de droit subjectif des individus comme pouvoir propre de leur volonté; ... il n'y a pas de droit subjectif des groupements sociaux quels qu'ils soient, tribus, cités, familles, nations, Etats. ... [O]n ne peut démontrer la réalité personnelle de ces collectivités, pas plus que la réalité de la notion de droit subjectif. ... Il n'y a pas plus de droit des collectivités qu'il n'y a de droit subjectif des individus.' Id., at 709.

[561] Traité I, at 524: '[S]eul l'individu humain conscient de ses actes peut être sujet de droit. Le droit est un ensemble de règles qui défendent ou ordonnent telles ou telles choses; défenses et ordres ne peuvent être adressés qu'à des volontés conscientes, par conséquent qu'à des individus humains conscients de leurs actes.'

[562] L'État, le droit objectif et la loi positive, at 255: 'Volonté une et collective, souveraineté nationale, souveraineté politique de l'Etat, mots sans valeur, qui ne servent qu'à voiler la brutalité des faits et l'arbitraire de la force.'

[563] Id., at 428.

[564] Id., at 424-426, 466, 672.

[565] Id., at 191-195. Also, Traité I (1927 ed.), at 72: 'Tout acte de volonté individuelle, déterminé par un but conforme à la solidarité sociale ou, ce qui est la même chose, à la règle de droit, est un acte juridique et crée une situation juridique subjective.'

aims to achieve a goal which is determined by social solidarity; conversely, the individual has to abstain from acts with anti-social objectives.[566] The *gouvernants* only 'translate' ('*constater*') objective law into positive legal rules. Because it is determined by social solidarity, law, instead of being the expression of power, can act as a limiting force on power. To sum up, it is established that the public or political will can *realistically speaking* only consist of the *individual* will of the *gouvernants*:

il n'y a d'autre volonté politique que la volonté individuelle des gouvernants; cette volonté individuelle des gouvernants est investie d'un pouvoir objectif, qui doit être réglementé et sanctionné par le droit.[567]

Every will, whether individual or public (with the public will being the individual will of the *gouvernants*), is subject to the law from which it also derives its powers and *duties*.

Although he rejected the existence of subjective rights, Duguit does therefore not deny the existence of the *legal subject*. However, he replaced its classical meaning of the holder of a subjective right by the simple notion that every individual human being is subject to the rules of objective law. Since only individual human beings are capable of acting upon a conscious will, objective law can only address individuals, which makes them the *exclusive* subjects of law. To accept any other legal subject, e.g., animals or a collective, would be unrealistic and metaphysical, as neither of these is capable of pursuing social goals. 'L'homme individuel, sain d'esprit, conscient de ses actes, est sujet de droit, est seul sujet de droit, est toujours sujet de droit.'[568] As such, by its nature, every human being is a legal subject: legal personality is a *natural reality*, not just a fiction or a fanciful conceptual structure erected by the human mind.

Finally, as to Duguit's third proposition, with the recognition of man as the exclusive legal subject, Duguit delivered another blow to the conventional conception of state personality and sovereignty. His challenge of these concepts cannot be separated from his legal-political ideal of democracy and his concern over the tendency of the personality concept towards metaphysics and mysticism.[569]

Enfin, faire de l'Etat la collectivité personnifiée et l'opposer à l'individu qui lui serait subordonné, c'est créer ou aggraver le conflit entre l'individu et la collectivité, entre l'intérêt individuel et l'intérêt collectif; c'est attiser les lutes sociales et préparer à brève

[566] L'État, le droit objectif et la loi positive, at 86-87. Also, on source of law, Traité I, at 170.

[567] L'État, Les Gouvernants et Les Agents, at 362.

[568] Traité I (1927 ed.), at 458; see also, id., at 451-481, where Duguit claimed that children and the insane are not subjects of objective law. Objective law addresses the conscious human will which these groups lack. If they violate the law, it will have no social consequences for them.

[569] L'État, le droit objectif et la loi positive, at 266: 'Toutes ces fausses doctrines de société organisme, de société entité métaphysique ou juridique, d'Etat personne juridique souveraine, aboutissent à l'insurrection de l'individu contre l'Etat ou à l'absorbtion [*sic.*] de l'individu par l'Etat, à l'anarchisme ou à la tyrannie collectiviste.' Also, Traité I (1927 ed.), at 18 and 633.

échéance le triomphe ou de l'anarchisme révolutionnaire ou du collectivisme tyrannique. Derrière les formules courantes des juristes, nous ne trouvons donc que le vide ou de dangereuses conceptions.[570]

In order to prevent 'l'écrasement de l'individu par l'Etat, l'absorption complete de l'individu par la collectivité,'[571] a new approach to the state and its sovereignty was required. Hence Duguit's position that: 'L'Etat n'est pas une personne juridique; l'Etat n'est pas une personne souveraine,'[572] *l'État c'est les gouvernants*. Only *individual human beings* can have legal capacity and personality, while the state has no legal capacity and is not a legal personality. The state is simply its *gouvernants* (rulers), the *gouvernants* who exercise the three functions of the state. Duguit's views on the relations between the political institutions were connected with the key element of his theory: the rejection of legal personality in general and state personality and sovereignty in particular.[573] Reducing the idea of the state to the reality of its *gouvernants*, grants the *gouvernants* the power actively to pursue and realise – if necessary by *force* – social solidarity and its social goals within the confines of the law. The factual element of *force* distinguishes the *gouvernants* from the *gouvernés*, but in their subordination to the law they are equal.[574]

La règle de droit s'impose donc à tous, à l'Etat comme au particulier, puisque *l'Etat n'est point la collectivité personnifiée et n'existe que par les gouvernants*, que les gouvernants sont des *individus*, et que, comme tells, ils sont soumis à la règle de droit. Cette règle oblige d'abord les gouvernants à ne rien faire qui porte atteinte à la solidarité sous ses deux formes.[575]

The *gouvernants* have been given *duties* and *competences* with which to pursue the social goals. Public power is the social force of the *gouvernants* which they are obliged to use in the service of society and solidarity, otherwise its use would be illegal.[576] Public or governmental power can only be justified by its objective, its social aim. The power to govern is thus the objective duty to govern in conformity with the demands of individual liberty and social solidarity. Duguit therefore defined the modern state as 'une fédération de services publics qu'administrent *les détenteurs de la plus grande force ayant* non plus le droit de com-

---

[570] L'État, le droit objectif et la loi positive, at 615; see also, L'État, Les Gouvernants et Les Agents, at 48 and 5: 'notions étroites et artificielles.'

[571] Traité I, at 631.

[572] L'État, Les Gouvernants et Les Agents, at 1. See also, L'État, le droit objectif et la loi positive; Also, Traité I, at 585-586.

[573] See, e.g., L'État, le droit objectif et la loi positive, at 227-241, 266-267.

[574] Id., at 185-186 and 242-255, what distinguishes the ruler from the ruled is that the ruler can use force – if necessary – to ensure the realisation of his will. This means that political power is not justified by the source from which it stems, like in the social contract theories, but derives its legitimacy from its proper use, i.e., in conformity with the principle of social solidarity.

[575] Id., at 262. Emphasis added. Also, Traité I, at 189, 672.

[576] L'État, le droit objectif et la loi positive, at 263 *et seq*.

mander, mais *le devoir* d'assurer le fonctionnement ininterrompu et productif de ces services.'[577] By defining the state as the collective of *individuals* who govern and subjecting these, like every other individual, to the rule of law, Duguit completely redefined the notion of the state, including that of the *Rechtsstaat*.[578]

This new concept of the state and law sprang from Duguit's fundamental objective of '*limiter juridiquement le pouvoir de l'Etat* et à fonder véritablement une règle de droit déterminant le sens et l'étendue des actes gouvernementaux.'[579] Here, law originates from the need to protect the individual against the (arbitrary) use of power by the *gouvernants*: 'l'arbitraire des gouvernants. ... de protéger les faibles contre les forts, les gouvernés contre l'omnipotence des gouvernants.'[580] To ensure this protection, the law imposes the objective duty upon the *gouvernants* to establish a political organisation, which would reduce the risk of the arbitrary and unpredictable use of power.[581] It is the state's primary obligation to organise 'la force et de régler ses manifestations, pour *protéger l'individu contre l'arbitraire* et imposer à tous, gouvernants et gouvernés, le respect du droit.'[582] Throughout his work, Duguit emphasises this objective. His response to the threat to the Third Republic's democracy posed by the *absolutisme des gouvernants* consisted of a practical political argument on the position of the Deputies and the President and a theoretical argument in which he redefined the state and law by drawing on a new concept of legal personality. His *individualist* and *realist* approach was as much an attempt to defend and develop *democracy*.

To sum up, individualism, realism, democracy and the rejection of the concept of legal personality are all interrelated in Duguit's theory of the state and law and conjoin in how law applies to the state, i.e., to *gouvernés* and *gouvernants* alike. By attributing *duties* rather than *rights*, all power is subjected to and limited by law. 'Les gouvernants sont des individus comme les autres; par conséquent, comme tous les membres de collectivité considérée, ils sont soumis au droit objectif de ce groupement. Et voilà ... *la subordination de l'Etat au droit*.'[583] In the context of the Third Republic and the widely felt concern over the decline of individual liberties and democracy, Duguit exhorted his contemporaries to:

> Bannons donc, une fois pour toutes, ces conceptions surannées de personnalités et de souveraineté de l'Etat, qui donnent naissance à des problèmes insolubles, à des discus-

---

[577] Traité I, at 589. Emphasis added.

[578] L'État, le droit objectif et la loi positive, at 97 and 259 *et seq.*; Traité I, at 670 *et seq.*

[579] Traité I, at 651-654. Emphasis added.

[580] L'État, Les Gouvernants et Les Agents, at 362-363; L'État, le droit objectif et la loi positive, at 468.

[581] L'État, le droit objectif et la loi positive, at 468.

[582] L'État, Les Gouvernants et Les Agents, at 3.

[583] 'L'Etat est une pure abstraction. *La réalité, ce sont les individus qui exercent la puissance étatique*; ... leurs actes ne peuvent s'imposer aux gouvernés que s'ils sont conformes au droit. ... la puissance politique a pour but de réaliser le droit; L'Etat est fondé sur la force; mais cette force est légitime lorsqu'elle s'exerce conformément au droit.' Traité I, at 670-680. Emphasis added.

sions interminables et vaines, qui ont toujours été et seront toujours le principe d'une action tyrannique et dictatoriale à l'intérieur et d'une politique agressive et conquérante à l'extérieur. Disons : les gouvernants sont des individus comme les autres, soumis comme tous les individus à des règles de droit fondées sur une solidarité sociale et intersociale; ces règles de droit leur imposent des devoirs, et leurs actes sont légitimes et s'imposent à l'obéissance, non pas parce qu'ils émanent d'une prétendue personne souveraine, mais quand et seulement quand ils sont conformes aux règles de droit qui s'imposent à leurs auteurs.[584]

This in a nutshell is the political and intellectual background against which Georges Scelle wrote on public international law. The truly *revisionist* scholar Scelle recognised that the application of Duguit's doctrines on international law would not just mean a renewal of international law, but actually include a true '*renaissance*.'[585] Breaking down the state to the level of the individual *gouvernants* and thereby freeing legal theory from the confines of the concepts of state personality and sovereignty is key to Scelle's scholarship.

3.5.3. **Scelle's concept of international law**

In the introduction to this contextual analysis of Scelle's conception of ILP, I have already briefly outlined my argument. Scelle established that individual liberties were being eroded, both nationally and internationally. Above, I have examined the crisis of democracy and individual liberties in Third Republic France. France had gone from being a republic of *citoyens* to a republic of (absolutist parliamentary) *gouvernants*. The general trend was to look to the political institutional structure to change its (mal)functioning and Scelle's emphasis on the need to restrain the *gouvernants* on international law to administer the restraints fits in with this trend. At the same time, however, Scelle formulated a response to the crisis of international law.

Worldwide, but in Europe in particular, democratic regimes were losing influence and international peace and security were increasingly threatened by totalitarian regimes which were rapidly gaining power. However, Scelle also noted the emergence of a new international reality with the foundation of the League of Nations and the International Labour Organisation and approved of this development of further international *institutionalisation*. International law sceptics argued that international law could not be law, as it lacked a legislature (to create it) and an executive (to enforce it). Scelle responded by explaining that 'law is not a command', but that 'objective law is the product of social solidarity' and by arguing that international law confers *competences* and *duties* upon the national *gouvernants* and thereby makes them *internationally* competent and effective. Scele based his legal theory on international institutionalisation on his famous principle of *dédoublement fonctionnel*.

---

[584] Traité I, at 733.
[585] La doctrine de L. Duguit, at 84. See *supra* footnote 483.

Scelle's approach was coherent and comprehensive. He claimed that international law directly addressed those in power and thus limited their use of this power and obliged them to respect individual liberties. It also gave them a duty to serve the cause of strengthening international solidarity. Scelle's conception of ILP in terms of *competences* is essential to his integral approach. Before examining how Scelle used the concept of ILP, I will first outline his concept of international law by means of the four elements previously identified in this chapter, namely international society, monism, the state and state sovereignty.

First, Scelle's view of the international society was based on the fundamental notion of *le fait social* and the conviction that the individual is also a social being, who would perish in isolation. Man's interests are best served if he is part of a political society. From this so-called *fait social* emerges the necessary social solidarity, the basis of any (political) society. Social solidarity is vital to the existence of a society and the survival of man.[586] It is clear that Scelle was influenced by Duguit in this respect.[587] Scelle distinguished the same two forms of solidarity as Duguit did: *la solidarité par similitudes*, '[elle] provient des ressemblances physiques, de la communauté d'origine, de la similarité des besoins et aptitudes, [etc etc] ... elle est l'élément communauté de base et se renforce par l'usage et la prolongation de la vie commune,' and *la solidarité par division de travail*,

qui apparaît, elle aussi, dès l'origine des sociétés, mais se développe plus lentement, constitue l'élément de différenciation et, par conséquent, d'organisation et de perfectionnement. C'est elle qui, se modelant sur les aptitudes individuelles, entraîne la distribution des tâches, spécialise les activités, multiplie la productivité, fait éclore les besoins nouveaux et cimente la solidarité globale, parce que la spécialisation rend les individus indispensables les uns aux autres et aboutit à la réglementation des compétences.[588]

The division of labour stimulates the process of integration and progress in every level of society, whether sub-state, state, or global. The principle of solidarity from which it follows can only be realised by individuals. Individuals alone can create a society. Groups can never be said to have a collective conscience or will, as they are incapable of solidarity.[589] The two forms of solidarity must be prop-

[586] Précis I, at 2; Précis II, at 1-2.

[587] Duguit outlined his ideas in the field of international law in sections 17 (La norme juridique intersocial) and 67 (Le droit public international) of, Traité de Droit constitutionnel (3rd ed., 1927), at 184-199 and 713-733. Scelle critically analysed these paragraphs in his work, La doctrine de L. Duguit, at 80-119.

[588] Précis I, at 2.

[589] Précis II, at 2: 'Les contraintes se traduisent en une somme de *représentations* dites *collectives* dont il faut bien comprendre qu'elles s'imposent individuellement à chaque conscience et n'ont pas pour siège on ne sait quelle conscience imaginaire attribuée au groupe lui-même. Ce qui peut faire naître cette illusion, c'est la conformité, voire l'identité de ces représentations individuelles. L'origine de ces contraintes est *biologique*, en ce sens que si elles ne sont pas observées l'ordre social disparaît, avec lui le phénomène de solidarité collectif et l'individu lui-même, pour autant que cette solidarité est nécessaire à son existence ou à son progrès.' See also, Précis I, at 3.

erly balanced before a functioning society, which benefits the individual members, can exist. Here, Scelle takes Duguit's reasoning one step further.

In order to maintain the balance, to secure the survival of the society and of the individual, social *constraints* must be imposed: '[t]outes les constraintes sociales sont donc originairement *d'ordre biologique*, puisqu'elles conditionnent à la fois la cohésion du groupe et la vie de l'individu.' Rules therefore spring from a biological necessity: '[l]e Droit est né : sa source est dans la nécessité biologique; la conscience de cette nécessité en fait une *règle normative* c'est-à-dire un impératif.'[590] By the term *biological* necessity, Scelle meant that because of man's dual nature (as both an individual and a social creature) society is the only means of his survival, the only way he can develop and prosper. Social constraints are absolutely necessary for the interdependent members of a society to survive and thrive, and if man were isolated from his social context, '*il meurt. ... Le fait social est donc un fait biologique.*'[591] In other words, law is an *existential* necessity.[592] For this reason, legal rules are biological in nature. Scelle therefore defines law as a natural phenomenon: 'un impératif social traduisant une nécessité née de la solidarité naturelle. C'est en ce sens qu'on peut dire que le Droit lui-même est *naturel*.' According to Scelle, there is no contradiction between a *société de fait* and a *société de droit*: '*Toute société de fait est en même temps une société de droit*.'[593]

Scelle also applied his reasoning to the international society and international law. The two forms of solidarity also exist at the global level, 'la solidarité par division de travail ... fait éclore les besoins nouveaux et cimente *la solidarité globale*.'[594] International law is the translation of the social constraints which the international society and its individual members need in order to survive and develop. As in any society, international legal norms have to reflect (global) solidarity and serve the needs of (global) social life in order to be law: 'La coutume, la loi, la jurisprudence ... sont l'expression de cette loi de l'être social qui est en même temps *la condition de l'existence humaine*. Il en est ainsi de la norme des sociétés internationales aussi bien que de la norme interne ...' Scelle contended

[590] Where Duguit used the term 'social', Scelle uses the term 'biological', but both cliamed that the source of law is necessity: without law, man will not survive. A post-1930s, post-WWII audience could easily become confused and disturbed by the use of the term 'biological' to define the foundation of law. We tend to associate this term with the absence of morality and with sympathy for *Blut und Boden*. Such associations, however, would be completely misguided in the case of the use to which Scelle put the term 'biological.' Here it intends to convey that law is *a matter of life and death*. Scelle moreover indicated that to recognise that the origin of law is biological only differed from Duguit's definition of the origin of law to a certain degree in that he, Scelle, merely took Duguit's reasoning one step further. La doctrine de Duguit, at 101.

[591] La doctrine de Duguit, at 103.

[592] Contrary to Kelsen, who, as we have seen, completely rejected causality as the unifying principle of any legal order, Scelle, because he considered law to be biological, also considered law to be *causal*. Objective law is by *necessity* born of social solidarity; in other words, the creation of law takes place through causality.

[593] Précis I, at 2-3.

[594] See *supra*, text to footnote 588.

that due to the reality of international interdependence, denying the existence of the international norms which express global solidarity is utterly impossible. With this claim, he did not close his eyes to the contemporary developments, but on the contrary considered them a warning against such a denial:

Nous vivons en ce moment même la démonstration dramatique de ce fait d'évidence. ... [L]es préjugés, l'ignorance et les passions des collectivités nationales sont tels que ... il semble que les gouvernements prennent immédiatement à tâche d'en violer les normes les plus simples et les plus essentielles. Le résultat est fatal. La société internationale et, en particulier, la société européenne périclite, et sa régression a pour contre-coup immédiat la décadence biologique et la mort des individus : chômages, troubles sociaux, disparition de la liberté individuelle, sous-alimentation, drames familiaux, suicides, paupérisme, anémie, folie, tels sont les résultats que nous pouvons chaque jour enregistrer comme les fruits de l'observation des règles élémentaire de la solidarité internationale, ou de la méconnaissance de la loi biologique de l'espèce.[595]

The contemporary international decline was caused precisely by the repudiation of global solidarity and the violation of international legal norms. Reading Scelle's critique of Duguit against this background, it appears that Scelle wished to solidify the foundation of international law and make it less dependent upon the individual will. After all, Scelle explained, if law, i.e., social norms, direct the individual to guide his will towards social goals and thus creates social action, this also means that social action in conformity with social norms, *in casu* law, depends on the individual's desire to act in pursuance of social goals. In other words, social acts are a matter of choice and law consists of social acts which are *voluntarily* produced. By claiming that law originates in biological necessity, Scelle defined law as *causal* and this makes law even more *objective* and thereby independent of the human will.[596] With his argument that the source of international law, like any law, is found in *la condition humaine*, Scelle distinguished himself from Duguit. Scelle criticised Duguit for '*exaggerating*' in the 3rd edition of his book in 1927 the role played by the sentiments of solidarity and justice in his conception of the source of law. Especially since at the international level, these sentiments are frequently hindered by '*les psychoses collectives*' which affect the development of international law: 'la conscience collective peut méconnaître la norme sociale, bien loin de lui servir de fondement.'[597]

---

[595] La doctrine de Duguit, at 104-105. Emphasis added.

[596] Id., at 101-102.

[597] Id., at 105: 'Nous venons précisément de le constater ci-dessus et c'est le cas très fréquemment dans les relations internationales où *les psychoses collectives* entravent le développement du droit ou entraînent sa violation. Cela prouve précisément que la conscience collective peut méconnaître la norme sociale, bien loin de lui servir de fondement. Quant à l'idée de justice, elle est extrêmement subjective, variable d'un peuple à l'autre et d'individu. En matière internationale on peut être à peu près sûr que toute conception nationale de justice est faussée d'avance par les préjugés et les intérêts immédiats. Cela ne signifie pas que le législateur ou l'expérimentateur social puisse faire abstraction de ces éléments. Conscience collective et sentiment de la justice, il lui faut bien les ménager, sous peine de compromettre l'efficacité de la norme et par

Rather than explaining the origins of international law by the sentiments of solidarity and justice at a time characterised by 'collective psychoses' and the 'ignorance and passion of national collectivities' which stood in the way of sound judgment, Scelle, by indicating the biological *necessity* of law for all *humanity*, intended to give (international) law an even stronger basis than that formed by the two sentiments Duguit used and which sometimes – actually even at the time – seemed to lack solidity. The political situation in most European democracies could be considered to point to democracy's imminent demise and this confirmed the importance of upholding the law. Feelings of normative solidarity and justice may be absent in mass conscience, but that does not mean that the law no longer exists: *the human condition* itself necessitates the existence of the law (of solidarity). The mere denial of law by the collective of individuals cannot therefore cause the law to disappear or alter its content. Like Duguit, Scelle clearly distinguished between objective law and positive law. He agreed with Duguit that the assumption that positive law is the legislature's translation of objective law was hypothetical: 'C'est une hypothèse nécessaire, *mais ce n'est qu'une hypothèse.*' Yes, it is important to recognise the necessity of this hypothesis for social stability, yet it is conceivable that reality invalidates it and necessitates its revision. Under the penalty of violence and social instability, law and institutions, constitutions and treaties have to conform to objective law. Objective law persists, even if it is not acknowledged as law by all members of the society or collective.[598]

Despite the times he lived in, Scelle still seemed to have faith in the human condition and its natural tendency towards progress. He believed that because the consequences of a total breakdown of the mutual exchange between individual members of state societies would be fatal, honesty, peacefulness and the continuity of international relations would of necessity have to survive.[599] In other words, the human condition necessitates the existence of law. According to Scelle, this was equally true for inter-societal, i.e., international, law. Humanity is thus not only a a society in fact, but, like every factual society, it is also a *société de droit* and international law is its law.

Consequently, Scelle's concept of *the* international or global society is *not* that of a society of states.[600] He considered this an 'anthropomorphic' idea. In his view, the global society is a society of *individuals*: '*la société humaine universelle.*'[601] It consists of inter-individual relations between the members of

---

là même la solidarité sociale. Ces éléments jouent donc également leur rôle dans la conception biologique du droit. Mais ce sont des éléments *secondaires* ...' Emphasis added.

[598] Id., at 105: '[Alors,] il est impossible de dire *a priori* que des règles normatives en opposition avec la conscience collective et le sentiment de justice dominant dans une société déterminée, soient par cela même contraires au Droit objectif. Il se peut parfaitement que la norme sociale scientifique soit l'œuvre d'une infirme minorité d'observateurs sociaux.'

[599] Id., at 107.

[600] Précis I, at 28.

[601] La doctrine de L. Duguit, at 88 and 117: 'Une société étatique, une collectivité intersociale, *une* société, *la* société internationale, sont toujours des groupes d'individus, et uniquement des

different states or non-state political collectivities, who are connected by means of international interdependence and global solidarity. From the opening quote of this section, we know Scelle only considered peace and order viable 'dans des *institutions* sociales élargies et se subordonnant les États.' As in the domestic order where institutions and procedures laid down in *constitutional* law regulate the use of *force*, the global society also requires '*l'organisation féderative*.' Scelle found that a federative organisation is a work in progress that aims to regulate power within society by means of the development of procedures and institutions. As such, he found '*tout système juridique est fédératif*,' the international legal system included.[602] There is a normative and an institutional side to the process of federalisation. Institutional federalism is a long, arduous and complex road aimed at the transformation of society through the establishment of institutions and regulations, especially in the case of the federalisation of the international society. Normative federalism – or international law – is the normative instrument for this transformation; it imposes itself on the individual members of the global society because, like all law, it is biologically necessary. At the international level, therefore, law also not only necessarily existed, but was *the* appropriate instrument or technique to transform the universal society into a more federalised, *institutionalised* global human society.

On the subject of monism, Scelle's normative federalism reveals him as an international law monist:

> la formule du fédéralisme normatif ... constitue l'expression même de la notion de droit international. Elle signifie qu'à chaque fois que des rapports internationaux s'établissent, les systèmes juridiques internes sont par là même instantanément modifiés, sans qu'il soit besoin d'aucun acte d'introduction des normes internationales dans le droit interne, et cela dans toute la mesure où la nouvelle règle inter-sociale est incompatible avec les systèmes composants.[603]

International legal norms address the individual members of the global society in general and the *gouvernants* in particular. As they apply to the *gouvernants* of the various collectives (e.g., states), the norms of the inter-societal (i.e., international) society become internal norms that also influence and adjust the internal social life of the society. For (international) normative federalism to transform into (international) institutional federalism (every society needs institutions for law to be effective), the legal system has to formulate and condition *competences* within the federal system. By the definition of *competences* and their attribution to the governors, the system differentiates between federal or global solidarity on the

groupes *d'individus*.' See also, Précis I, at 28: '*une société internationale est une collectivité d'individus, sujets de droit, appartenant déjà à des sociétés nationales. ... la plus grande d'entre elles: la société humaine ... est pourtant un fait universel et normal.*'

[602] La doctrine de Duguit, at 105-107.

[603] Id., at 108.

one hand and local solidarity on the other. The hierarchy of societies and legal orders dictates that the federal or global solidarity is superior: 'Ce principe de la *subordination nécessaire du droit interne au Droit international* est fondamental.' Scelle linked normative and institutional monism to form '*le monisme juridique integral*,' thereby establishing the necessary superiority in the hierarchy of the universal society and its legal order.[604] This absolute and entirely monist principle according to Scelle provided the only possible basis for a stable and logically satisfying construction of the *Droit des Gens*. In this monist construction of the universal community the essential function of law is to determine and distribute '*competences*.'[605] The organisation and legitimisation of the distribution of competences is laid down in international *constitutional* rules: they are the fundamental legal rules which are essential 'à la vie même et au progrès de la societé.'[606] Scelle's monism is, however, different and original in the sense that it is not the state persona, but the individual rulers, whom he considered to be the link between the legal orders. In other words, the concepts of state and sovereignty, elements three and four to be discussed here, were completely *revised* in this monist view of the global society.

As regards Scelle's position on the concept of the state, he followed Duguit where the latter had denied the existence of a state persona. The collective conscience and the idea that a collective is a *reality* are both fantasies.[607] *Realism* also compelled Scelle to stress that collectives are fictitious entities made up of *individuals*.

Nul ne saurait évidemment nier la réalité matérielle des phénomènes sociologique; mais ce serait une autre aberration que de vouloir transformer ces réalités *phénoménales* en réalités *personnelles*. Faire des structures sociologiques ou des institutions sociales des êtres collectifs dotés de conscience et de volonté, c'est se laisser aller à l'imagination anthropormorphique [*sic*.] et non plus se borner à la constatation scientifique. Si le substratum humain disparaît, le phénomène social s'évanouit.[608]

Scelle argued against the exlusive power of states which always tended to negate international solidarity or even undermine it. As such the positive law of states has often been an obstacle to the natural development of human solidarity and has thus prevented the reception of objective law.[609] In Scelle's theory, therefore, the state is perceived quite from how it was defined in the classical and restorative theories. It is perceived as the *hinge* (l'Etat-charnière) between the intra-so-

---

[604] Précis I, at 31-33. Also, La fonction exécutive, at 98.

[605] Précis I, at 7; Précis II, at 3.

[606] Précis II, at 4.

[607] La doctrine de L. Duguit, at 85: 'Duguit nous enseigne que les collectivités n'ont point de personnalité et que seul les individus peuvent être sujets de droit, aussi bien dans le domaine international que le droit interne.'

[608] Précis II, at 2. See also, Précis I, at 12; La doctrine de Duguit, at 90.

[609] Précis I, at 34.

cial and the inter-social.[610] It is a moment in political evolution; the national and the international phenomenon are two aspects of man's efforts ultimately to achieve global 'politico-juridical organisation.'[611] Like every political society, the state consists of an inter-social hierarchical collective containing a multiplicity of social groups.[612] It is not a legal person,[613] it has no independent soul and no personal will independent of the individual members of the state (or governmental) society. Of course, the state exists, but not as a 'personal reality', not as a real person. It exists merely as the reality of a social-political phenomenon[614] and as the collected competences of the *gouvernants*.[615]

Il n'y a en réalité ni personnalité étatique, ni droit subjectifs des Etats. Il ne peut y avoir que des *compétences* de gouvernants correspondant à des pouvoir et des devoirs ...[616]

Scelle agreed with Duguit that: 'l'Etat c'est *un groupe de gouvernants*.'[617] Rather than being a mere legal notion the state consists of factual elements on the basis of which international law recognises the competences of the *gouvernants*.[618] Of all collectives, the state is the most institutionalised and best organised. Defining the state as the *gouvernants* and at the same time establishing that the state is the hinge between the national and the international order, Scelle also establishes that the individual *gouvernants* are the *hinge*. This outcome was to be expected from Scelle's *monisme juridique integral*. It is through the attribution of competences to the national *gouvernants* that international law changes the domestic order.[619] The legal basis of this hinge function is the legal principle of *dédoublement fonctionnel des compétences gouvernementales*.[620] This principle means that international law attributes to national *gouvernants* and *agents* both national and international governmental competences, which also makes these national *gouvernants* and *agents* international *gouvernants* and *agents*. 'Pour mieux dire,' Scelle explained that:

---

[610] Précis II, at 5; also, for state as 'hinge,' Scelle, G., Some Reflections on Juridical Personality in International Law, *in* G.A. Lipsky (Ed.), Law and Politics in the World Community 53 (1953).

[611] Précis I, at 28.

[612] Id., at 10-13. Also, Précis II, at 5.

[613] Id., at 35.

[614] Scelle concludes that the state has political-historical and material features but cannot identify any legal criteria: ' il n'y a pas de critère juridique de l' Etat, parce que la compétence des sujets de droit a toujours une origine commune: le droit objectif...' Précis I, at 83.

[615] Précis I, at 10.

[616] Id., at 35. Emphasis added.

[617] Id., at 62.

[618] Id., at 83. Consequently, '[s]i l'on va au fond des choses, il s'agit uniquement, dans l'un et l'autre cas, de *constater l'existence de compétences gouvernementales* et il n'y a de reconnaissance *que de gouvernements*.' Id., at 103.

[619] Précis II, at 6: 'C'est dire que les compétences des sujets de droit des systèmes composants sont immédiatement et *ipso facto* conditionnées par la règle de droit du système composé.'

[620] Précis II, at 10 and 21; La doctrine de L. Duguit, at 93; also, La fonction exécutive, at 99 *et seq*.

le Droit international confère aux gouvernants et aux agents des différents Etats deux ordres de compétences, l'un interne, l'autre international, suivant qu'il est nécessaire de collaborer à la formation de l'ordonnance juridique interne ou à celle de l'ordonnance juridique inter social.[621]

Until federal (i.e., supra-national) institutionalisation has developed further, the national *gouvernants* and *agents* who have been given *international* competences by international law perfom all international social functions. With the principle of *dédoublement fonctionnel*, Scelle conceptualised the temporary stage in which the global society and its law found itself and gave it institutions and *gouvernants* and *agents*, the lack of which was often regarded as proof that international law did not exist and that the global reality was in fact anarchy. During this temporary (inter-state) stage in international development, until a truly federal institutionalised global society would come into existence, the universal monist system was largely carried by this principle of *dédoublement fonctionnel*. By putting international law at the summit of this hierarchical universal legal order, the sovereignty of the state was replaced with the sovereignty of law.

On the subject of sovereignty, finally, in the dispute between the revisionists and the restorers – '*la grande querelle des internationalistes actuels*' – Scelle found himself on the side of the revisionists: he agreed with their rejection of the traditional concept of sovereignty.[622] He considered it 'a fiction,' 'a logical impossibility,' and 'incompatible with objective law', as no-one and no-*body* had the right to impose their will on others.[623] Moreover, the traditional concept of sovereignty removes government acts from the rule of law and is therefore anti-democratic and contrary to the law: 'le concept ne peut aboutir pratiquement qu'à soustraire la volonté des gouvernants à l'emprise du Droit, à détruire la notion de compétence et, avec elle, celle de légalité.'[624] In other words, there is *no* subjective right of sovereignty; its existence would in fact imply a negation of law. In Scelle's theory, '*le Droit seul est souverain.*' Sovereignty belongs to international law. This law, which emerges from the global solidarity of humanity, is superior to all other law. The global society's *objective* constitutional *law* determines the distribution of *competences*. This is not the task of a sovereign ruler, but a 'social function' of international law.

La souveraineté étant un principe absolu ne pourrait s'entendre que de la société internationale globale, le Droit des gens ayant seul la compétence de la compétence, ce

---

[621] La doctrine de L. Duguit, at 94.

[622] Précis I, at ix.

[623] Id., at 13-14: 'La souveraineté est une notion d'ordre absolu qui implique le pouvoir pour un individu de faire tout ce qu'il veut et, par conséquent, d'imposer sa volonté à tous les autres individus. Or, ce pouvoir absolu n'existe pas en fait dans une société, car le pouvoir humain est toujours limité par les résistances du milieu. Mais la notion est, en outre, incompatible avec celle même de Droit. '

[624] Id., at 14.

qui implique non seulement sa *primauté* mais son *exclusivisme*. Il se confond ainsi avec le Droit tout court. C'est le *monisme juridique intégral*.[625]

In line with this reasoning, the notion of the *domaine reserve*, the traditional complement of sovereignty, must also be redefined: 'C'est simplement *l'ensemble des competences discrétionnaires* conferees aux gouvernants étatiques par le Droit international.'[626] Scelle turned things around, so to speak. Law does not spring from power, power is in fact competence attributed by law.

To sum up, Scelle cleansed international law of the collectivist notions of personality, national will and state sovereignty and instead defined international law in terms of the necessary regulation and determination of '*competences*:'

Le Droit international public, il n'est ainsi que l'ensemble des déterminations de *compétences* nécessaires à l'organisation des rapports juridiques entre individus membres des collectivités intersociales. Lorsqu'on a consenti à nettoyer son esprit des résidus dont l'encombrent les conceptions traditionnelles de personnalité collective, de volonté nationale, de majesté souveraine, de divinité locale ou étatique, et autres représentations anthropomorphiques que l'homme moderne a héritées de ses ancêtres paléolithiques, on s'aperçoit vite que les rapports internationaux sont avant tout des rapports individuels.[627]

Defining international law without making use of the traditional concepts of state personality and sovereignty and instead starting from a notion of the state as just another collective of *individuals* makes Scelle's concept of international law indeed a true *Droit des gens*: the law of the universal society of humanity. The biological origin of all law, the *condition humain*, is also the source of the *Droit des gens*.

Scelle responded to the sceptics who argued that international law did not really exist with the argument that international law *necessarily* exists. The other much-phrased objection against international law – its lack of effectiveness because of the absence of international (or federal) *gouvernants* and *agents* exercising the three public functions – he countered by means of the principle of *dédoublement fonctionnel*. International law is the *necessary* distribution of national and international competences over individual human beings. Next, I will examine how Scelle dealt with the parallel crisis of the individual liberties.

3.5.4. Scelle's concept of ILP: defending democracy and individual liberties

[L]es gouvernants étatiques [sont les] *principaux* sujets du droit des gens ...[628]

---

[625] Précis II, at 6. Also, Précis I, at 13.
[626] La doctrine de L. Duguit, at 113. Emphasis G.S.
[627] Id., at 118. Emphasis added.
[628] La Fonction Exécutive, at 91. Emphasis added.

> En réalité, la soi-disant conquête de la « personnalité » par l'individu, en droit public international, c'est *la conquête de la compétence pour agir contre les gouvernants*, la conquête du droit d'action en justice pour faire respecter la légalité par les gouvernants.[629]

It is fair to say that Scelle has become famous for arguing that only individual human beings have ILP: 'Les individus seuls sont sujets de droit en droit international public.'[630] But what we are interested in here is what Scelle actually meant by this unequivocal statement. What was he *doing in* using the concept of ILP the way he did? What was he *doing in* first outlawing the traditional conception of legal personality for being mystical, anthropomorphic, completely unrealistic, fictional, authoritarian and, not to mention, a psychological fallacy[631] and subsequently using it in relation to the position of the individual human being?

Scelle used the concept of (international) legal personality to defend the democratic system and to tackle the parallel crisis of the individual liberties. He constructed an approach to international law which was mainly intended to counter instances of *detournement de pouvoir* by the state *gouvernants*. Placed in the context of the *absolutisme des gouvernants* and the shortcomings of the French political institutional structure, it is understandable why Scelle so often referred to the *gouvernants'* tendency to abuse their power or use it arbitrarily.

> [Le droit positif étatique] est devenue ... un *droit positif anti-juridique*. La raison doit en être cherchée dans la psychologie exclusiviste des groupements et dans la psychologie autoritaire et égoïste des minorités gouvernantes. C'est cette psychologie que la science allemande caractérise par l'expression « volonté de puissance ». C'est la lutte de la force contre le droit. Mais cette constatation, précisément, donne tout son intérêt à la science du Droit international. Elle a pour but de renouer la chaîne mal soudée et souvent interrompue des solidarités superposées et, en ruinant la conception dualiste, de faciliter le développement de l'organisation juridique universelle.[632]

Selfish and authoritarian politicians formed a major obstacle to the realisation of social solidarity, both nationally and globally. Their actions had to be challenged and corrected: '*la pratique des hommes d'Etat est souvent contraire au Droit*. Mais les politiques font leur métier en faisant de la politique. Les juristes ne font pas le leur en s'inclinant devant les contingences, et en donnant comme droit objectif des pratiques contradictoires à la règle de droit.' Scelle refused to be an '*apologist[e] de la force*,' who defended 'le «Faustrecht»,' or the 'negation of law'.[633]

In response to this 'struggle of force against law,' Scelle argued in the first place that the state *gouvernants* were the *principal* subjects of international law.

---

629 Précis I, at 48.
630 Id., at 42.
631 Précis I, at vii-49; La fonction executive, at 93; see also, Précis II.
632 Id., at 34.
633 Id., at x; see also: at 61.

In the second place, he argued the strengthening of the legal position of the individual citizens *vis-à-vis* their *gouvernants* or rulers. The concept of ILP redefined as 'having *competence*' is essential to both these elements of Scelle's theory. *Competence* is the power to act recognised by, limited by, and guaranteed by law; it is the power to create legal situations: 'On appelle compétence *le pouvoir conféré aux individus membres de la société d'émettre des actes de volonté qui se réaliseront dans le milieu social.* C'est le pouvoir de créer des situations juridiques.'[634] As competence is the power to act by the force of will, only individuals can have competence and thereby be subjects of law.[635] Elaborating on Duguit's constitutional ideas,[636] Scelle argued that every individual, but the *gouvernants* in particular, has *competence.* Redefining ILP as 'having *competence*,' i.e., the legal power to act, means using ILP to constrain the power of the *gouvernants* and their *agents* and to strengthen the position of the individual *vis-à-vis* the *gouvernants* by the recognition of that individual liberties are the basis of the global society.[637] In brief, to act legitimately, the *gouvernants* and their *agents* had to respect 'le domaine de la superlégalité' of the *necessary* individual liberties.[638]

Scelle's definition of *gouvernants* shows that he, like Duguit, did not deny the significance of social force, but that he did aim to constrain it. Effective social power is the basis of social organisation; however, in itself it does not justify the attribution of *governmental competences.* Thereto, it is necessary that effective power is exercised to benefit social solidarity. The attribution of governmental competences is thus justified if there exists '*concordance entre l'efficacité de cette force et les besoins de la solidarité* au service de qui elle est mise.'[639] Factual social force is only used *legitimately* if it is used to accomplish the social solidarity objectives. If the efficacy disappears or the social objectives are no longer served, the juridical titles or governmental competences also disappear or may be withdrawn. If one has effective social force at one's disposal, one is endowed with the *objective duty* to use it to realise social solidarity in the exercise of social or public functions.[640] If used in this way, effective social power will be *recognised* as legitimate by the members of the political society and the necessary *competences* will be conferred upon the *gouvernants* and their *agents.* The kind of competence – discretionary or non-discretionary – and its purpose – to serve a

---

[634] Id., at 7-8.

[635] Précis I, at 9-10: 'Il ne peut donc y avoir de sujet de droit que là où il n'y a un être doué de volonté personnelle.'

[636] Traité I, at 724-725.

[637] Précis I, at 25. Also, La doctrine de L. Duguit, at 116.

[638] Précis II, at 12.

[639] Précis I, at 23.

[640] Id., at 24: 'Il est alors du devoir de ceux qui détiennent la force de prendre en main l'exercice des fonctions publiques. *Leurs titres juridiques sont dans l'efficacité de leur action*, dans sa conformité avec la solidarité sociale.'

private or a public interest – defines whether we are dealing with private individuals on the one hand or *gouvernants, agents* or *fonctionnaires* on the other.[641] *Gouvernants* are competent to act in the interest and on behalf of the individual members of the society on the basis of a discretionary competence. Officials and civil servants are generally given non-discretionary competences to serve the public interest.[642]

Individuals with (governmental) competences are subjects of law. The fact that common interest exists does not mean, however, that this is the interest of an independent entity which is completely separate from the members of the collective: '[l]es intérêts collectives ne cessent pas d'être des intérêts individuals.' As a matter of legal technique, the *gouvernants* have the competence to create legal effects for the *gouvernés*:

> les intérêts collectifs sont gérés par des *représentants*, c'est-à-dire que les effets de droit voulus par les représentants se produisent au bénéfice ou à l'encontre de tous les représentés. Il y a là un procédé de technique juridique, et rien de plus. Il n'y a pas d'autres *sujets de droit* que les *représentés* et les *représentants*, et pas d'autres compétences que celles des individus agissants. La collectivité ne peut pas plus être un sujet de droit que l'infans [sic.], la fondation ou l'animal.[643]

Earlier, we noted that Scelle, like Duguit, rejected the fiction of the state's (international) legal personality as well as the fiction of the state *organs* and the theory construed upon it.[644]

---

[641] Id., at 8.

[642] Contrary to Duguit, Scelle did not consider the monopoly of force to be the determining criterion for qualification as a *gouvernant*. Duguit distinguished between local and national rulers, whereby only the latter qualified as *gouvernants*. Scelle, however, decided that the *competence to control competences*, all of them law-imposed, determined who or what was a *gouvernant*. La doctrine de L. Duguit, at 111: 'Ceci pose, il apparaît que c'est *dans le contrôle des compétences* qu'il convient de chercher le critère juridique de la distinction entre agents et gouvernants.' The *gouvernant* is attributed a discretionary competence by public law, while the agent is subordinate to the *gouvernant* and has no discretionary say over how to accomplish the objectives set for him. Id., at 111-112; Also, La fonction exécutive, at 102. La doctrine de L. Duguit, at 112: 'C'est en ce sens que l'on doit dire que le gouvernant seul jouit d'une compétence réellement discrétionnaire. ... Cette définition s'applique aussi bien aux agents décentralisés qu'aux gouvernants locaux d'un Etat fédéral. Et nous retrouvons ici, dans l'Etat, la même loi de dédoublement des fonctions que nous avons constatée dans le milieu interétatique, parce que nous vérifions que le système étatique est lui aussi un système intersocial comme le système interétatique ou le système fédératif.'

[643] Précis I, at 11. 'La seule chose que le législateur puisse faire, c'est d'attribuer socialement *les effets* des actes accomplis par un individu, soit à cet individu lui-même, soit à d'autres individus, soit à des buts déterminés. ... ... Le législateur d'aucun pays ne peut investir de volonté ou de compétence des êtres fictifs ou des phénomènes. ... Ne disons donc pas que la personnalité morale existe juridiquement, mais seulement que le droit positif a créé, dans un désir de simplification, une façon vicieuse de parler.' See *supra* for Duguit on the requirement of a conscious personal will for the quality of legal personality.

[644] Précis I, at 12: 'L'introduction de cette fausse notion de personnalité morale dans le droit public nous paraît être une cause essentielle des retards et des déviations de son évolution. Il est spécialement ainsi en Droit international.'

The fiction of state personality and the 'dédoublement'[645] it causes, leads to concealed responsibility : 'd'abord, à faire disparaître ensuite la *responsabilité*. ... on cède à une mystique qui attribue des qualités immanentes à des êtres fictifs, mais qui bénéficie à *des personnes réelles devenues irresponsables et toutes puissantes* derrière l'écran qui les dissimule.'[646] With the fiction in place, the (omnipotent) *gouvernants* could hide behind the mask of the state person. Duguit's attempt to repair this injustice is reflected in Scelle's casting aside of subjective rights: 'Les *droits subjectifs* attribués aux personnes fictives : droit de souveraineté, de puissance publique, longtemps considérés comme de véritables droits patrimoniaux, et qui le furent originairement, deviennent le déguisement des *devoirs objectifs*.' In reality, there are only individual *gouvernants* endowed with governmental competences, which are not rights, but objective *duties*. In other words, '[l]a soi-disant *personnalité* morale *se résout*, en dernière analyse, *en des attributions de compétence*.'[647] In Scelle's perception, the distribution, determination and limitation of *competences* was the primary function of international law and the reason for its supremacy. It legally defined the power of the *gouvernants* and their *agents*.

La règle de droit s'impose également à tous les sujets de droit, gouvernants, agents et particuliers. Les compétences, qu'il s'agisse de la capacité des particuliers ou des fonctions confiées aux agents et gouvernants, ne constituent donc *jamais un droit subjectif* appartenant aux individus. Elles sont un *pouvoir objectif* conféré par le droit positif, dont l'utilisation est souvent même *obligatoire*, notamment lorsqu'il s'agit des agents et des gouvernants et qui, en principe, est *indélégable* par son titulaire à d'autres sujets de droit. Il n'y a pas de place, dans un milieu juridique, pour une volonté souveraine.[648]

In brief, Scelle first rejected the state's legal personality and its sovereignty and in its place put forward the attribution of competences. He then redefined legal personality as the state of having competences. Hereby Scelle used ILP to remove the mystery mask and *subject the gouvernants to the rule of law*. Individual *gouvernants* and their *agents* are subjects of international law. Below, we will return to the implications this has for the doctrine of responsibility.

Secondly, however, having defined ILP as the state where one has competence, the next step is to establish that every private individual is a subject of international law. Private individuals have the (discretionary) competence to pursue their private interests. Scelle also uses the term 'capacity', but conceptually this equals competence. The individual is not a subject of international law in the traditional sense that international law grants him natural subjective *rights*. In this case, in-

---

[645] Scelle also rejected the organic state theory. See, for 'dédoublement,' also *supra* section 3.4. on Hans Kelsen.

[646] Précis I, at 12. Emphasis added.

[647] Id., at 12-13.

[648] Id., at 14 and 35. See for Duguit's rejection of delegation, *supra* text to footnotes 545-546.

ternational law grants *individual liberties*.[649] In Scelle's view, individual liberties are neither *natural* nor *rights*. With their origin in objective law, individual liberties are *social*:[650]

Ces libertés nécessaires, n'existent donc que dans la limite où elles sont sanctionnées par le droit positif. Elles sont *sociales* et non pré-sociales et cela condamne nettement la théorie du *contrat social* et de l'état de nature. Le Droit n'est pas le résultat d'un abandon consenti par les individus sur une somme de facultés d'action ou de droits subjectifs leur appartenant préalablement à l'existence de toute société. C'est là renverser l'ordre des facteurs. Les *droits individuels* n'existent que dans et par la société. Ce sont des pouvoirs d'actions reconnus par le droit positif, *des situations objectives*.[651]

The perception that individual liberties confer the social power to act in conformity with the law is based upon the abovementioned principle of the sovereignty of law. Because it has supremacy, law determines the extent of the domain of necessary individual liberties: '[le Droit] *a la compétence de sa propre compétence* et c'est en celà que consiste ce qu'on appelle la souveraineté du Droit.' From this perspective, law also determines the domain of other social categories, such as, for example, morality, religion and economy. It determines what is legally relevant and what is not. 'Le domaine des autres disciplines est donc *juridiquement déterminé* et si, dans les limites qui lui sont ainsi tracéés [sic.], la volonté individuelle paraît être indépendante du Droit, c'est parce que le Droit lui-même lui a conféré dans ces domaines l'indépendance ou l'*autonomie*.' However, '*cette autonomie de la volonté n'est en réalité qu'une compétence*, un pouvoir d'agir ou de s'abstenir socialement reconnu, une compétence discrétionnaire.'[652] In fact, individual autonomy is a *discretionary competence* attributed and guaranteed by law and generally recognised as truly *necessary* to the individual for his existence and development.[653] According to Scelle, in every modern society, the public interest and solidarity require a sufficient amount of minimum individual autonomy: 'l'individu, sujet de droit, puise dans le droit positif une large compétence en tout ce qui concerne le développement de son initiative et de sa personnalité. C'est la *loi du progrès*.'[654] After all, how can

---

[649] Among these liberties are evidently the individual freedom of conscience, thought and religion, which oblige the society and especially the *gouvernants* to abstain from (intervening) action and to respect the private domain, but there are also liberties that do require social or governmental action.

[650] See also, Précis II, at 16: 'c'est le fait social qui est antérieur et supérieur à toute faculté juridique.'

[651] Précis I, at 26.

[652] Id., at 25.

[653] Id., at 26: 'On est d'accord pour reconnaître aujourd'hui que dans les sociétés arrivées à un certain degré d'évolution, une compétence discrétionnaire doit être laissée et garantie aux individus, dans un certain nombre de domaines. On parle alors des *libertés nécessaires*, et l'on fait état du degré de conscience personnelle et de maturité intellectuelle auquel est parvenu, après des millénaires, l'individu humain.'

[654] Précis II, at 17.

progress be made if, for example, individual life or the individual's freedom of conscience or movement is not guaranteed? This is why '*il n'y a pas de progrès humain sans un minimum d'émancipation individuelle et collective.*' The emancipation of the individual is an ongoing legal development to which end international law, according to Scelle, also increasingly features norms of universal objective law: '*Le Droit des gens est arrivé peu à peu à dégager les normes du droit objectif universel qui correspondent aux nécessités essentielles de l'existence et du progrès des communautés et des peuples.*'[655] The individual liberties which objective law guarantees to the legal subjects will, in Scelle's opinion, *necessarily* become part of international law because international peace and order require it.[656]

Thus the doctrine of the *individual liberties* supports the individual's emancipation *vis-à-vis* the *gouvernants*. Objective law confers upon the latter a *duty* to respect these liberties. Their power is limited, they are not allowed to will or do everything, and a domain remains that is private or inaccessible to them, namely the domain of the *individual liberties*. The doctrine of *necessary individual liberties* thus intends to protect the individual from the *gouvernants* if they abuse their power or use it arbitrarily:

> La théorie des libertés comprend l'exposé des règles *qui garantissent aux sujets de droit, dans les diverses collectivités du Droit des gens, l'usage individuel ou collectif d'un pouvoir d'action libéralement réglementé, parfois même largement discrétionnaire, dans les domaines essentiels de l'activité humaine.*
>
> Ces règles s'imposent d'abord aux gouvernants, et surtout aux gouvernants législateurs dont elles limitent la compétence, puis, par eux, aux agents et enfin aux particuliers qui doivent s'y conformer dans leurs rapports mutuels.[657]

Considering the French political context with its *absolutisme des deputes*, Scelle's contention that especially the competence of the *gouvernants législateurs* is restricted by international legal rules reveals what he was *doing* in defining the individual as a subject of law, not with rights but with individual liberties, namely formulating a response to the crisis of democracy and individual liberties.

On the basis of the doctrine of *individual* liberties, Scelle included the principle of democracy in his conception of international law and called it 'self-determination'. This principle is often defined as a collective right, but Scelle did not

---

[655] Id., at 18.

[656] Précis II, at 292: 'les soi-disant droits individuels et collectifs ne sont que des *compétences garanties* aux sujets de droit par la règle de Droit international commun, mais ... elles sont souvent mises péril par l'insuffisance du Droit des gens constructif, l'anarchie qui règne dans les relations entre les peuples, l'arbitraire des gouvernements. Cependant, l'expérience de plusieurs siècles de vie internationale paraît avoir démontré que la prospérité des nations et, par suite, la paix entre elles, sont conditionnées par l'octroi et la garantie de ces compétences juridiques. Ce sont elles, en effet, qui forment *la substance même* des rapports internationaux et qui, par conséquent, insufflent la vie aux sociétés internationales.'

[657] Id., at 16.

accept the concept of collective rights and considered them in reality to be *individual liberties* which are enjoyed or exercised collectively.[658] Whether it is exercised individually or collectively, self-determination is a *competence* of the *individual*.[659] What is known as people's right to self-determination is the legally guaranteed competence of the individual members of a political society to appoint their own rulers : '[*le droit des peuples à disposer d'eux-mêmes*] ... *n'est autre que la transposition en Droit des gens du* principe démocratique *de l'attribution et du retrait, par les gouvernés, des compétences gouvernementales*.'[660] Legal constraints are in individualised to apply to individuals *only*. After all, the individual is the only *real* being, the only entity with a conscience and a will.[661] Therefore, individuals are also the only ones upon whom *competences* can be conferred. The individual liberty to elect one's rulers is thus a competence recognised by international law in the principle of self-determination. With this principle, international law recognises the individual competence of the subjects of law to choose their own rulers and express their opinion on political situations.[662] *Democracy* is therefore a fundamental freedom of every individual member of a political society, a freedom that is guaranteed by international law:

Nous définirons donc le sens et la portée juridiques du droit des peuples de la façon suivante : *c'est la faculté juridique conférée par le Droit des gens positif aux sujets de droit membres de tout groupement politique, de se constituer en entité politique en instituant leurs propres gouvernants, ou de se rattacher à la communauté politique organisée qu'il leur plaira de choisir*.[663]

---

[658] Id., at 16-17. See also, Précis I, at 26-27: '[I]l n'y a pas de droits subjectifs en soi pour les collectivités: il n'y a pas plus de *contrat intersocial* que de contrat social, d'abord parce qu'une collectivité en tant que telle ne peut ni agir, ni vouloir, ni contracter, ensuite parce que les compétences attribuées aux représentants des collectivités supposent au préalable un droit intersocial. Mais le droit objectif peut attribuer certains statuts ou pouvoir d'actions aux individus membres des collectivités comme tels.'

[659] Précis II, at 18: 'Nous avons parlé de libertés individuelles *et collectives*. Cette terminologie ne doit pas faire naître d'équivoque. Les collectivités comme telles: minorités, nations, Etats, ne peuvent exercer de compétences ni jouir de libertés. Ce sont *leurs membres*, tous leurs membres ou certains d'entre eux agissant pour le compte de tous, qui se verront attribuer par le droit positif les compétences nécessaires à produire les situations juridiques voulues et qui les exerceront personnellement. Tous les membres, disons-nous, s'il s'agit de votations, plébiscites, réunions, associations, usage des libertés civiles et civiques. ... Certains d'entre ces membres, agents ou gouvernants, agiront seuls s'il s'agit de l'administration des biens affectés au but social collectif ou de l'exercice des fonctions sociales (self-government). La différence technique entre l'utilisation des libertés individuelles et des libertés collectives ne semble donc pas considérable du point de vue de l'analyse des actes juridiques. Elle se traduit pourtant par des modalités appropriées au but envisagé.'

[660] Précis II, at 294. Emphasis added.

[661] Précis I, at 9: « ... [la qualité de sujet de droit] est en effet un attribut social de la volonté. Il ne peut donc y avoir de sujet de droit que là où il y a un être doué de volonté personnelle. »

[662] Précis II, at 265: '... dans le principe du droit des peuples, ce qui détermine la compétence individuelle des sujets de droit de se prononcer sur la situation politique et sociale de la collectivité, c'est *le principe constitutionnel de la liberté individuelle*...'

[663] Id., at 262.

The *international* legal principle of self-determination requires that within the *internal* political order the governmental competences of the *gouvernants* were conferred upon them by the *governés* by means of an '*acte-condition*,' such as an election. It also makes clear that these competences are not rights, but duties. It obliges the rulers to rule well, i.e., in the interest of the governed. This ultimately means that they must actively pursue social solidarity. In case of significant changes to the state structure (e.g., secession) which affect the way in which governmental competences function, the governed – the individual subjects of law – are to be consulted and involved. International law thus stipulates that the legitimacy of any government is determined by the consent of the people. This, according to Scelle, therefore defines the legitimate basis of both national and international governmental power.[664] In this theory, international law validates democratic rule, instead of masking undemocratic internal practices with the help of ILP.

If the people expressly recognise the fact that the *gouvernants* and their agents use the social power legitimately in the exercise of public functions, a '*constitutionnalisation du pouvoir*' takes place and the *democratic* principle that the people are 'le déterminateur suprême des compétences gouvernementales' is respected.[665] International law thus recognises the legitimacy of the power of the *gouvernants* and invests them with governmental competences if both the factual criterion (effective social power exercised with a view to social solidarity) and the legal criterion (the consent of the people obtained through elections, for example) are fulfilled. The democratic principle, which demands that the *gouvernants* receive their power and authority from the *gouvernés* in order to be legitimate, has thus been transposed into international law as the principle of self-determination. The people's right is separated into the *individual* competences of the members of the political society, exercised collectively, to elect their *gouvernants*.

The principle of self-determination removes sovereignty from the *gouvernants*. In this scenario, international law grants the *gouvernés* the « compétence des compétences » which they in turn pass on to the *gouvernants*.

Non seulement il [le principe de l'autodétermination] fait passer la « compétence des compétences » des gouvernants aux gouvernés, – ce qui est bien la négation de la

[664] Id., at 261: 'Le principe du droit des peuples, dans l'ordre du Droit des gens, devait tender à s'introduire comme conséquence de la consolidation du principe démocratique en droit interne. Seulement, la désharmonie entre les deux ordres a subsisté dans la période de transition. C'est ainsi que l'on a vu des gouvernants annexionnistes, tout en procédant à des mutations de souveraineté forcées que le Droit international positif considérait comme régulières, chercher pourtant à se garantir contre l'imminence du nouveau principe, en faisant *ratifier* les cessions consenties par les gouvernants au moyen d'une consultation populaire ou parlementaire.'

[665] Précis I, at 24. Scelle continued: 'Arrivés à ce point limite, il faut bien constater que dans une société déterminée *la soumission du pouvoir à la règle de droit* est une question d'équilibre de forces et de moralité gouvernementale. On n'en doit pas moins maintenir que *la soumission des gouvernants au droit objectif* est l'axiome fondamental de la science politique.' Emphasis added.

souveraineté des premiers, – mais encore il est totalement *incompatible avec la notion de personnalité collective,* et notamment de personnalité étatique.

Si l'État, et l'État *seul*, en effet, est une personne juridique du Droit des gens, si sa volonté collective est seule susceptible de produire des effets de droit, il est *impossible* que des groupements intra-étatique ou *des individus opposent leur volonté à celle de l'État* ...[666]

The concepts of state personality and sovereignty could not be reconciled with the democratic principle of self-determination.[667] The idea of the state as a person and, moreover, the only possible international legal person, in Scelle's view resulted in the acceptance of the entirely undemocratic fact that the individual must remain silent. In a democracy, however, citizens have the liberty to speak up and raise their voices against their *gouvernants*. International law should contribute to democracy, not validate the lack of it.

Instead of using the concept of ILP, as it traditionally was, to conceal the negation of democracy, Scelle therefore used it to empower the individual to act and implement (objective) law.

Il n'y a pas d'autre personnalité juridique réelle que celle de l'individu doué de conscience et de volonté personnelle, et c'est dans l'utilisation des compétences par le sujet de droit individuel que réside le secret de la technique juridique.[668]

Le Droit objectif se réalise par le Droit constructif, par les institutions, donnant ainsi naissance au Droit positif qui est la traduction hypothétiquement exacte de la norme juridique. Tout acte social, c'est-à-dire volontaire, et par conséquent individuel, doit être conforme au Droit normatif et constructif. Il n'y a d'autres sujets de Droit que les individus. Ils sont dotés de compétences, c'est-à-dire de pouvoirs d'action conditionnant la mise en œuvre de la règle de Droit.[669]

The fact that in legal terms individual liberties impose obligations upon the gouvernants, rather than rights upon the individual, does not mean 'que les individus ne sont pas sujets de droit dans l'ordre juridique international:' it is simply a matter of legal technique.[670] The autonomy of the individual and (limited) governmental power are both competences and therefore, from Scelle's universal monist perspective, *gouvernants* and their *agents* and private individuals are '*directement* sujets de droit des gens.'[671]

In this skilfully constructed international legal defence of democracy and individual liberties, the concept of ILP is used first to challenge the conventional idea of the state and its position on the international stage (Scelle *removes the mask*)

---

[666] Précis II, at 260. Emphasis added.

[667] Scelle blamed these two concepts for the slow progress of international law in this respect. Précis I, at ix.

[668] Précis II, at 295.

[669] La doctrine de L. Duguit, at 117.

[670] Précis II, at 32.

[671] Précis I, at 48.

and, secondly, to submit the *gouvernants* to the rule of law and to emancipate the human individual (Scelle explains ILP as the quality of being legally competent).

Finally, I will discuss Scelle's theory that the state *gouvernants* are the *principal* subjects of international law. The term 'principal' implies two things. First Scelle, like Le Fur, compares the *gouvernants'* behaviour with that of feudalist lords. In other words, it is used to confront the *gouvernants'* tendency to put themselves above the law. Secondly however, the *gouvernants* are also in particular responsible for the efficacy of law.

... dans une société déterminée, l'organisation doit tendre à sanctionner la règle de droit et qu'elle y tend dans la mesure où l'anarchie fait place aux institutions. L'histoire diplomatique n'est bien souvent que celle de la défiguration et de la méconnaissance systématique de la règle de droit. Cela provient de ce que les gouvernants étatiques, principaux sujets de droit des gens, sont la plupart du temps assez forts pour se mettre au-dessus de la règle coutumière ou conventionnelle, comme jadis les seigneurs féodaux au-dessus du droit féodal.[672]

However, the position of the *gouvernants* seems to be explained best by the fact that they are invested with the power to create legal effects for the *gouvernés* and that they have an obligation to serve the common interests of social solidarity, both nationally and internationally. The state *gouvernants* are the essential subjects of international law, as on the one hand they are responsible for advancing the federalisation and institutionalisation of the global society and, on the other, the national *gouvernants* are also international *gouvernants* by means of the principle of *dédoublement fonctionnel*. The wide powers this conferred upon them called for their close supervision. The *gouvernants*' tendency to abuse their competence, to use their power arbitrarily, and to neglect their task to monitor each other in their relations with private individuals made it imperative these individuals were also granted *international legal personality*:

[les gouvernants et agents nationaux qui remplissent les fonctions internationales] [e]ux-mêmes *ignorent* souvent leur dédoublement fonctionnel. On aboutit ainsi au recours à la protection diplomatique, succédané de l'organisation supra-nationale, et qui n'est en fait qu'un *contrôle* de gouvernants et agents internationaux par d'autres gouvernants internationaux. C'est pour remédier à ces insuffisances et à ces abus que l'on tend aujourd'hui à donner au particulier, sujet de droit international, une compétence ou une personnalité juridique de droit public, aussi bien que de droit privé.[673]

And indeed, international law (le droit des gens) was rightly criticised for its lack of adequate control and sanctioning mechanisms.[674] This *contrôle de légalité sur les actes des gouvernants* was, however, urgently needed, both internationally

[672] La fonction exécutive, at 91.
[673] Précis I, at 47.
[674] Id., at 59.

and domestically, to halt the decline of international liberties. In order to remedy these insufficiencies, Scelle eliminated what were in his view the major impediments to the realisation of international law in general and the *contrôle de légalité sur les actes des gouvernants* in particular: 'les concepts de personnalité et de souveraineté.'[675]

Le concept de personnalité. Car dès l'instant que « juger » l'acte d'un gouvernant c'est *juger* en même temps l'Etat et la Nation, on se heurte à cet obstacle, quasi insurmontable en pratique, qu'est le sentiment collectif et la mystique nationale, les plus lourds impondérables. Mais si, repoussant la fiction, on parvient à se convaincre que, dans la réalité des faits, le litige se réduit au point de savoir si *un individu* sujet de droit, gouvernants sans doute, mais souvent gouvernant passager, a correctement interprété la loi de sa fonction et *dépassé ou non sa compétence*, l'obstacle se dégonfle et, dans la plupart des cas, le conflit émigre du point d'honneur au point de droit. [676]

By rejecting the old concept of ILP and subsequently attributing ILP to private individuals in general and to state *gouvernants* in particular, Scelle aimed to eliminate blind nationalist belief and mysticism from the conceptual world of international law. The old concept of ILP was a major obstacle to the evaluation of the legality of governmental acts, but Scelle re-conceived ILP in such a way that now governmental acts could be evaluated as to their legality or possible *detournement de pouvoir*. In case of illegal (inter)national governmental acts, the concept of ILP no longer hindered an adequate response.

Pourtant l'une des compétences *nécessaires* des gouvernants internationaux consiste à sanctionner le Droit, même à l'égard des autres gouvernants. Compétence nécessaire, car la solidarité internationale exige la prévention, la répression et la réparation des violations du Droit; mais compétence *concurrente* dans une société inorganisée, et par suite fertile en conflits. De là est née *l'intervention*, l'institution internationale qui comporte l'emploi de moyens coercitifs, dont le plus extrême est la guerre, et l'établissement des responsabilités.[677]

The concepts of personality and sovereignty stood in the way of a necessary practice of *intervention* by international *gouvernants* in case of illegal actions; intervention to enforce obligatory legal governmental action and to organise the responsibility for the realisation of social solidarity. The legitimacy of international intervention had to be based on objective law providing the *gouvernants* with the objective *duty* of realising law and social solidarity. Scelle pointed out that: 'la doctrine objectiviste du Droit des gens doit considérer l'intervention non pas seulement comme une compétence, mais comme une compétence *liée* des gouvernants, comme un devoir, *une fonction internationale*.' He admits that certains risk adhere to this, but 'le péril n'est point dans *le principe* de l'inter-

[675] Id., at 61. Also, La fonction exécutive, at 93.

[676] Précis I, at 61-62.

[677] Id, at 63.

vention. Il est dans *l'inorganisation du procédé* et l'absense de contrôle sur sa mise en œuvre.'[678] Scelle called for the organisation of (intervention as a means of) *contrôle de légalité sur les actes des gouvernants*,[679] and for the creation of the competence to enforce law collectively (if necessary by force) in order to maintain international public order and prevent conflict. The international society had to continue its efforts towards further federalisation up to the point where it would go from being an inter-state society to a supra-state or federal global society. Scelle considered the creation of the League of Nations a step in the right direction:

La société internationale actuelle, qui connaît déjà de multiples expériences fédéralistes, dont plusieurs s'enlisent déjà dans l'unitarisme étatique, a fait avec la Société des Nations un effort généralisé de fédéralisme constructif. Cet effort paraît actuellement péricliter sous la poussée des mystiques nationalistes et devant la résistance offensive des gouvernements autoritaires. Le fédéralisme normatif se développe cependant incessamment sous sa forme réglementaire (coutumière et conventionnelle) et sous sa forme juridictionnelle (arbitrage et juridiction obligatoires); mais il n'est pas douteux que c'est l'organisation de la fonction exécutive contre laquelle s'acharnent les résistances.[680]

However, the idea of a federal institutional structure was still controversial, in particular because of the *fonction executive* and the necessary measures of enforcement. But as in his opinion it was the only way to secure peace and order, Scelle strongly supported the development towards federalisation and argued that 'intervention' was necessary for regulating the attribution of competences and evaluating the legality of acts. This was a task of the international executive:

Mais gouverner, au sens étroit, c'est le rôle de l'exécutif. La fonction exécutive consiste à *procurer matériellement l'exécution du droit*, à assurer l'effectivité de l'ordonnancement juridique. Ce rôle essentiel à la sécurité sociale implique une *intervention constante* dans l'activité des agents juridiques ou sujets de droit, quels qu'ils soient : particuliers, agents et autres gouvernants. Il y a lieu tout d'abord de s'assurer de la régularité des investitures de compétence, soit que le gouvernant exécutif y procède lui-même (nomination), soit qu'il les vérifie (vérification des élections, successions et autres faits attributifs de compétence). Il y a lieu ensuite de contrôler de ces compétences pour empêcher les usurpations, les abus dans leur utilisation, ou, au contraire, prévenir les déficiences et refus d'utilisation lorsqu'elles sont obligatoires.

---

[678] Id., at 64. Also, La fonction exécutive, at 104: 'le principe de non-intervention, d'ailleurs si continûment et si totalement contredit par les faits dans les rapports internationaux, est incompatible avec toute technique juridique. Ou bien il n'y aura pas de fonction gouvernementale et exécutive internationale, ou bien il faut admettre que la compétence d'intervention est une compétence essentielle et même une compétence obligatoire des gouvernants internationaux.'

[679] The control of the agents and administrators, who only had non-discretionary competence, was hierarchically organised. They received instructions from the *gouvernants*. La fonction exécutive, at 102.

[680] Id., at 101 and 106.

Until the world was a federal organisation, the international executive, which was equally necessary in an inter-state system, had to be formed by the national *gouvernants*. Tthe concept of *dédoublement fonctionnel* thus provided the international legal system with internationally competent *gouvernants* who exercised the three necessary social functions of executive, legislative and judiciary. According to Scelle, 'c'est en vain qu'on voulu nier le caractère juridique du contrôle et l'intervention des gouvernants *vis-à-vis* les uns des autres.' On the contrary, '[j]uridiquement, tout gouvernement étatique, en sa qualité de gouvernement international, a le d'exiger le respect du droit international et son efficacité.' Scelle was quite pertinent on this issue: '[t]outes les fois ... qu'il s'agit de compétence liée ou réglementée, tout gouvernant de la communauté internationale a le droit d'exiger d'un autre qu'il s'abstienne de tout dépassement de compétence et qu'il accomplisse ses obligations.'[681] It is clear that the control of the legal use of competences is a necessity when one considers that the legal actions of *gouvernants* and *agents* 'have such profound and extensive social repercussions.'[682] Only by means of such control can governmental competences and individual liberties be guaranteed. This should prevent (if necessary by a threat of force) the *détournement de compétence gouvernementale*, but if any abuse still happens to take place, the international society will have to take action through its *gouvernants*. The international *gouvernants* have a duty to realise global solidarity, and to this end they have the right to monitor each other and the responsibility to prevent by intervention the escalation of any conflict and to respond by force if necessary to any violations.

Another important and more practical consequence of Scelle's theory is how it affects his view on the recognition or *non*-recognition of governments as a means of control. Having resolved the state person into separate individual state *gouvernants*, Scelle necessarily believed in the recognition of governments rather than states.[683] It must be verified through recognition whether governmental competences were legitimately invested in the gouvernants, i.e., whether the principle of democracy which is dictated by international law was respected.[684] Inter-

[681] Id., at 104-105.

[682] Id., at 107.

[683] Id., at 113: 'La reconnaissance étant le contrôle de la légalité d'une investiture, il ne peut évidemment y avoir de reconnaissance *que* de compétence d'agents ou de gouvernants, car les compétences sont des pouvoirs individuels. Un Etat ne pouvant avoir ni exercer de compétence, parler de reconnaissance d'Etat est sans signification juridique.' Emphasis added.

[684] Id., at 111: 'La compétence *de jure* naît de l'exercice normal d'une procédure de nomination ou d'élection, *prévue par le droit positif*. Quant au contenu, la compétence *de jure* est beaucoup plus large que la compétence *de facto*, et elle est garantie en droit positif. La compétence *de facto*, ayant pour base la nécessité, ne comprend d'autres pouvoirs juridiques que ceux qui sont indispensables à ses détenteurs pour remplir une tâche qui est par définition transitoire et précaire. ... ... Enfin, la compétence étant uniquement sur le fait de la détention de la plus grande force *ne saurait être garantie*. Elle est à la merci de la force comme elle est fondée sur la force. Pour qu'il en soit autrement, il faudra que le vice originaire se trouve purgé, soit par le procédé de la constitutionnalisation, soit par celui de prescription.' Moreover, Scelle maintains that 'le contrôle des investitures ne s'applique seulement à l'apparation de nouveaux gouvernants, mais *toutes modi-*

nationally, the government legitimises itself and its de facto power by governing in conformity with the requirements of social solidarity.[685] Legitimisation is thus a continuous process which is not terminated by the simple verification of the origin of governmental power. Recognition is therefore always conditional. Once they have been recognised, international *gouvernants* must continue to guarantee the legitimate use of their competences.[686] If, however, *détournement de compétence* still takes place, this requires action on the part of the executive, either through the imposition of a sanction or by creating an obligation to compensate or perform restititio in integrum.[687]

Although Scelle understood the general disappointment with the way the League of Nations performed its executive function, he also called to mind that 'tout esprit réaliste doit admettre que l'organisation sociale des peuples, c'est-à-dire *le fédéralisme institutionnel*, ne peut se réaliser que lentement et qu'il faut s'attendre à des à-coups successifs dans cette évolution.' In order to arrive at that stage, the League has to evolve from a society of nations into 'une société ... de gouvernements.' In Scelle's view, it was necessary that 'la société des Nations doit et peut évoluer vers une véritable société d'individus ou de collectivités comme le sont toutes les sociétés, et en particulier tous les systèmes fédératifs.' In other words, as long as the League of Nations 'sera gouvernée exclusivement par des gouvernants étatiques, elle ne sera pas gouvernée.' It was, however, not realistic to assume that international federalism could be accomplished by representatives of *national* interests, a successful transformation required 'dans les organes collectifs, de représentants des forces sociales internationales extra-étatiques aux délégués gouvernementaux.' This transformation which had ground to a halt as a result of the unprecedented contemporary crises nevertheless had to be stimulated, according to Scelle.[688]

If the transformation into a universal federal society was to be successful, international gouvernants would have to be made increasingly individually responsible for their actions. Scelle set aside the classical doctrine of the 'mystique du dommage collectif, de la responsabilité collective, etc. etc.' and explained that 'notre organisation sociale moderne s'enorgueillit d'avoir *individualisé* la responsabilité à la fois dans dans la personne de l'individu lésé et dans celle de l'auteur de l'acte dommageable.' The notions of sovereignty and personality had hitherto prevented any recognition of responsibility for government failure as they prevented state accountability – the state, after all, was above the law.

---

fications, quelles qu'elles puissent être, soit de la composition du collège gouvernemental international, soit de la répartition et de l'étendue des compétences au sein de ce collège. Il importe essentiellement, nous l'avons dit, à la stabilité de l'ordonnancement juridique, que nulle modification des compétences ne puisse se produire dans l'ordre gouvernemental sans qu'un contrôle collectif intervienne aussi rapidement que possible.'

[685] Duguit and Scelle both rejected the theory of the social contract and claimed that legitimate governance depended on social solidarity.

[686] La fonction exécutive, at 136 *et seq.*

[687] Id., at 156 *et seq.*

[688] Id., at 193-196.

Pour échapper à ce dilemme [sovereignty of law or sovereignty of state], on a dit qu'en Droit international la responsabilité est toujours contractuelle et non délictuelle. ... il n'y a jamais qu'une faute contractuelle. C'est une façon de rétablir une responsabilité objective : l'Etat accepte d'être responsable. Mais cette ingéniosité doctrinale nous paraît dépensée en pure perte. Le droit objectif n'est pas de nature contractuelle, surtout en matière de coutume. La seule réalité que révèle l'analyse, c'est que les *gouvernants* et *agents* étatiques peuvent parfaitement dépasser leur compétence et violer la règle qui la détermine. Il peut donc y avoir responsabilité pour faute, mais uniquement de la part *d'individus* et il faut donner à la responsabilité collective d'autres fondements.[689]

Scelle considered collective responsibility (based on social solidarity) as a '*responsibilité objective pour risques*,' which corresponds to a sense of justice.[690] However, objective responsibility is only the subsidiary principle of responsibility, as according to Scelle: 'Elle ne peut faire disparaître la responsabilité *subjective*, ou primaire, ni le principe de l'imputabilité.' In case of obvious *détournement de pouvoir*, when a *gouvernant* or agent abuses his competence, he should, as an individual subject of law, not be allowed to hide behind the state, but be held accountable personally. Still, Scelle did not believe in taking this point too far: 'Toutes fois qu'il y a *faute personnelle* et non pas, comme on dit, faute de service, cette faute doit être *imputée*, si l'on veut éviter le débordement de l'incompétence et maintenir la conscience professionnelle, dont l'absence est particulièrement redoutable lorsqu'il s'agit d'intérêts collectifs et de différends entre peuples.' Consequently, Scelle called for the support of initiatives in the field of international individual criminal responsibility. 'Il importe de dégager, toutes les fois qu'il est possible la responsabilité personnelle des gouvernants et agents internationaux.'[691] Individual legal personality in international law thus makes the individualisation of responsibility conceptually. There were more indications of a 'mouvement d'extention de la personnalité juridique des individus,' in Scelle's view, and he pointed at, among other things, the minorities' right of petition to the League of Nations Council and at the initiative of the International Law Institute to attribute ILP to Non-Governmental Organisations. Scelle concluded that the conquest of ILP by the individual is in fact *the conquest for the power and competence to stand up against the gouvernants*, the conquest for a right to enforce the *gouvernants*' respect for law.[692] By declaring that the *gouvernants étatiques* were the *principal* subjects of international law, Scelle

[689] Précis I, at 67.

[690] Id., at 68: 'Dans chaque Etat, les gouvernants et agents dirigent et gèrent les services publics, services publics nationaux qui sont souvent en même temps des *services publics internationaux*, puisqu'ils fonctionnent à la fois au bénéfice de la communauté nationale et de la communauté internationale. Les principes de responsabilité doivent être les mêmes dans les deux cas. ... Le principe de la responsabilité objective doit s'étendre à l'exercice de toutes les fonctions sociales: administratives, judiciaires, gouvernementales, législatives. Il n'y a en effet de *privilège d'intangibilité*, ou de souveraineté, pour aucune fonction, aucun acte juridique, aucun sujet de Droit.'

[691] Précis I, at 68.

[692] Id., at 48.

supported this conquest. Scelle used ILP to constrain the *gouvernants* and *agents* in their national and international governmental acts, to emancipate the private individual and empower him in his position *vis-à-vis* these *gouvernants* and *agents*, and to advance the institutionalisation and federalisation of the global society. As such, the concept of ILP – in its conventional meaning an obstacle in optima forma to the legal changes Scelle deemed necessary – was completely redefined and used anew as a means of progress.

3.5.5. **Conclusion**

Scelle's revision of ILP is more than the mere contribution from one among many international jurists to the contemporary debate on ILP and sovereignty, although it is that, too, of course. It is only when we situate his theory against the background of the intellectual and political crises of the Third Republic that it takes on its full significance, which in turn enables us to fully understand it. The problems of the Third Republic were different from the political problems which occurred in Kelsen's Vienna. There, the threat posed by the mass movements and multi-nationalism to the unity of the state made a concept of law with biological origins and causality as the unifying principle utterly impossible. Scelle's theory, however, is just as much in defence of democracy and the individual as Kelsen's. The actual political problems threatening democracy in France were largely considered a problem of the *gouvernants*, whose use of power was perceived to be a huge threat to democracy and individual liberties.

In a masterly fashion, Scelle put the concept of ILP to use. The notion of competence welds the whole hierarchical universal legal order together.[693] In the first place, he imposed it on the *gouvernants* and *agents,* whose competence was thus by definition conditioned by law, and subsequently, he attributed it to the private individual, whom he gave the competence to oppose governors and agents when they performed unjustifiable acts which prejudiced indiviudal liberties and rights.

By subjecting the individual *gouvernants* to the *droit des gens* and thereby imposing not only formal, but also substantive conditions on the international and national *gouvernants* (namely, the preservation and improvement of solidarity and society), the concept of ILP was used to link the individual to the 'oecumenical community of international law', which was to protect him as a subject of law and attribute to him the responsibility, i.e., *competence*, of developing his individual as well as his collective position. With humanity's solidarity at the summit of the hierarchy, the international legal order which springs from it conditions all underlying orders and societies. This was the integral response to the parallel crisis.

In Scelle's monist view, international law no longer lacked the three necessary public functions and rulers were individually bound by (international) law, just as individual liberties were protected by (the basis of) international law. The citizens

[693] La doctrine de L. Duguit, at 113. See also, Précis II, at 6.

were armed against the *détournement de pouvoir* engaged in by their rulers. Scelle's aim in recognising the ILP of individuals was to defend democracy.

3.6. Conclusion: Removing the Mask

In this chapter on the concepts of ILP as formulated by Brierly, Kelsen and Scelle, we have situated these writers' work against the political, intellectual and jurisprudential background of the Interbellum in order to reveal why they used the concept of ILP as they did.

When we examined the Interbellum political and intellectual context, the democratic crisis in modern European mass societies and the resulting threat to human individuality and freedom imposed themselves as the dominant issues at stake. Contemporary intellectuals oscillated between hope and fear. On the one hand, rationalists tended to recognise public opinion as the voice of reason, which deserved to be heeded both nationally and internationally. On the other hand, there was the deep concern over human individuality and new democracies threatening to fall prey to the irrationality of the masses. The psychology of modern mass man and what it implied for individual and social life and national and international politics dominated the intellectual debate. How to prevent man from relinquishing humanity and returning to the level of the horde? How to prevent (political) society from annihilating human individuality? How to prevent democracy from turning into mobocracy? The crisis of democracy and of the human individual self was addressed by artists, philosophers, sociologists, politicians and many more groups of people connected by an activity. These all struggled with the question of whether, and if so, how society could be governed by means of a stable democratic structure which accomodated the masses and at the same time preserved the individual's humanity. Jurists faced the same questions. International legal scholars not only had to address the crisis of their chosen branch of law, but also had to find a personal response to the problems as they lived and worked in these same societies and (sometimes) experienced the dangers first hand.

As regards the jurisprudential context of the three scholars whose work was examined in this chapter, it has become clear that the two separate movements of *restorative* and *revisionist* scholarship found different answers to the problems described. Both movements, however, dominantly featured the concept of ILP. Pitted against the established conventions of *restorative* scholarship, with traditional perceptions of the state, sovereignty and personality, *revisionist* scholars defended a complete renewal of international law theory and the modernisation of international law's identity. From positioning them in their context it has become clear that Brierly, Kelsen and Scelle all, if each in his own way, at the same time tried to formulate a response to the parallel crises of (the classical identity of) international law and of early modern democracy and human individuality.

They were united in their use of law as the means by which to resolve the *international* and *internal* political crises. They each advocated an *integrated* legal approach in which the concept of (international) legal personality was fundamental. Brierly, in the naturalist tradition, believed that man was a rational being. As such, man was also a morally conscious being, capable of separating right from wrong. Only the individual is able to recognise the authority of the law, but he will only subject himself to it if the law is just. The relevance of politics is limited. To preserve democracy and prevent it from falling prey to mass psychosis, the law, both domestic and international, has to be just so that individual citizens can acknowledge its authority and will remain untempted by unjust and non-legal forces. Conversely, Kelsen completely stripped his theory of law from elements of justice, but his reasoning was nevertheless purely normative. He claimed that by the application of legal norms to individual human beings the law identifies individuals in the mass. When the mass is subjected to a legal norm, this norm at the same time *identifies* (a group of) individuals. It is by the application of legal norms that one becomes an individual citizen, who stands out from the anonymous (mass) collective. Scelle also argued in favour of this singling out of individuals. He, however, wished to secure individuality to impose responsibility upon the absolutist political rulers. Scelle's conception of man as a *social* being – who can only survive as a member of a political society – formed the basis of his reasoning. According to Scelle, the human condition itself necessitated the existence of the law (of solidarity).

By using the concept of ILP in the way they did, Brierly, Kelsen and Scelle hoped to de-mystify international law by first eliminating old concepts and then redefining ILP. By arguing that only individuals can have ILP they attempted to defend democracy and the position of the individual. If they could just rid ILP of its anti-democratic and authoritarian image, the concept could prove extremely useful in supporting international peace and order. The meaning they gave to ILP, or what they were *doing in* using ILP as the exclusive attribute of the human individual, is best be captured in terms of the protection of human individuality and democratic political representation. ILP linked the individual with the international legal order, and this, according to the three scholars, was necessary to face the crisis of democracy and prevent the annihilation of the individual.

In other words, the concept of ILP clearly featured as – what in the introduction to this study was called – an 'evaluative-descriptive term:' it was indeed a 'locus of change.' Brierly, Kelsen and Scelle attempted to change the moral identity of the international society and its law: international law's modern moral identity had to take into account the protection of human individuality and democracy. This, at the same time, served to rehabilitate international law. By *removing the mask*, ILP was used to cleanse international law from anti-democratic and authoritarian tendencies and to change its moral identity so as to acknowledge human individuality.

Chapter 4
COLD WAR BI-POLARITY: ILP HANGING IN THE BALANCE

> In different ways, the United States of America and the Soviet Union have succeeded in constituting themselves into super-Leviathans and in rallying around themselves the rest of the States that matter. Thus, the process of centralisation has already reached the stage of a world diarchy. Whether the consummation of this evolution will take place in traditional ways or whether this supreme antinomy will be solved in a constructive spirit is *the* problem of our age.[1]

> [One of] the purposes of the United Nations [is]: To achieve international co-operation in ... promoting and encouraging respect for human rights and for fundamental freedoms for all ...[2]

4.1. INTRODUCTION

The second half of the 'Short Twentieth Century' ended around 1989-1991 with the Fall of the Berlin Wall, the demise of the Soviet Union and the end of the division of Europe as symbolised by the unification of Germany.[3] History had come to an end, Fukuyama argued, and liberal democracy had won the ideological battle that marked the 20th century, thereby 'constitut[ing] 'the end point of mankind's ideological evolution' and the "final form of human government".'[4] Acknowledging the collapse of Communism in Eastern Europe as a 'real historical break,'[5] which defined the early end of the 20th century, and taking it as the proper boundary of this chapter, reveals the feature that is most characteristic of the background of post-WWII international legal scholarship: i.e., the *omnipresence* of international (ideological) antagonism. The beginning of the period covered by this chapter is situated at the end of WWII, at a time when the future antagonists were still Allies in order to defeat Germany, Italy and Japan, but even then the threat of a Third World War already lurked in the background. This threat to the peace would hold the world captive all through the Cold War. The United Nations, which was created in order to preserve world peace, could not

[1] G. Schwarzenberger, Power Politics: A Study of International Society 257 (2nd ed., 1951). See also, at 426. Hereinafter: Power Politics.

[2] Charter of the United Nations, signed on 26 June 1945, Article 1.

[3] E. Hobsbawm, The Age of Extremes, 1914-1991 (1994). Hereinafter: The Age of Extremes.

[4] F. Fukuyama, The End of History and the Last Man xi (1992); Fukuyama quotes his article 'The End of History?' *The National Interest* 16 (Summer 1989).

[5] E. Hobsbawm, The New Century 4 (2000).

escape from the political and ideological rivalry between the United States and the Soviet Union either.

The coherence that the 'Cold-War' qualification suggests may be acceptable from a geopolitical perspective, as indeed 'a single pattern ... of constant confrontation of the two superpowers' existed, but this picture could still do with some refinement.[6] In many ways, it is too extensive and diverse a period to be able to characterise it by a single notion alone.[7] Scholars generally tend to divide this period between 1945 and 1991 into separate chunks. Whichever way it is viewed, i.e., from an economic, social, intellectual or international perspective, it cannot be denied that during the 1960s – early 1970s the tide turned, or at least long-term change set in. With the 1973 oil crisis, the time of economic growth and prosperity, which started in 1947, came to an end. The world's economy had developed into 'a single, increasingly integrated and universal world economy largely operating "transnationally".'[8] As a consequence, the economic recession of the 1970s and 1980s was indeed *global* in nature. These 'Crisis Decades' turned into 'a new era of decomposition, uncertainty and crisis – and indeed, for large parts of the world, such as Africa, the former USSR and the formerly socialist parts of Europe, of catastrophe.'[9] In the US and Western Europe, the late 1960s and 1970s were above all a time of social transformation, society rose up against the state and, more particularly, against its claims to internal as well as external supremacy of power. The protests were often intended to bring about the emancipation of less fortunate or discriminated against social groups and the advancement of democratic structures.

In the context of this study, however, the watershed relevant here is best located in the early 1970s, which saw the adoption of the UNGA Resolution 2625 (XXV) 'The declaration on principles of international law concerning friendly relations and co-operation among states in accordance with the Charter of the United Nations,' and during which the Helsinki process resulted in the 1975 Final Act and the continuation of the Conference on Security and Co-operation in Europe (CSCE). In spite of or maybe rather thanks to its legally non-binding nature, the political significance of the Final Act is eminent. After its conclusion, a gradual process of de-ideologisation set in between the 33 participating European States and Canada and the US, and with the subsequent CSCE conferences the new phase of international '*co-operation*' between the Cold War antagonists was consolidated.

From most perspectives, it would seem difficult to come up with one single characterisation for the years 1945-1990, as this was not a homogenous era from any point of view, not economically, not socially, not culturally, nor intellectu-

---

[6] The Age of Extremes, at 225-226.

[7] Id., at 225: the years between 1945 and 1990 'do not form a single homogeneous period in world history.'

[8] Id., at 9-10.

[9] Id., at 6.

ally. However, the reality that international legal scholarship faced was that of the Cold War with its constant US – USSR rivalry and the permanent threat of the escalation of the conflict into total destruction. While we have thus made our case for the diversity of the era, it is on the other hand fair to say that the global political bi-polarity with its ideological antagonism was indeed *the* problem of the time. In spite of the changes and international confrontations, an overall international stability did in fact persist, even if it was based on threats and fear.

Until the collapse of the USSR, international stability – which is not the same as security – was the result of the bi-polarity of power, the 'irreconcilable antagonism' between liberal capitalism and communism. The political balance and stability was due to mutual 'fear,' which had both internal and international ramifications.[10] The world's two superpowers defined themselves around the existence of the 'other'; the mechanism legitimising this definition of the self was 'fear' and as a consequence *anxiety* became an omnipresent imperative. This anxiety gradually decreased in intensity, but was always easily revived, as, for example, when the notion of the 'Empire of Evil' became part of the rhetoric of the Reagan era.

Throughout human history, neither collective nor individual life has ever been perfect and harmonious, which has instilled in man a perception of the world as perpetually in crisis. Many have experienced discontent over the missing harmony among all universal interests, and some have sought a means to achieve this harmony. Man's anxiety concerning the human condition is therefore a phenomenon to affect all ages. However, the period we are dealing with in this chapter was an era immediately following the unprecedented horrors of WWII and its termination through the use of two nuclear bombs. It was, moreover, itself a period of 'war.' During the Cold War, the fear that the ideological battle would turn into a global nuclear disaster pervaded all elements of daily life and thereby greatly contributed to the anxiety of modern man, in particular during the late 1940s and the 1950s. Related to this threat was a sense of disillusionment concerning (scientific) progress,[11] which also contributed to this modern form of anxiety. At the same time, many also experienced an *anxiety of freedom*, which was rooted in the uncertainty created by the immense realm of possibilities that had suddenly opened up, the responsibility of individual choice and man's tendency to work both good and evil. Poets, painters, politicians and legal scholars qualified *anxiety* as the mood of their time and as the *modern* human condition

[10] 'It is one of the ironies of this strange century that the most lasting results of the October revolution, whose object was the global overthrow of capitalism, was to save its antagonist, both in war and in peace – that is to say, by providing it with incentive, *fear*, to reform itself after the Second World War, and, by establishing the popularity of economic planning, furnishing it with some of the procedures for its reform.' Id., at 7-8. Emphasis added.

[11] In this respect, the public response, which was one of horror and fear, to the destructive power of the two nuclear bombs which had been dropped on Japan was an important factor. The ambivalence of scientific progress could not have been illustrated more clearly and it caused scientific research to become more accountable to society.

which they had to deal with in their work. Among those to characterise their time as another 'Age of Anxiety' were, for example, also McDougal and Lasswell.[12]

What does all this mean in terms of the historiography of international law and in particular of the use of the concept of ILP during this period? Contrary to the period discussed in the previous chapter, where the analysis of international legal scholarship also required knowledge of the *internal* crises of democracy, here it is justified only to take the *international* – by Cold War determined – reality as the basis for the contextualisation of the scholarship of Hans Morgenthau, Hersch Lauterpacht, Myres McDougal, and Wolfgang Friedmann and their use of ILP.

The anxiety over peace, power and human nature was characteristic of the reality in which international scholars lived and worked. The issues generally at stake in this 'era of confrontation and division' weighed heavily on them too. International scholars whose task and responsibility it is to make a contribution to peace through solid and independent studious effort could not escape the effects of this 'perilous epoch of threatened catastrophe.'[13] In the late 1940s, this anxious time of 'general disillusion,'[14] the focus of hope spread into different directions. Realist scholars took power as the basic principle of approach, but others, labelled Idealists, continued in a more moral-juridical vein. Just like in the reality of international life, the bi-polar rivalry is gradually enclosed in an international community (or institutional structure) oscillating between power politics and human rights, the early Cold War scholarly oscillation between Realism and Idealism gradually gave way to a rather pragmatic mainstream scholarship. A development which we find reflected in the work of the four scholars we elaborate on in this chapter.

In the first place, expectations shifted from law to *power* politics. The forces of barbarism eventually lost the war, but they had ruled the world for years. Humanity had shown the worst it was capable of, as human nature had displayed its darkest side and had proven that this side was still very much alive, even in so-called modern times. In hindsight, the optimism and idealism that abounded immediately after WWI and pervaded theories as diverse as, e.g., (Wilsonian) legalistic liberalism, the pure theory of law or the natural law doctrine, seemed to many scholars to have been profoundly naïve.[15] Law had proven a disappointment as *the* rational instrument for the perfection of (international) society, which many had hoped it to be. The reality was that not law but *power* had protected human freedom, that not pacifism but military *force* had defeated Nazism and had saved democracy. This is important to bear in mind when we study the work of post-WWII scholars. Today's ideas concerning 'power' have been greatly in-

[12] McDougal and Lasswell, The Identification of Diverse Systems of Public Order (1959), *in* McDougal et al., Studies in World Public Order (1960) at 41.

[13] Id., at 39. See also, M.S. McDougal, International Law, Power, and Policy: A Contemporary Conception, 82 *RCADI* (1953-I), at 139-140. Hereinafter: A Contemporary Conception.

[14] Power Politics, at 11.

[15] See, e.g., Schwarzenberger's qualification 'naïve day-dreaming,' Power Politics, at xv.

fluenced by the change that took place during the 1960s in how we perceived power. This might lead us to misunderstand the scholarly thinking which found its roots in the late 1940s and 1950s. We generally do not conceive of 'power' as a hopeful and positive concept or instrument, but rather as a capacity that tends to be cruel, oppressive and corruptive. Today, power is often depicted as 'dirty' and as failing to serve human freedom or the common good. In the years immediately after the Second World War, however, *power could also stand for hope*: '[the US and USSR] are centers of hope because they are centers of power.'[16] In reaction to the pre-WWII and contemporary idealism in international theory-making at the time, Morgenthau among others advocated a realistic approach.

Secondly, despite the truth of the above observations, some tried to retain a more optimistic outlook on the abilities of man and law to create and impose individual responsibility. The dark and tragic perception of man as a being driven by the constant search for power and security in order to prevent (pre-emptive) destruction by others which underpinned the realistic approach to international law and politics was regarded by some as an exaggeration and as unproductively pessimistic. The alternative – in the US, at least, in line with the views of Wilson and Roosevelt – was a kind of universal perspective which maintained that international institutionalisation would guarantee the protection of human rights, international peace and security and bring the dangerous game of power politics to an end. The fact that German war criminals were standing trial before an international judiciary in Nuremberg and being held individually responsible was seen as an instance where the law was at last able to punish evil. Individual responsibility featured as a key concept after the cataclysm of WWII, not only in the law, but also, for example, in philosophy. At the international level, the power of individual choice was now also being resorted to, which made of man a responsible being who was capable of choosing a better future. One of the scholars who followed this path was Hersch Lauterpacht, the only European scholar we will discuss in this chapter. During the late 1940s and the 1950s Lauterpacht did pioneering work in the field of human rights law and thought through the fundamental consequences of human rights for the international legal order. His realism was of a different kind: ideals may not be realised but at least they give direction to progress and as such function in and through reality. He moulded the idealism of the Interbellum period into specific institutional arguments and proposals for after the War.

However, the international reality of the Cold War, the generally felt disappointment in the United Nations (which was considered more of a political than a legal body) and the onset of the division of the world into 'spheres of influences' generally marginalised this view within foreign policy as well as within the scholarly debate. What did happen, though, and in this sense idealism was in a way realistic, was that in the reality of power politics and the battle of the ideologies ample use was made of the notions of human rights and democratic free-

[16] A.M. Schlesinger, Jr., The Vital Center: The Politics of Freedom 6 (1970 ed.), (1st ed. 1950).

doms, which soon transformed them into policy goals and ideological weaponry in international relations. Myres McDougal's perspective on international law during the Cold War was also steeped in the politics-and-power concept and he used the concept of 'human dignity' in this ideological context. Wolfgang Friedmann outlined the new international reality of the 1960s, which seemed to facilitate the emergence of a new phase in international law.

All four, these scholars had already worked and published during World War II, but their main work was carried out during the Cold War years that followed. Morgenthau and Friedmann were both born in pre-war Germany and fled the Nazi regime, eventually to arrive in the US. Lauterpacht was born in Poland and fled first to Vienna and then to Britain. McDougal was born and raised in the US. This chapter therefore has a Euro-American slant to it, which is rather symbolic of the century which started out as Euro-centric and with hindsight turned out to be in many ways American.

Between power politics and the appraisal of the rule of law, between realism and idealism, the concept of *ILP hung in the balance*. It was used in different ways by these four scholars, but was always affected by the era's *polarity* and *ambivalence*. The Cold War was a time governed by power politics of the purest kind, nonetheless, ultimately individual freedom and human dignity were to win the battle of ideas. Human rights became part of the ideological competition as within the US isolationism and internationalism were fighting for domination and valid and convincing international policy objectives were therefore needed to continue the quest for world leadership with the support of the American people. The USSR responded by launching their own human rights ideas, which focused on economic and social rights. Once they were part of international policy goals, human rights started to transform the language of international affairs and subsequently, when these new ideas were codified and documented, the international legal order itself. This political reality influenced pragmatic international legal scholars. In this field of tension between power politics and human dignity and liberty, international law slowly continued to develop and consolidate. The constitution of international human rights law and the early post-war developments in international criminal law were the seeds of hope that were to land in the fertile ground that presented itself at the end of the Cold War, when all the necessary potential was there for the reaping. During the decades until 1989, the concept of ILP – still hanging in this balance between idealism and realism – gradually developed into a concept of *inclusion*. It would be up to post-Cold War international life and scholarship to make it function as such in practice as well.

4.2. Context of Cold War International Legal Scholarship

4.2.1. **International political context: Cold War bi-polarity**

On 5 March 1946, Winston Churchill clearly expressed the (ideological) division that was to rule Europe and the world to the public, when he spoke the following famous lines as part of his 'Sinews of Peace' speech at Westminster College in Fulton, Missouri.

From Stettin in the Baltic to Trieste in the Adriatic an *Iron Curtain* has descended across the Continent. Behind that line lie all the capitals of the ancient states of Central and Eastern Europe. Warsaw, Berlin, Prague, Vienna, Budapest, Belgrade, Bucharest and Sofia, all these famous cities and the populations around them lie in what I must call the Soviet sphere, and all are subject in one form or another, not only to Soviet influence but to a very high and, in some cases, increasing measure of control from Moscow. ... Police governments are prevailing in nearly every case, and so far, except in Czechoslovakia, there is no true democracy.[17]

Nine days later, in an interview with *Pravda* on 14 March 1946, Joseph Stalin replied to this speech in a rather puzzling way.[18] In any case, as Gorbachev would explain in his 1992 Fulton speech, 'The River of Time,' '[in] my country [Churchill's] speech was interpreted as the formal declaration of the "Cold War."'[19] The *Iron Curtain* had come down and divided the world into 'spheres of influence'.

Such an extensive and complex period as the Cold War is impossible to describe adequately in a matter of mere pages. It has moreover already been the repeated subject of intensive and extensive study and debate. I will therefore not deal with the question of what caused it or who was to blame (the USSR, the US, or both) nor be drawn into the discussion whether the Cold War was the product of carefully calculated strategy or came about through an accumulation of misunderstandings, and so on and so forth. Here, in the outline of the international political background of international legal scholarship during the Cold War years we will focus very briefly on two developments. Firstly, the bi-polar rivalry and its dynamics of power politics, with the conventional and nuclear arms race as its most frightening manifestation. The world lost its Euro-centricity with the process of de-colonisation and the US' new role of Western leadership. Whether politically, economically, scientifically, technologically, culturally or intellectually, the centre of the Western world had definitely relocated to the US. Secondly,

---

[17] W. Churchill, *Sinews of Peace* speech, 5 March 1946, Westminster College, Fulton, Missouri. See, e.g., <http://www.missourinet.com/wow/1946speech.html>.

[18] Stalin's Reply to Churchill, March 14, 1946, (interview with *Pravda*), *The New York Times*, at 4, *in* Internet Modern History Sourcebook, <http://www.fordham.edu/halsall/mod/1946stalin.html>: 'In substance, Mr. Churchill now stands in the position of a firebrand of war. And Mr. Churchill is not alone here. He has friends in England but also in the United States of America. In this respect, one is reminded remarkably of Hitler and his friends. Hitler began to set war loose by announcing his racial theory, declaring that only people speaking the German language represent a fully valuable nation. Mr. Churchill begins to set war loose, also by a racial theory, maintaining that only nations speaking the English language are fully valuable nations, called upon to decide the destinies of the entire world.'

[19] M. Gorbachev, *The River of Time* speech, 6 May 1992, Westminster College, Fulton, Missouri. See, e.g., <http://www.missourinet.com/wow/1992speech.html>.

Western societies sprouted socio-political emancipation and cultural change. Human rights became 'universal' and the call for social change spread throughout the world as a result of increased international interdependence and solidarity. According to the Charter, the protection of human rights was one of the defining purposes of the United Nations. The institutions of the international society and the United Nations in particular gradually became the locus of international *co-operation*. The world's political and ideological conflict between the two superpowers undermined international life and the international community yet the formal structures were there ready to be used when co-operation was necessary for the facilitation of trade, communications, technological developments, and the resolution of common problems.

Firstly, the World's two poles of power contained each other during the Cold War. American hegemony prevailed in the West, while the Soviets enjoyed supremacy over the Communist world. This effectively divided the international community. The international power confrontation was managed through *Realpolitik*. The superpowers generally had greater faith in a balance of power approach than in transnational institutional co-operation, even though this meant having to deal with a sequence of crises.[20]

The series of well-known international crises that put a 'hot' face on the Cold War is long and every time one of these crises occurred people held their breath. Europe was relatively safe, divided as it was into power-spheres, which were more or less respected. The US for instance did not support or even interfere in the 1956 Hungarian Revolution. However, the US and the USSR were both involved in the Korean War (1950-53), the former officially (to a large extent due to the fact that China had turned Communist in 1949) and the latter unofficially, which made this war the first explosive global situation. A few years later, during the 1956 Suez War, the USSR demanded that the British and the French give up control of the Suez Canal. With Khrushchev as Stalin's successor, a period of détente or peaceful co-existence appeared to have arrived in 1953 with an agreement concerning Korea and the Soviet withdrawal from Finland. In 1960, however, an American U-2 plane pilot was captured after his plane had been shot down by the Soviet Union, and in 1961, the Berlin Wall was built. Then, during the Cuban Missile Crisis (1962), the two nuclear superpowers (the Soviet Union had succeeded in manufacturing its first atomic bomb in 1949) were involved in a direct confrontation and for days the world lived in fear of total nuclear destruction. Two years later, the Stalinist Brechnev forced Khrushchev to step down and ended the Prague Spring (1968) with Soviet tanks entering Czechoslovakia and ousting the regime of Alexander Dubček. After the détente of the early 1970s, tension unfortunately built up again. From 1965 until 1975, the US was entangled in the Vietnam War. Since the partition of Vietnam in 1954, the United States had supported the non-communist regime in South Vietnam, while com-

[20] The Age of Extremes, at 225 *et seq.*

munist North Vietnam had received significant support from China and the USSR. Gradually, the US involvement of what were euphemistically called 'advisors' lapsed into major warfare. Then, in 1979, the USSR occupied Afghanistan and during the 1980s the arms race was re-opened in spite of earlier talks on arms control. The US increased aid to anti-communist guerrilla groups in Cambodia, Afghanistan, Angola and Nicaragua. And only as recently as 1985 did the USSR begin its retreat from Third World countries until eventually it also withdrew its support of Eastern European communist parties.

The rivalry was also being fought out in space during these years. In 1961, the USSR put the first man in space. In 1969, the US landed the first man on the moon. However, the most frightening manifestation of the political and ideological rivalry between these Superpowers was the (nuclear) arms race. The military stand-off between the two powers was a nerve-racking process for the world at large, with the particular threat emanating from the nuclear arms race and its menace of Mutual Assured Destruction (MAD) in the case of the outbreak of a new world war. The MAD threat made '*the sense of oppression*'[21] an aspect of the daily reality of all individuals and therefore had an impact far beyond the strictly political arena. The Nuclear Test Ban Treaty, which was signed in 1963, did not do much to change this. During the 1970s and 1980s, the US and the USSR pursued policies of *co-existence*, and the breaking point of the (nuclear) arms race finally came in 1986 with the meeting between Reagan and Gorbachev in Reykjavik, Iceland, with the definitive melting away of the Cold War.

The ideological battle was not only being fought internationally but also domestically. In the USSR, Stalin suppressed so-called subversive elements through show-trials, prison camps and plain murder; it would be fair to say that he terrorised the population. Stalin's bloody regime, or any of the totalitarian regimes that succeeded his, for that matter, was not completely beyond compare to the way the US government worked at the time. In the US, during the 1950s, Senator McCarthy and the House Committee to Investigate Un-American Activities led the national American hunt for Leftist sympathisers, until ultimately it seemed as if every non-conformist person with liberal sympathies was under suspicion. This resulted in widespread (self-) censorship among artists, intellectuals and scholars.[22] The uproar created by these practices finally had an effect at the end of the 1950s and the general paranoia started to die down.

In any case, this bi-polarity of political and ideological antagonism between the superpowers brought an end of the Euro-centric world. The power blocks of liberal capitalism and totalitarian communism both confronted and contained each other during the Cold War. With their ideological antagonism, these poles dominated the dynamics of world politics. Both states made intensive use of internal and external propaganda in order to generate support. By the late 1940s,

[21] This qualification is my grandfather's. He was born in 1907 and I could discuss with him the atmosphere of the time while I was writing this chapter.

[22] The American Century, Vol. II, at 36-37.

propaganda had penetrated all aspects of social life. Sports, technology and (rocket) science, every conceivable field, even that of the Arts, was drawn into the political realm and turned into a weapon of ideological and psychological warfare. During the 1950s, for example, the United States used avant-garde Abstract Expressionism 'as a propaganda weapon during the Cold War.'[23] '[T]he unprecedented national and international success' of Abstract Expressionism was, as Guilbaut demonstrated in his study of the subject, 'due not solely to aesthetic and stylistic considerations, ... but also, even more, to the movement's *ideological resonance*.'[24] The artists' a-political attitudes were being interpreted politically, as evidence of the freedom of individual expression, the arts were included in propaganda and exhibited around the world as artistic products and emblems of democracy and capitalism and of the American mythical identity of individual freedom.[25] At the same time, Socialist Realism completely shaped Soviet official art.[26] The ideological rivals practised cultural imperialism and like the propaganda in other areas it was directed as much at their own population as it was at Europe. Paris lost its position as the world's cultural capital, to give way to New York as the new cultural and artistic centre of the Western world. Washington became the most powerful capital of the Western world, both politically and economically. Europe was effectively split in two and as the battleground for the superpowers it soon lost its central position on the world stage. The US continued its role of leader of the Western world and supported the economic reconstruction of Europe through the Marshall Plan. The 'German Question' thereby received an economic response at the international level. The UN moreover did not take up its seat in Europe but in New York City.

The colonial empires of Europe were being dismantled in a rapid process of national liberation and independence (1945-1960s). Both the US and the USSR

[23] S. Guilbaut, How New York Stole the Idea of Modern Art: Abstract Expressionism, Freedom, and the Cold War, at 11 (1983). Guilbaut, in a revealing contextual analysis, demonstrated the dialogue between art and politics, between the abstract expressionist movement and the specific history of the Cold War from 1946-1951, and the propagandist use of avant-garde art by, discussing the rejection of isolationism, the Soviet threat and the reaction of the American public. Hereinafter: How New York Stole the Idea of Modern Art. Also, C. Lindey, Art in the Cold War: From Vladivostok to Kalamazoo, 1945-1962 (1990), 'the cultural wing of the CIA realized that the promotion of American "free," advanced art could be used as a cultural weapon in winning over western intellectuals and artists to their cause. Helped by the New York Museum of Modern Art, numerous lavishly financed, well-organized exhibitions promoted American art in Europe.' Id., at 10.

[24] How New York Stole the Idea of Modern Art, at 2. Emphasis added. '[The artist] had become the guardian of the liberal democratic ideal (even though some progressive artists did continue to fight against nationalistic and isolationist conceptions of art and literature.' Even the magazine that gave voice to this section of the American Left, the *Partisan Review*, 'saw no radical alternative. The logic of *Realpolitik* would have to be accepted: a choice had to be made between the two ideologies without regard to the prospects for revolutionary change, which only two years earlier had still seemed within the realm of possibility.' Id., at 109.

[25] The American Century, Vol. II, at 34 *et seq*. 'The claim that they were free from ideology only made their art function more effectively as propaganda for various political agendas.' Id., at 41.

[26] See, for outline of the implications of the Cold War and its ideological antagonism for both the American and Soviet art of this era, Art in the Cold War, *op. cit*., footnote 23.

actively competed to bring the newly independent states inside their respective 'spheres of influence,' which evidently also contributed to the tension of the period. In the international community, the Western states were greatly outnumbered in absolute terms.

In other words, Europe finally and definitively lost its dominant position within international society. In 1952, Black wrote: '[i]t is doubtless a truism to state that Europe is on the wane, at least as a center of political power.'[27] Europe was in decline: bi-polarisation had caused the world to shake off Euro-centricity. The creation of the European Economic Community, and the resulting ongoing integration from 1956 onwards, is directly related to this truth.[28] Nonetheless, the Community did not succeed in positioning itself as the third superpower, and neither did China. In 1949, NATO was created to guarantee security to Europe and it institutionalised European military dependence. Fear of the Soviet Union kept the transatlantic alliance alive and well, as did the EC members' fear of a large and powerful Germany. '[T]he political collapse of Europe thus open[ed] a new era in American policy.'[29] Today, the United States perceives the twentieth century as theirs: 'The American Century.'[30]

Secondly, the growing global interdependence after WWII necessitated *co-operation* and transformed the international society and stimulated the creation of international law. Indeed, the number of international organisations increased significantly after WWII.[31] With the increasing necessity to protect and promote the global common interests, the international organisations, in general, and the United Nations, in particular, were the locus of co-operation and the vehicle of change. The UN's human rights objective was key to the creation of international human rights law as well as to the emerging recognition that in some degree the domestic situation, i.e., the relations between the state and its citizens, was a concern of the international community. The basic documents of the universal human rights regime were created within the United Nations system: '[s]ince its birth in 1945, the UN has served as a vital institutional spur to the development of the [human rights] movement.'[32]

The international human rights movement was not merely based on formal international support but also spurred by the domestic use of human rights lan-

---

[27] C.E. Black, Reflections on the Eclipse of Europe, 4 (2) *World Politics* 293 (1952). A review article of three books all dealing with the so-called 'collapse' of the European (political) system.

[28] The Age of Extremes, at 239-240.

[29] C.E. Black, Reflections on the Eclipse of Europe, 4 (2) *World Politics* 297 (1952).

[30] The Age of Extremes, at 15. See also, H.R. Luce, The American Century, *Life Magazine*, 17 February 1941. Also, following Luce, the exhibition in the Whitney Museum of American Art, New York, The American Century: Art & Culture 1900-2000.

[31] P.H. Kooijmans, Internationaal Publiekrecht in Vogelvlucht 147 (2000, 8th ed.).

[32] Alston and Steiner (Eds.), International Human Rights in Context: Law, Politics, Morality 118 (1996).

guage by grass-root organisations or (national and international) NGOs.[33] The role of NGOs, both those dealing with human rights and those active in other fields, only grew with the increase of global information and communication networks. On the one hand, an internal social effect of the international situation and the threat of nuclear war was the mushrooming of social or public interest movements. On the other hand, domestic public opinion as well as national social developments were factors of international change. The social upheavals of the late 1960s were manifest attempts to dislodge the age-old local social structures on the basis of a changing perception of authority and demands for the enhancement of democracy and the abolition of discrimination.[34] The transformation of the 1960s was an almost global phenomenon as the old society disappeared with the decline of the peasantry, rapid urbanisation, the expansion of the middle classes due to better job opportunities, increased levels of education and women's participation in the labour market, in fact, women's emancipation in general.[35] The social transformation went hand in hand with a revolution in the field of culture.[36] The baby boom had drastically changed demographics and made the sixties 'swinging,' the middle classes also through their sheer increase in numbers had become a politically significant factor, and society jerked to new patterns of authority and new norms. 'May 1968' was key to the social revolution of the second half of the twentieth century, although it did not itself constitute the revolution, but rather an occasion expressing the revolution.[37] In the US, the transformation became particularly visible in the way society was divided over the Vietnam War. This war became *the* occasion for young social activists to give voice to society's changing ideas and international solidarity, not only in the US, but worldwide. US student and peace movements protested for years against the American involvement in Vietnam. The social and cultural transformation contin-

[33] Id., at 456: 'NGOs operate subject to differing mandates, each responding to its own priorities and methods of action, bringing a range of viewpoints to the human rights movement. It is inconceivable that this movement, whatever its weaknesses, could have achieved as much in its first half century without the spur and inventiveness of NGOs.'

[34] During the 1950s, US civil rights movements organised numerous protest marches and mobilised society against injustice, especially racial segregation. Segregation in buses and public schools was subsequently abolished as a result of US Supreme Court rulings in 1956 and 1957. The fight against racism however needed to be continued until well into the 1960s, as social structures were slow to change. The however defeat of the old social patterns could not be halted.

[35] The Age of Extremes, at 287-319.

[36] Id., at 320-343. Pop-culture has been both an expression and a stimulus of the changes in social perceptions.

[37] Id., at 15. Hobsbawm: '[i]f their was a single moment in the golden years after 1945 which corresponds to the world simultaneous upheaval of which the revolutionaries had dreamed after 1917, it was surely 1968, when students rebelled from the USA and Mexico in the West to socialist Poland, Czechoslovakia and Yugoslavia, largely stimulated by the extraordinary outbreak of May 1968 in Paris, epicentre of a Continent-wide student uprising. It was far from revolution, ... [because] students alone ... could not make one alone.' The Age of Extremes, at 298. Though their dreams failed to bring about immediate revolutionary change, the events did contribute to long-term social evolution and the changed perception of authority.

ued during the 1970s. Former social hierarchies destroyed, both in Europe and in the US.

In other words, the social and political changes which these social movements clamoured for concerned both the national and the international level. Due to global interdependence, many problems required an international response. By the late 1960s the transformation of the international scene had taken off and the international community slowly started to shift from *co-existence* to *co-operation* through the formulation of new norms which created a basis for a slowly altering perception of sovereignty. The character of the treaties that were created during this time bears witness to this shift towards international co-operation and towards a more Humanist orientation of international norms to include human dignity and freedom. Within the ten years between 1965 and 1975 'the language of the international debate' was indeed 'reshaped,' and this had been largely stimulated by *ideological competition* and actual *global interdependency*. In 1960, the UN General Assembly declared that colonialism was a violation of fundamental human rights and that 'All peoples have the right to self-determination.'[38] 1966 saw the adoption of the International Human Rights Covenants and the International Convention on the Elimination of All Forms of Racial Discrimination. On 24 October 1970, the UN General Assembly adopted the Declaration on Principles of International Law concerning Friendly relations and Co-operation among states in accordance with the Charter of the United Nations.[39] Moreover, in the same year, the ICJ recognised that certain norms imposed *erga omnes* obligations.[40]

At the end of 1974, the UN General Assembly adopted the Charter of Economic Rights and Duties of States. In 1976, the International Convention on the Suppression and Punishment of the Crime of Apartheid entered into force,[41] as did the ICCPR and its Optional Protocol. In June 1972, the reintegration of Humanity and Nature spilled over into the legal realm when a UN Conference promulgated the Stockholm Principles on the Human Environment, proclaiming that the defence and improvement of 'the human environment for present and future generations has become an imperative goal for mankind.' In subsequent years a number of treaties for the purpose of containing environmental pollution followed. The 1974 Charter of Economic Rights and Duties of States intended to create a New International Economic Order which would be more favourable to the newly independent states.[42] These had in fact been the ones to initiate the

[38] UNGA Resolution 1514 (XV), holding the Declaration on the Granting of Independence to Colonial Countries and Peoples.

[39] UNGA Resolution 2625 (XXV).

[40] Barcelona Traction case, Judgment of 5 February 1970, ICJ Rep. 1970. The 1969 Vienna Convention on the Law of Treaties includes a recognition of *ius cogens*: derogation from these norms by treaty law is prohibited.

[41] UNGA Resolution 3068 (XXVIII), already adopted in 1973.

[42] UNGA Resolution 3281 (XXIX).

Charter, but Western states either rejected its content or simply withheld their support and thereby delayed the Charter's attainment of customary law status.

The political relevance of the Helsinki Final Act has already been emphasised. Its significance lies to large extent in the role it played in the building of mutual trust, which was necessary in order to be able to deal with increasingly global problems, such as for example environmental degradation, which required a common effort. The global legal order slowly evolved into an order which had the ability to recognise the common and global nature of the contemporary problems it faced. Ultimately, the CSCE conferences of the late 1970s and 1980s did contribute to furthering the cause of human rights.

Finally, the period of the Cold War basically came to a close when on 9 November 1989 the people tore down the Berlin Wall practically with their bare hands. Subsequently, *Solidaridad* came into office in Poland while in Czechoslovakia the former dissident Vaclav Havel was elected President of the Republic. Meanwhile, Soviet forces had left Afghanistan a year earlier. Officially, the Cold War ended with the CSCE Summit in1990 where the 'Charter of Paris for a New Europe' was adopted and it was declared that '[t]he era of confrontation and division of Europe ... has ended.' From then on, it was claimed, East-West 'relations [would] be founded on respect and co-operation. ... a new era of democracy, peace and unity in Europe [had begun].'[43]

4.2.2. Intellectual context: two responses to modern anxiety – realism and idealism

> Today, ..., we are living in an age filled with apocalyptic images of universal destruction. What is the significance of that split, symbolized by the "Iron Curtain," which divides humanity into halves?[44]

> Anxiety is the official emotion of our time.[45]

After Auschwitz, many concluded that the 'death of God'[46] had occurred or at

---

[43] CSCE Charter of Paris for a New Europe, 19-21 November 1990, section 'A new era of Democracy, Peace and Unity,' para. 2.

[44] C.G. Jung, The Undiscovered Self 3 (1957).

[45] The Politics of Freedom, *op. cit.* footnote 16, at 52.

[46] 'We belong to the part of the world where the dead pile up hugger-mugger in charnel houses. It's in Europe that this happens. That they burn Jews by the million. That they mourn them. America watches in amazement as the smoke rises from the crematoriums of Europe. ... It is not an island in the Malay Archipelago or in some Pacific region that these things have happened, it's on our own soil, the soil of Europe. The four hundred thousand skeletons of the German Communists who died in Dora between 1933 and 1938 are in the great European common grave too, together with the millions of Jews and the idea of God-with every Jew, every one, the idea of God.' From Marguerite Duras, *La Douleur* (1985), as quoted in, Documenta X – the book: Politics-Poetics (1997), at 101. Of course, it is Nietzsche who is best known for using the 'God is dead' metaphor and pointing at man as His murderer, but after the horrors of WWII this metaphor for the impossibility of a belief in a (Christian) God expanded. French existentialism stated this postulate in particular.

least his abandonment of this world and withdrawal to the 'catacombs.'[47] God was no longer the answer to man's uneasiness – his anxiety – in this world. Mankind and humanity had failed beyond comprehension. Modern man was now alone in a state of despair and in shock over humanity's most destructive and horrifying crimes to date that had taken place in the *Lager* on the European continent. Primo Levi's testimonies from the extinction camp Auschwitz evoke the horrifying reality of the *Shoah* in every detail.[48] Post-war anxiety gripped artists and intellectuals as well as the general public, both in Europe and in the United States. The menace of the atomic bomb, which had been dropped on Hiroshima and Nagasaki to end the War – that '*Obliterating bang*' – also acted as a powerful source of fear.[49] Technological 'progress' had produced an industry that had killed 6 million Jews in Germany, and the United States (with the USSR soon to follow) had developed weaponry capable of destroying the whole of mankind in a couple of hours. Soon post-war anxiety changed into pre-war distress.[50]

The despair and anxiety of the post-holocaust era moved intellectuals and artists to search for a new foundation to counter existential anxiety or *angst*. The philosophical success of religious and atheist Existentialism may partly be explained by the fact that it made such a comprehensive effort to deal with modern man's anxiety and its implications.[51] In the Arts, many expressed a sense of

---

[47] Besides atheist existentialism there was also a stream of religious existentialism among whom the well-known Jewish philosopher Martin Buber, who used this metaphor in *Gottesfinsternis* (1952). [The Eclipse of God.] The *I* in the *I-It* relationship is different from the *I* in the *I-Thou* relationship. The *I-Thou* relationship went to the 'catacombs' in this modern era. Man negated the reality of the Transcendence. His Ego had moved in between man and God, making a true meeting impossible.

[48] Primo Levi, If This is a Man. Original publication: Se questo è un uomo (1947).

[49] W.H. Auden, The Age of Anxiety: A Baroque Eclogue (1948), Faber and Faber Ed., at 73.

[50] *The Washington Post* noted in March 1948: 'The atmosphere in Washington is no longer a postwar atmosphere. It is to put it bluntly, a prewar atmosphere.' How New York Stole the Idea of Modern Art, at 168. See also, the British poet and critic Stephan Spender, who travelling around Europe in the months immediately after WWII describes the awareness of a new threat: 'The peoples of the world to-day exist in a state of anticipation of being precipitated into a new pattern of unity or a new chaos. ... The whole of civilization is enclosed in one idea: the idea of the potentiality which may recreate everything or destroy everything. This colours the mind of everyone who thinks. ... We are familiar with the end of the world. ... The idea of destruction exercises a fascination over many minds to-day. ... For it becomes evident that the inner life of humanity has attained the power to transform completely and totally the outer environment, so that the chaos or the order of that inner life must inevitably be reflected in man's future environment. Thus we find in literature a growing insistence on *being* rather than on making.' S. Spender, European Witness 91 (1947). Hereinafter: European Witness.

[51] In the aftermath of WWII, the French existentialist Jean-Paul Sartre, to whom it seemed without a doubt that God was dead, contended that amidst the 'absurdity' of life freed from religion man defines himself. The individual human being has no essential self, no core of being, he has to choose his essence, '*il se choisit*:' man *exists* and subsequently has to *create* his own *essence*, in other words, existence precedes essence. In Sartre's mind, man himself had to give meaning to his life, it was his own responsibility to create the *essence* of his life, and thereby the individual had effectively replaced God. Sartre recognised the anxiety of modern man – '*l'homme est angoisse*' – as inherent in his personal freedom and therefore man's destiny to live an anxious life. He is responsible for his

alienation and fear, emotions which were experienced as inherent in the existential situation of human freedom and personal responsibility.[52] The American values that had to be defended amidst the uncertainty and distress of the Cold War also penetrated the language of art. This led to the creation of an abstract and *international* art form: Abstract Expressionism, which developed further through the different and idiosyncratic 'handwriting' of Chromatic Abstractionists like Rothko and Newman, and Gestural or Action Painters, like Jackson Pollock.[53] 'These Chromatic Abstractionists shared with their Gestural colleagues a desire to address the dualism of fear and ecstasy [which] they believed constituted the human condition.' Abstract Expressionism was born 'of growing [American] confidence, yet tempered by the anxieties of the age.'[54]

'*Having invented a new Holocaust, And been the first with it to win a war*,'[55] even the United States had pushed modern rationality to its extremes and had lost its 'innocence' in the process. How should humanity go on now that it had '*lost the key to the garden gate*,' how should it proceed '*in a world that is fallen*'?

---

own actions and individual existence as well as for humanity at large, individual *responsibility* equally demands *engagement*, '*je dois m'engager*.' J.-P. Sartre, L'existentialisme est un humanisme, Lecture Sartre gave on 29 October 1945, (folio ed., 1996), at 77, 31 *et seq*., and 50. See, e.g., for an integration of existentialism in natural law theory, H.A. Rommen, In Defense of Natural Law, *Law and Philosophy* 105 (1964); and W. Friedmann, An Analysis of 'In Defense of Natural Law,' id., at 144.

[52] These artists wanted to depict the 'uncertainty [of] the human condition' through 'a new art [which was] global, apolitical, and expressive of the horror and fear that engulfed the world.' B. Haskell, The American Century: Art & Culture (1900-1950), Vol. I (1999), at 337 *et seq*., also, at 366 *et seq*. Also, L. Phillips, The American Century: Art & Culture (1950-2000), Vol. II (1999), at 20 *et seq*.

[53] The Chromatic Abstract language of, e.g., Rothko and Newman aimed 'to render pure, abstract states of consciousness ... they ignored neither the terror of modern life nor the 'moral crisis of a world in shambles.' Instead, they sought to defy humanity's tragic condition through images of renewal and transcendence. ... [Rothko's] paintings became "doorways to the spirit"' Footnotes omitted. The American Century, Vol. I, at 373. Also, The American Century, Vol. II, at 14-15, 24 *et seq*. With his gestural 'dripping' style, Jackson Pollock, for example, 'created a visual language that coupled images of primordial passion with those of spiritual harmony. The tangled tormented skeins of paint and lack of focal point in his work bespoke *entrapment* and *anxiety*; the lyrical grace and unconstricted energy of his calligraphic arabesques suggested freedom and ecstacy.' The American Century, Vol. I, at 364. Emphasis added. The entrapment refers also to Existentialism and its influences. Also, The American Century, Vol. II, at 14 *et seq*.

[54] The American Century, Vol. I, at 377 and Vol. II at 27. Vol. II, at 40: Synthesising the extremes of *angst* and *liberation*, 'it symbolized the power of individual liberty in a democratic society.'

[55] Robert Frost's *U.S. 1946 King's X*: 'Having invented a new Holocaust, And been the first with it to win a war, How they make haste to cry with fingers crossed, King's X-no fairs to use it any more!' R. Frost, Collected Poems, Prose, & Plays, at 362, (The Library of America ed.) 1970. 'The poem refers to the atomic bomb, developed by the United States during World War II and used against Hiroshima and Nagasaki in August 1945. The U.S. introduced a plan in the United Nations in June 1946 to institute international controls over atomic energy and the spread of atomic weapons; the following month the United States tested two atomic bombs in the Pacific.' Id., at 983. See also, on the fate of the world's smaller states, Frost's *No Holy Wars for Them*, id., at 361. Both poems were originally published in *Steeple Bush* (1947).

Who is this human being *really* who is capable of incarnating such Evil and whose '*passions pray but to primitive totems*'? [56] It would be wrong to characterise this post-holocaust era by a sense of nihilistic despair. However, the looming threat of total destruction and new chaos was inescapable to anyone who took care to reflect upon his time and life. In this era, challenged by the obtruding 'absurdity of life' in this world, the aching question was: if and how morality was still possible in individual, social, and international life and if and how human beings could resist the despair and obtruding anxiety and uphold and defend human dignity?

These questions were as much asked of international law scholars as of intellectuals in other disciplines. Morgenthau's realism and Lauterpacht's idealism yielded almost opposite views on law and its role in the preservation of peace, as they were based upon two equally different visions concerning mankind: where Morgenthau was rather pessimistic, Lauterpacht saw more reason for a morally constructive response.[57] The work of McDougal and Friedmann was not left unaffected either by the threat and fear of global catastrophe or the ideas concerning the (im)possibility of human progress and peace.

For the sake of a clear organisation in respect of the purpose of this chapter and in spite of the necessary flaws of generalisation, we will discern two movements or tendencies of mind in the immediate aftermath of WWII; another antinomy in this chapter. On the one hand, there were – here sketchily grouped as – 'realists,' who were sceptical about the possibility of morality if not at the individual level than definitely at the international level. They rejected the optimism of liberal thought and the faith in man' reason and his goodness. Since the human condition taints human action, man's ability to do good is very limited due to his dual (both good and evil) nature. The evil effects of man's behaviour are generally corrected less in social life. Consequently, within international life, in order to protect the peace and oppose totalitarianism effectively the balance-of-power politics and the willingness to defend human freedom and dignity by war were the only realistic response. On the other hand, there were those who rejected this recourse to power and instead proceeded with a more rationalist optimistic faith in human nature and its ability to produce morally valid action. Evil did exist but man had the ability to resist it by his faculty of reason. Here grouped as 'idealists,' they aimed to narrow the gap between reality and the ideal of a better world. If we continue along the same line for the sake of the present study, faith in human nature extended to a faith in law, in the possibility to establish a peaceful order and defend and promote human dignity and freedom by the (international) rule of law.

---

[56] The Age of Anxiety, *supra* footnote 49, at 49, 76, 125. Emphasis added.

[57] Spender pointed to the question or rather the choice that was being forced upon man: it was 'a choice between creation and destruction immediately after a period in our history, when it seemed that morals were simply an affair of private conduct and that no necessity of making a moral choice confronted the whole society.' This observation is particularly enlightening for our understanding of what is called the idealist response to the catastrophe of WWII. European Witness, at 92.

As to the realist response to modern anxiety, this is for instance found in the work of W.H. Auden (1907-1973) and Reinhold Niebuhr (1892-1971). In the *Age of Anxiety* (1948), W.H. Auden both poetically and lucidly expressed the anxiety of modern man and his fate of eternal failure. This long poem was motivated by the idea that a purely rational vision of man's nature was neither realistic nor tenable, and that this was particularly true after WWII. Man should *realistically* speaking be perceived as at best ambivalent by nature: uniting good and evil, reason and natural impulses,[58] free yet bound by failure and mortality, innocent yet capable of atrocities. Therefore, man lives in anxiety with the knowledge of both his freedom and his failure.[59] Rather than to bring about peace, rationalism had led the world to its doom, the new barbarism was born within modernity.[60] In this vivid description of the experience of modern anxiety as well as of human nature and modern socio-political life, Auden was significantly influenced by the religious existentialism of Reinold Niebuhr, an American theologian, who before he became professor of Ethics and Philosophy of Religion, served as a clergyman in Detroit, where the Ford industry was situated. There he had witnessed the effects of industrial and technological progress on human dignity. His socio-political ideas were not limited to American society alone, but included an international perspective as well. Niebuhr greatly influenced (American) intellectual and political life during the Cold War years by his active participation in the public debate on socio-political issues and his realist – power-based – responses to the problem of contemporary international life. Apart from Auden, Niebuhr influenced, for example, Arthur Schlesinger, Jr., and more importantly, for the objective of this chapter, Hans Morgenthau. According to the latter, Niebuhr was 'the greatest living political philosopher of America.' Niebuhr's thinking carried as much weight with atheist intellectuals because of his analysis of human anxiety within the contemporary modern society and his rejection of both idealistic rationalism and romantic naturalism.[61] He aimed to explain the experience of modern anxiety by the duality of human nature itself.

[58] Man is not just the embodiment of all that separates him from the animal, he also includes the animal as well: 'all the needs and conceits of / The poor muddled maddened mundane animal / Who is hostess to us all.' The Age of Anxiety, at 125.

[59] Man's state of anguish is the human condition: 'The sole essential a sad unrest / Which no life can lack.' Id., at 54. The ambiguity of human nature is 'the infinite impetus of anxious spirits.' Id., at 125. See also, on the individual's sense of loss and loneliness as well as on the 'impotence of reason to provide the meaning of existence' and how this mood was reflected in art, The American Century, Vol. I, at 353 *et seq.*

[60] The city symbolises Reason and the Mind: barbarism or fascism have emerged from rationalism, which is a thought that we will also find below in our discussion of Morgenthau. The city is also the World that has fallen. 'But the new barbarian is no uncouth Desert dweller; he does not emerge / From fir forests: factories bred him; / Corporate companies, college towns / Mothered his mind, and many journals / Backed his belief. He was born here. The/ Bravura of revolvers in vogue now / and the cult of death are quite at home / Inside the city.' The Age of Anxiety, at 24.

[61] With the object of this chapter in mind, emphasis is more on Niebuhr's critique of idealism and less on his critique of naturalism, however both are scrutinised in The Children of Light and the Children of Darkness: A Vindication of Democracy and a Critique of its Traditional Defence (1947),

Niebuhr demonstrated how both naturalism and idealism failed to explain this anxiety because they started from false –'superficial'– interpretations of human nature. His criticism thus focused on their perceptions of human nature. The true source of modern man's anxiety is his own contradictory nature, the ambiguity of the human condition:

[M]an, being both free and bound, both limited and limitless, is anxious. Anxiety is the inevitable concomitant of the paradox of freedom and finiteness in which man is involved. Anxiety is the internal precondition of sin. ... Anxiety is the internal description of the state of temptation. It must not be identified with sin because there is always the ideal possibility that faith would purge anxiety of the tendency toward sinful self-assertion.[62]

Man's *freedom* is an essential factor: man is anxious because he is aware of his limitations, but also enjoys seemingly unlimited possibilities. Anxiety is thus 'a permanent concomitant of freedom,' it consists of both creative and destructive elements. Anxiety relates to man's fear of 'meaninglessness,' which springs from the limits of his knowledge. The subsequent 'will-to-power,' one of the impulses of survival, thus springs from a need to compensate the insecurities of human life; it is an expression of insecurity.[63] Man is tempted to use his freedom yet seeks power to compensate the resultant insecurity. This desire for power to overcome anxiety drives him to act beyond his limits and will thus at the same time pose a threat to the social peace as it puts self-interest above the common interest. In other words, 'every thought, mood or action which proceeds from the self as anxious, finite, and insecure has some taint of sin upon it. ... Freedom from anxiety ... is an ultimate possibility which man as sinner denies in his action.'[64] Human anxiety is the inescapable precondition of evil and unjust action. Since anxiety is inherent in the duality of human nature, moral optimism is totally unjustified being based on 'the idealistic error of regarding the mind as essentially good.'[65] The idealistic rationalist confidence in the goodness of man is mistaken because it identifies the rational human mind with goodness while in fact rational

hereinafter: The Children of Light and the Children of Darkness, for their political implications. The Children of Light are the moral idealists and the naturalists are among the moral pessimists and cynics, i.e., the Children of Darkness. This naturalist current interpreted human nature as being made up of essentially natural vitality. The natural self is glorified as the highest self. The power of natural human vitalities (impulses of hunger, sex and survival) is emphasised while man's rationality and freedom of action is downplayed. Both the naturalist and the idealist approach ignored the *real* relationship between nature and reason. Man is within as well as without nature, blessed with reason, and conscious of his environment. His *spirit* enables him to 'stand outside of nature, life, himself, his reason and the world.' He is conscious of being part of the natural world, yet also able to transcend it, and therefore he can never feel at ease. This in Niebuhr's analysis is the source of man's existential condition of anxiety. 'He stands at the juncture of nature and spirit, and is involved in both freedom and necessity.' R. Niebuhr, The Nature and destiny of Man, Vol. I Human Nature 193 (1941). Hereinafter: Human Nature. Vol. II is hereinafter indicated as: Human Destiny.

[62] Human Nature, at 194-195. Footnotes omitted.

[63] Id., at 206.

[64] Id., at 294, 307.

[65] Id., at 13.

man carries within him the root of evil.[66] Reason is the weapon of the natural impulse of self-interest, as well as an instrument of justice, but it never serves justice *exclusively*. Even man's actions to serve justice are corrupted by self-interest. Reason can as easily be applied for the representation of evil and lead to totalitarianism. Unjust acts can hardly be prevented from the outside because human action out of anxiety and insecurity is driven by the (the will to) power. Human action is tainted with human egoism. In other words, the moral optimism of idealism is an illusion at the individual, national and international level, not to mention a dangerous indulgence (especially under the international circumstances). If not anchored in a realistic view of man, i.e., recognising man's dual nature, democracy would not stand a change, either at the national or at the international level.

In *The Children of Light and the Children of Darkness: A Vindication of Democracy and a Critique of its Traditional Defence* (1947), Niebuhr spelled out the (international) political consequences of his *realist* analysis of human nature. He was convinced that

> democracy has a more compelling justification and requires a more realistic vindication than is given it by the liberal culture with which it has been associated in modern history. The excessive optimistic estimates of human nature and of human history with which the democratic credo has been associated are a source of peril to democratic society; *for contemporary experience is refuting this optimism* and there is a danger that it will seem to refute the democratic ideal as well. ... Man's capacity for justice makes democracy possible; but man's inclination to injustice makes democracy necessary.[67]

In his view, a *realistic* vindication of democracy is less optimistic than the defences of the 'Children of Light' and less pessimistic than the non-democratic theories of the 'Children of Darkness.' The Children of Light were the moral optimists who sought universal harmony and adhered to a higher universal law in order to enforce this harmony. Their idealism was based on an exaggerated confidence in man's rational capacity for justice. Whether in the liberalist and individualistic version or in the collectivist and Marxist version of democracy, the underlying presumption is that human nature is inadequate and excessive either in its exaggeration of the individual's need for freedom at the expense of his (in fact, equally strong) need for community, thus infringing his true need to realise

---

[66] Id., at vii. '[Idealism] tend[s] to understand man too much from the standpoint of his rational faculties only and therefore to misunderstand him. [It] do[es] not understand the full dimension of his "spirit" nor yet the intimate relation between the human spirit and the human physical organism in its insecurity and weakness.' See also, for the necessary balance between moral optimism and pessimism, between confidence in and distrust of human reason, in respect of a realistic conception of democracy and a just society, Human Destiny, at 258-259.

[67] Children of Light and the Children of Darkness, at x-xi. Emphasis added. Id., at 11: 'Modern democratic civilization is, in short, sentimental rather than cynical. It has an easy solution for the problem of anarchy and chaos on both the national and international level of community, because of its fatuous and superficial view on man.'

himself socially, or in its neglect of man's individuality and his need to realise himself individually. However, neither was fundamentally aimed at destroying either the national or international community. The Children of Darkness or 'children of this world' were the moral cynics, who regarded man as totally self-centred and living with complete disregard for the whole. They '[knew] no law beyond their will and interest.... They [were] *wise*, though evil, because they [understood] the power of self-interest.' However, in their defiance of the common interest they accepted *evil* (i.e., 'the assertion of some self-interest without regard to the whole') as the basis of the socio-political order, whether that of the national or international community. Barbarism (Nazism or other forms of totalitarianism) springs from this evil, which at the international level means that the Children of Darkness challenge democratic civilisation by 'declar[ing] that a strong nation need acknowledge no law beyond its strength.' According to Niebuhr's analysis of the problem: 'Our democratic civilization has been built, not by children of darkness but by *foolish* Children of the Light, ... who underestimate [the] power [of self-interest] among themselves.'[68] They had done this at their own peril, as, after all, in pre-WWII Europe, liberal democracy had left the world unprepared and ill-equipped to deal with the looming danger.

A realistic democratic theory needed to accept the (individual and collective) 'will-to-power' and that by the search of that power naturally conflicts arise. The survival instinct that urges people to accumulate *power* cannot easily be defused, 'the egoistic corruption of universal ideals is a much more persistent fact in human conduct than any moralistic creed [including liberalism] is inclined to admit.'[69] The liberal democratic theory should be considered equally 'stupid' in its analysis of the *international* community: sovereign states pursue their own national interests and to assume that they will substantially transcend this egotism is totally unrealistic. The idea that any kind of moral universalistic concept could correct these impulses in any way, was in Niebuhr's view, a *foolish and sentimental* belief. Communities, whether sub-national or national, have survival impulses too, just like individuals. In other words, idealistic moral universalism had to be refuted for its dangerously naive approach to national and international political life. Some moral cynicism was actually to be preferred over the sentimentality of the secular moral idealists.[70]

Niebuhr formulated a realist political theory in which he argued that power was the best instrument for managing conflict between states. The reality of international life was 'chaos,' so Niebuhr believed, and 'the problem of overcoming this chaos and of extending the principle of community to world-wide terms' he considered 'the most urgent of all the issues' that the world was currently fac-

---

[68] Id., at 9-11. Emphasis added.

[69] Id., at 22.

[70] Id., at 41: 'The preservation of a democratic civilization requires the wisdom of the serpent and the harmlessness of the dove. The children of light must be armed with the wisdom of the children of darkness but remain free from their malice. They must know the power of self-interest in human society without giving it moral justification.'

ing.[71] This urgency was the result of the convergence of an old moral and a new technical force of universality. The sense of an existing moral obligation towards a universal community now coincided with the factual development of a 'phenomenal' increase in global *interdependency* due to technological advancement and the emerging global economy. While the idealists adhered to the establishment of a world community as an ultimate inevitability, the moral cynics emphasised the power of the particular (interest), the 'egoistic forces' of collectives and, especially, of nation states. Neither of the approaches was effective, in Neibuhr's opinion, in overcoming international anarchy. Niebuhr distinguished two schools of idealism. First there was the most naïve group, which held that 'it would be sufficient to embody a moral imperative into a universally accepted law.' This natural law approach of a kind of universal constitutionalism was, in his view,[72] particularly lacking in realism because of their idea that the redefinition of international law would suffice to extend the principle of community.[73] The more sophisticated idealists recognised the importance of power within social life and recognised the need of the world community for international institutions with specific authority, for example, the authority to judge or enforce order. However, both schools of idealists negated the *power of the particular*, the power of self-interest. The real problem was that

> It may be regarded as axiomatic that the less a community is held together by cohesive forces in the texture of its life the more must it be held together by power. This fact leads to the dismal conclusion that the international community lacking these cohesive forces, must find its first unity through coercive force to a larger degree that is compatible with the necessities of justice.[74]

'Fear of anarchy' is not convergent enough a force to actually bring unity closer. The universal community of mankind may be 'ultimately imperative,' but not without a prior battle and the corruption of the instruments of universality by the forces of particularity. Despite the two forces of universality, international anarchy is a much more realistic state of affairs than the idea of a global community is. Niebuhr concluded that power would be the predominant factor in the preservation of peace; the *balance-of-power* principle would rule within the international system. He claimed that 'world politics cannot rise higher than the balance-of-power principle.'[75]

---

[71] Id., at 153.

[72] Id., at 73-74, Niebuhr's critique is firm: 'Even if natural-law concepts do not contain the ideological taint of a particular class or nation, they are bound to express the limited imagination of a particular epoch, which failed to take new historical positions into consideration.'

[73] 'They imagine that nations insist upon absolute sovereignty only because ... "natural law" ... justified such sovereignty; and that therefore a new definition of international law, which denied the principle of the absolute sovereignty of nations would serve to annul the fact.' Id., at 163.

[74] Id., at 169.

[75] 'The international politics of the coming decades will be dominated by great powers who will be able to prevent recalcitrance among the smaller nations, but who will have difficulty in keeping

However, such equilibrium would be able to rein in international anarchy, if only for the short term rather than indefinitely.[76] It is the task of the international community to 'subdue chaos and create order,' and, secondly, 'to prevent the power, by which initial unity is achieved, from becoming tyrannical,' in other words: to preserve a 'proper balance' between freedom and order. The principles of order and freedom are conditioned by the exigencies of the context and require constant re-examination. 'Justice is introduced into a field of order if the organizing power is placed under both moral and constitutional checks.' This, however, is not easy in a world ruled by anarchy and Niebuhr considered it highly unlikely that the post-war superpowers would reach mutual agreement and create a world organisation, which would include constitutional checks upon their authority, simply because global interdependence was on the increase.[77] As only an order that respects freedom and implies justice can preserve peace, external checks are a necessity. They are however 'insufficient if some inner moral checks upon human ambition are not effective.' Although 'nations are more egoistic than individuals,' as Niebuhr tended to agree, certain inner moral checks exist even within states that curb their will-to-power. For the purpose of preserving world peace, these inner moral checks must also be 'strengthened.'[78] Consequently, for the sake of international peace, Niebuhr called for a culture of self-criticism within states and for mechanisms and institutions, which manage and process this criticism into a measure of restraint on the will-to-power. Politics should not be separated from morality, even though '[h]ypocrisy and pretension are the inevitable concomitants of th[is] engagement. But they do not arise where no effort is made to bring the power impulse of politics under the control of conscience.' Niebuhr engaged the US in such self-criticism where he stated that America lacked 'political and moral maturity' and as a consequence failed to assume its responsibilities.[79]

---

peace between each other because they will not have any authority above their own powerful enough to bend or deflect their wills. ... ... Whatever unity may be achieved in the coming decades must be attained by the coalescence of power and the development of a core of international community among the great powers.' Id., at 171.

[76] Id., at 173-175: 'the peace of the world may be maintained perilously and tentatively, for some decades, by an uneasy equilibrium between the three great powers, America, Russia, and Britain ... [and] it is quite easy to foreshadow the doom of such a system ... [since] every center of power will seek to improve its position.' Consequently, every change of position would provoke a response from another power, and so 'a mere equilibrium between them will not suffice to preserve the peace.'

[77] Id., at 178-181. Yet he retained some hope that a significant agreement might be reached: 'the evils of the policy of partitioning the world are so obvious, that we have some right to hope that a rigorous effort will be made to achieve a more basic and lasting accord. The best hope of justice lies in the fact that a stable order is not possible without introducing instruments of justice into the agreements which are to provide for order.' Id., at 181.

[78] Id., at 178-182. Niebuhr nevertheless remained dubious about the operation of such checks in certain states (e.g., Russia) that lacked the necessary democratic institutions and suppressed criticism.

[79] Niebuhr was a declared opponent of isolationism both during and after WWII. '[America] alternates between moods of complete irresponsibility and of cynicism. In the one mood it would dis-

In conclusion, the world community should neither be built by the children of darkness nor by the children of light but 'by men and nations sufficiently mature and robust to understand that political justice is achieved, not merely by destroying, but also by deflecting, beguiling and harnessing residual self-interest and by finding the greatest possible concurrence between self-interest and the general welfare.' Niebuhr further cautioned that since it was such an impossible task to create a world community it required 'faith not easily destroyed by frustration. ... [and which] understands the moral ambiguity of history... as permanent characteristics of man's historic existence.' Ultimately, Niebuhr concluded: '[t]he task of building a world community is man's final necessity and possibility.' Whereas man was free to transcend nature in order to reach for universality, at the same time the creation of universality was 'also his final impossibility,' because he was bound by the (natural) particular, by time, place, roots, and his mortality, his *dependency* upon nature. Thus, the world community would always remain 'the perpetual [ultimate social] problem as well as the constant fulfilment of human hopes.'[80] The ultimate realisation that the attainment of a world community is in fact an impossibility prevents us from being overly confident where human powers and universal (utopian) creeds are concerned, be they communist or world federalist. International tensions and conflict are here to stay: the only thing we can do is to manage them *realistically*, i.e., by *power politics*. Man has to fight for a just society in the knowledge that he will never attain it.

Secondly, the other trait of intellectual life in the West that we distinguish here may indeed be indicated by the term 'idealism.' However, attempts to reestablish morality and justice were not in all cases as naïve and unrealistic as we just saw idealism being suggested. After the totalitarian tyranny of the 1930s and 1940s and WWII, it is fair to say that natural law revived in political and (international) legal theory.[81] This return to natural law was rooted in the urgent need to reconnect morality with justice and law and politics, now that positivist philosophy had proven unable to prevent totalitarianism and the flagrant violation of justice. The Swiss theology professor Emil Brunner (1889-1966), who was, like Niebuhr, a

---

avow the responsibilities of power because it fears its corruptions. In the other mood it displays an adolescent pride of power and a cynical disregard of its responsibilities. ... If America achieves maturity, the primary mark of it must be the willingness to assume continuing responsibility in the world community of nations.' He believed that to practise an isolationist foreign policy was a sign of immaturity and that the US had to grow up and take responsibility, even when it was clear that the responsibility in question 'cannot be fulfilled without some egoistic corruption.' Id., at 184-186.

[80] Id., at 187-189.

[81] See, e.g., Kelly, at 418, where he suggests that Gustav Radbruch is 'the first apostle' of the new natural law. In the course of the 20th century, the gap between contemporary positivism and natural law has indeed narrowed by, e.g., the jurisprudence of H.L.A. Hart and his concept of the 'minimum content of natural law'. See also, S. Hook, Law and Philosophy (1964), at xii: at this symposium was observed that '[i]n reaction to certain historical events in the twentieth century which have outraged the moral consciences of men, the number who profess allegiance to natural law are now legion.'

rather 'public' theologian and as such among the most influential of the 20th century as well as being the driving force behind the establishment of the Swiss Institute of International Studies in 1943 in Zurich, went even further. He stated unequivocally that

> The totalitarian state is the practical consequence of the positivist philosophy of law. The positivist conception of law has done away, theoretically, with the idea of justice, the totalitarian state does so practically in ridiculing the *jus divinum* and abolishing the rights of man.[82]

Brunner also grouped Hans Kelsen among the positivists whom he criticised for having 'thr[own] out of their vocabulary the idea of human dignity and human rights.'[83] In the former's analysis, the gradual process of separating justice from its (religious) natural law basis could only give rise to totalitarianism. In passing, Brunner blamed Grotius for – rather than being 'the creator of natural law' – having started the deplorable process of 'the decay of natural law.'[84] His main point is that the formalist, positivist conception of justice – i.e., the negation of *jus divinum* – could only end in the emergence of totalitarian states which exalt their sovereignty. In order to prevent this from ever happening again, a new conception of justice had to be established: a conception that recognised the rights of man and rejected the idea that there are no limits to the sovereignty of the state. The practical consequences of the positivist philosophy – i.e., the monster of the totalitarian state – had revealed the 'true nature' of this philosophy as well as the need to reconnect justice to the law of nature. Brunner observed: '*Wir stehen zweifellos am Beginn einer neuen Epoche der Gestaltwerdung des Naturrechts.*'[85] Brunner set out to re-conceive justice and to re-connect it to the national and international legal order. Being a theologian, Brunner's contribution was evidently rooted in theological reasoning and connected to (Protestant, neo-orthodox) theological debate. Evidently, we will leave this (for our purposes preliminary) debate aside here.[86] However, a brief survey of Brunner's conception

---

[82] E. Brunner, Christianity and Civilisation 110 (1947). Hereinafter: Christianity and Civilisation.

[83] Id., at 100, 107-108, and 113: 'The positivistic school of law, which has prevailed in Europe for almost a century, is largely responsible for the legal chaos and the totalitarian monstrosity.' See also, E. Brunner, Gerechtigkeit: eine Lehre von den Grundgesetzen der Gesellschaftsordnung 247 (1943). Hereinafter: Gerechtigkeit.

[84] Christianity and Civilisation, at 109.

[85] Gerechtigkeit, at 321, 88, and at 63: 'Einer Zeit, welche die Ungeheuerlichkeiten des totalen Staates erlebt hat, steht, wenn sie an Gerechtigkeit denkt, die Feitheit im Vordergrund. Damit werden all die gedanklichen Motive wieder lebenig, die die neuere Staats- und Rechtsgestaltung in Bewegung gesetzt und überhaupt das neuzeitliche Geistesleben beherrscht haben. Es ist verständlich, dass gerade von da her auch ein neues Interesse am «Naturrecht» entsteht, an jener Idee, an der sich immer wieder das Postulat der ewigen, unveräusserlichen Menschenrechte entzündete.'

[86] See, for Brunner's view on man and the 'human essence' and the importance of his use of the psychological-anthropological 'I-Thou' relationship, which he took from Martin Buber's personalist existential philosophy, Routledge Encyclopediae of Philosophy, Vol. 2, 1998, at 30-34.

of justice rooted in natural law and his federalist ideas about the state and the international order will benefit our understanding of an influential representatives of the 'idealist' current of mind.

The revival of natural law was mainly driven by the intention to put natural or human rights on a firm footing and re-establish justice as a substantial notion. And indeed, the concept of justice as formulated by Brunner included the recognition of human rights. Brunner contended that human rights and liberties always exist side by side with the rights of the community to which the individuals belong; both set of rights have their origin in the natural order as it has been created. Human rights represent the equality of human dignity, which can be, but must never be, taken away from the individual human personality, and the community rights represent the inequality of men in their nature and duties – an inequality that is the precondition of any natural community. From this perspective, the state (which is such a natural community) is perceived as a divine institution, not as an institution derived from human rights. It is a naturally necessary institution, because within human nature lie selfish, anti-social, and anarchical tendencies. Without the state, order becomes anarchy and justice loses the battle to evil.[87]

In accordance with the created order, the state may demand from its citizens that they subject themselves to the state but 'vom Staate [muss] verlangt werden, dass er die Ur-Rechte des Menschen schütze; tut er das nicht, so ist er ungerecht.'[88] If the state fails to protect fundamental human rights, it is an *unjust* state. Having thus established that man's personal dignity has priority over the state and is independent from the state, it has become clear that human dignity and man's natural rights have their origin in natural law, the created natural order. Human rights are those rights that man has under *all* circumstances – and which may under *no* circumstance be violated.[89] On the other hand, by indicating that the state is obliged to protect human rights Brunner also placed natural law above the state and challenged the concept of state sovereignty. A *just* state respects and protects human rights and is *not* sovereign.[90]

In his attempt to seek out a new concept of justice, Brunner rejected both the individualist and the collectivist view on the relationship between the individual and the community. He rejected the individualist view because it considers individual freedom as supreme and disregards the fact that community *is* also essential to the individual. The collectivist view he rejected because it places the community above the individual and conceives of individuals as dependent upon

---

[87] Gerechtigkeit, at 85.

[88] Id., at 87: 'Seine Personwürde hat der Mensch nie *durch* den Staat, sondern *vor* dem Staat un unabhängig von ihm.'

[89] Id., at 75-76. Brunner gives the example of the freedom of the press: although this is undoubtedly a very important right, it is not a fundamental human right.

[90] Id., at 88: 'Und spricht man im Ernst von der *Souveränität des Staates*, wie der moderne Rechtspositivismus tut, so ist, wie und die neueste Zeit lehrte, der totale Staat da.' Also, Christianity and Civilisation II, at 117.

and subordinated to the community. In the (natural law) concept of the individual and the community Brunner advocated, the community does not have its origin in a social contract, but in creation itself, as man's desire to belong to a community is a natural human inclination. However, man's individuality is also part of the divine creation and its uniqueness should never be lost by merging into the collective. In Brunner's words: 'Gemeinschaft in Freiheit, Freiheit in Gemeinschaft.' This conception of man and community leads to federalism and natural law:

Die konkrete Gestaltung solcher freiheitlicher Gemeinschaft ist die föderative. Sie ist die Gemeinschaft von Freien. Aber dieses föderative Prinzip darf nicht im Sinn der Vertrags- und Vereinsgemeinschaft verstanden werden. Denn es geht hier um die Gestaltung ursprünglicher, nicht aus dem Vertragswillen der einzelnen abgeleiteter Gemeinschaft. Darum schliesst sie jenes Element in sich, das der moderne liberale Föderalismus nicht mehr kennt und versteht: das der echten, ursprünglichen, undelegierten Autorität.[91]

With 'ursprünglichen Autorität' as the source of community among individual human beings Brunner rehabilitates natural law as the representation of the Ideal – the ideal community based on the original authority of justice rather than power. The concept of nature which Brunner draws on in order to re-connect justice with natural law is that 'nature' as the 'natural order created by the divinity'. Nature is a theological as well as a *normative* concept, natural law is the law that emerges from human nature as it was created by God. However, it is *knowable* to everyone – irrespective of their beliefs – because these laws or norms are naturally forced upon every human conscience. Brunner observes in assent '*dass die Idee der Gerechtigkeit oder das Gerechttigkeitsgefühl etwas allgemein Menschliches ist.*' Every human being's sense of justice tells him to respect the laws of nature and to include among these laws fundamental human rights and community rights necessary to give each his due.[92] Brunner's concept of natural law stipulates that, besides the formal aspect, every legal action (legislative, judicial or otherwise) has to be directed towards justice, has to have a material component:

«Naturrecht» aber meint: Es gibt gewisse Grundprinzipien wie zum Beispiel die grundlegenden Menschenrechte, gewisse Grundsätze, die unter allen Umständen massgebend sind, wenn es zu finden gilt, was einem jeden als das Seine zukommt. ... die Gerechtigkeit bestehe darin, einem jeden das Seine zuzuteilen, das Grundprinzip alles Naturrechts. ... Wer das Suum cuique anerkennt, anerkennt im Prinzip das Naturrecht.[93]

Justice, however, is not static. The concept of justice presented here recognises the dialectic of both equality and inequality and of the static nature of law and the dynamic process of history. In other words, absolute justice belongs to the divine order, whereas in the human order of this world only relative justice exists. Con-

[91] Gerechtigkeit, at 89-99.
[92] Id., at 106-107.
[93] Id., at 101-102.

sequently, the state has to be understood as a necessary institution in this world that is unfortunately tainted by evil. The will-to-power of every human being and the tendency to use it (destructively) makes the state's monopolisation of power necessary and the state 'the presupposition of cultural life.'[94] The justice of this world is relative justice. Positive law in turn reflects the reality of this world of which it is a product. Because of man's evil streak, justice and the positive legal order necessarily deviate from natural law. However, rather than pursue absolute justice, Brunner is satisfied with 'Gerechtigkeits-realismus:' which means adapting justice to reality, in order to have at least a minimum of justice realised.[95] Brunner's examination of justice in the natural law tradition resulted in a concept of justice that included both individual and community natural rights, i.e., human rights. In Brunner's view, it is *realistic* to develop the socio-political order (both nationally and internationally) based on this concept of justice.[96]

Brunner developed a view on what a *just* social order means in terms of a state community and in terms of the international community. To be just, a social order has to recognise (individual and collective) human rights and be based on the federalist principle. This is the principle that stipulates that an order, either state or international, is constructed from below. A federalist order is neither centralist nor possessive of its citizens. The federalist state encompasses all other communities within its borders and has the monopoly of force. However, it is *not* sovereign, as it has to respect the fundamental human rights of natural law. Therefore, '[n]icht die Demokratie bewahrt uns vor dem totalen Staat, sondern der Föderalismus.' Federalism conforms to natural law because it represents the natural order, which was also created from below – 'Alle Ordnungen sind um des Menschen willen, und nie ist der Mensch un der Ordnungen willen. Beim einzelnen Menschen is darum anzufangen.'[97]

To be *just*, the construction of the social order has to start from the individual human being. This postulate even led Brunner to remark that '[w]o man im Ernst von Kollektivpersonen spricht,' – referring to the concept of 'real' collective personality in the German jurisprudential tradition – 'da ist man schon auf dem Wege zum totalen Staat.' This concept 'trotzdem er von so edlen Geistern vertreten wurde, [hat] ohne Zweifel den nationalsozialistischen Totalitarismus vorbereited.' In other words, for a *just* order: '[d]er Primat des einzelnen vor allen Kollektivgrössen: das ist der im christlichen Glauben tief verankerte Individualismus und liberalismus.'[98] The primacy lies not with the particular

---

[94] Christianity and Civilisation Vol. II, at 116.

[95] Gerechtigkeit, at 122. Id., at 118: 'Das relativ Gerechte ist, in der positiven Rechtsordnung, das Bessere als das absolut Gerechte, darum, weil, das absolut Gerechte als Rechtsordnung von vornherein nur ein Schein, eine Lüge und eine Vergewaltigung sein könnte.'

[96] In doing so, Brunner states that one must be utterly realistic: 'Realistisch aber ist nur der, der über der gegebenen Wirklichkeit nie die Grundlagen wahrhafter, schöpfungsmässiger Gerechtigkeit vergisst.' Gerechtigkeit, at 129.

[97] Id., at 159-160.

[98] Id., at 160.

community that is the state; the state is merely a necessary institution of this world. Its task is co-ordinative, protective and regulative, rather than creative or constitutive. The natural order preceded the state and therefore, in order to be *just*, the state must respect it by being organised federally and thereby respecting both individual and collective rights. When a state is *unjust*, it does not stop being a state. It is only when the state has no power, it ceases to exist.[99] However, a state that is merely based on power and negates justice will eventually cease to be.

Brunner considers that four steps need to be taken in order to establish a just order, both nationally and internationally, I will first mention the steps towards the justness of the state before we turn to international justice. As man is not all good and because a life in anarchy would necessarily be a horrible, cruel and dehumanising life, the first step must be building an organisation with a central will and the monopoly of power. The second step requires that the ruler of this organisation proclaims *law* instead of arbitrary dictates. The third step towards a just state is taken when the law thus proclaimed is also (relatively) *just* law,[100] i.e., is in conformity with and in support of the further realisation of the natural rights of the individual and the community. Finally, justice demands that power is justly distributed within the state. If all circumstances are right, democracy is indeed the best form of governance because every individual shares responsibility for the proper exercise of power by the state.[101] Quite realistically, however, it is observed that democracy alone is an insufficient antidote against totalitarianism. Thereto, social-economic justice should also be taken into consideration.[102] What does justice – represented in natural individual and community rights as well as manifest in the liberty of individuals and the common good – mean within international relations and international law? The four steps towards a just international order are not that different.

The first step towards a just international order is the confrontation of international anarchy. Again, Brunner warns against optimistic idealism and calls for a realistic assessment.[103] In general, the international conduct of states – especially great powers – is driven by the 'purely egoistic power principle.' This evil of egoism, either in the form of imperialism or of isolationism, dominates the political reality of international life and determines the '*urgency*' to end the anarchy.[104] The first step towards justice is by peace, i.e., the 'will-to-peace'. The will

[99] Id., at 231.

[100] Id., at 249. Also again on the reconciliation of the rational (natural law) system with the reality of this world in *Gerechttigkeits-Relativismus*.

[101] Id., at 237.

[102] Id., at 245.

[103] Id., at 273, 307.

[104] In theory, there are three ways to establish a peaceful international order: by means of a hegemonic power which subdues the world, by an international legal instrument like a peace treaty; or by power and law conjoined. The first possibility is not very peaceful, the second relies on an instrument that is in 'crisis,' and the creation of a supranational power on a legal basis is in fact quite unrealistic. Id., at 277-283.

to peace precedes the will to justice, so to speak. Peace is in the state's interest; the only realistic basis for an international order is that states for the sake of peace abstain from egoistic power politics and begin to respect the requirements of justice. This is not Utopian, because modern war means 'global' as well as 'total war'. The facts force states to want peace and to respect a minimum of justice. Subsequently, out of this will-to-peace international co-operation and institutionalisation will (have to) grow and state sovereignty will in a moral-practical sense be limited.[105]

The second step towards a just international order is *law*, international law. This is only one step away from the third requirement: *just* international law. Brunner calls for the *use* of the contemporary *fear* and *anxiety* to create the maximum of international legal instruments designed to preserve peace.[106] To be *just*, international law should moreover incorporate the *suum cuique* or 'each his due' principle: every nation its individual liberties and community duties. In this respect, Brunner also reflects on the right to self-determination and its limits[107] as well as the issues of unjust economic imperialism, the non-existence of an unlimited right to armament, and the moral-practical limitation of sovereignty for the sake of a just order. Absolute sovereignty is impossible because of the actual solidarity and interdependence among nations. Its limitation has to be voluntary and based on the recognition of the nations' duties towards the international community. Great powers are a hindrance to a just order. They should be the first to recognise the limitation of their sovereignty with the creation of a new world order.[108]

Finally, the application of the federalist idea of justice to the international order eventually requires a just (constitutional) distribution of power. However, to base the international order on this democratic idea under the actual circumstances of international life would indeed be Utopian, as Brunner agrees.[109] Nonetheless, ultimately only a just order can be a peaceful order; power has to serve justice, and as such, justice needs power. Internationally, the principle of state sovereignty greatly contributed to the failure of the League of Nations and its successor was not founded on the basis of the 'will of federation' either. In 1948, Brunner observes: '[a]lthough only a few years have elapsed since its formation, it must be admitted that this second attempt [the United Nations Organisation] has also failed for the present.'[110] In order to overcome international anarchy and to prevent 'the end of human civilisation,' a world state is no

[105] Id., at 283-285 and 293.

[106] Id., at 287.

[107] Id., at 291: 'Jedes Volk, das seine Fähigkeit bewiesen hat, einen selbständigen Staat zu bilden, und das diesen Willen dauernd hat, besitzt auch das Recht auf diese selbständigkeit. Nur eine Völkerorganisation, die ihm dieses Recht gewährleistet, kann den Anspruch erheben, einigermassen gerecht zu sein.'

[108] Id., at 292-295.

[109] Id., at 298.

[110] Christianity and Civilisation Vol. II, at 123.

option either. Only a federalist approach to the international community is somewhat realistic and could prevent a degeneration into tyranny.[111] The struggle for power and influence between the (two) superpowers, which endangered the life and freedom of humanity, could only be confronted by the 'will to peace' manifest in state behaviour and the gradual replacement of the international use of power by *just* international law and institutions.

To conclude, Brunner may be read as a representative of those contemporaries who held that law and justice should be in close relationship. The connection between positive law and natural law or justice was to be denied no longer. The state should be re-installed as the 'protector' of law (not merely its 'producer') and re-subjected to (natural) law, human rights included. Stimulated by international interdependency, international institutionalisation as well as the development of human rights law to represent and guarantee human dignity have indeed become normative concepts in the assessment of state behaviour.[112] 'Human Rights' became the main expression of modern post-WWII natural law language and their institutionalisation a truly defining development of the second half of the 20th century.[113]

This rather extensive elaboration on Niebuhr's and Brunner's thinking serves to clarify the background to Morgenthau's and Lauterpacht's position on international law and of the mutual criticism of realism and idealism at the time. Insufficient knowledge of this background of power-politics thinking could easily lead us to misunderstand Morgenthau's scholarship. Moreover, it also gives us a good impression of what Lauterpacht was up against in defence of his (more federalist and natural law) view of international law.

Artists often have their finger on the pulse of society and their work often conveys to us, perhaps centuries or decades later, the essence of their time. This is also true of two works made around the end of WWII by a painter, Francis Bacon (1909-1992), and a sculptor, Henry Moore (1898-1986), respectively, who were incidentally both British, which illustrate a difference in perspective on human nature and/or life. These works illustrate the dichotomy that maintained a precarious balance over time and slowly but gradually provoked change.

The first is Francis Bacon's *Three Studies for Figures at the Base of a Crucifixion* (*c.* 1944) in the Tate Gallery in London. It depicts man as a cruel beast against a background of an aggressive shade of orangey red. The entire painting

---

[111] Id.: 'A centralised non-federative, or, if I may use the phrase, a monolithic, world state would necessarily become a monster power of totalitarian character, whereas a federal structure always involves a certain risk for the peace of the world.'

[112] Like sovereignty, human rights law is however not absolute either since there is as we have seen no absolute justice. A system of positive law can only try to approach justice but should never be conceived of as a perfect static and eternal order deduced from some principles. Id., at 113.

[113] In 'the choice between making a heaven or a hell' of this world, 'the choice between creation and destruction,' this so-called idealist stream opted for the ideal of the first. European Witness, at 92.

expresses violence, horror and death, resulting in the loss of man's human identity.[114] When confronting this painting, the viewer can almost physically feel the degradation of humanity, coupled with a sense of fatality and despair. Francis Bacon put it as follows: 'Every man and woman's fate, whether they know it or not, is a marriage of heaven and hell. For him who applies it to human beings and pushes it to its extremes, how could realism develop into anything other than tragedy?'[115] With this painting, Bacon expressed this Energy of Evil, which is the capacity for violence and is one of the two states of the human soul. He expressed man's inclination to follow slavishly this energy because, as Blake put it, 'Energy is Eternal Delight.'[116] Bacon held a rather bleak and pessimistic view of man, which prompted an art critic to remark that '[h]is abiding concern for the irrational is evident in his imagery of the abnormal and the impaired, underscoring a darker view of a humanity only partially evolved from an ignoble, animal condition.'[117]

Around the same time, Henry Moore resumed sculpting and created the Northampton *Madonna and Child*, managing somehow to see beyond the sickness and evil that had contaminated humanity and finding the image of a woman and child who reflect a solemn pride, a calm strength, solid responsibility and serene dignity. As Fuller observed when he compared the work of Bacon and Moore:

> In a sense, we are compelled to choose between two antithetical visions of ourselves. We must decide whether, in a world apparently deserted by God, we prefer to see our fellow human beings as sacks of mutilated, spasm-ridden muscle; or as creatures still capable of composure, dignity, and profound spiritual strength.[118]

The struggle between these two visions of man was fought out and expressed not only in the arts, but in many other circles of post-war intellectual life. Over the years, Moore continued to express this spiritual strength, authenticity and serenity. Moore's sculptures of consoling female figures, in which one can discern

---

[114] 'One does not soon forget th[e] sensational images of hysteria and nightmare in paint [of the late forties and early fifties], which spoke so eloquently to our postwar distress. ... These and other idiosyncratic images of the forties and fifties bear witness to the trauma of World War II and the Cold War aftermath, but they also signify more broadly man's innate capacity for violence.' S. Hunter, Metaphor and Meaning in Francis Bacon, *in* L. Gowing and S. Hunter, Francis Bacon 30 (1989).

[115] Marlborough Gallery Catalogue, March-April 1967, at 24. With the image of 'marriage of heaven and hell,' Bacon referred to William Blake's poem of around 1790, which deals with the contradictions of life and human nature: 'Without Contraries is no progression. Attraction and Repulsion, Reason and Energy, Love and Hate, are necessary to Human existence. From these contraries spring what the religious cal Good and Evil. Good is the passive that obeys Reason. Evil is the active springing from Energy. Good is Heaven. Evil is Hell.' The Works of William Blake, Wordsworth Poetry Library ed., 178 *et seq*., at 179.

[116] Id.

[117] Hunter, see *supra*, footnote 114, at 32.

[118] P. Fuller, Henry Moore: An Interpretation 39-40 (1993).

bodies and landscapes at the same time (take, for example, the *Reclining Figure* (1957-58) at UNESCO headquarters in Paris), are interesting and evocative in their combination of natural and human forms, a reconciliation of humanity and nature.[119] The reclining female figure was a recurring theme in Moore's work, 'a symbol of consolation, reconciliation, and renewal: in her strange, undulating forms, she is at once woman, landscape, and cathedral.'[120] Here, Moore preferred to focus *not* on man's capacity for violence, but, rather more positively, on beauty, the sacredness of the human being and his capacity for 'composure, dignity, and profound spiritual strength.'

In brief, the broader intellectual and cultural context of international legal scholarship cannot be described and characterised without remarking on the anxiety of the age, which was indeed the anxiety of modern man and the deep concern over the world's ideological antagonism and superpower rivalry. No description of this era can be complete without indicating its ambivalence, with the forces of democracy pitted against totalitarianism, and individual responsibility struggling with national sovereignty.

4.2.3. **Jurisprudential context: the reinforcement of sovereignty or justice**

When for the second time in 30 years the world experienced a disaster of unrivalled magnitude, despite attempts to prevent such a disaster from ever happening again, there was hardly any room left for optimism. 'The great desillusion' (*sic.*) brought about a reduction in the role of international law as contained in the UN Charter and marked theory deeply.[121] Especially when compared with the standing of the Pact within the League of Nations, the Charter was a disappointment due to the minor role it assigned to the law and because of its incorporation of the *balance of power* principle. The desire to reconstruct international law reappeared among international jurists, although it was obviously marked by a completely different context from the one that had been present after WWI.[122] In the Cold War context, awareness of modern anxiety, ideological antagonism and

[119] Id., at 38: 'Moore's war drawings of figures somehow engulfed within the protective bowels of the earth relate immediately to his sculptural attempts to blend *human* and *natural* form, to see 'figures in the landscape and a landscape in the figures,' as John Read once put it.'

[120] Id., at 45.

[121] G.H.J. van der Molen, The Present Crisis in the Law of Nations, Symbolae Verzijl (1958) at 251. [Hereinafter, The Present Crisis].

[122] D. Kennedy, A New Stream of International Law Scholarship, *in* Beck and Arend and Vander Lugt, International Rules 233 (1996), Originally published in *Wisconsin ILJ* (1988). See also, E.H. Carr in his conclusion '[o]ur task is to explore the ruins of our international order and discover on what fresh foundations we may hope to rebuild it.' Carr, at 290. Also, Power Politics, at 11, 434. Schwarzenberger speaks of 'the main constructive task that lies ahead,' after World War II. 'For this reason the lessons to be derived from the failure of the League experiment have to be learned in full if similar mistakes and subterfuges are not to be repeated in experiments for post-war reconstruction.' Also, C. Eagleton, Organization of the Community of Nations, 36 *AJIL* 241 (1942). 'The task ... in rebuilding the law of the community of nations belongs primarily to international lawyers.'

superpower rivalry was nowhere as acute as in the discipline of international law. The existential questions, which dominated intellectual life in general, challenged international law scholars just as much. In his 1947 article entitled 'The Task of the International Lawyer' Eagleton claimed that: 'International law is at a critical stage today and its crisis is that of every human being.' The international lawyer's urgent task was to be constructive and to 'strengthen the shaky foundations of international law,' as Schwarzenberger also stressed in 1966.[123] He issued the warning that 'the whole of contemporary international law rests [on]: the inevitably unstable thermo-nuclear world equilibrium of power.'[124]

The international developments in Cold War (international) life were the very issues clamouring for a scholarly response from the international law discipline.[125] From the early stage Cold War international law scholarship was confronted with, on the one hand, a deeply divided world and, on the other hand, a universal organisation, which with its Charter and the Universal Declaration of Human Rights lay the ground for or could be the basis of a fundamental material normative change of international law. This paradox is reflected in international life – by a tendency to increase international power and influence and the parallel attempt to develop human rights law for the protection of the individual – as well as in post-1945 scholarship. Here, the two tendencies we discerned earlier in response to the reality of human nature and (international) politics, *realism* and *idealism*,[126] are again helpful for a general understanding of early Cold War scholarship. 'Realist' scholars tended to focus on the role of power in international relations. In the anarchical world of international power politics, the principle of sovereignty is essential for survival and the basis for a successful struggle for power. International law was (merely) an instrument of power politics employed wilfully by sovereign states. Broadly speaking, 'idealist' arguments contended that, firstly, besides power, *law* and *ethics* should *also* play a major role in international relations,[127] secondly, international law and justice are inseparable notions, thirdly, a universal legal community, i.e., a universal legal and institutional system, should exist and is actually a necessity for international peace and well-fare. The analyses of Morgenthau and Lauterpacht's use of ILP have to be seen in the context of the broad realist-idealist debate. This realist-idealist 'bi-po-

---

[123] C. Eagleton, The Task of the International Lawyer, 41 (2) *AJIL* 437 (1947).

[124] G. Schwarzenberger, International Law: The Ultimate Test, 6 *Indian JIL* 6 (1966). Hereinafter: The Ultimate Test.

[125] See also, W.G. Grewe, The Epochs of International Law (2000) at 639-658.

[126] Rather than reflecting my personal views, these notions – realism and idealism – reflect the debate of this era and the characterisations used at the time, by both the exponents as well as the opponents of the traditions.

[127] See, e.g., for influence of Emil Brunner on Max Huber's work, M. Huber, Prolegomena und Probleme eines internationalen Ethos, 53 *Die Friedens-Warte* 305-329 (1955/56); M. Huber, Der Einzelne in der Völkerwelt, *in* Das Menschenbild im Lichte des Evangeliums, Festschrift zum Emil Brunner, 153-170 (1950). See also, e.g., G.H.J. van der Molen, *in* Ethical Values in International Decision-Making (1960), at 43-51; See also, The Present Crisis and Van der Molen's Subjecten van Volkenrecht (1949).

larity' characterised early post-WWII scholarship, however, gradually, with the acceleration of international organisation and co-operation as well as the inclusion of human rights law in the positive international law framework, a more pragmatic mainstream international legal thinking dominated the 70s and 80s.[128] McDougal and Friedmann have been major contributors to this development.

Let us now see how the realist-idealist distinction, which we put to the fore here, featured in early Cold war scholarship and find, firstly, how realists tended to reinforce sovereignty while idealists argued the reinforcement of justice and secondly, but in line with this difference of perspective, the implications of this difference in outlook for their respective views on international organisation and human rights.

In the first place, the world's bi-polar power structure and the ensuing ideological conflict had a profound impact on legal doctrine. There were now 'two worlds,' as Nussbaum phrased it in 1950. He was still quite optimistic at the time; in his view: 'the amount of dangerous friction ha[d] been lessened,' since 'the psychological and material barriers against large-scale armed conflicts ha[d] been immensely strengthened.'[129] With the (balancing) bi-polarity in place, the ideological antagonism impregnated international law scholarship abundantly. In 1951, Schwarzenberger observed that a 'complete change in the intellectual climate' had taken place, affecting scholarship and resulting in the pressing need to support through the study of the international society a certain outlook on the situation:

> In the midst of the cold war, an attempt to study international relations as objectively as this is given to imperfect man may not appeal to the partisans on either side. Spokesmen of the 'other' camp may justly complain that I have made little secret of my unlimited antipathy to, and profound distrust of, totalitarianism in any form and disguise. Yet, ..., to avoid this criticism is not the kind of objectivity at which I aim. Everyone is entitled to his own judgments of value in these matters. The only duty which is incumbent on the scientific, as distinct from the propagandist, treatment of such controversial topics is to make articulate any predilections and antipathies of a subjective character. Conversely, those in charge of Western ideology-making have just as valid grounds of complaints. I have not made any conscious concessions to their thought-pictures nor to the requirements of their truth campaigns as distinct from the basic values which I share with them. To succumb to such temptation – which never existed – would amount to the betrayal of I the indefeasible trust of academic research in a free community: scientific integrity.[130]

---

[128] It is at also this stage that Lauterpacht is frequently cited to lend support to less sceptical approaches to international law and to give direction to its progress. In Friedmann's work, for example, we often find crucial references to Lauterpacht, as well as to Jessup, when it comes to the protection of the individual by (his position within) international law and to indicating the impact of human rights law on the structure of international law. Friedmann, The Changing Structure, at 234, 237, 245, at 240: Lauterpacht's International Law and Human Rights (1950) 'is the most important' contribution to the literature on the formulation of an international code of human rights.

[129] A Concise History, at 292.

[130] Power Politics, at xvii. See also, J.B. Whitton, Cold War Propaganda, 45 *AJIL* 151 (1951).

By 1968, Henkin observed that '[i]deological conflict [...] has increased instability, threatened the foundations of international law, reduced its content, and weakened its observance.'[131] Not only the international society was divided into two ideological camps, a Soviet communist and a Western capitalist camp, international law theory could not escape from the grips of ideological division either. Soon, there was Western scholarship and Soviet international law theory.[132] Moreover, with the process of de-colonisation a 'Third World' emerged and soon scholars who identified with the perspective of these newly independent countries contributed to the debate.

In spite of ideological differences, among the representatives of each of the three regional perspectives just mentioned we find *realists*. After WWII, the Western (scholarly) world was confronted with a Soviet conception of international law based on the principle of the *coexistence* of (economically) different systems. Soviet scholarship evidently reflected the official perspective of the totalitarian Soviet Union. Having become the 'other' Superpower, it was in the interest of the USSR to accept the existence of international law rather than arguing its 'non-existence' as it had done before WWII.[133] In service of the Soviet interests, communist scholarship set out to define international law as the law of the peaceful *coexistence* of *very sovereign* states bound by these norms.[134] With its emphasis on sovereignty and the will of the state, it was a rather 'conservative,' 'voluntarist' conception of international law.[135] Responding to this conservative conception as a fact of (international) life, Western international law theory and practice concurred substantially in the reinforcement of the 'inter-state' concept of the international society and international law. On top of this, many newly independent states equally embraced and proceeded to cling to the classical concept of sovereignty (as did the socialist states) in order to ensure their independence.[136] The fact that the non-western states gradually outnumbering the Western States seemed to be another reason for the latter to cling to the principle of sovereignty. In other words, the premise that the sovereign power of states had to be recognised as a reality of international life was generally being accepted by 'realists' everywhere.

---

[131] L. Henkin, How Nations Behave: Law and Foreign Policy 105 (1968). Hereinafter: How Nations Behave.

[132] See, for a comprehensive overview of Soviet international law theory, P.H. Kooijmans, Communistisch Volkenrecht: van non-existent recht tot recht van co-existentie, *in* J. Stellingwerff (Ed.), Marxisme en Revolutie 225-264 (1967). Hereinafter: Communistisch Volkenrecht.

[133] Id., at 225-236.

[134] Id., at 236 *et seq*.

[135] Id., at 249-250.

[136] '[T]he smaller nations, which are caught in a struggle to create national identity, are interested in developing, not restricting, notions of sovereignty. New nations have tried to use the doctrine of the sovereign equality of states as a legal bulwark against their more powerful neighbors.' R.J. Barnet, Coexistence and Cooperation in International Law, 18 (1) *World Politics* 89 (1965). See also, Daillier, P. and Pellet, A., Nguyen Quoc Dinh Droit International Public 62 (1994).

Hence, political power and the dogma of state sovereignty were again being recognised as lying at the root of international legal reasoning. Georg Schwarzenberger, a less sceptical realist than Morgenthau, may be quoted as an example of the realist conception: 'international law is both *subservient* to power politics and ... it flourishes best where it does *not interfere* with the struggle for power.'[137] He explained that the essence of power politics was that the groups which were members of the international society – i.e., *not* yet a community – 'tend to do what they can rather than what they ought.' He defined this brand of politics that was dominated by balance of power objectives in diplomacy and war as 'a system of international relations in which *groups* consider themselves to be ultimate *ends*.'[138] Sovereignty, (military) power, and influence were considered to be absolute necessities to survive in the international anarchy of the Cold War. Consequently, many jurists again considered the sovereign state as the sole true subject of international law and most of them rejected the idea that the individual was the only possible vessel for international legal personality. Among the realist scholars we may range Italian scholars, like Rolando Quadri and Gaetano Morelli, whose rather pure voluntarism constituted itself by stressing the sovereignty of states, international law to be purely inter-state law, and the conviction that the individual is merely an object of state interests not a subject endowed with international rights and duties.[139] In brief, the realist outlook on international life considered international law an instrument of power politics and turned to the reinforcement of state sovereignty.[140]

The *idealist* turn against state sovereignty was not really comparable to the revisionist post-WWI attack on the principle. Instead of attempting to dismiss state sovereignty, it was now being approached more positively and supportively. Against the realist approach of international life and politics, idealist approaches tended to conceive of the *individual* as the ultimate *end* of international law and

[137] Power Politics, at 224. Emphasis added.

[138] Id., at 13. Emphasis added.

[139] Quadri contended that human rights were a scholarly 'fantasy,' the idea that individual fundamental rights and liberties are inherent of human nature is not accepted. Moreover, positive international law does not recognise absolute human rights, which can be opposed by the individual to the state, either. In his (dualist) view, the individual had no rights and duties under international law. International law addresses *solely* states as a 'whole,' a 'unity.' The state, rather than duties, has rights. It was the only subject of international law, very Sovereign and independent. Never an organ of the international community, which was a society of peacefully co-existing sovereign states, not the community of the whole human race. R. Quadri, Diritto internazionale pubblico 398-409 (V ed. Napoli 1968). Morelli argued along the same lines, international law is inter-state law and dualism prevents international law from entering into the internal order. G. Morelli, Nozioni di diritto pubblico 110-119 (Napoli,1967).

[140] Schwarzenberger explained: 'The clinging of States to their sovereignty means that there are values which are more important to them than the well-being of international society or even international peace. ... Then it becomes the supreme object of statesmanship to safeguard at any price such cherished values, and the doctrine of State sovereignty is more than a relic of the past. The old bottles have been filled with a new and potent vintage.' Power Politics, at 100-101.

international relations.[141] Idealist scholars were convinced that justice and law are the right basis for international conduct. Justice operates in the function of the Ideal towards which legal action have to be directed: injustice cannot be law, law has to approach the demands of justice (or natural law) as closely as possible. In other words, the revival of natural law in political and (international) legal theory[142] was an Idealist endeavour. From Brunner we already learned the connection between modern anxiety and the return to natural law. The neglect of man's need for justice in formal positivist views on law was disastrous because man has this existential need to 'liv[e] and ac[t] *in* the order of justice.' If he does not, 'despair' and 'anxiety' will fall to him.[143]

The Dutch professor Gesina Van der Molen for example continued the quest for the reconciliation of international law with sovereignty, justice, and the individual. She regarded the 'increasing supersession of the law by politics in international life' as a 'symptom of the [contemporary] crisis in the law of nations.'[144] The fact that she did not confront this crises in a 'realist' manner does however not mean her argument was lacking realism. In 1949, Van der Molen called the 'civitas maxima' or universal world-state a dangerous utopia.[145] She did, however, argue in favour of a break with the traditional doctrine of absolute sovereignty. Sovereignty should be considered 'relative,' whereby the state is subjected to the international legal order. The international community (of states) should be viewed as an objective fact and a starting point for international organisation. The international community is the factual community of the 'entire human race,' the 'societas humana' or 'societas gentium,' – this family of nations 'is the realisation of a higher moral world-order, which has its origin in creation.' The law of nations was thus subjected to a higher morality. International law had to 'become again a universal community-law.'[146] The state was a means to the end of international justice, but not an end in itself. It was an intermediary between the international legal order and the individual. It was, however, the individual who was at the heart of this view, as Van der Molen called for a new international law of shared responsibility.

---

[141] See, e.g., P.N. Drost, The Individualization of International Law, Symbolae Verzijl 134 (1958).

[142] See *supra*, text footnote 81 and 82. As we also learned from Brunner's use of terminology, there was a debate going on about the use of the term natural law or rather whether it should be 'given up' and replaced by 'justice'. Brunner indeed preferred to 'justice' over 'natural law,' others like Rommen stuck to it. H.A. Rommen, In Defense of Natural Law, Law and Philosophy, at 105.

[143] Id., at 109-111.

[144] The Present Crisis, at 250.

[145] G.H.J. van der Molen, Subjecten van Volkenrecht 21-23 (1949), hereinafter: Subjecten van Volkenrecht. A universal world-state or 'civitas maxima' would reduce the level of individual freedom, Van der Molen argued, as the requirement of uniformity would threaten the specific constitution of the state based on and constituted by the specific character, culture and religion of its people. See also, G.H.J. van der Molen, Ethical Values in International Decision-making (1960) at 43-51.

[146] Subjecten van Volkenrecht, at 42-43.

> The real resistance to the devastating forces of today consists in the firm conviction that this law is more than a set of rules laid down in treaties and adopted by custom. These rules and principles are nothing but the crystallization of the inherent sense of justice that lives fundamentally in every nation and in every human being. Therefore, law and justice are inseparable concepts. The idea of justice must lie at the root of every rule of law. The idea of justice must be the constant touchstone for positive international law. ... ... The argument that international law is weak because it lacks the possibility of enforcement provided for in each national law order rests on a fallacy. International law is an imperfect legal order because it is the result of the still underdeveloped sense of justice felt by the subjects of this law, i.e., the peoples represented by the states. It is of the utmost importance *to strengthen this sense of justice ... ...*[147]

In the second place, the difference in objective – strengthening justice or sovereignty – had its effects on their attitudes towards international organisation[148] and human rights law: whether these phenomena were just another pair of weaponry in the struggle for power or indeed part of a *universal* law of nations. In the Cold War context of ideological and political division, the *universality* of international law was obviously questioned.[149]

On the one hand, the system of the peaceful co-existence of sovereigns evidently incorporated regional diversity as well as profound political and ideological division. Immediately after WWII, the universal validity of international law was inevitably called into question. In 1951, Wilk analysed the situation and observed the presence of a potentially serious threat to the common standards of the universal system of international law. He warned against the fact that this common basis was 'shrink[ing]' and that the 'disappearance' of these common standards would mean the arrival of 'a state, if not of virtual isolation, then of extreme hostility, of a revolutionary war in which even legal rules of warfare would have ceased to exist.'[150] Moreover, the accession of the newly independent de-colonised states to the international legal community and its implications for the universal nature of international law,[151] as well as the need for social justice within the international community, were being addressed in international

[147] The Present Crisis, at 254. Footnote omitted and emphasis added.

[148] See, for the subjection of international organisation objectives to national interests of power politics, Power Politics, at 93.

[149] See, e.g., K. Wilk, International law and global ideological conflict: reflections on the universality of international law, 45 *AJIL* (1951) at 648. See also, The Present Crisis, at 240; A.M. Stuyt, Gespleten Volkenrecht (1962). Detter de Lupis, The Concept of International Law 37-38 (1987), hereinafter: The Concept. See also, The Ultimate Test.

[150] Wilk argued that despite profound ideological differences there was still some basic agreement on the existence of some common standards of international law. At the same time he warned against the fact that universal international law could even soon 'break up' into regional or partial systems and negate the existence of an overall universal legal system. See, Wilk, *supra* footnote 149, at 670.

[151] See, e.g., G.M. Abi-Saab, Peaceful Change and the Integration of the Newly Independent States in the International Community, 32/33 *Yearbook of the AAA* (1962/63) at 175.

law scholarship.[152] Some subjected the 'Western' character of international law to heavy criticism.

On the other hand, however, the acceptance of the law of peaceful co-existence suggested that the gap between Communist and Western international law theory and practice were no longer completely unbridgeable.[153] Moreover, in spite of the superpower rivalry and the principle of state sovereignty and independence, actual *global interdependence* became the main imperative towards the organisation of international co-operation. Initially, this process was of a rather formal, institutional nature aimed at responding to the international anarchy implicit in the idea of mere international coexistence. However, soon a normative impulse emanated from the institutionalisation of co-operation.[154] The halting steps that were being taken in the direction of international cooperation were in the end sufficient to sustain the idea of the universality of international law and to further the codification of human rights project. The difference in perspective between 'Realists' and 'Idealists' is indeed well illustrated by their different attitudes towards the United Nations and Human Rights in the early years of the Cold War.

A 'Realist,' like, e.g., Schwarzenberger, turns against the 'naïve optimism' of those Idealists, who 't[ell us] that the United Nations is the world's only hope!' No, '[i]f this were true, the only reply would be: what a hope!'[155] Similarly, Realists were rather sceptical about the success of international human rights.[156] Being the new word for 'natural rights,' human rights belonged to the suspicious realm of 'natural law' rather than to positive international law and as such it would be a doomed enterprise in the divided world.[157] 'Realists' – conceiving law primarily as an instrument in the struggle for power – did not look at human rights very differently, human rights were to be used and function as instruments for power politics and in no case a reason for intervention. Schwarzenberger assuaged any hope: '[i]n a confederation such as the United Nations, which is based on the principle of heterogeneous universality, the Rights of Man pattern either remains optional or it degenerates into an ideological weapon in the contest of the world powers. In the post-1945 period, it has been the fate of these drafts to have suffered both of these iniquities simultaneously.'[158]

'Idealist' scholars however picked up on the normative spur without standing outside international politics (as they were accused of). Although the post-1945

[152] See, e.g., P.H. Kooijmans, Volkenrecht en Sociale Gerechtigheid (1965).

[153] Communistisch Volkenrecht, at 248,

[154] The institutional spur of the UN to the development of human rights law was already indicated.

[155] Power politics, at 715.

[156] Id., at 712: 'All the more futile are the long drawn-out attempts at divising a common denominator for human rights which are equally acceptable to democratic, authoritarian and totalitarian members of the United Nations.'

[157] Id., at 636-638. Being a non binding legal document, Schwarzenberger used the word 'mockery.'

[158] Id., at 734.

decades did indeed constitute a "new epoch" in the history of international law, pre-WWII (conceptual) developments in the fields of international institutions, human rights law and the right to self-determination simply continued to develop at their own pace during this time as well. Although it had germinated before the war, '[t]he human rights movement ... grew out of the disasters of World War II.'[159] The Nuremberg Charter, Trials (1945-6), and Judgments were evidently landslide developments for international individual responsibility and human rights issues.[160] Those 'idealist' scholars who were convinced that international organisation and human rights (maybe to some extent as instrument of power) in any case were a necessary way to deal with international problems and as such not merely an instrument but an *independent objective* of international life. With the establishment of the United Nations Organisation, 'human rights' became one of the official objectives of this universal international organisation. The Statute was one of the post-WWII legal documents that incorporated originally natural law concepts or meta-legal notions in positive international law. The inclusion of 'general principles' in the PCIJ 'sources-article' was prolonged into the Statute of the ICJ, the codification of human rights law, and the recognition of *jus cogens* by the ICJ, were to many scholars the right starting-points to acknowledge international law's development in terms of justice and universality.

In this context, the universality of the law of nations was less of a problem to the 'Idealist.' After all, he or she tends to understand the demands of justice to be naturally understood by every individual irrespective of the home-continent. Van der Molen, for example, took the idea of the universal human society as the foundation for her international law concept. The idea of the *societas humana*, the unity of humanity, was considered to be the basis of the legal international community and the ethical imperative of human rights law: 'the law of nations ought to become again a universal community-law, instead of an agglomerate of the subjective rights of individual sovereign states.' In other words, '[t]he states,' being the 'constituent parts of this international law-community,' may indeed be 'the principle subjects of the law of nations,' but '[s]econdary international personality can and must also be granted in a limited sense to the individual.'[161] Others however would continue the continue to argue that the individual was indeed the primary subject of international law and two of the predominant Post-WWII international legal developments – human rights and international individual criminal responsibility – gave them ample ammunition. In any case, the advancement of human rights law as well as the law and functioning of the United Nations had to contribute to the reinforcement of justice.

Finally, as the above may suggest, Cold War theoretical attention for the concept of ILP was relatively scarce. Faced with the dominant force of politics at the ex-

---

[159] Steiner and Alston (Eds.), International Human Rights in Context: Law, Politics, Morals v (1996).

[160] Id., at 99.

[161] Subjecten van Volkenrecht, at 43-44.

pense of the role of law, the theoretical arena mainly argued over the identity of international law.[162] Was it 'law as rules' (even though such rules proved hard to find) or 'law as process'? The dogma of state sovereignty claimed urgent attention and to a large extent overshadowed the issue of ILP in the post-WWII debate. For general public international law the theoretical discussion on ILP basically failed off after the ICJ's Advisory Opinion on the subject in the *Reparations for Injuries suffered in the Service of the United Nations* Case.[163] The concept of ILP continued to feature in the discussions on international institutions, but the thoughts devoted to it were more of a practical institutional than a theoretical nature.[164] The Court had turned to the Statute and ruled that the purposes and functions this constitutional document attributed to the UNO could only mean that it had 'a large measure of international personality.'[165] The ICJ thus established the view that IOs possessed a – from its Member-States – *derived* ILP as either explicitly or implicitly attributed by the organisation's constitution. Nonetheless, in the 1960s, Seyersted criticised this view and argued that IOs did have an *objective* ILP of its own, i.e., it has an original ILP attributed by international law not by its member states.[166] In this field of international organisations some debate continued,[167] but in more general international law scholarship, the concept was referred to as controversial yet easily left aside with a brief reference to or quotation of the Court's Opinion. We may conclude that with regard to In-

---

[162] See, for the debate on the question whether international law was really law, or just politics, e.g., How Nations Behave, at 84-94. W.G. Friedmann, The Changing Structure of International Law (1964) at 81; hereinafter: The Changing Structure. Also, The Concept, at 35-36.

[163] Case concerning *Reparations for Injuries suffered in the Service of the United Nations*, Advisory Opinion, ICJ Reports (1949) at 174.

[164] Blokker and Schermers observe that the [UN] system is little understood partly because there has not been much theoretical reflection in the field of international organisations,' and since '[s]uch reflection would need to depart from a comparative study of all types of contemporary international organizations.' Consequently, '[their] book aims to fulfil this role, at least with regard to the institutional law of international organizations.' Blokker and Schermers, International Institutional Law 8 (3rd rev. ed., 1995). Hereinafter: International Institutional Law.

[165] 1949 ICJ Rep.: 'In the opinion of the Court, the Organisation was intended to exercise and enjoy, and is in fact exercising and enjoying, functions and rights which can only be explained on the basis of the possession of a large measure of international personality and the capacity to operate at the international plane. It is at present the supreme type of international organisation, and it could not carry out the intentions of its founders if it was devoid of international personality. It must be acknowledged that its members, by entrusting certain functions to it, with the attendant duties and responsibilities, have clothed it with the competence required to enable those functions to be effectively discharged. Accordingly, the Court has come to the conclusion that the Organisation is an international person.'

[166] See also, for this view, International Institutional Law, at 978-979: the idea of the *objective* personality of IOs was predominantly developed by Finn Seyersted: not the Organisation's constitution determines whether the Organisation has ILP, i.e., the approach the ICJ had taken in the *Reparations* case, but the 'objective fact of its existence' determines the Organisation's ILP if this existence includes international (i.e., by sovereign states created) organs which may act 'legally independent' of those who created the organisation. In this view, IO's capacities are thus independent from its constitution.

[167] See, e.g., on the indivisibility of ILP, International Institutional Law, at 981-982.

ternational Organisations the concept of ILP fulfilled its (rather traditional) conceptual role in the sense that (again) it was used to enable in casu IOs to function as independent entities at the international plane: '[without such a legal status] [t]hey would lack the capacity to *participate* meaningfully in international and national legal life.'[168]

Contrary to what the initial 'idealist-realist' duality might suggest, post-war international legal scholarship was rather *pragmatic* in its approach.[169] It shied away from purely abstract theories in favour of the practical and the technical. Pragmatism is generally understood to be a perspective that qualifies truth in terms of practical success and relevance. In other words, legal thinking and concepts have to be useful; otherwise they are worthless (i.e., without truth). What is useful is determined by international practice, which explains why pragmatism goes so well with the realist view on international law and international relations. Sovereign power was evidently relevant, but was the concept of ILP useful too in post-WWII thinking about international life? Yes, 'idealists' would answer, it was useful in relation to the individual and the transformation of the international society what had to be established. The idealist themes of international organisation and human rights indeed touched upon the individual as a subject of international law. With human rights law more and more in place, pragmatic scholarship continued to find (derived) ILP quite useful for addressing new developments, like IOs and even MNCs. A realist answer to the usefulness of ILP was less affirmative: when questioning the usefulness of theoretical ideas to practical purposes and actual facts, an analysis must be made that includes an exploration of the social and political *context* in which the law operates.[170] In the struggle for power context, state sovereignty was much more important than ILP.

During these decades, the (rare) use of ILP in international law scholarship was determined either by the intention to reinforce sovereignty and by the struggle for power in international life or by the objective to reinforce justice by transforming international law into a universal law of nations with the individual human being as the ultimate end in itself. Ultimately, at the end of the 20th century, the idealist attempt to reinforce justice by developing international organisation and human rights law has been successful. The realist project has in a way contributed to this success by using these as instruments of international politics. Both contributed to the development of international law practice and theory towards pragmatic mainstream scholarship of the 70s and 80s. We will

---

168 International Institutional Law, at 975. Emphasis added.

169 See, for 'the turn to pragmatism,' M. Koskenniemi, From Apology to Utopia, at 157-159 nn.

170 See, e.g., H. Morgenthau, Politics among Nations (2nd ed., 1954) at 267-273; hereinafter: Politics among Nations. See also, M. McDougal, International Law, Power, and Policy: A Contemporary Conception, 82 *RCADI* (1953) at 151, 156, 164; hereinafter: A Contemporary Conception. See further, McDougal, Perspectives for an International Law of Human Dignity (1959), as published in McDougal et al., Studies in World Public Order (1960), at 990 *et seq*, 1004; hereinafter: Perspectives. Schwarzenberger used 'social environment' or 'the structure of its social background' instead of 'context,' Power Politics, at xvi and 202. See also, Henkin, How Nations Behave, at 94.

now examine the use of ILP in the work of Morgenthau, Lauterpacht, McDougal, and Friedmann. Their legal thinking was manifestly rooted in and visibly marked by the political context and tensions of their time, be it differently. Moreover, all four's ideas had a significant impact on international legal thinking in the post-WWII era.[171] We will start with Morgenthau and Lauterpacht, distinct exponents of realism and idealism, respectively. Both Morgenthau and McDougal, albeit in very different ways, searched for a realistic and empirical approach to international life.[172] McDougal's policy-oriented approach to international law combined notions of power politics and human dignity. Finally, Friedmann's response to the political and ideological conflict was to distinguish between 'the law of co-existence' and 'the law of co-operation' and to build further from there.

4.3. Hans Morgenthau (1904-1980)

[I]nternational politics is of necessity power politics.

4.3.1. **Introduction**

In the historiography of international law Hans Morgenthau is more than once depicted as a true American hawk, a classic example of pure scepticism among international legal scholars. As much as his realism is unquestionable, if we take Morgenthau's realist views on such a practical political issue like the Vietnam War into account, the image of a 'hawk' is more debatable. Already in 1965, i.e., at a very early stage of the debate, Morgenthau – then professor of political science and modern history at the university of Chicago – spoke out against US military involvement in Vietnam in a contribution to *New York Times Magazine* entitled: 'We Are Deluding Ourselves in Vietnam.'[173] The article did not go unnoticed: on 28 April 1965 Hannah Arendt wrote to Mary McCarthy:

The Morgenthau article made a certain stir and received a furious reply from [syndicated columnist Joseph] Alsop (pompous ignorance-Hans was hurt, really). I am worried about the whole situation and I have no confidence in Johnson. He thinks in terms of prestige only, does not know how else to think. Is terribly ambitious and very impatient with disagreement of any kind. Also quite primitive. His speech was a marvel of schizophrenia,

---

[171] See, e.g., M. Shaw, International Law (1991) at 54-57; R. Higgins, Problems and Process: International Law and How we use it (1994) at 1-16; Kooijmans' Internationaal Publiekrecht in Vogelvlucht.

[172] They argued that scholars had lost sight of – or simply ignored – the 'scientific findings and empirical facts' of international life. H.J. Morgenthau, Positivism, Functionalism, and International Law, 34 *AJIL* (1940) at 260; hereinafter: Positivism. They distanced themselves from abstract theorisation and, especially McDougal, from metaphysical assumptions. See, e.g., Politics among Nations, at 3; Positivism, at 260; A Contemporary Conception, at 137, 186. It may be noted here that Morgenthau was one of Kelsen's students in Geneva.

[173] H.J. Morgenthau, We Are Deluding Ourselves in Vietnam, *The New York Times Magazine*, April 18, 1965, at 24 *et seq*. Hereinafter: We Are Deluding Ourselves in Vietnam.

the first part saying the exact opposite of what the second supposedly outlined. I am not convinced he is in good faith. The academic community is almost unanimously against him, the people at large are quite apathetic despite all Gallup polls; nobody cares outside the Universities. ... What troubles me more than anything else is the sort of lying we have begun to practice. Morgenthau said the government's White Book [i.e., the State Department's February 1965 White paper *Aggression from the North*: the Record of North Vietnam's Campaign to Conquer South Vietnam] is simply a scandal. ... So ... cease bombing and start negotiating.[174]

In the newspaper article, Morgenthau argued that the United States had to get out of Vietnam. US military involvement had started as a policy to 'contain' Communism – the so-called Truman Doctrine – which Dulles applied far beyond the boundaries of the European continent and which turned into a 'dismal failure.' This was in the first place due to the fact that it was a military principle applied to the *political* threat of the expansion of Communism: in Asia and the Middle East the weakness and instability of governments and societies were fertile ground for Communism to rise to power in. Secondly, Morgenthau explained, 'even if China were threatening her neighbors primarily by military means, it would be impossible to contain her by erecting a military wall at the periphery of her empire.' Morgenthau's realistic approach, based on the past, present and future division of power in the region, bade him to conclude: 'For China is, even in her present underdeveloped state, the dominant power in Asia.'[175] If the US had a problem with this dominant role, it had to confront China itself, instead of its sphere of influence. However, Morgenthau maintained that 'practical judgement' was against it.[176] The United States, therefore, simply had to accept the predominance of China in Asia, an attitude which would serve the peace: 'military containment is counterproductive.' International relations with (Communist) governments in Asia should simply be assessed on the basis of power and interests.[177] The equation of the denomination 'Communist' with 'enemy of the free world' was obsolete, according to Morgenthau. Communist regimes were neither all alike, nor guided by the same national interests and US foreign policy would do well to ac-

[174] C. Brightman (Ed.), Between Friends: the correspondence of Hannah Arendt and Mary McCarthy, 1949-1975 (1995), at 180-182. McCarthy's reply seemed to express a more general feeling: 'I am still in a state of great anxiety about the U.S.' Id., at 183. Hannah Arendt informed her: 'Morgenthau has advanced to national figure or something of the sort. But seriously, he has been very good on the issue: I was not in Washington but heard he had been excellent. You are quite right about the new alignment: Johnson wanted the consensus, and by God he has it, but against him.' Id., at 217.

[175] We Are Deluding Ourselves in Vietnam, at 25.

[176] After all, to defeat China meant that it had to be conquered by millions of American foot soldiers, not just by dropping a nuclear bomb. Such an undertaking would be 'fraught with incalculable risks, so uncertain of outcome, requiring sacrifices so out of proportion to the interests at stake and the benefits to be expected.'

[177] 'For better or for worse, we live again in an age of revolution. It is the task of statesmanship to not oppose what cannot be opposed with a chance of success, but to bend it to one's own interests.'

knowledge this diversity, Morgenthau stated. He pointed out that foreign policy officials had ignored or at least been unable to deal with the specific needs and interests in the case of Vietnam, which was actually a traditional enemy of China. A Vietnamese 'Tito,' for instance, would not damage US interests. Foreign policy based on a balancing of power required a totally different approach. What America needed, Morgenthau explained, was 'a face-saving agreement' and not the further intensification of military involvement. The US had to stop basing foreign policy on public relations of prestige and instead focus on its merits, i.e., power and interests. With the 'White Paper'[178] the government was creating an imaginary world on which it subsequently based policy decisions as if they suited the facts. The reality, however, was that the Vietnam War was a *civil* war, not a war of 'foreign aggression.' To deny this truth was an act of utter *delusion*, making the US position 'untenable.' Based on his realist analysis, Morgenthau appealed to wisdom and the strength of restrain:

> Does not a great power gain prestige by mustering the wisdom and courage necessary to liquidate a losing enterprise? In other words, is it not the mark of greatness, in circumstances such as these, to be able to afford to be indifferent to one's prestige?[179]

Having seen an example of what Morgenthau's realism meant in practice, we should now turn to the roots of his realism, i.e., the developments of the late 1930s and 40s and the political philosophy of Reinhold Niebuhr.

When we take into consideration the general perception of power in the late 40s and early 50s and particularly Niebuhr's influence on Morgenthau's thinking, rather than labelling him a sceptic, I would prefer to stick to the more moderate notion of realist. In the idealist-realist debate, Morgenthau considered Lauterpacht as one of Niebuhr's 'the Children of Light.'[180] Morgenthau opposed most of what Lauterpacht stood for, i.e., the supremacy of law over power, world federalism, and particularly or, rather, fundamentally his rationalist or moral-legalist view on man and his social world.[181] Morgenthau described the contemporary ambivalence and the dilemma of modern man in the following terms:

---

[178] See *supra*, for explanatory comment, text to footnote 174.

[179] We Are Deluding Ourselves in Vietnam.

[180] See, for Morgenthau's criticism of Lauterpacht, Positivism, fn 10, 27, 31. The opposition should not be exaggerated to the extent that it would be suggested that Morgenthau did not recognise Lauterpacht's pragmatism too. This becomes especially clear when we read his references to Lauterpacht – often used to support his view – in Politics among Nations.

[181] Like Machiavelli, Morgenthau concluded for international governance to be realised would take a 'world government' and therefore international governance was basically a utopian idea. The UN, he felt, was a political power based organisation, not a world government. Morgenthau was the opposite of a world federalist. See, for Morgenthau on rationalism and faith in reason, e.g., H. Morgenthau, Scientific Man vs. Power Politics (1947), at 30: 'The belief in the redeeming power of the rule of law, which through its mere existence reforms the conditions of man, is only the classical belief in the autonomous powers of reason on another level of concretisation. The cry for a new piece of legislation as the first and last resort of social reform is but the echo of the appeal to reason pure and simple with which classical liberalism thought to exorcise the problems of social life.' Hereinafter: Scientific Man.

Two moods determine the attitude of our civilization to the social world: confidence in the power of reason, as represented by modern science, to solve the social problems of our age and despair at the ever renewed failure of scientific reason to solve them.

Morgenthau agreed that this mood of despair and anxiety was not new to human history and was indeed rooted in man himself, 'a creature which, being conscious of itself, has lost its animal innocence and security in religious, moral, and social worlds of its own.' The influence of Niebuhr's writings cannot escape the eye. To Morgenthau, what was 'new in the present situation' of modern man was not 'the existence of these anxieties in popular feeling but their strength and confusion, on the one hand, and their absence in the main currents of philosophy and political thought, on the other.' [182] Like Niebuhr, he meant to include them in his analysis.

Similar to classical and Interbellum *restorative* scholarship, Morgenthau's thinking was unmistakably state-centred and based in the (traditional) notion that 'international law owes its existence to the sovereignty of individual nations. To surround that sovereignty with legal safeguards,' he considered 'one of the main tasks of the rules of international law.'[183] That law is placed in the service of *power* was a core element of Morgenthau's thinking and evidently related to his criticism of Interbellum moralistic-legalistic approaches. We need to realise that Morgenthau's pragmatism,[184] his focus on the 'real' and the 'practical,' was rooted in his diagnosis of a contemporary 'crisis of civilization'[185] in general, and a 'crisis of Western political thought'[186] in particular.

The philosophy of rationalism has misunderstood the nature of man, the nature of the social world, and the nature of reason itself. It does not see that man's nature has three dimensions: biological, rational, and spiritual. ... [as such] it misconstrues the function reason fulfils within the whole of human existence ... As a political philosophy, rationalism has misconstrued the nature of politics and political action all together. ... the political and military catastrophes of the thirties and early forties and the political crises of the mid-forties bear too uniform a pattern to be attributed to accidents or to the shortcomings of individuals alone. They are but the outward manifestations of an intellectual, moral, and political disease which has its roots in the basic philosophic assumptions of the age. ... The very appearance of fascism ... ought to have convinced us that the age of reason, of

---

[182] Id., at 9. Niebuhr however did address them and therefore he was the 'the greatest living political philosopher of America.' See, for explicit references to Niebuhr's effective repudiation of rationalism, id., at 41, 33, 192. See also, Morgenthau's statement that 'The subject matter of this chapter [The moral blindness of scientific man] has been most illuminatingly treated in the books of Reinhold Niebuhr.' Id., at 200. See also, the bibliography of Politics among Nations (1954) in which quite a number of Niebuhr's writings, on political realism and (inter)national morality, are mentioned.

[183] Politics among Nations, *op. cit.* footnote 170, at 312.

[184] Id., at 3. See on the general shift to pragmatism, *supra* section 4.2.3.

[185] Scientific Man, at 12-13.

[186] H. Morgenthau, The Political Science of E.H. Carr, 1(1) *World Politics* 128 (1948). 'The experiences of the inter-war years revealed the weakness of the utopian approach to international politics and made its realistic analysis both possible and imperative.' Id., at 129.

progress, and of peace, as we understood it from the teachings of the eighteenth and nineteenth centuries, had become a reminiscence of the past. Fascism is not ... a temporary retrogression into irrationality ... it is truly progressive-were not the propaganda machine of Goebbels and the gas chambers of Himmler models of technical rationality?-and in its denial of the ethics of Western civilization it reaps the harvest of a philosophy which clings to the tenets of western civilization without understanding its foundations.[187]

In Morgenthau's view, rationalism was now intellectually, morally and politically bankrupt due to the fact that it was based on a false – because too optimistic – conception of human nature. Rationalism was ultimately to blame for the rise of fascism.[188] The idea of law as a panacea for world peace had been founded on this false conception of man and society. Only a strong sovereign state would be able to protect a nation's vital interests in the struggle for power and contribute to world peace. Without a balance of power, law is powerless. Today's perception of 'power' should not induce us to misunderstand Morgenthau. He understood power politics as necessary to counter the contemporary crisis and thus rejected 'the optimistic belief in the intrinsic goodness of the rational individual and the pessimistic conviction that politics is the seat of all irrationality and evil.'[189] Individual man he believed to be as corrupt as politics. A more valid philosophical alternative was necessary, based on a realist assumption of human nature: 'Man cannot hope to be good but must be content with being not too evil.'[190] Morgenthau thus aimed to lay down a theory of international politics which was designed to 'meet a dual test: an empirical and a logical one.'[191]

4.3.2. The identification of international law – a set of static, primitive and weak legal rules – as pretext

Hans Morgenthau, originally a lawyer by education and profession, constructed his book, *Politics among Nations*, a 20th century classic, around the concepts of power and peace. 'These two concepts are central to a discussion of world politics in the mid-twentieth century, when the greatest accumulation of power ever known gives to the problem of peace an urgency it has never had before.' Peace is perpetually threatened by the struggle for power, the normative devices functioning to restrain and civilise this struggle within the international society international morality, world public opinion, and international law are 'as they operate today, [in]capable of keeping the struggle for power within peaceful bounds ...'[192] On the other hand, Morgenthau did not glorify power politics. Re-

---

[187] Scientific Man, at 12-13.

[188] Id., at 14-16. The idea that 'science is able at least potentially, to solve all the problems of man,' both social and natural, is in his view erroneous and he believes it contributed to the rise of fascism. Id., at 11.

[189] Scientific Man, at 160.

[190] Id., at 165.

[191] Politics among Nations, at 3. See also, Positivism, at 260 *et seq.*

[192] Politics among Nations, at 20-21.

straints of power, like morality and law he felt were necessary to protect (international) society as well as its individual members from the terror of the most powerful. These restraints he considered, however, less effective than the balance of power in preventing war.

Morgenthau integrated his ideas on law into a theory on international relations in which he subdued the role of law in favour of power politics. Power is the determining force within the international community. Objectively, international law should restrict the naked force of state power. It is unfortunately too weak to rise to this task. In fact, it is merely used to rationalise or 'justif[y]' the power motivated actions of sovereign states, so Morgenthau argued.[193] Law is 'pretext,'[194] it is used to disguise the real goal of political action, which is the accumulation of power. National interests at stake determine whether and how international law is applied within international relations.[195] It functions above all as an ideology to support policy, for example, to sustain the *status quo*, to preserve a certain (powerful) position. As such, law is perceived as 'primarily a static social force.'[196] Its scope is thus limited; it is 'weak and ineffective,'[197] since it is subordinate to national interest.

On the other hand, 'to deny that international law exists at all as *a system of binding legal rules* flies in the face of all the evidence.' In Morgenthau's view, international law was still embedded in the system of Westphalia. He regarded international law as a system of *rules* created through the consent of the sovereign nation-states laid down in international treaties. Its existence depended, however, on two factual aspects as well: a balanced distribution of power among the members of the decentralised society and a necessary 'community of interests' among states. Because of states' general aspiration to power and their fierce defence of national interests, a community of universal interests and values rarely exists.[198]

Morgenthau's realism towards international law was based on his analysis of the international society. He attributed the weakness of international law to its 'decentralized' nature, caused by the 'decentralized structure of the international society.'[199] He rejected international law as a centralised system and as such succeeded in reconciling sovereignty and international law. The community of sovereign states is completely different from domestic societies, in which legal

---

[193] Id., at 80. Morgenthau's argument that law is simply used as pretext and justification should also be read against the background of the international law conception of the USSR and how it changed if and where required by a new communist ideology, which was promulgated after each internal power change. See *supra*, footnote 132, Kooijmans' article, Communistisch Volkenrecht, which is particularly revealing on this evolution of the Soviet international law concept.

[194] Politics among Nations, at 81.

[195] Id., at 258. 'The objectives of foreign policy must be defined in terms of the national interest and must be supported with adequate power.' Id., at 528.

[196] Id., at 83-84. International law may also function as an ideology of another policy.

[197] Id., at 288.

[198] Id., at 250-257.

[199] Id., at 251-252.

liberalism does work. International life, however, he felt was in a state of 'anarchy' and to deny this meant a prolongation of the ineffectiveness of international law. International law was still based on operating 'rationally' but had to do so in a world that tended to be 'irrational.'[200]

> The rule of law has come to be regarded as a kind of miraculous panacea which, wherever applied, would heal, by virtue of its intrinsic reasonableness and justice, the ills of the body politic, transform insecurity and disorder into the calculability of a well-ordered society, and put in the place of violence and bloodshed the peaceful and reasonable settlement of social conflicts. It is the legalistic spirit rooted in the abstract rationalism of liberal philosophy which brings him to this conclusion of international law as an illusion.[201]

International law would remain an 'illusion as a standard for political action,' as long as it was based on 'forgetfulness' of the *real* nature of the international society. And so, even though Morgenthau did not purport to deny the existence of international law altogether, the qualification of 'illusion' is clear. For many years to follow, he thus laid the foundation for the retreat of international law. At the same time, he considered it the 'intellectual and moral challenge' of his time to find an alternative 'standard for political actions.'[202] So emerged his *realist theory of international politics.*

4.3.3. **Morgenthau's use of ILP: impenetrability and exclusion**

Morgenthau believed a state's sovereignty over its territory to be 'impenetrab[le].'[203] This reveals that he held on to the traditional (Westphalian) concept of statehood. The state is 'the legal order that determines the conditions under which society can employ its monopoly of organized violence for the preservation of order and peace.'[204] At the summit of the legal order is the sovereign, not a supreme Norm, nor Reason. The sovereign (who is hardly distinguishable in a democracy)[205] commands rules, which are *legal* rules if not only commanded but also accompanied by the definition of the (possible) sanction. Society comprises many systems of rules of conduct, ethics, mores and law. The state is society's legal order, the state is society's legal person. Legal personality is one of the functions of the 'legal order of society'– i.e., the nation state – or, in other words, one of the functions of the state is to provide the nation with personality:

> The state provides the legal continuity of the national society. It thus enables the individual to experience the nation as a continuum in time and space, as a *personality* in

[200] Scientific Man, at 107, 96-97.
[201] Id., at 100.
[202] Scientific Man, at 107.
[203] Politics among Nations, at 289.
[204] Id., at 475.
[205] Id., at 305-306, on the location of sovereignty.

whose name men act, who demands and receives services and bestows benefits, to whom one can feel personal loyalties that are felt toward few other social groups except the family and the church.[206]

Without this function there would be no domestic peace. The state is a domestic legal order, and as such it is a legal personality on behalf of which men act. But what does this mean at the international level?

Internationally, law was practically less relevant. Since international legal rules are based on the principle of sovereignty, they are weak and ineffective:

[sovereignty] is not at all inconsistent with a decentralized, hence weak and ineffective, international legal order. For [it] is the very source of that decentralization, weakness, and ineffectiveness.[207]

The international legal principles of 'independence, equality, and unanimity' were, in Morgenthau's mind, merely 'synonyms' of sovereignty.[208] State sovereignty, being the legal term (and recognition) for the political factual situation of supreme power, means that the binding force of international law is state consent. The subjects of international law were thus the independent, equally sovereign states, which had consented to the law (and indeed created it).[209] Sovereignty was used to refer to a state's supreme authority in law-creation and law-enforcement within a defined territory. Only states that were sovereign could create international law. Morgenthau considered sovereignty as a legal concept to be based in the '*necessary*' international legal rule of 'mutual respect for the territorial jurisdiction of the individual state.'[210] This respect lay at the basis of his conception of international law.

In his discussion of sovereignty as a legal concept, Morgenthau largely ignored its conceptual relationship with the concept of international personality. Conservative or restorative scholarship used ILP to argue that sovereignty was a *shield* against any corrosion of supreme authority within the defined territory. Morgenthau too used the concept of sovereignty in this way. He did not make any separate use of *the concept of ILP* but *negated it by absorption.* Every sovereign state had rights and duties arising from 'necessary international law': there was the duty to respect other states' independence, as there was the right to be oneself respected. The same was true for state equality and the principle of unanimity or consent. Here we may refer to the interpretation Oppenheim gave of the concept of ILP as a number of fundamental rights and duties incumbent upon a state as recognised by the international community.[211] Morgenthau emphasised

[206] Id., at 475. Emphasis added.
[207] Id., at 286-288.
[208] Id., at 289-291.
[209] With the exception of 'the *jus necessarium* of the modern state system.' Id., at 288-289.
[210] Id., at 289.
[211] Oppenheim, para. 113 'International Personality'; at 261-262.

that sovereignty did not mean 'freedom from legal restraint,' or from international legal regulation where such had been consented to. Nor did it mean factual independence or 'equality of rights and obligations under international law,' as, after all, every state was bound by different international legal rules. Internationally, sovereignty was used as the concept indicating the 'legal status' of the state,[212] comprising some *necessary* international rights and duties. These were very much like the fundamental rights and duties of a state which Oppenheim distinguished as making up the recognised ILP of a state.

Consequently, ILP as a separate concept was largely redundant in realist theory. In an anarchic world of sovereign states, the subjects of international law were bound by international law only as long as it served their interests, as long as it was a tool for exercising supreme power and authority. At the international level, the 'impenetrability' of the sovereign state in combination with the state's legal personality as the nation's legal order placed a shield between the international legal order and the domestic order.[213] Recognised sovereignty – legal status – provided the state with its 'necessary' international fundamental rights and duties.

The issue of the status of non-state entities, such as international organisations, Morgenthau discussed in terms of 'sovereignty' instead of 'personality'. He rejected the idea of 'divisible sovereignty' as logically incompatible and politically undesirable. Other transnational ties Morgenthau judged to be 'infinitely weaker ... than the forces that unite peoples within a particular national boundary.'[214]

Morgenthau's emphasis on the balance of power and power politics, causing international law to be practically ignored and ILP conceptually absorbed by sovereignty, was of course intimately related to the world's political situation at the time. In the short run, the Cold War's bipolar system and its inflexible balance of power would simply continue to exist, Morgenthau asserted. Since a world state was unattainable and war was equivalent to total war and world destruction, the only instrument for the preservation of peace which Morgenthau considered realistic in the Cold War context was (a revival of) the old art of diplomacy. Diplomacy could be the manifestation of state sovereignty and the expression of power that might mitigate and civilise the struggle for power. However, to support the suggestion that Morgenthau was a realist rather than a sceptic, I will close with the following quote:

---

[212] Politics among Nations, at 293.

[213] See *supra*, chapter 3 on *restorative* Interbellum legal thinking. If one reads, for example, that sovereignty is ultimately vested in the nation, 'Sovereignty refers in legal terms to the nation as the recipient of the individual's ultimate secular loyalties, as the mightiest social force, as the supreme authority giving and enforcing laws for the individual citizen.' Id., at 312. The state is the nation's legal order and as such a legal personality. Sovereignty is not given to the state but vested in the nation – or to be more precise to the nation's (dormant) sovereign. Sovereign power is thus the source of law and not the other way around.

[214] Id., at 303-312.

> Diplomacy is the best means of preserving peace which a society of sovereign nations has to offer, but, especially under the conditions of modern world politics and of modern war, it is not enough. It is only when nations have surrendered to a higher authority the means of destruction which modern technology has put in their hands – when they have given up their sovereignty-that international peace can be made as secure as domestic peace. Diplomacy can make peace more secure than it is today, and the world state can make peace more secure than it would be if nations were to abide by the rules of diplomacy. Yet, as there can be no permanent peace without a world state, there can be no world state without the peace-preserving and community-building processes of diplomacy. For the world state to be more than a dim vision, the accommodating processes of diplomacy, mitigating and minimizing conflicts, must be revived. Whatever one's conception of the ultimate state of affairs may be, in the recognition of that need and in the demand that it be met all men of good will can join.[215]

Nonetheless, we have to conclude that (Morgenthau's) realism marginalised the importance of international law. With regard to the concept of ILP, its rather orthodox application catches the eye. In this approach, power politics governed the law and sovereignty governed ILP.

4.4. Hersch Lauterpacht (1897-1960)

> ... it appeared to me that any discussion of the international protection of human rights either in general or through the Charter of the United Nations and a Bill of Rights adopted in pursuance thereof must be deficient unless it takes place against the wider background of the problem of the subjects of international law and of the interaction of the law of nations and the law of nature in relation to the enduring issue of human government–the securing of the natural and inalienable rights of man.[216]

4.4.1. **Introduction**

When reading Lauterpacht's work on international law the image of a bridge springs to mind. A bridge conjoining positivism and natural law theory, a bridge connecting the Interbellum modernist past with the post-Cold War future and the legal tradition of the European Continent with the Anglo-American legal scene.[217] The historiography of international legal theory has placed Lauterpacht

[215] Id., at 534.

[216] H. Lauterpacht, International Law and Human rights vii (1950). Hereinafter: International Law and Human rights.

[217] 'The most unique of Lauterpacht's many services to the progress of international law was to maintain for a generation a broad and firm bridge between British and continental legal thinking.' He has been praised for his ability to 'draw in equal measure upon the fertile speculations of contemporary continental legal philosophy and upon the moral assumptions and pragmatic technique of the common law.' C.W. Jenks, Hersch Lauterpacht-The Scholar as Prophet, 36 *BYIL* 1-2 (1961); hereinafter: The Scholar as Prophet. Jessup stressed Lauterpacht's immediate and lasting influence on American international law students: 'he supplied a necessary mitigation of what tended to be an excessive positivism.' P.C. Jessup, 10 *ICLQ* 9-10 (1961).

in the natural law tradition and his early work has often been labelled idealistic.[218] In this respect, four preparatory directions: first, on the relation between positivism and natural law; secondly, on his place in the period covered by this chapter; thirdly, on the driving force of morality; finally, on natural law and the realist-idealist debate.

First, it has indeed quite rightly been pointed out that Lauterpacht's 'theoretical construction of international law is rooted in Kelsenite legal epistemology.'[219] Arguments expounding the 'impersonal sovereignty' of international law,[220] the fallacy of maintaining a strict distinction between public and private law and between the application of law and the creation of law (the doctrine of the gradual concretisation of the law),[221] as well as Lauterpacht's insistence upon the 'completeness of international law'[222] indeed bear traces of Kelsen's (hierarchical) thinking. Kelsen himself considered Lauterpacht one of his best students when he taught at the Viennese University Faculty of Law in early post-WWI years.[223] However, as evidenced by Lauterpacht's lifetime work, the latter disagreed with Kelsen's 'impatien[ce] of the cry that jurisprudence must serve the needs of life.'[224] To Lauterpacht, questions as to what law *should* be like were of equal interest and importance as questions as to what law actually *was*. In his view, the adoption of Article 38 of the Statute of the Court meant that modern positive (international) law as it *is* contained natural law values, recognised in the form of general principles, which incorporated directions as to how law *should* be. In other words, is and ought should not be treated separately. On the contrary, natural law is vital to the essence and legitimation of international law. This touches upon a fundamental and significant difference between the approaches of Kelsen and Lauterpacht: according to Lauterpacht, the ultimate source of law was not the hypothetical *Grundnorm*, but an ethical or moral postulate. The law of nature to

---

[218] See, e.g., The Epochs, *op. cit.* footnote 125, at 604; Shaw's International Law, at 50. More recently, Lauterpacht's combination of moral rationalism with a kind of 'institutional pragmatism' has been recognised, together with his 'hermeneutics of judging.' M. Koskenniemi, Lauterpacht: The Victorian Tradition in International Law, 8 *EJIL* 219, 221 (1997); hereinafter: The Victorian Tradition.

[219] I.G.M. Scobbie, The Theorist as Judge: Hersch Lauterpacht's Concept of the International Judicial Function, 8 *EJIL* 265 (1997).

[220] H. Lauterpacht, The Function of International Law 422 (1933); see also, id., at 346, 430-431. Hereinafter: The Function of Law. Lauterpacht also subscribed to Kelsen's identification of the state and the law and to the contention that consequently, 'there is no difficulty in accepting the view that the law may be a command merely by virtue of its external nature.' Id., at 420.

[221] H. Lauterpacht, The Private Sources and Analogies of International Law (1927), Hereinafter: The Private Sources. See also, The Function of Law.

[222] The Function of Law, at 51 *et seq.*

[223] H. Kelsen, 10 *ICLQ* 2-3 (1961).

[224] H. Lauterpacht, Kelsen's Pure Theory of Law (Lecture given in 1932), *in* E. Lauterpacht (Ed.), International Law: being the Collected Papers of Hersch Lauterpacht (1970-1978), Vol. 2, at 406. Lauterpacht was uncomfortable with Kelsen's Theory mainly because of 'the absence of any political or ethical tendency in the 'pure theory of law'.' He remarked that: 'It refrains *painfully* from making science an ideology of politics or an instrument in the struggle for power.' Id., at 404-405. Emphasis added. Hereinafter: Kelsen's Pure Theory of Law.

him was the foundation of all law. He concluded that '[t]he rejection of natural law is for Kelsen tantamount to the affirmation of the dignity and autonomy of man,'[225] but Lauterpacht 'decline[d] to follow Kelsen in this respect.'[226] In Lauterpacht's view, natural law was 'the reason of the thing.' To reject it would 'not always be consistent with the positivist idea.'[227] If we return to the image of the bridge, one might say that its supporting pillars included a Kelsenian pillar as well as a pillar of morality and the law of nature.

Secondly, shortly after World War II, Lauterpacht thoroughly re-constructed this natural law pillar in his article *The Grotian Tradition of International Law*,[228] which will prove to be a leading text in our quest for Lauterpacht's conception of international law and his use of the concept of ILP. This is not to imply, however, that the article heralded a break with Lauterpacht's former line of thinking. Lauterpacht made a significant contribution to international legal theory both before and after World War II. In the previous chapter, Lauterpacht has been mentioned as one of the scholars involved in the *revision* of international law, which attempted to reverse the crisis which international law found itself in.[229] Lauterpacht endorsed these efforts: '[A]ny exaggerated conception of the juristic personality of the State is disastrous for the progress of international law.'[230] Throughout this process, the concept of ILP was being used and redefined. As part of his defence of international law, Lauterpacht, like many *revisionist* kindred spirits, argued that the individual was the ultimate subject of international law. After WWII, he held on to this argument, but where previously it had been part mainly of a general *ontological* preoccupation with and renewal of international law,[231] Lauterpacht now used the doctrine of the subjects in connection with the recognition of human rights and freedoms in international law. Consequently, the question of the subjects of international law became the ultimate focal point of the late 1940s and early 1950s, especially in relation to the establishment and institutionalisation of international fundamental human rights and responsibilities. In his own assessment a new period in the history of interna-

[225] Id., at 424. See also, International Law and Human Rights, at 109.

[226] Id., at 428.

[227] Id., at 424-425.

[228] H. Lauterpacht, The Grotian Tradition of International Law, first published in, 23 *BYIL* 1-53 (1946), here as published, *in* E. Lauterpacht (Ed.), International Law: being the Collected Papers of Hersch Lauterpacht (1970-1978), Vol. 2, at 307-365; hereinafter: The Grotian Tradition.

[229] See *supra*, para. 3.1. We have discussed that the Interbellum period saw the concept of ILP featured in the attack upon 19th century and early 20th century *restorative* state theories. In order to refute the negation of international law, the metaphysical personification of the state with its dangerously mystical and totalitarian implications, needed to be rejected. See, The Private Sources, at 74-82, 299. See also, The Nature of International Law and General Jurisprudence, *Economica* 320 (1932), as published, *in* E. Lauterpacht (Ed.), International Law: being the Collected Papers of Hersch Lauterpacht (1970-1978), Vol. 2, at 3; The Function, at 431-434. See, on the danger of state sovereignty as the basis of international law, id., at 96.

[230] The Private Sources, at 80. Footnote omitted.

[231] It has been pointed out in the previous chapter that interbellum international legal scholarship was generally of an ontological nature. See *supra*, section 3.1.

tional law had begun with the adoption of the UN Charter: its provisions on human rights were 'epoch-making.'[232] Lauterpacht felt that the theoretical question of ILP was particularly urgent after the war because of its practical relevance in respect of the Nuremberg Trials and individual criminal responsibility.[233] In other words, his contribution to the human rights project and the regulation of individual responsibility under international law, two of the most important international legal developments of the post-WWII age, together with his theoretical work with regard to the fundamentals of international law, call for an analysis of his legal theory and in particular his understanding of the concept of ILP in the context of this chapter. To put in a caveat, it is impossible to do justice to Lauterpacht's multifaceted work here. Hence, Lauterpacht's leading role in the idealist-realist debate and in the development of human rights law will determine our focus here.[234]

Thirdly, as said, natural law philosophy was a continuing force in Lauterpacht's work, both before and after WWII. This moral foundation, which is such a characteristic feature of his legal thought, also appears frequently in the personal recollections of his colleagues and friends.[235] The analysis of Lauterpacht's post-WWII scholarship would not be complete without referring to McNair's statement on the anti-Semitism, the discrimination and the pogroms which Lauterpacht, who was Jewish, witnessed and experienced during his studies in Vienna and his life in Galicia before that.[236]

---

[232] International Law and Human Rights, at 3.

[233] Lauterpacht, The Subjects of International Law, 63 *LQR*. 438 (1947). Hereinafter: The Subjects-1947.

[234] See, for Lauterpacht 'as judge,' e.g., The Theorist as Judge; also, G. Fitzmaurice, Hersch Lauterpacht and his attitude towards the judicial function, 50 *BYIL* 1-12 (1979).

[235] One of his students described the unity between the man and his work as follows: 'He brought to everything he undertook the moral horizon and stature of the great prophets of his race. He leaves with us, an imperishable bequest to all who inherit his spirit, a sense of moral purpose, of moral earnestness and of moral urgency which represents the supreme need of our troubled age and world. His belief that the State exists for man and not man for the State, that the moral law applies in the same manner to public as to private conduct, that the use of force for the protection of private interests is alien to, whereas the judicial process is an expression of, the moral nature of man, that right is ultimately the only might, and that the protection of human freedom and human dignity are the only legitimate purpose of law and government, was not an academic conviction but a consuming fire ... .' C.W. Jenks, 35 *BYIL* x -xi (1960). Arnold McNair, who was his professor (and soon after became a close friend) at the London School of Economics and Political Science where Lauterpacht was a research student from 1923 until 1927 and then an assistant lecturer until he left for Cambridge in 1937, together with Lauterpacht's close friend Robert Jennings and pupils at Cambridge, most notably R. Baxter, S. Schwebel and W. Jenks, all pay tribute as much to Lauterpacht's contribution to international law as to his 'passion for justice,' 'human dignity and freedom,' 'his moral stature,' and his great gift for friendship and inspiration. See, McNair, 10 *ICLQ* 3-6 (1961); The Scholar as Prophet, at 101-102; Bourquin, 10 *ICLQ* 6-7 (1961); Verzijl, 10 *ICLQ* 7-9 (1961); P.C. Jessup and R.R. Baxter, The contribution of Sir Hersch Lauterpacht to the Development of International Law, 55 *AJIL* 98 (1961). R. Jennings, Hersch Lauterpacht: A Personal Recollection, 8 *EJIL* 301-304 (1997). S.M. Schwebel, Hersch Lauterpacht: Fragments for a Portrait, 8 *EJIL* 305-308 (1997).

[236] It should be noted that Buber and Lauterpacht both grew up in the Jewish communities in and around Lemberg (Lwow), Galicia. Martin Buber was born in 1878 and left for Vienna in 1898 to

At any rate, we may be sure that we can trace to the period, say, from 1914 to 1922, one of his main characteristics as a lawyer, namely, his insistence on the vital necessity of the legal definition and protection of human rights and his appeal to international law as a means of reinforcing the provisions of national laws passed for that purpose. ...
To the same source we can trace his insistence on the opinion – not universally accepted – that individuals can be said directly to possess international rights and be subject to international duties and thus enjoy personality in international law.[237]

On top of these experiences came the World War II and the *Shoah* in which his family was killed. Verzijl has mentioned Lauterpacht's keen interest in the former's concentration camp experiences,[238] and Jessup and Baxter refer to Lauterpacht's general silence concerning the Holocaust, which was set off by his urgent wish that international law be changed so as to be able to prevent people from being exposed to such bestialities ever again, which meant the development of individual responsibility for war crimes under international law.[239] Lauterpacht was closely involved in the preparations of the trials of a number of major German war criminals at Nuremberg between 1944 and 1946. It was his firm conviction that progress had to be achieved in international criminal and human rights law, as these were *the* essential conditions for international political progress and peace.

Fourthly, well aware of the ideological-political dichotomy[240] as well as the 'new' view on power,[241] Lauterpacht placed himself explicitly in what he too considered 'the tradition of *idealism* and progress.'[242] Lauterpacht warned

---

pursue his studies, which was a year before Lauterpacht was born. Still, they had the Jewish Galician background in common, which was characterised by Jewish nationalism (Zionism) *and* by Jewish *rationalism*. Lauterpacht's sympathy with the Zionist movement while he lived in Vienna has to be placed against its pre-WWII background. At the time, Zionism was to a large extent a *cultural* rather then political movement. Like Buber, many opposed the political Zionist dogma that every nation with its own state has only itself to answer to. Secondly, the Haskalah – 'Enlightenment' – movement, which referred to 'the intellect' and in which 'there is the strongest emphasis on the ability of the human mind to arrive at the basic truths of religion by unaided human reason,' had its origins in 18th century Germany and aimed to 'broaden the intellectual and social horizons of the Jews to enable them to take their place in Western society.' At the time, the Jews emerged from the Ghettos which aroused social tension and required them to 'accommodat[e] with modernity in a single generation.' From Germany the Haskalah ideal spread to freethinking spirits in Galicia, where it 'proved extremely attractive to a number of thoughtful Jews in the Galician towns of Lemberg and Brody.' L. Jacobs, The Jewish Religion, A Companion 410, 223-226 (OUP, 1995).

[237] McNair, see *supra* footnote 235, at 6.

[238] Verzijl, 10 *ICLQ* 7-9 (1961).

[239] C. Herzog, Sir Hersch Lauterpacht: An Appraisal, 8 *EJIL* 299-300 (1997).

[240] See, e.g., International Law and Human rights, at 296, 297-301.

[241] Lauterpacht noted that 'in the period immediately following upon the Second World War there was a growing conviction of the reality of power in international relations and a diminishing faith in the reality of law.' Or, put less mildly, 'there is no doubt that seldom in the history of the world has power been the object of greater veneration as in the years immediately following upon the Second World War.' Schlesinger, Morgenthau, and Lauterpacht seemed to agree on the explanation: the preoccupation with power was to a large extent caused by the fact that not the law but military force defeated Nazi-Germany, Japan and their allies.

[242] The Grotian Tradition, at 307 and 396 *et seq*. Emphasis added.

against the new appraisal of sovereignty and power, as he observed that 'the part power played in conquering lawlessness has tended to enthrone power as an end in itself.'[243] The appraisal of 'power' necessitated the asking of the fundamental question whether law should be considered an instrument of power or rather international political relations should be governed by the Rule of Law. The idealist-realist debate became quite passionate. One of Morgenthau's sympathisers, the British realist E.H. Carr, remarked that Lauterpacht dealt with 'the unwillingness of states' to submit to the judicial settlement of international disputes 'in true utopian fashion, as perverse and undeserving of the attention of an international lawyer.'[244] Realists often used Lauterpacht's scholarship to bash into. In 1941, Lauterpacht wrote a response to Carr's critique,[245] which remained unpublished. In 1953, he dedicated a lecture to the matter, entitled *On Realism, Especially in International Relations*, in which he argued that so-called 'idealism' was still a sound and wise path to go. Lauterpacht used firm language and sharply attacked the realistic school, suggesting that realism was 'an inducement to facile and complacent thinking; ... [and] intellectually dishonest;' as well as 'cynic[al],' 'opportunis[t],' and 'distrustful of principle.'[246] Lauterpacht rejected realism for all these reasons and more: for the denial of reason and the disapproval of moral judgment it displayed, for its acceptance of immorality as the normal attitude of the state,[247] as well as for the premise that 'there is no absolute international justice,' which branded the realist a 'moral relativist.'[248] An appeal to realism, in his view, completely disregarded the true capacity of the human will.

Lauterpacht was – so to speak – the Henry Moore of post-WWII international legal scholarship.[249] The work of both Lauterpacht and Moore feature a vision of man that focuses on human dignity and (moral) strength. Lauterpacht, like Moore, chose to reject the idea of *homo homini lupis*, because 'on that line of reasoning there is no salvation for humanity but irrevocable subjection to an order of effective force which [is] indifferent to the dignity of man ...'[250] It was, in Lauterpacht's view, the task of international lawyers to 'eschew the tendency to

---

[243] H. Lauterpacht, International Law after the Second World War, lecture given on 7 May 1950 at the Hebrew University of Jerusalem, *in* E. Lauterpacht (Ed.), International Law: being the Collected Papers of Hersch Lauterpacht (1970-1978), Vol. 2, at 160-163.

[244] E.H. Carr, The Twenty Years' Crisis 1919-1939, at 249 (1939). Also, at 53, 259-260, 263, 267-269.

[245] H. Lauterpacht, Professor Carr on International Morality, *in* E. Lauterpacht (Ed.), International Law: being the Collected Papers of Hersch Lauterpacht (1970-1978), Vol. 2, at 67-92.

[246] H. Lauterpacht, On Realism, especially in International Relations (1953), On Realism, especially in International Relations (1953), *in* E. Lauterpacht (Ed.), International Law: being the Collected Papers of Hersch Lauterpacht (1970-1978), Vol. 2, at 52. See also, for Lauterpacht's critique of realism, *op cit.*, Professor Carr on International Morality (1941)

[247] Throughout his work he called this the doctrine of double morality, see *infra* text to footnote 285. See, e.g., International Law and Human rights, at 5.

[248] On Realism, at 64.

[249] See *supra*, section 4.2.2, text to footnote 118.

[250] The Grotian Tradition, at 333-334. Emphasis added.

juristic pessimism and timidity in a period of political uncertainty and disillusionment.'[251] This does not mean that we cannot find traces in his work of the disillusionment which prevailed at the time and had been brought about by the Second World War and the unthinkable crimes that had been perpetrated when it raged or of the uncertainty and anxiety of the Cold War context, its power politics and the threat of the use of 'atomic energy as a potential weapon of war.' Knowledge of past massacres coupled with the contemporary nuclear threat was indeed a contributing factor to Lauterpacht's argument on the necessity of the general recognition of individual criminal responsibility under international law.[252] Moreover, his involvement in the preparations for the Nuremberg Trials made Lauterpacht appreciate the '*unusual degree of urgency*' attached to the '*seemingly theoretical controversy*' concerning the subjects of law and the doctrine of ILP. He thus implemented his scholarly task by taking one of the most orthodox dogmas – the traditional positivist doctrine that only states are subjects of the law of nations – and proceeding to argue that it was 'obsolete and unworkable.'[253]

As a consequence, Lauterpacht's scholarship is what I would like to call *foundational*, in the sense that he approached human rights from a fundamental international law perspective and was determined

> to show that the significant provisions of the Charter of the United Nations in the matter of human rights and fundamental freedoms are not an artificial innovation which is out of keeping with the essential purpose of international law, with the modern tendencies of its development, and with the sources from which it has drawn its vigour and its dignity. This applies both to the question of the subjects of the law of nations and, above all, to the place which the recognition and protection of human rights occupies in the scheme of international law conceived as the universal law of nations and based on the enduring *foundations* of the law of nature.[254]

Lauterpacht used the concept of ILP in two ways. Firstly, in a semi-traditional way ILP is attributed to states within the developing international federal community, and secondly, ILP is used to include the individual human being in the international community of positive law. Being attributed with fundamental rights by natural law, man is endowed with ILP by nature. This also implies the recognition of the law of nature as the source of all law, and this recognition in turn should be used to the furtherance of international organisation and justice.

---

[251] The International Protection of Human Rights, 70 *RCADI* 5-6 (1947-I).

[252] Lauterpacht, The Subjects of International Law, 64 *LQR* 110 (1948). Hereinafter: The Subjects-1948.

[253] The Subjects-1947, at 438-439.

[254] International Law and Human Rights, at 145. Emphasis added.

4.4.2. A neo-Grotian conception of international law

> Pessimisme is een nutteloos tijdverdrijf [Pessimism is a waste of time].
> *Bertrand Russell*

> We would rather retain natural law with its possible abuses than cut off the branch of law from the tree of justice.[255]
> *Hersch Lauterpacht*

After WWII, Lauterpacht necessitated a legal foundation for the 'new' fundamental rights of man. It is to the service of this purpose that the 'periodical revivifications' as well as Lauterpacht's own adherence to the legal theory of natural law should be attributed: 'the vindication of the rights of man.'[256] Kelsen's theory of law may have influenced Lauterpacht's ideas, but Brierly also left his mark. Lauterpacht praised Brierly for advocating the progressive revival of natural law in order to consolidate the moral foundation of international law at a time of 'transition and reassessment of values' after WWI.[257] In fact, Lauterpacht essentially did the same in his time.[258] Within the political aftermath of WWII and in the context of the realist/idealist debate, with the intention to re-establish faith in international law and its science, Lauterpacht felt compelled 'to sustain hope by drawing inspiration from works in which principle has asserted itself against makeshifts.' In *The Grotian Tradition of International Law*, Lauterpacht turned to Grotius' work for 'instruction' and 'a well-spring of faith in the law as it ought to be' and indeed he found an argument that 'satisfied the craving, in jurist and layman alike, for a moral content in the law.'[259] After all, in his age, Grotius essentially had the same problem defending the Law of Nations while holding on to his practical or realistic credibility.

> Th[e] intrusions of opportunism and realism did not decisively influence the character of *De Jure Belli ac Pacis*. But they are symbolic of the perennial problem with which the science of international law has been confronted almost from the outset. It has been exposed to the inducement to supply a rationalization of inferior and irrational practices; ... ... and to represent the transient manifestations of immaturity and anarchy in international relations as resulting necessarily and permanently from the nature of States the mutual relations of which, it is said, may be regulated by voluntary co-operation but not by a rule of law imposed and enforced from above. Grotius did not succumb to that tendency. This in fact explains much of the influence which he has wielded. For, in the history of politi-

[255] Kelsen's Pure Science of Law, at 428.

[256] International Law and Human Rights, at 111-112.

[257] Lauterpacht, Brierly's Contribution to International Law, *in* J.L. Brierly, The Basis of Obligation in International Law xv (1958).

[258] See, e.g., on the revival of natural law in 20th century and its causes, International Law and Human Rights, at 112-113.

[259] The Grotian Tradition, at 307 and 363-364.

cal ideas and human progress, it will be found that the attraction of the short cuts of sound realism is matched – and surpassed – by the appeal to faith and to principle.[260]

These words of Lauterpacht not only reveal why he went back to Grotius in 1946, they also aptly describes his mission: in the long run human progress would benefit most from an appeal to faith in (the principle of) international law. Moral claims are instrumental for the progress of international law. This is how Grotius and Lauterpacht held off succumbing to the realist tendency of scorning international law. Instead, like Grotius, Lauterpacht intended to enhance the authority of international law in its task to preserve peace and Lauterpacht's focus on human rights and individual responsibility was vital in this respect. By going back to Grotius,[261] Lauterpacht was able to raise the fundamental questions: who is man? what is the source of natural law? Subsequently, along the lines of the Grotius tradition, Lauterpacht outlined his conception of international law. Lauterpacht's son tells us that his father considered his 1946 article *The Grotian Tradition of International Law* the most important he had ever written.[262] And maybe this was both due to its relevance to the study of international law as well as to him personally, as it was mainly a quest into the fundamentals of his own legal theory and a confirmation of his faith in international law.

Lauterpacht thoroughly examined Grotius' rejection of the realist doctrines as laid down in *De Jure Belli ac Paci*, adding his own reflections throughout.[263] He concluded, for example, that after three centuries during which the right to war had been considered the supreme expression of sovereignty, now, in his lifetime, '[w]ar ha[d] ceased to be a supreme prerogative of States. The Grotian distinction between just and unjust war is once more part of positive international law.'[264] The right of absolute neutrality had vanished, moreover, under the UN Charter, which included a collective duty to secure peace and to punish aggression. Grotius' challenges of these realist doctrines have become part of what Lauterpacht felt to be the 'guiding ideas' of the Grotian tradition. The unity of its guiding (natural law) principles, and the ever strong 'moulding force' emanating from them,[265] have made *De Jure Belli ac Pacis* the foundation of the Grotian

---

[260] Id., at 362-363.

[261] Lauterpacht had of course studied Grotius before. In his book, Private Sources and Analogies of International Law (1927), hereinafter: Private Sources, Lauterpacht had briefly analysed Grotius' position on the question of private law as a source of international law. He explained that private or Roman law might be a source or evidence of the law of nature and as such, since Grotius 'certainly regarded [the law of nature] as the obvious source from which we may fill the gaps of the 'instituted' law of nations,' it could not be maintained that Grotius repudiated private law as a source of international law altogether. This outlook on natural law as the source of the 'completeness' of international law would be part of Lauterpacht's theory throughout his lifetime, but his study of Grotius' work – as published in 1946 – is of a different nature. The Private Sources, at 14.

[262] E. Lauterpacht, Editor's note to The Grotian Tradition, at 307.

[263] Such as the double standard of morality, absolute state sovereignty, the 'reason of state' ideology, the doctrine of unqualified neutrality, and the absolute right of war.

[264] The Grotian Tradition, at 349.

[265] Id., at 327.

tradition of international law, according to Lauterpacht, even though Grotius himself 'cannot [be] consider[ed]... as what is usually described as a 'Grotian' who has accomplished a workable synthesis of natural law and State practice.' Despite Grotius' definitional inaccuracy concerning natural law and the 'confusing eclecticism in the use of sources,'[266] it is this concept of *unity* that spoke to Lauterpacht so persuasively.[267]

As it is impossible here to deal with every specific doctrine, it will suffice to outline Lauterpacht's conception of law in the light of four core ideas of the Grotian tradition: 1) the subjection of states to the Rule of Law; 2) the law of nature as the basis (and continuing source) of international law; 3) the concept of human nature and the law; and 4) the identity of subjects, individuals and states.

First, *the* 'central' feature of the Grotian conception, all international relations are subject to international law. 'There are no lacunae in that subjection of States to the rule of law.'[268] Lauterpacht reaffirmed this principle immediately after WWII and again in 1950, when he once more explained that this was the only way towards human and international progress, even at a time of Cold War:

> The reality of that progress has been obscured by the more tangible and menacing reality of the division of the world into two opposing groups of States – a cleavage which seems to engulf hope and to rule out further improvement. The outlook is dark unless that ideological cleavage – otherwise legitimate and, subject to the respect of the sanctity of human personality, in some respects beneficent – is contained within the secure channels of the law.[269]

The future would be bleak, unless politics submitted to the law and unless the Cold War and its ideological divide were managed by international law instead of by power politics. The quotation above contradicts the criticism from the realists that idealists like Lauterpacht were blind to the political reality surrounding them and too naïve to take a stand. Lauterpacht was well aware of the realities of international life and was indeed closely involved in many of its aspects.[270] Lauterpacht's analysis differed significantly and fundamentally from that of the

---

[266] Id., at 311-315.

[267] He considered the great value of *De Jure Belli ac Pacis* to be its 'significant affirmation of the unity of all law and of the final place of international law in the general scheme of legal science.' Id., at 326.

[268] Id., at 327.

[269] H. Lauterpacht, International Law after the Second World War, lecture given on 7 May 1950 at the Hebrew University of Jerusalem, *in* E. Lauterpacht (Ed.), International Law: being the Collected Papers of Hersch Lauterpacht (1970-1978), Vol. 2, at 167.

[270] Declaration of Independence of the State of Israel, ILC (International Law Commission), European Convention of Human Rights, to mention only a few. Moreover, his rejection of, for example, the distinction 'between justiciable and non-justiciable disputes and between legal and political disputes' was mainly based on realistic calculations, as it was 'more largely grounded in the nationalistic concerns of governments than in legal theory.' See, P.C. Jessup and R.R. Baxter, The contribution of Sir Hersch Lauterpacht to the Development of International Law, 55 *AJIL* 98 (1961).

realists, because it was both ethically *and* politically grounded. In the Grotian conception, the international community is a political as well as moral unity.[271] Humanity may be organised in states, yet its *unity* of humanity is both a fact and source of morality. The universal law of humanity also applies to the relations among states, which are members of the international community. The moral unity of mankind prescribes that international law has not merely the Sovereign Will of States as its source but *also* the Law of Nature or Natural Justice. The international Rule of Law prevents the exclusion of the ethical from international law and thus intends to counterbalance the dominance of Sovereign power and 'contain' the struggle for power 'within the secure channels of [international] law.'

Secondly, in the Grotian perception, 'the Law of Nature [i]s an independent source of international law.' Considering the shortcomings of the international legal order, natural law, as an independent and 'direct' source of law, has a superior role to play: as a 'higher law' it 'must assert itself – i.e., the persuasive but potent *authority of reason* and *principle* derived from the necessary coexistence of a plurality of States.' In Grotius' treatise too:

> [t]he significance of the law of nature ... treatise is that it is the ever-present source for supplementing the voluntary Law of Nations, for judging its adequacy in the light of ethics and reason, and for making the reader aware of the fact that the will of States cannot be the exclusive or even, in the last resort, the decisive source of the Law of Nations. This aspect of the system of Grotius has become an integral part of the doctrine and of the practice of the modern Law of Nations.[272]

This is the role Lauterpacht also attributed to natural law: to correct or supplement positive international law and thus prevent it from being disconnected from justice. It is also a characteristic of the Grotian approach to conjoin positivism and natural law. In Lauterpacht's synthesis: 'positive international law ... incorporate[s] ideas of natural law and justice.'[273] Hence, Lauterpacht regarded the 'general principles' of Article 38 of the ICJ Statute as positive legal recognition of this supplementing role of natural law.[274] In the field of international law, natural law 'has acted as a lever of progress.'[275] It should continue to do so, to provide ethical and rational principles necessary to judge and enhance the quality of positive international law. In the Neo-Grotian concept, international law thus consisted of voluntary law and natural law, but 'the binding force even of that part of it that originates in consent is based on the law of nature as expressive of the social nature of man.'

---

[271] The Grotian Tradition, at 328-329

[272] Id., at 329-333. Emphasis added.

[273] Kelsen's Pure Theory, at 429.

[274] Natural law as a more direct source of law, freeing it from positivistic limitations, served Lauterpacht also in his argument on the doctrine of material completeness to prevent *non-liquet* orders, and in his conception of the international judge as a natural law-representative in the international community.

[275] The Grotian Tradition, at 333.

Thirdly, the Grotian tradition is marked by the idea that the source of this secularised form of natural law in human nature itself. We have already touched upon the different perspectives of the realists and the idealists concerning human nature. Lauterpacht qualified this theme of the concept of human nature as 'perhaps *the* problem of political thought.'[276] Hence, in order to counter the realist approach with a more optimistic view of human nature – since '[t]here is perhaps no political writer in whose system that conception of the nature of man is more prominent than in Grotius',' – Lauterpacht turned to Grotius' 'faith in the rational constitution of man and his capacity to see reason and to learn from experience.'[277] The conception of man as an essentially selfish power-seeking being, which made of 'the idea of a sense of moral duty rising supreme over desire and passion' 'a figment of imagination fatal alike to action and to survival,' was, according to Lauterpacht, 'the typical *realistic* approach of *contempt* towards the 'little breed' of man.'[278] Lauterpacht's outlook thus differed profoundly from Carr's and Morgenthau's view. Their opposite attitudes towards rationalism may be explained by their fundamentally different views on the causes of fascism and Nazism. Morgenthau saw fascism as the appalling but logical end of rationalism while Lauterpacht explained it through its complete irrationality. Lauterpacht held however that Nazi and Fascist 'totalitarianism and its denial of fundamental human freedoms drew their mystical inspiration from the philosophical revolt *against reason.*' In the canonical *International Law and Human Rights* (1950), he explained that against this background it was 'inevitable' that 'the desire to vindicate human rights should, once more, ally itself with the rationalist foundations ... of the philosophy of natural law.'[279]

In other words, Lauterpacht rejected the pessimistic vision of man in the realist conception of international relations for misconceiving men and states forever and exclusively struggling for power and their own self-interest. Lauterpacht believed just the opposite as being more realistic and true: 'that man in the long run rejects a political philosophy which makes the physical power of the state and not the dignity and rights of man the final value ...'[280] Man in this view was not in-

[276] Id. See also, International Law and Human Rights.

[277] The Grotian Tradition, at 333: '... the nature of man [is the nature of] ... a being intrinsically moved by a desire for social life, endowed with a ample measure of goodness, altruism, and morality, and capable of acting on general principles and of learning from experience. He admits man is an animal, but one different in kind from other animals. That difference consists in his impelling desire for society – ... for peaceful and organized life according to the measure of his intelligence. It is a difference the essence of which is the denial of the assertion that 'every animal is impelled by nature to seek only its own good'.'

[278] Id., at 333-334. Emphasis added. In 1953, Lauterpacht responded again to the non-abating criticism from the realist side: '[The realist] is pessimistic about the capacity of man to learn from experience, as indeed about the capacity of man to improve. For him human nature does not change; and human nature is bad. Contempt for the 'little breed' of men is a dogma of the [modern] realist.' On Realism, at 61-62.

[279] International Law and Human Rights, at 112.

[280] On Realism, 58-59.

trinsically moved by the blind desire for (increased) power, but by the desire for a peaceful society, i.e., not by egoism, but by solidarity, not by instinct, but by reason. It was his postulate to keep 'faith in the sovereignty of the rational human will' and in 'the power of man ... as a rational social being.' Like Grotius, Lauterpacht based his conception of (international) law on 'the social nature and *intrinsic goodness of man.*' However, the resulting 'element of morality and rationality ... is not limited to the conduct of individuals.'[281]

Fourthly, it is part of the Grotian tradition to extend '[the] all-pervading element of morality and rationality' to the international conduct of states. Or rather, the rules governing the conduct of individuals and states are 'essentially identical'. This Grotian teaching 'has proved a beneficent weapon in the armoury of international progress.' Lauterpacht recognised this 'essential identity' of all legal rules because of the simple fact that

> States *are composed of* individual human beings; it results from the fact that behind the mystical, impersonal, and therefore necessarily irresponsible personality of the metaphysical State there are the actual subjects of rights and duties, namely, individual human beings. This is the true meaning of the Grotian analogy of States and individuals. The individual is the ultimate unit of all law, international and municipal, in the double sense that the obligations of international law are ultimately addressed to him and that the development, the well-being, and the dignity of the individual human being are a matter of direct concern of international law.[282]

International law therefore had a moral content as much as municipal law, and the dictates of reason and of the general principles of law underpinned it just the same. '["A]fter all" States are individuals.'[283] They were not *like* but *composed of* individuals and therefore all law was ultimately addressed to individual human beings, hence, the identity of all subjects.

In line with this principle of identity and its intended object of progress, Lauterpacht did not accept the argument that morality weakens when man finds himself within a group. Lauterpacht rejected the double standard of morality doctrine, which validated a lower moral standard for state behaviour, and was the 'hall-mark of ... the realistic approach.'[284] This realist argument would have it that the individual delegates his or her vices to the group and that group behaviour (including state behaviour) was consequently always of a lower moral level than individual behaviour. Lauterpacht warned against 'exaggerating' the immoral inclinations of groups and stressed that:

---

[281] The Grotian Tradition, at 333-336. Emphasis added.

[282] Id. In the omitted footnote Lauterpacht pointed to the Nuremberg Judgment of 31 August 1946, in which 'we find an illustration of the practical implications of the problem.'

[283] Id., at 337.

[284] In this respect, Lauterpacht pointed to Niebuhr's book, Moral Man and Immoral Society, and E.H. Carr's The Twenty Years' Crisis. Lauterpacht also dealt with Niebuhr and Carr in his 1941 manuscript, Professor Carr on International Morality, at 80-82.

there has been a tendency to ignore the factors which operate in the opposite direction and to represent the existing manifestations of the 'double standard of morality' as inescapably inherent in State action in the international sphere.

Lauterpacht did acknowledge the psychological 'tendency towards the relaxation of the moral conduct of individuals acting in a group,' but the realist's lack of faith in man's capacity to act collectively in an intelligent and moral way and their denial of the sovereignty of the human will as 'an agency shaping the destiny of man' were unacceptable to him. He held that '[l]ike other manifestations of desire and instinct, they can be regulated and curbed by reason, by the impact of moral ideas, by law.'[285] Lauterpacht's faith in the rationality of man, the rule of law, and the *Rechtsstaat* stood firm.[286] However, '[d]emocracy, although an essential condition of freedom, is not an absolute safeguard of it. That must lie outside and above the State.'[287] The source of this safeguard of international law was ultimately the same. There could be no double standard of morality. Not only was there but one ultimate source, but also but one ultimate addressee: the individual. Since all international legal rules ultimately address individual human beings, they were, even when acting collectively, all subject to the same moral and legal standard.[288]

The 'essential identity' principle makes way for 'the binding force of promises' as the 'scientific basis – that of the law of nature and of the social nature of man – for the 'volitional Law of Nations,' i.e., international law based on agreement, whether expressed in a treaty or implied by custom. In modern terminology, the rule *pacta sunt servanda* ...' The 'sanctity of promises' as the source of obligation was, more than an ultimate hypothesis, the principal norm of natural law which was binding upon every individual. [289] The sanctity of promises was obviously essential for a peaceful social life and the recognition of the social and moral aspect of human nature. Lauterpacht thus held on to the belief that in man 'the element of moral obligation and foresight asserts itself triumphantly over un-

---

[285] The Grotian Tradition, at 337; Also, On Realism, at 61-62.

[286] The Grotian Tradition, at 337-338: '[I]n a group association which, like the State, is to a large extent the artificial product of law and force rather than of the more direct and intimate interplay of crowd emotions, there is even less justification for treating as permanent and inevitable the factors which tend to weaken moral restraints in collective activities of men. The modern State is not a disorderly crowd given to uncontrollable eruptions of passion oblivious of moral scruples. It is, as a rule, governed by individuals of experience and ability who reach decisions after full deliberation and who are capable of forming a judgment on the ethical merits of the issues confronting them.'

[287] International Law and Human Rights, at 123.

[288] With the complete rejection of the realist doctrine of the double standard of morality, the 'raison d'Etat' is equally rejected as a fundamental factor in international relations. Humanity as a legal and moral unity (organised in states) prescribes that the 'standards of justice' apply to individuals and states just the same. The Grotian tradition moreover denies the existence of an unrestricted right of war, the distinction between just and unjust war is – according to Lauterpacht – 'once more part of positive international law.' *En plus*, '[u]nder the Charter of the United Nations neutrality is no longer an absolute right' either. The Grotian Tradition, at 340-352.

[289] Id., at 353-354; also, at 331.

bridled selfishness and passion, *both within the State and in the relations of States.*'[290]

'States are individuals,' thus is one of the most crucial elements of the Grotian tradition and of Lauterpacht's international legal thinking. For 'Grotius's true attitude' towards the fundamental rights and freedoms of the individual, Lauterpacht points to the seeds of the international protection of the individual against a Ruler who is the enemy of his people. In Lauterpacht's post-WWII 'neo-Grotian' outlook however the protection of the fundamental individual rights and duties becomes *the* central theme. It proceeds from the Grotian concept of the international community, which is a community of individuals and states and governed by natural and voluntary law.[291] Hence, Lauterpacht's definition:

International law is the body of rules of conduct, enforceable by external sanction, which confer rights and impose obligations primarily, though not exclusively, upon sovereign States and which owe their validity both to the consent of States as expressed in custom and treaties and to the fact of the existence of an international community of States and individuals. In that sense international law may be defined, more briefly (though perhaps less usefully), as the law of the international community.[292]

The final remark here has to be on federalism: Lauterpacht's concept of the international community[293] as a *civitas maxima* was federalist in nature, i.e., the international community as the moral and legal unity of humanity composed of individuals and organised as a federation of states. In Lauterpacht's view:

It is the abiding lesson of history and a compelling postulate of reason that a world-embracing federation – of which regional federations may be a necessary stage – is, in the words of Immanuel Kant, the only means of attaining perfect internal government, which is, in turn, the essential condition of the realization of the moral and intellectual capacities of mankind. If that is so, then the idea of an all-embracing federation of States must be

---

[290] Id., at 336.

[291] Collected Papers, at 28-30: '[The existence of an international community] is directly germane to the question of its sources. For, ..., it is largely from the fact of the existence of an international community that there is derived the authority of those rules and principles of law – whether they are called 'general principles of law' or 'the reason of the thing' or 'the law of nature' or 'the modern law of nature' – which owe their validity to a source of obligation other than the express or implied consent of States.'

[292] Collected Papers, at 9.

[293] '[T]he international community is a community not only of States but also of individuals both as members *generis humani* and, on an increasing scale, as parties to transactions and legal situations transcending the borders of the sovereign States. ... in so far as individuals, who are the ultimate subjects of all laws, are subjects of rights and duties grounded in international law-and they are so to a considerable extent-they are in a distinct sense members of international society.' H. Lauterpacht, Collected Papers, at 30-31. The international community's existence was due to interdependence and solidarity of human interests, in spite of conflicts of interests. 'Th[e] solidarity of interests is ... the cause and the expression of the social nature of man which underlies all law. ... the interests of States are but the interests of the individual human beings of which they are composed ...' Id.

regarded not as an infinite ideal but as an object of a moral duty of positive action and as a practical standard of human endeavour.[294]

The organisation of the *civitas maxima* as a world federation of states is here, like with Brunner, linked to the international protection of human rights and a relative notion of sovereignty. To arrive at this federalist political organisation of humanity, it is unrealistic to expect and pursue the end of state sovereignty, Lauterpacht stated. However, being neither sacred nor absolute, sovereignty is, and can be further, limited by the direct relationship between the individual and the world federation, i.e., the protection of human rights by international law. In other words, 'the rational solution of the problem of international organisation' is *not* 'the immediate and total disappearance of the international personality of States,' but 'the gradual limitation of rights of sovereignty within an association of States based on the continued recognition of the distinct international personality of States.' This limitation of sovereignty by international human rights obligations attributed to the states 'can be achieved without interference with their international personality and status.' The direct relation of the world community with the individual human being – the moral and legal objective that world federalism postulates – requires the institutionalisation of the international community for the effective protection of the natural rights of man. To advance towards 'a true federation of the world under the rule of law,' such a 'gradual acceptance of institutions' is much more realistic than pursuing the adoption of a world federal constitution. Lauterpacht's federalism thus is a teleological view on international law and the 'recognition and protection of human rights may in itself become a significant contributory factor in the consummation of the organized *civitas maxima*, with the individual human being in the centre of the constitution of the world.'[295]

4.4.3. Federalism and the use of ILP: the sovereignty of man and justice

With the UN Charter a new era in human government had begun, Lauterpacht contended. Thanks to the UN Charter, the individual was now a subject of natural *and* positive law. Lauterpacht managed to approach the United Nations positively and to discover in it proof of fundamental and systemic progress of the rule of law:

[T]he Charter of the United Nations introduced an innovation of the most profound significance: it solemnly recognized 'fundamental human rights' and 'the dignity and worth of the human person' and made repeated provision for the promotion by the United Nations of "universal respect for, and observance of, human rights and freedoms." In thus bringing within the province of the United Nations the crucial aspect of the relation of

[294] H. Lauterpacht, State Sovereignty and Human Rights (Lecture delivered on 8 May 1950 at the Hebrew University of Jerusalem), *in* Collected Papers, at 426. Hereinafter: State Sovereignty and Human Rights. See also, e.g., The Subjects-1948, at 111.

[295] State Sovereignty and Human Rights, at 426-430.

man and State, the Charter opened up the possibility of a new era in human government.[296]

Lauterpacht distinguished two preconditions for the eventual and continuing success of this 'new era' in international governance. In the first place, a shift had to occur in moral sovereignty or 'moral authority' from the state to the United Nations, i.e., from the national to the universal level. Secondly, in more practical terms, international lawyers needed to contribute to this process in order to 'preven[t] the potentialities opened up by the Charter from being thwarted by obsolete dogmas of legal doctrine.'[297] In this context, for the sake of a new era and the enhancement of (natural) justice Lauterpacht used ILP in two ways. In the first place, as the concept that made the advancement of world federalism possible and secondly, as the concept that recognises the individual as a member not only of the natural community of mankind but also of the international community governed by positive international law.

First, we have just seen how Lauterpacht distinguished sharply between the concepts of sovereignty and ILP. He uses the concept of ILP to further the federalist agenda, i.e., the development of international organisation for the recognition and protection of the rights of man. The world as a federation of states is a world of ILPs endowed with rights and obligations, hence, with limited sovereignty. International institutionalisation is the most realistic and effective way to advance towards the federal world system:

> Of these institutions the protection, within an association of a federal nature, of the rights of man, acknowledged and effectively guaranteed by the association, seems to offer more distinct prospects of realization than schemes based on the renunciation of the international personality of States.[298]

The ILP of the state is preserved within Lauterpacht's argument. In fact, it is an essential concept in relation to the state: the limitation of sovereignty is actually a shift in the composition of the state's attributes from rights to duties. No matter in which composition, the state is endowed with these attributes, rights and duties, a different composition for example an increase of obligations under international law may indeed limit sovereignty yet the state remains an international legal person just the same. This shift in the composition of attributes, i.e., the restriction of state sovereignty, is caused by the organisation and further institutionalisation of the direct relationship between the individual human being and the international community in effective human rights law. In other words, the distinct ILP of states is preserved in the process of federal integration, i.e., actually the process

[296] H. Lauterpacht, The International Protection of Human Rights, 70 *RCADI* 5 *et seq.* (1947-I).
[297] The International Protection of Human Rights, at 5-6.
[298] State Sovereignty and Human Rights, at 430.

of institutionalising the direct relationship of man and the international community in an international human rights framework.

Although Lauterpacht called for the 'revision' of the notion of ILP explicitly in order to take account of the developments in modern international life and law and stop it from becoming 'a fiction obstructive of progress,'[299] he thus did not argue the 'obliteration' of ILP of states,[300] like some of his Interbellum fellow-Revisionists had done. He did however oppose the traditional doctrine of the subjects. In established classical international legal theory, the concept of ILP is discussed as 'an *emanation* of the doctrine of sovereignty.'[301] Based hereupon, it was stated that the *structure* of international law prescribed the recognition of states as subjects *only*. sovereign states consent to being subject to international law and by exercising their sovereign power choose to be international legal persons. This 'doctrine is an obstacle to the proper understanding and effectiveness of international duties.' Lauterpacht explained:

> Who is the subject of international duties? Is it the abstract, metaphysical personality of the State, or is it the individual human being in his capacity either as the representative of the State or as the ultimate unit of the international community? To say that the State – and the State only – is the subject of international duties is to say, in the last resort, that international duties bind no one; it is *to interpose a screen of irresponsibility* between the rule of law and the agency expected to give effect to it. ... ... [This interposition moreover] results indirectly in a diminished or qualified application in the sphere of international law of general principles of law as adopted among civilized communities and, in particular, of generally accepted standards of ethics.[302]

By making a sharp conceptual distinction between ILP and sovereignty, Lauterpacht preserved ILP: he did not use it in the conventional way as a 'screen of irresponsibility' yet used the concept to reinforce universal justice by arguing that ILP like states have to conform to the standards of ethics or justice too. 'In this as in many other matters,' Lauterpacht contended that 'progress is dependent on the return to Grotius, who stigmatized as an error the view of those who hold "that the standards of justice, which they insist upon in the case of individuals within the state is inapplicable to a nation or the ruler of a nation." (*Proleg*. 21) But such progress is, in turn dependent upon the wider acceptance of the view that the ultimate subjects of international duties are individual human beings.'[303] To this progress Lauterpacht intended to contribute, in the first place, rather than to institutionalise state irresponsibility, by using ILP as the quality that holds the state's responsibility to conform to the standards of justice.

---

[299] Collected Papers, at 472.

[300] State Sovereignty and Human Rights, at 427.

[301] The International Protection of Human Rights, at 9. Emphasis added.

[302] Collected Papers, at 280-283. In other words, the traditional and 'predominant doctrine' is the 'theoretical and practical foundation of the phenomenon of double morality.'

[303] Collected Papers, at 281-282. Note omitted.

Lauterpacht's pragmatism stands out. On the one hand, Lauterpacht believed that 'reasons of convenience and justice' required that 'the collective entity of the State' in most cases was 'the subject of responsibility.' His realism forced him to be pragmatic: 'in the normal course of affairs... international law is primarily a law between States.'[304] It would not be 'just' to impute responsibility to individuals acting on behalf of or as organs of the state 'in fulfilling normal [state] obligations of treaties or of customary international law,' unless the individual violated an international legal rule which was directly incumbent upon him. In general, responsibility for such duties performed under international law 'should be imputed to the State as a whole and ... the State should appear exclusively as the subject of international law for the purpose.' Lauterpacht here included considerations of 'justice' and 'the reason of the thing' and the preservation of 'peace' to support this type of responsibility of states.

On the other hand, however, with regard to responsibility for *criminal* acts, Lauterpacht did not postulate that the state as a whole should be held primarily responsible, but rather the organ or individual which/who put the criminal act in motion: 'the criminal responsibility of the State is of a *subsidiary* character.' The individual human being is the 'primary subject' of criminal responsibility.[305] In the context of the preservation of peace, the recognition of individual responsibility moreover 'tends to diminish the necessity for and the scope of collective punishment of States.' Collective responsibility was not under all circumstances 'inherently unjust,' it was 'at best, a rough instrument of justice, and there are compelling reasons for reducing the scope of its operation. It can be so reduced by the effective recognition of the individual as a subject of international duties.'[306]

Secondly, Lauterpacht indeed argued the recognition of individuals as subjects of international rights and duties. The traditional position against the recognition of individuals as subjects of international law upheld that since individuals do not participate in international law's creation and have no access to international courts to enforce their rights; they are objects rather than subjects of international law. In this conventional perspective, the individual, having neither international rights and duties nor a procedural capacity under international law, is not an international legal subject. Lauterpacht's opposition of the traditional position built

[304] 'Independent political societies function in the form of the corporate entity of the State, and it is appropriate that the general principles of law applicable to juridical personality and to corporate capacity for action should apply also in case of States. The legal structure of a limited liability company is as necessary in the relations of States as in private life.' The Subjects-1948, at 107.

[305] The Subjects-1948, at 109, and at 107: '[U]nless the subject of international duties is thought of as identical with the individual human being as distinguished from the mystical entity of the State, we open the door wide to that dualism of moral standards which, under the guise of 'reason of State,' has proved a disintegrating and destructive factor in the sphere of international morality and peace.'

[306] Id., at 107-111. Emphasis added. Collective guilt and responsibility were of course of great topical concern with regard to the discussions on 'the German problem.'

on the distinction between the question of the procedural capacity of a subject and the capacity of having ILP, i.e., the quality of being the subject of international rights and duties: 'The two questions are not synonymous.'[307]

To start with the procedural capacity, Lauterpacht in the first place contended that law was also law when it was not (yet) enforced. It is possible to have rights, even if you need a representative to have them enforced. The (non-) existence of a recognised procedural capacity to bring legal action does not impede the existence of rights and duties. The traditional positivist argument that the *structure* of the international legal system hampered the recognition of such a capacity in the individual was untrue,[308] according to Lauterpacht: 'there is nothing inherent in the structure of international law which prevents individuals ... from being parties to proceeding before international courts.'[309] For that purpose, he further argued, Article 34 of the ICJ Statute, which determines the Court's jurisdiction, should be changed into 'a less uncompromising and more practical definition,' so as to include the access of non-state entities, like private corporations and individuals.[310] Until this international procedural capacity will have become part of the system, Lauterpacht felt that the interests of the individual should be served by states acting on behalf of the general interest of the international community and that to that end the nationality of claims doctrine had to be abandoned.[311] The state is the intermediary between the individual and the international interest, and until the system has progressed, it represents the individual who is endowed with rights and duties under international law.

In brief, the individual's lack of procedural capacity under international law does not preclude him from having rights – from being endowed with ILP.[312]

Having distinguished procedural capacity from ILP, Lauterpacht argued that with the adoption of the United Nations Charter the individual had become a subject of rights under positive international law. For the first time in the history of *positive* international law, there was now a legal document recognising the individual's fundamental rights and freedoms.[313] Repeatedly, he stressed that the UN

---

[307] The Subjects-1947, at 455. Also, The Subjects-1948, at 97.

[308] International Law and Human Rights, at 4-5.

[309] The Subjects-1947, at 453.

[310] Id., at 453 *et seq.*

[311] Id., at 456: 'The State invoking the provisions of the treaty in favour of an individual who is not its national no longer acts on behalf of its own particular interest; it acts on behalf of the international interest in the welfare of the individual or groups of individuals concerned and of its own general interest in the maintenance of respect for treaties. Emphasis is thus given to the direct relation between the individual and the international interest. The same applies to treaties which regulate the condition of stateless persons.'

[312] See, e.g., for Lauterpacht's argument on what he felt was 'one of the central problems' at the time: an effective, individual right of petition in the international framework of human rights protection to correct this (procedural) shortcoming, State Sovereignty and Human Rights, at 416.

[313] See also, The Subjects-1948, at 101.

Charter contained implied *legal obligations* for states with regard to the recognition and protection of human rights:[314]

As a result of the Charter of the United Nations-as well as of other changes in international law-the individual has acquired a status and a stature which have transformed him from an *object* of international compassion to a *subject* of international right.[315]

By recognising the individual as a subject of rights, the UN Charter recognised the individual as a subject of international law. Having rights includes having duties, or so positive law and logic demand Lauterpacht rightly point out – 'the proposition that individuals can be subjects of international *rights* necessarily involves the corollary that they can be subjects of international *duties*'. Moreover, unless individuals have duties, the law would be a futile enterprise. This is particularly true as states are only individuals and one standard of morality applies. Lauterpacht quoted from the Judgment delivered by the Nuremberg Tribunal on 30 September 1946 to support this view: 'Crimes against international law are committed by men, not by abstract entities, and only by punishing individuals who commit such crimes can the provisions of international law be enforced.'[316] One may wonder if a more realistic assessment is possible. Positive international law (the Charter of the Nuremberg Tribunal and its judgments, as well as the UNGA Resolution on the prohibition of genocide) thus firmly established individual criminal responsibility[317] under international law and as such recognised the individual as an international legal subject, i.e., endowed with ILP.[318]

Moreover, the doctrine of the incorporation of international law as part of municipal law meant that 'in effect ... rights and duties created by international law are directly applicable to individuals through the instrumentality of municipal courts and that, to that extent, individuals are subjects of the law of nations,' also due to the fact that the positive municipal law of most states considered international law 'a direct source of rights and obligations of individuals enforceable by municipal courts.' As this was so widely accepted, Lauterpacht argued that it

[314] Id., at 101-102. Also, The International Protection of Human Rights (1947); International Law and Human Rights (1950); State Sovereignty and Human Rights (1950); Towards an International Bill of Rights (BBC radio talk, 1949).

[315] International Law and Human Rights, at 4. Emphasis added. Also, The Subjects-1948, at 112-113.

[316] The Subjects-1947, at 438-439. See also, The Subjects-1948, at 111. Emphasis added.

[317] Lauterpacht observed: 'Unless not only the State as such but also its organs are made personally responsible for complying with the measures laid down by the international authority, the effectiveness of the international regulation of *this vital problem* will be considerably impaired. The magnitude of the interests involved requires that that liability should be of a criminal character.' Subjects-1948, at 110.

[318] He also called to mind that older rules of positive international law, like those on piracy or warfare, had also addressed individuals directly. Especially in the case of the law of warfare, 'the apparently established doctrine breaks down altogether. The law declines, in this matter, to accept the artificial distinction between the State and those acting on its behalf.' The Subjects-1947, at 443. See also, The Subjects-1948, at 106.

could even be considered a rule of customary international law.[319] The monism of Lauterpacht's neo-Grotian conception of (international) law contended the rejection of the doctrine of the 'dualism of subjects,'[320] i.e., what we discussed as the 'identity of subjects' above.

Lauterpacht thus established that the traditional position that states were the exclusive subjects of international law was false and that positive international law itself recognised others than state entities as its subjects.[321] He explained that to distinguish 'whether a [non-state] person or body is a subject of international law' two elements are relevant: actual international practice and 'the *reason* of the law.' With these two pragmatic criteria, the *inclusion* of new subjects of international law is no longer hampered.[322] The reason of the law is the furtherance of justice and the protection of the individual human being. The creation of IOs – endowed with ILP – to further international co-operation and the protection of human rights conforms for example to this objective.

Finally, I would like to deal with the relation between universal justice and the use of ILP in Lauterpacht's work. Lauterpacht used ILP to *open up* a new era of international governance and intended to contribute to the development of international organisation and the effective protection of human rights. For an answer on the question *what* is the true *source* of the individual's ILP, we have to turn to the *reason* of international law – the protection of the individual's well-being, dignity and emancipation – rather than to positive law.

The '*reason* of (international) law' is one of the guiding principles for Lauterpacht's scholarship on international law, in general, and for the determination of the subjects of international law, in particular. The '*reason* of the law' principle demands an acute awareness of the needs of modern international life. Indeed, Lauterpacht observed that '[i]n modern international society the interests to be protected and regulated can no longer be entrusted *exclusively* to States. These interests call for the recognition of new subjects of rights and duties conceived as the *rational* means of international social welfare.' *Reason* prescribes that new subjects of law are included in the system and this should not be pre-

---

[319] He thus beat the positivist school on its own territory by providing evidence of both treaty and customary international law, sustaining that individuals – because they had rights and duties under international law – were subjects of international law.

[320] Id., at 443-444.

[321] Lauterpacht listed the following non-state entities as subjects of international law: insurgents (both recognised and non-recognised belligerents), the Holy See (during the years 1917-1929), the British Dominions before they acquired full sovereignty and thereby full ILP, and IOs like the UN, ILO, ICAO, International River Commissions, etc. These IOs are created by state consent and their ILP is either explicitly or implicitly laid down in the international treaty upon which they are based. ILP is implicitly attributed through the functions assigned and the tasks entrusted to the international organisation. It provides the necessary flexibility and is rooted in 'the reason of the thing' – the reason for the institution's creation. Cases of international arbitration between a private or public corporation and a state are also examples of the attribution of a degree of ILP to a non-state entity.

[322] Id., at 444. See also, The Subjects-1948, at 100 and 105.

vented by the misconception that the problem of the subjects is 'one of mere doctrine:'

[It] is rather one of not permitting the dead hand of obsolete theory to continue to lie heavily upon the development of international organisation. It is a question of meeting satisfactorily the requirements of an expanding and developing law not limited to the niceties of international intercourse but *concerned with the well-being of the individuals as the ultimate units of human society* and with the adequacy of the instruments which serve their needs.[323]

The doctrine on the ILP concept touches upon the fundamental objective of the law, which consists of protecting and regulating the needs and interests of the individual members of the international society: their individual well-being and dignity. Hence, the doctrine of the subjects is related the law's standard of justice:

[H]uman dignity and considerations of utility alike rebel against the idea of the State as the sole guardian of the interests of man. ... But it is *inadmissible* that the State should claim, in the conditions of the modern world, that it is entitled to *exclude* from this legal sphere individuals and non-governmental bodies which may be created for that purpose.[324]

...

[T]he claim of States to the *exclusive* representation and management of internationally relevant interests-a claim which is an accompaniment of the current pretensions of sovereignty-lacks justification and is a legitimate cause of resentment.[325]

The state's claim of exclusiveness, which made it 'an impenetrable barrier between the individual and the greater society of all humanity,' was incompatible with the *reason* of the state's existence, which was 'to safeguard the interests of the individual human being and to render possible the fulfilment, through freedom, of his wider duty to man and society.'[326] To use the dogma of state sovereignty and its twin doctrine of states as the sole subjects of international law as a joint instrument for *excluding* other entities from protecting human interests was, in Lauterpacht's view, *unjust*, contrary to human dignity itself, and in addition – and more pragmatically – contrary to effectiveness.

A contrario, one could say, his argument implied the *inclusion* of non-state entities with an appeal to human dignity itself and its effective protection, as *exclusion* was a 'legitimate cause of resentment.'[327] Natural justice, the needs and

[323] Id., at 450. Also, International Law and Human Rights, at 19, 69.

[324] The Subjects-1948, at 118. International Law and Human Rights, at 68. Emphasis added.

[325] International Law and Human Rights, at 68-69. Also, The Subjects-1948, at 118. Emphasis added.

[326] Id., at 68. See also, at 76-77.

[327] Id., at 68-70. See also, International Law and Human Rights, at 18-19. The Subjects-1947, at 450. 'In modern international society the interests to be protected and regulated can no longer be entrusted *exclusively to States*. These interests call for the recognition of new subjects of rights and duties conceived as the rational means of international welfare.' Emphasis added.

interests of man, both individually and collectively as mankind, demand inclusion to further the (Grotian) development of law and international organisation.

'The deeper significance' of the recognition of the individual as the subject of international rights and duties was for Lauterpacht its contribution to the (Grotian) progress of international law and the international society. As a subject of international law every individual was subordinate to international law, which meant one step forward in the realisation of the universal legal organisation of humanity into world federation under the Rule of Law. It was this long-term 'idealistic' objective that gave his scholarship direction:

[T]he gradual integration of international society in the direction of a supra-national Federation of the World-a development which must be regarded as the ultimate rational postulate of the political organisation of man-will be achieved by sudden and drastic changes in the legal organisation of mankind.[328]

The recognition of the individual as an international legal subject contributed to the increase of universal justice as it confirmed a principle of the Grotian tradition, i.e., the rejection of the double standard of morality, because it led to *one* 'universal code of ethics' being binding upon individuals as well as states.[329]

His natural law philosophy surfaced in Lauterpacht's subsequent remark that 'The question whether that innovation is constitutive or merely *declaratory* of a pre-existing higher law is of interest but not of decisive importance.'[330] However, perhaps not decisive in a world of positive law, it is indeed of interest and essence here, since it concerns the problem of the *source* of ILP: state recognition or the law of nature. The answer to this question demands a look underneath the surface of positive law:

[T]here is a deeper connexion between the two doctrines [of State sovereignty and subjects of law]. State sovereignty, the incarnation of the supreme will of the State as the exclusive source of the law, must disdain the idea of persons owing their quality as subjects of the law to a source independent of the will of States. That source is the fact that, in relation to both rights and duties, the individual is the *final* subject of all law. To that extent the practice of States inasmuch as it expressly confers rights and imposes duties upon the individual must-important as it is in showing the artificiality and the accuracy of the established doctrine in the matter-be regarded as essentially *declaratory*. This view, too, is incompatible with the notion of sovereignty as ordinarily conceived. It does not follow that it is a view which is not beneficent in practice and not in accordance with the *true purpose* of international law.[331]

What is this source of ILP – i.e., the source *constituting* the possession of the quality of a subject of international rights and duties – to which Lauterpacht re-

[328] The Subjects-1948, at 111.
[329] Id., at 111-112.
[330] Id., at 113.
[331] Id., at 118-119. Emphasis added. Also, International Law and Human Rights, at 69.

fers and that is independent of the will of states? It is the fact that the individual human being is the *ultimate subject* of all law. State practice and the newly created positive international law were *essentially declaratory*, and therefore not constitutive of these rights. The fundamental rights of man are inherent in his human nature. Natural law or justice stipulates these fundamental rights and duties. With the recent developments, positive international law as come to recognise these rights and thus constituted by their incorporation in positive law. 'The Charter of the United Nations, in recognising the fundamental human rights and freedoms, has to that extent *constituted* individuals subjects of the law of nations.'[332]

Considering the recognition of the two sources of international law – consent and the laws of nature or 'the reason of the thing' (i.e., the moral and legal imperative of humanity) – in the Grotian tradition we may observe that the Charter had a residual *declaratory* function. The legal relevance attributed to the international human society as the *reason* of international law affected the issue concerning the subjects of international law, because 'certain principles follow from the very existence and the assumed purposes of international society.'[333] Natural law principles emerged from this reality of a society of humanity. The Charter of the Nuremberg Military Tribunal in particular confirmed this position through the recognition of 'crimes against humanity,' as laid down in Article 6, and the judgment of the tribunal that 'the enactment of 'crimes against humanity' constitutes the recognition of fundamental human rights superior to the law of the sovereign State.'[334] There was indeed a law that is *superior* to positive international law: the law of nature.

Lauterpacht found that state practice had now accepted and codified that 'having regard to the *inherent purposes* of international law, of which the individual is the ultimate unit, he is in that capacity a subject of international law.'[335] The '*inherent purpose*' was what Lauterpacht had elsewhere called 'the reason of the thing'. If the independent source of international law was the fact that the individual was the *final* subject of all law, then the ultimate source of international law was the well-being and dignity the individual human being and any rule or action contrary to these conditions was illegal, i.e., contrary to international law.

---

[332] International Law and Human Rights, at 61.

[333] The Subjects-1947, at 444.

[334] The Subjects-1948, at 105. 'Crimes against humanity are crimes regardless of whether they were committed in accordance with and in obedience to the national law of the accused. Such acts are deemed to violate the sanctity of the human personality to such a degree as to make irrelevant reliance upon the law of the State which ordered them. To lay down that crimes against humanity are punishable is, therefore, to assert the existence of rights of man grounded in a law superior to the law of the State. Thus, upon analysis, the enactment of crimes against humanity in an international instrument signifies the acknowledgement of fundamental rights of the individual recognised by international law.' Id., at 104.

[335] Id. Emphasis added.

It seems like the issue in reverse: the subject becomes the source of law, whereas traditionally law would determine who is subject.[336]

The individual is the source of all law because of the '*absolute sanctity of human personality.*' Inalienable human rights severely impugned the absoluteness of sovereignty. Lauterpacht broke with the traditional doctrine that states were the exclusive recipients of ILP and thereby eliminated the often-cited obstacle to the evolution towards a world federation or community under the rule of law and the advancement of international law in the protection of human dignity and freedom.

In so far as the denial of the fundamental rights of man has been associated with the nation-State rights asserting the claim to ultimate reality and utterly subordinating the individual to a mystic and absolute personality of its own, the recognition of these rights is a brake upon exclusive and aggressive nationalism which is the obstacle, both conscious and involuntary, to the idea of a world community under the rule of law. Expressed in positive terms, such recognition, inasmuch as it amounts to a tangible international guarantee of the rights of man, is destined to become a powerful source, based on mutuality of interests, of international allegiance. An international legal system which aims at effectively safeguarding human freedom in all its aspects is no longer an abstraction. It is as real as man's interest in the guarantee and the preservation of his inalienable rights as a rational and moral being. International law, which has excelled in punctilious insistence on the respect owed by one sovereign State to another, henceforth acknowledges the sovereignty of man.

By proclaiming the sovereignty of man over the sovereignty of states, Lauterpacht argued that the (inalienable) fundamental human rights were 'superior' to positive international law, that they were 'rights superior to the law of the Sovereign State.' Lauterpacht declared 'the recognition of inalienable human rights and the recognition of the individual as a subject of international law' to be 'synonymous:'

---

[336] Lauterpacht justified this reversal through his belief that law was a mental phenomenon. Man was the only creator of and link between the real world and the world as it should be and thus the only entity to make positive law that approached justice. This is quite evident, for example, in the realm of human rights, which are inalienable because man is *man*, because his nature is the source of his fundamental rights. Law as a system has an ultimate source from which the whole order is derived by gradual concretisation. If the original source is formal, the law is defined in formal terms and rules are commands which are based on a hierarchically higher norm. If the original source is morality, or natural justice, the law will also incorporate a material component. As 'socially realisable justice' the legal order is composed of both positive law and corrective mechanisms to guarantee a sufficient level of morality. The individual human being is the only entity who has the capacity to grasp by approximation what is justice; he is the natural source for transforming moral norms into laws and policies. Hence, the individual is the vital link between morality and law. He is the only being endowed with reason and a conscience and therefore the only entity able to distinguish 'is' from 'ought.' The individual is able to seek justice and to translate it into practical arrangements and institutions. He alone can perform the rational mental act, either individually or collectively, by which law is created.

> [T]hey both signify *the recognition of a higher, fundamental law* not only on the part of States but also, through international law, on the part of the organised international community itself. That fundamental law, as expressed in the acknowledgement of the ultimate reality and the independent status of the individual, *constitutes both the moral limit and the justification of the international legal order*. Through them, it implies the promise that the organised international society *will not*, in turn, *degenerate into a tyrannical accumulation of power*. It is that danger which has been for many the reason of the determined opposition to the idea of an organised commonwealth of nations embracing all humanity. In that perspective the acknowledgment of *human rights and fundamental freedoms* on the part of the Members of the United Nations assumes *an added significance* of its own. The consequent recognition of *the individual human being as a subject of international law lends to the law* obtaining between sovereign States the beneficent complexion of a law of nations conceived as *the universal law of mankind*.[337]

The role/function natural law rules must (continue to) fulfil is that of 'the foundation of [the] ultimate validity' of positive international law. They need to be 'a standard of its approximation to justice.' Since natural rights and the law of nature are 'an expression of moral claims, they are a powerful lever of legal reform.'[338] It is for this reason that Lauterpacht would 'rather retain natural law with its possible abuses than cut off the branch of law from the tree of justice.'[339]

4.4.4. Conclusion

Lauterpacht's idealism was a realism of a different kind. It speaks from observations such as 'ideas are facts' or 'to deny the value of principle as a guide for human action is to deny the value of reason.'[340] To give direction and establish movement, ideas and ideals were essential. For the development of international law, the ideal to aim for: an international community – a *Civitatis maxima* – where every member of humanity could enjoy his rights and freedoms and live the social life desired by him, in peace, and as morally soundly as possible.

International law to Lauterpacht was the law of the international community, which ultimately comprised humanity, and humanity by its very nature comprised every individual. Therefore, all individuals were members of this international community of humanity and were as such endowed with natural rights and duties, in other words: with ILP. The source of fundamental human rights may be the law of nature, but their protection demands recognition and institutionalisation within positive international law. The UN Charter, which is binding upon its members, stipulates that member states have 'a legal duty not only to encourage and promote respect for these rights, but also to respect them.' '[A] legally authorized and effective machinery of direct impulsion' had to be es-

[337] International Law and Human Rights, at 70-72. Emphasis added.
[338] Id., at 74.
[339] Kelsen's Pure Science of Law, at 428.
[340] On Realism, at 63.

tablished.[341] This attitude again exemplifies how Lauterpacht's preoccupation with the recognition of the individual's ILP was based on *practical* concerns as well as on *foundational* considerations. Lauterpacht used the concept of ILP to argue the *inclusion* of non-state actors in the system, but he also used it in an attempt to enhance justice and the authority of international law.

Lauterpacht laid the foundations for progress in international (human rights) law during the post-WWII period. Unfortunately, he did not live to see the Covenants signed and implemented, but the value of his work for today's framework of human rights law and individual criminal responsibility can hardly be overestimated. With his post-WWII work in this field, he implemented the ideals of the interbellum revisionists, and made a strong theoretical as well as practical argument for individualising ILP and international law. He demonstrated that to accept ideals in order to direct action, whether within international affairs or international legal theory, might benefit actual developments and progress. The focus on human dignity and the institutionalisation of the protection of human rights and duties in international law was Lauterpacht's response to the urgent needs of international life. Power politics and ideological antagonism were so dominant that in his view only a strong and credible international law could sufficiently counterbalance them and submit all international affairs to the rule of law in order to ultimately guarantee the effective protection of individual freedom and dignity. His outspokenness in the debate between idealism and realism may have been labelled utopian, but was really rather pragmatic as a result of his introduction of the notion of 'the reason of the thing.'

Lauterpacht used the concept of ILP complete the transition from the mystical sanctity of the state-person's sovereignty to the 'Sanctity of the Human Personality.' The international protection of this sanctity and the emancipation of the human personality were difficult to establish during the Cold War. However, during the Cold War, realism and the development of international law could not have dome without so-called idealism. The two poles of international life and scholarship needed each other to continue and with the sufficient level of pragmatism in both managed to develop international law and human rights. Mainstream scholars like Friedmann took up the cause of legal progress and eventually, after 1989, it was given a serious chance to develop further into what Thomas Franck called, the 'Empowering of the Self.'

---

[341] State Sovereignty and Human Rights, at 417. The denial by the Commission of Human Rights of their right to hear and act upon individual complaints effectively meant the denial of the right to petition – this was unjustifiable in Lauterpacht's view: 'There is no prospect of the fulfilment of the purpose of the Charter in the matter of human rights and freedoms unless an effective right of petition is accepted as being of the essence of the system established by the Charter.' Id., at 421. 'The insistence on the right of the individual to lodge petitions is due to factors more *real* than any supposedly purely academic emphasis on the status of the individual as a subject of international law.' Id., at 424. Emphasis added.

4.5. MYRES SMITH MCDOUGAL (1906-1998)

4.5.1. Introduction

Political realism basically considered law to be largely irrelevant to international life. Power – or 'naked force' – was considered the only relevant factor. Foreign policy was to take only the national interest into account. International law was in crisis and one of the scholars who confronted this crisis and refused to accept the defeat of international law was Yale professor Myres McDougal, be it without losing sight of the significance of power. On the contrary, power is indeed one of the objectives or interests in foreign affairs.

In order to prove the relevance of international law, however, a totally different outlook was needed – comprising a different concept of law as well as a new vocabulary. McDougal rejected the 'pure power theory' of realists like Morgenthau and initially formulated his theory as a fundamental criticism of their position.[342] McDougal's disapproval of the realist approach may be summarised in three sentences (before dealing with his theory more extensively). First of all, according to McDougal, Morgenthau did not sufficiently recognise 'the increasing fractionalization of the nation state by functional groups,' and, moreover, 'greatly ... minimiz[ed] the degree to which today's 'community' or 'society' is in fact transnational.'[343] McDougal further rejected the realist conception of law as 'a static body of rigid rules.' He submitted that law was 'not merely a 'limitation' upon power but ... also a conscious, creative instrument in promoting both order and other values.'[344] And finally, concerning the realist attitude towards the relationship between law and political power, he remarked that:

> [they] profoundly misconceive law and power and greatly underestimate ... the role that law presently plays in the world power process and the role that, with a more effective balancing of power, it could be made to play in promoting and preserving the values of a free, peaceful, and abundant world society.[345]

4.5.2. International law as policy: authoritative decision-making processes

By way of elaboration, four elements of the above quotation will be addressed: McDougal's view on 'law and power,' the meaning of 'world power process,' his concept of international law, and, finally, the importance of 'values' within *the policy approach to international law.*

---

[342] McDougal agreed with Morgenthau that the balance of power in the world was important to the functioning of international law. As it was a fact of international life, it necessarily had to be incorporated into the ideas about international law. However, they approached the subject quite differently.

[343] McDougal, M.S., The Realist Theory in Pyrrhic Victory, 49 *AJIL* 377-378 (1955). See, for an illustration of Morgenthau's 'minimised' perception, Power among Nations, at 312.

[344] The Realist Theory in Pyrrhic Victory, at 377-378.

[345] A Contemporary Conception, at 160.

First of all, McDougal began his quest for a comprehensive theory which would be 'adequate to the crisis of [his] time' realising that law would be an 'illusion' if the concept of power – or 'effective control' – was excluded from the concept of law.[346] Traditionally the definitions of law tended to focus exclusively on the formal authority which enacts it. McDougal rejected traditional and contemporary legal theory's 'over-emphasis' on law as merely 'a system of rules.'[347] Contrary to Morgenthau, who distinguished law from power, McDougal argued that law and politics were closely related instead of 'distinct':[348] 'law is a policy process'. By rejecting the belief that law and policy were fairly distinguishable, McDougal broadened the concept of law beyond that of a merely formal definition of law as rules. Law as policy is a 'dynamic process'[349] and its obligatory nature is a matter of degree. This new concept of law brought along a vocabulary of its own.

Secondly, this planet needs a world public order that will structure and direct worldwide social human interaction – the 'world social process' – and that is actively involved in the pursuit and distribution of resources and values. The concept of 'process' is used here to indicate the continuous interaction among people involved in decision-making, i.e., in 'mak[ing] and enforc[ing] choices that affect the distribution of values among [the participants].' '[W]orld power processes' are those global social processes in which decision-making is controlled by power. *Power*: '... at the highest level of abstraction, ... may be most usefully defined as *participation* in the making of decisions that are attended by sanctions.'[350] The possibility of imposing sanctions indicates effective control.

Thirdly, those power processes that are also 'authoritative' decision-making processes are 'legal processes'. The nature of law may thus best be understood when viewed as a process of controlling and authoritative decision-making. Law is made up of policies that are produced by decision-makers, who are expected by the community to take certain decisions and formulate policy; who are, in essence, exercising 'formal authority'. *Power* becomes *formal authority* when the members of the community *expect* it to be exercised. In this approach, law is thus neither used nor suppressed by politics, but involves those decision-making processes of which 'effective control' and 'formal authority' are *both* constituent elements. Perceiving law as such a process, McDougal successfully avoided the promulgation of a purely formal concept of international law:

> international law, at highest level of abstraction, is most relevantly conceived as a combination of the two forms of power ... – as *formal authority* conjoined with *effective control*, as a *flow of decisions* in which community prescriptions are formulated, invoked, and in fact applied in the promotion of community policies.[351]

---

[346] Id., at 181-182.
[347] Id., at 143, 181.
[348] Id., at 155.
[349] Id., at 182-183, (contrary to Morgenthau's position on law as a static force).
[350] Id., at 172. Emphasis added.
[351] Id., at 181.

The formulation and application of these community policies occur on different levels within 'a hierarchy of interacting power processes.'[352] McDougal's concept of international law thus circumvented a few 'classical' issues:

a policy-oriented international law will not futilely debate either whether such prescriptions and applications are "really" international law or "really" national or municipal law, or whether international law is "supreme" over national law or national law is "supreme" over international law. ... [I]t will not seek in an infinite regress of verbalisms to discover some mystical "binding force" independent of particular decision-makers in particular contexts, for its prescriptions. Abjuring the metaphysical derivations and justifications of all the schools, it rather engage in empirical investigation ...[353]

Questions debated intensively before WWII, like whether a monist or dualist view on international law is more correct or – still topical – whether international law is truly binding, were thus avoided and were considered less important for proving the relevance of international law within international life. McDougal in his comprehensive approach sought different answers. He restored faith in 'rationality'. In his view, the relevant questions were those related to the construction of an international law which would provide the world's decision-making processes with 'rational criteria' for finding the right decisions and for formulating and establishing the right policies, and so, the *right* law.[354] Law is about serving a number of policy (political) objectives, which define the righteousness of the policies and as such, law is a relevant social and teleological enterprise.

Finally, the characterisation of law as a teleological enterprise gives rise to a need for elaboration on the fourth element enumerated above: the role of 'values' within the policy approach. McDougal's project was, *inter alia,* about finding the '*best*' international law.[355] The 'best' international law is *that* international legal system which is based on and most effectively promotes humanistic and democratic values, the determined objectives in this case. Law as an authoritative decision-making process needs objectives or, to use the policy-orientated vocabulary, 'goal values' to find direction. McDougal's 1953 Course at The Hague Academy starts with a quotation from Roscoe Pound's works. Reading Pound's words on international law, spoken in Leiden in 1923,[356] is quite illuminating to our under-

---

[352] Id., at 184. Also, M.S. McDougal, The Impact of International Law upon National Law: A Policy-oriented Perspective (1958), in McDougal et al., Studies in World Public Order (1960), at 171.

[353] Id., at 185-186. See, for the claim of scientific objectivity through the enlistment of empirical data, e.g., M. Shaw, International law (1991) at 54, 52-57.

[354] Id., at 163-164.

[355] Id., at 140.

[356] 'We shall not ask him ("the jurist of the immediate future") for a juristic romance built upon the cosmological romance of some closed metaphysical system. But we may demand of him a legal philosophy ... that shall enable international law to take in what it requires from without, that shall give us a functional critique of international law in terms of social ends, not an analytical critique in terms of itself, and above all that shall conceive of the legal order as a process and not as a condition.' R. Pound in 1923, as cited in, A Contemporary Conception, at 137. Dated wrongly at 1932. See *supra*, chapter 3, footnote 14.

standing of McDougal's work. Pound called for a departure from metaphysical conceptions of international law and for the formulation of 'a functional critique of international law in terms of social ends.' The idea at the heart of the policy-orientated approach to international law becomes entirely clear when viewed against the background of Pound's remarks, namely international law as the global flow of authoritative decisions aimed at realising a number of 'social ends' or 'major goal values'. McDougal discerned the following eight major values: 'power, respect, enlightenment, wealth, well-being, skill, affection, and rectitude.' International law is and must be involved in the preservation, promotion, distribution and 'sharing' of these values.[357] Its (ultimate) end is 'to promote a free world society ... and human dignity.' That is the challenge McDougal intended to meet with his policy-orientated approach to international law.[358] In other words, McDougal's project, the approach or theory he sought, was one that would 'best' establish an *international law of human dignity.*

By an international law of human dignity I mean the processes of authoritative decision of a world public order in which values are shaped and shared more by persuasion than coercion, and which seeks to promote the greatest production and widest possible sharing, without discriminations irrelevant to merit, of all values among all human beings.[359]

The role of goal values within the policy approach to international law may thus be concluded to be of essential and *defining* importance.

The explicit task or 'moral responsibility' McDougal assigned to legal scholars in general and to himself in particular, i.e., to 'test specific doctrines and practices for compatibility with conceptions of human dignity,[360] is particularly understandable in the aftermath of war, [361] and with 'the shadow of possible catastrophe hang[ing] over all ... heads.'[362] An international law of human dignity as a global institution with a universal scope was evidently not yet in place. In fact, it could be said that there was a risk that a 'law of human *in*dignity' would be established. McDougal felt that an 'overriding struggle ... between the totalitarian orders ... and the nontotalitarian, with a dominant democratic core ...' was taking place.[363] By arguing that international legal scholars should not fail to include

[357] Id., at 189, 188-191.

[358] Id., at 138, 140-141.

[359] Id., at 107.

[360] Id., at 140, 189. Also, at 157. '... it is the over-riding moral responsibility of legal scholars, as the appropriate skilled specialists of society, to identify or invent and to recommend the prescriptions, organisations, and decisions that favor the law of human dignity.' Id., at 140, 189-190. See also, M.S. McDougal and H.D. Lasswell, The Identification of Diverse Systems of Public Order (1959), *in* McDougal et al., Studies in World Public Order (1960) at 38-41; hereinafter: The Identification.

[361] See also, Falk et al., Myres Smith McDougal (1906-1998), 92 *AJIL* 730 (1998).

[362] A Contemporary Conception, at 138. For example, the nuclear destruction of the world.

[363] Perspectives, at 987.

values of human dignity in their conceptions of international law or in specific doctrinal arguments, as well as by arguing in favour of an international law of democratic freedom and individual well-being, McDougal took an ideological – anti-totalitarian – stand.[364] Any traditional expression of 'universalism' is a kind of 'make-belief,'[365] he argued, and he rejected the universality of international law as being an 'illusion.'[366] International law lacked universality due to diversity on essential normative issues. Having said that, international legal scholars should, however, not lose sight of 'the *future-oriented* nature of the challenge contained in the idea of universal legal order ...,' but, on the contrary, continue 'along the path toward a universal system.'[367] According to McDougal, global factual interdependence required law as a global institution.[368] Of course, it had to be a universal legal system of human dignity. To arrive at that, the existing diversity should not be hidden by 'obscurity,' but should be expressed.[369] Thus, ideological or political ideas form an integral part of McDougal's project in legal theory: he too was 'recommend[ing]' a particular 'policy alternative' to move the world forward. [370] I shall now address how all this relates to his conception of ILP.

4.5.3. **McDougal and ILP: beyond obsession**

McDougal's use of language is particularly idiosyncratic. How did he use ILP within his comprehensive theoretical framework? Sovereignty is used as an example of traditional concepts, which tend to hinder the establishment of an international order of human dignity. I would like to argue that his attack on the scholarly attitude of paying 'lip service' to the 'fact' of the universality of international law,[371] as well as his approach to the concept of sovereignty are at the same time part of a political move.

---

[364] See also, Grewe, at 648. '[T]he theory of international law developed in the 1950s and 1960s by the influential member of the Yale Law School, Myres McDougal, by advocating a »world public order« of »human dignity« also placed international law on an ideological basis which was unable to recognise any minimal foundation of common values between East and west – and thereby put in question the possibility of a universal international law.'

[365] The Identification, at 5-6. 'For some decades ... [t]he implicit assumption appears to have been that unless the universality of international law is established, there is no international law whatsoever; and further that the most effective means of moving the world towards a universal body of law is to assert its contemporary reality in fact. It is high time that the community of scholars abandon a conception of their role in history whose principal effect is to condemn them to inaccuracy and futility.' Id, at 38.

[366] Id., at 6.

[367] Id., at 5-6.

[368] A Contemporary Conception, at 137-138.

[369] The Identification, at 6.

[370] The Identification, at 39. Also, A Contemporary Conception, at 140.

[371] Id., at 6.

[T]he spokesmen of totalitarian powers are the ones who, professing to be more orthodox keepers of the faith than their bourgeois opponents, pay most punctilious to the supposed universality of international law. And why? Strange as it may seem at first glance, the most convincing interpretation is that the existing imperfections of the system can be used by them to help prevent further advances toward a world order with genuine measures of security. For it is in the name of such allegedly universal doctrines of international law as *sovereignty*, domestic jurisdiction, nonintervention, independence, and equality – all of which appear to fortify claims to freedom from external obligation – that the case is made to resist the institutional reconstructions which are indispensable to security. In this grave posture of world affairs it can only make sense to put aside the veil that is provided by false conceptions of the universality of international law. ... The discrediting of claims to universality which are in fact false is ... a first necessary step toward clarifying the common goals, interpretations, and procedures essential to achieving an effective international order capable of drawing upon the continuous support essential to global security by consent. By piercing the veil of pseudo-universality we may, further, diminish the degree of unwitting support that totalitarian powers obtain from the persisting failure of many scholars and leaders of the non-Soviet world to disclose the true state of affairs. Too many people, professional and lay, have failed to see that insistence upon universality as now "existing" serves as a tactical screen to disguise the strategic goal of advancing toward an imposed universalization of the totalitarian form of public order.[372]

In McDougal's view, the traditional doctrine of sovereignty tended to be used by proponents of (Soviet) totalitarianism and of the principle of non-intervention. Sovereignty was a basic but technical concept, which was mostly used by scholars who favour 'coexistence' and the preservation of the contemporary international situation.[373] McDougal considered the doctrine of 'peaceful coexistence' *misleading*, because it defined and applied fundamental concepts of traditional international law, *inter alia*, sovereignty, in such a way that they were made to serve 'the purposes not of peaceful cooperation, but rather of a temporizing tactic designed to obfuscate opponents while poising them for ultimate destruction.'[374] Sovereignty was a key concept in traditional theory, and as such considered ill-suited to a theory on the contemporary global situation. A new meaning was required, that was not merely exclusive (like the traditional doctrine prescribed) but also inclusive: in McDougal's opinion, sovereignty also meant *responsibility*.[375] Sovereignty incorporated two aspects: the 'exclusive competence' of the state as well as the 'inclusive competence' of the international community to protect common values of human dignity. Sovereignty had to 'honour' both the 'inclusive' and the 'exclusive' interest, and not *just* the 'exclusive'. In the international law of human dignity 'the concept of "sovereignty" ... will be interpreted as embracing only that competence which remains to States after due account is taken

[372] The Identification, at 7-8. Emphasis added. See also, Perspectives, at 988.

[373] Perspectives, at 1009.

[374] Id., at 988.

[375] Id., at 1010: 'In its attitudes toward territorial communities ... an international law [of human dignity] will, of course, respect the equality of states, ... but the equality it respects will be a genuine equality of shared power and responsibility ...'

of their obligations under international law,' McDougal pointed out, 'and not as a license for freedom from all restraint by shared authority.'[376]

The reality of sovereign state power was thus not ignored, but as a term of art, sovereignty nonetheless did not play a vital role in the language of the policy-oriented approach. This was a result of the attempt to distinguish the policy-orientated approach from traditional perspectives of international law. McDougal also admitted as much: '[a]n adequate framework of theory for guiding inquiry and choice would appear to require key terms *different* from, or in addition to, the authoritative words of great charters or other technical sources.'[377] Hence, as we have seen above, sovereignty was re-defined. The term 'formal authority' took over its role. The state was now defined 'as a territorially organized group with the highest degree of formal authority over an area' and *sovereignty* was defined 'as the degree of formal authority exercised in relation to internal and external participants in power processes.'[378] But, as we have also seen above, international law should be perceived as being rooted in 'formal *authority* conjoined with *effective control*.' In McDougal's view, sovereignty thus carried no meaning for international law if it was not at the same time interrelated with '*supremacy*, [i.e.,] the degree of effective power in relation to internal and external participants in power processes.'[379] Defining sovereignty as a relative concept (actors can have a *degree* of formal authority) subordinates the traditional concept to the policy approach's conceptual terminology. Sovereignty is interpreted in conformity with the overall objective of 'promot[ing] a rational, productive balance between competences,'[380] i.e., a balance between the *exclusive* competence of a state over its territory, both formal and effective, and the *internal* competence of the international community, which limits the formal authority of the state in conformity with its obligations under international law. Productive is the balance that succeeds in maintaining order and security as well as in promoting the values of human dignity. It acknowledges that both power and authority are needed to create international law and as such the contextual reality was thus fully represented in McDougal's thinking. The new terminology, however, enabled McDougal to distance himself from conservative conceptions that were also submitted by the Soviets. The usage of the term sovereignty, or mostly its non-use, as well as his re-definition of the concept, involved both a legal (theoretical) act as well as a political one.

Examining the concept of ILP used within McDougal's policy-orientated international legal thinking, we have to focus on that part of the theory dealing with the 'participants' in the world processes. Right from the start, when McDougal laid down his extensive research plan for the policy approach to international law, one of the central and fundamental questions he raised concerned the desig-

---

[376] Id., at 1009.
[377] Id., at 995. Emphasis added.
[378] A Contemporary Conception, at 194.
[379] Id., at 181.
[380] The Identification, at 26.

nation of the participants in the world processes. McDougal intended to take international legal theory *beyond obsession*.

One of the 'deep confusions' of contemporary international legal theory at the time was, in his view, its failure to present a comprehensive description of the participants in the power process of the international society.[381] The number and diversity of participants in world society was increasing and the concept of ILP was too traditional to deal with this transformation in a satisfactory manner.

Not only is the proper subject-matter of international law defined, as we have seen, as rules "governing the relations of nation-states" and the great bulk of attention in discussion confined to nation-states, but frequently explicit assertion is made that only nation-states can be regarded as appropriate subjects of international law. Since the decision of the International Court of Justice in the case on *Reparation for Injuries Suffered in the Service of the United Nations* it has ceased to be breach of etiquette to refer to international governmental organizations as at least partial subjects, but it is still common to question or castigate writers who are so bold as to suggest that the individual human being is himself a subject of international law. Most of the other group participants are largely ignored.

Theory tended to underestimate the new participants and since international legal arguments on ILP were generally rather exclusive, focusing on nation states as the (sole) subjects of international law, McDougal therefore persisted in using the notion of 'participant'.

Contemporary theory about international law, *obsessed* by a technical conception of the "subjects of international law", continues, however, greatly to over-estimate the role of the "nation-state" and to *underestimate* the role of all these other new participants.[382]

Again, the legal argument was both theoretically and politically motivated. The term 'participant' had this connotation of both legal and political elements. Power was defined as participation in power processes; being a 'participant' thus meant having access to these processes. McDougal argued in favour of a 'democracy of access,'[383] since an international law of human dignity demanded 'the widest possible sharing of power among responsible participants in an open society of freedom, security, and abundance.' He thus favoured the 'utmost pluralism:'

all effective participants in the world power process [should] be regarded as potentially permissible participants in international processes of authority, both for protecting their interests and for subordinating them to authority in securing of general community policy.[384]

---

[381] A Contemporary Conception, at 143, 160 *et seq*.
[382] Id., at 161. Footnotes omitted and emphasis added.
[383] The Identification, at 25.
[384] Perspectives, at 1010.

Considering the increase in the number of international participants a positive development,[385] I would like to argue that McDougal's virtual *negation* of ILP as an essential concept requiring theoretical attention, was in fact an act of *inclusion.*

Over the centuries, the concept of ILP has been used by international legal scholars either to *include* or *exclude* particular entities in or from relevant international processes, or, in other words, in or from the international community. The negation of ILP as a relevant conceptual topic, which needs to be addressed when proposing a completely new approach to international law, fits perfectly (though paradoxically) within this international scholarly tendency. McDougal considered the new participants within the world social and political process relevant to international authoritative decision-making. Negating the concept of ILP and strictly using the term 'participant' is an attempt *to get international theory beyond its obsession* (with the legal-technical aspect , which often tended to be rather exclusive) *and enhance democracy.*

Despite his general negation of the notion, McDougal nonetheless clarified on (at least) one occasion what his policy-orientated approach argument meant, if couched in the traditional terminology:

> Not merely states but also international governmental organizations, parties, pressure groups, private associations, and individual human beings are all appropriate subjects of an international law of human dignity.[386]

The traditional interpretation that states alone are the appropriate subjects of international law was now obsolete. Since the *Reparations* case, international organisations have been generally accepted subjects of international law, yet scholars who argue that the individual is a subject of international law are still 'castigate[d]' and any other participants are mostly ignored all together.[387] And this is so despite the fact that, '[t]he governmental forms of territorial organization, so exalted in importance by traditional theory,' as McDougal emphasised, 'are frequently but channels for the expression of decisions in fact made in some one or more of the many functional groupings,' just enumerated above. Indeed, for the utmost plurality in the world legal process, participation should be established to correct the underestimation of non-state participants and to establish a 'democracy of access,' and put an end to the 'blind[ness]' of international law. After all, in the end 'from the perspective of scientific description, the individual human being is the ultimate actor in all arenas.'[388]

---

[385] Id., at 996.

[386] Id., at 1010. See also, A Contemporary Conception, at 161.

[387] A Contemporary Conception, at 161.

[388] Id., at 161-162. McDougal: 'The world power process affords arenas for the individual both as an individual and in each specialized group capacity; individuals are protected in control of bases of power both as individuals and in each group capacity; and policies are continually being formulated and applied by varying specialized techniques on behalf of individuals both as individuals and in their various group capacities.' Id.

In conclusion, law as an instrument for the achievement of ultimate goals has been determinant in establishing the terminology and legal concepts necessary to make the instrument work. In McDougal's view, traditional concepts like sovereignty and ILP simply failed to rise to the occasion. For his partly politically motivated theoretical argument, McDougal needed concepts like 'participant,' which lacked a purely legal connotation but included political reality, and enabled international scholarship to transform not only its theories but also international life itself.

And so McDougal continued the process of inclusion, arguing the participation of a variety of actors into the world legal process and as such advancing democracy within the international society.

4.6. Wolfgang Friedmann (1907-1972)

4.6.1. **Introduction**

The choice to discuss Wolfgang Friedmann as the fourth scholar here was made on the basis of his functional approach to international life and law, which is particularly evident in his work during the early 1960s, which may be read as written by an exponent of the more pragmatic approach to international law that was used in mainstream international legal scholarship during the 1970s and 1980s. Already in 1938 Friedmann examined the foundations of international law and its 'present crisis' in the context of the 'disintegration of European civilization.'[389] Almost 30 years later, Friedmann again analysed the 'crisis of international law,' this time within the Cold War context.[390] This crisis of international law to which Friedmann alluded in 1965 came only one year after the publication of his canonical *The Changing Structure of International Law* (1964) in which he explained that the state of international law still 'justified a measure of cautious confidence.' However, he later observed that since then 'the "Cold war" ... ha[d] acquired a new and sharper intensity.' The 'continuing weakness' or 'paralysis' of the UN, especially where it came to superpower behaviour, in his view contributed to international law's crisis. Referring to a number of international incidents, Friedmann warned that if the power struggle between the superpower rivals 'intensified' and political and military tension mounted, the value and role of both international law and the United Nations would be truly jeopardised. Although subtly and pragmatically, he nevertheless urgently appealed to international lawyers to defend the value of law in international relations. After all, 'the very weakness of international law – the absence of a definite constitutional system with legislative, executive and judicial organs, and the looseness of many

[389] W. Friedmann, The Disintegration of European Civilisation and the Future of International Law, 2 *Modern L.R.* 194-214 (Dec. 1938).

[390] W. Friedmann, United States Policy and the Crisis of International Law, 59 *AJIL* 857 (1965).

norms,' had been its greatest advantage when international law had had to respond to major post-war challenges. It had managed to adapt its structure to 'the accession of a large number of new states to the family of nations,' had been able to respond to 'the problems of economic development' as articulated by these new members, and thirdly, had managed to 'cop[e] with the conflict of political and social ideologies which, in political terms, was expressed by the 'Cold War' conflict between Communists and the Western world, and, in economic terms, by the differences and conflicts between socialist and non-socialist systems.'[391] Friedmann had a clear eye for the Cold War context in which he lived and worked, yet his 1964 analysis has lost none of its validity in the long term, which is why it is appropriate to conclude this chapter with an analysis of his use of ILP.

It can be said that ideological conflict influenced Friedmann's thinking too. It contributed to his adoption of a functionalist approach based on a rule-orientated conception of law.[392] He focussed less on the issue of distinguishing law from politics; his main and overall concern was with the structure of international society. The changes he discerned in this structure caused him to argue in favour of a 'basic reorientation of our thinking in international law' in order to, at least, 'overcome the traditional distinction between public law and private law thinking, between diplomacy and political science thinking, on the one hand, and "black-letter law" on the other.'[393] This *reorientation* was guided by an instrumental conception of (international) law, an idea that was widespread among international scholars at the time, and is clearly visible in Friedmann's work:[394]

> He thought of law as a means of improving the condition of man, eliminating the defects in our societies, and moving in the direction of universal peace and welfare. But although he was an idealist and a reformer, he never lost sight of reality. He well understood the bounds of the possible. ... he thought of the welfare of all mankind as the goal to be pursued and had no use for narrow and myopic nationalism. His ideas and ideals were truly transnational.[395]

Friedmann thus considered law as an instrument, but not one of power politics alone. Rather, he saw law as an instrument to improve the condition of man, without, however, taking a natural law perspective.

In response to the debate on international life between "realists" and "idealists," Friedmann tended to recognise the significance of both these 'moving

[391] Id., at 858

[392] 'The functionalist approach is thus no miracle solution, but it affords an important means of by-passing the propagandist atmosphere of political international assemblies, and of bringing the nations together in practical tasks of mutual interest and benefit.' Friedmann, as quoted in R.A. Falk, New Approaches to the study of International Law, 61 *AJIL* 492 (1967).

[393] The Changing Structure, at 3, 70. Also, at 149.

[394] Id., e.g., at 3, 58-59, 94, 88-95. Also, Friedmann, Law in a Changing Society (1972, 2nd ed.) at 11.

[395] Hazard et al., In Memoriam: Wolfgang Gaston Friedmann (1907-1972), 67 *AJIL* 102-103 (1973).

forces,' i.e., of the 'national interest and the pursuit of national power' and of the pursuit of 'a stronger international legal order and the development from national to supranational institutions.'

> The recognition of the predominance of conflicting national interests in our time does not preclude, and it may even make even more urgent the search for means to alleviate this conflict through the progressive organisation of international order. [396]

Friedmann observed that the terms 'value' and 'interest' may be used 'interchangeably.'[397] With reference to Morgenthau, Friedmann explained that the 'national interest' is a rather flexible, context-dependent term, which may demand 'at one time ... the pursuit of absolute national sovereignty as it is at the other time [consistent] with the organisation of a regional union, an effective international order force, or even a world federation.' Concerning the general 'identification of the concept of "national interest" with "national security," "and specifically of security based on power,"' Friedmann remarked that it 'greatly curtails the flexibility of ... the interpretation' of the concept of national interest.[398] However, Friedmann also seemed to wish to reconcile the two approaches, i.e., power politics on the one hand and ideals on the other. Power is never an end in itself, but rather a means by which to attain a variety of goals (if one maintains a flexible notion of national interest). Citing Niebuhr and Carr, Friedmann observed that:

> Unlike the writers who appear to reject ideals in international politics in any sense other than as an 'ideology' (as used by K. Mannheim), *i.e.*, as a disguise of interests, the present writer accepts the *bipolarity* of politics, as resulting from a perpetual tension between "conscience and power," between "ethical and coercive factors."[399]

The moral aspect of international politics must not, however, be 'identified with saintliness as opposed to wickedness, or with pacifism as opposed to military nationalism,' but should be understood as the recognition 'that the pursuit of "ideals" is a real force in international politics, as it is in the life of individuals, but that such ideals may comprise the whole range of human ends, from the extermination of entire races as practised and aspired to by the Nazi philosophy, to the Stoic idea of the brotherhood of all men.'[400]

This is also one of Friedmann's problems with Natural Law theory: 'the question of what nature ordains depends on your point of view.' Moreover, it is 'the basic weakness of natural law – that, once you open the gates, almost anything can be declared as contrary to natural law and order, according to the philosophy

---

[396] The Changing Structure, at 45-46.

[397] Id., at 47, Friedmann went on to explain: 'The use of the term "interest" essentially serves to give the classification and balancing of values in all fields of law a subjective purposive flavour.'

[398] Id., at 48.

[399] Id., at 50.

[400] Id.

of the beholder.' In *An Analysis of 'In Defense of Natural Law'*, Friedmann builds a case against natural law, albeit mildly. He submits that: 'there is ... a great danger in the attempt to eliminate the deep and abiding conflicts of values, by an all-too-elastic and all-embracing concept of *jus naturale*.' On the one hand, Friedmann accepts that there is a (single) 'concept of "nature" that we may accept as truly basic and necessary to human life' and that:

this is a philosophy shared by Aristotle and Bentham, by St. Thomas [Jaspers, and, indeed,] Sartre, by Kant and Hegel: that man is a creature endowed with the capacity of reasoning as well as of choosing between alternative courses of action, rejecting those that by some standard he regards "bad" and accepting those that by the same standard he accepts as "good." [That] [p]erhaps we can deduce from this one practical consequence: that man cannot be a mere object of law, a chattel to be disposed of like an inanimate thing. [And therefore] we may perhaps say that to treat human beings as things, without legal capacity, without legal powers and rights, or to dispose of them as raw material for fertilizers, is a denial of "human nature."

On the other hand, relevant as this observation may be within the context of the present study, Friedmann's pragmatic outlook nevertheless prevents him from concluding that Natural Law can fulfil the function of law where law is to provide 'valid and compelling directives' in the case of actual, practical problems.[401] In his view:

The case against natural law is that its method of approach and its terminology disguise the need to decide between alternative values. It gives the illusion of certainty and of guidance where there is none. It is one way of shielding man from the loneliness of decision, as legislator, as judge, as statesman, or as ordinary citizen. But we cannot evade the choice. We must articulate our system of values whether instinctively or as an elaborate system of philosophy. If we do so, we will find that there are the competing demands of justice, security, and utility-as classically formulated by Gustav Radbruch-and that there are ultimate choices for the sake of which you may fight your enemy but which you cannot scientifically demonstrate .... "To decide oneself is to live" – as once said by Radbruch. Let us accept this choice, humbly but resolutely![402]

The paragraph cited rings with the echo of existentialism. The legal approach can never eliminate the problem of human choice. As man has the capacity of reason and morality – and is therefore capable of choosing – it is impossible to treat him as an object. Instead, he must be considered a subject, with legal powers and rights, who is continually required to choose between diverging values and conflicting interests. This antinomy of values extends not only to individual life, but to international life as well.[403]

---

[401] W. Friedmann, An Analysis of '*In Defense of Natural Law*', Law and Philosophy 147-149 (1964).

[402] Id., at 160. See also, The Changing Structure, at 77, where '[i]t is submitted that [the "natural law" approach] is not a solution but a camouflaging of the real problems.'

[403] The Changing Structure, at 79.

States act upon interests in the same way as individuals, which causes international conflicts to arise. In this context, Friedmann distinguished between international conflicts of interests and international conflicts of power, which might be the result. Conflicts of interests can further be disguised as conflicts of values. Friedmann spent a further paragraph emphasising the importance of this distinction, also in terms of international law:

The importance of the distinction for the structure of international law is that conflicts of power are, more or less adequately, regulated and adjusted by the traditional system of the *international law of coexistence*, whereas ideological conflicts, penetrating that social and economic organisation of the state as well as human values, such as the autonomy of individuals and social groups within the state, lead to the closer integration, and mutual antagonism, of like-minded groups of states.

Other than the international law of co-existence, the *international law of co-operation* and organisation 'requires a *community* of interests.' This is the key to the distinction, as, in Friedmann's words:

The challenge posed by the changes in the structure of the international society of our time does not mean the abolition of self-interest in international relations; it does, however, radically affect the *dimensions* and *objectives* of self-interest.

This is where the theory of international law needs to be supplemented. Morgenthau's realism may be more than adequate for an analysis of the law of co-existence, it does not, however, suffice for the 'international law of co-operation and organisation, as either an implementation or, in some cases, a spur to the forces and interests in mankind striving towards the implementation of common objectives.'[404] Friedmann, however, did manage to find a satisfactory mix of realism and idealism in his pragmatic and dynamic view of international law.[405]

---

[404] Id., at 52-58. See also, United States Policy and the Crisis of International Law, at 860: 'The need to preserve, on the one hand, some minimum rules of intercourse between all the nations of the world and, on the other hand, to absorb the increasing diversification and vertical extension of the fields of international collaboration in an expanding structure of international law has led to the growing articulation of two different types of international law: the law of coexistence and the law of co-operation. The international law of coexistence incorporates the minimum principles and standards under which states representing a great variety of political, social and economic systems may preserve a minimum of ordered relations. The law of co-operation represents the many diverse attempts to promote, through permanent international organizations or through *ad hoc* schemes the common interests of mankind in what Röling has called the "international law of welfare." And much of this law has developed on a regional rather than a universal level. The United Nations, as the world's most nearly universal organization, became the principal organized expression of the interests and concerns shared by all nations.'

[405] Friedmann's pragmatism is also visible in his approach to sovereignty, where he rejects the idea that there is no alternative and that the choice must be between national and international law. Instead he follows Hart in his position that national and international law are no longer 'absolute alternatives.' See, United States Policy and the Crisis of International Law, at 860 fn.

4.6.2. International law: co-existence and co-operation

The principal thesis of Friedmann's *The Changing Structure of International Law*, another classic of post-war international scholarship, is:

> that in international law it is today of both theoretical and practical importance to distinguish between the international law of 'coexistence,' governing essentially diplomatic inter-state relations, and the international law of co-operation, expressed in the growing structure of international organisation and the pursuit of common human interests.[406]

Friedmann devised his distinction to transcend the law of co-existence, which was really based on terror and the mutual threat of nuclear destruction. The law of co-existence represents the universal legal order concerned with *inter-state* relations, conflicts of power, and 'the regulation of ... the rules of mutual respect for national sovereignty.' In this respect, international law 'retain[ed] ... its validity ... [and] universality.'[407] However, Friedmann also recognised the existence of a non-universal law concerned with international *co-operation*. The law of co-operation was defined as that part of international law that is concerned with the common interests among states.[408]

The 'developing international "co-operative" law of international organisation' may best be characterised as an '*agent of [social] progress and evolution.*' Friedmann agreed with Morgenthau's analysis of the law of co-existence as 'static' and a 'natural ideological ally of the *status quo*,' but firmly rejected this characterisation with regard to the international law of co-operation.[409] Friedmann found yet another kind of development at a non-state level and of a non-universal scope: the extension of social and economic transnational co-operative relations. The law arising from the ordering of these social relations he also considered to be part of international co-operative law.

In his argument, Friedmann used a sociological approach. He stressed the international sociological phenomenon of (increasing) 'factual interdependence' and outlined the changes that were visible in the structure and scope of international society and the relations among its members. These changes, he argued, in turn required and caused changes in the structure and scope of international law. He distinguished, *inter alia*, a 'horizontal' and a 'vertical' development.[410]

---

406 The Changing Structure, at vii.

407 Id., at 60-61.

408 'Unlike traditional international law, which is predicated upon the assumption of conflicts of national interests, which it seeks to stabilise and regulate, co-operative international law [and organisation] requires a *community* of interests. ... The challenge posed by the changes in the structure of the international society of our time does not mean the abolition of self-interest in international relations; it does, however, radically affect the *dimensions* and *objectives* of self-interest. ... today only the concerted efforts of mankind, and not the clashing rivalries of nations in military build-up, cold war diplomacy and competition for the use of resources, can insure the survival of the human race.' Id., at 57-58.

409 Id., at 58-59.

410 Id., at 64.

The horizontal development, according to Friedmann, entailed the '*proliferation of sovereignties*' [411] caused by decolonisation and the accession of the decolonised non-Western states to the international community. Their membership of this community brought about a change in their legal status: from having been mere *objects*, they now became *subjects* of international law.[412]

By vertical development Friedmann meant the extension of international law 'from states to public and private groupings, as participants in the international legal process...'[413], i.e., the proliferation of participants. In addition to horizontal and vertical expansion, Friedmann also remarked on the expansion of international law in respect of the topics it governed. The international law of co-operation reached into new areas of social and economic life and with regard to these social and economic matters, the community of interests would at times be universal, at other times regional and at yet other times limited in some other way.[414] The new issues that arose were of a social, political and economic nature and were consequently highly sensitive as considered from different political and ideological perspectives. This subject-matter expansion of international law thus affected its universality, as '[t]he sensitivity of international relations to internal structure increases the deeper they go into the fields of human values.' Together with increased institution building in the field of international economic development (aid) and the urgent need to co-operate in order to preserve mankind and its natural resources, these main structural changes necessitated the 'reordering of international law.'[415] In the following section the focus will be on the participants.

4.6.3. **Friedman's use of ILP: inclusion**

> [L]aw has functions other than to prohibit or to command. It can also empower.[416]

The state, its sovereignty and the related international law of co-existence were, in Friedmann's analysis, 'increasingly inadequate' to meet the needs of contemporary international society.[417] For this reason, a law of co-operation was of ne-

---

[411] Id., at 61, 214. Emphasis added. Friedmann believed that the world might become divided between two political empires like Orwell predicted and called the growing number of UN members caused by the admission of 'petty sovereignties,' a 'bewildering and alarming flurry'. Id., at 214.

[412] See also, M. Abi-Saab, Peaceful Change and the Integration of the Newly Independent States in the International Community, 32/33 *Yearbook of the AAA* 172 (1962/63). Also, R.Y. Jennings, The Progress of International Law: an inaugural lecture 43 (1960). See, e.g., Oppenheim, 1905 ed., in order to be a subject of international law a state had to be civilised, by which he meant European civilisation.

[413] The Changing Structure, at 64.

[414] Id., at 61-64, 68-69, 152-187.

[415] Id., at 10-13, 176-181.

[416] See, for Barnet's review of Friedmann's book, The Changing Structure of International Law, R.J. Barnet, Coexistence and Cooperation in International Law, 18(1) *World Politics* 86 (1965).

[417] The Changing Structure, at 378.

cessity being put in place: the 'new international law'.[418] I will now focus on an aspect Friedmann deemed necessary for the re-ordering of international law to be able to proceed: 'the *inclusion*, as active participants and subjects of international law, of public international organisations and to a lesser extent of private corporations and human individuals.'[419] The increase in the number of subjects of international law was intimately linked to the expansion of the issues with which it was concerned and the character of international society: 'in sociological terms, a developing co-operative international law represents *community* aspects, rather than *society* aspects, in the relations between states and nations.'[420]

The importance of *inclusion* becomes obvious when related to Friedmann's interpretation of the concept of sanction. The reality of the new international law of co-operation was not so much constructed upon the traditional (punitive) concept of sanction, but on the interests served by participation: 'non-participation' was the true sanction and element on which the 'reality' of international law as well as its effectiveness was based.[421] In Friedmann's analysis, exclusion from participation was the new sanction of the new law.

Concerning the '*new subjects of international law*,'[422] Friedmann did not hesitate to stress that sovereign states were still the principal subjects of international law.[423] At the same time, he held that the subjects of international law were no longer *exclusively* states. International legal personality had been conferred upon (functional) international organisations, like the UN and its special agencies. The ILP of these organisations evidently 'derive[d]' from inter-state agreement.[424] These new subjects of international law constituted 'the legal organisation of the predominant and characteristic feature of post-war international organisation: functional co-operation.' The formation of international organisations by international agreement is an expression of the sovereignty of states. Nevertheless, this form of co-operation was resulting in a 'gradual hollowing out of national sovereignties.'[425] On the other hand, legal subjectivity – or ILP – is *granted* to an entity by sovereign states, it derives from their ILP. After all, Friedmann remarked, there was no such thing as an 'international entity ... capable of bestowing legal status of international validity.'[426] The fact that international organisations were accepted as having ILP was one of the main developments characterising the new international law.

---

[418] Id., at 62.
[419] Id., at 368, see also, slightly differently, at 71.
[420] Id., at 68.
[421] Id., at 81-95.
[422] Id., at 213-249.
[423] See, e.g., at 213-214, 235.
[424] Id., at 216-217, 288-289.
[425] Id., at 216.
[426] Id., at 181.

It is the consolidation of the legal status of public international authorities, as autonomous persons of international law, that the science and practice of international law has progressed most rapidly since the end of the last World War. ... the status of international organisations is now firmly established.[427]

Friedmann also raised the question whether private multinational corporations (MNC's) should be endowed with ILP. Sometimes public international law is applicable to an agreement between a state and a corporation (known as 'mixed agreement') and this creates a certain 'status of equality'. However, according to Friedmann, it was neither possible, nor desirable to grant ILP to private corporations, just as it had been given to international organisations. Still, Friedmann did not object to a 'limited *ad hoc* subjectivity' of corporations, 'to the extent that their transactions are controlled by the norms of public rather than private law'. This would not be unreasonable as these entities did 'participate' in the creation of international (economic) law. Their subjectivity had to be 'limited,' as they were not directly entitled to bring legal action before international authorities. Private corporations in association with states only in specific cases did not depend on inter-state activities for the protection of their international interests. With the increasing use of arbitration to resolve conflicts, the MNC and the state party 'are given equal standing before an impartial judicial forum.'[428] What Friedmann wished to cite as the source of such limited ILP was not entirely clear. ILP here seemed to derive from the state through the recognition that (specific) norms of international public law would govern the relationship between the parties.

The international law of co-existence treated the individual as an (insignificant) object: 'the isolated and helpless human being.' After WWII, the individual's human rights and his responsibilities under international law were discussed with increasing intensity and the law on these issues was consolidated within the existing framework. Scelle's postulate that *only* the individual was the true international legal person, Friedmann, however, rejected as contrary to the reality of international life. Nevertheless, the position of the individual in international law has changed significantly, in particular after WWII, mainly due to the formulation of international human rights documents. Apart from individual rights, individual responsibility has also increased under international law 'in the philosophy of the Nuremberg Charter and the subsequent trials.'[429] The legal status of the individual has changed due to the acceptance of *both* (enforceable) individual human rights and individual criminal responsibility, maintaining a 'proper proportion between the rights and duties of the individual' within international law.[430]

[427] Id., at 288.

[428] Id., at 223-224 and 231.

[429] Id., at 233-224.

[430] Id., at 249. 'To the extent that the individual is held entitled to assert certain claims to human dignity and the protection of vital human interests, on an international level, he can also be fairly held to assume a corresponding degree of responsibility for actions that directly interfere with such values.' Id., at 234.

This change of the status of individuals in international law is truly revolutionary:

> [T]he principle that, in certain exceptional circumstances, the individual may be held responsible for certain actions committed against aliens or even against his own nationals, is an important affirmation of the fact that it is ultimately individuals who compose mankind, and that the philosophy of international law is beginning to move away from the poisonous Hegelian and neo-Hegelian doctrines which postulate the state as the total integration of the *individual*, and the necessary repository of both his *freedom* and his *responsibility*.[431]

And so, international law finally arrived in the post-Hegelian age in which the individual human being is the ultimate addressee of international rights and duties, a situation that is firmly consolidated in today's international order.

Friedmann's thinking with regard to specific entities is particularly illustrative of the legal doctrine during the second half of the Cold War period. Friedmann's approach to international law, though comprehensive, was not theoretical in an abstract or conceptual manner. His approach was indeed very *functional*. Friedmann's sociological perspective was related to McDougal's policy thinking in that it, too, was geared towards social objectives and aimed at practical progress for the benefit and preservation of mankind. Friedmann, however, availed himself of the established legal vocabulary and did not hesitate to refer to international law as rules either. Sovereignty was on the one hand accepted as a reality, but on the other hand the concept was declared inadequate for meeting the demands of the new developments in international life. With the sovereign state no longer the only participant in the international legal process, Friedmann had to argue the inclusion of others. Although his discussion of 'the new subjects of international law' was necessarily still tentative and moderate in nature, his approach to subjectivity or ILP may nevertheless be seen as an example of how the concept was used in legal reasoning at the time and how it is basically still used today.

The concept of ILP was thus converted into a functional concept. During the 1950s and 1960s, more specific issues were raised in legal writing dealing with the source of international organisations' ILP,[432] namely whether this ILP (conceptually) *derived* from the ILP of the member states, either by explicit or implicit attribution, or whether it found an independent 'objective' source in its bestowal by international law itself. [433] The doctrinal debate on the basis of the ILP of international organisations has,[434] however, ground to a halt since the late

[431] Id., at 247. Emphasis added.

[432] See, for references on this matter, e.g., Schermers and Blokker, International Institutional Law: Unity within Diversity (1995) at 978-982.

[433] See, for Seyersted's idea of an *objective* international legal personality, *supra*, footnote 166.

[434] See, for the three different positions on the issue, International Institutional Law, at 978.

1970s,[435] as by then the implicit derivation theory had been commonly accepted. This is not surprising, as the ICJ had already adopted this view in 1949. ILP as a functional concept was thus used to enable international organisations to function and participate as independent actors in international legal life. It was applied to reconcile the contradiction between state sovereignty and independence on the one hand, and the need for international organisation and co-operation due to interdependence on the other. When international law was gradually shaking off the incapacity it had suffered from during the ice age that was the Cold War, the international framework of human rights was constructed and consolidated. The principle of non-intervention, which together with state sovereignty served as the basis of the Cold War international legal order, slowly started to erode in the UN context in particular, causing the two human rights Covenants to be adopted in 1966 to complement the Universal Declaration and UN resolutions.

4.7. Conclusion: a gradual process of inclusion

During the Cold War international life was dominated by power politics. Nevertheless, international law scholarship still oscillated between idealism and realism, rather than landing firmly in one camp, because it was influenced by the broader intellectual context as well. Early on, the debate was on whether it was best to reinforce sovereignty instead of the rule of law, or whether instead justice in international law had to be enhanced in order to give it more authority in international relations. An important component of enhanced international justice was of course the furtherance of the international protection of human rights. The practical development that human rights advocacy had become necessarily an element in the ideological conflict, gave rise to some ambivalence. However, it was precisely through this ambivalence that realism and idealism could meet in a different setting, as is evidenced in McDougal's work. Now that international cooperation was rapidly intensifying, Friedmann could realistically base his argument on the *fact* of interdependence and demand that international law adjust to the changes in international life. Rejecting natural law as a basis for international law, Friedmann reconciled universality and diversity, and the fact that he saw this need means that he recognised that they were conflicting elements. He united them by means of a conception of international law which embraced both the classical law of co-existence and the universal and regional law of co-operation.

The overview of how ILP was used within the Cold War context by our four international jurists furnishes proof of a moderate and gradual development towards *inclusion*. Initially, and this was largely owing to the strong traditional conception of sovereignty as the basis of international law, ILP tended to be perceived in a traditional, 'Oppenheim' kind of way as a collection of the rights,

[435] Id., at 980.

qualities or attributes of a sovereign state. As attempts were made to reinforce international law, sovereignty, though still firmly established as the foundation of the international system, began to receive less attention. New structures evolved as a result of increasing social and global interdependence, which demanded that international law change along with it. A pragmatic outlook has since dominated mainstream international legal thinking, especially over the past 35 years, as is in fact also illustrated by Friedmann's ideas and reflected in textbooks from this period.[436] Akehurst's remark on ILP is particularly illustrative of the existing attitude towards the concept: 'The position has changed in the last century, and international organizations, individuals and companies have acquired some degree of international legal personality; but when one tries to define the precise extent of the legal personality which they acquired, one enters a very controversial area of the law.'[437] This controversial area was however rarely entered. Although ILP had gained a place on the first pages of the textbooks as one of the most fundamental concepts of international law, it was still left ignored as undeserving of thorough theoretical treatment, with the label 'controversial' used to excuse the silence.

The discussion on ILP thus generally developed in a functional manner, by practical relevance, and connected with specific entities, which made it less a feature of international law theory.[438] The controversy concerning the (degree of) international legal personality of the individual as the bearer of rights and duties has gradually and significantly diminished. Human rights law and international criminal law recognised the individual's rights and duties under international law. Beyond doubt, the general trend consists of 'a drift away from the exclusive State paradigm'[439] towards the recognition of new subjects in international law and of the individual's international legal personality in particular.

In other words, within a context characterised by a balancing between the various 'poles' (i.e., the political-ideological superpower bi-polarity and the opposing views of realists and idealists concerning the best direction for international life to take) international law developed pragmatically, but decisively, both in theory and practice. Within this precarious balance between the old (i.e., the realist objective of strengthening sovereignty) and the new (the idealist aim of strengthen-

---

[436] Henkin: '... in fact, no modern nation has rejected "the system," and governments (if not academics) have stopped asking why they are subject of international law.' How Nations Behave, at 85 fn.

[437] M. Akehurst, A Modern Introduction to International Law (1987, 6th ed.) at 70.

[438] To some extent, a textbook exception: The Concept, at 15-43. Detter De Lupis' interpretation of ILP strikes one as Kelsenian: 'personality is, of course, a purely formal concept which does not confer, by itself, any specific rights of duties [*seq.*]; it merely serves as a focus of imputation.' Detter argues that if an organisation has been endowed with personality under municipal law by its founders, this 'indicates that it has also, whenever necessary, personality in the international sphere.' Id., at 21. '[T]here is ample evidence that individuals in many cases act as international persons.' Id., at 22. Detter explains the implication of her ILP interpretation for the conception of law and argues that the 'subjectivity test' for the definition of international law is a 'fallacy.' Id., at 40-43.

[439] The Concept, at 18.

ing justice) international legal scholarship used the concept of ILP to argue either the exclusion or inclusion of new subjects in the established structure of international law. The concept of ILP would continue to play this role until the end of the Cold War. It was the traditional concept used to argue in favour of the recognition or non-recognition – or, the inclusion or exclusion – of '*new*' actors as *legitimate participants* on the international plane and thus also to preserve or change the structure and identity of international law.

Chapter 5
THE CONCEPT OF ILP TODAY: THE END OF THE SUBJECT?

5.1. INTRODUCTION: A NEW AGE?

The post-Cold War era started with the promise of a new world order. Today, at the beginning of the 21st century, the promise has paled significantly. Looking back on the past ten years, it can be observed that even though the world has changed considerably, the eagerly awaited new world order has failed to materialise in any clear shape or form. How should the post-1990 decade or indeed the world we live in after the terrorist attacks on New York City and Washington on 11 September 2001 be defined? Have we entered a 'new era,' as Richard Holbrooke stated exactly one month after the attacks?[1] Has the post-Cold War period in fact been a second '*Interbellum*,' as he declared, and are we again to characterise the state of the world we live in in terms of ongoing warfare? Or have we entered, as Dominique Moïse termed it, the 'new, new world order'?[2] And what does this order have in store for us? When did 'today' start?

The defining difference between the Cold War era and the period since is the disappearance of the bi-polar structure. The bi-polarity and antagonism of the Cold War did not make for a safe and secure world; on the contrary, threats to world peace and the anxiety these caused were facts of life. However, in its own wicked way, bi-polarity and the 'balance of power' principle to some extent contributed to a stable world order which was at least not unpredictable. With the disappearance of international 'stability' and the balance of power principle as an ordering mechanism in international politics, political disorder threatened. In addition, the demise of Cold War predictability, which paradoxically had allowed at least some role for international law, might herald the beginning of a more lawless age. By contrast, it could also be claimed that with the idea of balance-of-power politics becoming superfluous, new (legal) opportunities dawned.

Ever since the end of the Cold War, various analyses and scenarios for the future have circulated and have stimulated debate. Sharply distinguished (perhaps too sharply) are, on the one hand, visions of a world in profound disorder, as opposed to, on the other hand, visions of the realisation of the Hegelian ideal of the universal state. Those prophesying disorder blame the global religious and cultural divide, the collapse of states, rising crime rates and the abandonment of politics and democracy.[3] Based on the hypothesis of the 'clash of civilizations',

---

[1] R. Holbrooke, The American Stake in Europe – the European Stake in the United States, Nexus Lecture 2001, 11 October 2001, Tilburg, The Netherlands, *in* 30/31 Nexus 83 (2001).

[2] D. Moïse, Welcome to the New, New World Order, *Financial Times* 13 September 2001, at 15.

[3] J.-M. Guehenno, The End of the Nation State (1995), transl. of *La Fin de la Démocratie* (1993).

Huntington for example predicts a world in disorder in which inter-state relations will take place in a 'largely lawless realm,' instead of being based on human rights and democratic values.[4] After extensive travelling around Africa where tyranny and anarchy have resulted from the social, economic, political and legal failure of states like Somalia, Liberia and Sierra-Leone, Robert Kaplan concluded that we are facing global anarchy now that the 'social fabric' has gone into decline worldwide.[5] A world ruled by crime is a world of anarchy and chaos, and Kaplan wondered: 'Was Democracy Just a Moment?'[6] However, as mentioned above, there are also those who paint a less pessimistic picture of a world in which political and economic liberalism have risen to victory and the Hegelian universal state will eventually be realised.[7] Fukuyama, a former student of Huntington's, reaffirmed the conceptual framework of his 'End of History' by picturing the ultimate 'unabashed victory of economic and political liberalism.' For this, Fukuyama drew on Hegelian thinking where human history is deter-

---

[4] S.P. Huntington, The Clash of civilizations and the Remaking of World Order (1996). Here, Huntington repeats an argument he made during the Cold War, namely that US foreign policy must be based on conservative realism in order to be able to protect the liberal society in America. According to Huntington, who was a life-long Democrat and foreign policy advisor to the Jimmy Carter administration, foreign policy must take a realistic view of human nature and the human condition. In his own words: 'That's it – that's what I am. As Arthur Schlesinger would say, I am a child of Niebuhr.' Robert Kaplan explains: 'Niebuhr's tragic sensibility constitutes a thread connecting all of Huntington's major works. It is the key to Huntington's definition of conservatism.' Kaplan himself acknowledged Niebuhr's influence too. R.D. Kaplan, Looking the World in the Eye, *The Atlantic Monthly*, Dec. 2001, Vol. 288 (5), at 68-82. Kaplan: '[I]n the late 1970s [Huntington] helped Zbigniew Brzezinski and Jimmy Carter to implement a human-rights policy designed to embarrass the Soviet Union, but he has remained sceptical about putting troops on the ground to build Western-style democracy in places with no tradition of it.' As we have seen in the previous chapter, human rights were a tool in the US-Soviet game of power politics.

[5] R.D. Kaplan, The Coming Anarchy, *The Atlantic Monthly*, Feb. 1994. Kaplan argues that the 'coming anarchy' (discernable now in Africa) will become a global phenomenon as (international) (drugs/diamantes) crime and extreme lawlessness will continue to grow and spread and nation states continue to weaken and fragment, while private military groups gain power and revolt. These are the issues the international society has to confront in order to prevent the further destabilisation of both African and non-African states and disintegration caused by the extreme fragmentation of power. Kaplan paints a dark and hopeless picture of West Africa, commenting on 'the withering away of central governments, the rise of tribal and regional domains, the unchecked spread of disease, and the growing pervasiveness of war.' From the local situation he extrapolates the global future. In his view: 'West Africa is becoming *the* symbol of worldwide demographic, environmental, and societal stress, in which criminal anarchy emerges as the real 'strategic' danger.' It suggests 'what war, borders, and ethnic politics will be like a few decades hence.'

[6] R.D. Kaplan, Was Democracy just a Moment?, *The Atlantic Monthly*, Dec. 1997, Vol. 280 No.6, at 55-80. 'Though the swing toward democracy following the Cold War was a triumph for liberal philosophy, the pendulum will come to rest where it belongs – in the middle, between the ideals of [Isaiah] Berlin and the realities of Hobbes. Where a political system leans too far in either direction, realignment or disaster awaits.' With reference to Reinhold Niebuhr, Kaplan emphasises the evil rather than the virtuous part of human nature in his approach of national and international politics. He claims that the US cannot 'establish democracy the world over,' because 'democracy emerges successfully only as a capstone to other social and economic achievements.'

[7] F. Fukuyama, The End of History?, *The National Interest*, 1989.

mined by human consciousness: 'th[e] realm of consciousness *in the long run* necessarily becomes manifest in the material world, indeed creates the material world in its own image.'[8] Given that economic behaviour has its roots in the realm of consciousness and culture, this behaviour is consequently caused or formed by the ideal. Fukuyama maintained that development in the realm of ideas has come to an end, as modern liberalism has proven to be the best ideology (or culture, or philosophy) available which it is impossible to improve on. This means that modern liberalism will eventually be universally victorious in the field of economics and subsequently in the field of politics. Fascism, communism and maoism have all become anachronisms and there is no other or new ideology available to contradict modern liberalism. It is the 'victory of the [Hegelian] idea of the universal homogeneous state' and the 'Common Marketization' of international relations.[9]

These scenarios have stimulated debate on the future of our world. If they have not done so directly, they have still served as the mostly bleak background to more detailed or focused arguments and research. The concerns raised by these images of our future have affected many discussions within various disciplines, and not in the least the international law discourse. The scenarios have in common that they try to characterise the new post-Cold War world, to analyse its dynamics and problems, to map the profound and immensely difficult dilemmas of the new age. The perpetual swing of the pendulum between 'the primacy of law' and the 'primacy of power,' between the more (conservative) realist and the more (liberal or Wilsonian) idealist outlook on international life, continues to occur in both international scholarship and international relations.

Have we entered a new age? And if so, when? Did it happen today? A decade ago? It is too early to tell. It is however a valid conclusion that with the end of the Cold War the world changed dramatically and that to discuss the years between 1990 and 2001 as a new era is not only common practice, but even legitimate. However, whether this age is truly new can only be proven by the passage of time. In another 10 years' time it may emerge that the period in question showed great promise, but that its inhabitants failed to establish a better and more just global order and that they were unable to enhance the legitimacy of international law or to solidify the authority of the United Nations.

Leaving aside the question of periodisation, I have to apply a caveat concerning the difficulties involved in giving a comprehensive overview of contemporary international legal scholarship. And this applies even more to any discussion of the (international) political and cultural-intellectual background of this scholarship.

---

[8] Id.: '[c]onsciousness is cause not effect, and can develop autonomously from the material world; hence the real subtext underlying the apparent jumble of current events is the history of ideology.'

[9] The world will reach its 'post-historical' stage and enter 'a very sad time' without art or philosophy. The 9/11 terrorist attacks have not changed Fukuyama's perspective. See, F. Fukuyama, De Geschiedenis loopt wel degelijk ten einde, *NRC Handelsblad*, 11 October 2001.

The general consensus is, however, that the times we live in are especially defined by two particular contemporary phenomena.

In the first place, the phenomenon of 'globalisation' is reshaping our world. Global interdependency has increased as a result of the integration of national economies into one global economic and financial system ruled by the dynamics of the free market and the liberalisation of world trade and stimulation of foreign investments. This global interdependency has slowly changed how and with whom we communicate and has brought about a confrontation between 'local' culture and a global (homogenising) cultural force. The position of the state is also challenged, as its sovereignty is eroding, both from within and from without. National societies are thus transforming, but above all it is the nature of – and the participation in – the international society which is shifting. The hype of 'globalisation' was to a large extent fuelled by high expectations, it was heralded as a new ideal, a panacea promising to bring global prosperity and prevent conflict worldwide. Since the late 1990s, however, the phenomenon has fallen subject to heavy criticism. Attention to its negative consequences and its impact especially on weaker economies and the poor has, however, not only been drawn by the anti-globalisation movement protesting in, for example, Seattle (WTO conference, 1999), Davos (World Economic Forum, 2001) or Genova (G8 summit, 2001). In 1998, UN Secretary-General Kofi Annan also declared that such a fortunate and beneficial interpretation of globalisation was a form of 'utterly wishful thinking.'[10] In order to be able fully to understand globalisation in all its aspects and consequences, it is necessary to study what he called the *politics* of globalisation and good governance: 'the belief in the ability of the markets to resolve all divisions neglected the reality of differences of interest and outlook; differences that *can* be resolved peacefully; but *must* be resolved politically.' In other words, the 'benign neglect,' during the heydays of globalisation, of the value of 'the politics of good governance, liberty, equity and social justice,' has to end and the political consequences of globalisation have to be looked squarely in the face. In our discussion of globalisation we will concentrate on the changing position of the state in relation to the emerging global civil society and deal with the question of politics and global democracy. A major and valid complaint made about globalisation concerns the democratic deficit of the global society and of its political institutions, the same deficit that rules most of its state members. The tension between the *political* and the *economical* poses a thought-provoking dilemma in respect of the organisation and institutionalisation of good governance and democracy in the global society.

The second phenomenon that distinguishes our era from any other is its intellectual atmosphere or how it has been identified by the puzzling notion of 'post-modernism.' Although our post-modernist detour must of necessity be brief, it is still necessary in order to increase our understanding of it. Post-modernism is an extremely heterogeneous movement, widely ranging from the arts and philoso-

[10] K. Annan, The Politics of Globalisation (1998), (SG/SM/6703).

phy to TV and children's computer games. Post-modernism is unsusceptible to definition, and so I give up any attempt at completeness in describing the phenomenon. Its common denominator is a challenging of principles, values, and/or ideas which prevailed during Modernism, or the period of European Enlightenment. Its criticism of liberal political theory is a distinct feature of the post-modern view. Post-modernism is an extremely broad intellectual-cultural movement, with roots in linguistic, cultural and critical literary studies. It has certainly and revolutionarily influenced the debate on social and political theory. As I am discussing this phenomenon for a better understanding of the context of contemporary legal scholarship, the focus will be on one of the core themes, which can be summed up in the popular post-modern statement: 'the death of the subject,' which symbolises a shift from the *creating*-subject to the idea of the *constructed*-subject. The discussion of the 'subject' is absolutely pivotal to contemporary debate in epistemology, ethics and politics, and in legal theory. It has also contributed to launching some intense discussions concerning the concept of identity. For this reason, we will briefly examine Foucault's attack of the subject and Ricoeur's response to this attack, which consists of a philosophical defence of the subject. Ricoeur's contribution to ethics will subsequently serve as the basis of our re-conceptualisation of ILP in the final chapter, when we need to touch upon the issue of (individual) responsibility. As regards the relevance of post-modernism for contemporary international law scholarship, it should be noted that Foucault's influence on the intellectual conventions of our time can hardly be overestimated. This influence is also noticeable in contemporary international law scholarship, which he affected in two ways. In the first place, he identified law as the repressive and therefore negative form of power. According to Foucault, law and legal concepts are the *negative* language of power. This conception of law has contributed to the general attitude among legal scholars that it is best to *skirt around* such legal concepts as ILP and it explains why legal language and traditionally used concepts are currently largely ignored within the international legal debate. Secondly, but related to the previous observation, Foucault rejects the traditional conception of the intellectual as a person in pursuit of universal truth and justice. Foucault argued that the idea of the 'universal intellectual,' the creature of justice and of law, 'the jurist' who never tires of countering power with law and universal values, has become obsolete. Today's intellectual is not the jurist, but the specialist, who is involved in very specific, local and concrete scientific research. Foucault's attack of the jurist has in my view contributed to the paradoxical state of contemporary international legal theory. On the one hand there is a revived interest in theory, yet on the other hand the available theoretical concepts of international law are not used. Like all other disciplines, international law scholarship proved unable to escape from the influence of ideas such as the marginalisation of universal modern values, the disqualification of the general, universal approach and the negative conception of law and legal language. This is why before I discuss contemporary scholarship, I first wish to deal with the context in which it is situated.

Even though their origins date back to the 1970s, after the Cold War both the phenomenon of globalisation and of post-modernism have generated lively scholarly debate in every possible discipline concerning their nature and their advantages and disadvantages. The most dominant post-modern approaches, such as structuralism, post-structuralism, and deconstruction, emerged in French philosophy in the early 1970s, entered legal theory in the 1980s and were introduced into international law scholarship in the late 1980s and early 1990s. The revival of theory was for a large part their doing.

As early as 1971, international relations theorists Keohane and Nye published a special issue of *International Organisation* in a successful attempt to boost theory concerning the ever less state-centred character of the international society and the emerging transnational society in which both states and non-state actors could participate and interact. As we have seen in the previous chapter, during the Cold War the scholarly debate on the subjects of international law reached its limits in the mainstream consensus that international law and ILP should be approached pragmatically. Although the significance of participation in transnational governance, so as to strengthen international law and the democratic nature of the international society, was acknowledged, at the same time it was undisputed that 'states are and must remain the overwhelming important subjects of international law.'[11] The Cold War context prevented international legal scholars from opting out of realistic and pragmatic approaches, causing the (moderate) state-centred reasoning to persist and preventing the emergence of new provocative conceptions.

At this point, now that international life has changed drastically, international legal scholars show a renewed interest in concepts and theory. Nonetheless, the rather restrained usage of the concept of ILP in contemporary international law discourse is puzzling. As Philip Alston already observed, compared with other disciplines, the concept of 'globalisation' has been relatively 'neglect[ed]' in international law literature.[12] This also applies to the concept of ILP. It seems to be ignored almost completely, or brushed aside with a simple 'ILP will get us nowhere,' (a response I often encountered at international law meetings and conferences) without even the courtesy of a final analysis or any kind of explanation. This is highly remarkable for two reasons: in the first place, because there is such widespread debate on the collapse or the failure of the state and the changes in state sovereignty and on the new position in international life of a diversity of non-state actors; secondly, in our post-modern times, where EVERYTHING has already been declared either 'dead' or 'ended,' the demise of the subject was proclaimed especially loudly. The concept of ILP was not even analysed expressly before it was declared defunct and no thought was spared to the fact that the concept comes into play naturally when international law has to confront the compli-

[11] W. Friedmann, The Changing Structure of International Law 213 (1964).

[12] P. Alston, The Myopia of the Handmaidens: International Lawyers and Globalization, 8 *EJIL* 435 (1997).

cated issues of legal theory and the accommodation of non-state actors within the system.

In my view, the *conventional doctrine of ILP has actually been (considered to be) an obstacle* for international legal scholars when they wish to discuss globalisation and, in particular, non-state actors from a legal perspective. Still, I will use contemporary international law scholarship and its views on globalisation and the changing role of the state and non-state actors to trace what little use is made of ILP in order to enhance our understanding of the scholarly context international lawyers operate in today. I will also concisely address the post-modern influences and the way they make themselves felt in international law literature and explain the premise I included above concerning the prevailingly negative outlook on law and the jurist.

The purpose of this chapter is therefore to explore the use of the concept of ILP today, or rather, as I already indicated in the first chapter, its *non*-use in international legal scholarship. Indeed, its negation at a time when international life is so globalised and hosts such a diversity of participants and operates in an atmosphere where intellectuals, scholars, etc. have, if not turned against the human subject, at least often attempted to reach beyond him, is surprising. To understand if ILP has any meaning today, and if so, what this entails, it will be particularly useful to explore the way in which ILP is used in the scholarship of Thomas Franck and Christine Chinkin. They both respond in their own way to contemporary international and intellectual life and formulate a vision of the international society and international law. What they have in common is that their endeavour is constructive and that their criticism, although profound, never borders on the cynical or downright sceptical. Their individual projects are in their own singular way attempts to improve international law, to make the international society more just, and most of all, to improve the individual life of many, where possible. This is done while maintaining a close connection with topical discussions in contemporary international law scholarship.

Thomas Franck's recent book deals with the topical issue of the construction of identity by today's individuals. In response to the current 'global identity crisis,' Franck offers a kind of social individualist vision of the future of a (global) social and political life based on the individual's right to re-define or re-identify the self. He addresses the implications of the empowered individual for the international law system and the chances of a 'universal constitutional democracy.' Christine Chinkin is a moderate representative of the feminist approach in international law discourse. Her emancipatory argument is, however, not restricted to women, but addresses suppressed groups in general.

After I have analysed whether, and if so, how ILP is used, I will comment on this practice and suggest that within international law theory we are shifting the focus from sovereignty towards a new paradigm of ILP. The juxtaposition of the demand for democratic legitimacy of global governance and the conviction that theory matters to international law provides us with the momentum to re-conceive ILP as an instrument to enhance the legitimacy of international law and the democracy of the global society by employing the concept as a conceptual missing link between the individual and international law, between morality and international politics, as the '*vocal cords*' of international law.

5.2. Context of Contemporary International Legal Scholarship

5.2.1. Globalisation and fragmentation: 'the age of non-state actors?'

The phenomenon of globalisation is of such immensity that any exhaustive survey is impossible. Globalisation already started during the Cold War. However, in the post-1990 world, which lacked the stability of the bi-polar structure, its consequences could emerge with greater force. Globalisation has both an economic and a political side to it, and on both sides the increasing influence of non-state actors challenges the traditional state-centred structure of the Westphalian order. This is why our time is often characterised as the 'age of non-state actors.'[13]

Economics

The claim that the state is in decline has been most forcefully made based on an economic perspective on globalisation. As capitalism had outlived communism and many national economies had shifted from planned to free market, the perception that *the invisible hand* of the market, i.e., the free market principle, was the new global ordering mechanism could become widespread. The process of global economic liberation – the creation of open markets and the breakdown of trade barriers – would constitute the salutary effect of globalisation. However, this outlook presupposed a socially responsible attitude on the part of the corporate world. In reality, there is a very real risk that the supremacy of economic interests will push aside social and political interests and cause a further shift of (global) power to corporate non-state actors, i.e., the MNCs or even private financial players with the financial power to cause dramatic devaluation.[14]

MNCs have always been powerful players in the international society and have since long been accepted as partners in the conclusion of 'internationalised' contracts with states. In such cases, many have argued, they are endowed with a kind of derived ILP.[15] Such contracts are governed by international law in order that possible conflicts may be settled by arbitration to minimise the risk of bias litigation. Thanks to their strong and long-standing lobbying tradition, MNCs have also gained significant influence on international trade negotiations. The process of globalisation has brought many new liberties and has eliminated numerous obstacles to the movement of goods around the globe and has facilitated investments in new locations and operation sites. However, since globalisation is

[13] J. Mathews, Power Shift – The Age of Nonstate actors, 76 (1) *Foreign Affairs* 50 (1997).

[14] E.g., G. Soros' subjection of Asian currencies to harmful speculation (e.g., Malaysia, 1997/8).

[15] See, e.g., Daillier and Pellet (and Nguyen Quoc Dinh), Droit International Public 674 (1994).

in many ways so beneficial to MNCs in terms of power and profits, this naturally gave rise to social pressure being applied to the global corporations where it was demanded that they do business in accordance with a new ethic, respecting labour standards, human rights[16] and the environment. MNCs should do what is possible 'within their sphere of influence,' as Kofi Annan has put it, to promote human rights and avoid their violation. This interaction between the business community and the United Nations is of course not new,[17] but the UN Secretary-General has developed an interesting new initiative with the *Global Compact*,[18] a non-legally binding framework for responsible corporate leadership and the global promotion of sustainable development. Its success depends on its *norm-creative capacity*, e.g., on whether the Nine Principles – 'a set of core values in the areas of human rights, labour standards and the environment' of which 'universality and legitimacy ... have the capacity to inspire *all* social actors to work towards change'– will develop into established international norms the corporate community will comply with and thus effectuate *actual* change. The Global Compact is a new interactive experiment in getting international norms adopted by corporations without inter-governmental negotiations, yet within the institutional structure of the international order. The (non-institutional) power of consumers is another, very significant, factor for global corporations, which have to seek public approval of their actions, to develop private initiatives ranging from the voluntary adoption of tightened 'codes of conduct'[19] to the publication of social and environmental sustainability reports in addition to their annual financial reports; [20] oil companies have not made up the rear in this respect.[21] It is fair to

[16] The point of departure for this argument is frequently the Universal Declaration of Human Rights Preamble's last paragraph, which states that the General Assembly, '*Proclaims* this Universal Declaration of Human Rights as a common standard of achievement for all peoples and all nations, to the end that every individual and *every organ of society, keeping this Declaration constantly in mind*, shall strive by teaching and education to promote respect for these rights and freedoms and by progressive measures, national and international, to secure their universal and effective recognition and observance ...' Emphasis added.

[17] The drafting of the United Nation Code of Conduct of Transnational Corporations has been in progress since 1977. See also the OECD Guidelines for Multinational Enterprises (2001). The UN has a rapporteur who has reported for example on the (environmental) damage, attributed to Shell, done to Ogoni-land in Nigeria.

[18] The plan was launched by the UN Secretary-General at the W.E.F. in Davos in 1999 in an attempt to address social and environmental issues of globalisation in cooperation with leading companies, and so, to 'correct' the negative consequences of the free market principle. Participating companies, the number has risen to the hundreds, have a kind of gentleman's agreement with Secretary-General Kofi Annan to implement, and annually report on their progress with regard to the Nine Principles. See, the UN website: <http://www.unglobalcompact.com/>.

[19] There is also a non-voluntary Code of Conduct laid down in a multilateral treaty negotiated under the auspices of the UNCTAD in 1973-4: 'Convention on a Code of Conduct for Liner Conferences.'

[20] Royal Dutch Shell published its first 'Health, Safety, and Environment' report in 1998. In these annual reports, international norms and standards, e.g., the Kyoto protocol or the OECD standards, are taken as targets for compliance.

[21] The Norwegian oil company Statoil has made the first deal ever with Amnesty International for courses on Human Rights and Conflict management for their managers who go abroad. In its board of directors Statoil has a vice-president for country analysis and social responsibility.

say that since the late 1990s, the debate on 'corporate (social) responsibility,'[22] 'corporate sustainability,'[23] or 'good corporate citizenship' has climbed rapidly to the top of the global governance agenda.[24]

From the global economic perspective, the state is in retreat, as in a globalised world the traditional state no longer constitutes the most natural form of economic organisation. It has been argued that the state has become an obsolete 'even impossible, business unit in a global economy.'[25] Indeed, the state's economic role and function has been changing and in some cases to the extent of partial withdrawal, for example, when it comes to the activities of the European Central Bank or the World Bank and the IMF. However, the '*Virtual State*'[26] has not arrived yet. On the contrary, as *Financial Times* Chief Economic Commentator, Martin Wolf, has explained: 'contrary to one common assumption, [today's] form of globalisation will not spell the end of the modern nation-state. ... As the source of order and basis of governance, the state will remain in the future as ef-

[22] This notion is now also widely used outside scholarly literature, e.g., in any self-respecting company's mission statement and in government statements. For instance, UK's Minister of State for e-Commerce and Competitiveness, D. Alexander, has declared that he is developing this notion. *See*, <http://www.societyandbusiness.gov.uk>.

[23] Another 'private' initiative is, for example, the Dow Jones' Stoxx Sustainability Index, which lists the Dow Jones companies that are leading in terms of *corporate sustainability*; these companies are assessed on the basis of a business approach that besides economic aspects, also includes environmental and social aspects that play a role in their operations and strategies, 'sustainability-driven companies position themselves for the future.' See, <http://www.stoxx.com/indexes/sustindexes.html>. See also, The Financial Times and FTSE Index.

[24] In the debate, Shell has even been challenged to exercise a kind of 'commercial statesmanship' in their employment of power, which emanates from their capacity to promote strategic interests even in instable situations, and should include, most of all, the courage to acknowledge and communicate on emotional and non-technical aspects of their strategies and operations. A.H.M. Brouwers, Shell moet zich staatsmanschap aanleren, *NRC Handelsblad*, 14 January 1997, a contribution to the polemic with the then President of Royal Dutch/Shell C.A.J. Herkströter, Multinationals willen debat met samenleving aan, *NRC Handelsblad*, 14 October 1996; also, C.A.J. Herkströter, Het schort aan richtinggevens leiderschap, *NRC Handelsblad*, 28 December 1996.

[25] K. Ohmae, The Rise of the Region State: the end of the nation-state 5 (1994). The Nation State will be replaced by 'regional States' as the 'true' units relevant within global economic relations and a global information society.

[26] R. Rosecrance, The Rise of the Virtual State, 75 (4) *Foreign Affairs* 45 (1996). The virtual state is a state which 'has downsized its territorially based production capability,' [it] 'specializes in modern technical and research services and derives its income not just from high-value manufacturing, but from product design, marketing and financing.' Id., at 46-47. See also, for a more realistic assessment of the implications of the information age for the future (of the state), Keohane and Nye, Power and Interdependence in the Information Age, 77 (5) *Foreign Affairs* 81 (1998). They stress the importance of the *credibility* of a state's politics and conclude: 'states are resilient, and some countries, especially large ones with democratic societies, are well-placed to benefit from an information society. Although the coherence of government policies may diminish in these pluralistic and penetrated states, their institutions will be attractive and their pronouncements will be credible. They will therefore be able to wield soft power to achieve many of their objectives. The future lies neither exclusively with the state nor with transnational relations: geographically based states will continue to structure politics in an information age, but they will rely less on material resources and more on their ability to remain credible to a public with increasingly diverse sources of information.' Id., at 94.

fective, and will be as essential, as it has ever been.'[27] Tax collection might be more difficult in a globalised world, but not impossible; we are not facing a fiscal crisis.[28] The World Bank has also stated that 'an effective state' – as 'partner, catalyst, and facilitator' is essential for economic and socially responsible development.[29] Good governance is necessary for healthy economic development, for example, the state has to create a stable and predictable legal climate to support investment and prevent corruption and capitalist excesses.[30] The transformation of the global economy into an 'information (or information technology) economy' has created the new reality that expertise or knowledge is (social) power, which has increased the pressure on global institutions to open up their structure to non-state actors.

Within the World Bank and the IMF, good governance has developed into one of the key notions.[31] Moreover, these global institutions have also increasingly been forced to account for the consequences of their actions, whether ecological, social, or humanitarian. This accountability is a partly unofficial (cultural) and a partly official (formal) development. The IMF, the World Bank, and, to a lesser degree, the WTO have significantly intensified their cooperation with civil society's non-state actors, or NGOs, and have implemented institutional adaptations as well.[32] Within the World Bank, NGOs are now increasingly understood to be 'partners' in the institutions' objectives and the creation of the independent Inspection Panel has indeed been a major institutional change. It enables 'any group of two or more people' or an NGO to challenge a particular World Bank-financed project for its negative impact on the local environment or human rights situation and thus for being in violation of World Bank policy.[33] This right of individuals is indeed a revolutionary move away from the conventional state-centred paradigm of international life. Here, like traditionally in the domain of

---

[27] M. Wolf, Will the Nation-State Survive Globalisation?, 80 (1) *Foreign Affairs* 178-190 (2001). See also, in the same issue, B.R. Scott, The Great Divide in the Global Village, at 160.

[28] Id., Wolf, at 185 *et seq.*

[29] The World Bank, The State in a Changing World, World Development Report 1997, at 1.

[30] The crisis in the US business and financial community with its huge corporate fraud cases in the spring and summer of 2002 has also fuelled the debate on a new ethic of corporate governance. President Bush called for a strengthening of the personal responsibility of CEOs and, on 30 July 2002, he signed the Sarbanes-Oxley Act to reform current American business practices. The legislation intends to improve corporate responsibility and increase the protection of shareholders and workers.

[31] Good governance is also a factor in the decision-making process in national debates and policy formulations for granting bilateral assistance.

[32] See, e.g., M. Williams, *International Organisations and the Environment Social Movement*, paper presented at the Non-State Actors and Authority in the Global System Conference, University of Warwick, 31 October – 1 November 1997. Also, J.A. Scholte, *The International Monetary Fund and Civil Society – An Underdeveloped Dialogue*, paper presented at the same conference. See for the new initiatives within/of the WTO, 'WTO and NGOs – Relations with Non-Governmental Organisations/Civil Society,' on their website.

[33] The Inspection Panel Operating Procedures as adopted on 19 August 1994, as posted on their website: <http://www.worldbank.org/inspectionpanel>.

human rights, NGOs play a vital role in bringing out and documenting harmful actions and violation of international norms.[34] NGOs have an arrived position within the global institutional structure as watchdogs and as experts, whose representation and participation in international law creating conferences has left its traces.[35] The NGOs' consultative status with the UN is undisputed,[36] moreover, the Organisation intends to develop UN – Civil Society relations further in order to enhance the fairness of global governance procedures and institutions.

It would be irresponsibly optimistic to think that trade and a capitalist philosophy are all that is needed to prevent war and conflict; democracy and a reasonable distribution of wealth are necessary conditions too, as Kofi Annan tends to remind us. The past neglect of such political values as good governance, the rule of law, social justice and human rights has contributed to social and political crisis in countries in Africa, Asia and Europe. Since the 'economic integration in an interdependent world is neither all-powerful nor politically neutral,' it is necessary to formulate a global political approach to the damaging consequences. Political and economic liberation should join forces to combat the downside of globalisation.

> Political liberty ... [i]s a necessary condition for lasting economic growth, even if not a sufficient one. Democracy must be accepted as the midwife of development, and political and human rights must be recognized as key pillars of any architecture of economic progress.[37]

In the global society, the 'universal pillars of democratic pluralism,' i.e., the rule of law, a legitimate government and the protection of human rights and freedoms, must be respected so as to prevent globalisation from turning into 'trade sovereignty', i.e., the priority of economic interests over politics and justice. And, 'as the sole international organisation with universal legitimacy and scope, the

---

[34] Amnesty International's essential role in the international protection of human rights is undisputed and well documented, but another example is Transparency International's contribution to the fight against corruption by means of raising public awareness, influencing business and governmental practices, and providing information on corruption and good governance through, *inter alia*, their TI Source Book, database, and Corruption Perception Index (CPI). In their article on TI, Wang and Rosenau show how TI has indeed played a key role as an 'an agent of *normative* change' in putting corruption on the global governance agenda. H. Wang and J.N. Rosenau, Transparency International and Corruption as an Issue of Global Governance, 7 (1) *Global Governance* 25-49 (2001). TI has also campaigned for an effective OECD Anti-Corruption Convention, adopted 21 November 1997. See also, <http://www.transparency.de>.

[35] The expertise NGOs have for example deployed at the international law making conferences in Rio (Negotiations on the Climate Treaty, 1992 Earth Summit), Ottawa (Negotiations on the Ban on Landmines Treaty, 1998), Kyoto (Negotiations on Global Warming, 1997) and Rome (Negotiations on the Statute of the International Criminal Court in 2000) has indeed confirmed that *knowledge bestows power*. The participation of NGOs in such law creating processes could even be more direct if they were hired to operate as members of government delegations.

[36] ECOSOC Res. 1296 (XLIV) on Consultation of NGOs.

[37] K. Annan, The Politics of Globalisation, Lecture at Harvard University, 17 September 1998, (SG/SM/6703).

United Nations has an interest – indeed an obligation – to help secure the equitable and lasting success of globalisation.' After all, 'the limitations on the ability of any state or any organisation to affect the processes of globalisation call for a *global*, concerted effort.' The United Nations are active in finding new institutional ways of establishing, coordinating and stimulating dialogue between state and non-state actors. The Global Compact is not an exception in this respect. In its 1995 report *Our Global Neighborhood*, the UN Commission on Global Governance proposed the introduction of a new right of petition for individuals and civil society organisations to bring threats to the security of the *people* to the agenda of the Security Council.[38] In May 2002, the first session of the Permanent Forum on Indigenous Issues took place. The Forum consists of sixteen independent experts, eight of whom are nominated by governments and elected by ECOSOC, while the remaining eight are appointed by the president of ECOSOC on the basis of 'broad indigenous representation.'[39] In other words, non-state actors are gradually gaining access to the traditionally inter-state system in various ways.

With the end of the fully state-centred Westphalian system in sight, the need for a *new architecture* of global political and legal structures is discussed. This new structure is to accommodate the plurality of players and enable them to contribute to the global society as well as to be held accountable to it. This means that the accountability for their actions of NGOs and MNCs must also be addressed. The relationship between the institutions of global governance, such as between the United Nations or the World Bank on the one hand and NGOs on the other, as well as the direct relationship between states and NGOs are slowly transforming international life. NGOs have also been criticised for the way they operate at times, especially when they rapidly mobilise public opinion on the basis of false or incomplete information. Their acquired role both instigates and requires debate concerning their capacities, responsibilities and position within the international system. NGOs are often praised for enhancing the representation of diverse interests and values in UN processes and for their (international) *norm-creating capacity* in general.[40] However, it must also be noted that NGOs are not representatives authorisad by democratic election, which raises the question of who controls the watchdogs? In any case, a new fabric is emerging in which states, IGOs and NGOs on the one hand operate interdependently and coordi-

[38] Our Global Neighborhood, The Report of the Commission on Global Governance (1995), at 260. The 'Council for Petitions' is one of many proposals for UN reform which emanate from the understanding that the 'multitude of new actors' is changing the world, both challenging and contributing to global governance.

[39] CHR Res. 2000/87 (27 April) as quoted in, M.J. Dennis, The 56th Session of the UN Commission on Human Rights, 95 (1) *AJIL* 218 (2001). See also, M.J. Dennis, Human Rights in 2002: The Annual Sessions of the UN Commission on Human Rights and the Economic and Social Council, 97 (2) *AJIL* 380-381 (2003).

[40] See, for UN partnership with civil society: <http://www.un.org/partners/civil_society/home.htm>.

nately, but on the other function in opposition with the question of accountability in dire need of solving.

Politics

With the end of the Cold War, international politics entered a new phase. No longer was the world sharply divided into the First, Second and Third World. States had to redefine their national interest and foreign policy. Earlier we mentioned the scenarios which were developed to characterise this new phase: the 'clash of civilizations' script or the 'impending anarchy' version. So how would global politics develop? The political side of the phenomenon of globalisation began to unfold with the disappearance of the international bi-polar political structure. After the USSR had disintegrated, formerly communist states sought to embrace economic and political liberalism. The end of the (extreme) balance of power politics furthermore led the former rival superpowers to abandon their respective spheres of influence and the (for example, African) countries in and over which they had fought their battles, leaving these states without resources to survive after which disintegration duly followed. Since the end of the Cold War,[41] profound questions have arisen concerning (the feasibility of the concept of) the state, the state's sovereignty and human (political) organisation. The end of the state has also been claimed from the political institutional perspective. A world in which global economic and political interdependency continues to increase might suggest that territory and political sovereignty as the organising or regulative principle are in decline. The political side of globalisation may be understood as the developments which undermine the political structure of states and challenge the traditional international community. In the political realm, globalisation goes hand in hand with *fragmentation.*

After 1990, several states – although often in ways that are incomparable – became fragmented or continued merely to subsist as failed states. Examples are the USSR, Yugoslavia, Czechoslovakia, Somalia, Ethiopia, Afghanistan and Sierra-Leone, to mention a few that have been subject to disintegration. In post-Cold War world politics, tribal and ethnic ideologies surfaced with such strength that numerous internal conflicts broke out and created a general state of lawlessness, instability and insecurity. This happened for example in Liberia, Rwanda, Congo and Sudan. In many (parts) of these countries, e.g., Kosovo, East Timor and Mozambique, the United Nations are doing an immensely important job trying to

---

[41] 'The collapse of the communist regimes between Istria and Vladivostok not only produced an enormous zone of political uncertainty, instability, chaos and civil war, but also destroyed the international system that stabilized international relations for forty years. ... The basic units of politics themselves, the territorial, sovereign and independent "nations-states," including the oldest and stablest, found themselves pulled apart by forces of a supranational or transnational economy, and by the infranational forces of secessionist regions and ethnic groups. Some of these-such is the irony of history-demanded the outdated and unreal status of miniature sovereign "nation-states" for themselves. The future of politics was obscure, but its crisis at the end of the Short Twentieth Century was patent.' Hobsbawm, The Age of Extremes, at 10-11.

re-establish social and political structures based on the rule of law and democracy, e.g., by organising free elections. Where before the lid could be pressed down on internal conflicts by the Cold War balance of power structure, it was now blown sky high and civil war broke out in many regions. Sub-state groups with a distinct national or ethnic identity explored their possibilities: should they decide to cherish their unique identity within the context of the traditional collective entity, like the Quebecois, or should they break away from the state and create an independent one of their, as the Kurds and Chechnyans chose to do? When the internal right to self-determination is denied, the fragmentation of the structure is the result. However, it would be incorrect to interpret this development as heralding the end of the nation-state, since the claims for statehood, based on nationhood or ethnic identity, actually rely on the state system. It does however mean that in these cases nationalism emanating from nationhood is a stronger force than nationalism emanating from statehood. Leaving the claim to statehood aside, the problems the international community has to confront now is the enormous violence displayed in these internal conflicts and the gross violations of human rights that occur in them. These things can partly be traced back to the unsatisfactory progress of good and democratic governance.

The international community is increasingly, albeit hesitantly, taking responsibility *vis-à-vis* the people who suffer most by exploring the doctrine of humanitarian intervention. This has also stimulated the discussion on the transformation of sovereignty and the extent of the *domaine reservé* and has triggered debate on the legitimacy of state power, which, in order to be legitimate, must hinge on respect for human rights, democratic values and political transparency. Seen in the light of these post-Cold War developments, it is fair to say that the position of the state, the scope of domestic jurisdiction and the degree of sovereignty are all shifting.

In the case of a total failure of governmental structures and when power has slipped to militant rebel groups, a serious problem arises, as 'non-state actors involved in armed conflicts, unlike states, are not legally bound to respect the provisions of international human rights treaties'[42] (although their position within Geneva Law is of course different if they are belligerents involved in an internal conflict as defined in the First Protocol).[43] Norway, in the framework of the UN Commission on Human Rights, has taken the initiative to negotiate a document on 'fundamental standards of humanity' in order to 'identify common rules of human rights and humanitarian law' which would apply to these non-state actors, i.e., armed groups involved in internal armed conflicts.

Forced by the international developments, the problem of the legal position of terrorist groups has also come to the forefront. Again in the context of the UN

---

[42] M.J. Dennis, The 56th Session of the UN Commission on Human Rights, 95 (1) *AJIL* 215 (2001).

[43] Protocol I (1977), Art. I para.4: 'armed conflicts in which people are fighting against colonial domination and alien occupation and against racist régimes in the exercise of their right of self-determination...'

Commission on Human Rights, European states have demonstrated their concern about the possibility that 'any status under international law' will be conferred upon terrorists. For this reason they again voted against the annually returning Turkish resolution in 2000, which denounces 'gross violations of human rights perpetrated by terrorist groups,' because a 'clear distinction must be made between acts which are attributable to states, and criminal acts which are not.'[44] In 2002, the EU abstained with respect to the terrorism resolution (CHR Res. 2002/35 of 23 April), explaining that '[a]s a matter of principle' it could not 'subscribe to the assertion that terrorist acts as such constitute human rights violations'' and that instead '[a]cts of terrorism can ... constitute, as has been the case in the events of the 11th of September, acts of aggression threatening international peace and security.'[45] These concerns are testimony to the sensitivity of the issue of attributing 'status in international law.' Legal status not only implies the accountability of new status holders under international law, but would also give them rights under the system. The international community continues to struggle with this question of how to conceive and perhaps incorporate non-state actor abuses of human rights within the system of international human rights law.[46]

After 11 September 2001, the monopoly of the state on force and intelligence has been strengthened in some respects, but in others, state power has weakened due to a sense of being constantly under siege from various directions. There is the globalisation of organised crime, evidenced by drug-cartels and the illegal trade in diamonds, and of course, internationally operating terrorist networks. However, rather than to fall prey to short-term observations, it is important to realise the long-term post-Cold War developments in world politics. In order to be successful, the economic and political aspects and consequences of the process of globalisation must be managed wisely, by which I mean that a responsible equilibrium must be sought, in an attempt to implement the principles of good governance also at the global level. The analysis of the French diplomat Guehenno can provide insight into these matters.

Guehenno argues that the fall of the Berlin Wall marked the 'end of democracy' and the state system, and the beginning of the 'imperial age' without an emperor. Contrary to Fukuyama, Guehenno envisions the end of democratic liberalism now that politics is losing its primacy and the idea of the coherent au-

---

[44] The 56th Session of the UN Commission on Human Rights, at 214-215.

[45] M.J. Dennis, The 58th Session of the UN Commission on Human Rights, March – April 2002, in 97 *AJIL* 366 (2003).

[46] M.J. Dennis, The 57th Session of the UN Commission on Human Rights, March – April 2001, in 96 *AJIL* 181-197 (2002), at 183: 'The Commission continued to struggle with the issue of abuses committed by nonstate actors, without state authority or sanction. Traditionally, human rights have been perceived as obligations of the state to protect and promote the rights and freedoms of individuals. Increasingly, however, states have been willing to characterize conduct by individuals or groups as violating human rights.' E.g., with regard to the position of women in and their protection by international law, international human rights law increasingly defines violent action by non-state actors against women (including domestic violence, rape, female genital mutilation, among others) as violations of international human rights and humanitarian law.

tonomous subject has fragmented.[47] His thesis is that we will witness the nation state's demise in a globally integrated and networked world in which territoriality – a defining and organising element of the nation state and its sovereignty – has been seriously undermined. His main concern is with the question of how politics should be employed if not territorially. The end of the nation state in fact means *the end of democracy and politics*, as it was always the state which defended democratic values and created room for solidarity and re-distributive justice. Guehenno warns of the threatening 'crisis of solidarity' which will occur if the traditional political organisation involved in political tasks fragments. Power has shifted away from the political institutions which make up the organisation of the sovereign state and is flowing towards a different structure, namely the network. We are leaving the 'institutional age' and entering the 'network age.' Networks hinge upon relations and a 'relational' empire will succeed where state societies have fragmented due to the erosion of the solidarity between its citizens and because of the centralised structure of the state society. In the resulting society which is characterised by chaos and clutter individuals lose their compass and their natural (territorially based) identity, so they will quest for a new identity for fear of becoming faceless and, consequently, turn to smaller communities.[48] Differences are emphasised in the search for new links and communities, based for example on religion, ethnicity, nationhood, ideals and interests, or the company. Not only power will change, so will violence.[49] Guehenno fears the defeat of politics by the (consequences of the) free market mechanism. Without politics and democracy, societies will fragment and the world will not only become decentralised, but also disorderly and violent. Sovereignty will no longer be a relevant concept and will need to be replaced by a functional notion that takes account of the world's openness and that will be effective in confronting urgent global problems. The post-national age will be seized by a *crisis of legitimacy* if democratic politics can no longer control and regulate power. Guehenno subsequently points out that in the vacuum left by the retreat of politics NGOs could

[47] The End of the Nation State, at 25, 30. 'In distinguishing clearly between the public and private spheres, the fathers of liberal democracy tried to reconcile the one-dimensional logic of interests with the humanist tradition that makes everyone into a subject: the citizen of modern times had a double life, but in each of the two facets of his existence, he preserved a certain internal unity. With the abandonment of the premise of the pre-eminence of the political, this break between public and private does but becomes banal, and this banalization pounds to bits the very idea of the subject, which is the other foundation of liberal democracy. Not only is there nothing that transcends the confrontation of particular interests, but these interests are being fragmented. An individual can simultaneously belong to a political party, a professional union, a consumers' group, and a company; he escapes conflict of interest only when he accepts an infinite division of himself.'

[48] Modern man sees the community 'as the natural framework within which everyone may rediscover his identity. Without any links to a territory, 'nomadic,' and nevertheless imprisoned in a function, without an overarching perspective to give a meaning to a given task, modern man, a social nodule infinitely reproduced and nevertheless always single, solitary, is condemned to find difference in order to share with others, as different as he is, a feeling of common heritage.' Id., at 45.

[49] See, in particular, id., at 111 *et seq*. '[T]he distinction between public violence and private violence ... [will be] blurr[ed].' Id., at 118.

play an increasingly important role. They could be the ones to fight for solidarity and relief in a world in which peace belongs to the past and unity is only expressed in the worship of the 'Golden Calf,' the supreme divinity of money.[50] However, Guehenno still sees a way out that would preserve liberty and our (democratic) values in the new global society: 'it is certainly a *question of adapting institutions to the new globality*, and of inventing new political forms, which cannot simply be a transposition to a continental or inter-continental level of the experience of the nation-states.' In addition, it is essential that we 'rediscover that a human community is not only a political notion but a philosophical and religious one' and that we 'rediscover what creates the bonds between humans that constitute a community.'[51]

This last remark refers to something that should not be ignored here either, namely the negative connotation of globalisation when we look at it from the individual's perspective. The anti-globalists or globophobes see the new world as fragmented, composed of international networks, it is true, but these networks lack a real centre which is able to regulate and correct when necessary. They are moreover concerned that global business objectives will enter the public sphere and interfere with governmental efforts undertaken in the public interest. This would reduce social and moral progress to the extent deemed feasible by profit calculation and deprive the people of their power and representation. Politics will be replaced by economics and 'the death of democracy' may well become a fact.[52] The idea that 'the public interest has lost out to the corporate interest' is not uncommon. Globalisation and a globalised world may be profitable from an economic perspective, but to the individual it may also be alienating and completely uncontrollable, which can produce a sense of powerlessness. After all, fighting for your beliefs in a global (economic) society so vast, complex and dominant must surely be futile? Reisman describes the paradox or dilemma we are facing as follows:

> [R]ational responses to this increasingly global condition require more transnational governmental structures and the transfer to them of competences reserved to the national bureaucracy. Each of these new creations, with its necessary transfer of competences, further reduces the range for personal involvement in the decisions that affect one's life. Hence a paradox: the search for political, military or economic security through the creation of transnational institutions simultaneously generates an insecurity, because the resulting interdependencies stir deep uncertainty and anxiety in many individuals about their dependence on processes that are beyond the influence of their primary political communities. When the overall value-status of the individual is also imperilled because of other economic or social changes, themselves the result of transnationalization of many sectors, latent feelings of insecurity are further aggravated.[53]

[50] Id., at 108.
[51] Id., at 139. Emphasis added.
[52] N. Hertz, The Silent Takeover: Global Capitalism and the Death of Democracy (2001).
[53] M. Reisman, Designing and Managing the Future of the State, 3 *EJIL* 412 (1997).

The individual is losing his way in a world that is ruled by the power of the market and by structures too vast to oversee. The human subject who decides his own essence and defines himself through action is on the verge of dying out. The individual political subject faces extinction as the state threatens to shed its function of serving as the primary political community.

Citizenship as the traditional definition of the relationship between the individual and the state loses significance in a global (political) world. Man wants to be free, but also to belong, to be independent and yet feel secure, and any organisation of political power (which is necessary to confront the power of the market) has to take these features of human nature into account. Man is not only a rational being, he is also a social creature who needs and seeks a socio-political community in which he can belong. For many, the positive side and romantic allure of the 'global village' is becoming obscured by the supremacy of capitalist philosophy and the resulting 'Coca-cola-ization' of taste and culture. This latter homogenizing force on the one hand provokes the emergence of a kind of 'global culture', while on the other it gives rise to active 'localism' for posing a threat to local culture and the human identity and individuality and for eroding the individual's influence on processes that determine his life to a significant degree. The global village tends to stretch man's natural *appetitus societatis* to its limits or, in other words, by globalisation man is ultimately confronted by the limits of individualism *in strictu sensu.* Being the social creature that he is man yearns to belong, and by belonging to political communities the individual is able to contain his feelings of powerlessness through the processes of recognition, representation and participation. The opposite trend of desiring to stand out, to distinguish oneself from homogeneous masses, keeps diversity and pluralism alive. As a consequence, today's globalism is part of a dialectical relationship with localism, a duality which only politics can regulate.

In conclusion, the rise of non-state actors which was stimulated by the economic process of globalisation and changing global politics constitutes the political institutional and cultural challenge of today: *how to adapt* the existing political institutions, both of the state and of the international community, to this new global order and in the process strengthen their stability, authority, fairness and legitimacy?[54]

5.2.2. Post-modernism and the fragmentation of the self: the end of the subject?

Post-modernism does not encompass a single homogeneous movement or

[54] The re-politicisation of world politics together with the democratisation of global governance has rapidly gained a place near the top of the global agenda over the past few years: 'globalisation's democratic deficit' needs to be urgently addressed by 'a global institutional response' to enhance the democratic legitimacy of global organisations. J.S. Nye, Jr., Globalisation's Democratic Deficit: How to Make International Institutional Institutions More Accountable, 80 (4) *Foreign Affairs* 2-3 (2001).

programme, nor is there consensus in the literature on how to define it. To what or whom should we turn for a better understanding of the attitude or *Zeitgeist* which is termed 'post-modern'? Could it be explained by popular culture, in a film like *The Truman Show* which fuses fact with fiction? Or should we follow the feminist idea that women are the non-existent sex or, when they do exist, it is only as 'the constructed-other' of men, giving them a suppressed and excluded identity, making women sexual objects with their sexuality defined only negatively?[55] We could turn to architecture and examine the 'deconstructivist' construction of the *Kunsthal* in Rotterdam. Yes, let's try contemporary architecture. It would be a good place to start, as it was one of the earliest and most original playgrounds of post-modernism. The post-modern revolt against modern architecture, which is perceived as 'the son of the Enlightenment', consists of a reaction against modernism's overly serious and excessively rational character and its attempt 'to reinvent itself totally on rational grounds.' In the words of the architect Charles Jenks, who stressed 'the essential double meaning' of post-modernism, post-modernism is both 'the continuation of Modernism and its transcendence.'[56]

The loosely knit intellectual movement of post-modernism is quite outspoken about its objective to move beyond Modernism. Modernism is thereby in broad terms identified with the mechanical worldview and the ideas that went with it and which were intended to provide certainty and stability. This view emerged in the 16th century with *Cogito ergo sum* as its leading dogma. This equation has determined and dominated the discourse ever since. Above all, post-modernism passionately challenges modern rationalism. This passion is rooted in a deep and bitter disappointment in the Enlightenment project, as it is believed that modern rationality eventually resulted in Nazism and the Holocaust and thus failed miserably as a guiding principle. Post-modernism completely rejects the alleged 'terror of reason' (in the sense of the absolute and timeless certainty that Modernism conceived reason to be), because reason taken to extremes excludes everything that is different. Consequently, a certain hostility *vis-à-vis* the Enlightenment ideals of social progress, the emancipation and liberation of the individual, the existence of universal values, the possibility of absolute knowledge and the supremacy of pure logical rationality (which were also all key principles of Modernism) can be felt in every discipline that has come under post-modern influences. Democracy is radicalised, rather than rejected, but it is also defined as a choice instead of as an institution of absolute and eternal value. It is in its revolt against modern reason that post-modernism is both an epistemological and a political movement.

Developments in contemporary architecture have both stimulated and illustrated the debate on art and culture and have even influenced social-political

[55] L. Irigaray, The Sex Which is Not One (1981), *in* L. Cahoone (Ed.), From Modernism to Postmodernism: An Anthology (1996), at 461.

[56] Ch. Jenks, The Death of Modern Architecture (1984) and What is Post-Modernism? (1986), *in* L. Cahoone (Ed.), From Modernism to Postmodernism: An Anthology, at 471, 475, and 478.

theory: 'The abandonment of the modernist box permitted theorists from many disciplines to focus on spatial conditions of unprecedented complexity and to use them to show that the certainties of the Enlightenment were giving way to a new, less teleological attitude of the present.'[57] The *abandonment of the modernist box* is indeed a common gesture among post-modernists, although their *whys* and *hows* are very diverse. As Jennifer Wicke rightly observed: 'There are more than thirty-one flavors of postmodernism, and sorting out the indices and differentia of these critical brands entails opening a theoretical Pandora's box.'[58] For this reason, we will keep the lid practically shut here and merely introduce briefly the contemporary challenge to Modernism. I will first discuss Foucault's conception of power and his announcement of '*la fin de l'Homme*' and subsequently Ricoeur's defence of the (philosophy of the) subject. This may seem like over-elaboration to the jurist interested in the *legal* concept of ILP, but, sticking to my methodological promises at the start of this study, I really believe that it is necessary to address the cultural-intellectual context here, too, even if this is difficult (as making observations about a period that is still going on is wont to be). Fortunately, the diversity of Post-modernism only makes it possible to dwell on one theme and two leading French intellectuals.

Central to post-modernism is the rejection of the Enlightenment ideal of the world's unity, the one harmonious order. The difficult relationship between the *fragmented* and the *whole* is not, to use the metaphor of architecture once more, restricted to the paradox evoked by a decorative element on a streamlined building.[59] It refers to a completely different worldview, which accepts and even highlights the uncertainties that Modernism tried to disguise or eliminate and which recognises that rules, whether aesthetic, cultural, epistemological, socio-political, moral or legal, are determined *locally*. In this post-modern realm of thought the universal and the absolute are negated. Post-modernism is fundamentally at odds with any notion of 'the whole', 'totality' or 'unity'.

Generally, the possibility of knowledge is approached with complete scepticism. The French philosopher, Jean-François Lyotard,[60] one of the leading fig-

---

[57] L. Phillips, The American Century: Art & Culture 1950-2000, at 284 (1999).

[58] J. Wicke, Postmodern Identity and the Legal Subject, 62 *Univ. of Col. Law R.* 456 (1991).

[59] In this respect, Jencks on his quest for 'the difficult whole' may be considered a moderate pathfinder of post-modernism, as he supports a 'relative absolutism, or fragmental holism,' which considers truth propositions to be 'time – and context – sensitive,' 'culture-dependent,' but also rejects the idea of absolute relativism as the total *im*possibility of *unity*. For Jencks, the transcendence of modernism lies in the realisation of the social, cultural, moral and ecological limits of modernism and in the awareness that 'all living and non-living things on the globe are interconnected, or capable of being linked.' If we forget that 'the world is a whole' we will destroy it. Jenks, *op. cit.*, footnote 56, at 471-478. Jencks rejects Lyotard's sceptical position in epistemology.

[60] Lyotard and Jencks are often consulted and quoted by others who seek some understanding of the phenomenon of post-modernism, probably because both have written essays entitled 'What Is Postmodernism?' The question may have been the same, but their answers are very different. See, for Lyotard, *infra* footnote 62. See, for Jenks, *op. cit.* footnote 56.

ures of post-modernism, has pointed out that we are experiencing a 'crisis of legitimacy' in our search for and understanding of knowledge. Today, 'the meta-narratives of modernism,' which served to distinguish between what was true and what was false, have lost their power to legitimise knowledge and provide social direction. However, Lyotard did not mourn the demise of the unifying (metaphysical) narratives now that the desire for unity had resulted in Auschwitz and totalitarianism in the 20th century. Instead, he concluded that unifying narratives were politically dangerous and unacceptable. Disagreement and incommensurability are the real conditions of the human quest for knowledge. There is no valid metaphysical idea or grand narrative: 'we can resort neither to the dialectic of Spirit nor even to the emancipation of humanity as a validation of postmodern scientific discourse.' Unity and coherence in knowledge has become impossible. With the end of modernism, according to Lyotard the legitimisation of knowledge can only occur by what he termed 'paralogy:' 'a move (the importance of which is often not recognized until later) played in the pragmatics of knowledge.' The anti-model of scientific pragmatism emphasises 'dissensus' and instability and claims that research should be based on rules that are completely '*locally* determined.'[61] Lyotard is not alone when he equates 'totality' or 'unity' with terror;[62] Foucault also rejected thinking 'in terms of totality,' i.e., by means of grand unifying theories, which he considered to be 'global, *totalitarian theories*.' Without a unifying paradigm, research must be fragmentary and always 'inconclusive.' A grand theory acts as an inhibition to research, because it predetermines the results.[63] Instead of pursuing the illusory idea of unity, we have to celebrate difference. All this leads to a kind of anti-worldview that denies coherence: 'the world is in fragments'.[64] This image refers to a different understanding of how we gather knowledge and create *meaning*: not through harmony, but through 'opposition' and 'dislocation'; meaning is neither found, nor given, but *constructed* through *discursive* practices. The idea that philosophy is a truth-providing – in the sense of *one* truth – discipline is rejected, while pluralism is celebrated: truth and meaning emerge in the juxtaposition of contradiction, uncer-

---

[61] Lyotard, The Postmodern Condition: A Report on Knowledge 60-61 (1986), transl. *La Condition Postmoderne: rapport sur le savoir* (1979). Emphasis added.

[62] J-F. Lyotard, Answering the Question: What Is Postmodernism? (1983), as published in Lyotard, The Postmodern Condition: A Report on Knowledge (1986), at 81-82: 'The nineteenth and twentieth centuries have given us as much terror as we can take. We have paid a high enough price for the nostalgia of the whole and the one, for the reconciliation of the concept and the sensible, of the transparent and the communicable experience. Under the general demand for slackening and for appeasement, we can hear the mutterings of the desire for a return of terror, for the realization of the fantasy to seize reality. The answer is: Let us wage a war on totality; let us be witnesses to the unpresentable; let us activate the differences and have the honor of the name.'

[63] M. Foucault, Power/Knowledge: selected interviews & other writings 1972-1977, at 78-81 (1980). Hereinafter: Power/Knowledge.

[64] 'The world – not only ours – is fragmented,' Castoriades wrote, but added 'Yet it does not fall to pieces.' C. Castoriadis, World In Fragments: Writings on Politics, Society, Psychoanalysis, and the Imagination vii (1997).

tainties and fragments, all on a tense footing with 'the whole', with which any relationship is denied. The construction of meaning by local confrontation includes the rejection of (cold and abstract) logical rationality. Indeed, it attributes a particular power of persuasion to pleasure and beauty, even in presenting theoretical (among which, legal) arguments. There is a perception that the search for or celebration of unity or one absolute truth is dangerous (as history had demonstrated) and this failure of Modernism distinctly resonates in social and political philosophy.[65]

Modern thinking starts from the idea of the human subject. It is therefore not surprising that the critics of Modernism have opened the attack on the *subject.* In the words of Guehenno: 'the very idea of the subject is pounded to bits.' The human subject of Modernism is definable and coherent, it is its solid starting point, both epistemologically (the human subject has knowledge of man and his surroundings) and morally (the human subject can understand life and give it meaning and direction). In response to this thread in Western thinking and, especially in France, in reaction to existentialism, anti-subjectivism emerged. The proposition of the *'end of the subject'* is a two-front attack, although the distinction between the moral political and the epistemological debate is largely superficial.

Modernism and the Ego are intimately connected: I *think* therefore I *am.* In Modernism, the conscious self became the centre of Western philosophy and epistemology. The human subject of Modernist thought was coherent, stable, rational, independent and cognisable. The Self exists because it thinks, i.e., man was defined by *ratio.* In this perception, man had the capacity to truly know himself and his surroundings and the knowledge thus accumulated provided him with absolute and universal *truths*, on which he based his actions, which were again directed by *ratio*, with the aim of enhancing order and harmony. Human reason would always guide man to do what was *right.* Modernists reified the self as consciousness, as the self created and re-created itself, its world and the meaning of both. It is to this presumption that post-modern thinkers react, often from the perspective of language.[66] Foucault in particular based his attack on an analysis of power operating *discursively* in society.

---

[65] See also, Cosmopolis.

[66] In the challenging of modernism, linguistics and psychoanalysis were broadly used. Generally speaking, the argument follows the following pattern: meaning emerges through structures and our mind works through binary linguistic structures; we use oppositions to differentiate, to define and to identify. Meaning is thus determined by linguistic oppositions. Language structures our consciousness and creates our sub-consciousness by separating the latter from the former. In post-modern thinking, our conscious self is generally understood as the product of language and not the other way around, as modern thinking claimed. Because language does, our thought processes also work in binary structures. When a statement is made, using language as it must, it is the language which makes the statement, not the individual who voiced it. *Meaning* is thus *not conveyed by* the *subject*, but by language itself. As meaning is always oppositional, we define by saying what it is not; we are actually incapable of defining or reasoning non-circularly. All context, whether that of a building or a text, is a determinant factor; however, the context of a text is simply other *texts*, not the author. The author has exited stage left together with the popular idea that it is not he who wrote the book, but

5.2.2.1. *Foucault and the 'end of the subject'*

Foucault's announcement that 'the human subject is dead' must be understood in relation to the human sciences, in which the human subject is the object of study.[67] Foucault objected to this studying of the human subject and contended that in the gathering of knowledge the focus should be on all that *constitutes* man. In his view '*man* is a recent invention ... [whose] appearance ... was the *effect* of a change in the fundamental arrangements of *knowledge*.' These fundamental arrangements of knowledge were formed by modern thought at the end of the 18th century.[68] As it is now becoming clear that it is not man who speaks or acts, but actually language and power, Foucault suggests we think about the disappearance of man. 'Ought we not to admit that man will return to that serene *non-existence* in which he was formerly maintained by the imperious *unity* of Discourse?' *Voila*, the cause of a great deal of controversy: '*la fin de l'Homme*.' Foucault poetically described the possibility of man 'erased, like a face drawn in sand at the edge of the sea.'[69] The announcement of man's death has caused a lot of confusion and concern. The image found its way to just about every discipline and various popularisations emerged, often rather inaccurate when compared to the original meaning of the image. Indeed, Foucault's anti-subject approach has radically influenced the human sciences research agenda and the agenda of several other disciplines. For many scholars, the *modern* subject is no longer acceptable

---

language itself. And so the world is not inter-subjective, and discourses are not either. It is all intertextual. We cannot escape language and so we cannot escape *the (inter-) textuality of life*. There is nothing outside language, not even universal values, which would be capable of liberating us from the linguistic prison we are trapped inside. A text has meaning because it is part of a network of texts and cannot refer to anything outside the text itself. A text is loaded with meaning and contradicting elements of truth, but it is not its creator who gave it meaning; *meaning* is only *constructed* temporarily and locally by the reader, irrespective of the author's intentions, motives or objectives. Moreover, we have to realise that our linguistic representations are social constructions which have developed through historical processes and are determined by political power in order to disguise prejudices and hierarchies. Our linguistic conventions are biased in their ordering and our vocabulary is embedded in various forms of hierarchy.

[67] What Foucault meant to say is that the human subject as the object of Modern thought, the subject which is the foundation and source of the human sciences, the cognisable self that has brought us a scaffolding of thought based upon itself, the subject involved in collecting knowledge and making meaning, *that* subject is fading away. His anti-humanist perspective is evidenced in his attempt to explain the existence of the human sciences and the fact that 'they are not sciences at all;' they merely serve the collection of *knowledge*. Hence Foucault's anti-humanism is anti-subjectivism in the sense that it wishes to account for developments, phenomena, for history – let us say – without reference to the human subject, also in order to account for the constitution of the human subject itself. M. Foucault, The Order of things: An Archaeology of the Human Sciences 366 (1970), translation of *Les Mots et Les Choses* (1966). Hereinafter: The Order of things.

[68] Thus, viewed from a cultural-historical perspective: at the end of the 18th century the emphasis shifted from God (or his representative on earth: the King) to the human subject as the basis of knowledge and truth and this new man gained the divine perspective of looking at himself as an object of study. Ever since, Modern thinking has defined man by his relation with God or King and for this reason the death of God has to involve 'the disappearance of man.'

[69] The Order of things, 386-387. Emphasis added.

as the basis for bringing us truth; new – *post-modern* – methods to gather knowledge, to find the available fragments of truth and to account for the phenomenon of man are needed. Foucault's re-direction has also profoundly marked political science and (international) legal theory where he argues that *man is constituted* by *power*, which he defined very differently compared to the classical concept of power as *sovereignty*. In fact, he rejected the classical definition. Here we will focus on 1) the rejection of the traditional (legal) conception of power in terms of sovereignty and legitimacy, 2) Foucault's new concept of power in terms of knowledge and truth and the related methodology of genealogy, and 3) the implications of this for the concept of the subject.

First, Foucault renounced the traditional liberal or *juridical* theory.[70] In this theory, power is a right based on a legal relationship: by cession the individual has given up his personal power for the establishment of sovereignty. Political power thus stems from a contract, the liberal idea of the original contract. As such, power is conceived in terms of *sovereignty* that springs from and is limited by law. Analysis of this kind of power thus focuses on whether it is used legitimately or employed *ultra vires*; it thus incorporates a negative connotation and approaches power as abusive, *illegal* and *oppressive*. The juridical form of power is, according to Foucault, a *negative* power relation, i.e., perceived as *oppressive* by nature. Liberalism has incorporated this negative attitude, since it defines human freedom as the absence of the sovereign's involvement. Foucault proposed to liberate power from its legal imprisonment. In his view, *law* – the *negative* language of power – was false and inadequate, because it ignored the fact that power can also be positive and productive. A contemporary definition of today's power mechanisms should also account for these aspects. The idea that power is merely *oppression* is much too *negative* and as such 'inadequate and possibly dangerous.'[71]

Legal and political theory, Foucault seems to argue, have traditionally either advocated or attacked the power of the Sovereign, which contributed to the fact that the general analysis of power was completely dominated by the issues of *sovereignty* and *legitimacy of power*. Foucault rejected in the clearest terms the idea that the juridical edifice of state sovereignty was the correct research model. In his view, power could not stem from a mythico-juridical event like the *contrat social*. He claimed that for too long political analysis had been dominated by legal conceptions, as was evidenced by political thinking about power and especially the notion of the sovereign personality:

---

[70] Power/Knowledge, at 88-89: Foucault rejected both the liberal and the Marxist theory: 'Broadly speaking, in the first case we have a political power whose formal model is discoverable in the process of exchange, the economic circulation of commodities; in the second case, the historical *raison d'être* of political power and the principle of its concrete forms and actual functioning, is located in the economy.' See also, for Foucault's denial of being a (para-) Marxist, id. at 58.

[71] Id., at 59.

political theory has never ceased to be obsessed with the person of the sovereign. Such theories still continue today to busy themselves with the problem of sovereignty. What we need, however, is a political philosophy that isn't erected around the problem of sovereignty nor therefore around the problems of law and prohibition. We need to cut off the King's head: in political theory that has still to be done.[72]

Foucault wished to direct the power discourse away from the question of whether power is rightfully exercised or legitimately disobeyed. He explicitly contrasted his work with the methods and fundamentals employed by *jurists*. Through beheading the King (sovereignty), Foucault intended to rid political theory of one of its traditionally most central and fundamental concepts.[73] Subsequently, to 'escape from the limited field of juridical sovereignty and state institutions,'[74] Foucault directed his research to power *outside* the *juridical* schema of *sovereignty* and into the micro-level of society, where the effects of power are most noticeable.

[It] would be the exact opposite of Hobbes' project in *Leviathan*, and of that, I believe, of all jurists for whom the problem is the distillation of a single will – or rather, the constitution of a unitary, singular body animated by the spirit of sovereignty – from the particular wills of a multiplicity of individuals. Think of the schema of Leviathan: insofar as he is a fabricated man, Leviathan is no other than the amalgamation of a certain number of separate individualities, who find themselves reunited by the complex of elements that go to compose the State, but at the heart of the State, or rather, at its head, there exists something which constitutes it as such, and this is sovereignty, which Hobbes says is precisely the spirit of Leviathan. Well rather than worry about the problem of the central spirit, I believe that we must attempt to study the myriad of bodies which are constituted as peripheral *subjects* as a result of the effects of power.[75]

While the modern analysis of power was preoccupied with the transformation of the individual will into the will of the state person and with *oppressive* (sovereign) power as an attribute of the state personality, Foucault's post-modern project intended to liberate power (and the study of power) from its *modernist legal box*.

Secondly, Foucault developed a new methodology and concept of power. He enumerated five methodological precautionary measures which had to be taken to

---

[72] Id., at 121.

[73] Of course, the legal-political theory of sovereignty has played a role at various times in history to transform society and the power structures within it and to legitimise new political constructions. Most recently, it took the guise of the sovereignty of the people in parliamentary democracies. Foucault indicates four such instances in which sovereignty was significant: 1) in the feudal monarchy, 2) in the justification of large-scale administrative monarchies, 3) in the struggle between Catholic monarchists and Protestant anti-monarchists, 4) in the (18th century) construction of the parliamentary democracy. Id., at 103.

[74] Id., at 102. Also, at 187.

[75] Id., at 97-98.

prevent incarceration in the modernist legal box and he investigated how power really operates within society. His method started with the reconciliation of two approaches that both incorporate the element of 'force': 'power as *repression*' on the one hand and 'power as war' or 'the conflict of *forces*'[76] on the other. He brought these two together into the concept of power as operating through the mechanisms of 'domination.' Repression is defined as 'a political consequence of war', i.e., the consequence of a force relationship. Therefore, repression is interpreted as *domination* or *submission* within a 'perpetual relationship of force.'[77]

Foucault then positioned these power mechanisms within discourses of *truth* and *knowledge*. Society, he said, is 'permeate[d], characterise[d] and constitute[d] [by] a manifold relations of power,' which 'cannot themselves be established, consolidated nor implemented without the production, accumulation, circulation and functioning of a discourse.' When dealing with relations between power and rightness, the discourse of truth is essential. Truth after all determines what is right, what is normal, and how one should behave or function within society. The power relations of *domination* and *subjugation* thus operate through the discourses of *rightness* and *truth* as 'the bearers of the specific effects of power.'[78] Power is exercised through the production of truth, but the production of truth is also subjected to power mechanisms, which, on the one hand, repress and subjugate and, on the other hand, release and liberate. Truth legitimises power, or put differently, power is in the hands of those who define truth. Texts, discursive practices are thus powerful tools. If discursive practices define truth and if they are embedded in techniques of domination and subjugation, if it is power that we intend to analyse, then let this be the new object of study, Foucault urged. In other words, the analysis of power leads to the analysis of truth discourses.

In order to be able properly to study power/domination mechanisms, Foucault indicated five methodological precautionary measures: i) any study had to focus on 'power at its extremities,' on power 'at the extreme points of its exercise, where it is always *less legal* in character';[79] ii) the analysis should not start from the conscious subject, i.e., not wonder who employs power, but focus on 'where it installs itself and produces its real effects.' These concrete effects operate at the most *local* and *concrete* level of discursive practices, that is where we find the 'material operators of power';[80] iii) 'Power must be analysed as something which circulates, or rather as something which only operates in a chain.' It is a process without beginning or end, it is more of a circular movement, which links up with us at the local level in a way that constitutes as well as subjugates. Power is exer-

[76] Id., at 90: To conceive power in terms of a force which functions in conflict with other forces boils down to the acceptance that politics is actually *war*, a state of perpetual war fought with other means. Even in times of peace warfare silently continues to regulate the relations of force, whereas 'the role of power is perpetually to re-inscribe this relation' in society and in us.

[77] Id., at 92.

[78] Id., at 93-94.

[79] Id., at 96-97. Emphasis added.

[80] Id., at 102.

cised, but not possessed; we employ power, yet at the same time we are its 'effect.' 'The individual is an effect of power, and at the same time, or precisely to the extent to which it is that effect, it is the element of its articulation. *The individual which power has constituted is at the same time its vehicle*';[81] iv) any analysis should be an '*ascending* analysis of power', starting at the 'infinitesimal mechanisms' of power at the most local level to see how these are hijacked by more 'general mechanisms and by global forms of domination' and thereby become mechanisms of *domination* and *exclusion* which operate at the narrowest individual level, yet serve economic advantages and political utility;[82] and v) the analysis should take into account that the mechanisms of power function through 'the production of effective instruments for the formation and accumulation of knowledge, ... *power*, when it is exercised through these subtle mechanisms, cannot but evolve, organise and put into circulation a *knowledge*, or rather apparatus of knowledge.'[83] Power is not a thing, but a relational phenomenon of domination and subjugation that operates at the most local and concrete level of society and within knowledge or truth discourses. This led to Foucault's conclusion that '[i]n reality power means relations, a more-or-less organised, hierarchical, co-ordinated cluster of relations.'[84]

The 'antithesis of power' has to be studied through the anti-method of *genealogy*, which is 'the study of the techniques and tactics of *domination*'[85] and subjugation within knowledge and truth *discourses*. Reference has already been made to the general post-modern aversion to the meta-narratives of modernism, the unifying paradigms. Similarly, Foucault argued that the validity of thought is not determined by a grand theory offering a 'pre-determined starting point and destination,' but that knowledge and truth are determined *locally*: theory is produced in 'an autonomous and non-centralised' way and therefore calls for an 'essentially local character of criticism.' Foucault argued in favour of returning to these local knowledges which existed before centralisation, i.e., before having been excluded from or included in a centralising theory. He believed in a return to the local '*subjugated*' knowledges, which had once been present, but were now 'disguised within the body of functionalist and systematising theory.' Subjugated knowledge can be different in nature, but basically it is any knowledge that

[81] Id., at 97-98. Emphasis added.

[82] Id., at 99. Foucault's main interest has been in the functioning of this process of the colonisation of local mechanisms by general mechanisms and even by 'the entire State system.' He directed his research to the micro-level of society to see how local domination came to serve social repression. His studies into sexuality and madness where aimed at understanding how these mechanisms of power became instruments of surveillance and exclusion due to 'their political usefulness' and economic profitability. It is only by studying such specific mechanisms and particular techniques of power that eventually 'we can understand how these mechanism come to be effectively incorporated into the social whole', i.e., how particular local mechanisms become part of the general repressive system of society.

[83] Id., at 101-102. Emphasis added.

[84] Id., at 198.

[85] Id., at 102. Also, at 187.

through some mechanism has been excluded from the truth (discourse). The recognition that theory is produced *locally* implies the *insurrection of subjugated knowledges*, which means digging out suppressed *historical* knowledge as well as liberating local, *popular* knowledge. The dismissal of totalitarian grand theories does not prevent an investigation into power and authority, as it must be questioned why these knowledges (power and authority) were 'disqualified as inadequate.' Of course a unifying theory must of necessity *include* and *exclude*, this is 'the tyranny of globalising discourses,' but why was *erudite* historical knowledge buried or why were certain low-ranking, local, *popular* knowledges disguised?[86] Through the insurrection of these historical knowledges and knowledges disqualified for their low ranking on the hierarchy of (scientific) knowledges, Foucault's critique unfolds to reveal 'a *historical knowledge of struggles*.' He intended his 'anti-science' as a 'genealogical' study aimed at re-discovering these struggles and their conflicts. Hence a *genealogy* emerges when such a struggle of knowledges is analysed; it is the product of a confrontation between subjugated knowledges and the centralising mechanism of a discourse. Through such an analysis the subjugated knowledges are liberated and empowered.[87] It reveals how the disqualification of knowledge operates within discourses and why. Who among the participants to the discourse are marginalised by such disqualification? In other words, whom does the discourse serve?

Knowledge is thus politically relevant or, rather, it plays a highly *political* role within society due to its role in the production of *truth* and the *power* that this entails. Foucault does not deal here with the traditional question of how discourse (e.g., the legal discourse or 'philosophy as the truth discourse *par excellence*') '[is] able to fix limits to the rights of power'; he considers the fact that power *needs discourse* (and *vice versa*) the really interesting issue. According to Foucault, the question should be 'what rules of right are implemented by the relations of power in the production of discourses of truth? ... We are subjected to the production of truth through power and we cannot exercise power except through the production of truth.'[88] Rather than approach *domination* in its traditional relation with '*right*', i.e., the legal realm, Foucault argues that the system of right should 'be viewed ... not in terms of a legitimacy to be established, but in terms of the *subjugation* that it instigates.' He remarked that the traditional view disguises the

---

[86] Id., at 80-83. Id., at 82: '[A] popular knowledge ... is far from being a general commonsense knowledge, but is on the contrary a particular, local, regional knowledge, a differential knowledge incapable of unanimity and which owes its force only to the harshness with which it is opposed by everything surrounding it.'

[87] Id., at 84: 'subjugated knowledges are opposed primarily ... to the effects of the *centralising powers* which are linked to the institution and functioning of an organised scientific discourse within a society such as ours.' Emphasis added. Id., at 85: 'in contrast to the various projects which aim to inscribe knowledges in the hierarchical order of power associated with science, a *genealogy* should be seen as a kind of attempt to emancipate historical knowledges from that subjection, to render them, that is, capable of opposition and of struggle against the coercion of a theoretical, unitary, formal and scientific discourse.' Also, at 117.

[88] Id., at 92-93.

real relations of 'domination' which are intrinsic to these relations of the 'system of right'. So, instead of theorising about 'the whole complex of apparatuses, institutions and regulations responsible for the application of the laws' and responsible for legitimising sovereignty, research should *shift* to the area of the relations of *domination* that are produced and reproduced by this system of right at the most concrete *locus*. The study of domination and subjugation within society should thus occur at the 'extremities.' *Right* is in this perspective not that which either legitimises or controls power, but it is *that* which instigates and institutionalises the methods of *domination* and subjugation. Foucault thus focuses on right and power in terms of *domination* in order to observe how it operates in the place where it truly *subjugates* and subjects: within the production of truth and knowledge.[89]

In other words, 'the *political* question ... is not error, illusion, alienated consciousness or ideology; *it is truth itself*.'[90] It is the question of how power works at the most *local* and *concrete* level; not so much at the legal level, but there where the state connects up with the existing cluster of relations, where power is also 'productive' and 'hold[s] good.' We accept its existence and its functioning, because power also 'traverses and produces things, ... induces pleasure, forms knowledge, produces discourse. It needs to be considered as a productive network which runs through the whole social body, much more than as a negative instance whose function is repression.'[91] *Power is discursive and productive of knowledge and truth.* Politics is a strategy to regulate and change the relations of force within society; every relation of force implies a power relation that in turn is not neutral, but refers to the political. Instead of politics conducted from a static set of prepositions (both substantial and procedural/institutional), Foucault calls for a 'new form' of politics or 'politicisation' based on the insights of the genealogical analysis of power.[92]

Thirdly, Foucault's anti-project aims to explain how *power constitutes subjects*. It is focused on the constitution of subjects 'as a result of the effects of power', on how *subjection* works at its most concrete and actual level: 'rather than ask ourselves how the sovereign appears to us in his lofty isolation, we should try to discover *how it is that subjects are* gradually, progressively, really and materially *constituted* through a multiplicity of organisms, forces, energies, materials, desires, thoughts etc.'[93] In order 'to arrive at an analysis which can account for the constitution of the subject within a historical framework,' Foucault needed 'to get rid of the subject itself.' The genealogical approach is intended as a break with the methodological tradition (Cartesian, existentialist or phenomenological)

---

[89] Id., at 96-97. Emphasis added.
[90] Id., at 133. Emphasis added.
[91] Id., at 119; also, at 184.
[92] Id., at 189-190.
[93] Id., at 97-98.

based on the subject and to provide instead 'a form of history which can account for the constitution of knowledges, discourses, domains of objects, etc., without having to make reference to a subject which is either transcendental in relation to the field of events or runs in its empty sameness throughout the course of history.'[94] The historical methodology of genealogy intended to deal with the phenomenon of power more adequately.

On the basis that *power* produces the human *subject*, Foucault's new method reduced the human subject to a product and thereby focused on the mechanisms of production. Foucault identified the individual subject as a *locus* of a fragmentary, incoherent self, constituted by the forces of *power*. This meant the end of the subject in its modernist form, the death of the Cartesian Ego, whose mind was more important than his body, his thinking more valuable than his feelings. The individual is no longer the *prime mover*: the *constructed* self has replaced the *constituted* subject. Evidently, this shift towards a more mechanical view of the subject has had radical implications for epistemological and philosophical thinking. Without the certainties of modernism, all *knowledge* becomes *arbitrary* and a plurality of relative, non-hierarchical views are all equally acceptable. It means the 'end of the subject' in its modern identity of creator (of meaning and the finder of truth) when the post-modernists identify the self as a *constructed* product. In rejecting the *subject*-dependent concept of power, which is created by 'will' or a combination of 'wills', Foucault conceived of a new view of *politics*, namely politics without an identifiable *subject* to direct the political process: between action and reaction, politics develop discursively and the only direction it takes is from the objective it is intended to serve. Politics is thus no longer produced *inter-subjectively*, but has become a *discourse of truth* in which numerous opinions operate, rather than just those of the few appointed members of the legislature.

However, faced with the practical political side of his end-of-the-subject argument, Foucault recognised that '[h]ere you can't escape the question of the subject, or rather the *subjects*, [c]ertainly, and this is what is preoccupying me.'[95] Foucault shaped a hypothesis starting from the following question: if power is not sovereign power, who then participate in the struggle for it? Foucault suggested that the struggle for power was a struggle of 'all against all'. In his view, there are no 'immediately given subjects of the struggle,' e.g., the proletariat on the one hand and the bourgeoisie on the other. 'We all fight each other. And there is always *within* each of us something that fights something else.'[96] Ultimately, the individual is a fragmented unit composed of 'sub-individuals', which is radically different from the coherent subject envisaged by Modernism. The bottom line is thus that Foucault considered the human body 'the locus of a dissociated Self,' which 'adopts the illusion of a substantial unity.'[97] And not only this, but

[94] Id., at 117.
[95] Id., at 207.
[96] Id., at 208. Emphasis added.
[97] The Order of Things, at 366.

we are also are all destined to fight each other and ourselves and so, without the constituent subject, the world is ready to come apart.

As such, the loss of human subjectivity is indeed the *end of humanism*, both epistemologically and morally-politically.[98] It is the loss of the self as a stable and coherent entity. Man's *in*coherence is applauded, rather than responded to by a philosophy that would enable man to re-establish a sense of wholeness by determining or finding 'meaning'. Contrary to the modernist project, which aimed to allay human anxiety, post-modernism celebrates the uncertainties and contingencies of life.

Two questions remain. The first is: if an individual is at the same time an effect as well as an element of the articulation of power, does that imply we are *never* powerless or never powerful and *capable*? The second question is: who or what should bear responsibility in the post-modern world where man has ceased to exist – power relations or linguistic structures? Or put differently: if we live in an age without a human subject, without at least some autonomy, what implications does this have for individual *responsibility*? It is with these two questions of capacity and responsibility that we turn to Ricoeur's alternative.[99]

5.2.2.2. *Saving* capacity *and* responsibility*: Ricoeur and the ethical and moral subject*

Foucault's contention concerning the disappearance of man is met with a combination of respect and disagreement by the French philosopher Paul Ricoeur, who spoke out in defence of the subject.[100] We will not merely examine Ricoeur here because of his response to Foucault's theory, but also because he offers the possibility of continuing in the idea of the *capable* and *responsible* human subject. As such, his ideas have both moral and legal implications which are worth contemplating and which will eventually also be helpful to our thoughts on the concept of ILP in the final chapter's evaluations and conclusions.

---

[98] It opposes, for example, the subject idea of existentialism, which considered the individual human subject the only entity capable of willing, of bearing responsibility, and creating meaning. It also considered it the only possible foundation in our quest for knowledge and in the moulding of history building of progress. However, it is also true that Sartre by his brand of humanism ended up supporting Stalin and defending the Gulags.

[99] See, for another significant defence of the notion of the subject in response to Foucault's theory of power and the end of man, J. Habermas, An Alternative Way out of the Philosophy of the Subject: Communicative versus Subject-centred Reason (1987), *in* L. Cahoone (Ed.), see *supra* footnote 55, at 589-616.

[100] Ricoeur clearly distinguishes between structuralism as a method of text analysis and structuralism as a philosophy. Structuralism in the first sense perceives text autonomously: the text is taken as an objective thing, '[it] escapes its author and signifies for itself.' Ricoeur accepts the structural analysis as a '*stage*' in his reasoning, but rejects the philosophical conclusion subsequently drawn on the basis of this practice, i.e., that 'the subject is eliminated from its position as the author of discourse'. Foucault's 'idea that man is a recent invention seems to [Ricoeur] sheer invention.' P. Ricoeur, Critique & Conviction 77-79 (1998). Emphasis added.

For some time, the fashionable idea was that Ricoeur was 'just another' philosophy professor, but not many scholars think so now. His has indeed been a 'reconnaissance tardive,' since recognition of his theory took well into the 1980s to become firmly established.[101] Perhaps it was because of his attempts to connect very different (and sometimes difficult to reconcile) philosophical perspectives or disciplines or perhaps because of his defence of the subject that his work was considered less *en vogue*. Moreover, going against the current of fashionable anti-universalist arguments, Ricoeur continued to defend the idea of the 'universal' and universal principles, although not without recognising that 'contextual' elements, like the diversity of cultures, societies, personalities and practical circumstances, also play a role.[102] In spite of his *séjour* at the interrelation of different perspectives or rather when this séjour started to make sense, as Charles Taylor has observed: 'on commence avec le temps à reconnaître que c'est ce travail d'interrelation qui constitue la véritable contribution à la théorie du sujet qu'a apportée la philosophie du XXe siècle, dont Ricoeur s'avère une des figures dominantes.'[103] In our quest for answers to the question of whether the end of the subject has indeed arrived, we must examine two of his works in particular: *Soi-même comme une autre* (1990, transl. Oneself as Another, 1992) and *Le Juste* (1995, transl. The Just, 2000). In 'The Just', Ricoeur defends the subject without ignoring the philosophical developments in the 20th century which undermined the paradigm Cogito ergo sum. He employs his knowledge of decades of philosophy in many different fields, turning the book into a journey during which calls our made at the ports of linguistic philosophy, action theory, hermeneutics and, during the final leg of the journey, at the port of ethics and moral theory. Here we must regretfully limit our focus to Ricoeur's explanation of the ethical identity of the self and to the consequent implication that the acceptance of moral responsibility is an *attestation* of selfhood and thereby of the existence of the human subject.

The question of the subject involves both political and philosophical (epistemological) theory, which are interlaced in the questioning and answering. Ricoeur

---

[101] F. Martel, Le voyage philosophique de Paul Ricoeur, *Magazine littéraire* (1997), at 357.

[102] Ricoeur explains that the desire to live together is universal, just like the claim to validity implied in the very idea of law, as this is why law obliges, is universal. However, as soon as laws and institutions are created, contextuality comes into play.

[103] Ch. Taylor, Une philosophie sans frontières, No. 390, Sept. 2000, *Magazine Littéraire*, Dossier: Paul Ricoeur, morale, histoire, religion: une philosophie de l'existence, at 30-31. Ricoeur acknowledges the strong influence Taylor has had on his own work on ethics. See, e.g., The Just, at xiv. As Taylor rightly observed: 'Annoncez « la fin de l'Homme » et vos titres montent en flèche, comme les nouvelles technologies au Nasdaq. Avec un peu de recul, l'intérêt de ces prises de position dramatiques est moins évident. On a plutôt l'impression d'avoir perdu beaucoup de temps.' It is suggested that Ricoeur's Protestantism is partly to blame for the fact that recognition came to him relatively late, although he has always 'insisted on a strict separation between philosophy and faith.' 'There is no doubt that this religious orientation is a significant part of the explanation for the long period of neglect of his work in France.' G. Gutting, French Philosophy in the Twentieth Century 364-365 (2001).

distinguishes two basic attitudes towards the problem of the subject, which he referred to as 'the exalted cogito' and 'the shattered cogito,' and to which he offers his 'hermeneutics of the self' as an alternative. The exalted cogito refers to a tradition in Western philosophy since Descartes that tries to find in the subject an absolute foundation of knowledge. With the image of the shattered cogito, however, Ricoeur characterised the tradition since Nietzsche which turned against this positioning of the 'I' as a valid foundation for knowledge, because this view ignored the fact that in order to be able to doubt, think and self-reflect the cogito needs the mediation of language. Since the use of language is not something literal, non-figurative, neutral or truthful in itself, there is no language that is completely free of deceit, no language that is not somehow suspect, and therefore any foundational claim of the cogito to certainty has to be rejected. Man's inner world is as much an interpretation as the outer world. Rather than seeing Nietzsche's anti-cogito as the inverse of the Cartesian cogito, Ricoeur regarded it as indicative of 'the destruction of the very question to which the cogito was held to give an absolute answer.'[104]

With his hermeneutic alternative, however, Ricoeur presented an argument 'opposing ... the ambition of placing [*I am*] in the position of ultimate foundation.' Rather than positioning the I, Ricoeur demonstrated that '[t]he *self* is implied reflexively in the operations (e.g., speaking or acting), the analysis of which precedes the return towards this self.' In other words, the self manifests itself when speaking and acting, because the act of speech and the act of acting refer to the self reflexively as the speaker or actor. For the identification of the subject, Ricoeur uses the 'detour' of the question of 'who?'. The *indirect* positioning of the self thus occurs by asking the self to identify itself: 'who is speaking?' or 'who is acting?' The self, *i.c.* the speaker or actor, identifies himself: 'I am.' *Who* deliver(s) the narrative of a life, either personally or together as a (historical and/ or political) community? *Who* takes responsibility for these actions and accepts moral imputation? Each question of *who* demands 'identification'. With every answer, self-designation occurs. 'I am,' 'I can,' I am *capable* of designating myself by speaking, acting and narrating. Or, 'Here I am,' 'I am the one you accuse,' which is an example of the identification of the subject of imputation. The personal identity unfolds its many layers: the identity of the speaker and the actor,[105] the narrative identity of the self,[106] and finally the ethical and moral identity of

[104] P. Ricoeur, Oneself as Another (1992), at 14. Hereinafter: Oneself as Another.

[105] In the nine studies of Oneself as Another, Ricoeur examines all four questions. The first two studies are exercises of the philosophy of language (semantics and pragmatics) and deal with the question, 'who is speaking?' As speaking is actually the performance of the act of speech, the subsequent two studies in action theory on the question 'who is acting?' are also closely related: 'by implication speakers are themselves actors.' Oneself as Another, at 17.

[106] The third question, 'who is recounting?' concerns the analysis of personal identity as 'narrative identity.' The idea of the narrative identity of the self is Ricoeur's dialectic reconciliation of permanence and temporality, of identity-*idem* (sameness) and identity-*ipse* (selfhood). The narrative identity of the self emerges from the narrative which is told with the use of our memories and experiences and the promises we made; our self and sameness tell of our personal identity. The narrative

the self.[107] The self that is designated in this way is neither an ultimate foundation, nor is it disintegrated to the extent that no trace of certainty or unity remains. However, the unity that emerges from Ricoeur's 'fragmentary' studies is merely the thematic unity of '*human action*' and the certainty that the 'hermeneutic of the self' provides is not absolute. However, more than the perspective of the anti-cogito was able to, attestation or 'testimony' provides the 'certainty' of trust; it saves the self by placing 'trust' in the 'reliabi[lity]' of the attestation of the self. Ricoeur thus arrives at a definition of attestation as 'the *assurance of being oneself acting and suffering*. This assurance remains the ultimate recourse against all suspicion, even if it is always in some sense received from another, it still remains *self*-attestation.' In brief, self-attestation 'will preserve the question 'who?' from being replaced by the questions 'what?' or 'why?'... at every level – linguistic, praxic, narrative, and prescriptive.' As long as we continue to ask 'who?' and continue to place 'trust' in the answer, the self can attest of it*self* and thus identify itself. Like 'I' can identify myself when speaking, acting, recounting or imputing, so you or he or she can be identified. This justifies the general conclusion that the capable human subject exists.

By the notion of attestation, Ricoeur offers an alternative to the contemporary negation of man's future by pointing to the power of trust, or 'trust in the power to say [and] do,' in the power to act, therefore.[108] As such, the hermeneutic *cer-*

---

identity accommodates both the *permanence* and the *change* of the identity of a person or community as it '*mediates*' between selfhood as sameness of character and selfhood as 'discontinuity and instability.' In other words, the character of the narrative is not the same as the character of the identity-*idem*. Personal identity is lost if selfhood is no longer upheld by sameness, i.e., if selfhood loses its 'corporeal anchoring in the world.' The narrative identity emerges from this dialectic of the same and selfhood, from identity and diversity, from permanence and change; it is a constructive mediator to the constitution of the self. The character of the narrative is the character of the 'emplotment,' the character of a life story. With the notion of emplotment, Ricoeur opposes the (post-modern) theme of contingency, the absence of any kind of unity and the resulting loss of meaning. In Ricoeur's view, the impossibility to determine connectedness in life by means of the causal-type model does not mean that contingency is all there is. By the notion of emplotment he offers a narrative conception of the connectedness of life. By emplotment, i.e., by the configuration of events into a narrative, an event is transformed into a meaningful part of the narrative. Id., at 142. The actions in the plot and its characters are necessarily related in the narrative, as predicates and actions are attributed to persons and 'the contingency of an event contributes to the necessity, retroactive so to speak, of the history of a life, to which is equated the identity of the character.' Id., at 147.

[107] For the attestation of the ethical identity of the self, the notion of 'self-constancy' is important. It gives permanence in time, independent of sameness and in spite of diversity and change. How can other people depend on us if we are not stable, coherent subjects? How can we trust the value of a contract if the subject changes? Ricoeur did not see the sameness of the body and character as the only expression of the *continued self*. He also identified '*keeping one's word*' as an expression of this permanence in time and yet this does not overlap with the self's sameness. Keeping one's word challenges time and as such it has permanence in time, even though it is independent of the permanence of character. It involves the selfhood of the self as a 'polar opposite' to the permanence of character, since it is not inscribed in the self as sameness, but simply relates to the 'who?' who has given his word. 'To keep one's word' expresses 'self-constancy' by 'the faithfulness to a word' and indicates the ethical attitude of being *accountable* to the other to whom the promise was given; it signifies honouring the *trust* that the other has placed in your faithfulness.

[108] Oneself as Another, at 22-23.

tainty of attestation is the 'ultimate recourse' when faced with announcements of the disappearing self. By choosing to preserve the question of '*who*?', Ricoeur refuses to follow the contemporary movement of replacing it with the question of '*what*?', which we saw Foucault do. While Foucault depicted individual identity as a product of historical and social influences and as the mere *locus* where these (power) forces congregate, Ricoeur defends a subject that may, it is true, at times be divided or lacking a centre, but that nevertheless attests of its coherence by narrating its own life story or by acting ethically, morally and politically. In brief, Ricoeur describes a constant process of self-definition by self-attestation. Admittedly, the self is indeed an *interpretation*, but to reduce it to a product of forces, like Foucault did, is unacceptable to Ricoeur.

This epistemological dimension of the hermeneutic of the self is evidently closely intertwined with the ethico-political dimension in the notion of attestation.

The *capable* subject which Ricoeur established is created in a *dialogue* with *another*. It is in this dialogue that the self is capable of identifying itself, i.e., in dialogue with oneself as another, with the near other, the 'you' of the inter-personal, or with the distant other or third person with which it lives through social institutions (hence institutional mediation). In relation with each of these 'others', the self can attest to its ethical and moral identity.

If someone is *counting on* a person, that person is 'accountable or responsible for' his actions to the first person.[109] As such, 'self-constancy' is an expression of one's ethical identity. The problem of identity – the question '*who am I?*' – cannot be fully answered until the 'capable person,' the person who can speak, act and narrate his own identity, also *attests* of his own position. Here, the capable subject is or becomes the 'self of responsibility' or the 'subject of moral imputation', which is the subject capable of pursuing *good* (ethics) and respecting *obligation* (morality). The identification of the subject of imputation by 'Here I am!' attests most clearly of the self. Because it springs into action from a position of befuddlement over the multiplicity of practical possibilities induced by the modern anxiety of 'everything is possible, but what am I to do' into self-attestation: 'Here is where I stand.' It is the *response* to the other who counts on it. In responding, one *attests of* one*self*. This is the answer to the problem of the self: the personal testimony, '*témoignage*,' of justice. The *unity* of the self becomes evident when confronted with the other, with situations of uncertainty, danger or conflict in which one desires to do *good*. The expression of the *good* and the *just* present a coherent and firm image of the self: 'this is me' – 'here I am'; it transcends the narrated (or constructed) self. By attestation the ethically and morally *capable* subject identifies himself and takes *responsibility*.

Ricoeur thus manages to save the human subject from extinction by portraying him as capable and responsible. The identification of the subject by self-attesta-

[109] Id., at 165.

tion finds its strongest case, according to Ricoeur, in the attestation of its ethical and moral identity: '[t]he *autonomy* of the self will appear then to be tightly bound up with *solicitude* for one's neighbor and with *justice* for each individual.'[110]

In other words, the capable subject emerges most clearly from the attestation of its ethical and moral identity. Here, ethics are qualified in the 'teleological' terms of the predicates of 'good' and distinguished from morals which are qualified in the deontological terms of the predicates of 'obligation'.[111]

These predicates apply first of all to those actions we judge and evaluate as good or bad, permitted or forbidden. They further apply reflexively to the agents themselves to whom we impute these actions. It is here that the notion of a capable subject reaches its highest significance. We ourselves are worthy of esteem or respect insofar as we are capable of esteeming as good or bad, or as declaring permitted or forbidden, the actions either of others or of ourselves. A subject of imputation results from the reflexive application to agents of predicates like "good" or "obligatory."

The capable subject is the subject capable of self-esteem and self-respect:

[S]elf-esteem and self-respect are not simply added to the forms of self-designation we have been considering. They include and in a way recapitulate these forms. In terms of what then, someone may ask, can we esteem or respect ourselves? As, in the first place, capable of designating ourselves as the speakers of our utterances, the agents of our actions, the heroes and narrators of the stories we tell about ourselves. To these capacities are added those that consist in evaluating our actions in terms of "good" and "obligatory." We esteem ourselves capable of impartially judging our own actions. Self-esteem and self-respect are in a way reflexively addressed to a capable subject.

However, besides the fact that the ability of self-esteem and self-respect designate the *capable* subject, it is these ethical and moral dimensions of the self that enable us to take the next step towards ethico-juridical imputation:

[T]here is a bond of mutual implication between self-esteem and the ethical evaluation of those of our actions that aim at the "good life" (in Aristotle's sense), just as there is a bond between self-respect and the moral evaluation of these actions, submitted to the test of the universalisation of our maxims of action (in the Kantian sense). Taken together, self-esteem and self-respect define the ethical and moral dimension of selfhood, to the extent that they characterize human beings as subjects of ethico-juridical imputation.[112]

---

[110] Oneself as Another, at 18.

[111] There is also a third level in the hierarchy of human action, i.e., the '*tragic dimension of action*,' which requires a response of practical wisdom. This comes into play when one is confronted with a totally new problem that, in order to be solved, requires practical wisdom – *phronisis* – because the notions of good or right are insufficient for its resolution and because one is required to take a position based on one's *conviction*.

[112] The Just, at 4.

What it means to live a life in conformity with the 'good' and the 'obligatory,' i.e., moral and legal duties, depends on the relationship the self is involved in. Relationships can be with: 1. oneself as another, 2. the near other, or 3. the third person or distant other, i.e., fellow citizens.[113] In relations with either of these others, the teleological and the deontological apply, or rather they demand that the subject pursue the good and conform to its duties and obligations. Ricoeur defines the desire to live a 'good' life in relation with these three others: 1. with oneself as another the desire is personal fulfilment; 2. with the 'near other' the desire is for reciprocity in friendship or, more generally, the inter-personal; and 3. with the 'distant other' the desire is 'a fulfilled life in and with others in *just* institutions.' We should not '*forget*,' Ricoeur underscores, that all in all the desire '*to live well with and for others in just institution*' is the foundation of moral and legal duties, rather than the fiction of the social contract, which has a more moral connotation.[114] The teleological of the good should never be cut off from the legal; a purely procedural foundation for justice would mean that the deontological loses its teleological roots.

The *legal* subject is the capable subject not in relation with itself or to the near other (the inter-personal otherness), but is the capable subject in relation with the distant other or 'institutional otherness.' The transition from the capable subject to the legal subject or 'subject of real rights' requires 'the relation to the third':

> Only the relation to the third ... gives us a basis for the institutional mediation required by the constitution of a real subject of rights – in other words, of a citizen.[115]

The transition from capacity to the actualisation of capacity requires the mediation of just institutions. Among these 'social institutions' or 'social systems' are, of course, the juridical and the democratic systems. These are 'orders of recognition.' The relationship of the subject with his fellow citizens is the constitution of the capable subject as the ethico-juridical subject.

> The social bond instituted by contracts, by agreements of every sort, which give a juridical structure to the giving of one's word as an exchange, is intercalated within the structure of trust. The principle that agreements should be kept constitutes a rule of recognition that surpasses the face-to-face relation of the promise made between two people. This rule encompasses anyone who lives under the same laws, and, if we invoke international or humanitarian law, humanity as a whole. The other is no longer "you," but the third party designated in a noteworthy way by the pronoun "everyone" [*chacun*], an impersonal but not anonymous pronoun.[116]

---

[113] Let us picture the following chart. From left to right we have oneself, near other, distant other, and from below to above: the good, the obligatory and the practically wise. At the lowest level of the chart, ethics have *primacy* over morality; from this Ricoeur derives 'the necessity for the ethical aim to pass through the sieve of the norm,' and 'the legitimacy of recourse by the norm to the aim whenever the norm leads to impasses in practice.'

[114] Oneself as Another, at 239.

[115] The Just, at 5.

[116] The Just, at 7-8.

It is in this relation to 'everyone' that justice must be done. The political and juridical level of the institution here conjoin in *the subject of justice*. Political institutions have to be just.

To the question 'who is the subject of rights?' Ricoeur has given two distinctive answers. In the first place, he is 'the same subject worthy of respect' and therefore ultimately the subject 'to whom human action [can] be imputed.' However, the capacities of the subject remain 'virtual', unless there is 'interpersonal and institutional mediation'. Only then can these capacities be actualised as rights, which are 'the rights of *humanity* in the precise sense of this term – that is, as rights attached to human beings as human beings and not as members of some political community conceived of as the source of positive rights.' However, '[w]ithout institutional mediation, individuals are only the initial drafts of human persons:'

> Their belonging to a political body is necessary to their flourishing as human beings, and in this sense, this mediation cannot be revoked. On the contrary, the citizens who issue from this institutional mediation can only wish that every human being should, like them, enjoy such political mediation, which when added to the *necessary* conditions stemming from a philosophical anthropology becomes a sufficient condition for the transition from the capable human being to the real citizen.[117]

The subject of rights or the legal subject is here defined as a 'citizen.' The legal and the political conjoin here. Although evidently the political is only one of many dimensions of a person's life, it cannot be positioned on the same level: 'the tie of citizenship is always presupposed by all the other [allegiances].'[118] We belong to the political all the time, not just at certain moments. Paraphrasing Hannah Arendt to whom Ricoeur admits to being greatly indebted he explains: 'It is as citizens that we become human.'[119] Belonging to a political community – possessing '*citizenship*' – is therefore fundamental to people's lives and to the constitution of the self. It involves the desire to live together in *just* institutions, both at the teleological level and elevated to the deontological level with the formalism that this requires. 'The question of *politics* gets reintroduced through a reflection on the *just* that some have sought to isolate from the tutelage of the problematic of power, sovereignty, violence, and political evil.'[120] The question of justice and the question of politics cannot be separated. The question of poli-

---

[117] The Just, at 9-10.

[118] Critique & Conviction., at 102-103: Ricoeur warns of the danger of minimalising this political dimension and the notion of being a *citizen*: '[T]oday, the risk is rather in the disappearance, or in the indecipherable character of political membership. If the state is lost .... I mean that membership in the political body is not of the same nature as membership in one of the other spheres that define our roles, our rights, our obligations, our advantages and our responsibilities. The 'city' in the political sense is not reducible to the sum of the 'cities' to which we belong, to the sum of allegiances that make up civil society.'

[119] The Just, at xvi.

[120] The Just, at xx.

tics entails the question of the organising structures of society and the social and political institutions, which have to be *just* as they have to establish the '*just distance*' between the self and third persons, the just distance between all citizens.

5.2.2.3. *Conclusion*

In this contextual detour on our way to address contemporary international legal scholarship, one of the major themes of post-modernism, namely 'the end of the subject,' was addressed through the thought-provoking propositions of Foucault and the alternative propagated by Ricoeur. One of the entities closest to our hearts – the self – came under the scrutiny of sceptics of the universal tendency in theory. The legal subject presupposes the notion of the human subject as a single, coherent, unitary and autonomous entity, which does not change with time and to which the law can be imputed. With the legal subject being so fundamental to law, it was impossible to ignore the proclamation of *la fin de l'homme* and the replacement of the modern identity of the subject by the notion of a mere locus of contingency, a fragmented self without essence.

Moreover, by addressing Foucault we also became aware of his relentless assault on the jurist as intellectual and on the law as the negative language of power. His firm rejection of the analysis of power and society in terms of sovereignty and legitimacy could not have been any clearer. In the next section we will address Foucault's influence on international legal scholarship in this respect. Foucault's beheading of the Leviathan plunged several legal scholars into shock as this act rendered their language and concepts suspect. The juridical became associated with things negative and obsolete. It was even reviled for being unfair, as these concepts are not innocent or neutral notions for describing the world, but sustain power. Therefore, post-modernists' assault on meaning is also an assault on power structures and existing authority, 'they lend themselves to the proof that the true purpose of our concepts is not to describe the world but to fortify our power over it. If you don't like the prevailing power, then ruin its concepts'.[121] The concepts of sovereignty, legitimacy and, as we will see, ILP are among those that have been declared concept 'non grata'.

Ricoeur offers an alternative that, while not blind to many of the new insights, still manages to preserve the notion of the human subject. He provides an answer to the deconstruction of meaning and the elimination of the subject. The self is not a complete fiction or illusion, because it is simply not true that the self cannot be referred to. However, in relations with others the self constitutes itself and forms external constraints which it considers it meaningful to live by. By arguing that the self attests of himself by esteeming and respecting others and himself, Ricoeur not only provides evidence of the human subject, but also by his 'little ethics' a model of thinking about the constitution of the self and, beyond that, about the institutions of society. Here, the legal is no longer ignored or rejected,

[121] R. Scruton, Modern Philosophy 478 (1994).

but included in the question of just institutions according to ethics and morality. Sovereignty and legitimacy are not obsolete notions, the anxiety of modern man is not ignored, the necessity to maintain society's social fabric and institutions in order to safeguard democracy is recognised. Unfortunately though, although we find traces of Ricoeur in the work of Thomas Franck, his influence on international legal scholarship is still close to negligible compared to Foucault's.

5.3. Contemporary International Law Scholarship: skirting round ILP?

In the previous chapter, we characterised the modern international law scholarship of the 1970s and 1980s as prevailingly pragmatic in nature. Normative issues concerning the world order were often confronted in a rather technical manner. With the end of the Cold War, however, new opportunities for international law and its theory seemed to arise.

The present study began by posing the question from which this research has sprung, namely why it is, surprisingly so, that in the mid-nineties the concept of ILP is largely ignored within international law theory. Why do international legal scholars today, rather than redefine traditional or available legal language and concepts like their predecessors did in their use of ILP, borrow so heavily from the language and concepts of other disciplines, like political theory, political economy and international relations?[122] Of course, this has resulted in many new insights, but it did cause one of the most fundamental *legal* notions, ILP, to be neglected. This neglect is even more surprising when placed against the background of *globalisation* where non-state actors have come to play a significant role in the emerging global civil society, as well as within the intellectual context of questioning the demise/survival of the *subject*. In this section I will first offer four possible explanations for the fact that ILP is ignored and proceed to locate ILP in the incidental instances when it is used.

---

[122] See e.g., A.-M. Slaughter, International Law and International Relations Theory: A Dual Agenda, 87 *AJIL* 205 (1993), at 239: 'Liberal international relations theory provides international lawyers with a conceptual apparatus to understand and analyze this phenomenon [i.e., the relations between liberal and non-liberal states] and gradually to build it into law.' Slaughter inter alia argues that international lawyers should 'revise their most fundamental conceptions of the international system' by applying 'liberal international relations theory' to international law. More generally her argument aims to present a dual agenda for joint research. See, for the follow-up article, Slaughter and Tulumello and Wood, International Law and International Relations Theory: A New Generation of Interdisciplinary Scholarship, 92 *AJIL* 367 (1998) which also indicates a contrary response of IL scholars 'newly insisting on the importance of law,' *inter alia*, in response to its apparent irrelevance in tackling global problems; see also, by way of illustration Slaughter on trans-governmentalism as the new mode of international governance, A.-M. Slaughter, The Real New World Order, 76 (5) *Foreign Affairs* 183 (1997). Here Slaughter argues that the State is not disappearing, but 'disaggregating into its separate, functionally distinct parts.' Id., at 184.

First, the *old* concept of ILP was unsuited to providing an adequate response to the contemporary or *new* phenomenon of globalisation. To start with a general observation of Alston's which I underscore: contrary to legitimate expectations, the developments following from globalisation which changed the position of the state and of non-state actor, have been 'relative[ly] neglect[ed]' in international *law* scholarship. It is true that 'globalisation' is commonly dealt with in a non-legal way, even in legal scholarship. In most disciplines or interdisciplinary studies it merely features as an economic phenomenon. Kofi Annan cautioned against continued neglect of the *politics* of globalisation and Alston rightly pointed at the failure of international law scholars 'adequately' to address 'the *implications for international law* of both the changing internal role of the state and the changing nature and structure of the global economy.'[123] This lack of close and thorough attention has naturally contributed to the disregard for ILP in contemporary scholarship. Since Friedmann, scholars have been dealing with NGOs and MNCs as 'new subjects of international law', but this has neither been developed to any significant extent in international legal theory, nor has it really served practice. The description of non-state actors in terms of entities functioning within the international legal order has completely failed to induce any fundamental theoretical analysis of the concept of ILP.[124] The perception of globalisation as responsible for accelerating or increasing global interdependence, i.e., the 'Friedmann argument' is generally repeated, but nobody bothers to reveal its deeper (philosophical) roots, or if they do, these roots are considered irrelevant.

Let us recall the general first reaction in academic hallway dialogue to the suggestion of taking ILP as an appropriate conceptual angle or model for thinking through the issues currently at stake in international life: 'ILP will get us nowhere.' The concept is associated with traditional, *old* international law. It is (intuitively) perceived as a concept belonging to *past* world orders, not to the new order of today. As I observed earlier, this reaction suggests that any remaining theoretical controversy has by now run its course and that the concept of ILP is rejected for its '*obvious* obsolescence.' Whether consciously or unconsciously, it seems as if the concept of ILP is considered an obstacle to progress and renewal in international law, rather than a tool with which to achieve these things. This concept, if it were dealt with explicitly or accepted as central or fundamental to the international legal framework, would hold back the development of interna-

---

[123] Ph. Alston, The Myopia of the Handmaidens: International Lawyers and Globalisation, 8 *EJIL* 435 (1997). Emphasis added.

[124] See e.g., R. Wedgewood's presentation on 'Legal Personality and the Role of Non-Governmental Organisations and Non-State Political Entities in the United Nations System' at the March 1998 Symposium of the Kiel Walther-Schücking-Institute of International Law on *Non-State Actors as New Subjects of International Law: International Law – From the Traditional State Order Towards the Law of the Global Community*, the editors of the Proceedings are R. Hoffmann and N. Geissler (Ass. Ed.), see for an extensive review article, M. Maclaren, Like Blind Men Feeling an Elephant: Scholars' Ongoing Attempts to Ascertain the Role of Non-State Actors in International Law, 3 *German Law Journal* (2002).

tional law and hinder its smooth adjustment to a world marked by *globalisation*. It seems that the concept of ILP is silently rejected in order to prevent international law from getting mired in the past and being denied a future. New concepts are therefore sought, like, for example, 'corporate citizenship' or concepts are borrowed from international relations and political theory. Concrete institutional reforms are proposed in response to claims that international institutions lack democratic legitimacy. Practice tries to find new ways to bridge this gap, but international legal discourse generally *skirts round* the traditional concept that at first sight seems the most obvious, either as a workable concept that only needs some rethinking, or as the first idea to go out the window, if not without a proper obituary.

Secondly, in addition to the concept's presumed inadequacy with regard to *globalised* international life, another issue is covertly or overtly pointed out as an explanatory factor for ILP's lack of success. It relates to another part of our contextual detour, namely our observations on contemporary intellectual life where a *negative* image of the *legal* and the *jurist* prevails. At conferences and academic gatherings, it has become evident that the influence of post-modern deconstruction and post-modernism's negative view of all things *legal* and its negation of the traditional role of the *jurist* as the ideal type of intellectual have influenced the direction taken by many international legal scholars who used to have a real eye for and a keen interest in *theory*. This seems to be part of, or a spillover from, a wider development. The general neglect of the legal field in current intellectual debate has even radiated to international legal scholarship.[125] Obviously, the human rights discourse continued on its own (modernist) path. However, we have seen how Foucault both described and prescribed a shift away from the legal and his influence and that of his fellow post-modern thinkers on the intellectual conventions of our time can hardly be overestimated.

With his attack on the juridical edifice of state sovereignty as the only model for the analysis of power and society, Foucault sent a ripple through theory which is still continuing to stir the waters. We have seen how firmly he rejected the traditional approach to power analysis in terms of legitimacy and sovereignty. The post-modernist movement and its 'critical' method of deconstruction influenced most disciplines during the 1970s and 1980s, but '[p]ostmodernist jurisprudence is a late player on the postmodernist stage: there was little participation by jurists in the postmodernist movement until the late 1980s'.[126] In fact, in international

[125] Ricoeur mentions a 'general neglect' of the questions of right and law, i.e., the questions of justice, in 20th-century philosophy when he considers the philosophy of history. He observes: 'it is with the sense of *resisting* a line of thought strongly encouraged by *the spirit of our times* that I have undertaken over the past few years to do justice to the question of right and law, to do justice to justice.' P. Ricoeur, The Just viii-ix (2000, transl. of *Le Juste*, 1995). Emphasis added.

[126] M.D.A. Freeman, Lloyd's Introduction to Jurisprudence, 6th ed., at 1147 (1994), see Ch. 14 'Postmodernist Jurisprudence.' See, for a post-modernist (deconstructivist) approach in international law theory: A. Carty, Critical International Law: Recent Trends in the Theory of International Law,

legal scholarship post-modernist thinking only really broke through in the late 1980s and early 1990s.[127] To prevent any terminological confusion, it must be said that within international law these scholars tend to identify themselves as proponents of the '*New Approaches to IL*' (or *NAIL*) or '*New Stream*', rather than as post-modernists. Nevertheless, they embrace the *discourse* analysis that is inspired by post-modernism. To the extent that this movement was influenced by claims as to the 'death of the subject', the rejection of general, universal and absolute knowledge and the inadequacy of modern concepts of power, identity and unity, it caused a shift towards the social and political ideas and categories *underlying* legal thinking. In a sense, a shift occurred turn from the legal to the pre-legal, from the more abstract and general level of the legal field to the *less legal* level of social and political assumptions that 'control modern discourse about international law.'[128] A purely *legal* discourse analysis is not so much distinguished from the sociological and political discourses as considered inseparable from them. The prevailing preoccupation with method and discourse analysis has indeed made legal theory *less legal* and among other things more historical, sociological, political, epistemological and hermeneutic in nature.[129] In brief, much emphasis is on approaching the legal sphere in new ways and with new methods that generally originated in other disciplines and thereby contribute to the less legal and *more epistemological* character of international legal scholarship. '[T]he problem of method' dominates the scholarly agenda[130] or, as Slaughter and

---

2 *EJIL* 66 (1991). Hereinafter: Critical International Law. Carty himself also applies the post-modern method of deconstruction in his historiography of recent post-modern (deconstructive) contributions to international law theory by, e.g., contemporary international law scholars David Kennedy and Marti Koskenniemi.

[127] See, e.g., two epoch-making works in this respect, D. Kennedy, International Legal Structures (1987), hereinafter: International Legal Structures; M. Koskenniemi, From Apology to Utopia: The Structure of International Legal Argument (1989), hereinafter: From Apology to Utopia. Both books seem to have marked the international legal scholarship of the 1990s onwards unlike any others. Koskenniemi points to the evident relevance of Foucault's thinking in respect of his own 'deconstructive' enterprise of writing a history of international legal argument *without* reference to the *subject* but with a focus on the 'deep-structure' of the argumentative positions, which are the 'constitutive assumptions' that underlie and control the discourse and give the arguments their similar structure. From Apology to Utopia, at XVII-XVIII. Id., in fn 2: 'The work of (the early) Michel Foucault is perhaps most evidently relevant to the undertaking of such an enterprise. See, *Foucault* (Archaeology) ... also (Power/Knowledge).' Also, id., at XX fn 6, 54.

[128] Id., at XVI.

[129] See, e.g., the opening lines of From Apology to Utopia, at XIII: 'This is not only a book in international law. It is also an exercise in social theory and in political philosophy.' At XV: 'One needs to explicate the assumptions about the present character of social life among States and on the desirable forms of such life which make it seem that one's doctrinal outcomes are justified even as they remain controversial. This does not mean that lawyers should become social theorists or political visionaries. But it does mean that without a better grasp of social theory and political principles *lawyers will continue to be trapped in the prison-house of irrelevance.*' Emphasis added. Koskenniemi's argument is indeed that international jurists operate with a set of assumptions – the deep structure – that give them their 'legal identity'. However, these assumptions are not at all legal, but social and political.

[130] From Apology to Utopia, at 464.

Ratner's title to their conclusion of the 1999 Symposium on Method in International law reads: 'the message is in the method.'[131]

However, the shift from the conventional political concept of power to the conception of power as non-subjective and related to knowledge, a circular network, also involves the more political objective of liberating suppressed opinions, like those of cultural minorities or marginalised groups, who are emerging from 'the dominant totalitarian discourse of liberal internationalism'.[132]

Indeed, in contemporary international law scholarship, the post-modernist projects are just as much methodological as *political*. This also contributes to the decreasingly legal flavour of international law discourse. In Carty's words on the postulate of the 'critical' post-modern approach to international law: 'the language of international law has to be understood historically as no more than a subsystem of the discourse of liberal *political* theory.'[133] *The legal is political*[134] and politics cannot be completely excluded from law or legal thinking. But this view of the legal sphere should not be considered a threat to peace.[135] By and large, in the spirit of our time, the modernist concepts of sovereignty, the state and ILP have been regarded with suspicion, at least until quite recently. The beheading of Leviathan has not only forced political theory into the local sphere, but also legal scholarship. Post-modern or critical international law scholarship questions the (binding) nature of law and as such the distinction between law and

[131] A.-M. Slaughter and S. Ratner, The Method is the Message, 93 *AJIL* 410 (1999). This report of the Symposium contains a valuable overview of currently used methodologies in international law.

[132] See, for a definition of and an express argument in favour of *liberal internationalism* as the appropriate analytical framework for the future, A.-M. Burley [Slaughter], Toward an Age of Liberal Nations, 33 *HILJ* 393 (1992), at 404-405: 'Liberal internationalism focuses on the economic, political and social reality behind the sovereign façade. It thus celebrates twentieth century efforts to recognize individuals as subjects of international law, a trend most evident in the growth of human rights law. it further applauds current efforts, led in the scholarly literature by Thomas Franck, to establish the right to vote in free and fair elections as a fundamental human right. ... The version of liberal internationalism advanced here, by contrast, maintains a healthy respect of state power. The sovereign state has hardly withered away. ... A more sophisticated liberal internationalism thus cautions against the alluring simplicity of formulas designed simply to privilege the individual against the state.' The focus should be on the relations between the state and society in the international system, '[t]he result promises neither utopia nor the end of history, but holds out hope of at least a small measure of progress toward individual rights and the global rule of law.'

[133] Critical International Law, at 66.

[134] Id., at XXIII: 'The line drawn in the midst of the universe of normative statements which has separated 'subjective' politics from 'objective' law will appear without foundation.' See also, the quotation in the previous footnote.

[135] The critical legal studies movement which emerged in the late 1970s and 1980s, particularly in the US, and is generally seen as an early and important strand of post-modern thinking in law, argued that law is only politics in disguise and that its appeal to objectivity is in vain as it cannot be separated from the political struggles within society. See for a comprehensive article on critical legal studies in international law theory, N. Purvis, Critical Legal Studies in Public International Law, 32 *HILJ* 81 (1991). The leading critical legal studies scholar from Harvard, Duncan Kennedy, is also one of the scholars to whom the leading international legal scholar David Kennedy admits to being indebted. See, International Legal Structures, at 9.

politics; legal language is by deconstruction exposed as social and political theoretical language and as a consequence legal concepts threaten to slip away. Discourse analysis aims to lay bare the underlying assumptions about the social world and where it should be headed: as a *political* project, discourse analysis mainly scrutinises *liberalism* as the political theory structuring international law (theory).[136] In his seminal article on post-modernism within international law, Anthony Carty explains that the methodological and the political are connected:

'Critical' international legal studies constitute a so-called post-modern approach to international law. This is to assert that the discipline is governed by a particular, historically conditioned discourse which is, *in fact*, quite simply the translation onto the international domain of some basic tenets of *liberal political theory*. It opposes itself to positivist international law, as representative of an actual consensus among States. The crucial question is simply whether a positive system of universal international law actually exists, or whether particular States and their representative legal scholars merely appeal to such positivist discourse so as to impose a particularist language upon others *as if it were a universally accepted legal discourse*. So post-modernism is concerned with unearthing difference, heterogeneity and conflict *as reality* in place of *fictional* representation of universality and consensus.[137]

In my view, the contemporary context is one in which the identification of law as the useless and *negative* language of power is the norm in academic and intellectual circles and traditional (legal) concepts are considered mere fortifications of power. This contributes to the general behaviour of legal scholars which is to *skirt round* the traditionally important legal concept of ILP in their attempts to avoid its true scrutiny from a *legal* theoretical perspective.

The jurist no longer embodies the ideal of the influential intellectual and to be intellectually respected the work of legal scholars needs to be specific, local, particular. Traditionally – and this is not merely true for French cultural and intellectual life – the respectable, ideal type of scholar and intellectual was a left-wing male, a 'spokesman of the universal,' as Foucault called him, and he added: 'to be an intellectual meant something like being the consciousness/conscience of us all.' It was the intellectual's task to represent universal truth and justice, 'so the intellectual, through his moral, theoretical and political choice, aspires to be the bearer of this universality in its conscious, elaborated form.' However, after WWII the 'universal intellectual' gradually lost terrain to the 'specific intellectual,'[138] who is involved in specified, local and concrete scientific research.

---

[136] Id., at XVI-II: 'It would be futile to assume that the assumptions which characterize modern social and political discourse are different, or separable from those which control legal discourse on these same matters. I have chosen to group those assumptions together under the label of *the liberal theory of politics*.' '[The liberal political theory] as I shall attempt to show, ... controls normative argument within international law in a manner which creates ultimately unacceptable material consequences for international life.'

[137] Critical International Law, at 66. Only first emphasis added.

[138] Power/Knowledge, at 126-127.

The 'universal intellectual' was 'derived from a quite specific historical figure: the *man of justice*, the *man of law*, who counterposes to power, despotism and the abuses and arrogance of wealth the universality of justice and the equity of an ideal law'. Foucault further observed that 'What we call today [in 1977] the intellectual ... was ... an offspring of the *jurist*, or at any rate of the man who invoked the *universality* of a just law.'[139] The specific intellectual is now necessarily an 'expert', e.g., of biogenetics, nuclear physics, ecology, whose knowledge is extremely relevant and influential. The specific intellectual's work is politically significant, he represents 'local scientific truth [within] ... the contemporary political struggles.' The new intellectual is no longer the bearer of universal values, 'but the strategist of life and death,' he who has the power to 'either benefit or irrevocably destroy life.'[140] Specific knowledge provides the expert with a form of power, as his participation in the discourse determines what is the 'truth'. Truth and knowledge produce power and are thus political.[141] Within these 'politics of truth,' the specific intellectual is powerful, and so Foucault stated, 'the role of the specific intellectual must become more and more important in proportion to the political responsibilities which he is obliged willy-nilly to accept ... [I]t would be a dangerous error to discount him politically in his specific relation to a local form of power.'[142] With these observations, the *jurist* as the ideal or 'powerful' intellectual has very subtly, but quite clearly been made redundant; he is no longer a participant in the power game of discourse. After all, it would not do to surrender to what is labelled 'the *nostalgia* of some for the great 'universal' intellectuals and the desire for a new philosophy, a new world-view'.[143] That would be sheer academic self-marginalisation. In the vanguard of international legal scholarship, writing a new legal theory about a universal society and the necessity of upholding universal values and norms is not exactly encouraged. In my view, this poses the risk that, rather than trying to strengthen the *legal identity*, it will become the custom to downsize it.

Koskenniemi also explained the value of his project in terms of identity: '[m]ost importantly, it makes it possible for the lawyer to see his particular *social*

---

[139] Id., at 128. Emphasis added.

[140] Id., at 128-129. The death of the author becomes evident from Foucault's observation that 'at present we are experiencing the disappearance of the figure of the "great writer."'

[141] The discursive product is governed by (locally operating) mechanisms of power/knowledge that define, categorise and thus exclude or include. This implies that the key political problem for the contemporary intellectual is 'not changing people's consciousness – or what's in their heads – but the political, economic, institutional régime of the production of truth.' Truth is regulated or governed by society's 'politics of truth,' i.e., what we accept to be true, what we accept as a valid way to produce truth, in other words: by the form of discourse and the scientific institutions involved in the production of truth. But it is also determined by which true statements we want to circulate within society and which of them we want to use in our education; which apparatus are involved in educating and disseminating the truth and, finally, how the produced truth relates to issues of social justice and morality.

[142] Id., at 131-133.

[143] Id., at 130. Emphasis added.

identity and practical tasks in a new light.'[144] In other words, rather than to perpetuate the notion that the professional *legal* identity is connected with the idea that 'objectivity' in law and in legal statements is possible,[145] the international jurist should accept its identity as *less legal* and more social theoretical and moral in nature. On the one hand, without intending to underestimate the value of self-reflection on the part of the international lawyer, one may wonder whether this will not cause our discipline and area of expertise to fall prey to self-absorption, or 'collective narcissism'[146] even and make it lose sight of actual international *legal* problems whose resolution also need a theoretical backing. On the other hand, the issue of 'objectivity' as defining the identity of law once more confronts the discipline with the most fundamental question of legal theory: what is the legal? Does international law exist? Post-modern international lawyer are said to have the task of 'resist[ing] phony, ... would-be universalist legal discourse in favour of the recognition of the *inevitably* restrictive and exclusive nature of individual State discourses.'[147] They have to be realistic and accept the diversity and plurality as almost unsurpassable; the 'mature anarchy' can at the most be managed incidentally, *only occasionally* in a legal form. In other words, the message is: accept the practically fictitious and illusory nature of international law.

Mainstream international scholars are accused of living in a dream world, only to serve their own *legal* identity and are alleged to lack the required understanding of the sophisticated arguments that are put forward. This may in part be true, as following the reasoning in question does indeed require a thorough studying of (sometimes counterintuitive) arguments in the areas of linguistic philosophy, social theory, hermeneutics and others. Another, more intuitive element (because rooted in conviction), however, also comes into play: international legal scholars are well aware of the indeterminacy of legal language and theory, of the conflictual plurality of legal perspectives in international life, of the thin line between the legal and the political, but still, against all odds, they try to advance international law and theory and resourcefully search for ways to improve it. This could be seen as evidence of international law in its liberal-political theoretical

[144] From Apology to Utopia, at XXIV. Emphasis added.

[145] Id., at 458.

[146] The Method is the Message, at 423.

[147] Critical International Law, at 67. Carty elaborates that the role of the international lawyers is 'crucial' and that their ambition should not be 'to substitute another pseudo-impartial legal order, but to facilitate the development of the process of inter-state/ inter-cultural dialogue and understanding which *may* allow a coming together, however temporary and fragile. What is called for is scholarly work of legal translation,' i.e., starting from the reality of the 'opposing,' 'contingent,' 'fragmentary nature of international society' the post-modern international lawyer should recognise that the legal language should first be deconstructed to reveal this reality of diversity and 'conflictual plurality' before they are accommodated, but without forcing them into a new universalist, compulsory construction. The 'legal translator' has 'to search out how a particular society forms a consensus on the place it accords to law, the *quality of obligation* it is willing to recognise. ... The supreme difficulty is simply that each society has its own manner of thinking and reflecting on the nature of obligation. There is here intense danger for international society, because each society will be aware of its identity as differentiated from other societies.' Id., at 68. References omitted.

structure, but one could also choose to characterise it differently, at a deeper level, as the ultimate attestation of these scholars. Their international law arguments are also testimony of their ethical and moral convictions. At the risk of exaggerating, I am prepared to contend that there are basically two options in life: to construct and to de-construct. Both options can be chosen against our better judgement and both can be deeply realistic. Most of us will choose one or the other at different times in our lives. They are not as different as they seem. Deconstruction may aim at eventual re-construction, but in a different manner and indeed, as Purvis points out, that is what some deconstructive, *New Stream* scholars have actually attempted.[148] In brief, it is obvious that post-modern and mainstream lawyers have difficulty with each other's language; in addition, post-modernists conclude with observations of indeterminacy, conflict, and incoherence, whereas mainstreamers take these things as 'facts of life'. They thus leave most of the 'pre-legal' (e.g., linguistic philosophical) findings behind in order to challenge urgent international problems and construct temporary legal moments which both describe and prescribe, which become part of a collective narrative, national or universal, and as such are taken along on the rest of the journey. There is indeed diversity, plurality and anarchy; however, this does not necessarily mean that the *universality* of the human condition should be denied.

The controversy over the *universal* and *contextual* is a characteristic of today's discursive reality. An exception to the fashionable denial of universal theorisation is made by, for example, Philip Allott who dares to speak of the 're-self-constitution of Humanity' and a 'New International Law,' without, however, ignoring the insights provided by social and political theory, psycho-analysis, biology, moral philosophy and much more. And although Foucault stated that 'the essential political problem for the intellectual ... is *not* changing people's consciousness,' this seems to be exactly what Allott is bent on doing. He seems engaged in some kind of neuro-linguistic programming, designed to 're-make' the *whole* of *humanity* and make us realise that we can change the world by thinking differently, or rather: 'To change the way in which we present the world to our minds is to begin to change the world.'[149] He argues that the function of international law is the self-constitution of the international society of the whole human race, in other words, by re-conceiving international law the international society will re-conceive, and thereby re-create, surpass and perfect itself.[150] Such an all-encompass-

---

[148] By way of an example Purvis points to Koskenniemi and Boyle, Critical Legal Studies in Public International Law, at 124.

[149] Ph. Allott, The Emerging Universal Legal System, paper presented on 20 September 2002 at the Seminar on Theoretical Approaches to The Relationship between International and National Law, Amsterdam Centre for International law, at 3.

[150] Allott develops the idea of 'the emerging universal legal system' as the product of the integration of 'the theory of international law in the theory of the universal phenomenon of law, and [of] the theory of the international society in the theory of the universal phenomenon of society.' This integration of theory includes the integration of 'values' and 'ideals.' Id., at 7: '*Value thinking*. The *free-thinking* human mind can create the new *human reality* of a new *human world* using its capacities of *right thinking* and *hypothetical thinking*. But all such creative activity involves the process of

ing vision of humanity's task for the future is rare in today's international law scholarship. Moreover, the individual, the non-state actor, the state, they are all capable of willing and acting, according to Allott, and in exercising their power they are accountable, both socially and legally.[151] In *Eunomia*, Allott explains his vision on the subjects of international law as follows:

> [I]nternational law must abandon the conceptual category of *subjects of international law*, the words which have been used to identify the participants in international legal relations. The law of the subordinate societies of international society, including the state-societies, applies to all those who participate in legal relations under the legal system. ... ... [and these] may be individual human beings or any other kind of person or society as determined by the legal system itself, as it chooses to delegate legal power in the social interest.
>
> Thus international law does not have *a priori* subjects of international law. The two supposed kinds of subject of international law – so-called *states and international organizations* – are only two among the countless participants in international legal relations. It can only be said that they are as numerous and various as the needs of international society demand and the actual legal relations of international law recognize.[152]

In such an all-encompassing universal society, the legal subjects of subordinate societies may also be subjects of the international society where international law

---

choice, the movement of the mind which leads to an act of willing and hence to practical action.' Id., at 10: 'Value is the language in which we express the struggle of our self-creating through *choice*.' It is the language we use to express our '*desire*' to re-constitute ourselves 'as individuals and as societies' and by the power of the 'ideal' we perpetually change reality and work in an attempt at 'human self-perfecting.' As society is an idea and an aspect of human consciousness, the mind, both private and public, has the power to change reality into a new self-constituted, 'self-surpassing,' 'self-perfecting' society reflected in a new law. Allott places the re-conceived, new, international law at the top of the universal legal system, as the law 'embrac[ing] the laws of all subordinate societies.' This new international society and new international law 'may at last be seen as, ... as having an overriding purpose and an overriding ideal – to serve as effectively as possible the common interest of humanity in its self-creating, self-sustaining, self-surpassing and self-perfecting.' Id., at 35.

[151] Id., at 15-16. However, in his social idealist perspective on international law, the subject is different from the Cartesian, modernist 'self;' in his mind, the subject as the foundation of our individual and social lives is not the atomic 'Cogito', but society, which is ultimately the social collectivity of humanity. Society is an idea and as such an aspect of human consciousness, it resides in the private and public mind: 'Society is a 'self' within the its own public mind. Society is also an aspect of the 'self' of each society-member and also an 'other' within individual consciousness. The Society-member is an aspect of the 'self' of the society and also an 'other' within social consciousness.'

[152] Ph.J. Allott, Eunomia: New Order for a New World 372-373 (1990); Allott's sense of realism forces him to agree that: 'As constitutional organs of the international society, the state societies and the international organizations formed by the state-societies play, within the current constitution of international society, an exceptional role in governing the public realm of international society and, in particular, in law-making, in the creating of new legal relations, both the legal relations of international law and the legal relations of their respective societies. *But*, especially in the international economy, the exercise of property-power by non-state actors, including legal property-power, is at least as important in determining the survival and prospering of the international society of the whole human race. It is at least as important that there should be social and legal accountability for the activities of the non-state actors as for the activities of the state-societies and of international organizations.' Emphasis added.

applies to them. Allott rejects the exclusive use of the conceptual category. He does so in terms which are really quite similar to the traditional ICJ statement. He claims that legal subjectivity is determined by 'the needs of international society' and by 'the actual legal relations of international law.' In brief, the conceptual category of *subjects of international law*, which is traditionally used to identify the participants in international legal relations, must not exclude a potential variety of new participants in international relations. However, as Allott rightly points out, the recognition of the participation of new subjects *demands* that, like it is the case for states and international organisations, 'there should be *social and legal accountability* for the activities of the non-state actors.'[153] The fact that Allott in his universal, general theory of law does see fit to forward an opinion on the subjects of international law moreover *a contrario* seems to support the assumption that the post-modern deconstructive method contributes to the fact that the concept of ILP is ignored within contemporary (critical) international law scholarship.

The third factor contributing to the general practice of legal scholars to *skirt around* ILP relates to the development mentioned above that international law scholarship cannot escape the influence of ideas, such as the marginalisation of *universal* modern values or the disqualification of *general*, *universal* approaches in theory (e.g., idealism or realism). *Global* theories have ruled the discourse long enough. In international law theory, the post-modern or critical approach linguistically argues the *absence* of *universality*, or 'the absence of a central international legal order as an impartial point to which state actors can refer, i.e., ... 'the disappearance of the referent. At the same time it favours a mature *anarchy* in international relations ...'[154] Other themes we touched upon when we dealt with the phenomenon of post-modernism, for example inter-textuality instead of inter-subjectivity,[155] 'indeterminacy of theory,' 'binary oppositions,' 'conceptual oppositions,' 'meaning is *relational*,' etc. etc., can also be spotted in the international legal discourse.[156] The revival of theory has included an attack on the traditional 'labels,' on the traditional schools of scholarship as 'not at all useful for attaining clarity on problems which have bothered modern international law-

[153] Id.

[154] Critical International Law, at 67. Emphasis added.

[155] See, e.g., International Legal Structures, at 7: 'By reading exemplary cases and scholarly arguments, I trace patterns and strategies of rhetoric which recur in a variety of different doctrinal areas. The approach which I take to these familiar materials is somewhat unorthodox. I do not analyze the relationship between international legal materials and their political and interpretative milieu. I am not concerned about the context within which arguments are made and doctrines developed. Nor do I concern myself with the meaning and distinctiveness of public international law doctrine. I focus rather upon the relationship among doctrines and arguments and upon their recurring rhetorical structure. I trace the references which one doctrine makes to another and the repetitions which characterize doctrinal materials widely dispersed through the field as a whole. It might be useful to think of this book as a look at public international law from the *inside*.'

[156] See, e.g., From Apology to Utopia, at XV, XIX;

yers.'[157] There cannot be one prevailing view or truth because the various schools depend on each other. 'Deconstructivist criticism intervenes to show that disagreement persist because it is impossible to priorize (*sic.*) one term over the other. ... the opposing positions turn out to be the same', as Koskenniemi explains.[158] Deconstruction in international legal scholarship aims to demonstrate the contradictions, indeterminacy, contingency and inconsistencies in international law and 'dig' them out by serious 'archaeological' work in order to reveal that no real consensus lies beneath the alleged consensus of positive international law. Does this imply a de facto denial of international law? This is at least the impression one is given, but at the same time this is vehemently and repeatedly denied. It would be fair to say that during the 1990s, international law scholarship, largely due to the influence of post-modern 'critical' scholars, like Marti Koskenniemi and David Kennedy, rather than approaching problems of international law from a theoretical perspective focuses on discourse analysis to demonstrate the *indeterminacy* of the international law discourse and how it is being held captive in its linguistic prison. In other words, because language determines our thinking (a popular post-modern theme) this language currently seems to prevent international legal scholars from advancing international law.[159]

A fourth question we must ask in order to understand why today's scholars *skirt around* the concept of ILP is how international law theory is affected by the philosophical negation of the autonomous subject (whether sovereign state or human individual); how does the abolishment of the distinction between object and subject influence international law thinking and how is their separation justified epistemologically?

The classic subject of international law, the state, has traditionally been conceptualised in relation with other states, together with whom they form the international community. The traditionally strained relations between sovereignty and international law are closely related to what is now considered as international law's entrapment: we depend on the pre-existing legal order to recognise the state, but the legal order in turns depends on its subjects (mostly states) to create and consent to obligations. The subject defines the object and the object defines the subject. The modern interrelation between object, subject and legal action is purely formal and inescapable due to the definitional interdependency. But what if we identify the objective and the subjective along post-modern lines, if we make the distinction between object and subject disappear? Will international law be robbed of its foundation? What in that case would be our new start-

---

[157] Id., at XV. Koskenniemi indicated in his introduction to From Apology to Utopia that (at that time) he considered international legal theory 'marginalized' and 'suspect'. Id., at XIII-XIV.

[158] Id., at XX-XXII, see also for influence of Foucault, id. fn 6 and 9.

[159] One could ask if this is not happening to the notion of non-state actors who are also trapped in their relation with their 'other,' i.e., the state. Is our discourse irrevocably stuck unless we change our language? Is the recognition that the legal discourse is actually part of the political discourse the only way out of this entrapment?

ing point, our basis from which our reasoning could start? Would it be the 'mature anarchy' Carty discussed? What would be the common denominator, the mediating language for inter-state relations, if not international *law*, if international law is disqualified for its indeterminacy and uncertainty?

After he has deconstructed international legal theory, Koskenniemi offers an alternative that *denies* the subject in order get passed the vain claims to objectivity of the Rule of Law. The argument that interpretation leads to 'authentic consensus' cannot prove objectivity, however, 'authentic consensus' is the nearest thing to objectivity we can achieve. To appease those horrified by his argument that all international law is just 'interpretation,' that it lacks certainty, that it is indeterminate and that it is without any objective, absolute values, Koskenniemi suggests a modest 'constructive effort' which is to accept that legal discourse may be *less legal* in the traditional *formalist* sense and *more political,* i.e., that it is inclusive of the political fundamental assumptions and objectives underlying the legal argument.[160] Accepting therefore the 'reality of conflict' and the impossibility of solving conflict in the international law debate by referring to a marker of absolute 'external rationality,' international law discourse should continue by recognising that 'normative problem-solution' is 'a conversation about what to do, here and now.' Rather than the pursuit of abstract 'totalitarian utopias' (cf., the Rule of Law project) this is a *concrete* process. *Conversation* has to be an 'open' process, which continuously examines the local and temporary 'authentic consensus.' The constructive effort entails that 'the critical project implies both an institutional and a normative ideal.'[161] The institutional ideal rests upon the normative ideal of '*authentic commitment*:'

[w]hat is involved in authentic commitment ("ethic of responsibility") has been usefully summarized by Moorhead Wright in three terms. It involves 1) the accountability of each for the choices one makes; 2) the exercise of discretionary power so as to take account and fairly assess the widest range of consequences of one's acts, and 3) responsiveness to the claims of others. The ideal of authentic commitment directs normative conversation away from abstract principles of natural law, away from formal rules and the liberal ethic

---

[160] From Apology to Utopia, at 485: 'The issues of consent and justice, permissibility of intervention, the types of groups which should possess self-determination, ways to prevent environmental degradation and to promote economic well-being, among a host of others, are real and difficult. The fact that they are dealt with by a specific style and method which attempts to contain these issues in a uniform style of specifically legal discourse is where the lawyer's problems lie. Having excluded sociological enquiries into causal relationships and political enquiry into acceptable forms of containing power, the lawyer has been left with a particularly idiosyncratic and limited arsenal of argumentative possibilities. The problem is not to do away with these issues but to extend the range of permissible arguments so as to grasp those issues closer to what is significant in them. ... Refusing to engage in sociological enquiries about causes and effects and to assess political weights to be given to particular arguments, the lawyer can only find itself in an argumentative deadlock.'

[161] Id., at 486-487. 'The institutional ideal of a 'conversant culture' implies a community in which people view each other – precisely because their choices are 'subjective' – as equals, equally human, equally facing a conflictual reality, and equally uncertain in their humanity about how to live. It imposes both openness and a search for agreement to our institutional practices.' Id., at 488.

of consent and the market-place. It recognizes that normative commitment may follow not only from whatever people might have consented to (although it does regard consent important) but also by virtue of the context in which they live. Authentic commitment means, in other words, respecting the conflictual character of social life. It tries to make life possible in conflict – indeed, it sees life in terms of constant coping, not in terms of assimilation into nostalgic utopia.[162]

It is, however, in my view not beyond dispute that the ideal of authentic commitment rejects abstract normative principles; it seems inconsistent in at least one way, now that the principle of bearing responsibility for one's actions is itself a normative principle in that it includes the idea that freedom or autonomy are not absolute, but limited by accountability to others. The values of the 'other' must be respected. To me this seems a form of inter-subjective normativity. In any case, it is argued that the construction and revision of society's institutions should occur on the basis of the ideal of authentic commitment. Koskenniemi praises the human capacity to transform a 'framework of ideas or institutions' and acknowledges the need of an ideal to provide direction: '[c]riticism without an ideal of community is without direction and degenerates into cynicism.' And so he uses the ideal of authentic commitment to re-establish the identity of the lawyer and thereby the identity of international law: in the conflictual reality of international life the international lawyer should be authentically committed, i.e., he should 'exist' in 'routine,' which 'denotes the visible, regular practices of social life' and 'constantly aims at transforming the contexts which shape it,' and he needs 'an intellectual directness towards context-transformation without losing touch of its embeddedness in routine.'[163] We have thus returned to the level of the author. While the lawyer may have been downsized in the enquiry into the deep structures of argument (the outcome of which was that lawyers were completely governed by language and linguistic patterns), he now seems to have been promoted to subject again; a subject who, although conscious of conflicting reality and of 'living in uncertainty', is committed to the ideal of community. However, law characterised the modern way, i.e., as valid on the basis of its objectivity, is unattainable, again because international law remains uncertain, conflictual and indeterminate. The contemporary international jurist cannot escape repeating the deep structural commitments; rather than serving the 'complete system', he can re-establish his identity by 'commitment to reaching the most just solution in the particular disputes which he is faced with.' In brief, '[r]ather than be normative in the whole ... he should be normative in the *small*.' Koskenniemi explains that this is 'a task of *practical reason*.'[164] By reasoning practically, the lawyer is able to

---

[162] Id., at 488. The final sentence is reminiscent of Foucault's rejection of any 'nostalgia' for the universal and for a new world vision.

[163] Id., at 490-491.

[164] Id., at 496-497. Emphasis added. 'It positively *excludes imperialism and totalitarianism*. Beyond that, however, it makes no pretention [*sic.*] to offer principles of the good life which would be valid in a global way.' Id., at 498: 'Engaging in practical reasoning, the lawyer shall have to recognize that solving normative problems in a justifiable way requires, besides impartiality and commit-

'imagine alternatives', Koskenniemi, like Unger,[165] believes. Finally, Koskenniemi's further remarks that the continuous debate on whether states or individuals are the 'true' subjects of international law 'fails to recognize the differences in our communal ties.' He continues:

> [a]ny attempt to overrule those ties will immediately seem like irrelevant utopianism or harmful totalitarianism. Indeed, it may be that the State/individual *opposition* contains no alternatives at all but that we think of individuals as autonomous and equal entities only because we have internalised a formal conception of statehood from the perspective of which individuals do appear in such a way. Alternatives to these two ways of looking at global life share in this error of trying to persuade us that they have finally understood its true essence, residing in some religious, economic, cultural, or other such "deep-structure". They tell us that conflict has to do with an opposition between "believers" and "non-believers", "rich north" and "poor south", "communist regimes" and "capitalist regimes", and so on. Yet, when these explanations are formulated and used in political programmes, they fail to respect the infinitely more varied character of collective and individual experience.
>
> The idea of one coherent explanation of the character of global social life and a coherent programme for world order needs to be rejected. ... The argument will remain indeterminate and political. And yet, only its remaining so will prevent it from being just another totalitarian apology.

In Koskeniemmi's view, the individual-state opposition in the discussion on the subjects of law is linked to the liberal deep structure of international law. Koskeniemmi imagined an alternative to these two options, without recourse to some other kind of meta-narrative, but by relying on a process of 'normative imagination' so that rather than 'to play the game better', it would be possible to 're-imagine the game, reconstruct its rules, redistribute the prizes.'[166]

In conclusion, although Martti Koskenniemi does not seem averse to a 'reconstructed' (perhaps less legal and more socio-political) conception of ILP and Anthony Carty even suggests that 'we need a [new] perspective on international legal personality,' while explaining the consequences of Koskenniemi's theory. Although Carty remarks that 'in [his] view there is no difficulty, in terms of the most rudimentary social theory, in jettisoning formalist approaches to legal subjectivity/personality,'[167] critical new international legal scholarship has still not

ment, also wide knowledge of social causality and of political value and, above all, capacity to imagine alternative forms of social organization to cope with conflict. It shall lead him to overstep the boundaries between practice and doctrine, doctrine and theory. The construction of contextual justice will demand an imaginative effort to rethink the contexts in which traditional roles have been formulated and in which their social effects have remained so unsatisfactory. The rethinking of contexts, again, makes it possible to imagine alternative social routines both for the lawyer and his "clients" while the very dynamism of the process excludes claims of objectivity and universal normative truth.'

[165] See *supra* chapter 1.

[166] From Apology to Utopia, at 500-501. Emphasis added.

[167] Critical International Law, at 82.

(expressly) addressed the re-thinking of the concept of ILP. To my knowledge, no 'New *constructive* Approach' of ILP has been formulated yet.[168]

In this section so far we have highlighted certain features of contemporary international law scholarship which may explain its reluctance to deal with ILP. However, as I mentioned at the beginning of this section, ILP is still used at times in the margin of international legal discourse and in the conventional textbook way. I will now give some examples of this.

The average textbook continues the pragmatic, functional approach and tends to dedicate one of its first general chapters to the 'subjects of public international law,' thereby also dealing with the concept of ILP. In general, such chapters identify international legal subjectivity and personality and persist in the traditional distinction between full and derived ILP. The individual is now an established subject of international law and if any controversy concerning ILP remain it is in relation to the status of NGOs (and MNCs).

In the French classic *Nguyen Quoc Dinh's Droit International Public*, it is for instance observed that 'La reconnaissance de la personnalité juridique internationale des personnes morales privées reste un thème de controverse doctrinale et constitue un problème toujours d'actualité.'[169] This observation dates from 1994, and even though since then the relations and borderline between the international business community on the one hand and the global civil society and global institutions on the other have continued to evolve, it still reflects well the state we are in. A tendency to recognise a greater social responsibility of corporations is articulated and the definition and scope of this corporate responsibility are the topic of discussion. Contributors to this discussion turn to international law for answers to these questions. Former US Deputy Assistant Secretary of State for Democracy, Human Rights and Labour, Bennett Freeman, argues that

[168] See for another example of ILP as the subject of deconstructive research, D.J. Bederman, The Souls of International Organizations: Legal Personality and the Lighthouse at Cape Spartel, 36 *Virg.JIL* 275 (1996): Bederman revisits ILP in a post-modern historiographic manner and by analysing the history of the International Commission for the Cape Spartel Light demonstrates the role of ILP in reconciling sovereignty and community in international institutions. His account shows how ILP functioned in the process of institutionalising functional international cooperation. In particular, it shows the power of ILP idiom as an idea and image, ']t]he idea that the Cape Spartel Commission as a juridical person, in both international and domestic law, was a powerful legal trope.' Id., at 331. By recounting the history of the Cape Spartel Lighthouse, Bederman illustrates some of ILP's history as well, i.e., its role in relation to international organisations and in particular of the power of ILP as an 'idea' and 'metaphor' in organising the study of these organisations, reconciling 'personhood' and 'community', and characterising their status under international law. It is however also the story of international law scholars as an early epistemic community who were influential to the extent that they were because of their expertise in the field of functional international cooperation and its legal aspects, in other words, a case of 'knowledge is power.' Id., at 376.

[169] See *supra*, Daillier and Pellet, at 673. See also, Shaw, who states that if the Draft Code of Conduct of the UN Commission on Transnational Corporations is adopted and applied directly to MNCs 'it would be possible to regard them as international persons.' M.N. Shaw, International Law 172 (1991).

corporate social responsibility is no longer a mere option for corporations if they wish to escape the backlash of globalisation (i.e., anti-globalism), it is 'an *imperative*.'[170]

In *Problems & Process*, Judge Higgins deals with 'how we *use* international law,'[171] and in keeping with the language of the school of international legal process as founded by McDougal, the traditional textbook chapter on 'the subjects of international law' here bears the title 'Participants in the International Legal System'. The notion of 'participant' removes the *obstacle* that the concept of the subject and ILP have over the years become and promotes the idea of the democracy of access. Higgins explains why the traditional conceptual distinction between subjects and objects is 'wrong' and has neither 'credible reality' nor 'functional purpose.' And so the notion of 'participants' can set us free from the 'intellectual prison' we have built ourselves and 'then declared ... to be an unalterable constraint.'[172] There are no international legal subjects and there are no international legal objects, the individual is neither object nor subject. International law is a particular decision-making process in which all kind of actors participate. Although Higgins does away with the subject, this does not mean that she goes as far as to negate or replace the concept of ILP. Participants can still be international legal persons. Contemporary international law discourse either uses the concept of sovereignty[173] to accommodate and sustain change or the notion of participant, often without further definition. The concept of ILP, however, is mostly avoided. Contrary to McDougal, however, Higgins seems to have a more pronounced role in mind for ILP. This conclusion may be drawn from her participation in the 1994 Annual ASIL Meeting when in response to Christine Chinkin's argument she said:

We claim to be talking about sovereignty, while in fact it appears that the subject is statehood or legitimate authority. ... ... Sovereignty is a relative concept in international affairs that changes through time, and it has become common-place to say that there has been tremendous erosion in the concept of sovereignty, relating particularly to the areas of human rights and now possibly humanitarian intervention.

In thinking instead about statehood today, there is a sense of *exclusion*, particularly among women and indigenous persons. From my perspective, these groups do not need

[170] B. Freeman, Corporate Responsibility and Human Rights, contribution to the first Global Dimensions Seminar on Corporate Responsibility and Human Rights of the Centre for the study of Global Governance, L.S.E., as posted at <http://www.globaldimensions.net/articles/cr/freeman.html>. See also, conference of The Royal Institute of International Affairs on Legal Dimensions of Corporate Responsibility, 23 November 2001.

[171] R. Higgins, Problems & Process: International law and how we use it (1994). Emphasis added.

[172] Id., at 49.

[173] See, e.g., E.M.H. Hirsch Ballin, Interdependent Sovereignty, paper presented at the IVR World Congress on Philosophy of Law and Social Philosophy, The Transformation of Legal Systems and economies in an Age of Global Interdependence, Pace University, New York City, June 24-30, 1999.

international sovereignty. They are interested in *international status* in order to acquire an external arena in which to articulate their claims for internal rights. It is for that reason that women in particular are interested in looking for an *international personality*; indigenous peoples, with their territorially based associations, might behave differently. Alienation is a general phenomenon, even within democratic societies. There is a sense of failure, even with democratic governments. Are there better role models? I do not understand why we are talking about "sovereignty" when the sub-issues are the ones identified here.[174]

The call that the debate on the inclusion or exclusion of certain parties should focus on international personality instead of sovereignty is valid, but not a matter of course, because using the notion of *participant* pushes rights and obligations to the forefront and tends to lay to rest the question of legal status in terms of ILP. However, Higgins uses ILP here in line with its function of *inclusion-exclusion* in the international society of non-state actors and the legal status this requires, which is really a suggestion to re-direct international law discourse from sovereignty to ILP.

To illustrate this line of reasoning, another exception to the general avoidance of ILP is the contribution to the global governance debate by global *politics* scholar Peter Willetts. He addresses the legal implications of the shifting status of NGOs within the United Nations from consultative body to *partner* of the UN in its economic and social objectives. He bases his argument that NGOs should be *included* as subjects of international law on *customary international law*. In his view, the NGO statute has become part of customary international law and the permanent right to participate in the General Assembly 'would not be a significant legal change ... [it] would merely be confirmation of the new status of NGOs as subjects of international law.'[175] Basing himself on UN practice during the 1990s, he draws the conclusion that international NGOs that are recognised by ECOSOC have now acquired ILP:[176]

The only accurate way to describe what has happened is to recognize that NGOs have become a third category of subjects in international law, alongside states and intergovernmental organizations. The new language of the 1990s, with the concept of social partners, is revolutionary because it implies an equality of status between governments and NGOs. The partners are equal in the sense that each has legal personality, but not in the sense that they have the same rights and obligations. The argument does not apply to national NGOs. ... An apparent difference between states and NGOs is that states may claim to

[174] R. Higgins, The End of Sovereignty?, Panel IV of the 88th Annual Meeting, *ASIL Proceedings 1994*, at 73-74.

[175] P. Willetts, From 'Consultative Arrangements' to 'Partnership:' The Changing Status of NGOs in Diplomacy at the UN, 6 *Global Governance* 205 (2000). He also observes the avoidance of this issue by international legal scholars: 'Some international lawyers do not bother to address the question of whether NGOs can also be subjects of international law. Others admit to the possibility but consider it to have very little application.'

[176] See, for an opposite opinion, P.H. Kooijmans, Internationaal Publiekrecht in Vogelvlucht, 8th ed., (2000), at 33.

have international legal personality *before* they are recognized, whereas an NGO does not acquire its rights in international diplomacy until it is recognized by ECOSOC. [177]

Willetts argues that NGOs have now gained the new official status of UN partners with ILP. International NGOs have the right to participate in most of the intergovernmental policymaking bodies of the UN, but obviously still lack the right to vote and to negotiate, although their right to participate in negotiations is acknowledged. ILP thus extends to the right to participate, even when this comes without the power to create international law directly. In practice, the difference is of course very subtle, as especially in the field of human rights law NGOs have had an enormous influence on the drafting of documents, simply because of their impressive expertise. The author is clear about his objectives: 'the relationships between governments and international NGOs within intergovernmental organizations are a contribution to *democratic global governance*.'[178] With the accommodation of international NGOs within the UN system and the consolidation of their extensive rights to participation, 'the interstate system has been transformed since 1945, both politically and legally, into a multi-actor system.'[179]

The *inclusive* line of reasoning is thus applied in relation to non-state actors, like NGOs and MNCs. The inclusion of NGOs is not really a *new* problem, nor is it approached in new theoretical ways. Within the United Nations framework and in the context of adjacent organisations, i.e., within the global institutional order, these non-state actors, whether they are NGOs or political organisations like the PLO, have taken up an increasingly important role and have obtained the connected rights and duties. In a descriptive analysis of this development, it emerges that these non-state actors are either attributed a degree of ILP or not, that is, they are either *included* or *excluded*. Whether ILP is an appropriate concept to assess the legal status of non-state actors or, indeed, whether it will 'get us nowhere' therefore depends on the concept of international law which the scholar answering the question adheres to.

The *prescriptive* value of ILP – the element of *inclusion* and the legitimisation of participation in the international society – continues to function only in the margin of the debate on non-state actors. NGOs and MNCs with ILP give rise to

[177] Id., at 206.

[178] Id., at 207. Emphasis added. 'Global governance [analogous to national democracies] requires governmental delegates, as the representatives of the countries, as having full authority over multilateral policymaking and international NGOs [groups of citizens] having the right to make sure their concerns are heard in global forums. ... NGOs have two additional roles that enhance democracy. So long as there are military dictatorships, autocratic feudal regimes, or corrupt oligarchies, the idea of global democracy is inappropriate and NGOs can claim to be surrogate *representatives of people* from undemocratic countries. Furthermore, NGOs make the political process transparent. The exposure of the Multilateral Agreement on Investment negotiations was the most dramatic example, but bringing issues from global diplomacy into the public realm in an aspect of all their work.' Id., at 207-208.

[179] Id.

the assumption that the participation of NGOs will make the legitimacy-producing mechanisms of international law more *just* and for MNCs it implies *responsibilities* under international law towards the people making up the international society. The importance of these underlying assumptions can hardly be overestimated, but the fact that the concept of ILP is generally left unmentioned when international jurists deal with these issues is perhaps at second glance less surprising than we supposed before. Of course, applying the traditional concept of ILP to the so-called 'new' actors on the stage still has a descriptive and a prescriptive (emancipatory) function, but real progress is achieved at the ground level, locally, where the procedures determine whether an NGO can have the capacity to speak in a particular meeting based on its expertise and where MNCs will admit that they have duties under environmental law and human rights documents. Could this imply that MNCs have ILP? From a pragmatic perspective on contemporary global problems, the question of legal status is *less relevant* than how and with which rights and duties these new participants can be effectively endowed.[180] A concept like 'corporate responsibility' may develop into a more effective notion for advancing compliance with international norms. This is something for practice to work out.

Undoubtedly, at a more conceptual level of the debate on 'new' actors, ILP is a suitable concept to be used as an evaluative, descriptive/prescriptive notion indicating that international law has or should have *identified* the actor as a *legitimate participant.*

What conclusions may be drawn from this general non-use and only occasional use of the concept of ILP in contemporary international law scholarschip? Is there an underlying coherent explanation? We started by asking '*why*?' and suggested four explanatory factors. Then we indicated how the concept still features when it is used. Now I would like to argue that both the non-use and the use of ILP have something in common or share a common intention: they are both appeals to *justice*. Whether ILP is regarded as an obstacle to *just* global institutions, as a concept too legal to be true, as a concept too much part of universal theory (in particular of the liberal political theory) about international law and international society, whether it is perceived as too formalistic or too intimately connected with the individual-state opposition in the subjects doctrine, the underlying explanation as to why the concept is not used may be found in an appeal to justice, which it seems unable to serve adequately. This is the case according to Allott's social idealist perspective, in which the abolishment of the 'conceptual category' of subjects of international law relates to the idea that a legal system can designate any individual or entity as a participant by delegating legal power in the 'social interest,' which is 'determined in and through the op-

[180] See also, P.H. Kooijmans, Internationaal Publiekrecht in Vogelvlucht, 8th ed., (2000), at 34-35.

eration of the total social process of society, including necessarily society's struggle with the dilemma of justice and social justice.'[181]

The same explanation seems valid for those instances when ILP *is* used expressly, namely in its application to the theory of *inclusion*, which also strats from the idea that increased and more diverse participation of non-state actors would make international institutions and international law more *just*, which frequently translates as more democratic in terms of global governance.

Evidently, justice can be perceived in many ways and the inclusion of democracy in such a concept might be too liberalist for post-modern tastes. For now, the conclusion that the concept of ILP is in our discipline consciously or unconsciously connected with considerations of justice will have to do. This means I will not enter into the various positions here. If we were to conclude that ILP will indeed get us nowhere in confronting today's problems involving globalisation, I wonder whether at another level this is not also an attempt to advance international law. However, the role I would like to suggest for ILP is a more theoretical one, namely to resurrect the subject, his capacity and responsibility.

5.4. THOMAS FRANCK'S STRUGGLE WITH ZEUS

5.4.1. **Introduction**

During the 1990s, Thomas Franck was engaged in a protracted struggle with Zeus. He reported on this battle by means of a sequence of articles in the *AJIL*,[182] finally to come to a conclusive victory in *The Empowered Self: Law and Society in the Age of Individualism* (1999). Franck's struggle with Zeus had the purpose of '*unchaining Prometheus:*' the Greek god who likewise rebelled against Zeus when he strove to 'endow each human with a divine spark.'[183] To this end, Prometheus stole fire from Helios' wagon and thereby went against Zeus' order that man should never be provided with this divine gift. Prometheus ended up being captured by Zeus and was chained at Scythia by Hephaistos, subsequently to be released by Zeus' son Heracles after Zeus had finally realised that really justice should emerge victorious, not violence. One of the most telling passages of *The Empowered Self* precedes even the book's dedication as Franck states that: 'Prometheus' eventual release may be seen to represent the reconciliation between the will of heaven and newly freed and assertive human beings. That a divine spark endows each person continues to be a powerful underpinning for modern individualism and the cause of human rights.'[184] Prometheus' release

[181] Eunomia, at 326.

[182] T.M. Franck, Clan and Superclan: Loyalty, Identity and Community in Law and Practice, 90 *AJIL* 359 (1996); Is Personal Freedom a Western Value?, 91 *AJIL* 593 (1997).

[183] Th. M. Franck, The Empowered Self: Law and Society in the Age of Individualism v (1999). Hereinafter: The Empowered Self.

[184] Id.

symbolises the liberation of the individual's fundamental right to choose his own identity, affiliations, and existence, to be fundamentally free in determining who he is. Today our 'right to fire' is our right to give complex answers when asked to define ourselves, now that we have been liberated from the 'old definitions' provided by nationalism, tribalism, ethnicity, or any other determinist view of human identity. Identity can only be chosen, not imposed. Franck liberated the divine spark in an attempt to provide a solid basis for individualism and the universality of human rights.

In his modern revolt against injustice, violence, and the denial of individual human freedom, Franck had to address and challenge a number of issues. After all, Prometheus' revolt against the Gods may have brought man the divine spark, but it also unleashed on mankind Zeus' angry response in the shape of *Pandora's box*. This is to warn us that the entry into the world of the divine spark, *in casu*, the spark of individual freedom and personal self-identification, may well be accompanied by all possible disasters and difficulties, comparable to the dark scenarios conjured up by Kaplan, Guehenno, Huntington, and others. Therefore, it should be stressed from the start that individual freedom must be balanced with individual responsibility and the world rule of law.

In the light of the international and intellectual context outlined above, the title of Franck's book, *The Empowered Self*, reflects its topical content and hints that it may well hold an apt response to the issue at stake today – the post-modern theme of identity and the self as related to the announced disappearance of the subject. However, Franck is neither a cynic nor a post-modern scholar,[185] instead he argues that what is emerging is '*post* post-modernism.' He responds to the post-modern arguments on international law, its lack of objectivity and determinacy, with a neo-liberal argument envisioning that what will emerge is not 'necessarily world government ... but, rather, a liberal global neo-community, a civil society based on socially and legally protected individualism.'[186]

5.4.2. **Franck's concept of international law**

Here we will concentrate on Franck's last work, but it must be noted that his theoretical argument on international law actually developed over the past decade, especially where he tackled a number of fundamental questions in two earlier works before arriving at an analysis of the emancipation of the individual in international law in *The Empowered Self.*

---

[185] Franck observes that the 'periodic recurrence [of cynicism] is unfortunate at several levels. At the level of the intellectual agenda, ... international law – because ... "how" and "why" questions are rarely asked – tends instead to generate dull, rather absurdly defensive, rule description and even more plodding prescription, as if the grand issues of domination, communication, obedience, and transformation lie forever beyond the attention span of serious international scholars. ... Disobedience is thought – albeit wrongly – to be the prevalent practice, and, thus the study of norms – either the is *or* the ought of a normative prescription – is irrelevant.' Th. Franck, The Power of Legitimacy Among Nations 7 (1990). Hereinafter: The Power of Legitimacy.

[186] The Empowered Self, at 98 and 100. Emphasis added.

The first of these earlier works, *The Power of Legitimacy Among Nations* (1990), deals with the ontological question of international law: 'Is international law, law like national law?'[187] and the even more relevant question: 'Why do powerful nations obey powerless rules?'[188] For what 'reasons' do sovereign states *obey* international law rules when there is no international coercive force? Franck observed that this legal philosophical – teleological – question had largely been neglected within international legal scholarship.[189] The lack of enforcement is mainly due to the absence of a world government with coercive power which could act as a sovereign that commands international law. However, Franck argues, contemporary legal theory also offers *non*-coercive factors for explaining (voluntary) obedience to law – which together form what is covered by the notion of *legitimacy* – and these factors are particularly interesting to international legal theory.[190] Franck's search for an answer to the issue of 'validation' initially directed him towards legitimacy instead of justice,[191] and caused him to formulate this hypothetical answer to his question: '*Because they perceive the rule and its institutional penumbra to have a high degree of legitimacy.*'[192] He thus develops an argument of a procedural type of legitimacy and defines the perceived power of legitimacy as depending on four 'validators' or properties which determine an international legal rule's pull to compliance: determinacy, symbolic validation, coherence, and adherence, they are 'the building blocks of Right process.'[193] In brief, the degree of legitimacy of a rule, a rule-making or implementing process, depends on these factors and thus a legitimate rule is clear, considerate of cultural context or elements, coherent in time and compatible with

---

[187] According to Franck, it is 'not'. In his mind, compliance is not based on the authority of the Sovereign but on the desire of the member of the international community to be accepted and respected. Franck determines that it is in a State's national interest to comply with community rules. '[T]he international legal system ... *is* a system of obligations for an emerging global community.' The Power of Legitimacy, at 33.

[188] The Power of Legitimacy, at 3.

[189] Franck also notes the *unjustified* 'closing of the international rule system to philosophical inquiry aided by the insights developed by the study of national and sub-national communities,' and thereby the unjustified 'alienation' of the national and international branches of legal philosophy. Id., at 5-6.

[190] Franck mentions Dworkin's triad of fairness, justice, and integrity or coherence, as well as Habermas' concept of inter-subjective discursive validation: authority as process, which has three characteristics: consent, openness, and participation. Franck regrets the lack of 'creativ[ity]' in international legal thinking on the subject of legitimacy. Id., at 15-17.

[191] As in Franck's view, justice can only be done to individuals, not to collectives like the State. Justice is not an aggregate concept, it only has meaning to the reality of individual life. Moreover, justice is an inadequate concept for the international legal system, which generally addresses States, and is also unsuitable for measuring the system's legitimacy, because justice is 'conceptually distinct' from legitimacy. Although both justice and legitimacy may pull to compliance legitimacy should be our first concern, according to Franck. Justice is a culturally dependent notion and difficult to work with in a pluralist global community. See, Franck's final Chapter 'Postlude: Why Not Justice?,' at 208-246.

[192] Id., at 25.

[193] Id., at 235.

other rules and principles, and adherent to hierarchy. This way it is able to communicate its meaning fully and is thereby capable of influencing the will and conduct of the states pulling to compliance. Here we have a purely voluntarist perspective on the global community and its law. The law should reflect the general will of the international community and it should function in accordance with the principles of 'right process.' Franck's argument aims to reconcile the realistic assessment of powerful sovereign states with the ideal of a world Rule of Law, in fact to reconcile national power with international law. The argument is therefore well suited to a liberal political programme. However, Franck does not shy away from the criticism of his 'liberal' position as coming from 'Critical' quarters. He is opposed to the idea of the indeterminacy of law: 'in practice determinacy is not an illusion.'[194] The degree of determinacy defines a rule's legitimacy. A rule may be elastic, but it has to be concrete to the extent that it defines what is prohibited and what is not. Of course, clarity is not enough and it may even need to be corrected if the outcome or result of the rule would be 'unjust, cavalier, unfair, even absurd.'[195] The same is true for the validity of its symbolic communication as well as its coherence or consistency; a rule should be 'authentic in its communication' and consistent with other principles which have been accepted as just and which are part of the hierarchical normative system. This normative hierarchy also exists in international law, as treaties are binding according to the higher norm of *pacta sunt servanda*, which emanates from the *opinio juris* and conduct of states.[196] The international legal system is thus based on the national interest which is served by belonging to the international community. It emerges by necessity and consists of principles and rules which are valid or legitimate because of the characteristics mentioned. To include justice as a factor in a pluralist society such as the global community would be to risk going down a road to chaos.[197] However, despite Franck's distinction between legitimacy and justice and his reluctance to formulate an international theory of justice, in the end he could no longer avoid making at least some reference to it, or else he would risk falling prey to an exaggerated position of formal positivism. Consequently, in his next book, Franck dealt with this relationship in terms of *fairness*.

---

[194] Id., at 56: 'The degree of elasticity of words and texts varies, and can be controlled as a deliberate strategy. Like legitimacy itself, textual determinacy is always a matter of degree, and the degree to which a rule exhibits determinacy varies from rule to rule. While no word formulas are entirely without elasticity, yet some are more elastic than others. The degree of determinacy directly affects the degree of a rule text's perceived legitimacy.' Here, Franck mentions the 'Crit' Duncan Kennedy, but at other instances he refers to and reflects on David Kennedy, Unger and Foucault too; id., at 248-249.

[195] Id., at 73.

[196] Id., at 187.

[197] Id., at 235, 236: 'The co-existence of radically different concept of right within an emergent global secular system often is made possible by emphasising the manifest legitimacy of secular rules while deliberately postponing to another day considerations of justice. ... In recognizing such lexical priority of legitimacy over justice, the global community is often different in degree from the secular considerations of justice.'

In the second of the earlier works preceding *The Empowered Self* Franck arrives in the 'post-ontological' stage of his argument, or it could be said that international law enters the 'post-ontological era.'[198] He continues his research in international legal philosophy. In *Fairness in International Law and Institutions* (1995) legitimacy and justice are no longer separated as strictly. Instead, Franck begins to acknowledge that *fairness* is a relevant factor for compliance with international law. Here, Franck defines the pull to compliance as depending on *both* legitimacy *and* fairness or, in other words, the notion of *fairness* comes to comprise two components: 1) *legitimacy* or procedural fairness (also process fairness), defined by the four indicators just mentioned, and 2) distributive *justice* or substantive fairness (also moral fairness). Franck no longer denies the moral roots of law: 'distributive justice is rooted in the moral values of the community in which the legal system operates. The law promotes distributive justice not merely to secure greater compliance, but primarily because most people think it is *right* to act justly.'[199] However, he also remains faithful to the postulate he formulated earlier as a reason *not* to include considerations of justice in an international law theory: justice operates only or merely has relevance in/for the life of individual human beings rather than that of states.[200] Therefore, in order to develop an international theory of justice, the individual has to be empowered and brought more to the forefront of the international legal system. This is reflected in the structure of the book, as after the first part, 'a critical analytical framework for a critique of international law,' Franck goes on to deal with 'fairness in *empowerment* of *persons* and *peoples*,' in which part he discusses the emergence of a right to democracy. In the third part of the book, Franck assesses 'fairness and institutional power,' examines 'the law and institutions of distributive justice,' and finally reflects on 'fairness about fairness: shaping a global discourse.' I would like to discuss four particular features of *Fairness* here, which will automatically lead us to *The Empowered Self*.

a. *Plurality*. Global interdependence and trans-national relations have been on the increase among a diversity of state and non-state participants alike. The increase in the plurality of actors has been contributing greatly to the changing nature of the international community. Franck's characterisation of today's global community reflects this change:

---

[198] Th. Franck, Fairness in International Law and Institutions 6-7 (1995). Hereinafter: Fairness. At 9: 'The new maturity and complexity of the system calls out for a critique of law's content and consequences. Its extensive coverage and its audacious incursions into state sovereignty demand a new emphasis on the system's values, aims, and effects.'

[199] Id., at 8. Franck adds: 'The moral pursuit of distributive justice should engage us because, like Socrates, our intellects should harbor an 'all-engrossing eagerness for answers to moral questions, beginning with the most urgent of all: how should we live?' The question of fairness encompasses that moral issue because fairness supposes moral compass, a sense of the just society. The law must create solutions and systems which take into account society's answers to these moral issues of distributive justice, for we are moral as well as social beings.'

[200] See *supra* footnote 191.

What was an anarchic rabble of states has transformed itself into a society in which a variety of participants – not merely states, but also individuals, corporations, churches, regional and global organisations, bureaucrats and courts – now have a voice and are determined to interact. Usually, they try to interact in accordance with recognized norms or principles. When they do not, they seek to explain why. In this newly socialized community, therefore, much of the attempt at interaction is discursive: an interlocutory process of exhortation, expiation, explanation, and exposition. ... The need to explain, to expatiate, is the deference which political power pays to the social potential of law. The adoption of norms seems to be the price which the individual actor – person or state – must pay to participate in an interactive community.[201]

Today's international community is thus a *discursive* and *interactive* society. However, although the 'global discourse' no longer occurs exclusively among states, it still tends to most of the time. This affects international law, as the perception of its fairness depends on its creation through this (fair/unfair) discursive process.[202]

b. *Legal transition.* The law of this global community is in transition, as Franck emphasised in his 1995 book. Like many of his fellow jurists, he saw the end of the Cold War with its promise of a new world order as 'heralding a forthcoming transformation in international law.'[203]

International law is only now beginning to think about the appropriate balance between the claims of the state, the individual, and the revived traditional and new groups. What sort of future do we want, what sort of governance should it have, and who or what will exercise power in it? In accordance with what kind of political process are claims to rights and goods to be reconciled and configured? We have barely begun to examine such problems and opportunities, standing as we now do at the cusp of a global triage that will fix our identities in the third millennium.[204]

Future international law and international law theory should, in other words, address these questions about international life and the position of its various actors, including the individual human being. In his next book (The Empowered Self), Franck would indeed address these issues. The variety of factors, i.e., the complexity of the problems of the new era, needed to be properly approached by means of a discursive process in order to create a balance between stability and change and to reconcile procedural and substantial fairness constructively. This would result in *fair* international law, the achievement of which was the biggest challenge of them all.

---

[201] Fairness, at 477.

[202] 'A discourse solely and exclusively reflecting the views of those who govern nations cannot be expected to produce rules which are fair, or can only be expected to do so haphazardly.' Id., at 484.

[203] Id., at 140.

[204] Id., at 243-244. As we see later on, Franck himself tackled this dilemma of balancing between the powers and rights of the state, non-state groups, and the individual in The Empowered Self.

c. *The moral community*. The fairness of international law depends on the fairness of the fairness discourse, whether it suits the requirements of 'due process' and the moral values of allocational fairness. But is it possible today to have a notion of fairness that is shared globally? Is there 'a *shared sense* of the *identity* of those entitled to a fair share'? To have an optimal fairness discourse 'there must be an ascertainable community of persons self-consciously engaged in a *common moral enterprise*.'[205] The emphasis is mine, as I wish to stress the bold character of Franck's enterprise (bold for raising the issue of humanity's *universal* moral challenges as well as the issue of identity) within such a sceptical intellectual context as ours. To think of the global community as a moral community and as a 'rule community'[206] is a true constructive challenge. Franck claims to have evidence that such a community is emerging. However, he does not consider moral or allocational fairness to have universal and absolute meaning. Rather, he agrees that it is a 'deep[ly] contextual' notion and thus 'relative and subjective.' What is needed therefore is *agreement* on 'a *fair* allocational formula,' which, in order to be fair, has to be based on an 'irreducible core of beliefs' or 'basic values.' In other words, common consent concerning a '*negotiated*' core of basic moral values has to provide solid ground for the fairness discourse,[207] including the discourse on the fairness of the global fairness discourses. Franck subsequently suggests the 'maximin principle' as a universally acceptable core principle of fairness, dictating that 'inequalities in the access to, or the distribution of, goods must be justifiable on the basis that the inequality has advantages not only for its beneficiaries but also, to a proportionate or greater degree, for everyone else.'[208] In Franck's view, this principle provides a realistic

[205] Id., at 10-11. Franck outlines two preconditions for an optimal fairness discourse, i.e., a fairness discourse to assess the fairness of the law, drawing from Rawls theory of justice. They are 1) moderate scarcity, the possibility to avoid a zero-sum setting; 2) a '*community*', as it requires shared values and principles to make a balanced decision or calculation of fairness. A community is based on the principle of reciprocity, as we have also seen Franck explain above in footnote 187. Its members function on the basis of the common interest as self-interest and the emerging expectation that each member will respect the other. Such a system of reciprocity shares this expectation, as it shares a system of moral values and obligations. To quote Franck: 'The laws in a community thus evince not only the generally held belief that each must do what he or she is legally required to do, but also that each will discharge towards all others those obligations arising from the shared moral sense.' Allocational fairness of 'goods' includes both concrete goods (material things or resources) as well as abstract goods ('peace, power, and liberty'), and therefore also includes the allocation of rights and duties.

[206] '[A rule community] must have agreed on a core of reciprocally applicable rules and it must also have agreed on a process for making and applying rules and resolving disputes about their meaning. In other words, a community is defined by having a corpus of rules which it deems to be legitimate and by having agreed on a process that legitimates the exercise of authority, one which conduces to the making of fair rules and fair allocations.' Id., at 12.

[207] Id., at 14-16. In this view, justice and moral principles are contextual and each relative to the other.

[208] Id., at 18. He explains: 'unequal distribution is justifiable only if it narrows, or does not widen, the existing inequality of persons' and/or states' entitlements.' Franck continues to draw from Rawls here.

and pragmatic theory of equality. Its effect would be 'relative equalization' and because it is moderate and still tolerant of inequalities it would be acceptable to most persons and states as a principle which closely approaches their own sense of morality. When we focus on the way international law is created and whether this is a *fair* process, the issue of representation and *participation* emerges. When we address fairness at the level of global governance – in the sense of 'how fair is the global fairness discourse?' – we find ourselves returning to a development outlined previously: the process of *inclusion*.

d. *Participation*. The final sentence of the citation above on the character of the current global community[209] explains that the actor with political power pays deference to the social potential of law by explaining his conduct in terms of the norms of the community. This is 'the price which the individual actor – person or state – must pay to *participate* in an interactive community.' Participation in the global community is based on the social force of law and the participants' recognition that being a member of this community is in their own interest. Participation in discursive interactions requires compliance with norms, it demands acceptance of the legal order and its claims to legitimacy. However the contemporary rise of non-state groups has given rise to frequent claims to another kind of fairness, namely the claim of inclusion in law-creating (negotiation) processes. These claims appeal to (a sense of) justice: the process that creates legitimate international law is unfair until, for example, certain human rights or environmental NGOs are represented. As we have already seen with Franck's elaboration of the notion of legitimacy in *The Power of Legitimacy Among Nations*, justice invades the question of legitimacy even though the intention is to separate them to the greatest possible extent. In *Fairness* however the reconciliation of justice and legitimacy is in the foreground. Justice-based claims intend to 'change existing entitlements and patterns of distribution', causing us to wonder whether the procedures and institutions that create legitimate international law are also *just*.

The idea of the 'democracy of access' and the importance to an international law of human dignity of a plurality of global actors participating in international processes was essential to Myres McDougal. Thomas Franck continues this line of thought, but in his own way and he criticises the 'fairness deficit' of international law. He discerns a global discursive society that encompasses many voices, both state and non-state, but in which only states participate in international legal processes. To counter this fairness deficit of international law (which has to be countered among other reasons because it impedes compliance with international norms) Franck argues that the participation of groups which are still not represented in the global discourse should be improved. The global fairness discourse is 'embedded in the decision-making processes of numerous treaty-based organizations and non-governmental institutions,' it takes place in the UN Security Council as well as the WTO or WB. These international legal processes and institutions of global governance have to be organised fairly as well. Franck addresses

[209] See *supra*, text to footnote 201.

the two main characteristics of the current institutions of international governance, firstly, the principle of 'one state, one vote' and secondly, the 'single voice' principle. In his view, both are unfair, the first for resulting in unfair equality,[210] but I will confine myself to the second.

In the global discourse forums concerning fairness *only* governments have a voice, and this '*exclusion* of so many voices ... undermines the fairness of the fairness discourse as currently constituted.' The unfairness of this *exclusion* of non-state groups from representation has not really been mitigated, as for instance 'all the unrepresented minorities within states ... lack voice in a purely state-centered system.'[211] The structure of the global system is unsuited to accommodating these voices in the forums of the fairness discourse. And so what is needed is 'the reconstruction of the global system' in order to address the unfairness. Such a reconstruction should also prevent a situation where claiming statehood would be the only way in which indigenous peoples could establish representation and participation in the global discursive community. Franck thus argues that extending participation and representation to peoples besides governments could enhance fairness. Since the fairness deficit is the result of the inadequacy of the 'discursive synthesis of legitimacy and justice,' the fairer allocation of participation rights may increase the moral fairness of the legitimacy process. The 'discontent' with the 'illegitimacy, injustice, and unfairness [of global institutions] must be addressed,' so Franck contends. Therefore, in order to maximise fairness, he proposes a reform of the UN system and the addition of a second chamber to the GA, the seats of which can be earned through elections by universal suffrage, with the number of votes based on the size of populations, for such a chamber would be representative of *all* people on the planet.[212]

Fairness, which is composed of legitimacy or right process *and* justice, is a balancing concept incorporating both progress and stability. After all, and here Franck refers in agreement to Koskenniemi's 'social conception' of law, it is the 'primary objective' of (fair) law 'to achieve a negotiated balance between the need for order and the need for change.'[213] 'Justice-based claims' seek '*a new and better order*;' dealing with 'distributive modalities and advance reasons for *change* in the existing entitlements and patterns of distribution.'[214] Legitimacy as right process demands a certain allocation of participating rights and obligations in order to arrive at a stable and orderly process and social life. Encompassing both justice and legitimacy, fairness forms a mediating notion to manage the dif-

[210] Fairness, at 48': 'the centripetal trend in tackling international problems is generating a centrifugal reaction which threatens to make discourse difficult, if not impossible. In that context, the principle of state equality, long a legal fiction, must be seen as wrong, first because it encourages secessionism which, in turn, makes fairness discourse more cacophonous, and secondly because it is an unfair organizing principle which infects the fairness discourse with a fundamental flaw of unfairness.'

[211] Fairness, at 481. Emphasis added.

[212] Id., at 477-484.

[213] Id., at 23.

[214] Id., at 477. Emphasis added.

ferent views on its two constituent parts and their mutual relationship. Justice and legitimacy meet or converge in the issue of participation within the global community and its fairness discourse.

In order to prevent confusion over Franck's concept of the global community it should be emphasised that in his view the emerging global community should not be viewed as 'an alternative to, or competing with the basic community which is the state.' Rather than alternatives the communities are complementary: '*Communitas* can be concentric and overlapping. Society is starting to perceive itself as a community of states and, simultaneously, as a community of persons.' Franck does therefore not intend to reject the concept of sovereignty or statehood, but to 'recogniz[e] in law what is increasingly evident in social and cultural practice: the striation of identity to accommodate multiple identifications.'[215] The next stage in Franck's quest or 'grander objective'[216] thus reveals itself as the issue of *identity* as related to the debate on the 'end of the subject' and the attack on the autonomous *self*. As such it is Franck's interpretation of what he perceives the legal scholar's task to be, namely 'to participate in the theoretical critique of international law's fairness.'[217]

5.4.3. Franck's construction of the *post* post-modern self: the world citizen

So far, the concept of ILP has remained outside this analysis of Franck's thinking. Neither of the works discussed uses the concept with any emphasis as to its particular relevance. It is there, but implicit in the background of his argument as the attribute of sovereign states which create international law. The theoretical critique touched upon so far is aimed at making international law fairer. In it, justice is included as a component of fairness. With the conviction now firmly in place that *justice* is a notion that makes sense in *individual* human life, fairer international law thus demands a more *individualised* international legal order. This is important to note, as it reflects the development of an ever-increasing attribution of relevance to the concept of individualisation in Franck's thinking on international law over the years. This development is closely related to the question of international justice and ultimately to the question of compliance. The claims to participation of non-state groups are justice-based by nature – they call for the representation of individuals by groups other than states. Franck warned that these groups had to be taken seriously in order to preserve an orderly international system. With these conclusions in *Fairness* on representation and participation in the international community, on the triangle of state, group and individual, and on the conviction that justice is an individual-based concept, which pointed to an emerging need for further individualisation, Franck first confronted the

[215] Id., at 13.

[216] Id., at 16: 'Step by step, slowly, we want to bring to the global agenda a heightened interest in making the expanding universe of international law *fair*'.

[217] Id., at 478.

post-modern deconstruction of the self and subsequently formulated a 'post post-modern' reconstruction in the form of a kind of universal constitutionalism. Franck contended that the individual subject had to be preserved. Because of the post-modern context in which Franck made this claim, he had to defend the autonomy and responsibility of the individual subject. He both based his legal theory upon this individualism and empowered the individual by means of this international legal theory.

Franck starts off by defending the *modern* subject against post-modern critique and de-construction. *The Empowered Self* may be read as a response to the contemporary argument that the individual subject does not exist, or as a challenge of the idea that the *modern self* is disappearing. Franck acknowledges that '[it] is against the inadmissibility of personal *choice*' that this book argues. It opposes the conception that '[o]ne's identity is situationally, not personally, determined' and disputes the line of reasoning that claims that '[t]o choose for oneself is meaningless, an affront to the very *idea* of identity.' In brief, he takes up position against the 'determinist view of human identity.' Whether determined by language or power, Franck objects to the entire idea of identity as the product of causality, of necessity and contingency, he rather adheres to the (Kantian-inspired) postulate of a free world in which individuals have the freedom to employ their will to construct their personal identity.

Franck then goes on to defend the individualist alternative which claims that the individual has the *right* to choose and to define her/his self. In this view, the 'coming global identity crisis' is an especially post-Cold War phenomenon: the geo-political schema has changed and is much less decisive in determining our loyalties. Now, there is room for redefinition. Franck discerns that basically all our 'certitudes' have come under scrutiny and are subsequently either preserved, rejected, or redefined. The assumption that it is possible to have '*any* defensible certitudes' is itself in dispute. Scholars who follow Foucault consider this 'less cause for anxiety than an exhilarating opportunity to unchain human consciousness, liberate it of old, false certitudes.' And Franck observes that:

> In the turbulent self-deconstructing times following the collapse of the old cold war order, Foucault would have been in his element, for definitional disarray is the order of the day. At the top of the list of things now needing *reconstructive* definition is *the self*.
>
> But such self-definition is not just a personal, psychoanalytic task. It is also a social, interpersonal task of the greatest political importance. Definition, by definition, unites and divides; it communicates and alienates; it integrates and disaggregates.[218]

Franck subtly points out that the times have changed since Foucault made his argument and that after deconstruction comes a time of reconstruction of the self. This reconstruction of the self is politically and socially relevant because it relates

[218] Id., at 3-4.

to how we perceive society now and how we envision its future, both domestically and globally.

Franck's submission that to choose one's personal identity, one's individuality, is now emerging as an international *right* supports and has as its aim in the empowerment of every single human being. It helps the individual in claiming the identity and rights which are necessary for *self*-determination. The individual's right to claim and reconstruct the identity of the self will defeat what Franck termed the current 'usurpers of identity', i.e., nationalists, tribalists, and communitarians. The thesis of *The Empowered Self* is that 'nationalism is in retreat. It no longer enjoys an exclusive licence to define personal identity.' According to Franck, '*individualism* has emerged, at the end of the twentieth century, as an increasingly preferred alternative to self-definition imposed by nationalism's genetic and territorial imperatives.'[219] To manage and support this development, Franck aimed for 'an individualism that empowers each person to define his or her own unique identity protected by a new regime of national and international laws.'[220] The importance attributed to the *individual* will and choice in this liberal philosophical position is given flesh in Franck's work by its translation into a 'rights-claim', the content of which Franck develops throughout the book.

The next step Franck takes after taking the individual and his right to self-identification as a starting point is to recognise that the individual defines his personhood by loyalties, affinities, and commitment to traditional as well as new *groups*. The underlying idea is that the individual's relationship with his state, nation or tribe, is not completely broken off, but is turning into a mere one of many relationships through which the self is defined. This catapults the question concerning the international position of 'groups,' which Franck raised at the end of *Fairness*, to centre stage. In the transforming global community, which is gradually shifting into a so-called post-Westphalian phase, there are three contenders for power, which Franck recognises as 'rights-claimants', within the international legal order, namely the state, the group, and the individual.

During the Westphalian age, only the state was recognised as an international participant and 'the individual ha[d] *meaning* solely through association with a state'. Today, in this new phase: '[s]tates are constrained, in law and practice, by the need to live in a community of states that requires them to act not 'naturally' but predictably: which is to say, normatively.'[221] The importance of the state for the definition of personal identity has decreased, Franck observes. The old concepts, like ethnicity, tribe, and nation state, may explain 'how we became what we are', but they are no longer the only concepts needed for a proper discourse on the reidentification of the self. This is why the world is in need of *new* 'cat-

[219] The Empowered Self, at 1-3.
[220] Id., at 44.
[221] Id., at 5. Emphasis added.

egories of identity'. The tendency to 'romanticize the 'authentic' group' among post-modern scholars aims to oppose the idea of the liberal democratic state, but this romantic bias bears the risk of leading to 'a 2,000-state global system.' This is not what we want, Franck explains, as such a proliferation of sovereignty would create an 'unmanageable' situation of fragmentation and disintegration. The challenge of today – in terms of rights and the role of law – thus consists of balancing 'reasonably' the (emerging) 'rights' claimed by all contenders, which together form the 'new triad' – the state, the group, and the individual.[222]

Groups, whether nations, indigenous peoples or tribes, have to be granted rights which acknowledge the inherent dignity of their members and the distinct identity of the group as a whole. Only then can a situation be prevented where for such recognition they would otherwise need to claim independent statehood. Self-determination should not be perceived as merely a claim to independence. If this were how the principle is exclusively explained, it would remain a threat to the international community of sovereign states. And it will remain a threat until self-determination is defined as the basis of the recognition, accommodation and participation of non-state groups, now that the individual increasingly constructs his or her identity by associating with non-state groups. Franck continues the line of argument which he started in *Fairness*. 'There are remedial steps that might be taken,' he says.

> One is to organize the global community to give voice to affinity groups other than states – for example, the interstate grouping of the aboriginal peoples of the Arctic region. The international system would thereby encourage social aggregation rather than disaggregation. A related move might introduce into international governance an element of participation by representatives not of governments but of *persons*. That would give some effect, at last, to the opening phrase of the UN Charter: 'We the peoples ...'. ... Another possibility is to give more voice to non-governmental organizations in interstatal forums ... . The international system could also be reformed by giving 'voice' to existing substatal political units.[223]

To tackle the problem of representation and participation within the global democratic discourse, Franck repeats the suggestion made in the final chapter of his previous book: a second UN Assembly. Direct public participation involves a radical change of the international system. It should promote the emergence of 'global politics' within which 'factions, minorities, and other affinity groups

---

[222] Franck deals with the group within the international system, the Interwar status of the minority group, and observes: 'To individualists, minority status is always a singular attribute, never a collective one. To communitarians, individual rights derive meaning solely from association with the group. By the end of World War II, these tensions became more palpable. What emerged was an intricate rights triad, as tensile and delicate in its ever changing balance as a Calder mobile. ... ... The post-war changes wrought by the advent of a United Nations human rights system ... [p]rimarily [put] ... emphasis ... on *individual* rights meant to shield persons against conformist pressures and repressions by both states and groups.' Id., at 235.

[223] Id., at 30-31.

could make themselves heard *without* secession and the pursuit of sovereignty, choosing instead to aggregate their interests through transnational political parties and coalitions'.[224] This could save the system from total inadequacy and breakdown and would see in the post post-modern phase in the definition of self-identity.

Consequently, a crucial theme in Franck's theory is the balance between the rights-claimants making up the triad. How should the various claims be balanced in case of a conflict? He suggests that the fundamental principle on which a reasonable balance should rely is the '*survival principle*,'[225] which entails that 'each of the three categories of claimants must be able to enjoy those rights essential to its survival.' However, for this we need an additional three subsidiary principles, the most important of which is the principle of 'the individual's residual moral supremacy,' which is effectuated in the international community's efforts to defend fundamental human rights and confront deviant regimes.[226]

Franck suggests that 'a person's rights are implicit and *inherent* in the objective fact of *being*. To put it another way: there are acquired rights and unacquired rights. States, groups, and individuals each may be holders of acquired rights, but only persons can also have unacquired rights.'[227] Franck empowers the individual by arguing that the latter – by the authority of 'moral intuition' – has 'inherent rights' which are '*prior to*, and *differ in kind* from, the acquired rights of groups and states.'[228] The individual's rights-based claims have *moral* priority over group-rights and state-rights.[229] Franck recognises the existence of inherent fundamental human rights which are not derived from the state, but find their source in the moral value of the personhood of every individual human being.

Persons' claim to rights emanates from the undeconstructible objective fact of personage and not from such contingent conditions as those of state sovereignty or group cohesion. From it follows that personal rights have a strong moral claim to priority over the rights of

---

[224] Id., at 37.

[225] Id., at 246 *et seq.*

[226] The other two subsidiary principles are the principle of 'local option,' which 'facilitates the synchronization of different systems of law to accommodate different identities within a common political space,' and the principle of 'assisted exodus,' which 'artificially creates a discrete territorial basis for treating autonomous or federated groups differently within a loose common polity.' The latter in a worst-case scenario may lead to ethnic cleansing but this is prevented by the adjustment of the moral supremacy of the individual's claims as compared to the claims of the state or the group.

[227] Id., at 252. Emphasis added.

[228] Id., at 283. Emphasis added. Id., at 253: 'a person's moral claim to rights derives from original, autonomous personage and not from the sorts of contingent external events that shape the rights claim of such entities as the state, society, or tribe. The rights of individuals in this sense may be said to have a natural or moral priority over the rights of a group or a nation, which is also to say that personal rights, in structural terms, have an irreducible(that is, irrefutable) functional utility and, in moral terms, claim an absolute value. ... ...and in [a] secondary, or derivative, sense the various forms of human society – the nation, the tribe or ethnie, etc. – are also 'natural' manifestations of individuals' irrepressible associational drive. But lexically, it is the individual who constitutes society.'

[229] Id., at 253.

states and groups: at least in situations of conflict not otherwise resolvable by clear guidance from normative law or political negotiations.[230]

Franck states that '[t]he international system increasingly recognizes and facilitates' this task of balancing the three types of claims and placing them in a reasonable equilibrium 'as a good in itself.'

As a final step in his reasoning, Franck then claims that the international community should also recognise another task, namely, the balancing of the 'freedom from' governmental interference with the 'freedom to' or 'commitment to universal social responsibility.' Linking personal freedom with social responsibility, and defining the former in relation to its moral and political corollary, entails the 'democratic reconciliation' of freedom and responsibility, which is necessary for the recognition of and contribution to an emerging universal constitutionalism. 'Social responsibility, in a liberal democracy, is widely accepted as the due that each owes all.' At the global level, it is '[o]nly now that basic human rights have been recognized universally' and that 'the international legal system [has] begun to acknowledge personal and societal *responsibilities*.'[231] Franck points to the recent transformation within international and regional institutions and to the fact that human rights norms are beginning to recognise and include a democratic participatory entitlement – the individual right of electoral participation – for which compliance mechanisms are even gradually being established.

In Franck's analysis the current insufficiencies at the global level of democracy, legitimacy, justice, and fair representation and participation, are all interconnected. Empowering the individual by recognising fundamental personal rights also aims to decrease the global democratic legitimacy deficit. 'All too evidently, international political institutions fall far short of this democratic legitimacy,' while such legitimacy is essential for the public acceptance of redistributive measures. The deficit of democratic legitimacy is caused by a lack of 'representation in the international institutions of governance.' The recognition of an international right to democracy is not only a manifestation of individualism, but also confronts the legitimacy problem faced by international institutions and law. Franck concludes: 'We have the building blocks. A new democratic impulse, together with growing respect for individual rights and an awakening sense of international social responsibility; together these can build foundations of universal constitutional democracy.'[232]

Franck indicates the direction the global community should move in. This does not mean, however, that conceptually all is clear. Franck simply notes the developments and recognises the significance of the claims of non-state groups to the current global transformation. Franck observes for instance that '[t]raditional corporations are manoeuvring for recognition as autonomous rights-holders: re-

[230] Id., at 283.
[231] Id., at 255-256.
[232] Id., at 284-285.

sembling, in part, the state, the group, and even the fictive person.' How he values this evolvement is not clear. With respect to the outlined developments, Franck only determines that '[i]nternational law is only beginning to think about the appropriate balance between the claims of the state, the individual, and the revived traditional and new groups.' Nonetheless, he still gives a glimpse of a possible future.

The contemporary challenge of the Enlightenment project and liberal political theory in international law together constitute the core of the post-modern approach to international law. Franck does not fail to address either the anti-liberal attack on his theory or the problem posed by the crisis of the *modern* self or the human subject and the resulting notion that the state can be the only participant on the international scene. Both these views are countered by Franck's approach to international law. Despite the echo of Kennedy's appeal in Franck's recognition that 'the search for new definitions must begin by a sceptical look at the old lexicon,'[233] he eventually confirms the ideals of Modernism, presenting a line of reasoning that begins with the individual right of self-identification and results in the establishment of a neoliberal global community.

The pressing question now of course is: does ILP play any role within this argument, and if not, why is that? Franck does not use the actual notion of ILP in this context. It is used only in passing and in the conventional manner, as related to the state. It seems that in his eyes the concept belongs entirely to the old lexicon and he uses it as such. Sovereign states have ILP, they create international law which may attribute rights and duties to non-state actors. But by recognising the individual as a self-determining being and leaving it for international law to endow this modern subject with rights and responsibilities, Franck envisions a new (theory about) international law in an attempt to move beyond post-modernism and into the realm of a global democracy of individuals who have assumed the (new) identity of international *citizens*: rights-holders and claimants under positive international law.

Today at the international level, international human rights law and norms have created a new shield that protects individuals against their governments, so Franck observes:

> An elaborate system of rules and procedures has come to afford protection for persons' lives, liberty, personal security, privacy, conscience, and equality of opportunity. It purports to protect individuals' freedom of speech, movement, choice of language, and participation in politics and other forms or punishment. These norms are intended to *shield* individuals even against their own governments: a *concept* hitherto virtually unknown in international law and state practice.[234]

---

[233] Id., at 6.
[234] Id., at 280.

According to Franck, the concept of shielding individuals from harm inflicted upon by their own governments has been 'hitherto virtually unknown.' This is true as far as practice is concerned. In everyday life the concept has only begun to apply since the last World War. The idea, however, was already present in inter-war scholarship, as we have seen for example in the work of Scelle. He used the concept of ILP in this way, i.e., by attributing ILP to individuals by which he sought to empower them against the French government!

Franck continues: 'individuals are now generally accepted as rights-holders and as claimants,' thereby recognizing that fundamental rights which are *not* derived from state sovereignty are now being attributed to individuals. Moreover, these rights ultimately have the moral priority over the rights of states and groups. In other words, the most fundamental building block of international law and of the emerging universal constitutional democracy is the individual. The individual enjoys international legal protection and is the ultimate source of legitimacy.

It is at least arguable that the notion of ILP has become too tainted by its usage in 'old' international law to be helpful in overcoming criticism from post-modern quarters. Perhaps it must be firmly relegated to the old inter-state reality. Like in domestic constitutional societies and the corresponding law, the individual has exchanged subject status for citizen status, which was 'a tectonic shift in the loyalty system,' and thus redefined the nation as a *citizenry*. With his argument, Franck envisions a similar shift which should occur within the global community, namely a move away from the Vattellian inter-state system in the direction of a universal constitutional democracy. This would result in the identification of the (post-modern) *self* as a world citizen – a member of the global citizenry – a *Weltbürger*.

> What is novel, then, is not the idea of *Weltbürgertum* itself, which is hardly new. Rather, it is the dawning of a notion that identity, whatever its manifestation, is a *personal* attribute – whether it be global solidarity, xenophobic tribalism, enlightened liberal nationalism, or whatever; and that an individual's identity is increasingly self-chosen, rather than imposed by accident of birth or some liege-lords' fiat. New is the dawning of a spirit of individual assertiveness: a refusal to accept, as absolutely determinative, the identities traditionally handed out to persons by those claiming to be ordained by God, history, or the law to tell us who we are.[235]

However, '[t]o celebrate the triumph of Kantian humanism would be to ignore the continuing vitality of the still-powerful, still-entrenched state system.' The 'end-of-the-State theories' turn a blind eye to reality. It is true that 'new multilayered loyalty references are emerging', yet '[a] balanced view of tendencies at the end of the twentieth century reveals that powerful centripetal and centrifugal loyalties coexist with resilient statist patriotism.'[236]

---

[235] Id., at 60.

[236] Id., at 61. Franck demonstrates that citizenship has become 'an instance of identity as a personal act of self-determination,' as individuals increasingly claim dual or multiple citizenship, and

In Franck's view, the capacity to choose one's own identity is a responsibility as well as a *right* which is (to be) guaranteed by (positive) international law. He claims that:

not the re-emergence – and tolerance – of multiple loyalty references, but the acceptance of a right of persons (and other entities, including transnational corporations) to compose their own identity by constructing the complex of loyalty references that best manifest *who they want to be.* ... [B]y national and international normative usage, they are being freed to design their own identities. It is an awesome responsibility, the ultimate freedom, and symptomatic of a promising reconfiguration of the dynamics of the international system.[237]

The shift from subject of international law to international citizen is (an essential) part of the transformation of the international legal system from a Vattellian inter-state system into a universal constitutional democracy in which the individual is not only imputed with international rights and duties but in which he is (directly) represented and in which he participates in the international institutions that create and apply international law. With the empowerment of the self in *legal* terms Franck aims for the transformation of the individual's international status from international subject to citizen. It is this change of *legal* identity that will counter the lack of democratic legitimacy within the international institutions of governance. It is the 'republican' perspective on freedom, legislation, and (universal) governance which Franck considers is the right direction to take. The state has not exactly withered away, but it is no longer '*the* central reference of every person's identity, loyalty, and enterprise' either.[238] Some shift has occurred from the state to the individual as the building block of the global community. The *shield* has been lowered, the voice of the individual may sound freely, and on the basis of personal autonomy the individual can commit to communities and groups besides the state. 'The individualist is an authentically *modern* phenomenon: a person who sets out to choose the components of his or her own, unique identity.'[239] The emerging individual human right to self-definition is the victory of Modernism.

5.4.4. **Conclusion**

Over the past decade, Franck has addressed a sequence of theoretical issues from compliance to legitimacy, to fairness, to justice, and eventually to the individual,

notes that 'at least some states are, indeed, moving in the direction of permitting individuals to exercise a greater degree of personal autonomy in designing their identity' in this respect. Id., at 61-75. A greater degree of autonomy, as, for example, expressed in the self-identification through the choice of (dual or multiple) citizenship does however not necessarily imply that society is becoming more atomic at the expense of the (sense of) community.

[237] Id., at 75.

[238] Id., at 76.

[239] Id., at 1.

the reconstructed self which he finally saw endowed with the divine spark. When the problem of *fairness* of international law, with its perceived lack of the intertwining elements of democratic legitimacy, fair participation and representation of persons and justice, is confronted, the practical support of *institutional* reform becomes indispensable. Franck refers to Habermas' position that 'successful institution-building may itself lead to, rather than be the prerequisite for, interactive and common ways of thinking and acting.' In other words, the (re)construction and improvement of global institutions will contribute to a globally shared sense of social community. 'Habermas' point is that there is a circular, mutually reinforcing flow between the 'institutionalization of citizens' communication' and the growth of communications itself.' Contrary therefore to the traditional assumption that a shared sense of community – or collective identity – precedes the establishment of common institutions, Franck agrees with Habermas that 'it is at least plausible to see ... actual co-operative practices as the progenitor of a gradually emerging discursive vocabulary, agreed principles and norms, common loyalty, shared identity, and at last, a culture of community....'[240] A person's identity can be composed of diverse traditional and non-traditional commitments, affinities, and loyalties which are all chosen based on an individual autonomous decision. As a result, 'a global system' is emerging which is 'increasingly characterized by overlapping communities and multivariegated personal loyalties yielding more complex personal identities.' Now that nationalism is 'losing its once-exclusive hold,' individuals claim the right to invent their personal identity and to move beyond the 'post-modern' situation where the identity of the self is an unconscious product of other forces outside the individual's personal will. However, although the 'liberation has begun' with 'the world becom[ing] an interactive system in which powerful new communities join states as the principal participants in the processes for making law, developing wealth, controlling crime, and providing health and recreation,' this liberation 'does not yet engage the majority of the world's people. It may never do so, leaving the world half-determinist and half-autonomous.' Nonetheless this is the 'direction,' which Franck foresees humanity will take, i.e., 'towards an eventual outcome in which the dynamism of growing individual freedom engulfs the lingering static forces that confine personal choice by mandating racial, cultural, national, linguistic, and religious particularity.' He expects that this development will result not 'necessarily [in] world government – some aspects of which, by necessity, are already in place – but rather, [in] a liberal global neo-community, a civil society based on socially and legally protected individualism.'[241]

The *new* liberal global community evidently requires not only individuals who define their personal self and express their identity in commitments to groups and communities, and who exercise their right to democratic governance, it also requires states to recognise individualism as a right to personal self-determination

[240] Id., at 96-98.
[241] Id., at 100.

and to acknowledge that freedom of conscience is a human right that is protected by international institutions and law. The individual as a holder of international rights is the result of the international human rights system as it has evolved since the end of WWII. The new system accommodates many different participants, including NGOs, and the individual has both rights *and* the capacity to file complaints, even against their own governments.[242] In his assessment of the international and regional system of human rights protection, Franck distinguishes four developments which affect the state, albeit not always adversely, as they may also contribute to the containment and controllability of conflict. In the first place, he identifies a 'significant progress towards the recognition, by international and regional law and institutions, that individuals are legitimate and globally recognized claimants and rights-holders.' This is accompanied by a 'growing global and regional recognition that the protection of personal rights cannot be left solely to states but must also be the responsibility of global and regional institutions.' Thirdly, in order to enable them to function adequately, a diversity of non-state actors, such as NGOs, must be included in the processes. Finally, functional international institutions 'increasingly include human rights factors in their political, economic, and fiscal calculations,' an example of which is given by the World Bank.[243] The international legal system has changed profoundly over the past decades due to these developments of international human rights law. The *state* has had to *retreat* under the pressure of both internationalism and individualism. Human rights law contributed to the increased autonomy of the individual by providing growing possibilities for the assertion of individuality and for claiming rights within regional and international institutions.

Franck's argument that the individual right to democratic governance is 'rapidly becoming' a norm protected by (standards of) international law and institutions does indeed fulfil this objective.[244] The process of fairness entails the transformation of democratic entitlement from a domestic to a universal *legal* standard, i.e., 'global normative entitlement.'[245] The 'victory of personhood' fills the gaps left by the retreating state, and so this development adds up to the over-

---

[242] Id., at 199: 'While less than triumphant, the new international system of human rights norms, in its first fifty years, has embarked on all states accountable for many wrongs against most persons. Especially significant is the extent to which these new rules open the way for the previously excluded individuals and non-governmental groups to participate in monitoring compliance. Persons are not only the holders of legal entitlements but also, in some instances, can be the authorized initiators of legal and political actions against violating states and governments.'

[243] Id., at 220.

[244] Id., at 84: 'The *right* to electoral democracy builds on [the associative and discursive entitlements which are already formulated in conventions], but seeks to extend the ambit of protected rights to ensure meaningful *participation by* the *governed* in the formal political decisions by which the quality of their lives and societies are shaped. As with other rights, it is necessary to define the entitlement, to establish instruments of compliance verification, and to enforce the right against violations. The international system is beginning to assume some *responsibility* for these tasks.' Emphasis added. See also, Th. M. Franck, The Emerging Right to Democratic Governance, 86 *AJIL* 46 (1992).

[245] Fairness, at 137.

throw of the Vattelian system. It is in the individual's *interest* to be both free and responsible, as freedom and responsibility together provide opportunities for equality or equal treatment. It is the essence of the individual that he/she freely expresses him/herself and has inherent rights, and in the discursive age the individual is finally empowered to use his/her unique voice.

The 'discursive interaction' is the '*Zeitgeist*' of modern international life. In other words, in order to 'have a voice' and to 'interact' in this new global society, the individual and, in some cases, non-state groups should have the right to participate in the global discourses. Franck's argument ultimately leading up to the empowerment of the individual can be briefly summarised as follows. Starting from the individual's autonomous personhood, the person's will to self-identification is subsequently defined in legal terms as the individual's right to self-determination, which involves choosing one's own commitments and loyalties. With the right to express one's individual autonomous self – and possibly reidentify the self – and the increasing capacity of the international and regional institutions to protect the individual's fundamental human rights, including the right to democratic governance, comes the transformation of the individual's status as an international legal subject into a citizen of the global community. The individual is now empowered to stand up against its own government, against the governments of other states and against non-state groups. In the triad of state, group and individual, the legal relationships are neatly balanced, but with the retreat of the state and the advancing international legal order, the individual is emancipated by earning rights as well as responsibilities. This is the point where the divine spark that burns within each individual has to prove its strength. The shielding mask provided by sovereign state power will gradually be lowered with each further step towards a global constitutional democracy in which every world citizen participates freely.

Why not conclude with some lines from Shelley's poem, *Prometheus Unbound* (1820)? They aptly summarise Franck's expedition to the heart of the theory of international law, where he made ILP as the shield of the state disappear and established the right to democracy, individual freedom and self-definition. Finding the individual a subject, he turned him onto a citizen, self-governing, lord of his own castle:

> ... ...
> The loathsome mask has fallen, the man remains
> Sceptreless, free, uncircumscribed, but man
> Equal, unclassed, tribeless, and nationless,
> Exempt from awe, worship, degree, – the King
> Over Himself; ... ... [246]

[246] Percy Bysshe Shelley, *Prometheus Unbound* (1820), lines 193-197, *in* D. H. Reiman and S.B. Powers, Shelley's Poetry and Prose (1977), at 194.

5.5. Christine Chinkin: Opening up the Agora

5.5.1. Introduction

In the description of post-modernism given above, we came across a feminist variation on the post-modern theme. This variation develops the idea that the female sex only exists as 'the constructed-other' of the male sex and that thereby female identity is always defined negatively. The feminist critique of international law aims to demonstrate that also within international law '[m]en and maleness are assumed to be the norm from which women and femaleness are to be differentiated. Women are construed as the 'other', the deviant from the norm.'[247] From this perspective, international law is not neutral and in order to challenge the system's lack of neutrality, the feminist approach strives to 're-think' international law and break down its masculine gender bias, which should eventually result in a change and reconstruction of the international community and its law so that from then on it will take account of gender and *include* 'women's voices' within its structures.[248] As such, the feminist approach to international law aims to contribute to making international law more *just* or rather making it 'a more useful framework for international and national justice.'[249]

> [The] feminist approaches to international law can contribute to the modern Grotian project. They offer ways of recasting the role of international law so that it can transform ideas about justice and order in the international community. ... Feminist theories allow us to interrogate the nature of the 'order' and the boundaries sponsored by the international legal system and to seek to undermine the illusory necessity of concepts and rules built on sexed and gendered hierarchies of difference.[250]

The feminist contribution to the Grotian project consists of revealing the existing limitations within international law – which have been erected as a result of international law's masculinity and constantly reproduced by the system and its concepts – and neutralising them, of transforming international law so significantly that the ideal of justice being served is as beneficial to women as it is to men. 'The boundaries of international law' have to be 'redraw[n] so that it responds to these injustices [towards women].'[251] The possibility of redrawing these bound-

---

[247] Charlesworth and Chinkin, The Boundaries of International Law: A feminist analysis 2 (2000). Hereinafter: A feminist analysis.

[248] Here the term gender is used to 'dra[w] attention to aspects of social relations that are culturally contingent and without foundation in biological necessity. The term also has the advantage of particularly emphasising relationality, that is the connection between definitions of masculinity and femininity, thereby avoiding the implication that only women should be involved in an investigation of gender. Sex, on the other hand, is typically used to refer to biological differences between women and men.' Id., at 3.

[249] Id., at 1.

[250] Id., at 20-21.

[251] Id., at 21.

aries depends largely on the enhanced participation of women and thus on the adequate representation of their interests. This feminist theory of international law, which continues in a way the scholarly process of the *inclusion* of new participants, *in casu* women, aims to make the international community and its law more just to women, which means transforming international law's ideal of justice to take account of the experiences and well-being of women. This objective also determines the feminist methodology.

An attack on the neutrality of the law is evidently also an attack on its identity and authority. In their seminal article, *Feminist Approaches to International Law*, Charlesworth, Chinkin and Wright, who are considered the forerunners of feminist jurisprudence within international legal scholarship, explain that: 'Feminist jurisprudence builds on certain aspects of th[e] critical strain in legal thought. It is much more focused and concrete, however, and derives its theoretical force from immediate experience of the role of the legal system in creating and perpetuating the unequal position of women.'[252] A distinct characteristic of the feminist methodology is indeed its objective of laying bare the gender bias present within international law concepts, structures, procedures, definitions, etc. and in the way they are applied. The world needs to know that 'International law is a thoroughly gendered system.' It departs from the basic observation that 'men of all nations have used the statist system to establish economic and nationalist priorities to serve male elites, while basic human, social and economic needs are not met.' The feminist attack on the state and the inter-state system is thus directed against the male-elite monopolisation of power and its domination of both domestic and, consequently, also international governance systems. These systems incorporate and institutionalise discrimination as well as a contemptuous and paternalist attitude towards women.[253] In the eyes of these feminist scholars, the identity of the state is masculine, which suppresses the representation of female interests in the international law discourse.[254] The male perspective dominates and subjugates,

---

[252] Charlesworth and Chinkin and Wright, Feminist Approaches to International Law, 85 *AJIL* 613 (1991). Hereinafter: Feminist Approaches. See, on the failure of international legal theories to address the unequal position of women, A feminist analysis, at 23 *et seq.* See, on the diversity of feminist legal theories, id., at 38 *et seq.* Charlesworth and Chinkin explain their choice of method: 'The silence of international law with respect to women needs to be challenged on every level and different techniques will be appropriate at different levels of the excavation. For this reason we adopt the method described by Margaret Radin as 'situated judgment' – using a variety of analytic strategies rather than a single feminist theory.' Elements of the current 'post-modern' *Zeitgeist* or phenomenon cannot be ignored: the use of binary oppositions (subsequently labelled either male or female), the rejection of a 'grand' theory, and the acceptance of incoherence. 'In some contexts, we rely on 'liberal' feminist techniques to point out that modern international law has failed to deliver on its promises of neutrality and equality and to challenge its illusory universality. Women have been almost completely excluded from international law-making arenas and it is important to document this and then to argue for the need of proper representation and participation.' Id., at 50.

[253] Feminist Approaches, at 615.

[254] A feminist analysis, at 125.

Foucaultian conceptualisation resonates.[255] The feminist project thus has a dual purpose: first it strives to expose the masculinity of the accepted doctrines within international law, which generally ignore the injustices being done to women, and subsequently it intends to serve the political objective of the world-wide empowerment of women in order to enhance their (political) representation and participation. As the feminist theory is still very much a legal theory, it aims to realise these goals by legal means. Theory matters (and has to matter) to the practical life of women.[256]

In *A feminist analysis*, Charlesworth and Chinkin explain their choice of method as follows: 'The silence of international law with respect to women needs to be challenged on every level and different techniques will be appropriate at different levels of the excavation. For this reason we adopt the method described by Margaret Radin as 'situated judgment' – using a variety of analytic strategies rather than a single feminist theory.' Elements of the current 'post-modern' *Zeitgeist* or phenomenon cannot be ignored: the analysis in binary oppositions (subsequently labelled either male or female), the rejection of a 'grand' theory, and the acceptance of incoherence. *Modern* international law has failed women; it has been unable to uphold its promise of objectivity, neutrality and universality.

> In some contexts, we rely on 'liberal' feminist techniques to point out that modern international law has failed to deliver on its promises of neutrality and equality and to challenge its illusionary universality. Women have been almost completely *excluded* from international law-making arenas and it is important to document this and then to argue for the need for proper representation and participation of women. ... Feminist analysis must thus explore the unspoken commitments of apparently neutral principles of international law and the ways that male perspectives are institutionalised in it.[257]

Hence, the feminist approach we focus on here is actually a combination of a variety of feminist perspectives which were chosen because of their shared objective, but which at different moments and in different contexts require a different approach. Not all problems women experience can be tackled from one perspective or technique, as this would ignore the diversity present among women, or rather 'the multiplicity of women's stories and the range of their cultural, national, religious, economic and social concerns and interests.'[258] Within this multi-layered approach, the notion of 'women' is thus used as a category, while

---

[255] Feminist Approaches, at 632: 'the most productive analysis of inequality is in terms of domination and subordination. Thus, equality is not freedom to be treated without regard to sex but freedom from systematic subordination because of sex.' See also, A feminist analysis, at 21.

[256] A feminist analysis, at 1: 'the absence of women in the development of international law has produced a narrow and inadequate jurisprudence that has, among other things, legitimated the unequal position of women around the world rather than challenged it. In this sense, the absence of women in international law is a critical feature of the traditional canon – its boundaries depend upon it.'

[257] Id., at 50. Emphasis added.

[258] Id., at 52.

acknowledging the existence of this diversity and multiplicity or the contextual – 'situational' element. The categorisation is mostly 'essentialist' and necessary to change international law and theory.[259]

The feminist analysis with its objective of transforming international law includes a phase of 'deconstruction,' where the gendered, *in casu* masculine and patriarchal, nature of international law is revealed. This is then succeeded by a second phase, that of 'reconstruction', which should lead to a point beyond modern international law. This second step 'requires rebuilding the basic concepts of international law in such a way that they do not support or reinforce the domination of women by men. Non-domination of women would allow the major aims of the UN Charter – the maintenance of international peace and security, the self-determination of peoples and the protection of fundamental human rights – to be defined in new, *inclusive*, ways.'[260] It should be observed that this role of feminist theory is still only largely hinted at, and has yet to mature fully.[261]

With regard to the subjects of law, the feminist approach considers the crisis of the human subject as really a crisis of the *masculine* (white, western, middle-aged, heterosexual) subject and sees it as an opportunity for women to be included in the decision-making processes. The *reconstruction* or recognition of subjectivity as gendered, be it masculine or feminine, but in any case particular rather than universal, is a prerequisite for the *inclusion* of the female subject.

One cannot speak of one single uniform school of feminist jurisprudence, but among the scholars who are at the forefront of this movement within international law is Christine Chinkin. In this section we will focus on her work in particular, which was partly co-written with Charlesworth. It will be shown how Chinkin's theory continues the development of what we have earlier called the process of inclusion, as her arguments concerning the participation of women in the international legal system aim to bring about exactly this, the inclusion of women, making *the female voice heard*. The concept of ILP however seems to be too much of a masculine concept to serve this purpose or at least too connected with the distinction between public and private, which is essentially aimed at *ex-*

[259] Id., at 55.

[260] Id., at 60-61. Emphasis added.

[261] At the end of the 2000 book, the conclusions still very much read like a map of questions still to be investigated, a jurisprudential and political agenda: 'In our view, feminists should tackle international law on a number of levels at the same time. We should use existing mechanisms and principles wherever possible to improve women's lives. We should also work to reform the letter of the law so that it more adequately responds to concerns of women. We must insist that equal participation of women in the international legal system and its institutions is a condition of their legitimacy. Beyond this we can contribute to the Grotian project of redrawing the boundaries of international law by challenging and questioning the 'objectivity' of the international legal system and its hierarchy based on gender. We must critically interrogate the categories we use as if they were somehow natural or inevitable. Standard dichotomies such as war/peace, order/disorder or security/insecurity have operated in international law to filter out the experiences of women. As Carol Cohn has pointed out, a radical shift in perspective and boundary drawing will only occur through a "commitment and ability to develop, explore, rethink and revalue those ways of thinking that get silenced and devalued."' Id., at 336.

clusion, to be of use for the *inclusion* of female voices. Below, I will first focus on the feminist conception of international law and how the distinctions mentioned function within it.

5.5.2. The sexed and gendered nature of international law

To use a label such as the one in the heading of this section to characterise the nature of international law may cause some discomfort to international legal scholars (even when they are of the female sex), as they are trained with the idea that international law is objective, impartial, neutral, and therefore authoritative. However, what the feminist approach aims to demonstrate is that the concepts and categories of international law as well as the assumptions and experiences on which it is grounded are generally masculine. The feminist theory provides a sensible and insightful analysis of international law and of the way in which international law scholars tend to reinforce and reproduce (if often unconsciously) the shortcomings of international law and as a result fail to remedy its issues with legitimacy and justice.

In order to expose these sexist shortcomings, the feminist approach uses a set of dichotomies, which substantiate the male/female distinction as public/private dualism and thereby as the determining factor for the identity of international law. The distinction between the public and the private sphere has traditionally been a dominant or defining feature of western liberal political thinking. This distinction is reproduced at the international level by the concepts of sovereignty and domestic jurisdiction. The sovereign state was perceived as operating among its peers in the public sphere of the international community, while in the private sphere they were not allowed to interfere. Consequently, modern international law has been constructed upon this sharp distinction between the internal/external – private/public – life of the state, which automatically reproduced the internal *unequal* distribution of power among men and women. As we have seen it was especially during the inter-war period that conventional international legal scholars used the concept of ILP to mark this distinction between the internal and the external or the private and the public. Chinkin's arrows, however, are pointed at the maleness of the state rather than at the concept of ILP. The feminist claim that the nature of international law is masculine has a practical organisational dimension besides its more legal theoretical and normative aspect. We will address the first aspect on our way to the second, which constitutes one of Chinkin's particular concerns, namely the question how public/private distinctions operate within international law and hamper international justice by excluding women. This central concern reflects how the 'organisational' and the 'normative' dimensions of the masculine nature of international law are linked.

From the feminist perspective, the *masculinity* of international law can be attributed to both its organisational and its normative structure. In general, women are 'either unrepresented or underrepresented in the national and global decision-making processes.'[262] As long as the general *exclusion* of women's voices, both Western and Third World, from the organisational structure of international law continues, the male perspective will dominate international law. The doctrine that states and IOs – within both of which 'the invisibility of women is striking' – are the primary subjects of international law contributes to its male domination. States are masculine and patriarchist, and international organisations, which are institutions for the functional cooperation of these same states, share the state's defects as regards the un(der)representation of women. Women are un(der)represented in the professional corps of these institutions, as they are on UN Committees and special bodies, which leads to ignorance and inaction concerning problems that are particularly experienced by women. This exclusion from participation in both national and international politics is one of the issues which international feminist scholars are striving to tackle.

The participation and representation of women in international law-creating and decision-making processes are in the feminist analysis also considered to affect the legitimacy and authority of international law.[263] However, to 'claim that women bring different attributes to public life to men also raises thorny theoretical issues. Arguments for women's equal participation in decision-making based on the special qualities they might bring to the process often rely on the assumption that women have a 'different voice' to, and a different way of arriving at, moral judgements than, men.' But, 'these are controversial assertions and may perpetuate myths about women's nature, rather than developing an understanding of the power relations that attribute particular characteristics to women.' Nonetheless, it cannot be denied that due to the lack of adequate representation and participation of women within the global political processes 'the realities of women's lives under the present unbalanced system do not contribute in any significant way to the shaping of UN policy.'[264] Rather than claiming that the participation of women will bring a different kind of morality – a 'feminine morality' – to the floor, it is claimed that female interests and experiences, diverse as these may be, have to be represented in order to promote international law's equal concern for women and thereby to justify its claim to 'universal validity.'[265] The feminist jurisprudence of Christine Chinkin can be said to be very much in touch with the reality of women's actual lives. As such, it is highly pragmatic. Chinkin is no feminist *l'art pour l'art*, and does not treat us to a free-floating legal theory.

Feminist jurisprudence furthermore confronts one of the traditional controversies surrounding the legitimacy of international law: its claim to universality. Within the UN system, participation and representation are organised on the basis of nationality and regionality. In order for international regulations to have uni-

---

262 Feminist Approaches, at 621-622.
263 A feminist analysis, at 194.
264 Id., at 193.
265 Feminist Approaches, at 616.

versal authority all regions and nation states must be generally represented. However, according to feminist scholars, the universality claim is false as long as sex and gender are not recognised as additional relevant factors. The UN, like other organisations, is responding by applying 'gender mainstreaming,' which means that the organisation is attempting to make gender an issue at *all* institutional *levels* and an aspect of all its *policies*. However, the next step threatens to become overdue: it is time to translate policies into action.[266] Issues of sex and gender have to become part of the discourse on the reform of the UN and must be given a place in the discourses occurring in other global institutions, such as the WB, IMF, and WTO. These all need to develop a much keener eye for women's concerns, interests, and life experiences.

> While increasing the participation of women in the UN is only one aspect of the broader project of enhancing the UN's future, it is essential for increasing the UN's effectiveness and accountability and involves two distinct but related tasks. First, women must participate equally in the UN and other global political structures. Second, the international power structures themselves must be challenged and reconstructed to accommodate the half of humanity currently on their margins.[267]

What can law do to contribute to fulfilling these tasks without being overly optimistic, because this is after all essentially a non-legal enterprise? Within the UN, mainstreaming requires an active effort from human resources management and the formulation of new appointments for SG special representatives on women's issues. A lot depends of course on the domestic situation regarding equality in the member states, i.e., on the level of participation of women in national politics and diplomatic services. The active participation of women's NGOs within the UN system is another response to the participatory issue. The second task, the transformation of international power structures for the purpose of improving the political participation of women, in addition requires the adaptation of policy and research agendas, as examining these at a more conceptual level will reveal how certain values and objectives are thoroughly male gendered because of having been exclusively based on male experience. It is important to note, however, that the successful tackling of the gendered and sexed nature of international law and international institutions at every possible level depends on a very basic practical fact: if the 'nexus between sex and gender and the division of labour into public and private spheres were broken, if women and men shared household and workplace responsibilities, the conditions for equal political *participation* in international organisations would be in place. At the same time, this could make the need for *representation* of women's interests less significant: the breakdown of the gendered public/private distinction would lead to 'a world in which gender should become less relevant and the abstractions of humanity more meaningful ... [rather than] a world in which women have to speak continuously as women – or

[266] A feminist analysis, at 196.
[267] Id., at 198.

men are left to speak as men.'[268] The suggestion here is that the public/private distinctions have to be broken down before we can accomplish the equal political participation of women.

Because the public/private dichotomy is gender-based, the masculinity of modern international law has further been brought about by the fact that this dichotomy largely determines the normative structure of international law. The dichotomy, which is central to western liberal theory, reproduces or institutionalises the public sphere as the domain of men and the private sphere as the domain of women. Moreover, on top of having this descriptive function, the dichotomy also operates normatively: the public domain is traditionally held in higher esteem than the domestic sphere. The public domain is allegedly where *it really happens* and is therefore considered supreme to the domestic sphere of housewifely drudgery.[269] Normal male behaviour, which is suited to life in the public sphere, is active, assertive, aggressive, ambitious, responsible and competitive by nature. This is why men's (political) participation comes naturally, while according to the same natural scheme, women are passive, emotional, reactive, and submissive rather than participatory. It is a profound feminist concern that as long as the normative structure operates on the basis of the public/private distinction, international law will continue to exclude women and disregard their interests and experiences: '[t]he normative structure of international law has allowed issues of particular concern to women to be either ignored or undermined.'[270]

The public/private distinction comes in many guises, as the feminist analysis has revealed, and translate themselves into an equal number of gendered dichotomies within international law thinking, for example where the state as a public institution is set off against family and home, and into numerous variations on male-female (binary) oppositions like non-intervention/intervention, war/peace, order/chaos, objectivity/subjectivity, responsibility/powerlessness, supremacy/subjection, civil and political rights/social and economic rights, state/non-state actors, citizenship/spouse and motherhood, etc.[271] These dichotomies rationalise the normative structure and operate as including/excluding mechanisms, silencing women's voices and serving the (perpetuation of the) masculine character of international law's normative structure.

In order to correct this shortcoming of international law and make it more just, the feminisation of international law aims 'to transcend *gendered* public/private dichotomies, incorporating and responding to women and their concerns.' Thereto the public and private may be perceived as follows: 'If the 'public' is un-

[268] Id., at 200. Quote from A. Phillips. Emphasis added.

[269] Id., at 57: 'Distinctions between public and private divisions such as international/national or state/civil society are seen to characterise the reality of the international community; at the same time, they are also connected with political choices about whether or not to intervene legally.'

[270] Feminist approaches, at 625. Similarly, the male rationalist nature of legal reasoning tends to exclude 'other forms of 'private' knowledge such as morality.'

[271] A feminist analysis, at 49.

derstood ... as involving susceptibility to political debate and dialogue, while the 'private' is the sphere from which people can withdraw from public scrutiny (not simply the area excluded by the public), women's experiences will not automatically be excluded or marginalized by the use of public/private dichotomies.'[272]

The feminist critique of the public/private distinction is connected to its political function/identity by its 'centrality to liberal theory' and its 'strong grip on legal thinking.' In the feminist view, the liberal private/public distinctions operate to legitimise the subjugation of women.

> The language of the public/private distinction is built into the language of the law itself: law lays claim to rationality, culture, power, objectivity – all terms associated with the public or male realm. It is defined in opposition to the attributes associated with the domestic, private, female sphere: feeling, emotion, passivity, subjectivity. Moreover, the law has always operated primarily within the public domain ... while direct state intervention in the family and the home has long been regarded as inappropriate.[273]

Domestically, the public/private distinction is considered 'the fundamental basis of the modern state's function of separating and concentrating juridical forms of power that emanate from the state.'[274] Internationally, this distinction is reproduced in, for example, human rights law: by defining that the violation of women within the private sphere of the home by others than state officials does not qualify as a human rights violations, because international law considers human rights violations to be public or male-realm concerns, international law fails in its protection of women. Feminist jurisprudence uncovers how international law is gendered by the dichotomy: in the male public sphere, a violation of personal integrity is a violation of human rights, while in the female private sphere it is not. This reflects the fact that the existing order turns a blind eye to in particular women's experiences of violence in the domestic sphere inflicted upon them by non-state groups or individuals for the purpose of dominating them. The state on whose territory such violence against women occurs is not responsible under international law unless the violence is perpetrated by one of its agents. To find a way to remedy this severe shortcoming of international law, '[a] feminist perspective on human rights would require a rethinking of the notions of imputability and state responsibility and in this sense would challenge the most basic assumptions of international law.'[275]

Chinkin consequently takes up this challenge and rethinks state responsibility from a feminist perspective. This exercise demonstrates what it means to transcend the public/private dichotomy. In Chinkin's view, the public/private distinction rationalises state responsibility to such an extent that it is obstructing the

[272] Id., at 59.
[273] Feminist Approaches, at 627.
[274] Id., at 627.
[275] Id., at 629.

concept from being of use to women. Chinkin then criticises among other things the Draft Articles on State Responsibility for upholding the public/private distinction too strictly and as a result insufficiently reflecting the contemporary 'penetration of the private sphere' by the public sphere, a development which can indeed be seen to be taking place under the influence of developments in human rights law and jurisprudence. In this respect, the duty of states to exercise due diligence and prevent violations of human rights law is widening. An example of responsibility for a failure to exercise due diligence is the responsibility for an 'omission to penetrate the [traditionally] private sphere of *non*-responsibility under international law.'[276] Chinkin contends that these developments should at least be addressed in the Draft Articles and concludes that:

> State responsibility is a legal construct that allocates risk for the consequences of acts deemed wrongful by international law to the artificial entity of the state. The human link is provided by the doctrine of attributability, but this maintains the fiction of public and private actions of individuals, which nevertheless begs the question of how they are determined. Why should the state only be responsible for the internationally wrongful acts of state organs? The state claims jurisdiction over the totality of functions within its territorial control; it might therefore be appropriate to assert its responsibility for all wrongful acts emanating form it, or from nationals subject to its jurisdiction. Who does denial of state responsibility for the actions of non-state actors protect – the state, individual freedom of action, or the most powerful who are able to remain outside the scope of international regulation? Does preserving the private space of non-attributable acts enhance or impede the achievement of an international rule of law? Such questions require nuanced and contextual responses that are little assisted by too much emphasis on a distinction between public and private spheres of action.[277]

One of these questions raises the issue of who or what gains from the denial of state responsibility for actions carried out by agents other than states and thus points to the problem of international law's legitimacy which is adversely affected by the fact that 'the most powerful ... are able to remain outside the scope of international regulation.' This explains Chinkin's argument that state responsibility has to be broadened to include the exercise of due diligence in actions by non-state actors. After all, the objective is to serve the international rule of law.

One of the most powerful non-state actors acting globally is the multinational corporation (MNC), which brings us to the issue of corporate responsibility and human rights law in the context of the globalisation debate. This debate has sprung up only quite recently and asks the question whether corporations have rights and duties under international law, in particular, human rights law, or in other words whether international law should create a system which obliges corporations to uphold human rights. Reports of a Global Dimensions Seminar mention how Chinkin developed an argument of inclusion on the basis of the preamble of the Universal Declaration of Human Rights, which proclaims that

[276] Ch. Chinkin, A Critique of the Public/Private Dimension, 10 *EJIL* 394 (1999).
[277] Id., at 395.

'*every organ of society*, keeping this declaration constantly in mind, *shall* strive by teaching and education *to promote respect* for these rights and freedoms and by progressive measures, national and international, to secure their universal and effective recognition and observance, both among the peoples of the Member States themselves and among the peoples of territories under their jurisdiction.' She contended that this proclamation also implies an obligation for corporations, which are just as much organs of society. And as such it imposes upon them both a negative and a positive duty: first to refrain from violations of human rights and second 'to be active and to influence other actors and governments.' The argument that international human rights law bestows corporate responsibility upon MNCs is also based on the rethinking of the basic international law assumption that separates the public and the private: by developing a doctrine of international corporate responsibility the public realm of international law penetrates the private life or corporate economic sphere of MNCs. The particular boundary of international law that is based on the gendered dichotomy of intervention/ non-intervention is also redrawn here. However, changing the basic assumption is not the same as changing the actual system. Corporate compliance will need to be regulated and developed further.[278] The currently much-used self-imposed codes of conduct worry Chinkin in the sense that they might undermine the more obligatory regulation through international human rights instruments. Moreover, an international voluntary code like the UN Global Compact should not be used to justify corporate behaviour that violates 'local standards.'[279] Chinkin does not in so many words articulate the argument that MNCs are international legal persons which may be held accountable and responsible under international law, but this is what her reasoning comes down to and she does include 'multinational corporations' in the group of 'entities that have acquired ... [a] degree[e] of international legal personality.'[280] The public sphere is forced to acknowledge the international legal status of global private actors.

Let us now conclude with a few remarks on the women's rights strategy.

The feminist project on empowering women by means of the notion of women's rights and the rights-based discourse is supported widely. Still, within

[278] Chinkin distinguishes three overlapping categories of human rights violation, i.e., direct, indirect, and collusive, and points to six potential international legal mechanisms, which Weissbrodt identified earlier, as a useful means for the regulation of corporate human rights violations. The human rights instruments, like the Universal Declaration, the UN Global Compact, industry or commodity group initiatives, framework agreements between multi-nationals and workers associations and between trade union coalitions and other interested bodies, and self-imposed company codes of conduct (Three types of Company Codes of Conduct are distinguished: Minimum standards for conditions of work, Increased company involvement in human rights in the community, and Ethical criteria for investment), and finally international regulation could be arranged by NGO or union model codes of conduct.

[279] Summary of Discussion, Global Dimensions Seminar 'Corporate Responsibility and Human Rights' at the United Nations, New York, 1st June 2001, as published on website: <http://www.lse.ac.uk/collections/globalDimensions/>.

[280] A feminist analysis, at 20.

feminist jurisprudence some reservations have also been made concerning the fact that recourse is sought to the concept of rights. To have significance at the international level, rights must first be rethought so as better to fit women's interests and experiences. 'Feminist critiques of rights have been remarkably rare in the literature on *international* women's rights,' Chinkin and Charlesworth observe. In their view, 'campaigns for women's rights to be recognised as human rights can play a useful, strategic role in advancing women's equality, particularly when used in conjunction with other political and social strategies, but ... the limited nature of rights must be acknowledged.'[281] The value of the concept of international women's rights is its empowering function, now that the human rights discourse offers ample possibility for actively enhancing the social and political position of women. As such, '[t]he significance of rights discourse outweighs its disadvantages.' Women become international claimants or 'obligation-holder[s],' rather than merely 'victims or dependents.' Consequently, as 'human rights discourse is the dominant progressive moral philosophy and a potent social movement operating at the global level, it is important for women to engage with, and contest, its parameters.'[282] The Convention on the Elimination of All forms of Discrimination Against Women (CEDAW, 1979) 'attempts to overcome the public/private dichotomy ... in international law' by asserting that women have 'equal rights to participate in public decision-making bodies at all levels.'[283] Recourse to human rights concepts for the purpose of empowering women and making them 'visible' both nationally and internationally, has significance as one of several feminist techniques for tackling women's unequal position. Moreover, by bringing international human rights law into the private sphere, international law advances in its transcendence of the public/private dichotomy.

5.5.3. Chinkin's use of ILP: the inclusion and empowerment of the female subject

It has already been observed that Chinkin's feminist jurisprudence is actually very pragmatic. Although it recognises that there are psychological differences between men and women, the new legal theory is not constructed upon psychological assumptions concerning the female self. To be sure, the end of the subject is a recognised theme, but more in the sense of the end of the monopoly of the male subject. It is the end of the subordination of the female subject that is sought.

---

[281] Id., at 208-210.

[282] Id., at 212. Women's rights are part of the international legal framework of human rights, both within the general instruments and the women-specific instruments, like the CEDAW. Especially the right of women to equal treatment and non-discrimination on the basis of sex is canonical.

[283] Id., at 217. Moreover, it 'explicitly affirms women's right to equality in a limited way within the 'private' arena of the family, unlike other human rights instruments which designate the family as a unit to be protected.' Id., at 218.

Rather then defining the difference between men's and women's voices as rooted in the differences between personal male/female identity or selfhood, it is defined in terms of experiences and interests. The African conception of the self as related to others, as opposed to the traditional and modern European perspective of the self as a free and autonomous entity, has not been able to act as a real alternative, since it too has failed to create a more equal situation for women on the African continent. In fact, male domination and female subordination are as much part of the power structures there as they are in western societies. Chinkin recognises that issues such as the male and female conception of the self and the female view on personhood are also a topic of debate within legal discourse. However, in her international feminist perspective the emphasis is on the gendered assumptions concerning international legal concepts and categories, rather than on the identity of the feminine self.

When rethinking the 'self' in international law, i.e., the 'self' as in 'self-determination', which is the right of peoples to a certain independent political status and which includes the right to economic, social and cultural development, one should in the first place recognise that to take the 'self' as 'a single relevant' entity is actually 'masking the fact that the most powerful identity is usually a construct of the most powerful players in the group,' and as a result, this self is most often male. Self-determination is the 'cornerstone of all human rights guarantees' within international law and for it to serve justice and benefit women equally, the 'self' part of the concept has to be reconstructed as a concept embracing both men and women. Reconceptualising the right of self-determination 'would embrace the idea of a secure and fulfilled existence within a freely chosen democratic political and economic framework.' It should thus incorporate the public and the private, the political and the socio-economic dimensions of self-determination and thereby embrace not only civic and political rights but also social, cultural, and economic rights. 'The equal participation of women and men in the choices of political and economic forms would be crucial to its legitimacy.' 'Women *as women*' are not recognised as group which has a right to self-determination, 'because of the historical linkage of personhood with manhood.'[284] This is the reason that neither the State, nor the 'people', both 'male' concepts,[285] are able adequately to represent 'the diversity of women and their interests' on the international stage. These concepts should therefore not be accepted as the 'sole representatives of women at the international level'. Women should be empowered to 'presen[t] their interests directly.'[286] The women's rights strategy is one tactic to correct the situation; the recognition of the participation of women's NGOs in global institutions is another. The recognition of the *female* subject un-

[284] A feminist analysis, at 163.

[285] The male sex of the state is for example expressed in the image of a defined and controlled territory, and 'indigenous minority peoples, do not qualify as full subjects of international law' because they do not govern a defined territory. Having full ILP or being a full subject of international law is reserved for the state only.

[286] Id., at 170.

der international human rights law, as well as the inclusion of private actors, like NGOs, that pursue the empowerment of women and promote their political, socio-economic and cultural status, may well be argued in terms of ILP.

In the course of the debate on *The Transformation of Sovereignty*[287] at the 1994 ASIL Annual Meeting, Christine Chinkin answered a question in the context of globalisation and non-state actors, namely: 'Why talk about Sovereignty?,' as follows:

> Sovereignty matters most to weaker, more vulnerable groups in society. By talking in terms of sovereignty, women and indigenous groups, for example, can acquire representation and legitimacy. Why "sovereignty"? Are there more useful concepts to describe the present transformation in international relations?[288]

Sovereignty is used as the conceptual basis for the increased plurality pervading international representation and participation, and is transformed into an instrument for making international law more legitimate. Chinkin's answer made it very clear that sovereignty is still the appropriate concept to emancipate, empower, and include certain entities in the international (legal) community. Sovereignty in this sense is a competence or status, and has become deterritorialised. As such, it has acquired a new role – that of an instrument of *inclusion* – which is the complete opposite of the *excluding* role it has traditionally fulfilled, partly because of its firm link with territory. However, is this new use of sovereignty the most fitting instrument for the conceptual establishment of emancipation and inclusion? In response to Chinkin's comment at the ASIL Annual Meeting, Higgins suggested that ILP should be used instead. Higgins stressed that rather than talk about the transformation of sovereignty, the debate should concern itself with statehood and *legitimate authority* at the international level. Such a debate would in turn connect the empowerment and *inclusion* of non-state participants to the notion of *international legal personality*. Higgins then suggested that where issues of participation, international rights and democratic values were concerned, international legal scholars had better enlist the concept of ILP. Six years later, in *A feminist analysis*, the following observation was made:

> While globalisation may be seen as a process of creating global homogeneity, it has also been accompanied by polarisation and division. International law-making and international dispute resolution are becoming increasingly specialised, with separate regimes and institutions developed for different areas but which also affect each other in diverse ways. Participants in the international legal system have increased beyond states and international governmental institutions to include what is sometimes described as 'international civil society' – individuals, groups of peoples, NGOs, multinational corporations and other entities that have acquired varying degrees of international legal personality.[289]

---

[287] The 88th annual meeting of the ASIL in 1994 was dedicated to this theme.

[288] Id., at 73.

[289] A feminist analysis, at 20.

This demonstrates that ILP may be used as a relative and derivative concept for establishing the international legal status of new participants in the international legal system and its institutions. This is at the same time ILP's traditional function within international law, i.e., admitting new entities upon the international stage by 'confer[ring] 'public' status on an entity with consequences for jurisdiction, representation and ownership.'[290] It draws the line between the 'public' and the 'private' realm, and as such the concept of ILP contributes significantly to the masculinity of international law as based on public/private distinctions.

ILP reprocesses the public/private dichotomy as a distinction between the internal and the external, as after all international law is almost exclusively concerned with the external, international life of the state. The concept of ILP is used to separate and shield the internal from the external. As such it is slightly suspect because of its connection with the 'public' – male – part of the dichotomies. The fact that 'the state is considered the most complete expression of international legal personality,' confirms the traditional link between ILP and the state's membership of the international public sphere and acts as barrier to non-state actors in their efforts to attain similar international status:

> The monolithic view of statehood upon which traditional international law doctrine depends significantly limits the scope of international law. One consequence is that it establishes a model for full international personality that other claimants for international status cannot replicate. Moreover, the idea of statehood constructed by international law creates a barrier between the entity of the state and those within it.[291]

However, bestowing ILP on private – non-state – actors also offers an opportunity to transcend the gendered dichotomy. Although this idea is not articulated expressly – nowhere is it explicitly argued that ILP should be attributed to private actors – it is still very much featured in the conceptual background. For example, with regard to corporate responsibility within international law, MNCs are to a certain degree equated with international legal persons. Further, the recognition of the participation of NGOs in the international sphere is another example of the shifting boundaries of international law; their acquisition of a degree of ILP illustrates the new perception of the public/private dimension of international law. However, the feminist relationship with ILP remains a difficult one, since ultimately ILP is derived from the masculine concept of statehood and can just as easily be used to exclude private actors from the international arena, arguing that only states can have any real status within international law.

5.5.4. **Conclusion**

Chinkin's feminist critique of international law demonstrates that it is largely structured by gendered binary oppositions. It tackles the public/private di-

---

[290] Id., at 31.
[291] Id., at 125.

chotomy in order to put an end to the stifling of female voices and include women in the global organisational structure of the international community and its law, i.e., to terminate the exclusion of women from participation and representation. The transformation of the law necessary for attaining this objective should make international law more active and better equipped in responding to the injustices women have to suffer. Improved female participation and representation should give international law more validity and authority. It is to serve the legitimacy of international law and the ideal of justice that international law pursues.

Feminist jurisprudence employs the deconstructive method to reveal the masculinity of international law. It resonates with the language of post-modern politics and employs the international liberal theory to uncover that male domination and female subordination are constantly being reproduced. Finally, Chinkin uses the law and legal concepts reconstructively in order to pull down the barrier between the public and the private, which actually leads beyond modern international law.

Another recent phenomenon defining (international) life, that of globalisation, is not ignored either. The rising numbers of non-state actors and the emergence of a global civil society bring to the forefront questions concerning their legal status and their responsibility under international law, which Chinkin proceeds to deal with. She addresses and answers these questions, which really go to the legitimacy of international law, as international law does not sufficiently accommodate the representation and participation of these non-state actors either, by offering the general argument of inclusion. Chinkin's theory may therefore be said to fit the tradition of the objective of *inclusion* in general, regardless of whether women or non-state actors, such as NGOs, indigenous peoples, or MNCs are concerned.

Feminist projects aim to include and empower the female subject using rights-based language and reasoning. One of the objectives is to gain recognition for women's rights within the system of international human rights. The individual may have already attained the status of a recognised subject of international law, however, but the gender of this subject tends to be masculine. In order for the *female subject* to be fully recognised, international women's rights have to be developed further so as to make women ever stronger claimants and right-holders.

Like the work of Thomas Franck, feminist jurisprudence deals with the issue of the legitimacy of international authority by examining the legitimacy of procedures and institutions. Prerequisites for procedural legitimacy are broad participation and neutrality. The feminist argument has as its objective the full recognition of women as (female) subjects of international law and, taken one step further, it aims, in the same vein as Franck, to achieve the recognition of this particular group as world *citizens*, whose interests would then not only be represented within the international arena, but who would also truly participate in the creation and application of international law and international policies. Although ILP plays no explicit role in Chinkin's theory, conceptually it functions in it in the traditional way of the concept used for the inclusion of new actors as legitimate participants in the international community and international law. The feminist approach is useful for laying bare the gendered nature of international law and the inequality between men and women as regards issues of justice. The female subject must be empowered, both in her own right and collectively, so as to make women visible and audible on the international stage. The concept of ILP, which is a male concept used to confer public status, is here used to blur the public/private dichotomy. However, in spite of the feminist language and method, the conceptual usage of ILP in this way naturally furthers the process of inclusion and is essentially a continuation of the pragmatic conventional way of using ILP.

5.6. Conclusion: has 'the loathsome mask' fallen?

With the present chapter we have come to the conclusion of this substantive inquiry into the use of the concept of ILP within international legal scholarship since the late 17th century. Today, during the early years of the 21st century, we may wonder why this concept is currently seemingly being ignored, even though we live in an age of non-state actors and at a time preoccupied with issues of identity and selfhood or the human subject.

After having addressed both the phenomenon of globalisation and that of postmodernism we have gradually been able to demonstrate how contemporary international legal scholarship cannot be understood without referring to these contexts. The consequent re-contextualisation of the work of Franck and Chinkin within contemporary international legal scholarship made their dual purpose even clearer: they both aim to go beyond the stage of deconstruction and arrive at a reconstruction that results in a fairer and more legitimate international law.

The concept of ILP will continue to play its functional role in international legal theory where the discussion on non-state actors is concerned. There it is however used in the rather conventional manner of the descriptive-prescriptive concept intended to include or exclude actors in or from international law. It is used to *legitimise participation* in the international legal arena. It will doubtless continue in this role, even though it is trapped in the same dilemma as applies to the source of international law: in order to exist, must ILP first be recognised in some form, explicitly or implicitly, by means of some action or legal document, by the community of states, or is ILP an indication of the *inherent* rights and duties of states, which exist even before international law expressly grants or imposes them, in other words, a kind of natural legal personality as the counterpart of natural sovereignty? And if we apply the latter possibility analogously to individuals, could it be that every individual human being has ILP by nature, now that human rights have come to be recognised as inherent rights that one has simply because one is human? From the position that is taken concerning ILP it immediately becomes clear what the position will be on international law itself. Our historic overview has made that abundantly clear. Gradually however the global discursive community may adopt different notions or it may be that in the future the positivist view on law will prevail and ILP will be the concept that is used to indicate the legal status of both NGOs and MNCs under international law, as created by state consent, with an appeal to the necessary defence of for example international values and norms of justice, democracy, and the well-being of future generations.

However, the real advancement or conceptual redefinition of ILP may be found in the attempt to recognise the traditional problem of obligation as an entrapment, to step away from mainstream solutions and return to our rich heritage of natural law approaches. From the 'critics' of the theoretical spectrum comes the position that international law discourse has to tackle the problem of obligation. To avoid the scepticism inherent in the deconstructive method of the 'critical' scholars, a different method is required for finding an appropriate source for the binding nature of international law. Our rich tradition of international legal scholarship offers the natural law movement, which – if one wished to describe it in unfairly brief terms – assumes that the source of law may be found in ethics and morality. What we need is a new concept of ILP which is rooted in a theory of justice and would mark the crossing between the moral and ethical realm on the one hand and the legal order on the other. Or rather, it should form a link between this moral/ethical and legal realm and affirm that the latter originates from the former. It could be characterised as an anti-voluntarist position, which would at the same time attempt to avoid pure idealism by taking the hermeneutics of the self as a valuable starting point.

The critical scholar Anthony Carty seems to suggest something similar although it is unclear what exactly his intentions are when at the end of his observations on *From Apology to Utopia* he remarks: 'If what is needed is a social theory which avoids reductionism we need a perspective on international legal personality which allows us to 'explore the embeddedness of facts and ideas in each other'.'[292] Is it possible to conceptualise ILP and international law without construing the binding force of international law as bridging the gap between sovereignty and state Will on the one side and objective norms on the other? To avoid a choice between politics and morality, the very same aspects that law attempts to reconcile? Ultimately, a theory of international law and ILP has to deal with this dilemma. In the final chapter I will therefore have to take a stand: I will attempt to rethink ILP from a justice perspective. This may seem strange compared to the way the concept is currently being used, but let us recall that Leibniz also created ILP out of his views on universal justice.

Has the 'loathsome mask' really fallen? In the work of Franck and Chinkin it has to a considerable extent. Both shifted away from the state-paradigm and intended empower the individual by an argument that ends up formulating a kind of world *citizenship*.

---

[292] Critical International Law, at 81.

Chapter 6
EVALUATION AND CONCLUSIONS: ILP AND UNIVERSAL JUSTICE – FROM MASK TO VOCAL CORDS

6.1. Introduction

This book began with an explanation of what motivated me to undertake this quest for the meaning of ILP and I drew attention to two developments which took place in the context in which this study subsequently evolved. First, there is the fact that today international life and the international atmosphere are experienced and described very differently from how they were during the first years after the end of the Cold War, when a 'new world order' was expectantly proclaimed. This development has particularly affected the general perception of the state and its role, both nationally and internationally. Secondly, I had to admit that it was not merely I who shaped this project, but that the project also shaped me to a significant degree, in the sense that it caused me to oscillate between the idea that only states were the original legal persons in international law and the idea that only individual human beings can be the true and original legal persons in international law. This question is so charged with elements of moral and political philosophy that I felt compelled to quote Kelsen to indicate its effect on this study, as it evolved into more than just a specifically legal problem due to the '*Zusammenhang zwischen Fachdisziplin und Weltanschauung*.' This is the place to return to this question. Who are the international legal persons of today or, in other words, how should one perceive the present international community and its members; is it a *ball masqué* or have we progressed to the stage of *dé-masqué*?

It is one of the purposes of this book to search for 'alternatives.' The inquiry into the history of the notion of ILP, the historical study of international legal thinking about this concept, was started in order to gain a perspective from which we could assess our own conceptions and broaden our 'horizons of expectation', so that subsequently we would be able to imagine 'alternatives.' And has the historical study provided us with this ability to conceive of alternatives? The history of the concept of ILP has here unfolded in four 'episodes.' The contextual approach assisted the analysis of what the particular *issue at stake* was in each episode. Rather than approach the history of ILP as a continuous response to 'a canonical set of questions', I chose the contextual analysis as it recognised that *questions change* (with time and with authors) and that, notwithstanding the (intellectual) continuity of the teachings of the (international legal) discipline, answers do, too. Therefore, situating the conceptual history of ILP in a sequence of contexts intended to enable a study of the use of ILP in each particular context (the horizontal developments), rather than in a canonical sense (the vertical developments) and to help find an interpretation of the meaning of ILP that was well-founded. In interpreting the historic meanings of ILP, the contextual approach has enabled us to distinguish between the effect of the conventions of the time and the intentions of the author who responded to these conventions. As such this study of the concept of ILP has necessarily become the study of the work of ten international legal scholars who used the concept of ILP in a variety of situations and with a diversity of intentions. In spite of the purpose of this study and the methodology I selected, it is still possible to detect the presence of one overall development, like the title of this chapter, 'From Mask to Vocal Cords?', suggests, although it must be underlined that each chapter is the story of a particular position in time.

The continuity that may be uncovered is *not* in the claim that ILP is a static term whose meaning was defined at some point and which has since then been handed down through international law history, as this would imply falling into the hermeneutic trap of preconditioned thinking. In fact, ILP has been used to refer to many different entities and to support very different arguments. It is rather the case that from the sequence of episodes described we slowly see the story emerge of a concept which was not only fundamental to international law thinking, but was also used by the scholars we have examined to define the identity of international law.

The conclusion is that the concept of ILP has mainly functioned as an 'evaluative-descriptive term' and has as such been used as a 'locus of change' in the language of international law. Let us recall Skinner's comments on evaluative-descriptive terms: 'It is essentially by manipulating this set of terms that any society succeeds in establishing and altering its moral identity.'[1] Our study has indeed shown that in each of the four episodes in history analysed in this book international legal scholars used ILP either to consolidate the established order or to alter the (moral) identity of the international society and of international law. It has been a 'locus of change' in many arguments and, where it was not, it was the 'locus for the defence of status quo'. I propose to briefly re-visit and summarise the outcome of the episodic studies here before we turn to a tentative re-conceptualisation of ILP.

6.2. An episodic narrative of the conceptual history of ILP

Although the term person or *persona*, which in ancient Greek was used to indicate the mask of the comedian and thus to identify the role he played, has a much longer history in terms of etymology, Leibniz coined the term for international law language. He introduced it at the end of the turbulent 17th century to reconcile political realism with moral idealism, to reconcile sovereignty with justice. Leibniz's *universal jurisprudence* included an integral vision for both the Ger-

[1] See *supra*, chapter 1, text to footnote 83.

man Empire and the European political order in general. It was established that using ILP enabled Leibniz, on the one hand, to preserve the universal political, moral and legal structure and, on the other hand, to adjust these 'old' structures to the new developments, i.e., to recognise the sovereignty of the Princes and prise open the doors to the European society which had to accommodate them. As the legal counterpart of (relative) sovereignty, the concept of ILP functioned to legitimise the participation of the German Princes in international life, but by the same legal move established their *responsibility* to conform to the justice-based rules of the law of nations. In this perspective, sovereignty is limited by the law of nations and responsibility is defined as its corollary; the two exist conjoinedly in the concept of ILP, i.e., personality under the law of nations. As a concept which indicates the *legitimacy* of an actor's *participation* in international life, ILP could contribute to the clarification of international diplomatic communication and benefit European stability. In Leibniz's universal jurisprudence, the recognition and legitimisation of the new actors' participation at the international plane implied that these powers were subjected to the law of nations, which was rooted in justice and, as a consequence, they were assigned the legal *duty* of furthering universal *justice*.

Although our findings are quite specific, i.e., limited to the uncovering of the origin of one particular concept, they nonetheless beg to correct the historiographical narrative of international law in general as it is traditionally (re-)told in our scholarship: (modern) international law has its origins in 1648 when the European order of (modern) sovereign states was (instantly) erected. However, this traditional narrative gives rise to two historiographical problems, of which one concerns the facts of practice and the other concerns ideas and scholarship. First, the political reality in Europe and the Holy Roman Empire in the second half of the 17th century was by no means settled. Europe was still undergoing the transition from the universal political structures to the national polities and this transition was (sometimes) painfully reflected in the (diplomatic) relations between the rulers. Secondly, the traditional narrative disqualified the valuable legacy of the law of nations and nature as being pre-modern and thereby excluded it, and unfairly so, as it was still attested to by Leibniz (and to some extent by Wolff). The exclusion of this legacy reinforces the identity of international law as a law defined by the subjects it is binding upon, i.e., sovereign states, and by absolute sovereignty based on (military) power. As a consequence, any 'alternative' conception of the (future) identity of international law, i.e., as a law of nations that is not based on the internalised barrier between the international and national order, is prevented from coming into being. Leibniz's late-17th-century thinking gave us a different, complementary identity of (modern) *ius gentium*: a law of nations that is binding upon those entities which are able to employ international power and are therefore obliged to take into account the common interests of a universal human society and pursue universal justice.

The second stop on our historical journey was the Interbellum period and the work of Brierly, Kelsen and Scelle. These revisionist scholars arrived in a world of 19th-century conventions. In international legal scholarship, these conventions consisted of an idealised, reified and deified state-person whose sovereignty over its subjects was absolute. The state-person determined the identity of international law. In Europe, democracy was in crisis and each of the three scholars lived under particularly critical circumstances. Their reaction to the idolatry of the state was radical and their work highly original. Their ideas would continue to mark international law scholarship for the rest of the 20th century. While they were all situated in the general European contexts of accumulating political tension, which was present both inter-state and intra-state, and experienced the general intellectual oscillation between a deep-seated fear of the masses and the hope that the public opinion might represent reason, they each also came from more specific backgrounds.

Brierly regarded ILP as the locus of change to go from an anthropomorphic identity of international law to an anthropocentric one. He used the concept of ILP to demythologise the state. He separated ILP from state sovereignty and attributed it to the state *institution*. In this way, he connected the individual to the international legal order. This move was marked by the practical political context, but was also profoundly moral in nature. In Brierly's natural law approach to international law, ILP was deconstructed as an orthodox dogma and re-established as a legal *technique* to link individual human beings with international law. Brierly was unequivocal in his plea in favour of a return to what he called the Grotian concept of the international legal community – a community of the *genus humanum* – and the re-unification of law and justice.

The analysis of Kelsen's conception of ILP was particularly revealing. It challenged the interpretation of the '*Lebensfremdheit*' of his scholarship, as well as the not uncommon view that his theory of law developed in complete isolation from reality. One may disagree with his legal theoretical views, but when viewed against the background of the political and intellectual context of Vienna in Kelsen's days, it simply cannot be argued that his thinking failed to take account of social-political reality. Quite the contrary, in fact. Kelsen also used ILP to demythologise international law and to de-deify the state, albeit through a very different methodology. He conjoined epistemology and ethico-political thinking in the re-definition of the state as *Zurechnungspunkt* – the point of attribution of rights and duties. However, by using ILP as a rather more technical concept or tool of cognition, it also became a relational concept: legal personality was identified by a legal order and so was the state-person. Consequently, the legal personality of the state was merely a point of attribution, after pausing at which international law continued on its way (well into the so-called internal or domestic legal order) and ultimately addressed the individual human being. The individual was the final destination of attribution, but at the same time, it was also the starting point for a democratic creation of a 'state will.' By the novel identification of state with law, every individual person became both subject and legislator.

Being a legal person meant being a citizen. The redefinition of the concept of legal personality as the point of attribution of a legal order was used to link the individual with the international legal order. Kelsen's argument works at many levels, for example, it works to defend international law, to develop an epistemological reduction and to uphold democracy and individual freedom. Again, ILP was the 'locus of change'. Through its profound redefinition, the old moral identity of the orthodox theory of law and state began to crumble and a new moral identity was developed. With the resolution of the duality between law and state, the dissolution of the dogma of sovereignty and the conception of ILP as *Zurechnungspunkt*, Kelsen's Pure Theory blurs the strict boundary between the international and the national legal order and implies a teleological view of the law: towards the organisational unity of a universal legal community.

The analysis of Scelle's conception of ILP plunged us into the political troubles that beset the French Third Republic. The contextualisation of his scholarship, and his remarks on ILP in particular, brought to the forefront Scelle's reaction to the parallel (both national and international) regression of democracy and individual liberties. He used ILP, not only to demystify, but also to downsize the state. Or rather, he redefined the state as its rulers and he brought each of these individually under the rule of law as the primary international legal persons. This was indeed a response to the parallel crisis. Scelle had created a concept of international law as the law of the universal society of humanity. *La condition humaine* was the ultimate source of *le droit des gens*. Therefore, the concept of ILP featured as a purely individual attribute, which was used to empower the individual against those in power. It was used to define the competence of those in power and to make the inclusion of the principle of *dédoublement fonctionnel* possible.

Again the concept of ILP was used as a locus of change. Each of these three *revisionists* rejected the classical conceptions of sovereignty and personality, which they considered only confirmed the authoritarian and anti-democratic tendencies. Rather than using ILP to reconcile sovereignty with international law, the concept was used in the confrontation of the crisis of democracy and the threat to the individual it involved. Ultimately, the individual was the true subject of international law. Rather than to suppress the individual, the attribution of ILP to the individual was intended to contribute to his emancipation. The incorporation of the democratic ideal in the conception of international law, together with the redefinition of the position of the individual within international law, aimed to bring about the revision of the moral identity of international law: the law of a universal community or (developing) world state.

These three approaches to the integrated crisis of international law and Western democracy and the threat this posed to the individual human being were perhaps fundamentally different, but a common feature is present in the way the three scholars confronted the crisis and in their use of ILP in this endeavour. What they had in common was that they confronted a *political* crisis with a *legal* response and that they were intent on *removing the mask* and appealed to some kind of *universal* legal structure.

The examination of the third episode, the Cold War, revealed that the (widespread) 'radicalism' of the Interbellum decades did not repeat itself in post-WWII international law scholarship. The international balance of power and ideological antagonism caused legal theory to freeze. Many were disappointed by the failure of (international) law to protect freedom and peace. Instead, it had been power and force that had successfully protected democratic values. In the Cold-War context and in the midst of the realist-idealist debate, Morgenthau basically ignored ILP in his marginalisation of international law. Instead, he focused on the state and its power: sovereignty (as a legal concept) simply ruled. If used in passing or merely implicitly, ILP was referred to in relation to the state in the traditional way: the state had a(n Oppenheimian) set of international rights because of its sovereignty. In realist scholarship, ILP was the 'locus of status quo', i.e., a *status quo ante*. The reinforcement of sovereignty as a legal concept meant the marginalisation of ILP as an independent concept: the conceptual role of ILP was replaced by the legal conception of sovereignty. Consequently, an 'orthodox' version of international law and international law thinking was preserved which recognised the reality of power politics and this had a *weakening* effect on international law.

Although the ideals of Interbellum revisionist scholars continued to inspire, for example, the codification of individual human rights, the Cold War situation nevertheless caused a reptilian pace in international legal theory. However, Lauterpacht in this same context still made a fundamental contribution to international law theory. The developments in the field of human rights and international individual criminal responsibility enabled him to claim that individual human rights were the foundation of international law and the source of the sovereignty of the state. Reaching beyond the *inclusion* of the individual in the international legal order, Lauterpacht as a neo-Grotian jurist intended to further universal justice at the most fundamental level. His inclusion of the individual as a member of the universal community of humanity endowed with inalienable rights and duties by natural law (i.e., the source of fundamental rights) was intended to change the identity of international law: the 'recognition of the individual human being as a subject of international law lends to the law obtaining between sovereign States the beneficent complexion of a law of nations conceived as the universal law of mankind.'

It has been demonstrated that the Cold War was an ambivalent era in the sense that, on the one hand, international life was determined by power politics and, on the other hand, an elaborate framework of international human rights law was gradually erected. McDougal's scholarship reconciles both developments in his 'law is process' approach. McDougal also negated ILP, but this was actually an act of *inclusion* aimed at the enhancement of the democracy of access. The notion of *participant* which he used was not contaminated by the old connotation of *exclusion*. The notion of participant was also used to recognise that the individual was the ultimate actor.

Still, the concept of ILP slipped further and further into theoretical disuse. However, Friedmann did not ignore ILP. He noted that despite the ambivalence of the times, changes had still been wrought to the structure of the international society and international law and his report of international law's circumstances and potential in the late 1960s makes distinct use of the notion of ILP. Friedmann wished to propel international law forward from a law of co-existence to a well-established law of co-operation and in this process the designation of new subjects of international law played an important role. Friedmann intended law to function in such a way that it would initiate both legal and social change. To contribute to this function of law, the notion of ILP was used as an instrument for the *inclusion* of new subjects in the international legal order.

Mainstream international legal scholarship generally took a practical approach to the doctrine of ILP and used it either to include new subjects or seal off the system and preserve the status quo. In practice, the *Reparations for Injuries* case has resolved the issue for most scholars: the international legal system determines which entities have ILP and what the scope is in each case. This did not, however, bring the issue to the next level. It is in this practical (including/excluding) role that the concept of ILP has generally been functioning in international law scholarship since the 1970s until today. Not much theoretical discussion occurred, despite the fact that the concept of ILP featured in the first fifty pages of every international law textbook. Its conceptual relevance is widely acknowledged but the discussion of its source or foundation and thus the question of which is the most original international legal person are no longer really addressed. The pragmatic and practical conception is supported and sustained.

The final episode of this study remains open-ended in a way. This episode has not yet come to an end, and who is to say what lies beyond? Nevertheless, it has been examined whether, at this time when globalisation and the 'end of the subject' debate challenge international law scholars and contribute to the (re-)surfacing of international legal theory, the concept of ILP has come to the end of its conceptual history. Will it from now on only exist in its functional, well-established way? Or will it be forced back into use by today's challenges and thus acquire new meaning?

It has been concluded that, even though the concept of ILP is still allotted the usual space in the introductory sections of international law textbooks and the question of 'new subjects' is fuelled by the development of globalisation, the debate in the vanguard of international law scholarship has replaced ILP with notions such as 'non-state actors' or 'international participants' which are now used to discuss the position within international institutions and international law of, e.g., civil society actors, NGOs or MNCs. Within theory, the concept of ILP is associated with the 'old' international law and as such, it appears to have negative connotations of obsoleteness. Although interest in international legal theory has been increasing since the early 1990s, this has not stimulated the conceptual development of ILP. We have tried to explain this by acknowledging the influence of the (Foucaultian) suspicion of legal language, which approaches power in terms of sovereignty and legitimacy. Instead, international legal theory turns to concrete and local mechanisms in the global framework to analyse the status of a particular non-state actor. A vision on such a fundamental and traditional concept as ILP would require some kind of general, universal concept of international law, but generality and universality have been sworn off as undeserving of any intellectual respect by a significant number of scholars.

Hence, at a time impregnated with (Foucaultian) suspicion of subjectivity or the subject, international legal theory has been avoiding the concept of ILP within international law. Scholarship – under the command of the New Stream – deals with the structures of international law arguments, the flaws in the traditional historiography of international law and the box we are all (supposedly) trapped inside. Against this scholarly background, Thomas Franck attempts to reach *post* post-modernity. He starts where Foucault (in Franck's view, prematurely) left off: the need to rethink and redefine our identity, now that our old certainties and differences have collapsed. Since the end of the Cold War (international) life has changed tremendously, especially in terms of loyalties and certainties, and self-identification has indeed become a *political* task. Franck intends to liberate the spirit of individual assertiveness, but the right to self-identification goes hand in hand with the duty to engage both socially and politically. This *responsibility* is the counterpart of the right of the self to define itself. To enter a new phase, and for the development of a universal interactive community that functions *fairly*, international institution building is a necessity. To counter the fairness deficit of international law and to do justice to the plurality of actors in today's global system, however, Franck did *not* use the notion of ILP. It did not feature in his argument on the inclusion of participants and the improvement of democracy by granting wider access, or in his contention that the legitimacy of international law needs to be enhanced. In other words, *without* recourse to the legal notion of ILP, Frank develops the idea of the universal human society which is progressing towards a global constitutional democracy in which the individual subject is a world citizen. The right to personal self-determination is grounded in positive international law and the furtherance of the global community. In other words, Franck's argument is a skilled continuation of the established idea of the 'changing structure of international law and society.' ILP is absent as a notion more than as a concept, but the inclusion argument is advanced pragmatically in that it recognises the increase of (international) rights-holders and the need for enhanced participatory fairness. But as this story of the state of international law in the age of individualism unfolds, the concept of ILP is not the explicit 'locus' for the argument of change, or rather it is surpassed as Franck's argument of inclusion is a rights-based argument. His appeal for procedural and substantive fairness is an appeal directed at those creating international law and distributing participation rights, i.e., states. Franck's argument certainly touches upon the moral identity of international law, as does Christine Chinkin's.

By her feminist critique of international law, Christine Chinkin argues that the subject of international law is exclusively male. She appeals to *justice* in her demand that international law is stripped from its masculine gender bias and transformed so as to recognise the *female* subject and to *include* female voices. The perception of the identity of international law as 'objective' is wrong; international law is sexed and gendered and as such often ignores the particular needs of women and fails to defend their fundamental rights. In respect of the use of the notion of ILP, Chinkin explains that on the one hand it is used in its – by now – traditional international legal function: as a relative and derivative concept for establishing the international legal status of new participants in the international legal system and its institutions. On the other hand, admitting new entities upon the international stage in this way means that 'international personality confers "public" status on an entity with consequences for jurisdiction, representation and ownership.' As such it confirms the dividing line between the 'public' and the 'private' realm, and as such it also contributes to the masculinity of international law as based on public/private distinctions. However, bestowing ILP upon a private – non-state – actor also offers the opportunity to transcend the gendered dichotomy and it appears as if this is implied in the background. Nonetheless, the relationship with the concept of ILP is still troubled as far as Chinkin is concerned: can what emerged as a masculine concept ever benefit women? When ILP is attributed to NGOs or MNCs, it is used quite pragmatically and functionally, with the objective of including these non-state actors in the international state (and therefore male) structures and institutions and *legitimising* their *participation*. Its rejection of the *injustices* of international law makes Chinkin's project both a moral-political and a legal undertaking which advocates women's participation in the form of full female citizenship in a global community and calls upon the existing international legal structures to improve the position of women worldwide. International law will lose authority if it does not manage to respond to these injustices.

How are we to interpret and value the conclusions concerning the episodes described? Most importantly, they stimulate thought concerning alternative futures. They help us imagine an alternative conceptual role for ILP, alternative to the traditional conception of ILP as based on and developed in conjunction with the (absolute) sovereignty of the modern state.

At the end of the first chapter, the question was raised whether we have come to the end of the conceptual history of ILP and the preliminary answer given there was 'Yes and No.' The traditional concept of ILP has played out its role, so the question may be answered in the affirmative. It is true that in practice, as a functional concept, ILP will continue to be an essential tool in, among other things, the creation and functioning of international organisations, explanations of international law in textbooks, etc. But in international law *theory*, the traditional conception of ILP defined primarily as the quality of a sovereign state and secondly as a derived quality of international actors has stopped being the subject of (heated) debate. ILP has found its purpose where it is used as a rather pragmatic concept or tool which indicates that an entity exists 'in the eyes of international law.'[2] Today, ILP is generally no longer conceived of as springing from or deriving from state sovereignty as it was for quite some time in the past. By the attribution of international legal rights and duties, (new) actors come 'into sight', become 'visible', as international legal persons and are being included in the international (legal) community. In this functional role, ILP continues to be a fundamental concept of international law, i.e., fundamental to structure and unity. ILP will thus continue to function and indeed remain indispensable to international legal practice, and to our mental ordering of international reality. Theoretical debate should focus more on the identity of international law, the penetrating gaze of which is so decisive for the recognition of the international legal person.

For the actual problems and challenges that international law (theory) faces today, our thinking is ordered to go *beyond* the concept of ILP, to go beyond the question whether or not an actor has ILP and should be included in the international legal system. For these kinds of issues ILP as a conceptual tool seems to be too crude. After all, a claim to ILP and inclusion is a claim that is a response to a question 'if' an actor should be included; 'if' certain actors for the sake of international fairness should be included in international law and institutions. However, for the globalised world we live in today and the challenges it poses, this question is simply too general, too broad. The question has shifted from 'if' to 'how.' We no longer find, for example, any debate concerning the ILP of MNCs and what would be the actual use and effect of granting it to them; today, any discussion with similar objectives takes place in terms of corporate responsibility. The discussion has (very pragmatically) moved on and has left the concept of ILP behind. This is where I tend to say, 'Yes, we have come to the end of the conceptual history of ILP.' The concept has arrived at its practical functional destination and as such it remains essential to international law. The concept seems to lack, however, the necessary sophistication for answering the question of *how* non-state actors should be included in certain structures, as this requires specific procedural arrangements for every global organisation or structure.

This does not mean that nowhere in contemporary international law scholarship entities claim or are refused ILP anymore: ILP may still be claimed and/or granted in the spirit of fairness and/or justice, although, for the reasons I have just given, this occurs less and less often. As a concept of legitimate participation – i.e., the recognition that a certain actor should be part of the international (legal) community – it is still (subliminally) present in our consciousness. As such, it is inevitably related to perceptions of how the international community and its institutions should be organised, i.e., what is the best (most realistic, efficient, fair, just, etc.) way to structure the international (legal) community. It is at this more abstract, more philosophical, level that our answer should be 'No, we have not come to the end of the conceptual history of ILP.' Rather than ignore the concept,

[2] Article 2, Montevideo Convention (26 December 1933).

we should embrace it as a locus of change in our thinking about international law and its identity today. We should allow ourselves to imagine an alternative future that hinges on a key element of ILP's conceptual history, i.e., its relationship to responsibility and justice. We can rethink the concept of ILP by drawing upon its origins: ILP was born from a confrontation between moral idealism and political realism and emerged as a concept intimately linking the responsibility to pursue justice with the right of international participation.

Obviously, this conclusion opens up many new possibilities and is, in that sense, a beginning rather than an end. It could be the subject of a whole new study, however, I must limit myself here to a few suggestions for possible alternative conceptions of ILP, which recognise the historical usage of ILP in a moral political role, i.e., mediating between the individual, the state and the global community. It is in this role that the conceptual history of ILP could find continuity.

6.3. The concept of ILP revisited: the metaphor of the vocal cords

So where do we go from here: *Ball masque* or *dé-masqué*? Since the end of the Cold War, the international community has faced the challenges of failing states and an *atopos* of chaos which threatens individual human beings and their rights. Recently added to these challenges is the fight against international terrorism which is now considered a top priority. In view of these developments, concerns about the capability of states to ensure their citizens' safety and emphasis on the states' obligation under international (human rights) law to protect its citizens tend to replace the discussion on the 'end of sovereignty?' or the 'end of the state?'. It is acknowledged that there is a need for stable states to preserve and defend the rule of law. Contemporary challenges raise the question whether we are attending the funeral of international law rather than that of the state. But this problem of reconciling sovereignty with universal justice is, as we have seen, by no means new. After all, Leibniz already tried to reconcile realism with idealism, self-interest with the interests of some sort of international community. In his attempt to reconcile natural law with positivism, to recognise (sovereign) power but only when it coincided with the responsibility to conform to the demands of justice, Leibniz showed he had a clear eye for the political *reality* in Europe and the Empire, but this did not cloud his vision concerning the *normative*. This caused Leibniz to be rightly placed in what is called the Grotian tradition.

At a time when international law was similarly under fire, Lauterpacht mapped out the principles of the (neo-) Grotian tradition. Among these he ranged the sovereignty of law over power, justice as the basis of international law and the identity of subjects or rather the identity of morality, whether applied to states or individuals. Like Grotius, Lauterpacht constructed his conception of international law on the basis of man's rational and social nature. He considered man a rational and moral being, 'intrinsically moved by a desire for social life' and endowed with the capacity 'of acting on general principles and of learning from experience,' in short, not a being with only his own best interests at heart. Lauterpacht also tried to link realism with idealism, to connect theory and practice, to conceive of a law that would mediate between power and the normative or the ideal, and in that sense he too was a representative of the Grotian tradition.

One element of this tradition that I would like to elaborate on is man's desire for the social life or what could also be called the desire to belong. This works on the basic premise that all individuals are connected, that autonomous human beings naturally associate with each other. This basic premise reminds us that there is an alternative view to the (liberal) idea that individuals are isolated and only create societies out of self-interest. It is the pre-modern view which held that without society man cannot live, as man wants to associate with others and to belong. In other words, the primacy of the autonomous individual in political theory cannot imply the marginalisation of human association; on the contrary, man is a social being and society is a necessity of human life.

This idea also formed the basis of the political ideas of Grotius, Leibniz, Wolff and Kant, but their 17th and 18th-century naturalism soon became marginalised by 19th-century positivism or liberalism, which raised the idea of the autonomous individual to the international level and trumpeted the victory of the autonomous sovereign state as a free and independent entity which lived in a society of equally sovereign and independent states. As we observed, a choice presented itself between the Vattellian and the Kantian conception and the international society decided to choose the Vattellian or realist option. My reminder of that particular feature of the natural law tradition, the portrayal of man as a social being, is not an invitation to wallow in utopianism. On the contrary, it is actually an attempt to connect realism and cosmopolitanism in a reasonable manner. The concept of ILP could serve as the locus for this connection, in the same way that it has been the locus for dialogue between the two in the past. This dialogue manifested itself in oscillating views. On the one hand, there was the idea of a society of sovereign states and, on the other, the notion of a society of humanity. On the one hand, there was realism, which conceives of international relations as power politics and, on the other, there was idealism, which always uses some version of the idea of the universal human society. Just like international law generally takes care to mediate, or should at least mediate, between politics and morality, so ILP is or could be the locus where such mediation actually takes shape.

We may conceive of ILP as a connecting concept, because even if the individual is perceived as the original or primary subject of international law, it is still true that at the international level the state is the habitual actor or legal person in mainstream international life. Besides the traditional perspectives (an international community exclusively made up of *masked* states or a universal community (*dé-masqué*) consisting of individuals who are considered the only bearers of ILP), a third concept thus emerges. Namely, although the state is the international legal person who acts, it does so representing its citizens. The ILP which enables it to act is derived from its citizens. This line of reasoning can be broken down into several steps. First, we must deal with the relationship between the individual and the collective in social and political terms. Second, we must establish the essentially social nature of man and his political participation as a precondition of his existence. Third, the concepts of international community and humanity must be defined and linked to the function of international law and institutions. Finally, I will argue that the innate right to (international legal) personality brings with it the correlative responsibility or duty to secure this right for the international community.

First, let us revisit Brunner. On the one hand, he recognised the importance of individualism, of the (spiritual and moral) emancipation of the individual from the collective. On the other hand, he did not take this belief as far as liberalism did, as he considered that man also needs community life. An increase in individualism is beneficial up to the point where it leads to the dissolution of the community, which would bring isolation and anarchy and could result in the de-humanisation of life. If the tendency towards that kind of individualisation persists, only coercion can finally hold the social order together. The underestimation of the value of a healthy community life in its various forms coupled with the underestimation of the normative value of the human need to belong has resulted in a serious (political) risk of upheaval that threatens the domestic and international public order today as the world experiences that fundamental transition towards a new order.

The basis of any realistic conception of justice and law must be a realistic conception of man. In my view, Brunner's idea of the 'person-in-community' qualifies as such. Yes, it is a position in between individualism and collectivism, and it necessarily embraces the 'polarity of individual man and social community,' the duality of the individual personality, the paradox of human life. But while this position may be branded ambiguous, at least from this perspective law must protect both individual human rights and the rights of the community of which the individual is a member. This latter function of the law requires not only individual rights, but also individual responsibilities or duties for the 'person-in-community'. Because from this perspective, contrary to the collectivist approach, the collective has no rights. It has no higher moral value or source of rights than the individual. If this were different, man would lose his individuality by merging into the collective. His only identity would be that in relation to the collective: purely functional. But for Brunner, the rights of the community are legally speaking really individual duties. Rather than that, as Brunner explains, 'the rights of the individual are limited by the rights of the community,' individual rights are limited by a responsibility towards the community.[3] There is no subordination.

[3] See, for a human rights system which includes the concept of individual *duties* as well as rights and consideres 'that the enjoyment of rights and freedoms also implies the performance of duties on the part of everyone,' the African Charter on Human and Peoples' Rights, adopted in 1981, entered into force in 1986.

The term 'communal personalism' reflects well the difference with 'individualistic liberalism.' Yet it 'stands firm on the side of individualistic liberalism against all attempts of anonymous society or tyrannical state to degrade the person into a mere instrument of collective power.'[4] In other words, because of his individual rational and social nature, the individual human being living in a socio-political community has both rights and *responsibilities*.

Underlying these rights and responsibilities is the capacity to be the bearer of these rights and duties. A concept which captures this duality of human life (collectivity and individuality) is the concept of person or citizen as used in the *republican* tradition. We have already seen in the previous chapter that today the idea of citizenship is being re-examined. For an alternative to the political theory of liberalism, which takes the citizen as a formal concept, a fiction that is conceptually separated from the individual as a social and moral agent, we turn to the conception of individual freedom as political participation. Here, the concept of person is not formed by the idea of the 'social contract', but by the conception of man as a social and political creature.

Second, political participation is an existential condition of human life. Hannah Arendt explained that the question of human nature is unsolvable or unintelligible to man himself. She thus shifted our political thinking from human nature to the human condition and to the condition of all political life: *plurality*. 'Human plurality, the basic condition of both action and speech, has the twofold of *equality* and *distinction*.' We are as able to understand each other as we are to disagree and by our actions and our words we live among and together with each other: 'With word and deed we insert ourselves into the human world ...' We thus take up life in the public realm by choice, in freedom. It is the condition of all men who want to live 'the life that is given to them' that they affirm their presence in the world as both *doers* and *speakers*. As such, they disclose or 'reveal their unique personal identities' to this world, and this disclosure is man's individual appearance in the world.[5] This appearance or revelation of the self is only possible in a social life '*with* others.' It fully depends on 'sheer human togetherness.'[6]

This appearance of the self is a kind of re-birth, it is man's *political* birth and it depends on action accompanied by speech (as action).[7] It is only in the *public*

[4] Christianity and Civilisation Vol. II, at 111-112.

[5] H. Arendt, The Human Condition (1958), 2nd ed. 1998, at 175-179, 7-11.

[6] Id., at 180. Grotius was also aware that for his very existence man depended on the social and even defined human nature by this *appetitus societatis*. Grotius of course dealt with human nature, whereas Arendt deals with the human condition, but both consider the social element crucial.

[7] 'Without the accompaniment of speech, at any rate, action would not only lose its revelatory character, but, and by the same token, it would lose its subject, as it were; not acting men but performing robots would achieve what, humanly speaking, would remain incomprehensible. Speechless action would no longer be action because there would no longer be an actor, and the actor, the doer of deeds, is possible only if he is at the same time the speaker of words. The action he begins is humanly disclosed by the word, and through his deed can be perceived in its brute physical appear-

realm that the agent can disclose himself in the action, the public realm is the stage on which the actor and his action are spotlighted and wrapped in the 'shining brightness' necessary for the appearance. Conversely, therefore, the agent cannot reveal himself where 'human togetherness is lost,' for instance, in times of war when words become propaganda against the enemy instead of a revelation of the '"who," the unique and distinct identity of the agent.'[8] In addition, therefore, to the requirement of human togetherness, another requirement is that the agent of the action is identifiable. When he speaks, his audience must turn their attention to him, turn in his direction and realise who is speaking.[9] The *identification* of the agent is required for an act to have *meaning*.

Elsewhere in this book it is described how historically the meaning of ILP has been related to the idea of participation in international life. In this light, Arendt's idea that speech is a political act, because through it we may participate in the political processes, is particularly useful. Man's humanity has since Aristotle been defined as political; man is the *zōon politikon*; Arendt focuses on Aristotle's second definition: man as a '*zōon logon ekhon*,' i.e., 'a living being capable of speech.'[10] These definitions define human life in the *polis*, the political way of life. Speech makes matters political and speech makes man political. The political is, after all, the realm of plurality. But the idea has developed to mean that *without being a political participant man is not human.* A life without speech and action, without any participation in the political realm, is no longer a human life, for it would be a life without fellow men and (therefore) devoid of meaning. Political participation is thus not a right of man, but more fundamentally a *conditio sine qua non*. (Democratic) governance and politics need speech and action. They require political participation in the discursive public realm and the *res publica* is the public realm of freedom. Freedom here means that by nature one is free to participate in the pursuit of the common good rather than free from government interference. In this republic (in the sense of political community) plurality is vital and it must be protected in order to ensure its continued existence. The individual has autonomy, but in return must participate in political life. In this view, happiness is determined by both man's private and his public life. Every political community depends on the political actions (thought, speech) of its members to thrive and survive. To exist means to live politically, being human means being a citizen. *Citizenship* is a defining element of man's *humanity*.

Third, it is for this reason – that citizenship is a defining element of man's humanity – that the human society in general must protect the humanity of its indi-

ance without verbal accompaniment, it becomes relevant only through the spoken word in which he identifies himself as the actor, announcing what he does, has done, and intends to do.' Id., at 178-179.

[8] Id., at 180.

[9] See, on politics and theatre, id., at 187-188: 'the theatre is the political art par excellence; only there is the political sphere of human life transposed into art. By the same token, it is the only art whose sole subject is man in his relationship to others.'

[10] Id., at 26.

vidual members; humanity has a duty to guarantee the individual's political identity, as this defines him as human. To avoid it sliding off into unbounded idealism or turning into a utopian fantasy, the concept of humanity has to be given legal reality. Throughout this book, we have heard international law scholars explain what they understood to be the universal human society and/or the international community of states. In my mind, the two are interrelated and inseparable. The human condition – i.e., the 'equality' and 'diversity' of mankind – is a universal reality, it is what unites the whole of mankind as 'humanity;' in this sense, the universal reality of humanity is based on 'the human status' itself. When we turn to the issue of 'crimes against humanity,' it becomes evident that 'humanity' would become devoid of meaning if some crimes were not conceived of as crimes against the international community of states, as crimes against humanity in general, because these crimes (among which expulsion and genocide) are indeed 'crimes against the human status' itself. They are an attack on the human condition itself by aiming for the *elimination* of *human diversity*. As such, they are truly 'crimes against *humanity*.'[11] Leaving the discussion about which crimes should be considered as such to one side, I would like to follow up on the underlying idea. I second the notion that there is a universal political sphere which is organised in international institutions and organisations that – in principle – derive their authority from the political societies or states, which in turn derive their governmental authority from the representation of their citizens. The international community is best understood as the sum of international legal and political structures, institutions and organisations which were created to coexist and co-operate with the purpose of reaching their various (common) objectives. The international community is therefore the political organisation and institutionalisation of humanity or the legal and political order of the universal human society. The element of political representation is however essential to this conception of the international community.[12] For the protection of its human status, humanity has to rely on the international community which structures and institutions should therefore be sufficiently (political) representative of humanity's equality and diversity.

Some would deny that an international community exists and refer to the heterogeneity among nations and peoples, but I would say that the international community, i.e., the community of political societies mainly organised as states, exists through international law and international institutions of which the United Nations is currently the best available representation. In other words, interna-

---

[11] See, the epilogue to H. Arendt, Eichmann in Jerusalem: A report on the banality of evil, 247 (1963). Emphasis added.

[12] If the international community as the political and legal structures and institutions of humanity is insufficiently representative of humanity's plurality, the question of how to accommodate the non- and/or under-represented arises. It is in this light that we should see the issue of "new" or "non-state" actors which move towards inclusion in the system. As we concluded above, this is an issue which has to a large extent surpassed the question of "whether" and should now be treated in a more functional manner, "how" such inclusion should be arranged.

tional law and institutions have a role to play in the development of humanity's (political) community.

International law and institutions are the *loci* of the international community where international politics and international morality are to be reconciled and negotiated. At the basis of such mediation should be the protection of the human status and the recognition that it is the international community's responsibility to guarantee humanity's equality and diversity. Here, it is foreseeable that international morality will collide with the self-interest of power politics and it is at this standoff that international law plays and should play its part. International law thus incorporates a regulatory and an aspirational dimension. It is not required that humanity should organise itself in a single world-encompassing state, but the inherent plurality of humanity makes (international) politics a necessity. International politics is necessary but not sufficient for the protection of humanity. International politics needs international law to reconcile politics' inclination to being self-serving with the basic moral premise of the protection of the human status. As the world's political societies are mainly organised as states, international law should be an expression of the fact that these states do recognise the fundamental and supreme value of humanity and the human status and that their protection concerns them directly. Through international law, states acknowledge their common responsibility to protect 'humanity', if necessary by the involvement of international law organisations and institutions.[13] It cannot be denied that this argument is profoundly normative, but it cannot be accused of being completely detached from legal or political reality either. After all, in 1970, the International Court of Justice confirmed that there are norms[14] for which

> all States can be held to have a legal interest in their protection, they are obligations of *erga omnes*.
>
> Such obligations derive, for example, in contemporary international law, from the outlawing of acts of aggression, and of genocide, as also from the principles and rules concerning basic rights of the human person including protection from slavery and racial discrimination. Some of the corresponding rights of protection have entered into the body of general law (*Reservations to the Convention on the Prevention and Punishment of the Crime of Genocide, Advisory Opinion, I.C.J. Reports* 1951, p. 23); others are conferred by international instruments of a universal or quasi-universal character.[15]

---

[13] International law has in fact incorporated this recognition of peremptory norms in codified, positive law documents. Kooijmans has shown how the international community has developed or is 'steadily' developing into what Dworkin called a 'community of principle,' i.e., the international community does indeed have a set of undisputed principles at its core, principles which are recognised as norms of *ius cogens*, like, e.g., the prohibition of genocide. P.H. Kooijmans, International Law: Placebo or Medication?, *in* W.J.M. van Genugten et al. (Eds.), Realism and Moralism in International Relations 88-90 (1999).

[14] See also, id, at 89.

[15] *Barcelona Traction* case (Belgium *v.* Spain), 5 February 1970, paras. 33 and 34, ICJ Reports 1970, at 32.

In other words, the (legal) interest of state A is affected if genocide is committed in state B. This is the international legal expression of the moral proposition that when humanity is affected by crimes against it, the members of the international community are equally affected. For the second step of the normative argument, namely that a *responsibility* (obligation) arises for the international community to respond, the concept of ILP comes into play.

Fourth, the concept of the (international legal) *person* may be used to solidify the argument in legal terms and to take it to the next stage of sustaining the responsibility of the international community to protect what is called 'the principles and rules concerning basic rights of the human person.' The concept of ILP can help us turn the fundamental relationship between the individual, the state and the international community around. It enables us to reconnect to the origins of the law of nations, but with the adjustment that here international law and ILP are conceptualised on the basis of the natural unity *and* diversity of humanity and at the intersection of both politics and morality.

The concept of person is also used to indicate man's humanity, i.e., the human condition. In the Kantian tradition, the concept of person is defined in relation to the distinction between 'end' and 'means.' A person is distinguished from a thing because his/her existence is in itself 'an end.' Mulholland explains this tradition by saying that:

> the best way to understand the concept of end in itself and with it, the distinction between persons and things, is through the notion of autonomy: that is, in the idea that each human being is an equal participant in the determination of valid law governing the interrelations of persons. The status of bearer of rights is the status of one who must be counted in the determination of moral rules. The reason why each person must be counted is that any decision to exclude someone from participation, i.e., to make someone a thing, must be unilateral and therefore in the process of determining rules, biased. The point is made in Kant's concept of autonomy. Kant sees clearly that the principle of autonomy does not indicate the basis for an accumulative concept of society. Decisions are not to be made by majorities. Nor does my autonomy permit me to legislate for mankind without regard for the legislation of others. Rather, autonomy presupposes collectivity. I can give laws to others only if I acknowledge that they give laws to me. This shows that autonomy presupposes a relation to something else, the autonomy of others. My very lawgiving contains the condition that I am part of a collectivity.[16]

Mulholland establishes an 'innate right to be a person,' i.e., 'the right to have rights,' on the basis of the so-called 'impartiality principle' which is constituted by the idea of 'collective autonomy.' It is an innate right in the sense that it is an 'unacquired or 'natural' right. The constitution of the impartiality principle unfolds as follows:

---

[16] L.A. Mulholland, The Innate Right to be a Person, *in* G. Lafrance (Ed.), Éthique et droits fondamentaux / Ethics and Basic Rights 132 (1989).

The idea of collective autonomy can be understood as constitutive of impartiality in the determination of principles of rights. a) Each individual must be represented as having independent judgment on the rules that govern everyone. b) Any accepted principle must be collectively acknowledged.[17]

The idea of collective autonomy does not base the existence of a political society on the fictions of the state of nature and the social contract, but takes account of the reality that political societies are 'historically produced.' '[T]he idea of collective autonomy, i.e., that everyone collectively provides the ethical ground for the laws of political society,' acknowledges history's erratic but undeniable input, but also 'presents history and society as an object of reflection.' Because of this reflection on the significance of history and on 'the basic political/legal framework' of a society,

the position that is characterized by the idea of collective autonomy is that of a participant who, along with other participants, is constantly involved in the process of correcting and adjusting the rules of the game, with an eye on the historical conditions that produced its present character.[18]

The *participant* who reflects on the basic political and legal framework at the same time enjoys the perspective of an 'autonomous agent outside the socio-historical context.' In other words, the individual is an independent moral agent. 'The reflection characterizes a position of independence from, but in relation to, the political whole.' The idea of collective autonomy can thus be a method for the determination of moral values. Mulholland explains that, contrary to Rawls' model, which is constructed on the basis of the idea of the 'state of nature', the present model requires that we 'ask whether the principles that govern society are consistent with persons maintaining their standing as persons, distinct from things, which characterizes them as participants in the procedure.' In other words, a person is a morally independent agent who participates in the procedures regulating the political society. The rules and principles produced by the collective of participants cannot exclude participants impartially.

That being a person is an innate right can be proven by the Kantian test of universalisability which dictates that any rule denying the capacity to participate (rules, therefore, which reduce persons to things) cannot be justified under the impartiality model. If participants exclude co-participants from the procedures, they fail the test of universalisability, because these rules/procedures have not been adopted in an impartial manner, i.e., with everyone participating. Exclusion is a violation of impartiality and a denial of personality. 'The only way of ensuring that a prevailing set of rules is impartial is to include the rule that all human beings are fundamentally equal persons.' The right to be a person is an innate right which is foundational to justice, without this natural right the pursuit of jus-

[17] Id.

[18] Id., at 133.

tice is not possible: just rules have to be the product of impartial (inclusive) procedures. Impartial rules are necessary for society to 'consistently regard its basic structure as just.' Thus, 'the equal right to be a person is a constitutive feature of a system of rights in a political society, and hence ... this right should be reflected in the constitution of any state.'[19] To sum up:

> ... there is a kind of natural right to be a person. Notice that the right is not derived. There is no moral principle that can be appealed to in order to establish this natural right. A human being has the right to be a person because he/she is human, and nothing less is constitutively involved in the determination of impartial principles. The argument for the right depends on examining the epistemological requirement for the fundamental rules governing society.[20]

Having established that there is a natural right to be a person and that it is *unjust to exclude some human beings from the status of person in the civil community*, let us now take this line of reasoning one step further and argue that there is also an innate right to be an international legal person. It has been established that 'the title to be a person is dependent only on being human and is thus supra-legal.'[21] Even though the idea of collective autonomy is first and foremost a method for determining moral values, it also establishes that 'human beings must have equal status in the determination of interpersonal moral principles' and even recognises 'the ultimate sanction' for the violation of the right to be a person:

> Any government which violates the innate right cannot claim to have moral authority over those which it prevents entirely from having rights. Hence, the principle requiring the innate right overrides governmental authority. Accordingly, because there is an innate right (to be a person), there is a right to coerce political authority through rebellion.[22]

Ultimately, therefore, the denial of personality may give rise to a right to rebel and may thereby indeed have important international legal implications. Drawing on Arendt, we could continue this line of reasoning as follows: every human being by virtue of his humanity has the natural right to be a person, or, in other words, the right to be a person, to be a participant, is defined by humanity and must as such be protected by humanity. Where the essence of humanity, the human condition, is involved, the protection is the responsibility of the 'supranational.' For the final step from the supra-legal to the institutionalised supra-

[19] Id., at 134.

[20] Id., at 135.

[21] Id., 'All human beings must be considered persons in the determination of principles of justice since a) such principles must be impartial, and b) problems of justice are defined as conflicts between possible bearers of rights. That is, they concern conflicts of judgement over who should get certain advantages and disadvantages. To deny rights to some individual or group is to make a judgement to the effect that he or they may not have them but this is to be partial in the decision. The other must be allowed as much title to exercise judgment, on the matter.'

[22] Id., at 135-136. This is not an uncommon thought in international law, it reminds us of Grotius' remarks in this direction.

national, from humanity to the institutionalised community, a connection is again sought below with Arendt and, to a lesser extent, Ricoeur.

In the previous chapter, I have described how Ricoeur, who was greatly indebted to Hannah Arendt for his political thinking and '*petite éthique*,'[23] defended the capable and responsible subject against contemporary suspicion. Ricoeur subsequently indicated in clear terms what actually creates the *legal* subject. Ricoeur also holds the view that to belong to a legal/political community is essential to man's humanity. He agrees that to be human means to have a natural right to be a person, i.e., to be a *citizen*. The transition from (capable) subject to *legal* subject requires 'the institutional otherness:' i.e., a relationship with the 'third person' or 'distant other,' who is 'the other' of social or institutional relations (*l'altérité institutionnelle*).[24]

Only the third [interpersonal form of otherness and institutional form of association, i.e., the interpersonal and institutional otherness], situated in the background of the relation to the you, gives us a basis for the institutional mediation required by the constitution of a *real subject of rights* – in other words, of a *citizen*. This double necessity- that of the mediation by otherness in general and that of the distinction between the other as a "you" and the other as a third party – can be established on the plane of fundamental anthropology to which we appealed in order to elaborate the notion of a capable subject.[25]

The subject of rights is in the first place the 'subject worthy of respect,' which we have seen defined in the previous chapter. The subject worthy of respect is the subject capable of answering to the question 'to whom can human action be imputed?' The human subject precedes the state in its existence and has not become a person by social contract. As a subject capable of speaking and acting, of assessing actions as good or bad and of judging acts impartially, the capable human subject is the *subject of rights*, namely the subject of 'rights *of humanity*,' which are 'rights attached to human being as human beings and not as members of some political community conceived of as the source of positive rights.'[26] For these (innate) rights of humanity to become effective, interpersonal and institutional otherness is required, in other words: political and legal institutions are needed. The socio-political institutions and legal systems are mediators to ensure that each gets his due; they are dispensers of *justice*. This institutional mediation confirms that human persons are subjects with rights; it makes of them *legal* persons. To be a legal person is a necessity for living a humane life.

For the final step, we have to bring together the concept of person, the law of nations and the international community as the institutional mediator of humanity. The right to be a person or legal subject is the natural right to belong to and participate in a legal-political community; it is, in short, the right to citizenship.

---

[23] P. Ricoeur, Le Juste 13 (1995).
[24] Id., at 34.
[25] P. Ricoeur, The Just 5 (2000, transl. D. Pellauer).
[26] Id., at 9.

In a constitutional democracy under the rule of law, man is a citizen. For his benefit, the political organisation of the state must function as or provide the institutions that connect the individual to the political, as the legal political institutions which enable persons to participate in the political society and its rule-creating processes. In a globalised world, the political is as much international as national. If the state does not fulfil its responsibilities and obligations towards its citizens (for example, by reducing them to things instead of persons through the gross violation of civil and political rights) and thereby destroys its own governmental authority and legitimacy, the individual is denied his natural right to be a person, i.e., to participate in and be connected with the political society he lives in.

The duty that is the correlative of this natural right is of course in the first place the state's. However, because the natural right in question is so significant, the international community also has a responsibility, more particularly, in cases where the state fails and is no longer able to provide the institutional mediation to which every human being is entitled. It can do so in the shape of the United Nations, which is the body providing institutional mediation not only for the international community as a community of states, but also for the international community as the legal and political order of *humanity*.

If a state fails to fulfil its responsibilities towards its citizens and anarchy overtakes the country, the international community, the global discursive society, has to listen to those whose basic rights are denied. *It must (temporarily) provide the necessary institutional structure to reconnect the individual to the political and thereby 'transform' him back from thing to person; in other words, it has to provide inclusion.* The individual has the innate right or natural right to be a person, to be a subject of the rights of humanity, which means that he has the natural right to be part of a structure that provides institutional otherness – the right to participate in the legal and political institutions and structures of a society, i.e., in a body politic. If a state functions well and its citizens are represented properly by the government, the ILP which the state derives from its citizens remains with the state. The state is then the legitimate representative of its citizens at the international level with the authority to pursue their interests. However, if the state fails, collapses or falls victim to civil war or the oppression of minorities, the ILP of that state is withdrawn or returned to the people it was supposed to represent. In situations such as these, humanity, by way of its international community, has to *open up* its institutions and law, even if only temporarily, to *include* these human beings and by this international recognition to *reaffirm* their '*personality*.' This is why in my view we should conclude that the individual as a member of humanity has the natural right to be a person and must thereby ultimately be considered the first and original international legal person, now that it has emerged that the institutionalised international community has the correlative responsibility to protect this natural right. The well-functioning state has full ILP, but only derived from its citizens.

As such, ILP as a concept finds itself at the crossroads of the moral, political and legal. In classical international law, ILP was the *mask* worn by the state on the international stage, just like in the original meaning of the Greek word '*persona*' the comedian wore the mask of the character he portrayed. With the personification of the state, ILP indeed functioned like a mask, a shield at times, or a façade at others, that divided the international from the internal situation. However, I would prefer to think metaphorically of ILP now as of *vocal cords*, so that we may re-conceive the concept as the capacity to speak and act, and, in a broader sense, the capacity to be a political participant, with a natural right to such participation. In cases where the state fails to function as a choir filled with different voices, a choir which is brave enough to allow a certain well-placed dissonant at times, but where instead the voices of certain minorities, or of a whole people, or of the entire female population, are silenced and suppressed, the international community has a duty to invite and accommodate these groups on stage and to be an audience to them or their representatives, like NGOs, or to make their voices heard through other channels, like the United Nations Permanent Forum on Indigenous Issues or Global Compact. Let us recall Hannah Arendt's comment that:

> The fundamental deprivation of human rights is manifested first and above all in the deprivation of a place in the world which makes opinions significant and actions effective. Something much more fundamental than freedom and justice, which are rights of citizens, is at stake when belonging to the community into which one is born is no longer a matter of course and not belonging no longer a matter of choice, or when one is placed in a situation where, unless he commits a crime, his treatment by others does not depend on what he does or does not do. This extremity, and nothing else, is the situation of people deprived of human rights. They are deprived, not of the right to freedom, but of the right to action; not of the right to think whatever they please, but of the right to opinion.

It took the calamities of war and genocide for us to become aware of 'the existence of a right to have rights,' such as the right 'to live in a framework where one is judged by one's actions and opinions,' and the 'right to belong to some kind of organized community.' The loss of this right to have rights and to belong to an organised community (what Arendt calls a 'human right') 'entails the loss of the relevance of speech (and man, since Aristotle, has been defined as a being commanding the power of speech and thought), and the loss of all human relationship, the loss, in other words, of some of the most essential characteristics of human life.' The loss of this human right can therefore not be put on a par with simply 'the loss of specific rights', but could include 'the loss of a community willing and able to guarantee any rights whatsoever.' Many have succeeded in keeping their human dignity, even in concentration camps and camps of extermination. 'Man, it turns out, can lose all so-called Rights of Man without losing his essential quality as man, his human dignity. Only the loss of a polity itself expels him from humanity.'[27]

---

[27] H. Arendt, The Origins of Totalitarianism 297, ch. 9, (Harcourt, New Edition, 1973).

... humanity, which for the eighteenth century, in Kantian terminology, was no more than a regulative idea, has today become an inescapable fact. This new situation, in which "humanity" has in effect assumed the role formerly ascribed to nature or history, would mean in this context that the right to have rights, or the rights of every individual to belong to humanity, should be guaranteed by humanity itself. It is by no means certain whether this is possible. For, contrary to the best-intentioned humanitarian attempts to obtain new declarations of human rights from international organizations, it should be understood that this idea transcends the present sphere of international law which still operates in terms of reciprocal agreements and treaties between sovereign states; and, for the time being, a sphere that is above the nations does not exist.[28]

This does however not imply that we should appeal to world federalism. A world government would be exposed to the same risk of regressing towards totalitarianism if it equated 'the right thing' with 'what is good for' humanity. 'A conception of law which identifies what is right with the notion of what is good – for the individual, or the family, or the people, or the largest number – becomes inevitable once the absolute and transcendent measurement of religion or the law of nature have lost their authority. And this predicament is by no means solved if the unit to which the "good for" applies is as large as mankind itself.' The question remains, however, if to identify 'right' with the law of nature will prove to be enough, because more important than the natural rights of any individual human being is 'his political status,' which means his right and responsibility to participate and communicate:

The paradox involved in the loss of human rights is that such loss coincides with the instant when a person becomes a human being in general-without a profession, without a citizenship, without an opinion, without a deed by which to identify and specify himself-*and* different in general, representing nothing but his own absolutely unique individuality which, deprived of expression within and action upon a common world, loses all significance.[29]

Such exclusion from the global human society, this excommunication from humanity and the denial of membership of political communities which enables humans to partake fully of their humanity, brings with it '[t]he danger ... that a global universally interrelated civilization may produce barbarians from its own midst by forcing millions of people into conditions which, despite all appearances, are the conditions of savages,'[30] or rather of slaves. Man must never be stripped of his political status. An individual human being who is excommunicated from the polity or public sphere is denied a connection with humanity, but this connection is at the same time his only passport into the political:

The human being who has lost his place in a community, his political status in the struggle of his time, and the legal personality which makes his actions and part of his des-

[28] Id., at 298.
[29] Id., at 302.
[30] Id., at 302.

tiny a consistent whole, is left with those qualities which usually can become articulate only in the sphere of private life and must remain unqualified, mere existence in all matters of public concern.[31]

Membership of a polity or the right to be a citizen takes priority over all other rights, because it is a requirement for man to be man.[32] One cannot be completely deprived of one's legal personality, although it can be limited (just as, of course, it can be elevated to a higher level). The point is, though, that legal personality can never be lost, and if a human being or beings is/are individually or collectively denied a political community, this does not automatically result in the loss of their political status. Instead, this status or right must then be met or integrated in the international community, which in some cases certain UN initiatives have in fact done. ILP is the concept that establishes this duty in order to prevent a "civic death." If a state does not live up to the demands of human rights law and thus fails to perform its primary function as a political community, another community, namely the international community, has to fill the void. ILP will then flow back to its initial source: the individual subject. The correlative responsibility of the international community can take many forms, and which one it actually assumes depends, among other things, on the extent of the state's failure. The response of the international community must be proportionate and should therefore be balanced against the principle of sovereignty. However, in the course of the present line of reasoning, state sovereignty has been implicitly redefined and reconciled with international law.[33] State sovereignty is no longer the concept that implies the unlimited power of the state or anti-social international conduct on its part, but now includes responsibility. This responsibility is in the first place that of the state, or rather the government, towards its own citizens and secondly a responsibility for humanity in general. In some cases, the international community may help a polity to fulfil its responsibility towards its citizens or temporarily step in to provide an institutional framework. As such, transitional international administration is not necessarily illegitimate; quite the contrary in fact. However, it requires a primarily facilitating approach, which, for example, confirms the right to self-determination and accommodates the wishes of the people. It must not result in the imposition of a foreign administration. However, it cannot afford to lose adequacy in the securing of peace, order and a functioning polity either. Only when these conditions have been fulfilled can the natural right to be a person be upheld and justice be served. I will have to leave any detailed discussion of form and extent aside here, but views on the legitimacy of interna-

[31] Id., at 301.

[32] As Ricoeur explains: 'Sans la médiation institutionnelle, l'individu n'est qu'une esquisse d'homme, son appartenance à un corps politique est nécessaire à son épanouissement humain et, en ce sens, elle n'est pas digne d'être révoquée.' Le Juste, at 39-40.

[33] See, for a more explicit re-conception of sovereignty in relation to ILP, J.E. Nijman, Sovereignty and Personality: a process of inclusion, *in* G. Kreijen et al., State, Sovereignty, and International Governance 142-144 (2002).

tional administration may benefit from the conceptual shift suggested above.[34] The International Transitional Administrations with UN involvement (such as the ones in Kosovo, East Timor or Mozambique) are an excellent example of how (a representative part of) the international community (operating through the UN) may directly administer territories or assist the authorities in establishing functional governments in the aftermath of conflict and the exclusion of its people from the political society, perhaps because this society has collapsed altogether. Legitimate ITA arrangements are temporary means of accommodating the natural right to be a person, after all, the responsibility of the international community is to re-institute the polity and democratic self-governance. Such transnational interference in local matters of course touches upon the doctrine of intervention and the concept of state sovereignty. But the re-conception of sovereignty which was implied above helps sustain the newly developing doctrine on the international community's 'responsibility to protect'. At the heart of the new approach to (humanitarian) intervention is a conceptual shift that closely resembles our line of argument. It, too, argues the reinterpretation of sovereignty in order to include the responsibility to protect. This responsibility is first and foremost one of the state, but if the state fails to fulfil it, the responsibility shifts onto the international community, which will then be called upon to prevent, to react and to rebuild.[35] Again, any detailed discussion on how such interventions could be operationalised must unfortunately be left aside here, but the starting point must be that international law and the international community, the UN and all other international institutions in general are the loci where any development in this direction should take shape and be made operational. Obviously, this challenge may also require institutional adjustments.

We have seen how throughout its conceptual history ILP has been used for ethico-political reasons and in attempts to reconcile justice with the reality of power. When we define ILP as a natural right to political participation, as the right to have rights, this includes the right to live in a world governed by *just* institutions. To fulfil its obligation to guarantee the individual human being's ILP in case of state failure, humanity will have to develop its institutional and legal structure into more *just* versions of itself. Man's desire for a *good* life includes the desire to *just* institutions, which enable him to make his voice heard. The *vocal cords* enable man to speak out and act politically. The law with its judiciary system provides society with places where the 'word' is more powerful than violence, where the word triumphs over violence. In this sense law is different from the political, as it is situated halfway between morality and politics. However, the innate right to political participation of the individual is also limited by the individual's duties towards the society and polity of which he is a member, i.e.,

[34] See also, e.g., David Harland, who, based on the *traditional* concept of sovereignty, had to conclude that 'full legitimacy for an international administration ... is impossible.' D. Harland, Legitimacy and Effectiveness in International Administration, 10(1) *Global Governance* 19 (2004).

[35] Report of the International Commission on Intervention and State Sovereignty, The Responsibility to Protect (2001).

duties to his fellow citizens. The corollary of the right to participate is the duty to take moral and political responsibility. Leibniz reconciled justice with power by using ILP to guarantee both participation and responsibility, and this is reflected in the idea that the natural right to be an international legal person has as its corollary the responsibility of the self to respect the other person. 'The concept of ILP: from mask to vocal cords?' indeed reflects, as Kelsen has put it, the transformation from a substantive concept into a more functional or relational concept and as such it becomes an indispensable methodological concept.

To sum up, the right to legal personality is part of man's human identity and humanity is under an obligation to defend it if the 'primary' political community fails to provide the necessary conditions. It therefore follows that the individual is the legal personality *par excellence* of international law, i.e., the law of mankind. Yes, states are international legal persons, but they are *secondary* persons; individual human beings are the *primary* legal persons in international law. The individual is both the source and the final destination of the law of nations. ILP forms the *cords* between the individual human being and the universal human society, and because of it, the international community and international law must guarantee the right to have rights, the right to political participation, i.e., the right to speak out and raise one's *voice*. This could be the new function of ILP.

It is thus suggested here that we re-conceive ILP by using it to express that the natural right to be a person is an international right which finds its correlative duty or responsibility vested in the international community. As such, it is the responsibility of the international community to guarantee humanity's humanity, i.e., to protect the individual human being from *exclusion*. Let us use the natural right to be an international legal person to indicate that *de-capacitating* and *silencing* the human subject is against the law of nations and is sanctioned by the international community in pursuance of its responsibility to respond adequately and appropriately to protect the human person.

CONSULTED LITERATURE

Abi-Saab, G.M., Peaceful Change and the Integration of the Newly Independent States in the International Community, 32/33 *Yearbook of the AAA* 172 (1962/63).

Allott, Ph.J., Eunomia: New Order for a New World (1990).

Allott, Ph., The Emerging Universal Legal System, paper presented on 20 September 2002 at the Seminar on Theoretical Approaches to The Relationship between International and National Law, Amsterdam Centre for International law.

Alston, Ph., & Steiner H.J. (Eds.), International Human Rights in Context: Law, Politics, Morality (1996).

Alston, Ph., The Myopia of the Handmaidens: International Lawyers and Globalization, 8 *EJIL* 435 (1997).

Alvarez, A., Exposé de Motifs et Déclaration des grands principes du Droit International Moderne (1936).

Alvarez, A., La Psychologie des Peuples et la Reconstruction du Droit International Le Problème de la Paix (1936).

Akehurst, M., A Modern Introduction to International Law (6th ed., 1987).

Annan, K., The Politics of Globalisation, Lecture at Harvard University, 17 September 1998, (SG/SM/6703).

Anzilotti, D., Cours de Droit International (1929).

Archibugi, D. & Michie, J., Technological Globalisation or National Systems of Innovation? 29(2) *Futures* 121 (1997).

Arendt, H., The Human Condition (1958), (2nd ed. 1998).

Arendt, H., Eichmann in Jerusalem: A report on the banality of evil (1963).

Arendt, H., The Origins of Totalitarianism (Harcourt, New Edition, 1973).

Ariew, R., G.W. Leibniz, life and works, *in* N. Jolley (Ed.), Cambridge Leibniz Companion 18 (1995).

ASIL Proceedings, The Transformation of Sovereignty (1994).

Auden, W.H., The Age of Anxiety: A Baroque Eclogue (Faber and Faber ed. 1948).

Austin, J., The Province of Jurisprudence Determined (1832), (W.E. Rumble Ed.).

Austin, J.L., How to do things with words (1962).

Baker, R.S., Woodrow Wilson and World Settlement (1923).

Barnet, R.J., Coexistence and Cooperation in International Law, 18 (1) *World Politics* 89 (1965).

Barthélemy, J., Le Role du Pouvoir Exécutif dans les Républiques Modernes (1906/7).

Barthélemy, J., La crise de la démocratie contemporaine (1931).

Barthélemy, J., Traité de Droit Constitutionnel (1933).

Batchelor and Fer and Wood (Eds.), Realism, Rationalism, Surrealism, Art between the Wars (1993).

Bederman, D.J., The Souls of International Organizations: Legal Personality and the Lighthouse at Cape Spartel, 36 *Virg.JIL* 275 (1996).

Benda, J., The Enemies of Democracy in France, 13 *Foreign Affairs* 284 (1934/5).

Berman, N., Modernism, nationalism, and the rhetoric of reconstruction, XIII *Current Legal Theory* 33 (1995).

Bersier Ladavac, N., Hans Kelsen (1881-1973) Bibliographical Note and Bibliography, 9 *EJIL* 391 (1998).
Black, C.E., Reflections on the Eclipse of Europe, 4 (2) *World Politics* 293 (1952).
Blake, W., The Works of William Blake (Wordsworth Poetry Library ed.)
Blokker, N., & Schermers, H., International Institutional Law: Unity within Diversity (3rd rev. ed., 1995).
Borchard, E.M., The Access of Individuals to International Courts, 24 *AJIL* 359 (1930).
Bourquin, M., Règles Générales du Droit de la Paix, 35 *RCADI* 1 (1931-I).
Bourquin, M., Tribute to Hersch Lauterpacht, 10 *ICLQ* 6 (1961).
Boyle, J., Ideals and Things: International Legal Scholarship and the Prison-house of Language, 26 *HILJ* 350 (1985).
Bragger, J.D., Constitutional Laws of 1875, *in* P.H. Hutton (Ed.), Historical Dictionary of the Third French Republic, at 237.
Brightman, C. (Ed.), Between Friends: the correspondence of Hannah Arendt and Mary McCarthy, 1949-1975 (1995).
Brierly, J.L., The Shortcomings of International Law (1924), *in* Lauterpacht and Waldock (Eds.), The Basis of Obligation in International Law and other papers 68 (1958).
Brierly, J.L., The Judicial Settlement of International Disputes (1925), *in* Lauterpacht and Waldock (Eds.), at 93.
Brierly, J.L., Matters of Domestic Jurisdiction (1925), *in* Lauterpacht and Waldock (Eds.), at 81.
Brierly, J.L., International Law as a Subject of Education (1926), *in* Lauterpacht and Waldock (Eds.), at 127.
Brierly, J.L., The Law of Nations: An Introduction to the International Law of Peace (1928). The Law of Nations (5th ed.).
Brierly, J.L., The Basis of Obligation in International Law, *in* Lauterpacht and Waldock (Eds.), The Basis of Obligation in International Law and Other Papers by the late James Leslie Brierly 1 (1958). This is the original English version of the course 'Le Fondement du caractère obligatoire du droit international' as delivered in 1928, 23 *RCADI* 467 (1928).
Brierly, J.L., The Legislative Function in International Relations (1931), *in* Lauterpacht and Waldock (Eds.), at 212.
Brierly, J.L., The Rule of Law in International Society (1936), *in* Lauterpacht and Waldock (Eds.), at 250.
Brierly, J.L., Règles Générales du Droit de la Paix, 58 *RCADI* 1 (1936-IV).
Brierly, J.L., The Outlook for International Law (1944).
Brown, G., Leibniz's moral philosophy, *in* N. Jolley (Ed.), The Cambridge Companion to Leibniz 411 (1995).
Brown, S., The Seventeenth-century intellectual background, *in* N. Jolley (Ed.), The Cambridge Companion to Leibniz 43 (1995).
Brownlie, I., Principles of International Law (4th ed., 1990).
Bronowski, J., The Ascent of Man (1980). (1st ed., 1973).
Brouwers, A.H.M., Shell moet zich staatsmanschap aanleren, *NRC Handelsblad*, 14 January 1997.
Brunner, E., Gerechtigkeit: eine Lehre von den Grundgesetzen der Gesellschaftsordnung (1943).
Brunner, E., Christianity and Civilisation (1947).
Brunner, J., Oedipus Politics, Freud's Paradigm of Social Relations, *in* M.S. Roth (Ed.), Freud: Conflict and Culture 80 (1998).
Bull, G. (Ed.), Michelangelo, Life, Letters, and Poetry (1987).

Camfield, W.A., Max Ernst: Dada and the Dawn of Surrealism (1993).
Canetti, E., Die Fackel im Ohr, Lebensgeschichte 1921-1931 (1980 ed., Carl Hanser Verlag).
Carey, J., The Intellectuals and the Masses (1992).
Carr, E.H., The Twenty Years' Crisis: 1919-1939 (1939).
Carty, A., Critical International Law: Recent Trends in the Theory of International Law, 2 *EJIL* 66 (1991).
Cassese, A., Remarks on Scelle's Theory of 'Role Splitting' (dédoublement fonctionnel) in International Law, 1 *EJIL* 210 (1990).
Cassirer, E., Substanzbegriff und Functionsbegriff: Untersuchungen über die Grundfragen der Erkenntniskritik (1910).
Cassirer, E., The Myth of the State (1945).
Castoriadis, C., World In Fragments: Writings on Politics, Society, Psychoanalysis, and the Imagination (1997).
Cavaglieri, A., Règles Générales du Droit de la Paix, 26 *RCADI* 311 (1929-I).
Charlesworth & Chinkin, The Boundaries of International Law: A feminist analysis (2000).
Charlesworth & Chinkin & Wright, Feminist Approaches to International Law, 85 *AJIL* 613 (1991).
Chinkin, Ch., A Critique of the Public/Private Dimension, 10 *EJIL* 387 (1999).
Chinkin, Ch., Summary of Discussion, Global Dimensions Seminar 'Corporate Responsibility and Human Rights' at the United Nations, New York, 1st June 2001.
Churchill, W., Sinews of Peace speech, 5 March 1946, Westminster College, Fulton, Missouri. See, e.g., <http://www.missourinet.com/wow/1946speech.html>.
Collingwood, R.G., The Idea of History (1946, rev. ed. 1993).
Condorelli, L., Scholie sur l'idiome scellien des manuels francophones de droit international public, 1 *EJIL* 232 (1990).
Cotterrell, R., The Politics of Jurisprudence, A Critical Introduction to Legal Philosophy (1989).
Daillier, P. & Pellet, A., Nguyen Quoc Dinh Droit International Public (1994).
Davies, N., Europe: A History (1997).
Dennis, M.J., The 56th Session of the UN Commission on Human Rights, March – April 2000, 95 *AJIL* 213 (2001).
Dennis, M.J., The 57th Session of the UN Commission on Human Rights, March – April 2001, 96 *AJIL* 181 (2002).
Dennis, M.J., The 58th Session of the UN Commission on Human Rights, March – April 2002, 97 *AJIL* 364 (2003).
Descamps, E.E.F., Le Droit International Nouveau, l'influence de la condamnation de la guerre sur l'évolution juridique internationale, 31 *RCADI* 393 (1930-I).
Detter de Lupis, I., The Concept of International Law (1987).
De Visscher, Ch., La Technique de la Personnalité Juridique en Droit International Public et Privé, 17 *RDI et Législation Comparée* 475 (1936).
Documenta X – the book: Politics-Poetics (1997).
Dominicé, C., L'ordre juridique international entre tradition et innovation: recueil d'études (1997).
Drost, P.N., The Individualization of International Law, Symbolae Verzijl 134 (1958).
Drucker, P., The End of Economic Man: The origins of Totalitarianism (1939).
Duguit, L., L'État, le droit objectif et la loi positive (1901).
Duguit, L., L'Etat, Les Gouvernants et Les Agents (1903).
Duguit, L., Traité de Droit constitutionnel (3rd ed., 1927).
Dupuy, R.J., Images de Georges Scelle, 1/2 *EJIL* 235 (1990).

Dupuy, R.J., The United Nations Facing the Crisis of the Nation State, *in* Nandasiri Jasentuliyana (Ed.), Perspectives on international law 201 (1995).
Eagleton, C., Organization of the Community of Nations, 36 *AJIL* 229 (1942).
Eagleton, C., The Task of the International Lawyer, 41 *AJIL* 435 (1947).
Einstein, A., Letter of 30 Juli 1932, in Freud's *Gesammelte Werke*, Vol. XVI, at 12 (1950).
Eliot, T.S., The Waste Land (1922).
Eliot, T.S., Four Quartets (1995, reprint 1944 ed.).
Erich, R., La Naissance et la Reconnaissance des États, 13 *RCADI* 427 (1926-III).
Eyffinger, A., Europe in the Balance: An Appraisal of the Westphalian System, 45 *NILR* 161 (1998).
Falk, R.A., New Approaches to the study of International Law, 61 *AJIL* 477 (1967).
Falk, R.A., et al., Myres Smith McDougal (1906-1998), 92 *AJIL* 729 (1998).
Fer, B., et al., Realism, Rationalism, Surrealism, Art between the Wars (1993).
Findekeller, C.D., Letter to Leibniz, 30 December 1692, *in* Acad. Ed., I, 9er Band, at 225.
Finkelkraut, A., La tolérance, notre dernier tyran?, The Pierre Bayle Lecture, 20 November, 1998.
Fisher, D.J., Reading Freud's *Civilization and Its Discontents*, *in* LaCapra and Kaplan, Modern European Intellectual History 271 (1982).
Fitzmaurice, G., Hersch Lauterpacht and his attitude towards the judicial function, 50 *BYIL* 1 (1979).
Fortescue, W., The Third Republic in France 1870 – 1940: Conflicts and Continuities (2000).
Foucault, M., The Order of things: An Archaeology of the Human Sciences 366 (1970), translation of *Les Mots et Les Choses* (1966).
Foucault, M., Power/Knowledge: selected interviews & other writings 1972-1977 (1980).
Franck, Th.M., The Power of Legitimacy Among Nations (1990).
Franck, Th.M., The Emerging Right to Democratic Governance, 86 *AJIL* 46 (1992).
Franck, Th.M., Fairness in International Law and Institutions (1995).
Franck, Th.M., Clan and Superclan: Loyalty, Identity and Community in Law and Practice, 90 *AJIL* 359 (1996).
Franck, Th.M., Is Personal Freedom a Western Value?, 91 *AJIL* 593 (1997).
Franck, Th.M., The Empowered Self: Law and Society in the Age of Individualism v (1999).
Freeman, B., Corporate Responsibility and Human Rights, contribution to the first Global Dimensions Seminar on Corporate Responsibility and Human Rights of the Centre for the study of Global Governance, L.S.E., as posted at <http://www.globaldimensions.net/articles/cr/freeman.html>.
Freeman, M.D.A. (Ed.), Lloyd's Introduction to Jurisprudence (6th ed., 1994).
Freud, S., Warum Krieg? (1932), *in* Gesammelte Werke, Vol. XVI, at 12 (1950).
Freud, S., Group Psychology and the Analysis of the Ego (Standard ed. J. Strachey, 1959).
Freud, S., Civilization and Its Discontents (1930), (Standard ed. transl. J. Strachey, 1961).
Friedmann, W.G., The Disintegration of European Civilisation and the Future of International Law, 2 *Modern L.R.* 194 (1938).
Friedmann, W.G., Legal Theory (2nd Impression Revised, 1947).
Friedmann, W.G., An Analysis of 'In Defense of Natural Law', Law and Philosophy 144 (1964).
Friedmann, W.G., The Changing Structure of International Law (1964).
Friedmann, W.G., United States Policy and the Crisis of International Law, 59 *AJIL* 857 (1965).
Friedmann, W., Legal Theory (5th ed., 1967).
Friedmann, W.G., Law in a Changing Society (1972, 2nd ed.).

Friedrich, C.J., The Age of the Baroque 1610-1660 (1952), reprinted *in* Rabb (Ed.), The Thirty Years' War (1972, 2nd ed.).

Frost, R., Collected Poems, Prose, & Plays, at 362, (The Library of America ed.) 1970.

Fukuyama, F., 'The End of History?' *The National Interest* 16 (Summer 1989).

Fukuyama, F., De Geschiedenis loopt wel degelijk ten einde, *NRC Handelsblad*, 11 October 2001.

Fuller, P., Henry Moore: An Interpretation 39-40 (1993).

Gierke, von, O., Das Wesen der menschlichen Verbände (1902).

Giraud, E., La Crise de la Démocratie et le Renforcement du Pouvoir Exécutif (1938).

Gorbachev, M., The River of Time speech, 6 May 1992, Westminster College, Fulton, Missouri. See, e.g., <http://www.missourinet.com/wow/1992speech.html>.

Greiffencrantz, von, C.J., Nicolai, Letters to Leibniz, May & July 1693 and February-March 1694, Acad. Ed., I, 9er Band, at 452-453, 531-532, and Acad. Ed., I, 10er Band, at 272-274 and 324-327.

Grewe, W.G. (Ed.), Fontes Historiae Iuris Gentium (1988).

Grewe, W.G., History of the Law of Nations: World War I to World War II, 2 *EPIL* 839 *et seq.* (1995).

Grewe, W.G., The Epochs of International Law (2000).

Gross, L., The Peace of Westphalia 1648-1948, 42 *AJIL* 20 (1948).

Grotius, H., De Jure Belli ac Pacis libri tres (1625), transl. by F.W. Kelsey, The Classics of International Law series (1925).

Guehenno, J.-M., The End of the Nation State (1995), transl. of *La Fin de la Démocratie* (1993).

Guilbaut, S., How New York Stole the Idea of Modern Art: Abstract Expressionism, Freedom, and the Cold War (1983).

Gutting, G., French Philosophy in the Twentieth Century (2001).

Habermas, J., An Alternative Way out of the Philosophy of the Subject: Communicative versus Subject-centred Reason (1987), *in* L. Cahoone (Ed.), From Modernism to Postmodernism: An Anthology (1996), at 589.

Harland, D., Legitimacy and Effectiveness in International Administration, 10(1) *Global Governance* 19 (2004).

Harley, J.E., The League of Nations and the New International Law (1921).

Haskell, B., The American Century: Art & Culture 1900-1950 (1999).

Hazard J.N. et al., In Memoriam: Wolfgang Gaston Friedmann (1907-1972), 67 *AJIL* 102 (1973).

Hegel, G.W.F., The Philosophy of Right, (1967, transl. Knox).

Hehir, J.B., The Uses of Force in the Post Cold War World, presentation delivered at conference at the Woodrow Wilson Center, June 1996, <http://www.clausewitz.com/CWZHOME/hehir.htm>. See, for revised version, Strategy and Ethics in World Politics, *in* R.L. Hutchings (Ed.), At the End of the American Century: America's Role in the Post-Cold War World 110 (1998).

Heilborn, P., Subjecte des Völkerrechts, *in* K. Strupp (Ed.), II *Wörterbuch des Völkerrechts und der Diplomatie* 684 (1925).

Heilborn, P., Les Sources du Droit International, 11 *RCADI* 1 (1926-I).

Henkin, L., How Nations Behave: Law and Foreign Policy (1968).

Herkströter, C.A.J., Multinationals willen debat met samenleving aan, *NRC Handelsblad*, 14 October 1996.

Herkströter, C.A.J., Het schort aan richtinggevens leiderschap, *NRC Handelsblad*, 28 December 1996.

Hertz, N., The Silent Takeover: Global Capitalism and the Death of Democracy (2001).
Herzog, C., Sir Hersch Lauterpacht: An Appraisal, 8 *EJIL* 299 (1997).
Higgins, R., Problems and Process: International Law and How we use it (1994).
Hillmann, R.P., Quincy Wright and the Commission to study the Organization of Peace, 4(4) Global Governance 489 (1998).
Hirsch Jr, E.D., Three Dimensions of Hermeneutics, III (2) *New Literary History* 245 (1972).
Hirsch Ballin, E.M.H., Interdependent Sovereignty, paper presented at the IVR World Congress on Philosophy of Law and Social Philosophy, The Transformation of Legal Systems and economies in an Age of Global Interdependence, Pace University, New York City, June 24-30, 1999.
Hobbes, Th., Leviathan (Penguin class ed., 1981).
Hobsbawm, E.J., The Crisis of the Seventeenth Century, *in* T. Aston (Ed.), Crisis in Europe (1560-1660), Essays from *Past and Present* (1965).
Hobsbawm, E.J., The Age of Empire 1875-1914 (1994).
Hobsbawm, E.J, Age of Extremes: The Short Twentieth Century 1914-1991 (1994).
Hobsbawm, E.J., The New Century (2000).
Holbrooke, R., The American Stake in Europe – the European Stake in the United States, Nexus Lecture 2001, 11 October 2001, Tilburg, The Netherlands, *in* 30/31 Nexus 83 (2001).
Hook, S., Law and Philosophy (1964).
Huber, M., Der Einzelne in der Völkerwelt, *in* Das Menschenbild im Lichte des Evangeliums, Festschrift zum Emil Brunner, 153-170 (1950).
Huber, M., Prolegomena und Probleme eines internationalen Ethos, 53 *Die Friedens-Warte* 305-329 (1955/56).
Huizinga, J., How Holland became a Nation (1924), *in* Verzamelde Werken 2 (1948).
Huizinga, J., In de Schaduwen van Morgen: een diagnose van het geestelijk lijden van onzen tijd (1935), transl. by Huizinga, In the Shadows of Tomorrow (1936).
Hunter, S., Metaphor and Meaning in Francis Bacon, *in* L. Gowing and S. Hunter, Francis Bacon 30 (1989).
Huntington, S.P., The Clash of civilizations and the Remaking of World Order (1996).
Hutton, P.H. (Ed.), Historical Dictionary of the Third French Republic 1870-1940 (1986).
Irigaray, L., The Sex Which is Not One (1981), *in* L. Cahoone (Ed.), From Modernism to Postmodernism: An Anthology (1996), at 461.
Israel, J.I., The Dutch Republic: Its Rise, Greatness, and Fall 1477-1806 (1995).
Jabloner, C., Kelsen and his Circle: The Viennese Years, 9 *EJIL* 368 (1998).
Jacobs, L., The Jewish Religion, A Companion (OUP, 1995).
Janik, A., and Toulmin, S., Wittgenstein's Vienna (1973).
Jaspers, K., Man in the Modern Age (1957, orig. publ. in 1932 entitled: Die geistige Situation der Zeit). First English transl. published in 1933.
Jaspers, K., Leibniz, *in* The Great Philosophers Vol. III (Engl. ed., 1993).
Jellinek, G., Allgemeine Staatslehre (1905).
Jenks, Ch., The Death of Modern Architecture (1984) and What is Post-Modernism? (1986), *in* L. Cahoone, From Modernism to Postmodernism: An Anthology (1996), at 469.
Jenks, C.W., Hersch Lauterpacht, 35 *BYIL* x (1960).
Jenks, C.W., Hersch Lauterpacht-The Scholar as Prophet, 36 *BYIL* 1 (1961).
Jennings, R.Y., The Progress of International Law: an inaugural lecture (1960).
Jennings, R.Y., Hersch Lauterpacht: A Personal Recollection, 8 *EJIL* 301 (1997).
Jessup, P.C., Tribute to Hersch Lauterpacht, 10 *ICLQ* 9 (1961).

Jessup, P.C., and Baxter, R.R., The contribution of Sir Hersch Lauterpacht to the Development of International Law, 55 *AJIL* 98 (1961).
Jones, E., The Life and Work of Sigmund Freud (1957).
Josephus Jitta, D., The Renovation of International Law (1919).
Jung, C.G., The Undiscovered Self (1957).
Kant, I., Perpetual Peace (1795), *in* H.S. Reiss (Ed.), Kant Political Writings (2nd ed., 1991).
Kant, I., The Metaphysics of Morals (1797), *in* H.S. Reiss (Ed.), Kant Political Writings (2nd ed., 1991).
Kaplan, R.D., The Coming Anarchy, *The Atlantic Monthly*, Feb. 1994.
Kaplan, R.D., Was Democracy just a Moment?, *The Atlantic Monthly*, Dec. 1997.
Kaplan, R.D., Looking the World in the Eye, *The Atlantic Monthly*, Dec. 2001.
Kaufmann, E., Règles Générales du Droit de la Paix, 54 *RCADI* 309 (1935-IV).
Kelly, J.M., A Short History of Western Legal Theory (1992).
Kelsen, H., Hauptprobleme der Staatsrechtslehre (1911).
Kelsen, H., Über Grenzen zwischen juristischer und soziologischer Methode (1911).
Kelsen, H., Zur Theorie der juristischen Fiktionen (1919), *in* Klecatsky and Marcic and Schambeck (Eds.), Die Wiener rechtstheoretische Schule: Schriften von Hans Kelsen, Adolf Merkl, Alfred Verdross 1215 (1968).
Kelsen, H., Das Problem der Souveränität und die Theorie des Völkerrechts (1920).
Kelsen, H., Von Wesen und Wert der Demokratie, 47 *Archiv für Sozialwissenschaft und Sozialpolitik* 57 (1920/21).
Kelsen, H., Das Verhältnis von Staat und Recht im Lichte der Erkenntniskritik (1921), *in* Klecatsky and Marcic and Schambeck (Eds.), Die Wiener rechtstheoretische Schule: Schriften von Hans Kelsen, Adolf Merkl, Alfred Verdross 95 (1968).
Kelsen, H., Der Begriff des Staates und die Sozialpsychologie. Mit besonderer Berücksichtigung von Freuds Theorie der Masse, VIII *IMAGO-Zeitschrift für Anwendung der Psychoanalyse auf die Geisteswissenschaften* 97 (1922).
Kelsen, H., Der soziologische und der juristische Staatsbegriff (1922).
Kelsen, H., Gott und Staat (1922/23), *in* Klecatsky and Marcic and Schambeck (Eds.), Die Wiener rechtstheoretische Schule: Schriften von Hans Kelsen, Adolf Merkl, Alfred Verdross 171 (1968).
Kelsen, H., The conception of the State and Social Psychology, V *The Internat. J. of Psycho-Analysis* 5 (1924), transl. of 1922 IMAGO article.
Kelsen, H., Allgemeine Staatslehre (1925).
Kelsen, H., Les Rapports de Système entre le Droit Interne et le Droit International Public, 14 *RCADI* 227 (1926-IV).
Kelsen, H., Der Staat als Übermensch: Eine Erwiderung (1926).
Kelsen, H., Der Staatsbegriff und die Psychoanalyse (1927), *in* Klecatsky and Marcic and Schambeck (Eds.), Die Wiener rechtstheoretische Schule: Schriften von Hans Kelsen, Adolf Merkl, Alfred Verdross 209 (1968).
Kelsen, H., Von Wesen und Wert der Demokratie (2nd rev. ed., 1929).
Kelsen, H., Théorie Générale du Droit International Public, Problèmes Choisis, 42 *RCADI* 117 (1932-IV).
Kelsen, H., The Pure Theory of Law, 'Labandism', and Neo-Kantianism. A Letter to Renato Treves (1933), *in* S.L. Paulson and B. Litschewski Paulson (Eds.), Normativity and Norms, Critical Perspectives on Kelsian Themes 174 (1998).
Kelsen, H., Introduction to the Problems of Legal Theory (1992), transl. of the 1st ed. (1934) of the *Reine Rechtslehre: Einleitung in die Rechtswissenschaftliche Problematik*, S. Paulson and B. Litschewiski Paulson (Eds.).

Kelsen, H., Peace through Law (1944).
Kelsen, H., General Theory of Law and State (1945).
Kelsen, H., Kausalität und Zurechnung (1954), *in* Klecatsky and Marcic and Schambeck (Eds.), Die Wiener rechtstheoretische Schule: Schriften von Hans Kelsen, Adolf Merkl, Alfred Verdross 663 (1968).
Kelsen, H., Tribute to Hersch Lauterpacht, 10 *ICLQ* 2 (1961).
Kennedy, D., International Legal Structures (1987).
Kennedy, D., International Law and the Nineteenth Century: History of an Illusion, 65 *Nordic JIL* 385 (1996).
Kennedy, D., A New Stream of International Law Scholarship (1988), *in* Beck & Arend & Vander Lugt (Eds.), International Rules 230 (1996).
Kennedy, P., The Rise and Fall of the Great Powers (1987, Vintage Books ed. 1989).
Keohane, R.O. & Nye Jr., J.S., Power and Independence in the Information Age, 77(5) *Foreign Affairs* 81 (1998).
Kissinger, H., Diplomacy (1995).
Knabe, L., Introduction to Entretien de Philarete et d'Eugène sur la question du temps agitée à Nimwegue touchant le droit de Souveraineté et d'Ambassade des Electeurs et Princes de l'Empire, Acad. Ed., IV, 2er Band, at XXI.
Knubben, R., Die Subjekte des Völkerrechts (1928).
Koch, J., Tussen Habsburg en Hitler: Cultuur en politiek in Oostenrijk, 1918-1938, *in* P. Op de Coul (Ed.), *Tekens van Moderniteit: Wenen in het Interbellum* 11 (1998).
Kooijmans, P.H., The doctrine of the Legal Equality of States: an Inquire into the Foundations of International Law (1964).
Kooijmans, P.H., Volkenrecht en Sociale Gerechtigheid (1965).
Kooijmans, P.H., Communistisch Volkenrecht: van non-existent recht tot recht van co-existentie, *in* J. Stellingwerff (Ed.), Marxisme en Revolutie 225 (1967).
Kooijmans, P.H., International Law: Placebo or Medication?, *in* W.J.M. van Genugten et al. (Eds.), *Realism and Moralism in International Relations* 87 (1999).
Kooijmans, P.H., Internationaal Publiekrecht in Vogelvlucht (2000, 8th ed.).
Koskenniemi, M., From Apology to Utopia, The Structure of International Legal Argument (1989).
Koskenniemi, M., Lauterpacht: The Victorian Tradition in International Law, 8 *EJIL* 215 (1997).
Koskenniemi, M., The Gentle Civilizer of Nations: The Rise and Fall of International Law 1870-1960 (2002).
Krabbe, H., L'Idée Moderne de l'État, 13 *RCADI* 509 (1926-III).
Landauer, C., J.L. Brierly and the Modernization of International Law, 25 (5) *Vanderbilt J. of Tr.L.* 881 (1993).
Lasson, A., System der Rechtsphilosophie (1882).
Lauterpacht, H., The Private Sources and Analogies of International Law (1927).
Lauterpacht, H., Kelsen's Pure Theory of Law (Lecture given in 1932), *in* E. Lauterpacht (Ed.), International Law: being the Collected Papers of Hersch Lauterpacht (1970-1978), Vol. 2, at 404.
Lauterpacht, H., The Nature of International Law and General Jurisprudence (1932), as published, *in* E. Lauterpacht (Ed.), International Law: being the Collected Papers of Hersch Lauterpacht (1970-1978), Vol. 2, at 3.
Lauterpacht, H., The Function of International Law (1933).
Lauterpacht, H., Règles du Droit de la Paix, 62 *RCADI* 95 (1937-IV).

Lauterpacht, H., Professor Carr on International Morality (1941), *in* E. Lauterpacht (Ed.), International Law: being the Collected Papers of Hersch Lauterpacht (1970-1978), Vol. 2, at 67.
Lauterpacht, H., The Grotian Tradition of International Law, 1st published in, 23 *BYIL* 1-53 (1946), here as published, *in* E. Lauterpacht (Ed.), International Law: being the Collected Papers of Hersch Lauterpacht (1970-1978), Vol. 2, at 307.
Lauterpacht, H., The International Protection of Human Rights, 70 *RCADI* 1 (1947-I).
Lauterpacht, H., The Subjects of International Law, 63 *LQR* 438 (1947).
Lauterpacht, H., The Subjects of International Law, 64 *LQR* 110 (1948).
Lauterpacht, H., Towards an International Bill of Rights (1949), *in* E. Lauterpacht (Ed.), International Law: being the Collected Papers of Hersch Lauterpacht (1970-1978), Vol. 3, at 410.
Lauterpacht, H., International Law after the Second World War (1950), *in* E. Lauterpacht (Ed.), International Law: being the Collected Papers of Hersch Lauterpacht (1970-1978), Vol. 2, at 159.
Lauterpacht, H., State Sovereignty and Human Rights (1950), *in* E. Lauterpacht (Ed.), International Law: being the Collected Papers of Hersch Lauterpacht (1970-1978), Vol. 3, at 416.
Lauterpacht, H., International Law and Human Rights (1950).
Lauterpacht, H., On Realism, especially in International Relations (1953), *in* E. Lauterpacht (Ed.), International Law: being the Collected Papers of Hersch Lauterpacht (1970-1978), Vol. 2, at 52.
Lauterpacht, H., Brierly's Contribution to International Law, *in* J.L. Brierly, The Basis of Obligation in International Law xv (1958).
Le Bon, G., La Psychologie des Foules (1895).
Le Fur, L., La Théorie du Droit Naturel Depuis le XVIIe Siècle et la Doctrine Moderne, 18 *RCADI* 259 (1927-III).
Le Fur, L., La démocratie et la crise de l'Etat (1934), *in* Les Grands Problèmes du Droit (1937).
Leibniz, G.W., Severinum de Monzambano (1668-1672), *in* Acad. Ed., IV, 1er Band (1667-1676), N.32, at 500.
Leibniz, G.W., Georgius Ulicovius Lithuanus (1669), Propos. XLII, *in* Acad. Ed., IV, 1er Band (1667-1676) N.1, at 3.
Leibniz, G.W., Securitas Publica (1670), *in* Acad. Ed., IV, 1er Band (1667-1676) N.5, at 133.
Leibniz, G.W., Entretien de Philarete et d'Eugène sur la question du temps agitée à Nimwegue touchant le droit de Souveraineté et d'Ambassade des Electeurs et Princes de l'Empire (1677), *in* Acad. Ed., IV, 2, at 289.
Leibniz, G.W., Caesarini Fürstenerii de Jure Suprematus ac Legationis Principum Germaniae (1677), Acad. Ed. IV, 2ter Band (1677-1687), N.1, at 3. Here, in an English transl.: *Caesarinus Fürstenerius* (1677), in LPW, at 111 *et seq.*
Leibniz' drawing and poem, *Devise sur la Reconvalescence du Roy*, April 1687, *in* Acad. Ed., IV, 3er Band, N. 128, at 841-842.
Leibniz, G.W., Letter to P. Pellisson-Fontanier, 3 July 1692, *in* Acad. Ed., I, 8er Band, at 127.
Leibniz, G.W., Letter to Wilhelm de Beyrie, April 7, 1693, *in* Acad. Ed., I, 9er Band, N. 241, at 391.
Leibniz, G.W., Letter to Abbé Jean-Paul Bignon, October 1693, *in* Acad. Ed., I, 9er Band, N. 396, at 590.
Leibniz, G.W., Codex Juris Gentium diplomaticus (1693), in the transl. of P. Riley (Ed.), Leibniz Political Writing (1989).

Leibniz, G.W., Memoir for Enlightened Persons (mid 1690s), *in* LPW at 85.
Leibniz, G.W., Felicity (c. 1694-8?), *in* LPW, at 83.
Leibniz, G.W., Portrait of the Prince (1679), *in* LPW.
Leibniz, G.W., Excerpts from three letters to Th. Burnett (1699-1712), *in* LPW, at 191.
Leibniz, G.W., On Natural Law, *in* LPW, at 77.
Leibniz, G.W., Letter to Landgraf Ernst of Hesse-Rheinfels (1683-91), *in* LPW, at 185.
Leibniz, G.W., Monadology (1714), transl. G.R. Montgomery, Discourse on Metaphysics and the Monadology (1992).
Leibniz, G.W., Opinion on the Principles of Pufendorf (1706), *in* LPW, at 71.
Leibniz, G.W., Observations on the Abbé de St Pierre's 'Project for the Perpetual Peace' (1715), *in* LPW, at 181.
Levi, P., If This is a Man. Original publication: Se questo è un uomo (1947).
Lewis, H., The Politics of Surrealism (1988).
Lindey, C., Art in the Cold War: From Vladivostok to Kalamazoo, 1945-1962 (1990).
Lippmann, W., The Phantom Public (1925).
Livingstone, M., Retrospective George Segal (1997).
Louter, de, L., La Crise de Droit International, 26 *RGDIP* 76 (1919).
Luce, H.R., The American Century, *Life Magazine*, 17 February 1941.
Luchaire, J., Principes de la Coopération Intellectuelle International, 9 *RCADI* 307 (1925-IV).
Lyotard, J.-F., The Postmodern Condition: A Report on Knowledge 60-61 (1986), transl. *La Condition Postmoderne: rapport sur le savoir* (1979).
Lyotard, J.-F., *Answering the Question: What Is Postmodernism?* (1983), as published in Lyotard, The Postmodern Condition: A Report on Knowledge 71 (1986).
MacDonald Ross, G., Leibniz (1984).
Maclaren, M., Like Blind Men Feeling an Elephant: Scholars' Ongoing Attempts to Ascertain the Role of Non-State Actors in International Law, 3(10) *German Law Journal* (2002), <http://www.germanlawjournal.com>.
Mannheim, K., Man and Society in an Age of Reconstruction (The English ed. was published in 1940, original German publication was of 1935).
Marlborough Gallery Catalogue (March-April 1967).
Martel, F., Le voyage philosophique de Paul Ricoeur, *Magazine littéraire* (1997), at 357.
Mathews, J.T., Power Shift 76(1) *Foreign Affairs* 50 (1997).
Mayeur, J.-M., La vie politique sous la Troisième République 1870-1940 (1984, éd. du Seuil).
McDougal, M.S., International Law, Power, and Policy: A Contemporary Conception, 82 *RCADI* 133 (1953-I).
McDougal, M.S., The Realist Theory in Pyrrhic Victory, 49 *AJIL* 376 (1955).
McDougal, M.S., The Impact of International Law upon National Law: A Policy-oriented Perspective (1958), *in* McDougal et al., Studies in World Public Order (1960), at 157.
McDougal, M.S. & Lasswell, H.D, The Identification of Diverse Systems of Public Order (1959), *in* McDougal et al., Studies in World Public Order (1960) at 3.
McDougal, M.S., Perspectives for an International Law of Human Dignity (1959), *in* McDougal et al., Studies in World Public Order (1960), at 987.
McNair, A.D., Tribute to Hersch Lauterpacht, 10 *ICLQ* 3-6 (1961);
Merkl, A., Die politische Freiheit als Gegenstand wissenschaftlicher Erkenntnis, *in* Klecatsky and Marcic and Schambeck (Eds.), Die Wiener rechtstheoretische Schule: Schriften von Hans Kelsen, Adolf Merkl, Alfred Verdross 736 (1968).
Métall, R.A., Hans Kelsen. Leben und Werk (1969).

Moïse, D., Welcome to the New, New World Order, *Financial Times* 13 September 2001, at 15.
Molen, van der, G.H.J., Subjecten van Volkenrecht (1949).
Molen, van der, G.H.J., The Present Crisis in the Law of Nations, Symbolae Verzijl (1958) at 251.
Molen, van der, G.H.J., *in* Ethical Values in International Decision-making 43 (1960).
Morabito, M., Histoire constitutionnelle de la France (1789-1958), (7th ed. 2002).
Morelli, G., Nozioni di diritto pubblico (Napoli,1967).
Morgenthau, H.J., Positivism, Functionalism, and International Law, 34 *AJIL* 260 (1940).
Morgenthau, H.J., Scientific Man vs. Power Politics (1947).
Morgenthau, H.J., The Political Science of E.H. Carr, 1(1) *World Politics* 127 (1948).
Morgenthau, H.J., Politics among Nations (2nd ed., 1954).
Morgenthau, H.J., We Are Deluding Ourselves in Vietnam, *The New York Times Magazine*, April 18, 1965, at 24 *et seq.*
Mulholland, L.A., The Innate Right to be a Person, *in* G. Lafrance, Éthique et droits fondamentaux / Ethics and Basic Rights (1989).
Müller, K., & Krönert, G. (Eds.), Leben und Werk von G.W. Leibniz (1969).
Murdoch, I., Metaphysics as a Guide to Morals (1992, Penquin ed. 1993).
Musil, R., Tagebücher, Aphorismen Essays und Reden (1955 ed. by A. Frisé – Gesammelte Werke).
Musil, R., Prosa, Dramen späte Briefe (Herausgabe by A. Frisé 1957).
Nye, Jr., J.S., Globalisation's Democratic Deficit: How to Make International Institutional Institutions More Accountable, 80 (4) *Foreign Affairs* 2 (2001).
Niebuhr, R., The Nature and Destiny of Man, Vol. I: Human Nature, Vol. II: Human Destiny (1941).
Niebuhr, R., The Children of Light and the Children of Darkness: A Vindication of Democracy and a Critique of its Traditional Defence (1947).
Nijman, J.E., Sovereignty and Personality: a process of inclusion, *in* G. Kreijen et al., *State, Sovereignty, and International Governance* 109 (2002).
Nippold, O., Le Développement historique du Droit International depuis le Congrès de Vienne, 2 *RCADI* 1 (1924-I).
Nussbaum, A., A Concise History of the Law of Nations (1950).
O'Connell, D.P., International law (Vol. I, 1970).
Okri, B., Astonishing the Gods (1995).
Ohmae, K., The End of the Nation State: The Rise of Regional Economies (1995).
Op de Coul, P. (Ed.), Tekens van Moderniteit: Wenen in het Interbellum 8 (1998).
Oppenheim, L., The Future of International Law (1921), (transl. of a 1911 German text).
Oppenheim, L., (R.F. Roxburgh Ed.), International Law: A Treatise (1920).
Ortega y Gasset, J., The Revolt of the Masses 54-55 (1950 ed., 1932 transl.).
Pagès, G., *in* Rabb (Ed.), The Thirty Years' War 33 (1972, 2nd ed.).
Parker, G., Europe in Crisis 1598-1648 (1979).
Parker Follett, M., The New State (1918).
Parker, N.G. and Smith, L.M. (Eds.), The General Crisis of the Seventeenth Century (1978).
Phillips, L., The American Century: Art & Culture (1950-2000), Vol. II (1999).
Politis, N., Le Problème des limitations de la souveraineté et la théorie de l'abus des droit dans les rapport internationaux, 6 *RCADI* (1925-I).
Politis, N., How the World Court has functioned, 4 *Foreign Affairs* 447 (1925-6).
Politis, N., The Status of the Individual in International Law, *in* The New Aspects, at 18.
Politis, N., The New Aspects of International Law (1928).

Pound, R., Philosophical Theory and International Law, 1 *Bibliotheca Visseriana* 73 (1923).
Pufendorf, S., L'Estat de l'Empire d'Allemagne de Monzambane (1669), this is a French transl. of Pufendorf's work: Severinus de Monzambano, De statu imperii Germanici (1664).
Pufendorf, S., *On the Law of Nature and Nations* (1688), transl. *De Jure Naturae et Gentium* (1672) in the Classics of International Law ed. (1934).
Pufendorf, S., under the pseudonym Basilii Hyperate, '*Historische und Politische Beschreibung der geistlichen Monarchie des Stuhls zu Rom*' (1679).
Purvis, N., Critical Legal Studies in Public International Law, 32 *HILJ* 81 (1991).
Quadri, R., Diritto internazionale pubblico 398-409 (V ed. Napoli 1968).
Ray, J., La Communauté Internationale d'après les Traités du XVIe Siècle à nos Jours, 3 *Annales Sociologiques*, Ser. C, (1938).
Redlob, R., Théorie de la Société des Nations (1927).
Reeves, J.S., International Society and International Law, 15 *AJIL* 361 (1921).
Reeves, J.S., La Communauté Internationale, 3 *RCADI* 1 (1924-II).
Reibstein, E., Völkerrecht: eine Geschichte seiner Ideen in Lehre und Praxis, Vol. I, (1957).
Reiman D.H., and Powers, S.B. (Eds.), Shelley's Poetry and Prose (1977).
Reisman, M., Designing and Managing the Future of the State, 8 *EJIL* 412 (1997).
Ricoeur, P., Oneself as Another (1992).
Ricoeur, P., The Just (2000, transl. of *Le Juste*, 1995).
Ricoeur, P., Critique & Conviction 77-79 (1998).
Riley, P. (Ed.), Leibniz Political Writings (2nd ed., 1988).
Riley, P., Leibniz' Universal Jurisprudence: Justice as the Charity of the Wise (1996).
Rommen, H.A., In Defense of Natural Law, *in* Law and Philosophy 105 (1964).
Rood, A., Alchemie en Mystiek, Het Hermetische Museum (1997).
Rosecrance, R., The Rise of the Virtual State, 75(4) *Foreign Affairs* 45 (1996).
Roth, B.R., What ever happened to Sovereignty? Reflections on International Methodology, *in* Ch. Ku & Th.G. Weiss, Toward Understanding Global Governance (1998).
Rousseau, Ch., Georges Scelle, 65 *RGDIP* 5 (1961).
Russel, J., Max Ernst: Leben und Werk (1966).
Rutherford, D., Philosophy and Language, in N. Jolley (Ed.), Cambridge Leibniz Companion, at 224 (1995).
Sartre, J.-P., L'existentialisme est un humanisme (1945), (folio ed., 1996).
Scelle, G., La doctrine de L. Duguit et les fondements du droit des gens, 1-2 *Archives de Philosophie du droit et de Sociologie juridique* 83 (1932).
Scelle, G., Précis de Droit des Gens, Principes et Systématique, Vol. I, Introduction, le milieu intersocial (1932).
Scelle, G., Précis de Droit des Gens, Principes et Systématique, Vol. II, Droit Constitutionnel International (1934).
Scelle, G., Théorie et Pratique de la Fonction Exécutive en Droit International, 55 *RCADI* 87 (1936-I).
Scelle, G., Some Reflections on Juridical Personality in International Law, *in* G.A. Lipsky (Ed.), Law and Politics in the World Community 49 (1953).
Schindler, D., Contribution à l'étude des Facteurs Sociologiques et Psychologiques du Droit International, 46 *RCADI* 229 (1933-IV).
Schlesinger, Jr., A.M., The Vital Center: The Politics of Freedom (1970 ed.), (1st ed. 1950).
Scholte, J.A., The International Monetary Fund and Civil Society – An Underdeveloped Dialogue, paper presented at Non-State Actors and Authority in the Global System (2000).

Schrecker, P., Leibniz's Principles of International Justice, VII (4) *J. of the History of Ideas* 484 (1946).
Schwarzenberger, G., Power Politics, A Study of International Society (2nd ed. 1951).
Schwarzenberger, G., International Law: The Ultimate Test, 6 *Indian JIL* 6 (1966).
Schwebel, S.M., Hersch Lauterpacht: Fragments for a Portrait, 8 *EJIL* 305 (1997).
Scobbie, I.G.M., The Theorist as Judge: Lauterpacht's Concept of the International Judicial Function, 8 *EJIL* 264 (1997).
Scott, B.R., The Great Divide in the Global Village, 80 (1) *Foreign Affairs* 160 (2001).
Scruton, R., Modern Philosophy (1994).
Séfériadès, S., Principes Généraux du Droit International de la Paix, 34 *RCADI* 181 (1930-IV).
Segal, S., Les fondements du droit dans la doctrine de M. Georges Scelle, IX *Rev. Int. de la théorie du droit* 186-187 (1935).
Seneca, L.A., On Benefits, (Loeb Classical Library, 1935).
Shaw, M.N., International Law (3rd ed. 1991).
Sheldon, Leibniz's message to us, VII (4) *J. of the History of Ideas* 386 (1946).
Simons, W., Introduction to Pufendorf's *On the Law of Nature and Nations* (1688), transl. *De Jure Naturae et Gentium* (1672) in the Classics of International Law ed., (1934).
Simonovitch, M., Les Théories contemporaines de l'Etat (1939).
Siotto-Pintor, M., Les Sujets du droit International autres que les Etats, 41 *RCADI* 245 (1932-III).
Skinner, Q., *Meaning and Understanding in the History of Ideas*, *in* J. Tully (Ed.), Meaning and Context 29 (1988).
Skinner, Q., *A Reply to my Critics*, *in* J. Tully (Ed.), Meaning and Context 231 (1988).
Skinner, Q., *Motives, intentions and the interpretation of texts*, *in* J. Tully (Ed.), Meaning and Context 68 (1988).
Skinner, Q., *Some Problems in the Analysis of Political Thought and action, in* J. Tully (Ed.), Meaning and Context 97 (1988).
[Slaughter], Burley, A.-M., Toward an Age of Liberal Nations, 33 *HILJ* 393 (1992).
Slaughter, A.-M., International Law and International Relations Theory: A Dual Agenda, 87 *AJIL* 205 (1993).
Slaughter, A.-M., The Real New World Order, 76 (5) *Foreign Affairs* 183 (1997).
Slaughter, A.-M., & Tulumello, A.S. & Wood, S., International Law and International Relations Theory: A New Generation of Interdisciplinary Scholarship, 92 *AJIL* 367 (1998).
Slaughter, A.-M., & Ratner, S., The Method is the Message, 93 *AJIL* 410 (1999).
Spender, S., Vienna (1934).
Spender, S., European Witness (1947).
Spiropoulos, J., l'Individu et le Droit International, 30 *RCADI* 191 (1929-V).
Stalin's Reply to Churchill, March 14, 1946, (interview with *Pravda*), *The New York Times*, at 4, *in* Internet Modern History Sourcebook, <http://www.fordham.edu/halsall/mod/1946stalin.html>.
Stolleis, M., Geschichte des öffentlichen Rechts in Deutschland, Vol. 1 Reichspublizistik und Policeywissenschaft 1600-1800 (1988).
Stuyt, A.M., Gespleten Volkenrecht (1962).
Tanca, A., Georges Scelle (1878-1961), 1 *EJIL* 240 (1990).
Taylor, Ch., Une philosophie sans frontières, No. 390, Sept. 2000, *Magazine Littéraire*, Dossier: Paul Ricoeur, morale, histoire, religion: une philosophie de l'existence, at 30-31.
Thierry, H., The Thought of Georges Scelle, 1 *EJIL* 193 (1990).

Toulmin, S., Cosmopolis: The Hidden Agenda of Modernity (1990).
Triepel, H., Les Rapports entre le Droit Interne et le Droit International, 1 *RCADI* 77 (1923).
Vaihinger, H., Die Philosophie des Als Ob, System der theoretischen, praktischen und religiösen Fiktionen der Menschheit auf Grund eines idealistischen Positivismus (1913).
Valéry, P., La Crise de l'esprit, XIII *La Nouvelle Revue Française* 321 (1919).
Vattel, de, E., The Law of Nations or the Principles of Natural Law applied to the Conduct and to the Affairs of Nations and of Sovereigns, as published, *in* Classics of International Law (ed. 1916).
Verdross, A., Le Fondement du droit international, 16 *RCADI* 247 (1927-I).
Verdross, A., Eine Antinomie der Rechtstheorie, *Die Wiener Schule*, at 1379.
Verzijl, J.H.W., International Law in Historical Perspective, Vol. 2 International Persons (1969).
Verzijl, J.H.W., Tribute to Hersch Lauterpacht, 10 *ICLQ* 7 (1961).
Vinogradoff, P., Historical types of International Law: lectures delivered in the University of Leiden, *Bibliotheca Visseriana* (1923).
Vollenhoven, van, C., Sprongen in de Ontwikkeling van het Gewoonterecht (1912), *in* Mr. C. Van Vollenhoven's Verspreide Geschriften 32 (1934).
Vollenhoven, van, C., De Drie Treden van het Volkenrecht (1923).
Vries, de, J., Economy of Europe in an Age of Crisis (1600-1750), (1976).
Waldock, C.H.M., James Leslie Brierly (1881-1955) – a Biographical Note, *in* Lauterpacht and Waldock (Eds.), The Basis of Obligation in International Law and Other Papers by the late James Leslie Brierly (1958).
Walter, R., Hans Kelsen – Ein Leben im Dienste der Wissenschaft (1985).
Walter Jones, J., Leibniz as International Lawyer, 22 *BYIL* 3 (1945).
Wang H., & Rosenau, J.N., Transparency International and Corruption as an Issue of Global Governance, 7 (1) *Global Governance* 25-49 (2001).
Wedgewood, R., 'Legal Personality and the Role of Non-Governmental Organisations and Non-State Political Entities in the United Nations System' at the March 1998 Symposium of the Kiel Walther-Schücking-Institute of International Law on *Non-State Actors as New Subjects of International Law: International Law – From the Traditional State Order Towards the Law of the Global Community*, the editors of the Proceedings are R. Hoffmann and N. Geissler (Ass. Ed.).
Wheaton, H., Elements of International law (6th ed., 1855).
Whitton, J.B., Cold War Propaganda, 45 *AJIL* 151 (1951).
Wicke, J., Postmodern Identity and the Legal Subject, 62 *Univ. of Col. Law R.* 456 (1991).
Wilk, K., International law and global ideological conflict: reflections on the universality of international law, 45 *AJIL* (1951) at 648.
Willetts, P., From 'Consultative Arrangements' to 'Partnership:' The Changing Status of NGOs in Diplomacy at the UN, 6 *Global Governance* 205 (2000).
Williams, M., The World Bank, The World Trade Organization, and the Environment Social Movement, *in* R.A. Higgott & G.R.D. Underhill & A. Bieler (Eds.), Non-State Actors and Authority in the Global System 241-255 (2000).
Wilson, G.C., The Modernization of International Law, XIX *Am.Pol.Science Review* 268 (1925).
Wittgenstein, L., Philosophical Investigations (1953).
Wolf, M., Will the Nation-State Survive Globalisation?, 80 (1) *Foreign Affairs* 178-190 (2001).
Wolff, von, Chr., The Law According to the Scientific Method' (or rather Jus Gentium Methodo Scientifica Pertractatum) first published in 1749.

Wolff, von, Chr., Jus Gentium Methodo Scientifica Pertractatum (1764), Classics of International Law (ed.), 1934.
Woolsey, T.S., Reconstruction and International Law, 13 *AJIL* 187 (1919).
Zeldin, Th., France 1848-1945, Vol. I, Ambition, Love and Politics (1973).

Cases:

Case concerning the *S.S. "Lotus"*, 1927 PCIJ (ser. A) No. 10.
The *Island of Palmas* case, 1928 PCA. (RIAA Vol. II (Netherlands *v.* USA)).
Case concerning *Reparations for Injuries suffered in the Service of the United Nations*, Advisory Opinion, ICJ Rep. (1949) at 174.
Case concerning *Barcelona Traction*, (Belgium *v*. Spain), Judgment of 5 February 1970, ICJ Rep. (1970).

International and National Documents:

Nota Herijking van het Buitenlands Beleid, Tweede Kamer der Staten-Generaal, Vergaderjaar 1994-1995, 24337, nr. 2 (1995).
Handelingen van de Tweede Kamer, Vergaderjaar 1996-1997, aanhangsel, 1607, Vragen van Weisglas d.d. 1 juli 1997.

UN Commission on Global Governance, Our Global Neighbourhood (1995).
UN Secretary General's report, 'Renewing the UN: A Programme for Reform,' 16 July 1997, (A/51/950).
World Bank, The State in a Changing World, World Development Report 1997.
ICISS, Report of the International Commission on Intervention and State Sovereignty, The Responsibility to Protect (2001).

Peace Treaty between the Emperor and Sweden/ Osnabrück, *in* W.G. Grewe (Ed.), Fontes Historiae Iuris Gentium: Sources Relating to the History of the Law of Nations, Vol. 2 (1988).
Peace Treaty between the Emperor and France/ Munster, *in* W.G. Grewe (Ed.), Fontes Historiae Iuris Gentium: Sources Relating to the History of the Law of Nations, Vol. 2 (1988).

Montevideo Convention, i.e., Convention on Rights and Duties (Inter-American), 26 December 1933.
Charter of the United Nations (26 June 1945).
Universal Declaration of Human Rights, (UNGA Resolution 217 A (III), 10 December 1948).
UNGA Resolution 1514 (XV), 14 December 1960, Declaration on the Granting of Independence to Colonial Countries and Peoples.
UNGA Resolution 2625 (XXV), 24 October 1970, Declaration on Principles of International Law concerning Friendly Relations and Co-operation among States in accordance with the Charter of the United Nations.
UNGA Resolution 3068 (XXVIII), 30 November 1973, International Convention on the suppression and punishment of the Crime of *Apartheid*.

UNGA Resolution 3281 (XXIX), 12 December 1974, Charter of Economic Rights and Duties of States.
CSCE Charter of Paris for a New Europe (November 1990).
Vienna Convention on the Law of Treaties (23 May 1969).
African Charter on Human and Peoples' Rights (entered into force in 1986).
Geneva Protocol I (1977).

OECD Guidelines for Multinational Enterprises (2001).
UN website: <http://www.unglobalcompact.com/>.
UNCTAD Convention on a Code of Conduct for Liner Conferences (1973-74).
The Dow Jones' Stoxx Sustainability Index, <http://www.stoxx.com/indexes/sustindexes.html>.
The Inspection Panel Operating Procedures, website: <http://www.worldbank.org/inspectionpanel>.
Transparency International has also campaigned for an effective OECD Anti-Corruption Convention, adopted 21 November 1997. See also, <http://www.transparency.de>.
ECOSOC Res. 1296 (XLIV) on Consultation of NGOs.
Our Global Neighborhood, The Report of the Commission on Global Governance (1995).
UN partnership with civil society: <http://www.un.org/partners/civil_society/home.htm>.

INDEX OF NAMES